# Philosophies
# Men Live By

Second Edition

## Robert F. Davidson

HOLT, RINEHART AND WINSTON, INC.
New York  Chicago  San Francisco  Atlanta  Dallas
Montreal  Toronto  London  Sydney

The courtesy of the publishers in permitting use of copyright material from the following sources is gratefully acknowledged:

DeWitt, Norman W., *St. Paul and Epicurus*. University of Minnesota Press, Minneapolis. © 1954 by University of Minnesota. Excerpts from *The Stoic Philosophy of Seneca* by Moses Hadas, translator. Copyright © 1958 by Moses Hadas. Reprinted by permission of Doubleday & Company, Inc. *The Importance of Living* by Lin Yutang. Copyright © 1937, 1965 by The John Day Company, Inc. Reprinted by permission of The John Day Co., Inc., an Intext publisher, and William Heinemann, Ltd., Publishers. *A Preface to Morals* by Walter Lippman. Copyright 1929, 1957 by Walter Lippman. Reprinted with permission of Macmillan Publishing Co., Inc. *The Portable Dorothy Parker*. Copyright 1926, renewed 1954 by Dorothy Parker. Reprinted by permission of The Viking Press, Inc., and Gerald Duckworth & Co., Ltd.. *The Portable Nietzsche*, selected and translated by Walter Kaufmann. Copyright 1954 by The Viking Press, Inc. Reprinted by permission of Viking Press, Inc. Aristotle's *Politics*, trans. by Benjamin Jowett. From *The Oxford Translation of Aristotle*, ed. W. D. Ross, vol. 10, 1921. By permission of The Clarendon Press, Oxford. *I and Thou*. Reprinted by permission of Charles Scribner's Sons from *I and Thou* by Martin Buber, translated by Walter Kaufmann. Copyright © 1970 Charles Scribner's Sons. By permission of T. & T. Clark, Ltd. for the British market. Immanuel Kant, *Groundwork of the Metaphysic of Morals*, translated and analyzed by H. J. Paton. By permission of Harper & Row, Publishers, Inc., and Hutchinson Publishing Group, Ltd. *Reconstruction in Philosophy* by John Dewey. Enlarged edition copyright © 1948 by Beacon Press. Original edition copyright 1921 by Henry Holt & Co. Reprinted by permission of Beacon Press. *Marx's Concept of Man* by Erich Fromm. Copyright © 1961, 1966 by Erich Fromm. Reprinted by permission of Frederick Unger Publishing Company, Inc. *Early Writings of Karl Marx*, trans. T. B. Bottomore. Copyright 1946. Reprinted by permission of Pitman Publishing Ltd., T. B. Bottomore and C. A. Watts and Co., Ltd. Immanuel Kant, *Critique of Practical Reason and Other Writings in Moral Philosophy*, translated by Lewis W. Beck. Copyright 1949 by The University of Chicago Press. By permission of The University of Chicago Press. Excerpts from *Irrational Man* by William Barrett. Copyright © 1958 by William Barrett. Reprinted by permission of Doubleday & Company, Inc., and Heinemann Educational Books, Ltd. *Nietzsche: An Introduction to the Understanding of His Philosophical Activity*, by Karl Jaspers, translated by Charles F. Wallraff and Frederick J. Schmutz. By permission of University of Arizona Press, copyright 1965. *Concluding Unscientific Postscript*, by Søren Kierkegaard, translated by David F. Swenson and Walter Lowrie (copyright © 1941, 1969 by Princeton University Press) for the American Scandinavian Foundation. Reprinted by permission of Princeton University Press and the American Scandinavian Foundation. Stuart Hampshire: *Spinoza* (Pelican Original, rev. ed., 1962). Copyright © Stuart Hampshire, 1951. By permission of Penguin Books, Ltd. From *Markings* by Dag Hammarskjöld. Translated by Leif Sjoberg and W. H. Auden. Copyright © 1964 Alfred A. Knopf, Inc., and Faber and Faber, Ltd. Reprinted by permission of Alfred A. Knopf, Inc., and Faber and Faber, Ltd. Friedrich Nietzsche, *Thus Spake Zarathustra* and *Beyond Good and Evil*, Vols. 11 and 12 of *The Complete Works of Friedrich Nietzsche*, Oscar Levy, General Editor (1909–1911). By permission of Russell & Russell, Publishers, New York. Alan W. Watts, *Beat Zen, Square Zen and Zen*. Copyright © 1959 by Alan Watts. Reprinted by permission of City Lights Books, San Francisco. *The Words* by Jean-Paul Sartre. Reprinted with the permission of the publisher, George Braziller, Inc. Copyright © 1964 by Jean-Paul Sartre.

**Library of Congress Cataloging in Publication Data**

Davidson, Robert Franklin, 1902–
   Philosophies men live by.

   Includes bibliographical references.
   1. Philosophy—History.  2. Philosophy—Introductions.  I.  Title.
B74.D38   1974    109     73–21684

**ISBN 0–03–011851–4**

# Preface

The marked change in the mood of college students today, as well as significant developments in the concerns of the philosopher, have made a revised edition of *Philosophies Men Live By* both necessary and desirable. The reception this text received at the hands of students and instructors during the years since it was originally published has been most gratifying. Its major purpose, in the revised as in the original edition, is to provide an introduction to philosophy that students will find both relevant and stimulating.

With this in mind, a determined effort is made to present the insights of the great philosophers in terms that are meaningful to the beginning student. The concerns of the philosopher are related to the experience and interests of college students in the present generation, and the point of view of this generation of college students is also discussed. Technical terms, beyond the vocabulary of the student with no previous training in philosophy, are avoided insofar as possible.

Brief comment upon a large number of figures in the field of philosophy, typical of the traditional introductory text in this field, as a rule serves only to confuse the student. Hence this also has been avoided. Instead a selection has been made of some sixteen or eighteen outstanding philosophers, each of whom is presented in enough detail to make his position clear and to indicate its significance. Each position is treated sympathetically in order to enable the student to feel its enduring appeal. And in each case enough biographical detail is also provided to portray the philosopher as a real person and to show the relation of his background and experience to the philosophy he professed.

The philosophers discussed have been grouped in a topical rather than a chronological sequence. In this way the enduring philosophies men live by (hedonism, rationalism, utilitarianism, naturalism, pragmatism, existentialism) can be made more intelligible and appealing. Any such effort to present the ideas of the great philosophers in a way that the beginning student will find meaningful necessarily calls for simplification and popularization. And this, of course, is always fraught with danger. To avoid possible misrepresentation, large use is made of statements by the philosophers themselves. This enables the student not only to become familiar with the spirit of each philosopher, but also to feel a direct contact with the thought of the individual being discussed. Attention is also concentrated upon the more significant and influential works of each philosopher. This gives the student some sense of familiarity with the great philosophical masterpieces and, in many cases perhaps, may stimulate him to read such "great books" in their entirety.

It would be impossible, of course, to eliminate completely the point of view of the author in a vital discussion of philosophies men live by. A determined effort has been made, however, to achieve objectivity in the portrayal of each position. The underlying purpose, made clear throughout the volume, is to stimulate each student to think through for himself the philosophies discussed and to develop increased insight and maturity in his own view of life. There is no intention of leading the student to an uncritical acceptance of the author's views or the ideas of any of the philosophers discussed.

It is a pleasure to be able to express here my appreciation to those who have contributed in various ways to the present volume. In particular, I am grateful to several of my former colleagues and students for their assistance. Professors Thomas A. E. Hart and Martin Curry, formerly members of the University of Florida faculty, and Mr. Thomas Beason, a recent graduate of St. Andrews Presbyterian College, have read the revised manuscript in its entirety. Their thoughtful suggestions have improved appreciably the presentation and interpretation of the material included here. I am also much indebted to Professor Joseph G. Moorman, who read the manuscript for the publishers, and to Mr. John Tugman, and Ms. Heidi J. Leibowitz in the editorial office of Holt, Rinehart and Winston, Inc. Their assistance in the revision of the manuscript has made it a far better book than it otherwise could have been. For the ideas and points of view expressed here, however, I am myself, of course, entirely responsible.

In the actual preparation of the manuscript itself, the work of Phyllis Durell and Sally Rist has been invaluable. They have shown not only skill and competence, but good nature as well, in providing legible copy from the frequently disorganized material with which I supplied them. My debt to the many scholars whose critical studies have clarified the philosophies discussed in this volume is, of course, too apparent to require further recognition.

R.F.D.

*Gainesville, Florida*

# Contents

To know the chief rival attitudes toward life as the history of thinking has developed them, and to have heard some of the reasons they give for themselves, ought to be considered an essential part of liberal education.

Who can decide offhand which is absolutely better, to live or to understand life? We must do both alternately, and a man can no more limit himself to either than a pair of scissors can cut with a single blade.

*William James*

## CHAPTER 1

# The Role of the Philosopher

*The Sophists and Socrates*

Does the philosopher have anything to say—anything important, that is—to the young men and women whose lives now seem involved in one crisis after another? That we live today in a time of crisis needs no elaboration. Evidences are too apparent on every hand. There are, of course, recurring social and personal crises (Watergate, Vietnam, drug addiction) to which we have more or less become accustomed. It has been suggested, however, by the more deeply disturbed among us that we are also witnessing the decline and fall of modern European civilization, and along with this a widespread confusion in the world community as well.

The specific occasion for this, in the minds of many at least, lies in the advanced technology and technologically dominated civilization developed during the past century in the Western nations. This technology, which initially made possible our capitalistic economy, also soon enabled the nations of Western Europe to establish an imperialistic domination over the underdeveloped countries of Africa and Asia. In our time the African and Asian world has rebelled, first against Western economic imperialism, and more recently against the claim to ethnic superiority of the white races. This rebellion, together with the widespread appeal of Marxism to developing peoples, has produced world conflict, either overt or covert, on an unprecedented scale. There is thus some reason to believe that we are now seeing the disintegration of another great civilization, and with it something of the same kind of social and political confusion that marked the breakdown of the Roman and medieval civilizations.[1, *]

We are confronted today, however, not only with this crisis in our civilization, but with an equally grave crisis in human life itself. In America

* Footnotes that indicate the source of quoted material begin on page 427.

especially we see a growing disenchantment with the established order of things. The basic values of human personality as we conceive them—man's integrity; his freedom to think, to speak, and to live as he likes; his worth as an individual—are being subjected to such increasing restraint today that our very existence as persons seems threatened. This is not a crisis that can be solved by further developments in science or technology. Indeed, such developments are among the major causes of our present difficulties, if works like Charles Reich's *The Greening of America* or Theodore Roszak's *The Making of a Counter Culture* are at all reliable.

What we face is an existential crisis, a crisis that concerns the very nature and meaning of human life itself. And for this reason it is a situation in which the philosopher can and should offer significant assistance. Without the development of a way of life in which the concerns and the worth of the individual find meaningful expression, we cannot hope to deal successfully with the dissatisfactions that so deeply disturb young men and women today. Traditionally it is in just such a situation as this that philosophy has been most useful—more so than science or politics, in a different way than art or poetry or religion. For the philospher alone undertakes to cultivate the kind of insight and perspective essential for success in this search for the most satisfying experiences in human life. Only religion is as directly concerned as philosophy with this quest for life's meaning and its more enduring satisfactions. And for this reason the insights of religion have a significant place in a consideration of philosophies men live by.

### Philosophy and Religion

For a faith to give their lives direction and to sustain them in time of need, men in every age have looked to religion and the Church. Today many still turn to the traditional faith of their fathers for an answer to age-old questions concerning the meaning of human life, questions made increasingly urgent by the present crises in our personal lives and our civilization. One cannot but be impressed by the widespread appeal and influence of an evangelist such as Billy Graham, not only for an older generation but among the young as well, or by the "Jesus people" who appear among the younger generation in the most unexpected places. The popularity of such plays as *Jesus Christ Superstar* and *Godspell* provides further evidence of religion's appeal. Religion, however, is fundamentally inspirational and devotional in its emphasis. The Church seeks to direct our loyalty to the best that we know and to channel our idealism along socially constructive lines. But religion undertakes to provide no carefully reasoned answers to the problems that face us in our more reflective moods. Its emphasis is upon faith and commitment rather than upon thoughtful analysis or experimentation. The God of religion is a personal experience, not an intellectual hypothesis.

For the more thoughtful as well as the more perplexed of our day, the faith of the church thus has not proved entirely adequate. Such men and women must eventually turn to the philosopher for a more satisfying consideration of the issues of life. Yet to one who is deeply religious the philosopher's attitude will often seem suspect, when not downright irreligious. The thoughtful and critical—indeed, at times the questioning and skeptical—spirit of philosophy may well appear a real danger to religious faith. As William Temple (1821–1902), sometime distinguished Archbishop of Canterbury pointed out, an almost inescapable tension does exist between the spirit of religion and that of philosophy. It is not easy for an individual to combine both attitudes successfully in his own experience. By the philosopher, the basic convictions of the religious life must necessarily be treated as questions for objective and impartial examination. Yet a man cannot easily examine with detachment the object of his own religious faith. He cannot worship with devotion on Sunday a being that on Monday he must treat as merely an intellectual hypothesis.[2]

Although no hard and fast line can be drawn between the domain of philosophy and that of religion, the aim and the spirit of each then does differ. Where religion appeals to faith and to authority, philosophy insists upon an appeal to reason and to experience. Where religion is concerned with inspiration and with loyalty to high ideals, philosophy demands a continued examination of the premises upon which one acts. Where religion seeks certainty in one's convictions, philosophy provides conclusions that are only tentative and open always to revision. In those moments, however, when the faith or the inspiration engendered by high religion seems on the verge of being destroyed by doubts that inevitably assail us all, there is good reason to turn to philosophy. The discerning philosopher may well furnish a more comprehensive and satisfying interpretation of life than religious faith alone can suggest or than a cold and dispassionate scientific account of existence can provide.

## The New Naturalism

There are indications that a new philosophy of living is in fact taking shape among the youth in this country, on college and university campuses as well as among many groups outside the bounds of higher education. This is suggested at once, of course, by the quite marked change in personal appearance and life style that has occurred. It is to be seen in the new freedom in dress (which is most obvious perhaps among young women) and in the equally visible appeal of longer hair and beards among young men. It is evident in the new music, the rock festivals, that attracted thousands of young people to Woodstock or Altamont. It is apparent also in changing attitudes toward sexuality and marriage, and perhaps as strikingly as any-where in the whole question of recreational drug-taking, in particular the use of marijuana.

This new philosophy of living is as yet, of course, not clearly defined. It still expresses itself rather largely as a revolt of youth against the moral ambiguities of their parents and the social point of view of the "Establish-ment." But there have been numerous efforts recently to give more specific statement to the new point of view. In 1969 Theodore Roszak described the thought of half a dozen contemporary figures who seemed to him most influential in *The Making of a Counter Culture*. The following year, Charles A. Reich's *The Greening of America* proved to be an immensely popular examination of the major influences shaping the new philosophy of youth. Philip Slater's *The Pursuit of Loneliness*, an equally discerning though somewhat less widely sold discussion of the "new culture," was also published that year.

At about the same time a rather extensive study of the political and personal attitudes of today's college student was being made for the Rocke-feller Fund under the direction of Daniel Yankelovich. In 1972 his study was published under the title *The Changing Values on Campus*. Yankelovich calls the point of view now widely accepted by college students "The New Naturalism." This is quite an apt designation for the same philosophy Roszak identified in *The Making of a Counter Culture*, which was described in more concrete terms in *The Greening of America* as "consciousness III," and which *The Pursuit of Loneliness* simply called the "new culture."

Fundamentally, the new naturalism can be seen as a renewed interest on the part of young people today in man's attitude toward nature and what is natural. What is "natural" is expected to be enjoyable and is deemed to be good; what is artificial or essentially unnatural is bad. Yankelovich identi-fied some eighteen different meanings of the "natural" as this is interpreted by college students. "Some of the meanings are obvious, others are subtle," he writes. "Some are superficial expressions of life-styles which students try on and then abandon like so many one-night stands. Other meanings are fundamental to man's existence. Some meanings are intimate and personal, others are broadly political. Some will endure, others will fade from the scene. Compositely, these meanings add up to a new world view, a philoso-phy of life and of nature capable of transforming man's relationship to himself and his society."[3]

Many expressions of the new naturalism are, of course, quite familiar. The most obvious is simply looking and feeling physically natural. This means rejecting such manipulations as make-up, shoes, bras, formal suits and ties, artificial hair styles, shaves, and closely cut hair. Closely akin to this is a new emphasis on enjoyment of the senses and sensory experience rather than a concern with logical reasoning and conceptual scientific knowledge. This has led to a greater interest in one's body, as opposed by an older one-sided emphasis upon the cultivation of the mind, together with a new freedom in sexual frankness and in the use of drugs or techniques to become "turned on" or "tuned in." This new freedom has brought a rejection of moral conventions that prevent the spontaneous expression of emotion and desire.

The new naturalism likewise finds expression in the growing movement to live physically close to nature, in the open, off the produce of the land, and to escape from the artificial and man-made conditions in our cities, even though they provide comforts that an older generation now sees as necessities. As portrayed in *The Greening of America*, "Members of the new generation seek out the beach, the woods, the mountains. They do not litter these places with beer cans. . . . They do not go to nature as a holiday from what is real. They go to nature as a source. The salt water of the sea is the salt in their blood; the freedom of the sea is their freedom. Nature is not some foreign element. Nature is them."[4] This emphasis upon harmony with nature includes the new concern for the preservation of the natural environment and an interest in ecology. It leads to a rejection of the kind of "progress" that requires technological mastery of nature, and replaces the beauty of the natural environment with the "asphalt jungle" of six-lane highways or obscures the beaches with high-rise apartments and condominiums.

At a somewhat less obvious level, this new philosophy accepts living in groups rather than as isolated individuals as natural for human beings. Community is taken to be the desirable social ideal, a community in which each individual is accepted as he is and for himself, where each person is given ample opportunity for full self-development rather than being forced to conform to some traditional social pattern. The emphasis is put on cooperation rather than competition in all social and economic activity and on the mutual sharing of creative experiences. Young people with this viewpoint are no longer willing to take jobs that are monotonous and unappealing. They reject the whole notion of getting ahead in the world as an appealing goal. The ideal of success in business or professional life, which for the past several generations was generally accepted as a fundamental aspect of the American way of life, no longer seems meaningful or appealing to them. Here perhaps more than anywhere else the "new naturalist" philosophy runs counter to that of the "Establishment."

The major intellectual concern of the new naturalism seems to be with self-knowledge, with the discovery of one's natural self, rather than with objective scientific knowledge. The mysterious element in man and in nature also is intriguing. And quite as significant is an agreement with the existentialists that "truth" is discovered and known immediately by participation, by involvement in living, rather than through the analytical approach of modern science or statistical generalizations of a scientific world view. As seen by its most enthusiastic advocates, this new philosophy is destined indeed not only to change the life style and culture of the younger generation, but to bring about a much-needed revolution in the political structure and social thought of our country.*

### Developing One's Philosophy

Here the question everyone must face is a question of holding a vague, inconsistent, half-conscious, blindly accepted, and probably foolish philosophy, or building one that is based upon the best available information about ourselves and our world. Gradually, unconsciously, but surely, we all absorb from home, from friends and associates in school and college, from the texture of life itself, those attitudes and convictions that provide the framework of our own working philosophy of living. These values shape our view of life as naturally and inevitably as the things we have to eat and wear shape our preferences for food and clothing. Even though television may well be creating a "global village," to use Marshall McLuhan's expressive phrase, a person who lives in Mississippi will still, as a rule, have a sense of values different from that of a person who has grown up in New York City. A young American and a young Chinese can no more be expected to have the same definition of democracy than the same tastes in food and drink.

It is of such deeply rooted, unreasoned convictions and values as these that our working philosophy consists, even as we begin to examine life more thoughtfully and objectively for ourselves. Indeed, the very process by which we conduct a more mature self-examination is itself shaped by these underlying convictions of ours. There is no such thing as complete objectivity in philosophy.

Moreover, one can always understand an important issue more easily and deal with it more effectively when his own interests and emotions are not deeply involved. Thus, as Americans it was not difficult for us after the Second World War to see that the French were quite out of touch with the realities of a new day in their policies in Southeast Asia. Even after almost ten years of destruction and futile warfare, however, we did not see nearly so clearly how true this was of our own policy in Vietnam. We may be able to deal much more intelligently, therefore, with the conflicting philosophies that are proposed today if we first examine much these same philosophies in situations comparable to but not our own.

---

* Thus in *The Greening of American* Charles Reich writes: "There is a revolution coming. It will not be like revolutions of the past. It will originate with the individual and with culture, and it will change the political structure only as its final act. It will not require violence to succeed, and it cannot be successfully resisted by violence. . . . It promises a higher reason, a more human community, and a new and liberated individual. Its ultimate creation will be a new and enduring wholeness and beauty—a renewed relationship of man to himself, to other men, to society, to nature and to the land. This is the revolution of the new generation. . . . It is both necessary and inevitable, and in time it will include not only youth but all people in America." (p. 2)

Without question, then, the history of philosophy can help illuminate our present search for the best that life has to offer. Does the new naturalism provide a college student with the most desirable and satisfying philosophy in today's world? Or are there other alternatives that a person should consider carefully before allowing his views to be shaped by current attitudes? An acquaintance with the thought of the great philosophers should make it possible for us to be more intelligent and more explicit about what we seek and value today. We can learn much from what the great minds of the past have believed about the nature of man and of the world in which he must work out his destiny. Available also are valuable insights concerning what goes to make up the good life and the good society.

Truth, of course, does not come to us from the authority of the past. It can be reached only through a searching examination and testing of various alternatives, which must be a continuous contemporary concern. But this is not an undertaking we can carry on successfully in ignorance of the insights that constitute our intellectual heritage. Let us not forget at the outset, however, that it is with our own personal philosophy that we are primarily concerned. Unless this is the case, we are not dealing realistically with philosophy but are engaged at best in historical reflection. Yet until we do broaden our understanding and sharpen our insight, what we like to call "thinking" may well be merely a matter of reshuffling old or new prejudices.


## Invitation to Philosophy
### The Sophists

Not without good reason has consideration of the meaning and spirit of philosophy traditionally begun with the Greeks. Throughout much of the ancient Greek world, but especially in Athens during the fifth century B.C., there were social and intellectual tendencies at work much like those in our own age, which made philosophical inquiry and reflection almost inevitable. By 450 B.C. the old economic and political order in Athens was falling to pieces; the privileges of the established aristocracy were being sharply challenged by a rising democratic movement; the traditional religious mythology and worship of the Olympian deities no longer exercised authority over the minds of the more thoughtful.

For a generation Pericles, one of the great figures of ancient history, dominated the government of the city and became the generous patron of literature, philosophy, and the arts. From all parts of the Mediterranean world, men were attracted to Athens by its growing cultural and economic opportunities. Periclean Athens may be likened perhaps to the Paris of a generation or two ago. Both cities were centers to which the brilliant and aspiring young men of the age were drawn and in which there developed an atmosphere particularly stimulating to creative thought and endeavor.

Numerous men of superior insight and ability are to be found among the Athenians in the Age of Pericles. But no one so well exemplified the spirit of philosophy as did Socrates, and none raised in so provocative a fashion as did the Sophists the problems that confront every student of philosophy. These men asked the same questions about life, about morals, and about religion that we are now asking, and surprisingly enough we find them suggesting answers that have been proposed by many today as the last word in modernity. It is revealing to see that these problems are not new but perennial. It is instructive to examine the situations that produced such views of life, as well as the difficulties to which they led. Indeed, a more tempting invitation to the study of philosophy can hardly be imagined than that provided in the thought of the Sophists and Socrates.

### The Sophists

The earlier philosophers of Greece, able men such as Pythagoras, Parmenides, and Heraclitus, lived during the century before the age of Socrates and the Sophists. These philosophers were concerned largely with the nature of the physical universe. The forces at work in the world about them, and the principles by which the universe was governed, held their attention and stirred them to philosophical reflection. But by the middle of the fifth century b.c. the concern of Greek philosophy had shifted from such broadly scientific speculation to an interest in morals and politics. Especially was this true in Athens. Among the able foreigners drawn to that city were many wandering teachers, known simply as "men of wisdom" (*Sophists*), who focused attention with a new directness and clarity upon the enduring issues of human life.

These Sophists did not form a closely knit school. They came and went as individuals, attracted to Athens from Asia Minor and Italy by the greater freedom and opportunity of the Athenian society. As a group, however, they did have much in common. They were interested not in speculation about the physical universe but in the practical problems of successful living. Their major conviction might well be stated in the words of Alexander Pope: "The proper study of mankind is man." Wisdom as they saw it did not mean abstract scientific knowledge; it meant an understanding of human beings and of the skills necessary to get along successfully in one's relationships with his fellow men. At their best the Sophists were widely traveled, observant, and discerning. They brought to Athens a new appreciation of the culture of other lands and stimulated among the Athenian youth a greater interest in philosophical thought, in law, and in social institutions.

Only the sons of the wealthier families could afford the high fees charged by the more able Sophists, but to such young Athenians these Sophists had much to offer. In the growth of democracy in Athens, as in our own country, one can see "a long and bitter struggle by the poor, on the one hand, to bleed the rich either by force or by law, and, on the other, by the rich to resist by force or law such bleeding," writes B. A. G. Fuller in his very readable *History of Greek Philosophy*. In these circumstances, "a young man who wanted to get on and make a success of his career need not be over-scrupulous about right and wrong, truth and falsehood, or even common sense and hard facts. All that he needed was a bit of blarney and a flair for playing upon the weak spots in his audience. Votes were to be caught and influence obtained in the Assembly, not by a display of sound statesmanship, but by the clever use of catch phrases and oratorical appeals to passion and prejudice."[5]

For the price of admission to their classes, the Sophists would teach their pupils how to accomplish any end, no matter what its nature. In the eyes of the masses, therefore, they soon began to appear as champions of the privileged classes. To use an analogy from our own society, they might well be likened to great corporation lawyers or political lobbyists, whose cleverness enables the wealthy always to win their cases in the courts or to get desired legislation passed. When Plato, a generation later, portrayed the Sophists in his dialogues, this seems to have become the popular estimate of their character and aim, and Plato's account of them has made it the generally accepted position ever since. Such an estimate, however, fails to do justice to the critical insight and the stimulus to philosophical thought provided by the earlier and abler representatives of the movement, especially by such men as Protagoras, Hippias, and Gorgias.

### Moral Relativism

Protagoras (481–411 B.C.), unquestionably the greatest of the Sophists, early gained fame as a teacher in Asia Minor. Drawn to Athens around the middle of the fifth century B.C., he became a friend of Pericles and a noted figure in the intellectual life of the city. Influential connections and high fees enabled him to gain wealth as well as fame, and he exerted great influence upon the thought of the day. One of Plato's dialogues, known as *Protagoras*, is in itself a tribute to the influence of the "Great Sophist."

Protagoras traveled widely and became familiar with the customs of many lands and people. An acute observer, he noted that although a great variety of moral and religious beliefs existed, the people in each country unquestioningly accepted their own practices and standards as right, and condemned those views that differed from their own. Such observation led him to philosophy: What makes a thing good and what bad? Is there, then, anything that is really right or wrong? What do we mean when we say that a belief is true? These were the questions Protagoras asked, and his answers sound surprisingly contemporary. In examining the institutions and customs of his age, he seems, indeed, to have anticipated the attitude of the modern sociologist. Morals, he concludes, are but the social traditions, the *mores* of the group. All moral standards are relative. What is right for the Egyptian is right simply because it enables him to live well in that civilization. It need not be right for the Greek. What is good for the Athenian is good because it works well in Athens. The task of the scientific observer is to describe what he finds, and Protagoras reports that he can discover no universal moral principles.

Are some things, then, always right and others always wrong? Is there an enduring moral ideal that is everywhere valid and desirable, whether one be a Greek or an Egyptian, a Russian or an American, a resident of New York or of Tennessee? To such questions Protagoras finds himself compelled to give a negative answer. His *moral relativism* is implied in the famous dictum: "Man is the measure of all things, of things that are that they are, and of things that are not that they are not." All our standards, he finds, are relative; they depend upon one's situation and training. We cannot get beyond our own experience and social environment. The real measure of right and wrong, of good or evil, is actually the extent to which our interests and desires are furthered or hindered. A thing is good if it works. If it works well for the individual in the social group to which he belongs, there is no other criterion, moral or religious, by which it can legitimately be judged. Thus Protagoras reveals himself as an early pragmatist.* In somewhat the spirit of William James (1842–1910), noted American philosopher and exponent of modern pragmatism, Protagoras accepts *the good as the expedient in the way of conduct and the true as the expedient in the way of belief.*

In such moral relativism there are obvious dangers to orthodox morality and religious belief. But in his own practical philosophy of living Protagoras is a conservative. If all moral standards are relative and not absolute, how should one live? The intelligent thing to do, Protagoras maintains, is to accept the customs and beliefs of your own community and live in harmony with them. Recognize that these practices are right and good only insofar as they enable you to get the things that you want. But recognize also that open flouting of the accepted standards of the day will simply bring you strife and unhappiness. The wise man when in Rome will do as the Romans do and so promote his own happiness and success in life, which, Protagoras concludes, is the only thing that really matters.

Somewhat to his own sorrow, Protagoras does not seem to have followed this philosophy consistently. According to a tradition, not too well authenticated, one night at the home of a friend he read an essay of his entitled *On The Gods,* in which the relativism that he accepted in the field of morals was applied also to religious faith. An army officer among the guests was scandalized at this procedure and had Protagoras indicted for impiety. The

---

* F. C. S. Schiller, in *Studies in Humanism,* Part II, provides a vigorous defense of the Sophists, and especially of Protagoras, who is taken to be the first great humanist among the Greek philosophers. There is in his thought "a depth of moral insight with which nothing else in the orthodox Greek ethic can at all compare," Schiller writes (p. 36).

authorities found the philosopher guilty of the charge, confiscated and burned all the copies of his essay they could lay their hands on, and were about to seize Protagoras himself. Confronted with the choice of death or exile, he managed (about 411 B.C.) to make his escape by way of a boat bound for Sicily. But the ship was wrecked on the voyage and Protagoras was drowned. His fate, as here portrayed, does confirm the practical wisdom of the more cautious policy that the philosopher himself had earlier advocated.

### Moral Skepticism

A younger generation is almost always impatient with what appears, in its eyes at least, to be the conservatism of its elders. It was not long, therefore, before the philosophy of Protagoras produced more radical results in the ideas of two younger Sophists, Gorgias and Thrasymachus. With devastating logic the relativism of Protagoras was in their hands developed into a thoroughgoing and politically disturbing skepticism.

A native of Leontini in Sicily, Gorgias is depicted by tradition as a silver-tongued orator, more distinguished perhaps for brilliance and subtlety as a speaker than for profound insight, but able to attract disciples in abundance and to command generous fees. In 427 B.C. he was sent to Athens to seek assistance for his native city in its struggle with Syracuse. His eloquence at once won him fame, and the desired aid was soon dispatched to Leontini. It was, as it happened, greatly to the interest of Athens to curtail the growing power of Syracuse, a fact that undoubtedly served to reinforce Gorgias' persuasiveness. In any event Athenian society made such an impression upon the visitor from Sicily that he almost forgot the plight of his home town. He decided to stay, for the time being at least, in Greece, and there he spent most of the remaining years of his life, delivering the speeches that made him famous and teaching the new Sicilian style of logic and rhetoric with marked success. In his old age he retired to Thessaly, where he is reputed to have lived to be nearly one hundred years old.

In what has come down to us (a rather technical discussion of the issues raised by Protagoras), Gorgias is said to have advanced three justly famous propositions that throw into sharp focus the implications of Protagoras' moral relativism. Later Sophists did not hesitate to point out their meaning in concrete and disturbing fashion.* In his first proposition Gorgias makes it

---

* See, for example, the views of Callicles as described by Plato in *Gorgias*. There is some difference of opinion among scholars concerning Gorgias' philosophy. An attempt is made here to present the skeptical spirit later associated with his teaching. The three propositions advanced in his essay *On Being*, or *Nature*, of which a fragment has been preserved, are as follows: I. Nothing exists. II. If anything exists, it is incomprehensible. III. If it is comprehensible, it is incommunicable. (See also K. Freeman, *The Pre-Socratic Philosophers*, pp. 359–361.)

clear that if one accepts the relativism of Protagoras there actually is no such thing as right or wrong. If a course of action were really right, then it ought always and everywhere to be followed. If we do things merely because of social convention or to further our own ends, then such acts are not right but only expedient. As soon as one becomes emancipated from the bonds of tradition and custom, he sees with Protagoras that all moral standards are relative and changing. He must then admit, if he is intellectually honest, that "right" and "wrong" have no enduring significance. There is only that which promotes one's own interest and that which obstructs it. To pretend that such is not the case is mere hypocrisy.

Let us suppose for the purpose of argument that there actually is a universal standard of right or truth, Gorgias suggests. According to his second proposition, even if it did exist, we could never know that universal truth. Our thinking as well as our conduct is determined by the circumstances of our own lives, and we have no way of rising above these limitations. Experience is our only teacher, and as our experiences differ, so will our concepts of morality and religion. If we grow up in America, our thought is shaped by the social conventions and religious ideas of this country. If we grow up in Nepal or in Tunisia we naturally absorb the views prevalent there. We are creatures of our environment and our experience, Gorgias maintains. We have no divine faculty of reasoning that enables us to escape such limitations.

Were he alive in our own day, Gorgias would undoubtedly point out that the Chinese and the Russians with their background accept Communism just as naturally as we accept the free-enterprise way of life. The statistics we use to prove superiority of one system convince us only because we believe already. They do not reveal what is right or true universally, but rather they reveal the quality of our own experience. Our arguments will carry as little weight with the Communist who knows only modern China as his argument does with successful businessmen in this country.

But is it not possible that there may be an occasional genius, gifted or intelligent enough to rise above these limitations of circumstance and experience? Perhaps so, Gorgias admits; but in his third proposition he points out that such an individual, if by chance there were one, could never *communicate* this new insight successfully to anyone else. The overwhelming majority of men necessarily accept their own customs and convictions in preference to any new doctrine. They will always be bound by the limits of their own experience and their own age. One who claims a new insight into religion or morality or politics will not be welcomed with open arms or even given an unprejudiced hearing. Rather he will be condemned, even by the best-intentioned people, as a dangerous radical. Neither the fate of Socrates nor that of Christ was then at hand for use as illustration, but from our point of vantage today one finds in Jesus' crucifixion as well as in Socrates' execution rather disturbing confirmation of Gorgias' third proposition.

## Moral Realism

If Protagoras may with some justice be treated as the ablest exponent of pragmatism among the Sophists, then Gorgias as here interpreted is the radical empiricist. A third Sophist, Thrasymachus, takes the matter one step further and shows what such relativism and skepticism lead to when adopted as a practical social philosophy. Noted for his vigorous style in debate and also for his sharp tongue, Thrasymachus was likewise much interested in politics and social philosophy. It is here that his chief interest for us is to be found.

The position adopted by Thrasymachus is portrayed with a good deal of force, if not with too much sympathy, in the first book of Plato's *Republic*. All attempts to find a moral standard equally valid for rich and poor, strong and weak, are here sarcastically rejected by Thrasymachus. He who looks realistically at life sees clearly, according to this Sophist, that only might is right. The interests that prevail in the hard world about us, in politics, in economics, in the relation of race to race, are the interests of the strong. They prevail not because they are right in any universal or absolute sense but because they are powerful. We commonly accept what is legal as right; but the laws of every land turn out, upon examination, to be in the interest of those in power. The rest of us obey the laws not because these laws are right in any absolute sense, Thrasymachus argues, nor even because our best interests are served thereby, but simply because we have to obey. Laws are enforced as well as made by those who have power, and they do both for their own interests.

Should we object to his assertion that might makes right, Thrasymachus could certainly cite many contemporary economic and political developments in defense of his thesis. The right of the British Empire for nearly two centuries in India, for example, he could easily point out, was based solely upon the power of the British to maintain themselves there. This was clear enough to Gandhi, if not to Winston Churchill. Look also, Thrasymachus might say, at what happened in Russia or in China as political power passed into the hands of the commoners there. Prior to the Revolution, the laws in Russia established the privileges of the Czar and the aristocracy. As soon as the other classes became powerful enough, however, new laws were passed to safeguard *their* interests and privileges. Now, to the majority of Russians at least, these present laws are the laws that are right, not the old laws that no longer command the necessary power to be enforced. This is equally true in China; nor would Thrasymachus admit that the situation in our country is basically different. Our own legal system in America, he would insist, clearly reflects the interests of the white middle class, the owners of industry and the investors of capital, who are powerful enough to control the legislatures that pass the laws and the courts that enforce them. If political power in America should pass into the hands of organized labor or of black revolutionary groups, new laws reflecting their interests would surely be enacted. Some of the more conservative among us, indeed, are concerned that this is already taking place to a rather alarming extent.

One does not understand, then, what moral relativism actually involves until he has examined with some care the radical empiricism of Gorgias and the political realism of Thrasymachus to which the doctrines of Protagoras led these later thinkers. Obviously the philosophy of the Sophists was anything but an innocuous pastime; and there is little wonder that the Athenian Establishment was alarmed as these ideas spread rapidly among the youth of that city. At the very least, the Athenian youth were being encouraged to question the accepted moral standards and religious beliefs of their elders, and were becoming unduly critical of all political authority. At worst, the disciples of the Sophists were promoting a self-centered individualism, encouraging each man to seek his own interests without regard to the welfare of his fellows and with no loyalty to any high ethical or religious ideal. An older generation in every age, whether our own today or that of Athens 2,500 years ago, is always disturbed by attitudes of this kind among those who are still young.

Yet the Sophists raised questions that cannot simply be brushed aside— questions, indeed, that go to the very roots of the moral and political confusion of our own age and for which we are still seeking answers today. They began a devastating attack upon the bondage of tradition and custom in every sphere of life, thus providing for us, as for the Athenian youth in the age of Pericles, an almost irresistible impetus to philosophical reflection. Once having gone this far, the inquiring mind cannot easily return to the security of unquestioned beliefs and convictions. Old dogmas in politics, in morality, and in religion no longer satisfy. One is forced to develop a more consistent and carefully reasoned philosophy of living or else be content with the skepticism and individualism advocated by the Sophists.

### Philosophy as the Love of Wisdom
#### Socrates (469–399 B.C.)

Among those young men of Athens who were aroused from dogmatic slumber by the teaching of the Sophists, there was no more picturesque figure than Socrates. With bald head, great round face and protruding eyes, thick lips, and a snub nose, Socrates was anything but handsome. His personal appearance was soon forgotten, however, when one came under the influence of his personality and his conversation. And of conversation there seems to have been no end; it was the main business of life for Socrates. Born an Athenian, the son of a sculptor or stonecutter, Socrates lived his life almost literally in the market place of his native city. His youth was spent in the golden age of Athens, the Age of Pericles; and the pride of the young philosopher in his Athenian citizenship is not surprising nor was it exceptional. His devotion to Athens served as a determining influence in Socrates' life. It gave him an outlook quite different from that of wandering teachers of wisdom such as Protagoras or Gorgias, who came and went through the portals of Athens during Socrates' seventy years of residence there.

Almost any day Socrates' ungainly figure could be seen in the market place of the city. He spent his time discussing the basic problems of morality and politics that the Sophists had raised. In these issues Socrates' interest seems never to have flagged. How he himself lived one can hardly tell. He early abandoned his father's trade for the pursuit of philosophy; but he scorned the practice of the Sophists, who charged ample fees for their teaching. He ate when his friends invited him to join them, and he literally took no thought of the morrow. His concern with philosophical inquiry almost completely replaced his interest in his own material welfare and in that of his family as well. One can well understand the tradition that Socrates was not quite so popular with his wife Xanthippe, who did not find his life style particularly appealing, as with his fellow Athenians.

Drawn by his skill and insight in argument, his boldness in challenging all pretense and in debunking the establishment of his day, and withal by his rare humility of spirit, the youth of Athens flocked about Socrates. All of life's insistent questions were illumined by this master of his craft, who felt so deeply that "the unexamined life is not worthy of a man." But the enthusiasm of Socrates for his philosophical mission stirred up enmity quite as frequently as it made disciples. He insisted upon a critical examination of every belief and fearlessly unmasked ignorance and hypocrisy wherever they existed, even in the outlook of the more prominent public figures among his contemporaries. Few people can bear without malice the public exposure of their own limitations. Instead of being angry with themselves at their shortcomings, these Athenians "are angry with me," Socrates observed. "This confounded Socrates, they say; this villainous misleader of youth!"[6] Yet the subject of this abuse seemed completely unconcerned about the hard feelings he aroused. He went his way, doing what he believed to be right, and his hold upon his disciples was so great that one can hardly disentangle today the simple truth from the work of imagination in the accounts of Socrates that have come down to us.

### The Historical Sources

Plato, the greatest of the group of disciples about Socrates, has made Socrates the hero of his dialogues and by his own artistic genius has undoubtedly complicated the matter still further. In the earlier of these dialogues, such as *Apology*, *Crito*, and *Euthyphro*, there seems good reason to believe that the figure of Socrates is portrayed with a large degree of historical accuracy. In *The Republic* and other later dialogues, on the other hand, Plato seems more and more to have used Socrates as the mouthpiece of his own philosophy, a philosophy true to the spirit of the master perhaps, but the expression in particular of Plato's own mature insight. *Gorgias, Protagoras, Symposium,* and *Phaedo* stand in a somewhat intermediate position, reflecting the outlook of Socrates to some extent no doubt but much of Plato as well.

Xenophon, also a contemporary, has given us, in his *Memorabilia*, a markedly different picture of Socrates. Here we find a man of good intentions, loyal to the commonplaces of prudential morality, and in general something of a bore. One can hardly imagine such a teacher stirring up either intellectual or moral turmoil. If the genius of Plato enhances the charm of Socrates even in the earlier dialogues, it is obvious that limitations in Xenophon's own insight are reflected in the figure of Socrates portrayed in the *Memorabilia*.* On the other hand, Aristophanes' comedy *The Clouds* depicts Socrates as a typical Sophist, proprietor of a "thinking shop," where the respect of youth for their elders was destroyed and a self-centered individualism was made man's one avowed aim in life. And Socrates was actually condemned to death for much the same skeptical and irreligious attitude that characterized the teaching of the Sophists.

Philosophy had already come into disrepute in Athens at the hands of the Sophists, and it is not strange that Socrates, who adopted many of their more effective techniques, was soon classed among them by the general public. Yet, beneath the apparent similarities in their outlook, it is not difficult to see an essential difference between the philosophy of Socrates and that of the Sophists. Aristophanes clearly was writing to amuse—perhaps also by innuendo and caricature to defend the established order of his day. He was not concerned with careful distinctions that seemed irrelevant to his own purposes.

### Socrates and the Sophists

Socrates' critical approach to the conventional outlook of his day did have much in common with that of the Sophists. After a brief and disappointing youthful interest in speculation about the physical universe, he too

---

* For those interested in pursuing this question further, a judicious nontechnical discussion is available in F. M. Cornford's *Before and After Socrates*, pp. 56–64. A much more radical position is taken by Anton-Hermann Chlorest in *Socrates: Man and Myth* (Routledge and Kegan Paul, 1957), who contends that Plato, because of his artistic temperament and creative ability, is probably less true to the historical Socrates than are the other sources.

turned to a determined search for deeper and more lasting satisfactions in human life. He felt as strongly as did the Sophists that no progress could be made in morals, in politics, in understanding the good life, without a searching reexamination of old beliefs and customs.

Most people cannot think clearly simply because they do not know what they are talking about, Socrates insisted. We must begin, then, by defining our terms. This principle is basic to the Socratic philosophy. In the early dialogues of Plato, Socrates is constantly at work pushing his search for an exact, logical definition of terms. Again and again he lures an unwary opponent into suggesting a definition of piety, of courage, of justice. Then by skillful questions he shows the logical inconsistencies in the proposed definition and the need for clearer thinking. So successful, indeed, was he in using this procedure that it came to be known as the Socratic *dialectic*. Socrates believed, as definitely as did the Sophists, that one never discovers what is right or wrong, what is really good or evil, simply by accepting uncritically or following blindly the conventions and traditions of the day. The beginning of wisdom for every individual lies in an intelligent and critical examination of all generally accepted beliefs and attitudes.

His practice of cross-examining others, of forcing them to define their terms more precisely and by this method revealing their ignorance or incompetence, Socrates justifies by an interesting device. The oracle at Delphi had told his friend Chaerephon that no one in Athens was wiser than Socrates, so Plato has him declare in the *Apology*. Certain that the oracle must have made a mistake, Socrates set out to discover someone wiser than himself. But talking with one man after another, he found that all of them, even those most renowned for their wisdom, were dealing only in words. A little skillful questioning quickly revealed their complete lack of understanding of those basic concerns that so interested Socrates. Whereas all the others supposed themselves to be wise, however, he alone realized his own ignorance. Where they were complacent in their acceptance of superficiality and pretense, he at least recognized that he did not know. The oracle, then, was right after all in pronouncing him the wisest of men. "The truth is, O men of Athens, that God only is wise," Socrates concluded; "and by his answer he intends to show that the wisdom of men is worth little or nothing. He is not speaking of Socrates; he is only using my name by way of illustration, as if he said, He, O men, is the wisest, who like Socrates knows that his wisdom is in truth worth nothing."[7]

Thus the first step in building a sound philosophy of living, Socrates maintained (in agreement with many of the more discontent of our age), lies in getting rid of the confused mass of social convention and opinion that passes for knowledge—that is, in a critical reexamination of all accepted habits of thought and conduct. But beyond this point the Socrates of the early dialogues does not go. Rather he continues time after time to insist in tantalizing fashion upon his own ignorance. Just when he has shown beyond further question the confusion and contradiction in a conventional idea of piety, or courage, or goodness, and one awaits with interest his own convincing account of what is true or right, the dialogue abruptly ends.

It may have been that Socrates' insistence upon his own ignorance was genuine—that at all costs he wished to avoid unwarranted dogmatism or unsound generalization in his own philosophy of living. It is quite possible, however, that he had very definite convictions of his own, which he refrained from stating for pedagogical reasons. It is a poor teacher, as Socrates so ably demonstrates, who does all the thinking for his pupils. The first condition of genuine understanding is the effort to do one's own thinking, to depend no longer upon someone else to provide the "right answers." Socrates' insistence upon his own ignorance and his continued refusal to define basic moral principles may in large measure be seen, then, as an effective device for forcing his followers to think for themselves rather than merely to depend upon him for a ready-made philosophy. Small wonder that he stands among the great teachers of all time.

In one sense, Socrates may perhaps justly be called an agnostic. Time after time he professed himself ignorant as to what constituted the right course of action, the specific truth. He insisted that his own claim to wisdom lay only in the fact that he had the good sense and intellectual integrity to admit that he did not know all the answers. This moral agnosticism, however, whether genuine or consciously adopted, was far different from the moral relativism and skepticism of the Sophists. For no philosopher has ever been more convinced than was Socrates that there is a valid standard of right and wrong, of good and evil, and that knowledge of what is right and good is attainable. Deep down in every mind, covered by a litter of superficial opinion or ignorant prejudice, there are, according to Socrates, moral standards to which all men agree or can be led to agree. As he went about uncovering prejudice, questioning old conventions, stimulating men to think for themselves, his purpose was not to destroy moral conviction. Rather it was to provide what seemed to him the sound rational basis upon which alone moral certainty and true religion were possible. If in method Socrates seemed akin to the Sophists, in purpose and in underlying principle his philosophy of living was directly opposed to theirs.

Right and wrong, good and evil, truth and error seem relative and dependent upon social convention only because we do not stop to examine our ideas carefully, analyze our facts, and then define clearly what we have in mind, Socrates was convinced. It is the task of philosophy to help us recognize the superficial and unessential, discard what is only relative or merely individual, and commit ourselves unreservedly to those enduring principles that the human mind alone can discover. Knowledge, then, is the key to virtue. And virtue is impossible without understanding.

*Knowledge Is Virtue*

Of all the doctrines that go back to Socrates, the belief that knowledge and virtue are essentially related is perhaps the most characteristic. In the more trying periods of civilization, courage is the virtue men admire. This was the case in ancient Rome, and we ourselves are again living through an age in which courage at times seems of paramount importance. An industrial and technological society, on the other hand, has too frequently been willing to accept acquisitiveness as its cardinal virtue. For virtue, when properly understood, is simply *that trait of character upon which the achievement of the good life depends*. Now, as seen by Socrates, it is upon knowledge more than anything else that the good life depends. Only the man who knows what he is doing can do what is right. Morality consists not in a thoughtless or blind obedience to conventional standards but in the intelligent direction of life. Those who blindly follow their passions and instincts are living little better than animals; only he who lives intelligently is living as a man. "The unexamined life," Socrates kept insisting in one situation after another, "is not worthy of a man."

If virtue and knowledge are to be identified, so also are sin and ignorance. Every man naturally seeks his own good, Socrates points out, and does what he believes to be to his own advantage. We may think that we often do what we know to be wrong, but actually no one voluntarily acts in a way he considers to be against his own best interest. He does wrong because he is ignorant, because he does not *know* what the consequences of his conduct will be. No youth embarks upon his first petty robbery with the clear precognition that it will lead ultimately to a life of crime or a prison sentence. Instead, where others have failed or been caught, he believes that he can beat the game. No one tries LSD or heroin for the first time, knowing that in the long run the drug will undermine his health or ruin his life. Actually it is ignorant expectation that leads him to such action. We recognize clearly that for others the usual consequences of dishonesty and deceit will be disgrace and suffering, but for ourselves we constantly make exceptions. We lull ourselves into a fatal self-deception by believing that things will be different for us: that just this once, in these circumstances, we can get away with it. What we call sin, then, is for Socrates actually ignorance. One cannot really *know* the good, which means understanding clearly why it is good, and then prefer the evil, he insists.

It is the intelligent, then, not the naive and unsophisticated, who seek to do what is right. Morals, when correctly understood, are not undesirable restraints imposed upon us by some external authority but are principles of conduct designed to enable us to achieve the greatest satisfaction human life can afford. As Socrates points out, *the good is actually that which men will want to do, if only they know what they are doing.*

"KNOW THYSELF," the motto inscribed over the temple of Apollo at Delphi, Socrates adopted as the cornerstone of his philosophy and sought to make the guiding principle of his life. No sound philosophy of living is possible, he insists, until we examine critically the underlying attitudes and beliefs by which our own conduct is shaped. No man can hope to attain wisdom until he has come to see clearly how superficial, ignorant, and prejudiced most of his thinking really is. Dependable self-knowledge is impossible without first getting rid of the sham and hypocrisy that, for most of us, serve as a barrier against any honest searching of the soul or any deep insight into human nature.

### The Philosopher's Mission

The role of the philosopher as Socrates interprets it is not merely to help the individual lead an intelligent and satisfying life. In accord with the Greek view of his day, Socrates conceived of man as essentially social. For him, as for his Athenian contemporaries, personal and social morality were but aspects of one larger whole. To live as a human being a man must be part of a larger community; he must live as a citizen of the state. Yet, as Socrates looked around him at the Athenian democracy of the day, he observed that nowhere were his fellow citizens more ignorant, more uncritical, more bound by outmoded tradition and custom than in politics. Time after time men gained important office in the state and exercised authority over the lives of others with no better qualification than a desire for power and prestige or an ability to flatter the multitude.

Socrates concluded, therefore, that the primary mission of the philosopher is a social one. It is his task to help build a better society. With this mission in mind he depicted himself as the "gadfly of the State," constantly engaged in stinging the sluggish public into an awareness of the issues before it, much as the horsefly stings a sluggish mare into activity. Socrates' constant questioning of the leaders in public life was not designed simply to reveal their ignorance or to secure prestige for himself. It was, rather, his way of forcing upon his fellow citizens a more thorough consideration of the basic issues of public morality—of justice, of patriotism, of good government. This task he considered his chief duty as an Athenian. It was, moreover, for Socrates fundamentally a religious as well as a political mission. When, as a result of his insistent criticism of conventional ideas and practices, Socrates was facing death, he made this comment to his fellow Athenians: "Know that this is the command of God; and I believe that no greater good has ever happened in the State than my service to the God. For I do nothing but go about persuading you all, old and young alike, not to take thought for your persons or your properties, but first and chiefly to care about the greatest improvement of the soul."

Even at this critical moment, moreover, it was not his own life in which Socrates was primarily interested but rather the welfare of the community as a whole. "And now, Athenians, I am not going to argue for my own sake, as you may think, but for yours," he declared. "For if you kill me you will not easily find a successor to me, who, if I may use such a ludicrous figure of speech, am a sort of gadfly, given to the State by God, and all day long and in all places, I am always fastening upon you, arousing and persuading and reproaching you. You will not easily find another like me, and therefore I would advise you to spare me."[8] In our day the philosopher has perhaps too readily turned over to the newspaper columnist or the television commentator the role played by Socrates in arousing public opinion and shaping the conscience of the community.

### The Philosophy Socrates Lived By

The general character of Socrates' philosophy of living is well indicated in the foregoing account of the meaning and task of philosophy as he saw it. Our clearest insight into his philosophy is found not in what he said but in how he lived, and Plato in the *Apology* has drawn for us a justly famous picture of the way Socrates lived—and died—by the philosophy he accepted.

After the disastrous outcome of the war with Sparta, democratic government was reinstated in Athens in 403 B.C. Its leaders were in no mood to put up with the old philosopher who had stirred up so much unrest, no matter how good his motives may have been. Socrates was brought to trial for his life, accused of corrupting the youth of the city and of disbelief in the gods of the state. A slight compromise with conviction might well have brought him freedom; a refusal to compromise meant martyrdom. The working philosophy by which one's conduct is guided stands out nowhere so dramatically as in a situation such as this. Loyalty to inner conviction, to the voice of an enlightened conscience, no matter what the cost, runs through Socrates' speeches in the *Apology* like a golden thread. In words that are characteristic, he expresses this fact to his fellow Athenians:

> If you say to me, Socrates, this time you shall be let off, but upon one condition, that you are not to inquire and speculate in this way any more, and that if you are caught doing so again you shall die;—if this was the condition on which you let me go, I should reply: Men of Athens, I honor and love you, but I shall obey God rather than you, and while I have life and strength I shall never cease from the practice and teaching of philosophy, exhorting any one whom I meet and saying to him after my manner: You my friend;—a citizen of the great and mighty and wise city

of Athens,—are you not ashamed of heaping up . . . money and honor and reputation, and caring so little about wisdom and truth and the greatest improvement of the soul, which you never regard or heed at all?[9]

Having refused to make any compromise to save his life—indeed, having taken the occasion of his trial not for pleas of mercy but instead for a vigorous reaffirmation of the philosophy by which he had lived for some seventy years—Socrates was condemned to death by the Athenian jury. To those on the jury who had voted for his acquittal, he spoke these final words: "The difficulty, my friends, is not to avoid death but to avoid unrighteousness . . . Wherefore, O judges, be of good cheer about death, and know of a certainty that no evil can happen to a good man either in life or after death." Here indeed is the cardinal conviction in accord with which life was lived and death unflinchingly faced by Socrates: *Know of a certainty that no evil can happen to a good man either in life or after death.*

Socrates' unswerving loyalty to what he believed to be right was based upon his faith that there is a moral order in the universe by which man's destiny both here and hereafter is determined. This was not a view of life that he undertook to demonstrate by rational argument. It was an enduring faith that gave his life nobility and great influence, and made him the exemplar without parallel of the spirit of philosophy at its best, of philosophy as a way of living in accord with the dictates of wisdom. It is here, moreover, that Socrates' most convincing answer to the moral relativism and skepticism of the Sophists is to be found, an answer whose deeper implications he left to be worked out by the long line of philosophers who followed him, from Plato and Aristotle to Spinoza and Kant.

### The Death of Socrates (399 B.C.)

Each year the Athenians sent a ship to the festival of Apollo at Delos, and during its absence the city was not to be polluted by the execution of any who might be under sentence of death. This ship had been made ready for departure on the day before Socrates' trial, so the death penalty imposed upon him was not carried out until its return thirty days later. During the month, Socrates might easily have escaped from prison. He was strongly urged to do so by a group of his friends, led by Crito, who had already made the necessary arrangements with his jailer.* But Socrates refused to accept their offers of help. If laws are necessary for the welfare of citizens of the state, then the law ought to be obeyed just as surely when it is to a man's disadvantage as when it is advantageous, he maintained.

At length the ship returned from Delos, and the next morning Socrates' friends came early to the prison, knowing that he soon must die. That last

---

* Plato makes this episode in Socrates' life the central feature of his dialogue *Crito*.

day has been portrayed in unforgettable fashion by Plato. Socrates spent it discoursing with his companions on the immortality of the soul, urging them to be of good cheer, since no man who had adorned his soul "in her own proper jewels, which are temperance, and justice, and courage, and nobility, and truth," had anything to fear from death. Having said farewell to his wife and children earlier in the day, he bathed as sunset drew near and when the hemlock was brought him, he drank it without hesitation. Phaedo, one of the small group with Socrates to the end, then says:

> Hitherto most of us had been able to control our sorrow; but now when we saw him drinking, and saw, too, that he had finished the draught, we could no longer forbear, and in spite of myself my own tears were flowing fast, so I covered my face and wept over myself; for certainly I was not weeping over him, but at the thought of my own calamity in having lost such a companion. Nor was I the first, for Crito, when he found himself unable to restrain his tears, had got up and moved away, and I followed; and at that moment Apollodorous, who had been weeping all the time, broke into a loud cry which made cowards of us all.
>
> Socrates alone retained his calmness. What is this strange outcry, he said. I sent away the women mainly in order that they might not offend in this way, for I have heard that a man should die in peace. Be quiet, then, and have patience. When we heard that, we were ashamed and refrained from our tears.[10]

Gradually the poison took effect. Socrates remained unmoved, but death was not long in coming. "Such was the end of our friend," Phaedo concludes, "whom I may truly call the wisest, the justest, and best of men whom I have ever known."

### The Enduring Quest

No single figure in the field of philosophy has been so creative and so provocative as Socrates. As well put by Sir Francis Cornford, "Socrates was one of that small number of adventurers who, from time to time, have enlarged the horizon of the human spirit."[11] Despite the fact that he wrote nothing, he left upon the minds of those who heard him and who associated with him daily in the market place of Athens an indelible impression. Almost every new direction taken by philosophy during the century that followed his death drew its inspiration from him, and the exponents of each new point of view claimed him as their spiritual father.

Among the young men of his own day attracted to Athens by the fame of Socrates, Aristippus of Cyrene became a confirmed hedonist and advocated the pursuit of pleasure as the only acceptable philosophy of living. But in so doing he considered himself still Socrates' disciple. In the life style of the master, in Socrates' willingness to enjoy the ordinary pleasures of life and his spontaneous gaiety and lack of moral snobbery, Aristippus found the inspiration for his own hedonistic philosophy. On the other hand, Antisthenes, also a well-known member of the group associated with Socrates, was so impressed by the master's careless poverty and unconcern for the things of this world that he almost made a religion of it. The Cynic school, which Antisthenes founded, openly defied the social and moral conventions of the day in an uncompromising effort to follow the way of nature that the Cynics took to be the heart of Socrates' philosophy.

It is Plato, however, who is generally regarded as the greatest of those drawn to philosophy by the life and the teaching of Socrates. In his most influential work, *The Republic*, Plato undertakes to make clear what the quest of the good life involves when one is completely loyal to the insights of reason. And for Plato this exposition is a direct outgrowth of what he took to be the major concern of Socrates—so much so, as a matter of fact, that scholars still debate about how much in Plato's dialogues is his own and how much represents reliable accounts of what Socrates actually did and said.

In such fashion as this, then, the creative spirit of Socrates gave early impetus to that enduring quest for a satisfying meaning and purpose in human life which is still of paramount importance in our time. As we seek, in an age that has seemingly freed itself almost completely from the inhibitions of the past, to build for ourselves a philosophy of living that is intellectually tenable as well as sufficient for the deeper needs of the human spirit, we find ourselves confronted with the same questions that Socrates raised so provocatively with his disciples. Is the pursuit of pleasure the sure and direct way to happiness? Or are the hedonists who take this position deceived by passion and emotion? Does the life of reason afford the human spirit permanent satisfaction? Or is reason in itself incapable of providing the full realization of our human capacities? Are there in the very nature of things enduring ideals and values to which man must devote his life, if he is true to the best he knows? Or are we confronted with a universe that is indifferent or even hostile to all that we hold most worthwhile in human life?

These are questions that the disciples of Socrates debated in Athens. They are the questions with which the great philosophers of the ages are concerned. And they are questions for which we ourselves still seek satisfying answers.

# One
## THE PURSUIT OF PLEASURE

The end or purpose of life is simply the true enjoyment of it. This seems so simple simply because it is so.

LIN YUTANG

A Book of Verses underneath the Bough,
A Jug of Wine, a Loaf of Bread—and Thou
    Beside me, singing in the Wilderness—
Ah, Wilderness were Paradise enow!

OMAR KHAYYAM

Nature has placed man under the governance of two sovereign masters, *pain* and *pleasure*. It is for them alone to point out what we ought to do, as well as to determine what we shall do.

JEREMY BENTHAM

CHAPTER **2**

# Popular Hedonism

---

## *The Cyrenaics, Epicurus, and Lin Yutang*

Ours is an age in which men and women desperately want to be happy. There has never been a time in this country when the enjoyment of life has been more generally and more openly seen as its central aim and purpose. The philosophy attributed to the younger generation today, as interpreted for example in *The Greening of America*, is a doctrine of present happiness: "listen to music, dance, seek out nature, laugh, be happy, be beautiful . . . live fully in each moment, love and cherish each other,"—these are the important things.[1] It is worth remembering, however, that in the United States we have always accepted happiness as a basic aspect of our way of life. Life, liberty, and the pursuit of happiness were God-given rights for those founding fathers who in 1776 formulated our Declaration of Independence and stated there the principles upon which the new American nation was to be established. Now for the first time perhaps in man's history people do have at their disposal the economic means and the leisure to enjoy the best that human life on this planet has to offer. There is ample evidence that in large number Americans today are seeking to take advantage of the opportunity.

An understanding of what makes us happy is something that everyone initially takes for granted. We may recognize our lack of knowledge in the field of modern science, may even admit to poor taste in art or literature and to very limited ethical insight, but most of us have no doubt about our ability to achieve happiness if we but had the necessary means to do so. Only when life confronts us with frustrations that seem inescapable do we begin to realize our need for greater understanding. Actually, happiness is as puzzling as truth, as subtle as beauty, and quite as difficult to attain as virtue. It has been the concern of the ablest philosophers over the centuries; and of none more directly than those known as hedonists.

The happy life, so the hedonists maintain, is one marked by the enjoyment of the greatest amount of pleasure and marred by the least pain, and *hedonism is the philosophy that accepts the pursuit of pleasure as the chief and enduring concern of human life*. (The term itself is derived from the Greek word for pleasure, *hedoné*). Most of the virtues in the catalog of morals men must learn to desire, or discipline themselves to attain, but pleasure is desired by all men naturally and without reflection. Indeed it seems the normal and instinctive good established by nature for mankind. The real problem, the hedonists insist, is not to decide what constitutes the good life. This we all know well enough: it is the life that affords us maximum enjoyment. What we need to know is how to obtain the greatest pleasure and how to avoid the pain that seems woven into the very fabric of living, no matter where or in what circumstances our lot is cast. This the philosopher must help us determine, if he is to be of genuine assistance.

As hedonism is the natural philosophy of the ordinary, unsophisticated man and woman, so also it should be the view of life accepted by the philosopher if he is true to the facts of experience. But where the pursuit of pleasure by the majority of mankind is thoughtless, inconsistent, and frequently self-defeating, that of the philosopher should be intelligent, well planned, and sure of success. So at least those argue who accept a hedonistic philosophy; and able advocates of its major tenets are to be found in every age and culture. We shall do well, therefore, to examine carefully its sources of strength and appeal, as well as any serious limitations it may contain.

## Aristippus and the Cyrenaic Philosophy

To Aristippus, a wandering Sophist of Cyrene (ca. 430–350 B.C.), we owe perhaps the earliest and the most forthright statement of hedonism. His philosophy reflects clearly the circumstances and the personality of its author. The town of Cyrene, founded on the coast of Africa by Greek colonists, lay on the edge of a plateau about ten miles from the Mediterranean. Screened from the hot sands of the desert by high mountains but open to the mild sea breezes, this territory abounded in all sorts of flowers and fruits. At the time of Aristippus' birth, Cyrene had grown into a rich and splendid city. The gleaming marble of its temples, the stately buildings and colonnades of its Acropolis, rivaled those in Athens. A prosperous Mediterranean trade brought wealth in abundance into the coffers of the city, and its strategic location enabled it to enjoy comparative peace and security.

Aristippus had all the advantages that circumstances such as these afford. A genial and clever youth, he was fond of worldly pleasures but was also intelligent and resourceful and seems to have gotten along well with people of all sorts. If chance had not brought him under the charm of Socrates and thus led him to philosophy, he might easily have distinguished himself in politics or achieved prestige in the social life of the day.

During a visit to the Olympic games, however, Aristippus heard from a friend a glowing description of Socrates. He was so intrigued that he could scarcely wait to get to Athens and meet this stimulating and interesting person. He was soon numbered among Socrates' most active followers, a member of the little circle of intimate companions drawn together about the master. He seems to have done some teaching on his own during this period, for which he is reputed to have charged fees, as the Sophists did, thus antagonizing his comrades. Not long after the death of Socrates, Aristippus also adopted the typical mode of life of the Sophists, traveling from place to place, teaching as he went and collecting high fees from his pupils. Coming back in time to Cyrene and falling under the seductive appeal of his native city, however, he decided to remain and establish there a school of philosophy. The hedonism he expounded has taken its name from the city in which he lived and taught.

### The Cyrenaic View of Life

It is not easy at first to recognize the influence of Socrates in the direct and uncompromising pursuit of pleasure that Aristippus advocates. One sees more clearly, perhaps, a reflection of the ease and luxury of Cyrene or of the early life that Aristippus himself had lived as a man of the world who liked to enjoy himself and knew how to do so. But Socrates, despite his independence of mind and depth of conviction, enjoyed life thoroughly. He dined and wined gladly with his friends and, as depicted in Plato's *Symposium*, discoursed on love with as much insight and ardor as any of his contemporaries. Upon this enthusiasm of Socrates for the simple joy of living, his lack of any pretense or snobbery, his careless gaiety, Aristippus seized as the key to happiness and to philosophy. Socrates was a living example of how to be happy though good. His serenity and content were won not by shunning pleasures but by being interested in everything that went on, by finding something enjoyable in whatever happened, by refusing to be over-serious even in the face of death itself.

So, at least, Aristippus reasoned, and he set out to clarify in a way that all could understand these suggestions, vague, tentative, and incomplete, that he found so appealing in the life style adopted by Socrates. Socrates had insisted that the better you are, the better time you are having. Aristippus concludes that the better time you are having, the better you are. It does not take a wise man, reflecting upon the meaning of life, to see that all men, consciously or unconsciously, are seeking pleasure, he points out. The pursuit of pleasure and the avoidance of pain are the two driving forces in the behavior of all creatures. What, then, could be more simple, more normal, more healthy, than to obey this imperative of Nature and frankly seek to enjoy ourselves? Pleasure is our natural goal in life; let us, therefore, have as much and as intense pleasure as we can get.

Since pleasures of the senses are the most intense of all pleasures, they are to be preferred to other types. They alone provide the kind of thrill, the intoxication of spirit, that makes life really enjoyable. For the Cyrenaic, moreover, the pleasures of the moment are more desirable than those that may perhaps be obtained in the future. Of the present alone we are certain. The future may never come (for us at least). Even if it does, it will undoubtedly be quite different from what we now anticipate. If we are wise, however, we will control this pursuit of pleasure, not be controlled by it. "It is not abstinence from pleasures that is best, but mastery over them without ever being worsted," Aristippus is reputed to have said. This principle is undoubtedly among the more significant as well as the more difficult to attain in his philosophy of living.

Unfortunately nothing written by Aristippus has survived. In *Lives and Opinions of Eminent Philosophers*, an early third century A.D. work by Diogenes Laertius, essays by Aristippus are mentioned. Some of these were then in circulation; and various revealing incidents, which portray the hedonism of the philosopher in practice, are also recounted here. The account of Laertius is the earliest description of the philosophy of Aristippus and so is of genuine historical value. But it is meager and disorganized, and by no means a satisfactory treatment. Among contemporary interpretations, the spirit of the Cyrenaic position and the major tenets of the philosophy of Aristippus are especially well portrayed in B. A. G. Fuller's *History of Greek Philosophy*, to which the present discussion is much indebted.

### The Philosophy of the Rubaiyat

Nowhere has Cyrenaic hedonism been expressed with such haunting beauty as in Edward FitzGerald's translation of the *Rubaiyat.* These verses, the work originally of Omar Khayyam, Persian astronomer and poet of the twelfth century, stand among the classic portrayals of life devoted to the pursuit of pleasure. There are moments when the appeal of the *Rubaiyat* is undeniable, although as much of this appeal lies no doubt in the charm of the poetry as in the soundness of its philosophy. In any event, Omar Khayyam as interpreted by FitzGerald clothes the hedonism of Aristippus in its most alluring garb. The Cyrenaic philosopher could ask no better presentation of his view of life.

For the *Rubaiyat*, as for Aristippus, the road to happiness lies in the direct and uninhibited enjoyment of pleasure. Life is short, the future uncertain, and the present itself fast slipping away. Pleasures must be seized while there is yet time; and pleasures of the senses are to be preferred, for in them we find immediate and undeniable satisfaction. He who hesitates has no one to blame but himself. So, at least, the early stanzas of the *Rubaiyat* assure us in imagery that is now quite familiar:

Before the Phantom of False Morning died
Methought a Voice within the Tavern cried,
    "When all the Temple is prepared within,
Why nods the drowsy Worshipper outside?"

Come, fill the Cup, and in the fire of Spring
Your Winter-garment of Repentance fling:
    The Bird of Time has but a little way
To flutter—and the Bird is on the Wing.

A Book of Verses underneath the Bough,
A Jug of Wine, a Loaf of Bread—and Thou
    Beside me singing in the Wilderness—
Oh, Wilderness were Paradise enow!

Some for the Glories of this World; and some
Sigh for the Prophet's Paradise to come.
    Ah, take the Cash, and let the Credit go,
Nor heed the rumble of a distant Drum!

The present world, this hedonist insists, is the only one we can count on. It is in this life that we must find the happiness that so appeals to us, if we are to find it at all. Heaven and Hell are not somewhere in the future, but are qualities of experience here and now.

Oh threats of Hell and Hopes of Paradise!
One thing at least is certain,—*This* life flies;
    One thing is certain and the rest is Lies;
The Flower that once has blown forever dies.

Strange, is it not? that of the myriads who
Before us pass'd the door of Darkness through,
    Not one returns to tell us of the Road,
Which to discover we must travel too.

I sent my Soul through the Invisible,
Some letter of that After-life to spell:
    And by and by my Soul returned to me,
And answer'd, "I Myself am Heav'n and Hell:"

Heav'n but the Vision of fulfill'd Desire,
And Hell the Shadow of a Soul on fire,
    Cast on the Darkness into which Ourselves,
So late emerged from, shall so soon expire.

Not only is life uncertain and fleeting. Our destiny is shaped by a power far greater than our own puny desires and ambitions. Man is only a pawn in the hands of fate. He has no real freedom, and it is futile as well as foolish to strive against the forces that move us on. God, if god there be, is not troubled by human hopes and fears.

> We are no other than a moving row
> Of Magic Shadow-shapes that come and go
>     Round with this Sun-illumined Lantern held
> In Midnight by the Master of the Show;
>
> Impotent Pieces of the Game He plays
> Upon this Chequer-board of Nights and Days;
>     Hither and thither moves, and checks, and slays.
> And one by one back in the Closet lays.
>
> The Ball no question makes of Ayes and Noes
> But Here or There as strikes the Player goes;
>     And He that toss'd you down into the Field,
> *He* knows about it all—HE knows—HE knows!
>
> The Moving Finger writes; and, having writ,
> Moves on: nor all your Piety nor Wit
>     Shall lure it back to cancel half a Line,
> Nor all your Tears wash out a Word of it.

In such a world there can be no such thing as moral responsibility. The things man does, he has to do. The God who created him as he is can certainly not blame man for enjoying the pleasures that by nature he is led to desire. Such a doctrine would be unthinkable!

> What! out of senseless Nothing to provoke
> A conscious Something to resent the yoke
>     Of unpermitted Pleasure, under pain
> Of Everlasting Penalties, if broke!
>
> What! from his helpless Creature be repaid
> Pure Gold for what he lent him dross-allay'd—
>     Sue for a Debt he never did contract,
> And cannot answer—Oh the sorry trade!
>
> Oh Thou, who didst with pitfall and with gin
> Beset the Road I was to wander in,
>     Thou wilt not with Predestined Evil round
> Enmesh, and then impute my Fall to Sin!

As he envisions the culmination of life, however, doubts do seem to trouble even so confirmed and forthright a hedonist as the author of the

*Rubaiyat.* Perhaps, indeed, he has missed what was most worthwhile after all. Or has he? While his repentance never seems entirely sincere, Omar Khayyam is forced to admit that an unrestrained pursuit of pleasure does not completely satisfy the deeper desires of the human heart.

> Indeed the Idols I have loved so long
> Have done my credit in this world much wrong:
>     Have drown'd my Glory in a shallow Cup,
> And sold my Reputation for a Song.
>
> Indeed, Indeed, Repentance oft before
> I swore—but was I sober when I swore?
>     And then and then came Spring, and Rose-in-hand
> My thread-bare Penitence apieces tore.
>
> And much as Wine has play'd the Infidel,
> And robb'd me of my Robe of Honour—Well,
>     I wonder often what the Vintners buy
> One half so precious as the stuff they sell.
>
> Would but some wingéd Angel ere too late
> Arrest the yet unfolded Roll of Fate,
>     And make the stern Recorder otherwise
> Enregister, or quite obliterate!
>
> Ah Love! could you and I with Him conspire
> To grasp this sorry Scheme of Things entire,
>     Would not we shatter it to bits—and then
> Re-mold it nearer to the Heart's Desire!*

* These verses are from the fifth (1889) version of FitzGerald's translation, published after his death.

### The Cyrenaic Spirit in Our Day

One does not have to look far, indeed, to see that the spirit of Aristippus and the *Rubaiyat* does still have an appeal. For many men and women in our age, both young and old, the pleasures of the moment and the pleasures of the senses far outweigh less tangible future satisfactions. Rock music, football games, and marijuana easily make the appeal of mathematics, economics, or philosophy seem to a number of students quite dull by comparison. In drive-in movie theaters and paperback novels, increasing unrestrained portrayals of sexual indulgence make sexual gratification appear the sure as well as the natural way to immediate enjoyment of life. At no time, moreover, is the appeal of the philosophy of Aristippus greater than to a nation involved as ours has been in a long and apparently meaningless war. In such times, for many young men and women the future is quite uncertain, the accepted values of social life are unobtainable, the pleasures of the moment and the pleasures of the senses well-nigh irresistible. Into the strenuous and dangerous life of military service the Cyrenaic attitude has always fitted easily and naturally. Intense and immediate pleasures afforded by wine, women, and song seem too often the one sure compensation for constant hardship, deprivation, and discipline. At times indeed only mood-altering drugs provide a sure escape from the boredom and frustration that civilian as well as military life has produced in recent years. Unquestionably the Cyrenaic philosophy of living has proved attractive to many of the more culturally mobile of the younger generation, as well as to a greater number among their dissatisfied elders.

The most widely known popular expression of such Cyrenaic hedonism in our country today is perhaps the *Playboy* philosophy of Hugh Hefner. It is true that Hefner has at times sought to give his position a significance somewhat broader than the hedonism of Aristippus. A glance at the playmate of the month in *Playboy* magazine, however, or at a few of the quite obvious cartoons included there, is surely enough to indicate an unmistakable Cyrenaic concern with pleasures of the senses and pleasures of the moment in the hedonism portrayed so explicitly in succeeding issues of *Playboy*. Something of the appeal of this philosophy could clearly be seen in the number of Hefner's playmates whose pictures appeared on the walls of male students in college and university dormitories some years ago.*

Disturbing doubts about the adequacy of such unrestrained hedonism assail many today, however, even as they did Omar Khayyam. We are tempted at times to give ourselves without hesitation to the pleasures of the senses, and for the moment to forget the morrow. But unfortunately tomorrow has a way of showing up, despite our desire to forget it. And inevitably one is forced to ask himself whether the dissipation of the night before was worth the headache of the morning after, even on the premise of the hedonist that pleasure is the most important thing that life affords. Indeed, questions such as these proved quite disturbing to Epicurus, one of the ablest of the early exponents of hedonism. The intensity of sensual pleasures is frequently more than counterbalanced by the pain that follows in their wake, Epicurus observed. And instead of remaining the master of his pleasures, the Cyrenaic too easily become their slave. The more prudent hedonism of Epicurus certainly deserves our careful consideration.

*One of the more serious problems raised by the *Playboy* version of hedonism is pointed out by Theodore Roszak in *The Making of a Counter Culture*: "Finally, as a neat little dividend, the ideal of the swinging life we find in *Playboy* gives us a conception of femininity which is indistinguishable from social idiocy. The woman becomes a mere playmate, a submissive bunny, a mindless decoration. At a stroke, half the population is reduced to being the inconsequential entertainment of the technocracy's pampered elite." (p. 15)

## Epicurus and the Epicureans

It is in the teaching of Epicurus (341–270 B.C.), cultured Greek philosopher of the ancient world, rather than in the thought of Aristippus, that hedonism has found its most acceptable statement as a way of life. Born in Samos, a city in Asia Minor where his father had gone as an Athenian colonist about ten years earlier, Epicurus was able to retain his Athenian citizenship. This made him liable for the two-year period of military service expected at that time of all Athenian youth, and in 323 B.C. at the age of eighteen he returned to Athens to complete this required training. As it happened, these were critical and disturbing years in the life of the city. Death had just terminated the career of Alexander the Great, and the Athenians, who had chafed under the domination of the Macedonian emperor, lost no time in organizing an armed revolt against his regent in their city. But in less than a year the patriotic Greek forces were decisively beaten and the young Epicurus was taught a lesson in the futility of political ambition that he never forgot.

As a young man Epicurus studied with leading exponents of the philosophies of Plato and Aristotle, both already well established in his day. He was from the beginning openly critical of the doctrines of the Platonists, however, and later also he broke with the followers of Aristotle. Nowhere does he express any debt to the men with whom he studied during this early period, and later he even refers to himself as self-taught. For such ostensible ingratitude he has often been severely criticized, but, as one of his recent defenders points out, Epicurus considered himself a moral reformer with a new message of salvation, and such men customarily feel themselves absolved from debts of gratitude to others. "The presumptuous attitude of Epicurus was not only excusable as befitting a rebel and a reformer; it was also virtually imperative for him as the founder and head of a sect. Self-assuredness and even arrogance is rather demanded of a leader by his disciples than resented, however exasperating it becomes to his rivals."*

### The School in Athens

Despite its political misfortunes, Athens was still the center of intellectual and cultural activity in the Hellenistic age. The two great schools of ancient philosophy, the Academy of Plato and the Lyceum of Aristotle, were

* Norman W. DeWitt, *Epicurus and His Philosophy* (University of Minnesota Press, 1954), p. 15. In recent years there has been a somewhat surprising interest in Epicurus. In addition to the above volume, DeWitt has also published another, *St. Paul and Epicurus*. A quite sympathetic study in France by A. J. Festugière, *Epicurus and His Gods*, appeared in an English translation by C. W. Chilton (Oxford: Basil Blackwell, 1955); and a detailed study by George K. Strodach, *The Philosophy of Epicurus*, was published in 1963.

both located there and were attracting the ablest thinkers of the day, even though Plato had been dead for more than a generation and Aristotle for a decade. As Epicurus' fame as a philosopher increased, it was natural that he felt strongly the attraction of the influential city of which he himself was a citizen. In 306 B.C., therefore, he purchased a home and a garden in Athens and established there a new school of philosophy.

This was a judicious move. Epicurus was now thirty-five years old; his philosophy had been worked out in some detail, and his own influence as a teacher was well established. If he wished to challenge successfully the leaders of rival philosophies, now was the time and Athens was the place. The Garden of Epicurus, as his school soon became known, was in many ways similar to the Academy and the Lyceum. Like them, it included two pieces of property: a residence for the philosopher where he and many of his abler disciples lived, and a separate place for lectures and more popular discussions with his followers. Epicurus soon gathered about him here a group of enthusiastic friends and followers. Drawing apart under his leadership from the political turmoil and the economic unrest that disturbed the Hellenistic world at that time, this group formed a thoroughly congenial fellowship of kindred spirits.

Indeed, the Garden of Epicurus became famous in antiquity for its example of goodly living and pleasant companionship quite as much as for its philosophical thought. A unique feature of life in this fellowship, moreover, was the presence of women. The school of Epicurus was one of the few institutions in the Greek world of that day where women could associate with men on a basis of equality, and this situation quite naturally gave rise to some disturbing rumors. A modern French author, however, describes the situation with commendable objectivity: "These young women would find in the Garden a company where they would be treated as equals, where their dignity as human beings would be conceded. This would be for them an entirely new experience. It is true that the courtesan in Athens at the end of the fourth century was not despised, but even so her condition was far from that of married women. She remained above all an object of pleasure."[2]

To the members of this little society Epicurus seems at all times to have been most generous. While he rejected the notion of a common purse for the school, he contributed from his own means to the needs of the group and was widely known for his sympathy and reasonableness. Completely loyal to the precepts of the master, whom they came to venerate almost as a god, his disciples committed his "golden maxims" to memory verbatim and accepted them as the inspired scriptures of their philosophical faith. Always in rather delicate health, Epicurus seems to have been long subject to gout and for many years even unable to walk. These infirmities of the flesh he bore calmly and courageously, at least according to the reports of his followers, and not until his seventy-second year did death at last bring to an end his philosophical reflection and discourse.

*Epicureanism*

For Epicurus philosophy was a very practical concern, a way of living, not an abstract system of thought. Much of the appeal of his philosophy, both to his early disciples in the Garden in Athens and to later ages, lies in its simplicity and common sense. He defines philosophy as "the daily business of speech and thought to secure a happy life," and, as a good hedonist, Epicurus has no question that pleasure is the major and essential ingredient in happiness. "Pleasure is our first and kindred good," he writes. "It is the starting point of every choice and every aversion, and to it we come back and make feeling the rule by which to judge of every good thing. . . . Wherefore we call pleasure the Alpha and the Omega of a blessed life."[3]

For the use of his disciples Epicurus outlined the essentials of his philosophy in forty *Cardinal Principles*, which fortunately have been preserved by Diogenes Laertius in his *Lives and Opinions of Eminent Philosophers*. His chapter on Epicurus reproduces verbatim a number of Epicurus' letters and numerous fragments from his philosophical texts and, by so doing, has saved these documents for us. The most appealing statement of the hedonism of Epicurus is to be found in these letters, rather than in his more formal theory. There is no better introduction to the Epicurean philosophy than his letter to Menoeceus, a young disciple to whom he is giving initial instruction in the way of life that will bring greatest happiness.*

> Let no one delay to study philosophy while he is young nor weary in philosophy when he is old, for no one is either short of the age or past the age for enjoying health of the soul. And the man who says the time for philosophy has not yet come or is already past may be compared to the man who says the time for happiness is not yet come or is already gone by. So both the young man and the old man should philosophize, the former that while growing old he may be young in blessings because of gratitude for what has been, the latter that he may be young and old at the same time because of the fearlessness with which he faces the future. Therefore the wise plan is to practice the things that make for happiness, since possessing happiness we have everything and not possessing it we do everything to have it.
>
> Both practice and study the precepts which I continuously urged upon you, discerning these to be the ABC's of the good life. First of all, believing the divine being to be blessed and incorruptible, just as the universal idea of it is outlined in our minds, associate nothing with it that is incompatible with incorruption nor alien to blessedness. It is not the man who would abolish the gods of the multitude who is impious but the

* This letter has been given a fresh translation by Norman W. DeWitt in his *St. Paul and Epicurus*. DeWitt likens it to the letter of St. Paul to his young friend and disciple Timothy, and even suggests that Paul was familiar with Epicurus' letter when he wrote to Timothy.

man who associates the beliefs of the multitude with the gods; for the pronouncements of the multitude concerning the gods are not innate ideas but false assumptions. . . .

When . . . we say that pleasure is the aim [of life], we do not mean the pleasures of profligates and those that consist in high living, . . . but we mean *freedom from pain in the body and turmoil in the soul*. For it is not protracted drinking bouts and revels nor yet sexual pleasures nor rare dishes of fish and the rest—all the delicacies that the luxurious table bears—that beget the happy life but rather sober calculation which searches out the reasons for every choice and avoidance, and expels false opinions, the source of most of the turmoil that seizes upon the souls of men.

Meditate therefore by day and by night upon these percepts and upon the others that go with these, whether by yourself or in the company of another like yourself, and never will your soul be in turmoil either sleeping or waking but you will be living like a god among men, for in no wise does a man who lives among immortal blessings resemble a mortal creature.[4]

### The Intelligent Pursuit of Pleasure

If a life that contains the greatest amount of pleasure and the least pain is every man's goal, such a life cannot be achieved, Epicurus points out, simply by the impulsive pursuit of immediate and intense pleasures. It is here that the Cyrenaic makes his major mistake. Only a little reflection is needed to realize that for every dissipation or overindulgence we pay with greater pain on the morning after. The ideal Epicurean is the man who is wise enough to avoid cheating himself with short-lived pleasures that cost too much, prudent enough to choose simple pleasures that last longer and cost less, and intelligent enough to banish all envy or ambition that troubles his soul. Such a man will live—much as did Epicurus himself—the quiet, cultured life of a country gentleman, surrounded by congenial friends, far removed from the disturbing turmoil of politics or the harassing anxiety of economic strife and competition.

In the thought of Epicurus we find, then, a much more restrained and prudent hedonism than in the bold irresponsibility of the Cyrenaic. Epicureanism is indeed more legitimately a *philosophy* of living, a pursuit of pleasure guided by reason rather than by passion. The consistent Epicurean, not the Cyrenaic, is really the master of his pleasures rather than their slave. For the Epicurean, man's intelligence controls emotion and desire, subjecting momentary passion and impulse to a well-conceived ideal, and pointing the way to the happiness that accompanies freedom from pain in the body and turmoil in the soul.

It is in his attitude toward pleasures of the senses that Epicurus disagrees most markedly not only with the Cyrenaic but also with all less thoughtful hedonists. "And again self-sufficiency we believe to be a great good," he writes to Menoeceus, "not that we may live on little under all circumstances but that we may be content with little when we do not have an abundance, being genuinely convinced that they enjoy living most who feel the least need of it; that every natural appetite is easily gratified but the unnatural appetite is difficult to gratify. So plain foods bring a pleasure equal to that of luxurious diet when once the pain due to need has been removed; and bread and water bring the utmost pleasure when one who is hungry brings them to his lips."[5]

Health of the body and tranquility of the spirit are here the essential ingredients of lasting happiness. And for Epicurus the greatest obstacle to happiness is not pain or poverty, or the absence of the luxuries that many associate with the good life. It is rather whatever tends to disturb our serenity and peace of mind, whatever causes fear, anxiety, or worry. Pleasures of the mind rather than of the body, and enduring pleasure, not the pleasures of the moment, are the surest sources of happiness. Pleasant fellowship and stimulating conversation among congenial friends, in an association free from all anxiety over social ills or soul-disturbing inquiry into realms of hidden truth—here is to be found enjoyment at its best for the intelligent hedonist, and this Epicurus made possible for the followers who gathered around him in the Garden near his Athenian estate. As recently pointed out by a distinguished authority on Greek life and thought, " 'Eat, drink and be merry, for tomorrow you may die' is really a travesty of Epicureanism. The revels in the Garden seem mainly to have centered on mathematics, which can be pursued without emotional involvement and entail no hang-over."[6]

Above all other pleasures, however, Epicurus places the enduring delights of friendship. "Of all things that wisdom provides for the happiness of life as a whole, by far the greatest is the possession of friendship," he writes. "We ought to look around for people to eat and drink with, before we look for something to eat and drink; to feed without a friend is the life of a lion and a wolf." "The well-born man occupies himself chiefly with wisdom and with friendship; of these the one is a mortal good, the other an immortal good."[7]

The pleasures that accompany friendship are singled out above all others, it is important to note, not because pleasures of the mind are in themselves superior to pleasures of the senses. All pleasures are equally good, according to Epicurus. It is the amount of pleasure that is important. The intelligent hedonist simply seeks to secure for himself the most pleasure in life and the least pain. He will frequently choose to suffer momentary pain if it enables him to gain more lasting pleasure, and he will always avoid an overindulgence of physical appetite or desire that brings an unpleasant consequence. The temporary pain of a surgical operation, for example, is more than compensated for by the permanently improved health it can produce. Epicurus describes quite explicitly the conduct in this regard that wisdom dictates:

Even though pleasure is our first and native goal, for that reason we do not choose every pleasure whatsoever but ofttimes pass over many pleasures when a greater annoyance issues from them. And ofttimes we consider pains superior to pleasures, and submit to pain for a long time when it is attended for us with a greater pleasure. While, therefore, all pleasure because it is naturally akin to us is good, not all pleasure is worthy to be chosen, just as all pain is evil but all pain is not shunned. It is by measuring one against the other, and by looking at the conveniences and inconveniences that all those matters must be judged.[8]

### The New Hedonism

When the city state was the dominant political institution in Greece, man was seen by the Greek philosopher as essentially a political animal. Above all else he was a citizen; service to the city was his highest achievement and in such service he found a lasting satisfaction. When this framework of the city state was shattered by Alexander the Great, however, a serious crisis in Greek life and thought occurred. As the conquests of Alexander overturned the world of Pericles and Plato, the little Greek cities lost their autonomy and the Greek citizen lost the freedom to shape his own destiny in any real sense. To provide man's life with meaning and purpose a new philosophy was needed. This Epicurus undertook to formulate.

If a man was to find freedom in the world in which Epicurus lived, he must find it within himself. To Epicurus, this much was crystal clear. In marked contrast to the constant concern of Socrates with the improvement of ills in a democratic society, and also to Plato's careful delineation of the ideal philosopher-king, Epicurus warns his followers not only of the dangers of ambition, of desire for wealth, for power, and for honor, but also of the futility of involvement in political life. The individual had nothing to hope for in life but his own contentment, and if contentment flows from peace of mind he must avoid all the involvements that destroy his tranquility of spirit. He who wished to be independent of circumstance should then learn to be self-sufficient. To be happy one must find the sources of happiness within himself. Above all he must be able to conquer the desires and the fears that produce "turmoil in the soul." The extension of the name of happiness to this state of contentment that came with health of the body and tranquility of spirit was the major innovation of the new hedonism of Epicurus.

### Science and Determinism

The determinism found in the *Rubaiyat*, which would deny to man the freedom to govern life intelligently, Epicurus explicitly rejects. He saw clearly that, unless man had both the foresight and the freedom to plan his conduct intelligently, the rational pursuit of pleasure and the achievement of happiness was not possible. There were two grounds in his day upon which the belief in determinism rested. One was scientific, the other religious. We still meet these today. The man of wisdom, in Epicurus' opinion, will recognize the limitations of scientific knowledge and will also see the irrationality of subscribing to a fatalism that takes away human freedom.

Epicurus was quite familiar with the scientific outlook of his age, in particular with the atomic materialism of Democritus, and made large use of this in developing the hedonism for which he became famous. Despite a number of essays and letters dealing with science, however, Epicurus exhibits no special originality of scientific insight. He gathered his facts with an eye fixed not on nature but on the hedonistic ethic to which he was committed and for which he was seeking support. "We must understand clearly," he writes, "that the knowledge of celestial phenomena, considered either in connection with other doctrines or by itself, has no other object but peace of mind and a sure confidence which is also the aim of all other studies."[9]

Nevertheless, Epicurus' insight as a moral philosopher was acute enough to recognize the necessity of postulating human freedom if genuine moral responsibility and successful control of conduct is to be expected. He saw in the scientific outlook of his day ample grounds for denying the determinism to which science then as now has customarily been committed, and he insisted accordingly upon a meaningful place for human freedom in the intelligent directing of conduct. While his reasoning in this matter is not now entirely convincing, Epicurus' position does have genuine ethical significance.

"Destiny, which some introduce as sovereign over all things," he writes, the wise man "laughs to scorn, affirming that certain things happen of necessity, others by chance, others through our own agency. For he sees that necessity destroys responsibility and that chance or fortune is inconsistent, whereas our own actions are free, and it is to them that praise and blame naturally attach. It were better indeed to accept the myths concerning the gods than to bow beneath that yoke of destiny which the natural philosophers have imposed."[10]

### Epicurus and the Greek Religion of His Day

As are most philosophers who undertake to establish a new interpretation of human life and destiny, Epicurus was critical of the traditional religion of his day. For this reason he was branded an atheist by those who disagreed with his ideas, and in succeeding generations Epicurean hedonism has continued to disturb the devout. There may well be good reason for this, but as one looks at the Greek religion of his day it is hard not to share in some measure the contempt that Epicurus felt for its influence on human life and human happiness. "The jaundiced tradition that denounces Epicurus as an atheist is sheer slander," writes one of his abler defenders. "In point of fact he regarded himself as a religious reformer who was recalling mankind to a more pure and lofty conception of the divine being."[11]

Without tranquility of spirit happiness is not possible, Epicurus insists. Yet of all the things that disturbed the minds and spirits of his contemporaries, fear of the gods and fear of death were in his judgment the most serious. His efforts to deal with these two religious concerns are among the more interesting aspects of his philosophy. In the scientific outlook that he accepted Epicurus found no basis for a belief in immortality, but this did not seem to him a reason for fear of death. If anything, it should have the opposite effect. His advice in this matter is quite contemporary in tone:

> Accustom yourself to the belief that death is nothing to us, because all good and evil lies in consciousness and death is the loss of consciousness. Hence a right understanding of the fact that death is nothing to us renders enjoyable the mortality of life, not by adding infinite time but by taking away the yearning for immortality. For there is nothing to be feared while living by the man who has genuinely grasped the idea that there is nothing to be feared when not living. So the man is silly who says he fears death, not because it will pain him when it comes, but because it pains him in prospect; for nothing that occasions no trouble when present has any right to pain us in anticipation. Therefore death, the most frightening of evils, is nothing to us, for the excellent reason that while we live it is not here and when it is here we are not living.[12]

In dealing with the anxiety that fear of the gods produced, Epicurus was equally ingenious. If happiness is that quality which makes life good and desirable, he argues, then clearly the gods are indescribably happy. Otherwise they would not be gods at all. Furthermore, their happiness cannot depend upon human worship or praise; it would then be too uncertain and transient. Nor could the gods be constantly concerned with the direction of human life, or the correction and punishment of human error. This would impose upon them a life of toil and worry completely incompatible with happiness. Thus Epicurus reaches his conclusion that the gods in their own enjoyment of happiness have no concern at all with mortal beings, and interfere in no way either for good or evil in man's day-to-day conduct or his destiny. "The blessed and immortal nature knows no trouble itself nor causes trouble to any other, so that it is never constrained by anger or favor. All such things exist only in the weak," Epicurus asserts as the first of the forty *Cardinal Principles* of philosophy that he prepared for his disciples.[13]

### The Influence of Epicurus

In one form or another hedonism has attracted men and women in all ages and in all walks of life. For some seven centuries, three before the birth of Christ and four thereafter, the philosophy of Epicurus was one of the influential views of life in the ancient world. During the Hellenistic age, the chief opponents of the Epicureans were the leaders of the schools founded by Plato and Aristotle. In the early Christian era, the Stoic philosophers and then the Christians themselves were its major adversaries, competing with Epicurus for the allegiance of men and women throughout the Roman world. The extent to which his works were known and used during the early years of the third century A.D. is clearly indicated by the extensive collection of the writings of Epicurus included by Diogenes Laertius in his *Lives and Opinions of Eminent Philosophers*.

The thought of Lucretius, a Roman poet of a somewhat later day, was also shaped in significant fashion by the philosophy of Epicurus. His important work, *De Rerum Natura* (On the Nature of Things), is among the best-known pieces of literature that have come down to us from that period. And what FitzGerald's translation of *The Rubaiyat* did for the hedonism of Aristippus a century ago, this poem by Lucretius did for the philosophy of Epicurus in the Roman world a century before the Christian era.

### Lucretius, the Roman Poet of Science

Of Lucretius himself surprisingly little is known. A few things about the poet, however, can be readily inferred from the poem itself. We find here the picture of an educated and aristocratic Roman, familiar with both the palaces and the country houses, the ostentation and the vulgarity of the day, as well as with the widespread boredom that accompanied the life of the wealthy in the first century B.C. This was the atmosphere in which Lucretius lived and the kind of world in which the philosophy of Epicurus would have great appeal. Lucretius's friendship with Memmius, a Roman patrician to whom he addresses his poem, likewise suggests that he himself came of a family of good standing in Rome. The best evidence places his birth about 95 B.C. and his death, as a relatively young man, at 55 B.C. By 54 B.C. both Marcus Tullius Cicero and his brother had read *De Rerum Natura* and had written to each other about the poem. Beyond this there are only the conjectures of the curious in later ages.

In Lucretius's poem itself there is to be seen a marked hatred of conventional superstitions, a commitment to scientific thought and accuracy of observation, a profound sense of the beauty of nature, and complete confidence in natural law—all attitudes that have great appeal today. We must be careful, however, not to interpret Lucretius from a contemporary point of view. He should rather be seen as an unusually intelligent and gifted Epicurean of the first century B.C.

The inspiration for his philosophy he owes directly to Epicurus, Lucretius asserts in an unusually eloquent passage in *De Rerum Natura*:*

### In Praise of Epicurus, "the teacher whom he held Divine"

Into thick darkness came of old bright light
You do I follow, you, who brought the light
To show us what is good and bad in human life,
You do I follow, glory of the Grecian race,
And in your footsteps firmly plant my own.
Not that I want to rival you; affection makes me want to imitate.
How can a swallow vie with swans
Or kids with little tottering limbs
On race track vie with mighty practiced horse?

You are the father of my mind, discoverer of Nature.
From your books, O seer renowned,
You give a father's precepts in philosophy;
As bees in blooming meadows suck each flower,
So your golden words repeatedly
We feed on and find them golden,
Worthy of eternal life.

In stating his view of how a man should seek to direct his life, Lucretius gives apt poetic expression to the thought of Epicurus. The intelligent man will not engage as most men do in a constant struggle for power or wealth. The gratification of avarice, ambition, and lust brings no lasting satisfaction. The only enduring happiness is to be found in satisfying our natural desires in moderation, not in excess, and in banishing the insecurity and fear of death that mar our enjoyment of life. For attaining tranquility of spirit, the study of nature, and of nature's constant and dependable laws, affords the surest promise. From such a study comes a satisfying emotional and intellectual acceptance of universal law by which all things are governed with order, regularity, and consistency. And for Lucretius such understanding alone provides the peace and tranquility that man seeks.

### The Joy and Peace That Comes from Philosophy

O sweet it is when on the mighty sea,
The wind stirs up great billows,
One's own foot firm on steady earth,

* The passages quoted here are from a recent translation of Lucretius—A. D. Winspear, *The Roman Poet of Science, Lucretius* (The Harbor Press, 1956).

To watch another's troubles.
Not that we find delight in others' strugglings,
But that it's sweet to look on ills
From which oneself escapes.
Sweet, too, to look
When cavalcades of war contend upon the plain;
And one is safe, oneself.

But far surpassing everything in bliss it is
To occupy the high serene, embattled eminence,
The ivory tower
Whose muniments are thought and high philosophy,
The wisdom of the wise.
Here you look down and see, like tiny ants,
Men scurry to and fro, wandering here and there
Seeking to find the hidden path of life,
Well-spent, well-ordered.

You see them battle with their wits,
Pit lineage 'gainst lineage,
Working day and night with sinews and with mind,
To gain the crown of wealth, the pride of power.
Men's wretched minds, men's blinded hearts!
In darkness deep, in peril sore,
This little life of ours is passed.

Actually life would be tolerable enough, and often quite happy, were it not for the universal fear not so much of death as of the future that awaits us after death. This is a cardinal tenet of Lucretius's poem as of the philosophy of Epicurus. And for this fear of death and what the gods may do to us, religion is largely to be blamed. A scientific philosophy alone is able to free us from such fear and to restore that tranquility of spirit so essential to human happiness, Lucretius insists quite in the spirit of Epicurus:

*Now I Must Cast Away That Fear of Death*

Now I must tear up by the roots and cast away
That fear of death,
That fear that sullies mortal life from end to end
And pours the murk of death on everything,
Leaves no man's pleasure pure and unalloyed.

And so this darkened terror of the mind must be dispelled
Not by the rays of sun or gleaming shafts of day,
But by Nature's laws, by looking in her face.

Death then is nothing, affects us not at all,
Since soul is held to be of mortal stuff.
And just as in the past we knew no ill

When Punic hosts from all sides rushed to war
When all the earth beneath the lofty shores of sky
Trembled in dreadful battle,
And men could doubt which side was doomed for fall
And loss of empire on land and sea alike;
So, when we're dead,
When soul and body out of which we're formed, one entity,
Are torn apart in death,
Nothing can touch our sense at all or move our consciousness
(For we shall not be alive to know).

From this we learn there's naught to fear in death;
That once a man is dead he cannot be in misery,
That there's no difference if he never had been born,
When death immortal once has snatched away our mortal life.

Why do you weep and groan at death?
If life was good for you
And all its joys have not drained off
Like water poured in cracked receptacle,
And left untasted,
Why do you not, like guest at feast of life,
Slip peacefully away, with mind serene, poor fool,
Grasp quiet and nothingness?

Does that seem sad, does that seem grim?
It seems to me more tranquil far,
Than any kind of sleep.[14]

### Hedonism for Our Age
### Lin Yutang: The Importance of Living

Before concluding our discussion of the Epicurean philosophy, let us look with some care at a more recent statement of hedonism that ably portrays its meaning and appeal for our own age. No popular writer has presented the general point of view of Epicurus and the Cyrenaics with greater persuasiveness than has Lin Yutang (1895—). His volume, *The Importance of Living,* although published more than a generation ago, not only interprets hedonism in concrete and graphic fashion, but also indicates clearly its many similarities to the new naturalism of our day. Likewise throughout this volume the spirit of Taoism and of Eastern philosophy is everywhere apparent, giving to the hedonism of Lin Yutang something of the appeal that Eastern thought holds for many people today.

An urbane and cultured Oriental who has made his home in New York City in recent years, Lin Yutang is a distinguished contemporary interpreter of the mind and spirit of China. Familiar alike with the Confucian classics of his own country and with the urban and industrial civilization of America, he has led a full and rich life in which the spirit of the East and of the West have met in quite unusual fashion. Lin was made head of the Arts and Letters Division of UNESCO in 1946, and shortly thereafter was appointed Chancellor of Nanyang University in Singapore. There, however, he found himself forced to devote most of his time and energy to combating the rising tide of Communism. After a few years of such unrewarding activity, he resigned in disappointment and frustration, returning to New York City to live.

Author of numerous works in Chinese, Lin Yutang has published more than twenty-five books in English, among them novels, essays, and anthologies interpreting Chinese life and philosophy. Best known to American readers are *My Country and My People, The Wisdom of China and India,* and *The Importance of Living.* Published in 1937, *The Importance of Living* is a highly readable account of the philosophy to which Lin was gradually led in the course of a full life. It is not the work of a professional philosopher, but rather of one who reached his conclusions at first hand from life as he lived it and saw it lived.

### The Enjoyment of Living — *not really like Zen I don't think.*

As with earlier hedonists, the end or purpose of life as Lin Yutang here sees it is simply the enjoyment of life. "This seems so simple simply because it is so," he says. It is not a conscious purpose, arrived at through the study of philosophy. It is the natural attitude that we all begin with toward life. Some men look for a divine purpose in life, a purpose that God sets for all humanity, and others feel compelled to seek a high purpose that an individual should set for himself. But in Lin's opinion neither attempt really gets very far. When he asks what can be the purpose of human life except the full enjoyment of it, however, he finds the problem amazingly simple and the answer quite clear.

The practical question that every man faces is what to do with the fifty or sixty years he has between youth and death. It is a question very much like that of how to spend his vacation, or even the next weekend. The only answer that a sensible hedonist can see is that he should order his life so that he can find the greatest enjoyment of it. The problem of living is a problem not of getting to heaven but of getting along in this world. When questioned about what they are going to do in heaven, or how they will be happy there, most Christians have only the vaguest notion and talk of wearing crowns and white robes, or singing hymns and playing harps. Unless heaven can be made much more vivid and convincing for him, Lin Yutang sees no reason for striving to go there at the cost of neglecting the enjoyment of this earthly existence.

When faced with a choice between pleasures of the senses and mental or spiritual enjoyment, Lin Yutang refuses to admit that a distinction is possible. "All human happiness is biological," he writes; "it is largely a matter of digestion. Let us admit of course that true happiness is only happiness of the spirit, but unless the body functions well, there can be no tranquility of spirit."[15] This is simply to say that the pleasures of mind and spirit cannot be separated from those of the senses. In real life they are inextricably joined together.

Mental pleasures, Lin Yutang points out, are real only when they are felt through the body. Look at the so-called higher pleasures of the mind—literature, art, music, religion, and philosophy—and see what a minor role the intellect plays here as compared with the senses and feelings. The best literature and art, Lin asserts, simply recreates life and so gives us its atmosphere and color, the fragrance of the pastures or the stink of the city gutters. So poetry is but truth colored with emotion; music is sentiment without words; and religion, wisdom expressed in fancy. There is no reason for art and poetry and religion unless they restore in us a freshness of vision, a greater emotional glamor, and a more vital sense of life. Even for philosophy, when it reflects life as it actually is, the same thing is true. [There is real danger lest in philosophy we lose the feeling of life itself and wander into a world of bare and cold abstraction.] But this is not a philosophy that is sound and healthy. Only by placing living above thinking can philosophy recapture some of its original freshness and naturalness of insight, Lin Yutang insists.

All of this leads Lin Yutang to call his philosophy naturalism or materialism. His is a naturalism that would reestablish our confidence in the senses and in the pleasures of sense. He does not reject the life of the spirit, but simply recognizes the biological view of life as fundamental. There is no such thing as a soul without nerves, without taste, without a sense of color and motion, he maintains. Spirituality is based on a material, earthbound existence. The two cannot be separated. It is hard even to imagine what angels would be like without wings.


### On the Nature of Happiness

When thus interpreted, the enjoyment of living covers many things. Some are obvious, such as the enjoyment of a good meal, a gay party, an outing on a beautiful spring day. There are less obvious things—the enjoyment of poetry and of art and religion, the contemplation of clouds, of winding rivers and falling cataracts, the pleasures of friendship, of conversation, and of home life. The feast of life is before us, Lin Yutang urges. The only question is what appetite we have for it. The appetite is the important thing. Most people, indeed, fail to realize how simple and how natural it is to be happy. "Let us not lose ourselves in the abstract," Lin writes, "but get down to facts and analyze for ourselves what are the truly happy moments of our life."

First, then, all happiness for this contemporary hedonism is *sensuous.* We cannot find happiness by stressing things of the spirit apart from the senses:

> Just as it is impossible for me to say whether I love my children physically or spiritually when I hear their chattering voices or when I see their plump legs, so I am totally unable to distinguish between the joys of the flesh and the spirit. Does anybody ever love a woman spiritually without loving her physically? And is it so easy a matter for a man to analyze and separate the charms of the woman he loves—things like laughter, smiles, a way of tossing one's head, a certain attitude toward things?[16]

At one point, however, we do find Lin Yutang in disagreement with the new naturalism of the contemporary scene. "There is a soul-uplifting quality about lipstick and rouge and a spiritual calm and poise that comes from the knowledge of being well-dressed," he observes in commenting upon the feminine enjoyment of life. Is he wrong about this?

Here in any case is the first lesson in a hedonistic philosophy: We must lose our contempt for the body and our fear of the senses. The pleasures of sense are not merely good and desirable in themselves. They are the foundation upon which all happiness in life must rest.

Likewise, happiness lies in *the enjoyment of the present*—the present day, the present moment, the present life. For the hedonist, "This earth is the only heaven," as Lin Yutang puts it in an expressive phrase. If we know that this earthly existence is all we have, we will try the harder to enjoy it while it lasts. We will make up our minds to live sensibly and make the most of what we have instead of allowing a vague hope of immortality to detract from our wholehearted enjoyment of life. And what is true of this world is true also of this day and hour. The joy of the day is made up of the joys of the hour, and the joys of the hour of the joys of the moment. Time is the one thing that when lost we cannot replace, and yet we let anyone take up our time who wants to. "There is always plenty of life to enjoy for the man who is determined to enjoy it," Lin Yutang maintains. If a man does not enjoy this earthly existence, it is his own fault. It is because he does not love life sufficiently or allows it to be turned into a humdrum and routine existence.

Leisure also is necessary for happiness. This is one of the most characteristic principles in the philosophy of Lin Yutang, and one that he expresses in a wide variety of ways, many of them, until quite recently at least, uncongenial to the American mind. "Leisure in time is like unoccupied floor space in a room," he writes. We must have unoccupied space in a room to make it habitable. It must not be all cluttered up like a storeroom. So our leisure hours make life endurable. Too many Americans, as Lin Yutang sees them, allow their lives to become so full and cluttered up that they lose the opportunity and the perspective necessary to enjoy the beauties of life. The three great American vices for this Oriental hedonist are efficiency, punctuality, and desire for success. These are the values that keep the American always at work, that make him so nervous, so tense, and so unhappy. His insistence upon always going somewhere and doing something leaves him no time to *be* something. Character takes time to grow.

Finally, and in some ways most important of all, happiness comes in *being natural;* Lin Yutang pointed this out several decades before the youth culture in our own country acclaimed this discovery. Lin Yutang calls his a biological view of life. He simply accepts the fact that man is an animal and recognizes that no one can be blamed on that account. One of the great achievements of science, he feels, is in making it clear that we are more like monkeys than like angels. And we can be happy only when we act as nature has made us, not when we try to remake ourselves into something quite different. In developing his naturalism, however, Lin Yutang makes what is certainly one of his most discerning statements about human happiness: "No one's life can be happy unless beyond the superficial attainments of the external life, the deeper springs of character are touched, and find a normal outlet."

### A Hedonist's View of Education

Nowhere does the viewpoint of the hedonist strike closer home than in Lin Yutang's philosophy of education. The goal of education is not breadth of information nor the accumulation of facts and details, he maintains. That is the easiest of all things to accomplish. The truly educated man is one who has the right loves and hatreds. He has taste or discernment. The aim of education, therefore, is the development of good taste in appreciation and in conduct. But good taste, discernment, and understanding do not come to the mind crammed full of historical facts and figures. Taste requires, rather, a capacity for thinking things through; an independence of judgment; an unwillingness to be taken in by any form of humbug, social, political, or academic.

This emphasis is sadly lacking in most of our schools, as Lin Yutang sees them. Our modern educational system, it seems, has rather tried to discourage thought. Education has become "a mechanical, measured, uniform and passive cramming of information," instead of the pleasant pursuit of knowledge that it should be. We have tried to educate people in masses, as in a factory, instead of as individuals. And so we have developed a standardized product that is certified by a diploma. To have diplomas, we must have grades, and to have grades, we must have standardized tests, and to have tests there must be the memorizing of facts and dates and places. But in this fashion we can never get good taste and discernment and independence of thought, in Lin Yutang's judgment. The ideal pursuit of knowledge is like the exploration of a new continent. It is "an adventure of the soul," a positive, growing individual pleasure in understanding. One cannot work to get good grades, to satisfy one's parents, to get a good job, to earn a higher salary later in life, and hope to get an education.

The discovery of a favorite author, according to Lin Yutang, is the most critical event in any person's intellectual development. Only in this way can one get any real good out of reading. One must be independent and search out his own masters, rather than be made to conform to a tightly organized program of study. The conscientious student who sets out to work because he ought to, not because he wants to, ends by "studying bitterly" and becoming a "hard grind." No one can really learn anything from a book when he hates the author. Instead, every man must find an author who is just right for him and then proceed to devour every word that this author writes. Thus he truly steeps himself in his literary love and derives from his reading sustenance for his soul. After a few years the spell will be over and he must seek a new literary lover; after three or four such experiences he emerges a changed person. He has acquired that breadth of sympathy and understanding, that good taste and discernment, which have made of him an educated man. And, above all, the process has been a thoroughly enjoyable one, not the unappealing academic routine provided by too many institutions of higher learning.

With this philosophy, it is not hard to understand why Lin Yutang found his work as a university president in Singapore quite frustrating.

### The Religion of a Pagan

Early Greek hedonists like Epicurus and his followers saw in the religion and mythology of their day an undesirable concern with another world, a fear of death and of the wrath of the gods, that took away from this life much of its pleasure and joy. In our conventional Christianity, Lin Yutang when writing *The Importance of Living* found much the same sort of defects. It was concerned too much with theological doctrine, too little with life, too much with salvation, too little with human happiness. The mixing of religious devotion with scientific theory he also found unacceptable in contemporary Christianity. It is no business of religion whether the age of man on this planet is thousands of years or millions, whether he came into being by a long process of evolution or sprang full-grown from the earth. Only in the realm of morals, of conscience, and of spiritual experience does religion have a dignity and worth of its own. The Christian Church, Lin Yutang insisted, must cease to preserve ancient folkways or to dabble in astronomy and biology. It must return instead to the simple teaching of Jesus about reverence for human personality and love of one's fellow man, if it hopes to gain the respect of intelligent people today. Disassociating himself definitely from the Christian faith at that time, Lin Yutang called himself a *pagan*. The religion of a pagan, as he defines it, clearly reflects the spirit of Taoism and ancient China. It also provides an excellent expression of what hedonism at best can make of religion:

> A Chinese pagan, the only kind of which I can speak with any feeling of intimacy, is one who starts out with this earthly life as all we can or need to bother about, wishes to live intently and happily as long as life lasts, has a keen appreciation of the beautiful and the good in human life wherever he finds them, and regards doing good as its satisfactory reward. He feels a slight pity or contempt for the "religious" man who does good in order to get to heaven and who, by implication, would not do good if he were not lured by heaven or threatened by hell. As I look at it at present, the difference in spiritual life between a Christian believer and a pagan is simply this: . . . the pagan lives in this world like an orphan, without the benefit of that consoling feeling that there is always someone in heaven who cares and who will attend to his private personal welfare. It is no doubt a less cheery world; but there is the benefit and dignity of being an orphan who by necessity has learned to be independent, to take care of himself, and to be more mature, as all orphans are.[17]

### Popular Hedonism and Its Critics

The appeal of the pursuit of pleasure as portrayed by an urbane hedonist like Lin Yutang few would deny. This appeal is undoubtedly enhanced by the literary charm of the writing of Lin Yutang. If a man does not find it necessary "for the good of his own soul" to seek a philosophy that is more inspiring, then let him at least live as an intelligent hedonist, a cultured Epicurean who prudently chooses those pleasures that contribute most to the enjoyment of living. Let him emulate that wise disenchantment of the Chinese pagan who does not expect too much of life, who is seldom disillusioned because he has few illusions, and seldom disappointed because he has no extravagant hopes. And even those for whom Epicureanism may finally prove unacceptable certainly need not lose sight of its valuable insights into human life.

### *From Pagan to Christian*

The reaction of Epicurus and of Lin Yutang against conventional religion is not only understandable but quite valuable in pointing to faults of which established Churches are too often guilty. But, as one reads Lin Yutang's account, it is easy to see how the inadequacy of a narrow interpretation of Christianity helped produce his "pagan" point of view. Born into the family of a Chinese Protestant pastor and sent by his father to a theological seminary in China, he was forbidden to attend the Chinese theater, never allowed to listen to Chinese minstrels, and entirely cut off from the great heritage of the Chinese classics. When later in life he rediscovered this Chinese literary and cultural heritage for himself, it seemed a wonderful new world as thoroughly congenial to his own Oriental spirit as Western Christianity was foreign.

It is certainly of some interest, however, to note that some twenty years after he wrote *The Importance of Living* Lin Yutang found a less narrow and traditional Christianity quite acceptable. In *From Pagan to Christian*, published in 1959, he portrays in symbolic fashion the path that led him shortly after his return from Singapore to become a member of the Madison Avenue Presbyterian Church in New York City. "I have come by religion the hard way," he writes here; "I think this is the only way, and I do not think there is any other way to give it the necessary validity. For religion is, first and last, an individual facing up to the astounding heavens, a matter between him and God." "I have dwelt in the mansions of Confucian humanism, and climbed the peaks of Mount Tao and beheld its glories, and have had glimpses of the dissolving mist of Buddhism hanging over a terrifying void, and only after doing so have I ascended the Jungfrau of Christian belief and reached the world of sunlight above the clouds."[18]

### The Critics of Epicureanism

The Epicurean has insisted that our philosophy of living must bring genuine and lasting enjoyment as we put it into practice. Can any philosophy that does not do this hope to meet the test of experience successfully? Who is willing to condemn an act for no better reason than that it is pleasant? However, many philosophers do question the adequacy of hedonism on other grounds. Genuine happiness and a full realization of the best that life has to offer cannot be achieved, they maintain, by the means that the Epicurean has suggested. We shall do well to look carefully at positions these philosophers advocate before surrendering ourselves to hedonism's obvious charm and appeal.

In the world in which we live today, however, a more serious difficulty facing the hedonist philosophy may well lie in its social outlook. Only by depending upon others to do the hard and unpleasant work of this world for him, the severest critics of hedonism argue, is it possible for anyone to practice this philosophy. For until someone is willing to assume the strenuous and harassing burdens of political life, there can be no stable society in which to pursue a life of calm detachment. In the Graeco-Roman world of Epicurus' day, when there seemed nothing that an individual could do to halt the rapid disintegration of the Greek commonwealth before the rising power of Rome, even his critics recognize that the Epicurean ideal did have a valid appeal. Only by withdrawing from the turmoil and uncertainty of political strife could the Greek philosopher and his disciples see any chance of personal happiness. The complexities and frustrations of our technologically dominated society have, as a matter of fact, affected many of our contemporaries in the same way. But is not this philosophy of living at best only a temporary expedient, even a confession of failure, the critics of hedonism ask? Can it provide guidance for an age when a better world should be in the making, or challenge able and intelligent young men and women to play a part in this undertaking?

Certainly we must with Lin Yutang examine carefully other philosophies that claim to provide a surer sense of values, a clearer awareness of what is worthwhile in life, of what really counts in the long run, than does popular hedonism, ancient or modern. In the end, however, each student must decide for himself whether or not such claims as these prove convincing.

## CHAPTER 3

# Altruistic Hedonism

*The Utilitarians*

The Epicurean pursuit of pleasure, despite its appeal, is open to criticisms that do raise serious questions about its acceptability. Is it possible, however, that these refer to defects not in hedonism itself but rather in an egoistic hedonism where men think primarily of themselves and so lose sight of more valuable sources of pleasure? That such is the case is the view of an able group of nineteenth-century British philosophers known as *Utilitarians*. These philosophers adopt a position, definitely hedonistic in principle, that undertakes to remedy the social inadequacies critics see in Epicureanism.

For example, Epicurus and the Cyrenaics regard the pleasures of each individual as his main concern in life. If one thinks of other people at all, it is only because of the pleasure he himself derives from their friendship. The utilitarian philosophers, on the other hand, maintain that the greatest good of the greatest number should always be our serious concern. The disciples of Epicurus withdrew from the disturbing events of the world about them to enjoy with tranquil spirit the pleasures of mind and body. The Utilitarians were outstanding leaders of the nineteenth-century movement for social reform in England. They lectured widely, wrote innumerable pamphlets and books, edited a journal, and organized a political party, all with the purpose of improving the economic and political conditions of their day. Because of such concern with the welfare of others as well as with one's own pleasure, Utilitarianism is often described as *altruistic* hedonism. This in itself is enough to suggest that the aim of the utilitarian philosophy will command our respect. If altruistic hedonism can successfully combine an immediate enjoyment of living with an interest in the welfare of one's fellow men, then it may well prove to be a desirable philosophy for an age of social unrest such as ours. In any event, in seeking an acceptable social philosophy, one should certainly examine Utilitarianism with some care.

### Jeremy Bentham, Father of Utilitarianism

Jeremy Bentham and John Stuart Mill, the two ablest exponents of Utilitarianism, were both child prodigies. They were reading Latin, Greek, and philosophy when other boys their age were still enjoying fairy tales. And they spent their youth in the company of distinguished scholars and social reformers instead of the company of the eligible young ladies of their own generation. At the age of thirteen, Bentham found his religious sensibilities offended and his mind troubled by doubts when he was required to affirm his belief in the Thirty-nine Articles of the Anglican Church before being allowed to matriculate at Oxford University. He did enter Oxford, however, and upon his graduation proceeded to study law in London. Because of his marked ability, his father had hopes that Jeremy would become a distinguished jurist, but the son took little interest in the practical side of his profession. Despite this fact, his father, with commendable paternal affection, continued to support him and found some compensation for his early disappointment when Jeremy's first book, published anonymously not long after its author's twenty-eighth birthday, was immediately ascribed by the public to various eminent writers of the day.

Bentham (1748–1832) spent almost the whole of his life either in London or at his home in the country nearby. Like Epicurus, he soon gathered around him a group of devoted friends and admirers who accepted his views almost without question and were eager to help in spreading his philosophy. His outstanding book, *The Principles of Morals and Legislation* (1789), was written as a background for a new penal code he was advocating. He organized the efforts of his friends behind the proposal and incurred heavy personal expense in promoting it. But all to no avail. The program was finally turned down by the British government. This experience aroused in Bentham a deep-seated distrust not only of the current Tory political leaders of his day but also of the motives of politicians in general. Despite his concern for social reform, Bentham, like many other philosophers, was largely a recluse. He was occupied chiefly in elaborating theories on paper, expecting that they would go into effect almost automatically as soon as their logical validity was demonstrated. His close friends looked upon him as a man of profound wisdom, and approved almost as a matter of course whatever he proposed. It was a great disappointment to Bentham when he discovered that all men, and especially practical political leaders, were not equally discerning.

In time, however, the younger men around Bentham came to realize that books and pamphlets, no matter how logical or brilliant, were not enough to achieve lasting political action or social reform. They decided, therefore, to organize a political party. Calling themselves the Philosophical Radicals, they worked out a practical political platform, and soon elected to

Parliament a number of able spokesmen for their program. The very considerable influence this group exerted during half a century was due in the main not to their numbers but to the exceptional ability and social vision of these exponents of practical Utilitarianism. Bentham himself, as a matter of fact, did not call his philosophy by this name. He preferred a somewhat more cumbersome phrase, "The greatest happiness principle." The term Utilitarianism was adopted by John Stuart Mill at first to describe the views of a small literary group among Bentham's disciples and only later, when the name "Philosophical Radicals" proved politically inadvisable, to designate the political party and its philosophy. In time Utilitarianism became the accepted name for Bentham's philosophy as well as for Mill's own position.

### The Principle of Utility

It was Bentham's hope that he could make ethics as exact and precise as the physical sciences. To this end he omitted all literary artifice in his writing and sought rather to achieve the precision and clarity of the lawyer or the mathematician. Consequently, his books read more like legal documents than like literary masterpieces, and his hedonism can derive no support from the charm or brilliance of its presentation. An unequivocal acceptance of the tenents of hedonism is clear, however, in the opening words of Bentham's *Principles of Morals and Legislation*:

> Nature has placed man under the governance of two sovereign masters, *pain* and *pleasure*. It is for them alone to point out what we ought to do, as well as to determine what we shall do. On the one hand the standards of right and wrong, on the other the chain of causes and effects, are fastened to their throne. They govern us in all that we do, in all we say, in all we think; every effort we can make to throw off our subjections, will serve but to demonstrate and confirm it. The principle of utility recognizes this subjection and assumes it for the foundation of that system the object of which is to rear the fabric of felicity by the hands of reason and law.

Epicurus himself could have asked no more clear and forthright avowal of the dominant place of pleasure and pain in shaping our lives. Indeed, the moral philosophy of Bentham contains little more than a careful restatement of Epicureanism, with the egoism of Epicurus modified somewhat by the necessities of social life. The principle of utility itself is thoroughly Epicurean. "By utility," Bentham writes, "is meant that property in an object whereby it tends to produce benefit, advantage, pleasure, good or happiness (all this in the present case comes to the same thing) or to prevent the happening of mischief, pain, evil or unhappiness, to the party whose interest is considered."[1]

No philosophy could be simpler and more direct. A chair, for example, has utility because at a lecture we derive pleasure from sitting down rather than standing for an hour or two. A cushioned chair has greater utility than a hard chair because we get greater pleasure (that is, we are more comfortable) when sitting in the cushioned chair. Hence, when two chairs are vacant, one cushioned and the other hard, we naturally and without unnecessary reflection sit down in the cushioned chair. All choices in life, when clearly analyzed, are really of just this sort, in Bentham's opinion. The kind of clothes one decides to wear, or not to wear, the friends we associate with, our attitude toward the use of marijuana or another social drug, our decisions about what is important in education or in politics, can all be understood in terms of the utility involved. The advantages, the satisfactions for us, in each alternative determine our choice.

### The Meaning of Right and Wrong

For Bentham the right action in any circumstance, then, is the one that on the whole produces the best approximation to the desired results for all concerned. It is not our motives but the consequences of what we do that counts. Upon this natural and obvious principle our morals should be based, he maintains: "Any sort of motive is either good or bad on the score of its effects." A thing is judged to be right or wrong in terms of its outcome and, more specifically, in terms of the pleasure it produces or the pain it permits us to escape. The *principle of utility* is defined, accordingly, as "that principle which approves or disapproves of every action whatsoever, according to the tendency which it appears to have to augment or diminish the happiness of the party whose interest is in question." "Of an action that is conformable to the principle of utility one may also say either that it is one that ought to be done, or at least that it is not one that ought not to be done," Bentham writes. "One may also say that it is right that it should be done, at least that it is not wrong that it should not be done. When thus interpreted, the words ought, and right and wrong, and others of that stamp, have a meaning: when used otherwise, they have none."[2]

If this view of right and wrong is accepted, the only moral problem is that of determining what conduct produces the greatest pleasure or brings the least pain. Epicurus had rejected the more naïve Cyrenaic view that the pleasures of the moment and those of the senses are to be enjoyed without thought of the future. This he condemned as unintelligent even for a hedonist, and turned instead to intellectual and lasting pleasures that involved as little pain as possible. The only difference between one pleasure and another for Epicurus is a difference in the *amount* of pleasure it affords. If friendship is preferred to refinement of eating or drinking, it is because friendships give us more pleasure in the long run. One pleasure is in itself no better or more desirable than another; that is, there is no *qualitative* distinction among pleasures; the only differences are *quantitative*.

This general Epicurean point of view Bentham does not question. He is interested only in a more exact standard for measuring pleasures. This standard he refers to, in the language of mathematics, as his "hedonistic calculus." Seven factors must be taken into account in such a calculation: the *intensity* of the pleasures or pains involved; their *duration*; their *certainty* or uncertainty; their *propinquity* or remoteness—that is, how near or how far away they are; their *fecundity*—that is, the tendency of a pleasure to produce other pleasures, or of a pain to lead to other pains; their *purity*—that is, the freedom of pleasures from attendant or subsequent pain, or of pain from pleasures; and their *extent*—that is, the number of persons whom they affect. To popularize his "calculus" and give it a somewhat more general appeal, Bentham devised the following rhyme:

> Intense, long, certain, speedy, fruitful, pure—
> Such marks in pleasures and in pains endure.
> Such pleasures seek if private be thy end:
> If it be public, wide let them extend.
> Such pains avoid, whichever be thy view.
> If pains must come, let them extend to few.

"To take an exact account, then, of the general tendency of any act, sum up all the values of all the pleasures on the one side, and then of all the pains on the other," Bentham writes. "The balance, if it bears on the side of pleasure, will give the good tendency of the act, if on the side of pain, its bad tendency."[3] It is not to be expected that each of us will follow through a careful analysis like this each time we decide to do something, Bentham admits. But it should always be kept in mind; and the more nearly we approximate it, the more rewarding our choice and our social contribution will be. The only new thing about the Hedonistic calculus in Bentham's opinion was the exact formulation it gave to the usual practice of mankind. For this is essentially what we all do in less exact fashion.

## Law and the Good Society

Thus far the philosophy of Bentham is not only hedonistic but largely Epicurean. It was only when he turned from private to public morality that Bentham began to modify the tenets of Epicurus; but it is actually here that we find his chief interest in life. As a matter of fact, his greatest contributions were made in the social sciences and in legal philosophy rather than ethics. Bentham was convinced that good government must promote the greatest happiness of the greatest number, not the interests of the privileged few. All men, in his opinion, are by nature egoistic. They think first and basically of their own good. Yet unless they can be made to think also of the

→ then by NATURE, MEN ARE IN SOME WAY, IMMORAL. )

good of others, a stable and well-ordered society is not possible. Hence it is the function of law to see that a man does consider the good of others as well as his own good.

How is the intelligent legislator to accomplish this, Bentham asked? His answer contains a shrewd combination of hedonism and altruism. Legislators must pass laws to make sure that men suffer enough pain when they disregard the welfare of others that this will outweigh any pleasure they may derive from an antisocial act. Thus, a youth may decide to commit a robbery in the hope that it will give him money with which to enjoy himself. But if he is convinced of speedy and certain legal punishment for such an act, he may well be deterred and so maintain a more socially desirable conduct. There must, however, be a *certainty* and a *duration* of the pain involved in such punishment that will clearly *outweigh* the *intensity* and *propinquity* of the anticipated pleasure, Bentham points out. Here his hedonistic calculus is of obvious value to the legislator. The same principles would, of course, operate for Bentham in the rules and regulations by which a wise administration directs the affairs of corporation employees, political campaign workers, or students on a college campus.

In what we call the "laws of nature," Bentham finds the principle of utility at work in just the way it should be exemplified in the laws of the state. Let a man overeat, and the pains of indigestion—intense, long, and certain—soon outweigh the memory of the earlier pleasures he enjoyed. Let him try to get along without adequate sleep; his senses become dulled and his health falters. Pleasures follow as the natural consequence of the *right* action, pains as the natural consequence of *wrong* action. In our social relations and even in religion the same situation is to be seen. When we disregard the interests of others, they resent it and by the pressure of social chastisement seek to cause us enough pain to change our attitude. Few experiences can bring more intense suffering than the loneliness of the college freshman ostracized by his fellows because he has failed to conform to some college tradition or accepted social attitude. The Christian Church likewise strengthens with divine approval acts that help others. It stresses the divine displeasure and punishment that attend acts that injure others, and thus seeks to offset any pleasure men might find in such acts. Excommunication, Heaven, and Hell were for long effective instruments in stimulating adherence to social mores and in preventing acts harmful to others.

Bentham thus identifies four *sanctions* of the principle of utility: the legal, the natural or physical, the popular or moral, and the religious. It is the function of the law to give what additional support is needed to the natural, the moral, and the religious sanctions of utility. Recognizing that nature has placed man under the dominance of two sovereign masters, pleasure and pain, the intelligent legislator will use this fact to see that people take into consideration the welfare of others as well as their own. In this fashion the good society can be built upon purely hedonistic principles.

### Bentham's Altruism

Interest in the welfare of others was essentially a matter of practical philosophy for Bentham. He gave the best years of his life unstintingly to improve the lot of the underprivileged, but the theory by which he justified this endeavor pictures all men as moved only by the pursuit of pleasure. In his proposed legislation Bentham exhibited deep concern for the general welfare, the good of the greatest number. In his hedonistic philosophy, however, it is not always easy to find real justification for this concern. At best his Utilitarianism embodies a sort of enlightened self-interest, more refined and purified, more socially conscious than that of Epicurus or Lin Yutang, but nevertheless an egoistic, not an altruistic, hedonism. For a statement of Utilitarianism that is genuinely altruistic in spirit, it is necessary to turn to Bentham's greatest disciple, John Stuart Mill.

## The Development of Mill's Thought

John Stuart Mill (1806–1873) ranks among the ablest as well as the more distinguished figures in British philosophy. Hardly anywhere can one find a man whose life was so explicitly shaped by a specific philosophy. In large measure this was the work of his father, James Mill, a recognized leader among the group of younger men attracted to Bentham. More interested in Bentham's political and social principles than in his ethical theory, James Mill soon became an outstanding exponent of the "democratic radicalism" accepted by this younger group. But his greatest practical contribution both to political thought and to philosophy was undoubtedly the experiment he conducted in educating his brilliant son.

### The Making of a Philosopher

In his *Autobiography* John Stuart Mill has provided a detailed account of the educational experiment undertaken by his father. Compared with the way in which parents today customarily treat their children, it reads almost like a record of penal servitude at hard labor. At the age of three, Mill began to learn arithmetic and Greek. At eight he took up Latin. Soon he was reading the great Greek and Latin classics in the original. Homer's *Iliad* was his favorite, but within a few years he had read the *Odyssey*, the Greek dramatists, all of Thucydides, much of Plato, Virgil's *Aeneid*, Lucretius, the *Orations* of Cicero, and many less famous works as well. The contrast between a typical day in Mill's life and what most of us can remember at his age is enlightening. He arose each morning at six, studied for two or three hours before breakfast, and followed breakfast with another five hours of concentrated study. In the evening he returned to his studies for another two or three hours.

This exacting educational program was conducted entirely by Mill's father. James Mill took the necessary time from a strenuous life for work with his son, deliberately shielding him from association with other boys of his own age, whose childish fancies aroused little sympathy in the father's mind. James Mill's method was designed to make his son a first-rate thinker who would become the major prophet of Utilitarianism, and in this he succeeded remarkably well. As the son subsequently pointed out:

> Most boys or youths who have had much knowledge drilled into them, have their mental capacities not strengthened, but overlaid by it. They are crammed with mere facts, and with the opinions or phrases of other people, and these are accepted as a substitute for the power to form opinions of their own: and thus the sons of eminent fathers, who have spared no pains in their education, so often grow up mere parroters of what they have learnt, incapable of using their minds except in the furrows traced for them. Mine, however, was not an education of cram. My father never permitted anything that I learnt to degenerate into a mere exercise of memory. He strove to make the understanding not only go along with every step of the teaching, but, if possible, precede it. *Anything which could be found out by thinking I never was told, until I had exhausted my efforts to find it out for myself.*[4]

### The Crisis in Mill's Intellectual Development

One cannot help being impressed by what Mill was able to accomplish during his youth; yet his early life and education seems almost directly to contradict the hedonistic notion that pleasure is the chief end of living. Nor is it surprising that when he was about twenty Mill suffered a mental crisis that today would probably call for psychiatric treatment. His own account of this experience is a revealing one:

> From the winter of 1821, when I first read Bentham, and especially from the commencement of the *Westminster Review,** I had what might truly be called an object in life; to be a reformer of the world. My conception of my own happiness was entirely identified with this object. The personal sympathies I wished for were those of fellow laborers in this enterprise. I endeavoured to pick up as many flowers as I could by the way; but as a serious and permanent personal satisfaction to rest upon, my whole reliance was placed upon this; and I was accustomed to felicitate myself on the certainty of a happy life which I enjoyed, through placing my

* The literary review founded by Mill's father and the radical group of younger men around Bentham to provide suitable expression for their political and social philosophy.

happiness in something durable and distant, on which some progress might be always making, while it could never be exhausted by complete attainment.

But the time came when I awakened from this as from a dream. It was in the autumn of 1826. I was in a dull state of nerves, such as everybody is occasionally liable to, one of those moods when what is pleasure at other times becomes insipid or indifferent; the state, I should think, in which converts to Methodism usually are, when smitten by their first "conviction of sin." I seemed to have nothing left to live for. At first I hoped that the cloud would pass away of itself; but it did not. A night's sleep, the sovereign remedy for the smaller vexations of life, had no effect upon it. In vain I sought relief from my favourite books, those memorials of past nobleness and greatness from which I had always hitherto drawn strength and animation. I read them now without feeling, or with the accustomed feeling *minus* all its charm; and I became persuaded that my love of mankind, and of excellence for its own sake, had worn itself out.[5]

Fortunately Mill's condition was not as serious as he feared. Only after a good many months did his spirits improve, but gradually they did. Experiences in which he formerly had no interest, music and poetry, especially the poetry of Wordsworth, proved particularly appealing to him at this time and gave Mill a much sounder understanding of human nature. As a result of his own early training, however, Mill was always inclined to take things rather seriously. He never quite reached the point where he could forget himself in simple enjoyment or in the pure animal exuberance of youth.

### John Stuart Mill and Harriet Taylor

It was during this period that Mill became acquainted with the young woman who after a friendship of twenty years became his wife. He first met Harriet Taylor at a dinner party, and the mutual attraction that was at once apparent developed rapidly into a relationship that would have caused talk in any age, even our own. It is not difficult to imagine the reaction in the Victorian age that witnessed the couple's unusual friendship.

Mill was twenty-four when he met Mrs. Taylor in 1830; she was twenty-three. His life had been preoccupied almost entirely with intellectual and literary matters and devoid of romantic interests. A love affair, while hardly predictable, is not difficult to understand in retrospect. He was young, handsome, and already a man of considerable importance. The wife of a respected gentleman, and the mother of two children, Harriet Taylor was young, attractive, and quite intellectually curious for a woman of that day. Her husband was devoted to her but was older and much more conservative in his social and cultural tastes. As is aptly pointed out in a recent study of

Mill, "the great romance contained, therefore, all the traditional elements of the eternal triangle—the dull but devoted husband, the beautiful but bored wife, the gallant but gullible lover."[6] The friendship between Mill and Mrs. Taylor grew gradually but steadily. Mill began at first to discuss his writing with her and soon, upon this pretext largely, was spending all his free hours at the Taylor home. Eventually even John Taylor realized that this relationship was more than mere friendship. He tried to convince his wife that the affair had gone beyond proper limits, and several of Mill's friends also undertook to persuade him to end the relationship. These efforts had but one effect upon Mill and Mrs. Taylor. They appeared together in public less frequently but saw more of each other in private.

After several years of this, John Taylor suggested to his wife a trial separation of six months, hoping that given an opportunity to see the situation more objectively she would break off the affair with Mill. Mill supported the idea, feeling confident that Mrs. Taylor would make a final break with her husband and seek a divorce. Both men were wrong. Harriet Taylor went to France for the six months. Mill followed and the two were together constantly, free from the restrictions imposed in the more conservative British society. At the end of the period Mrs. Taylor, to everyone's surprise, returned to her husband and then for another fifteen years continued her romance with Mill as it had been before. The search for a resolution seemed hopeless in an age when divorce was a breach of propriety that brought to those involved a most offensive notoriety.*

This almost intolerable situation was finally terminated in 1849 when John Taylor died of cancer. Mill assisted Mrs. Taylor in making arrangements for the funeral but did not attend. An immediate marriage was in that day thought unseemly *because* their relationship had been so intimate and so obvious to all. Harriet Taylor's somewhat peculiar sense of propriety likewise made a respectable period of mourning necessary. A little over two years after John Taylor's death, she and Mill were married in a quiet civil ceremony on August 21, 1851.

### A Woman's Influence

It would be a serious mistake to see this relationship only in terms of the typical romantic affair between a young and bored wife and an able, distinguished man. Almost all that Mill wrote during the most creative period

---

* This episode in Mill's life, so different from the rest of the interests and activities of the man later called "the saint of rationalism," has naturally occasioned a good deal of discussion. A carefully edited collection of their letters by F. A. Hayck, entitled *John Stuart Mill and Harriet Taylor: Their Correspondence and Subsequent Marriage* (University of Chicago Press, 1951), provides interesting insight into their personal and social life. A not unexpected reaction to this is to be found in *John Stuart Mill and the Harriet Taylor Myth* by H. P. Pappe (Melbourne University Press, 1961).

of his life, from 1830 to 1860, was read and criticised by Harriet Taylor. In his opinion, at least, she made a contribution to his thought that added greatly to its appeal and validity. The nature of this is well illustrated in Mill's account of her influence upon his *Principles of Political Economy*, completed in 1847. Concerning this work, Mill writes:

> What was abstract and purely scientific was generally mine; the properly human element came from her: in all that concerned the application of philosophy to the exigencies of human society and progress, I was her pupil, alike in boldness of speculation and cautiousness of practical judgment. But while she thus rendered me bolder in speculation on human affairs, her practical turn of mind, and her almost unerring estimate of practical obstacles, repressed in me all tendencies that were really visionary. Her mind invested all ideas in a concrete shape, and formed to itself a conception of how they would actually work: and her knowledge of the existing feelings and conduct of mankind was so seldom at fault, that the weak point of any unworkable suggestion seldom escaped her.[7]

Not often indeed has a man avowed such a debt to the woman he married as Mill did to Harriet Taylor. Never has a philosopher written in more glowing terms of his wife's character and ability: "I soon perceived that she possessed in combination, the qualities which in all other persons whom I had known I had been only too happy to find singly. Alike in the highest regions of speculation and in the smaller practical concerns of daily life, her mind was the same perfect instrument, piercing to the very heart and marrow of the matter; always seizing the essential idea or principle. Her intellectual gifts did but minister to a moral character at once the noblest and the best balanced which I have ever met with in life." Although the objective evidence does not entirely bear out Mill's evaluation of Harriet Taylor's ability and perception, the fact that he himself believed it is significant. It seems clear also that she brought to her relationship with Mill a warmth and affection otherwise lacking in his life that proved to be essential for his mental and physical well-being.

### Mature Achievement

Since it provides the one element of human interest in Mill's adult life, one can easily give too much prominence to his relationship with Harriet Taylor. Whatever insights into his personal attitudes we may find in this relationship, his involvement in it certainly did not in any way limit Mill's extraordinary achievement and influence. After writing regularly in *The Westminster Review* for a number of years, he became its sole owner and editor in 1837. Six years later he decided to sell the journal and give more of his time to the development of his own ideas. His early training had convinced him of the importance of clear and accurate thinking, and for nearly thirteen years he worked upon his first major book, A *System of Logic*. Published in 1843, this was generally regarded as his greatest single achievement. It ran through many editions and was for years the standard work in the field. Its reputation was due especially to the skill with which Mill defended the inductive method in logic, a method employed so successfully in the scientific thinking of his day. With Francis Bacon and John Dewey, he stands as an able proponent of the necessity of relating logic and life if one's thinking is to be significant and effective.

A brief essay, *Utilitarianism* (1863), is Mill's one direct contribution to ethical theory. This was later combined with the essays *On Liberty* and *Representative Government* in a small volume that ranks among the classic discussions of political and social philosophy. The essay *On Liberty*, published originally in 1859 and prominent in recent Women's Liberation reading lists, was, Mill tells us, more directly and literally a joint work with his wife than anything else that bears his name.

Despite the large amount of writing that he did, both political and philosophical, Mill also retained a responsible post for more than thirty years with the East India Company, serving finally as Chief Examiner of India Correspondence, the highest office next to that of Secretary in the Company's home service. When the East India Company was dissolved by Parliament, Mill was offered a seat in the council set up to supervise the affairs of India. This he declined, however, preferring to devote his energies to the intellectual interests in which by that time he had so distinguished himself. During these later years he wrote numerous essays on political and philosophical subjects, but none so important as those already mentioned. His highly readable *Autobiography* was published in 1873 shortly after his death, and in the following year a small volume entitled *Three Essays on Religion* appeared. In these essays Mill insisted, in accord with his empirical philosophy, that religion must be interpreted in terms of human experience. It is what religion means in life, not the problems posed by theology, that he finds significant.

### The Philosopher in Politics

Upon his retirement in 1858 from his duties with the East India Company Mill intended to devote himself entirely to writing. He had a comfortable pension and, with the royalties from his published works, could look forward to some years of relative leisure. He and his wife decided upon a brief holiday on the Continent, and on November 1, 1858, they were in Avignon. Then, quite suddenly two days later, Harriet Taylor died. The death of his wife was a great blow to Mill. For a time he was a virtual recluse and he devoted himself to his writing with almost feverish intensity.*

Early in 1865 a group of electors from Westminster proposed to Mill, much to his surprise, that he stand as a candidate for Parliament from that district. The proposal did not seem to him a practical one. His political philosophy makes interesting reading when compared with our practices in politics today:

> I was convinced that no numerous or influential portion of any electoral body, really wished to be represented by a person of my opinions; and that one who possessed no local connection or popularity, or who did not choose to stand as the mere organ of a party, had small chance of being elected anywhere unless through the expenditure of money. Now it was, and is, my fixed conviction that a candidate ought not to incur one farthing of expense for undertaking a public duty. What has to be done by the supporters of each candidate in order to bring his claims properly before the constituency, should be done by unpaid agency, or by voluntary subscription.[8]

Mill felt it only just and courteous, however, after a group of electors had sought him out of their own accord and offered to bring him forward as their candidate, to allow them to make the final decision:

> I therefore put their disposition to the proof by one of the frankest explanations ever tendered, I should think, to an electoral body by a candidate. I wrote, in reply to the offer, a letter for publication, saying that I had no personal wish to be a member of parliament, that I thought a candidate ought neither to canvass nor to incur any expense, and that I could not consent to do either. I said further, that if elected, I could not undertake to give any of my time and labour to their local interest. I made known to them, among other things, my conviction (as I was bound to do, since I intended, if elected, to act on it), that women were entitled to representation in Parliament on the same terms as men.[9]

There is much to be said for the dedication of the group of electors that decided to accept him as their candidate despite these conditions. A well-

---

* After the death of his wife, her daughter, Helen Taylor, became Mill's constant companion and to a surprising extent gradually took her mother's place in his life. Mill's comment in his *Autobiography* indicates clearly his feelings in this matter. "And, though the inspirer of my best thoughts was no longer with me," he writes, "I was not alone: she had left a daughter, my step-daughter, Miss Helen Taylor, the inheritor of much of her wisdom, and of all her nobleness of character, whose ever growing and ripening talents . . . have already made her name better and more widely known than was that of her mother. . . . of what I owe in the way of instruction to her great powers of original thought and soundness of practical judgment, it would be a vain attempt to give an adequate idea." (p. 169)

known literary man was heard to say that the Almighty himself would have no chance of being elected on such a platform.

To his surprise as much as anyone's, Mill was elected to Parliament by a small majority over his Conservative opponent, and he served as a member of the House of Commons during the three sessions that passed the Reform Bill of 1865. He not only supported this bill with conspicuous ability, but moved an amendment to the Reform Bill to admit to suffrage all women who possessed the qualifications required of male electors. Although the amendment was defeated, Mill's support of it was effective enough to arouse wide public interest and to get under way the movement that later developed into the National Society for Women's Suffrage.

In the spring of 1873, feeling somewhat weary and exhausted, Mill returned to Avignon with Helen Taylor to relax in the warm sunshine and the memories of that city. After overexerting himself one day, he developed a high fever and on May 7, 1873, he died in Avignon. He was buried there beside his wife.

Generally recognized during his later years as one of the distinguished men of his age, Mill moved in the world of letters with some of the most celebrated authors of Victorian literature. Thomas Carlyle was his close friend; Charles Dickens and Robert Browning were younger than he by about seven years, and Charlotte Bronte, George Eliot, and John Ruskin by only a little more. In the world of politics he held an equally enviable position. Gladstone was two years younger than Mill and Disraeli only two years older. These men were not only his contemporaries but his associates and colleagues.

### The Utilitarian Heretic

Heresy has been attacked more vigorously during the pre-Marxian era by the orthodox in religious rather than in philosophical circles. Anyone, however, who professes to believe in the major tenets of a faith but so modifies these tenets (though it be in an effort to be honest and reasonable) as to give up what is distinctive in them is classed as a heretic. From this point of view, Mill may justly be termed a utilitarian heretic. Within the first fifteen pages of his essay *Utilitarianism*, he actually abandons the main principles of Bentham's moral philosophy. The egoistic view of human nature and conduct, the appeal to enlightened self-interest, the quantitative calculus of pleasure and pain upon which Bentham put such store—all these Mill discards. Almost all that remains of the ethical theory he inherited is a tenuous commitment to hedonism, but even this no longer contains the major ideas usually associated with such a philosophy of living. The breadth of his own sympathies, and his concern to do justice to the facts of life as he saw them, inevitably took Mill beyond the utilitarian system of his predecessors. The position he adopts is as discerning and appealing as almost any that one can find. Its practical results in his own life tend to suggest as much. Yet the effort to present his philosophy in strictly utilitarian and hedonistic terms lands Mill in serious logical difficulty when not in downright contradiction.

Actually Mill, like Bentham, was less interested in the theoretical problems of philosophy than in the vital issues of social and political life. He also had great respect for his father and for Bentham.* This loyalty to them made him seek as best he could to minimize the differences between his own thought and theirs, even where he realized that the difference existed. In *Utilitarianism* Mill commits himself quite explicitly, therefore, to the hedonism of Bentham and Epicurus:

> The creed which accepts as the foundation of morals, utility or the Greatest Happiness Principle, holds that actions are right in proportion as they tend to promote happiness, wrong as they tend to produce the reverse of happiness. By happiness is intended pleasure and the absence of pain, by unhappiness, pain and the privation of pleasure. All desirable things (which are as numerous in the utilitarian as in any other scheme) are desirable either for the pleasure inherent in themselves, or as a means to the promotion of pleasure and the prevention of pain.[10]

Those who attack the Epicurean philosophy because it recognizes no higher end in life than pleasure, and thus seems to treat man as little better than a beast, are to Mill obviously misguided.

> When thus attacked, the Epicureans have always answered that it is not they but their accusers who represent human nature in a degrading light, since the accusation supposes human beings to be capable of no pleasures except those of which swine are capable. Human beings have faculties more elevated than the animal appetites, and when once made conscious of them, do not regard anything as happiness which does not include their gratification. There is no known Epicurean theory of life which does not assign to the pleasures of the intellect, of the feelings and imagination, and of the moral sentiments, a much higher value as pleasure than to those of mere sensation.[11]

### Qualitative Differences in Pleasures

As intelligent and social human beings, we do find many satisfactions that mean more to us than the pleasures of the senses. No amount of good food can compensate for the loss of a friend. Omar's jug of wine simply cannot compare with the satisfaction of a job well done, the sense of commitment to a cherished ideal, the enjoyment of beauty in nature or in art. "Now it is an unquestionable fact that those who are equally acquainted

---

* Of special interest in this connection is Mill's essay on Bentham, published in the *London and Westminster Review*, August, 1838, shortly after Bentham's death.

with, and equally capable of appreciating and enjoying, both, do give a most marked preference to the manner of existence which employs the higher faculties," Mill points out. "No human creatures would consent to be changed into any of the lower animals, for a promise of the fullest allowance of a beast's pleasure; no intelligent human being would consent to be a fool, no instructed person would be an ignoramus, no person of feeling and conscience would be selfish and base, even though they would be persuaded that the fool, the dunce, or the rascal is better satisfied with his lot than they are with theirs."

It is true that a person whose capacities of enjoyment are low has the greatest chance of having them fully satisfied, Mill admits. But the person of high endowments will not want to change places with him on that account. "It is better to be a human being dissatisfied than a pig satisfied; better to be Socrates dissatisfied than a fool satisfied. And if the fool, or the pig, is of a different opinion, it is because they only know their own side of the question. The other party to the comparison knows both sides."[12] This is among the best known and most frequently quoted statements in Mill's essay. One is reminded of an illuminating comment by Anatole France: "The joy of understanding is a sad joy, yet those who have once tasted it would not exchange it for all the frivolous gaieties and empty hopes of the vulgar herd."

It is necessary, therefore, to recognize the fact that some *kinds* of pleasure are more desirable and more valuable than others, Mill argues: "It would be absurd that while, in estimating all other things, quality is considered as well as quantity, the estimation of pleasures should be supposed to depend on quantity alone." But if Mill is right, then the orthodox Epicurean is wrong. If some satisfactions are in themselves so worthwhile as to be far preferable to other kinds of pleasure, Bentham's elaborate hedonistic calculus is no longer of value to us. The achievement of happiness is now clearly not simply a matter of adding pleasures together, or of avoiding pain. There is, Mill recognizes, a quality of human experience at its best in which we find enduring satisfaction quite different from the enjoyment of pleasure at the physical level. His able analysis of human experience shows clearly the limitation of orthodox hedonism, as does his own continued devotion to the common good rather than to the pursuit of individual pleasure.

## Devotion to the Common Good

Hedonism has been criticized not only for accepting the pursuit of pleasure as man's chief end in life but also for an inherent selfishness or egoism. Mill's valiant effort to counteract this second weakness of traditional hedonism makes it even clearer that he himself can hardly be called a hedonist. The utilitarian standard of conduct, he maintains, "when rightly understood, must be not the agent's own greatest happiness, but the greatest amount of happiness altogether."

I must again repeat, what the assailants of utilitarianism seldom have the justice to acknowledge, that the happiness which forms the utilitarian standard of what is right conduct, is not the agent's own happiness but that of all concerned. As between his own happiness and that of others, utilitarianism requires him to be as strictly impartial as a disinterested and benevolent spectator. In the golden rule of Jesus of Nazareth we read the complete spirit of the ethics of utility. To do as you would be done by, and to love your neighbor as yourself, constitutes the ideal perfection of utilitarian morality.[13]

*— Not HEDONISM*

X

There would seem to be little objection that one could offer to a moral ideal such as this except to question seriously whether it is, as a matter of fact, hedonism at all. The good of others, not the pursuit of one's own pleasure, has clearly become Mill's major concern, and one's happiness, whenever it is achieved, is now a by-product of other, more fundamental aims. Mill makes an effort to justify his continued commitment to hedonism, it is true. "The utilitarian morality does recognize in human beings the power of sacrificing their own greatest good for the good of others," he writes. "It only refuses to admit that the sacrifice is itself a good. A sacrifice which does not increase, or tend to increase, the sum total of happiness it considers wasted. The only self-renunciation which it applauds, is devotion to the happiness, or to some of the means of happiness, of others."[14] This effort to suggest, however, that in working for the happiness of others instead of his own one has not given up the pursuit of pleasure as his chief concern in life would hardly convince confirmed or consistent hedonists such as Epicurus or Omar Khayyam.

It is, moreover, his social interpretation of human nature that provides Mill with his most persuasive argument for the central doctrines of his philosophy. The firm foundation of Utilitarianism, he writes, lies in "the social feelings of mankind; the desire to be in unity with our fellow-creatures, which is already a powerful principle in human nature, and happily one of those which tend to become stronger from the influences of advancing civilization."[15] Promoting the common good brings us happiness because we are by nature social beings, deeply involved in the life of the community. Neither the thinly disguised self-interest that Bentham has suggested nor the direct pursuit of pleasure recommended by Epicurus but, rather, a genuine and increasing interest in the welfare of others is the motivating force in man's social life, Mill maintains. *— but it becomes increasingly hard and futile to help others.*

### Education and Social Reform

*— which leads in another way to Epicureanism.*

As might well be anticipated in view of his own early experience, Mill felt that society must look to education as its chief hope for improvement, and his discussion of the nature of education anticipates much that is being said today. Desirable attitudes, convictions, and moral ideals can be developed through education, and our concern for others increased, Mill points out. But education of this sort involves much more than formal training provided by schools: "the main branch of the education of human beings is their habitual employment." Men who in their daily lives are the mere tenders of machines can never have access to the cultural riches of our civilization through which alone the full development of human personality is achieved. Each man must have an opportunity in his daily job for personal development, Mill maintains. Human personality is of too great worth to be degraded by the ill effects of our social institutions. Mill's point of view here, one might note, is in agreement with an important aspect of Karl Marx's philosophy, an aspect that is now attracting a considerable attention.

In his later years, Mill advocated two measures in particular that held great promise, he felt, for the achievement of a better society. These were the enfranchisement of women and the promotion of cooperative enterprise. It is interesting to note how far in advance of his contemporaries he was here. He may well have had a somewhat exaggerated notion of the political and social impact of these two measures. Experience with women's suffrage has not indicated that the world immediately becomes a better place in which to live as a result of the influence of women in politics. Nor did the cooperative movement greatly modify our free-enterprise economy in America, despite a number of efforts some years ago to promote it. Both these proposals, however, as Mill rightly saw, provided increased political and economic opportunity for *the fuller development of human personality upon which his philosophy placed such importance.* The modern American woman may not be completely emancipated. Certainly the proponents of Women's Lib do not think so. But she does enjoy a much fuller life than was possible in an earlier day when women were little more than the property of their husbands.

Despite his consistent and vigorous support of democracy and of universal suffrage, Mill himself also recognized clearly that there were dangers in both. Democracy certainly demands greater intelligence and greater self-control on the part of all citizens than does any other form of government, and Mill constantly urges that through improved education men and women should become better fitted for their political responsibilities. Only at a relatively late stage in their political development do people become capable of successfully governing themselves, he feels. But once they are capable of doing so, self-government not only makes them happier but also enables them to become better persons—more intelligent, more virtuous, more responsible, in a word more fully human than they otherwise could be. Unquestionably, the problems of democracy upon which Mill concentrated at the beginning of the nineteenth century are those, as one interpreter points out, that have actually turned out to be crucial in the twentieth.[16] While he obviously failed to solve these problems, Mill certainly recognized them and dealt with them in a way that has relevance for us today.

## On Liberty

Mill's essay *On Liberty* (1859) provides the clearest and most forceful statement of the social philosophy to which he gave allegiance. This essay he himself regarded as the best and most eloquent of his works. It may well prove to be the most influential thing he wrote. Nowhere, indeed, can one find a more uncompromising commitment to the ideal of freedom that underlies the traditional American and British way of life. Today, when we see human freedom so seriously endangered not only by totalitarian governments, but by the Corporate State in our own country that so disturbs Charles Reich in *The Greening of America*, it is both desirable and encouraging to reread Mill's eloquent essay in its defense.

In Mill's opinion liberty is so truly the foundation of all social happiness that any encroachment upon it is not only dangerous but eventually disastrous. The greatest good of society as a whole can only be achieved, he is convinced, by allowing each individual to exercise his own freedom unrestrained, so long as he does not harm others. Only in this way, moreover, is the fullest development of each individual possible. In this discussion of liberty, as a matter of fact, Mill specifically identifies the principle of self-development rather than the pursuit of pleasure as the basic tenet of his philosophy as a whole. The fundamental aim of life, he maintains, as "prescribed by the eternal and immutable dictates of reason," is the fullest and most harmonious development of man's powers to a complete and consistent whole.[17]

## The Case for Freedom of Thought and Speech

One very simple principle, Mill writes in the introduction to *On Liberty*, is entitled to govern the dealings of society with the individual—namely, "that the sole end for which mankind are warranted, individually or collectively, in interfering with the liberty of action of any of their number, is self-protection." The individual's own good, either physical or moral, is not a sufficient warrant.

> He cannot rightfully be compelled to do or forbear because it will be better for him to do so, because it will make him happier, because, in the opinion of others, to do so would be wise, or even right. These are good reasons for remonstrating with him, or reasoning with him, or persuading him, or entreating him, but not for compelling him. To justify that, the conduct from which it is desired to deter him must be calculated to produce evil to someone else. The only part of the conduct of anyone, for which he is amenable to society, is that which concerns others. Over himself, over his own body and mind, the individual is sovereign.[18]

Mill argues the case for freedom of thought and discussion with rare insight and persuasiveness. No one, he maintains, is in a position to say absolutely that a view with which he disagrees is undeniably false. Whoever does so is actually claiming infallibility for himself. There have been some tragic cases in history when well-meaning individuals silenced other people whom they felt to be dangerous to the common good. Socrates was put to death by his fellow Athenians because he refused to give up his right to criticize the established democracy of his day. Jesus was condemned by his own people because he refused to be silent concerning the defects of the established religion. History has vindicated both men and has instead condemned those who denied to them the liberty to disagree with the accepted ideas of their day. When today we silence people with whom we disagree, we claim a similar infallibility, Mill insists, and are guilty of the same error as were those who condemned Socrates and Jesus. We are turning to force, rather than reason, to lead us to truth—and there is as little ground today as in the past for expecting this to be successful.

Let us suppose, however, that we can be sure that an opinion is actually false. Should it then be silenced? Mill maintains that even in such circumstances it should not be. Not only does the individual who believes it have a right to his opinion, but also it is good for others to have it expressed. "He who knows only his own side of the case, knows little of that," Mill writes. If we do not know what we reject, we really do not know what we believe. Nor is it enough to hear positions with which one does not agree stated by others who also do not accept them. This will never enable a man to escape his own prejudices.

> That is not the way to do justice to the arguments, or bring them into contact with his own mind. He must be able to hear them from persons who actually believe them, who defend them in earnest, and do their utmost for them. He must know them in their most plausible and persuasive form; he must feel the whole force of the difficulty which the true view of the subject has to encounter and dispose of; else he will never really possess himself of the portion of truth which meets and removes that difficulty. Ninety-nine in a hundred of what are called educated men are in this condition; even of those who can argue fluently for their opinions. Their conclusion may be true, but it might be false for anything they know: they have never thrown themselves into the mental position of those who think differently from them; and considered what such persons may have to say, and consequently they do not, in any proper sense of the word, know the doctrine which they themselves profess.[19]

Obviously, when Mill says he believes in liberty of thought and discussion, he means it. And his belief, like that of Socrates, rests upon a confidence in man's ability to think clearly if given the necessary facts and the opportunity. No one will insist that men be allowed to think for themselves unless he has such a confidence that ultimately truth is to be reached in this way— and that error is to be overcome not by force but by clearer thinking.

In times of relative peace and prosperity, it is not too difficult perhaps to accept this position. When a government is faced with the loss of its power and prestige, however, the appeal to force seems much simpler and more certain of immediate success than does the appeal to reason. This is especially true when we have the largest guns or the newest atomic weapons. In this situation Mill's warning that confidence in force alone will in the end prove deceptive is a timely one. Here, certainly, he stands in the tradition of the great philosophers, and he has a message for us that should not be over-looked, whether in the formulation of American foreign policy or in the interactions of the Establishment and members of a counter-culture.

### The Dilemma of Altruistic Hedonism

Enough has been said to indicate the broad appeal of Mill's philosophy as well as to make clear his difficulties in defending the hedonism of Epicurus and Bentham. When he undertakes to compress within the con-fines of a purely hedonistic pursuit of pleasure the interests and achievements that bring lasting happiness, he seems to be faced with an inescapable dilemma. This dilemma raises the most serious objection to his Utilitarian-ism, one that has made it finally unacceptable to most philosophers despite its many appealing features.[20]

#### Hedonism or Altruism?

As a hedonist, the utilitarian is committed to the pursuit of pleasure, and his own pleasure is necessarily his greatest good. As an altruist, on the other hand, his primary concern is the welfare and happiness of others. In many instances, as Mill points out, we do find pleasure not merely in the company of others but in helping others. The basically social nature of human personality makes this both natural and understandable. Thus far there is no obvious conflict. But the consistent hedonist, Mill's critics point out, is forced to go one step further. Whether he analyzes the motives of a mother who makes personal sacrifices for her family or the attitude of a rich man who devotes his time and energy to bettering the lot of the less privi-leged, the hedonist must maintain that such action occurs because the individual involved expects to derive more pleasure from it than he would from purely selfish conduct. Now one of the strange paradoxes of life is that the person who decides to help others only in order to get pleasure for himself usually finds the experiment disappointing. Actually, Mill himself agrees that it is the person who helps others because he is interested in their welfare rather than his own who finds unsought but lasting satisfaction in what he does.

There are times, moreover, when the welfare of others can be promoted only at the sacrifice of our pleasures—times, that is, when our own pursuit of pleasure can be continued only by renouncing our interest in others. A nation attacked at war, especially, when its very sovereignty is threatened, illustrates clearly this dilemma of altruistic hedonism. In such a situation, the critics of utilitarianism point out, men and women cannot continue to enjoy leisure and luxury themselves and at the same time promote the nation's good. A choice has to be made between these two aims. And if this is true in the country as a whole in such times of national crisis, it is particularly true for the young man or woman called to serve in the armed forces of the country. A young man who gives up his chance for an education or a good job, a wife or fianceé, and goes willingly to face hardships, danger, and perhaps death, is obviously finding it necessary to put his loyalty to other values above his private pleasures. While the issue was not quite the same, one might well argue that loyalty to values other than pleasure equally motivated those young men who, in our recent involvement in Vietnam, chose exile or imprisonment rather than military service in a war they believed to be wrong. There are satisfactions, of course, that come to the young man or woman who makes such choices. But are they satisfactions that can be encompassed in the hedonistic pursuit of pleasure? In many of the more serious and crucial decisions in life, it is difficult then to see how one can be both a hedonist and an altruist; that is, how one can follow the utilitarian philosophy consistently. And in such cases we must ask ourselves whether it is the hedonism of Epicurus or the altruism of Mill that men acclaim more highly, and that we ourselves find more appealing.

We have only to look, as a matter of fact, at the philosophy by which Bentham and Mill lived, rather than that which they professed, to find their own preference clearly apparent. The source of the satisfactions that gave their lives meaning and brought them a measure of enduring happiness was certainly not an egoistic pursuit of pleasure but an altruistic interest in the common good—a genuine concern for the removal of injustice, for the welfare of the underprivileged, for political and social reform. This concern, indeed, frequently led them to sacrifice most of the pleasures listed in the catalog of the orthodox hedonist. Mill himself, when he was reexamining his own philosophy of living at the time of his early emotional crisis, stated this with unusual clarity:

> I never, indeed, wavered in the conviction that happiness is the test of all rules of conduct, and the end of life. But I now thought that this end was only to be attained by not making it the direct end. *Those only are happy (I thought) who have their minds fixed on some object other than their own happiness*; on the *happiness of others*, on the *improvement of*

*mankind*, even on some art or pursuit, followed not as a means, but as itself an ideal end. *Aiming thus at something else, they find happiness by the way.* The enjoyments of life (such was now my theory) are sufficient to make it a pleasant thing, when they are taken *en passant*, without being made a principal object. Once make them so, and they are immediately felt to be insufficient. They will not bear a scrutinizing examination. Ask yourself whether you are happy, and you cease to be so. The only chance is to treat, not happiness, but some end external to it, as the purpose of life.[21]

Upon the insights stated here Mill might well have built a much sounder philosophy than the modified Utilitarianism that he chose to defend. As suggested earlier, however, he was disturbed primarily by evils he saw in the social and political life of his day, and was satisfied with a much too superficial analysis of Epicurean hedonism. He never undertook a careful examination of the significant difference between the relation of pleasure and happiness in the philosophy of Bentham and Epicurus and that relation in his own thought, as stated so clearly in the quotation above. Had he done this, he would almost certainly have adopted a position much closer to the philosophy of Aristotle than to the hedonism of Epicurus. When Aristotle is discussed in a later chapter, it should become apparent that in his thought rather than in Utilitarianism one may well find a consistent philosophical basis for the altruism of Mill and Bentham.

## CHAPTER 4

# Pessimism

*Arthur Schopenhauer*

Although not himself a hedonist, Schopenhauer has an important contribution to make to our understanding of hedonism as a practical philosophy of life. For an uncompromising commitment to following through the implications of hedonism, as he saw them, led Schopenhauer to pessimism. Every man's convictions, of course, are the outgrowths not of logic alone, but also of the circumstances of his life—sometimes largely of home environment or early associations, at other times more obviously of the conditions of the world in which he lives. In Schopenhauer's case, it may well seem that all things conspired together to make him a pessimist. Before we undertake an examination of his thought, therefore, a look at the man himself and the world in which he lived will be revealing.

## The Man and His Age

Europe in the first half of the nineteenth century was suffering all the disasters and ravages of war and of postwar unrest. It knew the terror of the French Revolution, Napoleon's dream of empire, the constant march of French armies across the continent for a decade or more, and finally, in 1815, the Congress of Vienna. There, under the shrewd leadership of Prince Metternich of Austria, the forces of reaction attempted to stamp out every vestige of democratic and liberal sentiment born in the early enthusiasm of the French Revolution. We are today again in a position to appreciate the meaning of such destruction, disillusionment, and disaster. As did the ambition of Napoleon a century and a half ago, so in our age the thirst for power, first of Hitler and the Nazis and later of the Russian and the Chinese totalitarian regimes, again brought fear, internal strife, and prostration to weaker peoples the world over. Now, as then, powerful nations, including our own, are guilty of wanton destruction as they seek to impose upon conquered or war-torn populations a political ideology they do not want.

Every such major conflict brings in its wake a wave of reaction and disillusionment. In the decade after the First World War, Europe and America felt this spirit of cynicism and despair. The age of Schopenhauer knew it after the Napoleonic era. Inevitably it is becoming apparent again in our own day. It is not difficult for those who are young to become pessimistic or cynical as they see humanistic ideals and aspirations, for which millions have sacrificed their lives, gradually becoming engulfed in a spirit of self-interest, vengeance, and aggrandizement on the part of powerful nations. In the thinking of such an age, the problem of evil becomes dominant. The tragedy of human society seems but a reflection of the chaos of the universe itself. To many, a divine order appears impossible, and God, if there is a God, is seen as unconcerned or impotent to aid mankind in the hardships and hope-lessness of life. It was in such an age that Schopenhauer lived. Small wonder that the prevailing despair of Europe found reflection in the mood of the philosopher.

### Early Influences

His paternal heritage, as well as his youth and early manhood, fitted Schopenhauer in a particular fashion to respond to the spirit of his age. Born in Danzig in 1788, he began life with every prospect of fortune and happiness. His father, a wealthy merchant of aristocratic Dutch lineage, moved his business and his family to Hamburg when Schopenhauer was only five years old. Heinrich Schopenhauer traveled extensively, and he quite frequently took his young son along. When Arthur was ten years old, he spent two years with a French family. When he was about fifteen, he spent a winter in the home of a clergyman in England. There Schopenhauer picked up a good knowledge of English, a decided distaste for the constant round of morning and evening prayers that he was forced to undergo, and a genuine admiration for the British character. A winter in Paris the next year left him with a marked enthusiasm for the theater, if not for the French. In the travel journal he kept during these two years, two contrasting impressions stand out: the beauty of nature, on the one hand, and the misery of human life on the other.

The atmosphere of business and finance in which Schopenhauer grew up left its mark upon his philosophy. Despite the fact that he hated the countinghouse, and forsook it permanently two years after his father died in 1803 (apparently by his own hand), one can see a realism in Schopenhauer's treatment of human nature and a bluntness in his philosophy that clearly reflect his early experience in the business world.

Schopenhauer's mother was a popular novelist of the day. Having married for social position rather than for love, as she frankly confessed, she soon tired of her rather prosaic husband, who was twenty years her senior. At his death she sought a more exciting life in the sophisticated intellectual and literary circles of Weimar. There a brilliant company was gathered, with Goethe at its head, and her house soon became one of the social centers in the city. However, she was no more happy in the company of her son, who joined her in Weimar soon after he left his father's business, than she had been with her husband. The two finally arranged to live apart, he coming to call upon her only on her afternoons "at home," a guest among other guests.

But even his mother's extreme expedient did not succeed. Things went from bad to worse, and finally one afternoon in a moment of anger she pushed her son down the stairs of her house. Schopenhauer left Weimar soon after. He was now twenty-one; he had inherited his share of his father's estate and was financially independent. Although his mother lived for another twenty-four years, he never again made an effort to see her.

His stay at Weimar was not entirely unprofitable, however. While there he did meet Goethe among his mother's guests and was publicly congratulated by the great poet for his writing. He also became acquainted with a distinguished oriental scholar, Friedrich Meyer, who introduced Schopenhauer to the philosophical literature of India. He found the oriental religious outlook increasingly appealing, and Schopenhauer's later thought is largely influenced by insights drawn from the Buddhist view of life.

### Academic Interests and Activities

Not until he was twenty-one did Schopenhauer at last begin formal academic work at the University of Göttingen. He first enrolled as a medical student and devoted himself to courses in science. But before long he turned to philosophy, remarking to a friend that as life was a great problem he had decided to spend his in reflecting on this problem. Kant and Plato were his favorite philosophers and influenced him most directly, but his interests were broad and general rather than technical or scholarly. He was an eager reader with wide literary sympathies, and a keen observer, with the insight of one who enjoyed a rich and varied portrayal of life and saw swiftly rather than studied exhaustively. His sense of humor also was keen, leading him to single out the comic and the ridiculous in whatever he saw or read. Obtaining his doctorate when he was twenty-five, Schopenhauer at once began work on the book that was to establish his reputation in philosophy.

In five years *The World as Will and Idea* was completed. Schopenhauer sent his manuscript to the publishers in 1818 with the modest claim that here was an original and highly significant work that "would hereafter be the source and occasion of a hundred other books." Actually Schopenhauer was right, but the world was not ready for his masterpiece and it attracted very little attention at that time. The young philosopher was furious when he learned that the greater part of the first edition was finally sold for waste paper. He wrote such bitter letters to the publishers that they severed all further relations with him. A winter in the warm Italian sunshine, however, helped somewhat to overcome the pessimistic mood into which Schopenhauer had been plunged by this disappointment.

After a good deal of negotiation, Schopenhauer was appointed a lecturer in philosophy at the University of Berlin in 1820. But with almost unbelievable egotism he deliberately chose to lecture at the same hours that were assigned for the lectures of Hegel, at that time the outstanding figure in German philosophy. Consequently he soon found himself talking to empty seats. For several years he continued to have his name printed in the university's catalog along with the announcement of his course of lectures, but nobody came to hear him. It took another two years in Italy for him to recover from this unpleasant experience. Even that was not enough, however, to prevent sarcastic comments upon professional philosophers, to whom he referred as Sophists, from appearing in subsequent editions of *The World as Will and Idea*.

### Human, All Too Human

In 1825 Schopenhauer returned to Berlin, interested apparently in seeing what he could do to settle an old lawsuit against him. Always acutely sensitive to noise, he had been disturbed one day when still connected with the university by three women chattering away on a landing outside his room. When one of them refused to go away, the philosopher took his walking stick and put her out by force. Unfortunately for him, she fell down the steps in the process, was injured slightly, and brought suit against Schopenhauer for assault and battery. Despite all that he could do, he had to pay five-sixths of the costs in the case and a compensation of five thalers a month to the woman for the rest of her life. When she finally died, he inscribed upon the death certificate, in characteristic fashion: *Obit anus, abit onus* (The old woman dies, the burden departs).

A few years later Berlin was visited by a cholera epidemic. Frightened by a dream that foretold his death if he remained in the city, Schopenhauer departed in haste and did not stop until he reached Frankfurt. There he spent the remaining years of his life, living quietly in two rooms with his pipe and his flute. A bronze statue of the Buddha and a small bust of the philosopher Immanuel Kant stood together on his writing desk; he had no friends or companions except a small poodle, the only creature to which

Schopenhauer ever seems to have felt real attachment. He named the dog Atman, a term taken from the pessimistic Hindu religion of India, in which Schopenhauer had by then become deeply interested. The boys of the neighborhood preferred to call his poodle *"der junge Schopenhauer,"* a nickname not too hard to understand when one looks at the philosopher's picture.

Schopenhauer was one of those individuals in whom genius expresses itself early and who are content thereafter largely with the elaboration of early ideas. He was only thirty when he published *The World as Will and Idea*; during the next forty years he deviated in hardly the slightest detail from the philosophy expressed in it. His later essays are humorous and readable, full of wisdom and insight, but they are nevertheless only elaborations or applications of the convictions stated in his one great work.

During the last years of Schopenhauer's life an increasing public interest in his philosophy tended to mollify somewhat the gloom of his youth. The growing popular awareness of science, and especially of the biological sciences, drew attention to Schopenhauer's concept of the *will-to-live*, a cardinal aspect of his interpretation of Nature as well as of human nature. Darwin's famous *Origin of Species*, published in 1859, gave convincing scientific support to the thesis that life is strife and struggle, a principle upon which Schopenhauer had based his own philosophy some forty years earlier. An article on German philosophy in the *Westminster Review* in England ranked Schopenhauer among the more significant scholars of the day, as did similar articles in French and Italian journals. And the freshness, vigor, and realism of his philosophy gradually attracted many intelligent readers outside academic circles, men and women concerned with life itself rather than with abstract or technical treatises on the subject.

A little circle of welcome flatterers gathered around the old philosopher at Frankfurt. Visitors came to see him from London, from Vienna, from Prussia, even from America. Students made pilgrimages to his home; army officers felt the fascination of his pessimism; Leipzig University offered a prize for the best essay on his thought; lectures on his philosophy were given in the German universities; and his *Essay on Women* not only caused men to smile but brought him increased attention from the sex he so maligned. On his seventieth birthday he received messages of congratulation from all over the world.

Schopenhauer loved the admiration of these people. An old man now, with clear, blue eyes and a somewhat sarcastic smile, he smoked his pipe, played his flute, talked wittily and entertainingly on almost every subject and had his portrait painted for posterity. Life he now found not nearly as gloomy and sad as he had pictured it in his youthful essays. This recognition came to him none too soon, however. One morning in September, 1860, with the will to live pretty well exhausted, Schopenhauer, after having his breakfast at the usual hour, died quietly and peacefully as he sat on his sofa.

He had only to die, moreover, to establish his philosophical reputation securely—a somewhat sardonic commentary on his own pessimism. His name has now become an accepted symbol of whatever is gloomy and disillusioned in the thought of our own age as well as his.

## The World as Will

No single aspect of a workable philosophy of living is more important than its estimate of man's place and worth in the total scheme of things. Is man but a cosmic accident, "a planetary eczema that soon will be cured," as one writer has put it? Or is man the center and climax of a divine creative activity, as the Judeo-Christian faith maintains? Is the universe itself the expression of moral order, the medium through which a divine purpose is at work in human life? Or is the universe but a blind mechanism, unconcerned with human life and destiny and unaware of the nobler aspirations of the human spirit? In its broadest outreach the aspect of philosophy that deals with questions such as these is known as *metaphysics*. When stated in technical or scholarly terms the subject matter of metaphysics can become exceeding abstract and beyond the realm of interest for the ordinary reader. But obviously, in its practical bearing upon the philosophy by which one lives, nothing is more influential than the metaphysical scheme a person accepts. It colors one's outlook on human nature, on the worth of life, on the trustworthiness of science, and on the acceptability of religious faith.

Schopenhauer's approach to metaphysics is neither academic nor difficult to understand:

> Temples and churches, pagodas and mosques, in all lands and all ages, in splendor and vastness, testify to the metaphysical need of man, which strong and ineradicable follows close upon his physical need. Certainly whoever is satirically inclined might add that this metaphysical need is a modest fellow who is content with poor fare. It sometimes allows itself to be satisfied with clumsy fables and insipid tales. If only implanted early enough, they are for a man adequate explanations of his existence and supports of his morality. . . .
>
> With the exception of man, no being wonders at its own existence; but it is to them all so much a matter of course that they do not observe it. Only after the inner being of nature has ascended, vigorous and cheerful, through the long and broad series of animals, does it attain at last to reflection for the first time on the entrance of reason, thus in man. Then it marvels at its own works, and asks itself what it itself is. Its wonder, however, is the more serious, as here it stands for the first time consciously in the presence of *death*. With this reflection and this wonder there arises therefore for man alone, the need for a *metaphysic*; he is accordingly an *animal metaphysicum*. . . .

[I]t is the knowledge of death, and along with this the consideration of the suffering and misery of life which gives the strongest impulse to philosophical reflection. If our life were endless and painless, it would perhaps never occur to anyone to ask why the world exists and is just the kind of world it is, but everything would just be taken as a matter of course. In accordance with this we find that the interest which philosophical and also religious systems inspire has always its strongest hold as the dogma of existence after death.[1]

### On Reason and Human Nature

The typical error of the philosopher has been in treating man as the *rational* animal, Schopenhauer maintains. This idea naturally appeals to philosophers, but it takes very little observation or psychological analysis to see that it is not correct. Although reason may well be man's most valuable possession, it is actually but a sort of surface crust upon human behavior. We all make some pretense of being rational and intelligent, to be sure. We do so to maintain our prestige with our fellows, perhaps to impress those upon whom we look as inferior, even to deceive ourselves at times. But beneath all such rational reflection there is a dominant *will*, a persistent vital impulse or desire that molds our thinking to its own purpose, Schopenhauer points out. Intellect may seem at times to direct the will. Actually it is only an instrument to accomplish the purposes of impulse and appetite. Thinking is an aspect of living. We *think* initially in order to *act*, only later to understand.

In all animal natures the *will* is primary and substantial, the intellect is secondary, indeed a mere tool for the service of the former. . . . The *intellect* becomes tired; the will is never tired. After sustained work with the head we feel the tiredness of the brain, just like that of the arm after sustained bodily work. All *knowing* is accompanied with effort; *willing*, on the contrary, is our very nature, whose manifestations take place without any weariness and entirely of their own accord. . . . [I]f rest is persistently denied to the intellect it will become fatigued and may pass into complete incapacity, into childishness, imbecility and madness. . . . The will, on the contrary, is never lazy, is absolutely untiring, it never ceases willing and when during sleep it is forsaken of the intellect it is active as the vital force, cares the more uninterruptedly for the inner economy of the organism and sets in order again the irregularities that have crept into it. For it is not, like the intellect, a function of the body, but the *body is its function*.[2]

Examine your conduct honestly, Schopenhauer suggests, and you will see at once that you do not want a thing because it is good; instead you find it good because you want it. "Thus we speak of good eating, good roads, good weather, and so on; in short, we call everything good that is just as we wish it to be." Other animals seek what they want without cloaking their desires in elaborate philosophies. Only man finds it necessary to seek good reasons to justify himself in doing what he wants to do.

This process of *rationalization* has received much attention at the hands of contemporary psychology. Sigmund Freud in particular is often given credit for recognizing its important place in human conduct. Little was added by Freud, however, to Schopenhauer's discerning analysis of the matter. "Nothing is more provoking," Schopenhauer writes, "when we are arguing against a man with reasons and explanations, and taking all pains to convince him, than to discover at last that he *will* not understand, that we have to do with his will." Hence the uselessness of logic as a practical device. No one was ever convinced by argument of that which he did not want to believe. In college classrooms, it is true, students until quite recently did usually appear to accept the conclusions presented to them with faultless logic by their professors. But in any discussion of controversial issues it was quite evident that their own self-interest, their concern with the matter of grades, not the logic of the professor, was responsible for this acceptance. To convince a person, you appeal not to logic but to desire and self-interest. Only the philosophers who have been shut off too much from the everyday world of affairs, where the nature of man is revealed in behavior, describe human beings as *rational*. So, at least, runs the argument of Schopenhauer.

Reason, he concludes, holds a definitely secondary place in human nature. It is at best but the servant of will, at worst the tool of desire. Reason enables man to get what he wants more effectively than does unaided appetite at the animal level. It seldom enables him to change the dominant force of desire. Not only do we think in order to get what we want; we actually believe what we want to believe, not what is objectively demonstrable, and we refuse to believe what is contrary to our desires. In facing the unpleasant aspects of our world, reason simply gives way to imagination and to hope, Schopenhauer maintains:

> Plato very beautifully called hope the dream of the waking. Its nature lies in this: that the will, when its servant the intellect is not able to produce what it wishes, obliges it at least to undertake the role of comforter, to appease its lord with fables, as a nurse, a child, and so to dress these out that they gain an appearance of likelihood. Now in this the intellect must do violence to its own nature, which aims at the truth. Here we see clearly who is master and who is servant.[3]

### The Will to Live

If man is dominated not by intellect but by will, what is will? Schopenhauer leaves us in no doubt on this point. He does not mean what is popularly called "will power," that is, the higher forms of conscious choice or moral obligation. By *will* he means simply the active appetites and desires of living, wanting, longing, self-asserting. Will, as we know it in man and as we see it expressed in animal life below the human level, is simply the *will to live*, the biological drive inherent in life itself. In simplest form, the will to live expresses itself as hunger. Nothing is so important to a starving man as food; no effort is too demanding, no deception too unforgivable, to satisfy this basic appetite. The human body itself, according to Schopenhauer, is but an expression of this underlying will to live. Pushed on by that force which we vaguely call life, the blood builds its own vessels by wearing grooves in the body of the embryo; the grooves deepen, close up, and become arteries and veins. The will builds the brain as an instrument for its own purposes in the struggle for existence just as surely as it builds hands and feet or the complicated digestive tract. "Teeth, throat and bowels are objectified hunger; the grasping hand, the hurrying feet, correspond to the more indirect desires of the will which they express."

In the relation of the sexes, however, the will to live finds even more clear and direct expression, and this relationship as a result dominates Western thought as well as conduct. This Schopenhauer pointed out almost a century before Freud made it the commonly accepted point of view. The present revolution in our moral standards, with its atmosphere of greatly increased sexual freedom and with what at times seems almost an obsession with sex in our novels and movies and in magazines such as *Playboy* and its numerous imitations—all simply confirms Schopenhauer's point of view. Nor would he be surprised that books like *The Sensuous Woman* and *Everything You Have Always Wanted to Know About Sex* appeared regularly on the weekly lists of most popular works of nonfiction. Schopenhauer's description of this aspect of human nature is quite graphic:

> The sexual impulse proves itself the strongest assertion of life by the fact that to man in a state of nature, as to the brutes, it is the final end, the highest goal of life. Self-maintenance is his first effort, and as soon as he has made provision for that, he only strives after the propagation of the species; as a merely natural being he can attempt no more. Nature also, the inner being of which is the will to live itself, impels with all her power both man and the brute toward propagation. Then it has attained its end with the individual, and is quite indifferent to its death, for, as the will to live, it cares only for the preservation of the species, the individual is nothing to it.[4]
>
> . . . If one considers the important part which the sexual impulse in all its degrees and nuances plays not only on the stage and in novels, but also in the real world, where, next to the love of life, it shows itself the strongest and most powerful of motives, constantly lays claim to half the powers and thoughts of the younger portion of mankind, is the ultimate goal of almost all human effort, interrupts the most serious occupations, sometimes embarrasses even the greatest minds . . . destroys the most valuable relationships, demands the sacrifice sometimes of life or health, sometimes of wealth, rank and happiness, nay, robs them who are otherwise honest of all conscience, makes those who have hitherto

been faithful, traitors; accordingly, on the whole, appears as a malevolent demon that strives to prevent, confuse, and overthrow everything; then one will be forced to cry, Wherefore all this noise? . . . Why should such a trifle play so important a part, and constantly introduce disturbances and confusion into the well-regulated life of man?

But to the earnest investigator the spirit of truth gradually reveals the answer. . . . It is no trifle that is in question here; on the contrary, the importance of the matter is quite proportionate to the seriousness and ardour of the effort. The ultimate end of all love affairs is really more important than all other ends of human life, and is therefore quite worthy of the profound seriousness with which everyone pursues it. That which is decided by it is nothing less than the composition of the next generation. . . . It is not a question of individual weal or woe . . . but of the existence and special nature of the human race in future times, and therefore the will of the individual appears at a higher power as the will of the species.[5]

## The Will as Will of the Species

The will to live that moves the individual so powerfully and dominates his conduct so completely is not for Schopenhauer, then, an expression primarily of a man's individual desire or passion. Will in the individual springs, rather, from the life force in the human race as a whole, of which the individual is but a limited and partial expression. It is with mankind, not simply with this particular man or woman, that the will to live is concerned.

The aim of nature is directed to the maintenance, and therefore to the greatest possible increase, of the species. . . . What draws two individuals of different sex exclusively to each other with such power is the will to live, which exhibits itself in the whole species, and which here anticipates in the individual which these two can produce an objectification of its nature. . . . The growing inclination of two lovers is really already the will to live of the new individual which they can and desire to produce, nay, even in the meeting of their longing glances its new life breaks out, and announces itself as a future individuality harmoniously and well composed.[6]

Propagation of the species, then, is not only the dominant motive but the ultimate purpose of every living organism. Only so can the will to live conquer death. To ensure the success of this conquest, the will to reproduce is placed almost entirely beyond the control of the intellect. Here intelligence has little chance against the deeper purposes of the will, as many parents have learned to their sorrow when attempting to reason with sons or daughters concerning members of the opposite sex to whom they are attracted.

## The World as Will

Such is our philosopher's view of human nature and conduct. But man, for Schopenhauer, is not an isolated phenomenon, unrelated to the larger universe around him. Rather he is the clearest expression of its inner nature. In human nature we find our best clue to the nature of the universe itself, our soundest metaphysical insights. Two approaches can be made to understanding any object, Schopenhauer points out: one is external, the other internal; one is the way of rational analysis and scientific thought, the other the way of immediate, intuitive understanding. As we examine ourselves in the first fashion, externally, rationally, and scientifically, we can know only the physical organism and the world of matter of which it is a part. But the immediate, intuitive insight that we have into human nature reveals to us the dominant, vital *will to live* as the reality beneath the physical and material externality, shaping and molding it according to its own deeper desires and purposes.

Had we the ability to look beneath the surface, to obtain such an inside, intuitive knowledge of the rest of the universe, we would find just the same thing that we find in man. As a matter of fact, we are not able to do this, so we must be content with that knowledge of the external universe which science can grasp. The world of matter and of physical objects as science portrays it is thus actually a product of thought and rational analysis. It is constructed by reason and so is actually an idea in the human mind, Schopenhauer maintains.* But there are indications enough that beneath the external appearance, behind the material and physical world that we know only as *idea*, there is at work the same dynamic, living *will*, the *World-Will*. The indications that confirm this Schopenhauer describes in his accustomed graphic fashion:

> If we observe the strong and unceasing impulse with which the waters hurry to the ocean, the persistency with which the magnet turns ever to the north pole, the readiness with which the iron flies to the magnet, the eagerness with which the electric poles seek to be reunited, and which, just like human desire, is increased by obstacles; if we see the crystal quickly take form with such wonderful regularity of construction, which is clearly only a perfectly definite and accurately determined impulse in different directions, seized and retained by crystallization; if we observe the choice with which bodies repel and attract each other, combine and

---

* It is this fact that accounts for the title Schopenhauer gave to his major work, *The World as Will and Idea*. The position taken here by Schopenhauer is based directly upon the critical philosophy of Immanuel Kant, whose influential work *The Critique of Pure Reason* altered the course of German philosophy. Kant's position is considered in detail in Chapter 11. Our present concern is with the original aspects of Schopenhauer's philosophy, not its Kantian foundation.

separate when they are set free in a fluid state; lastly, if we feel directly how a burden which hampers our body by its gravitation toward the earth, unceasingly presses and strains upon it in pursuit of its one tendency; if we observe all this, I say, it will require no great effort of the imagination to recognize, even at so great a distance, our own nature. That which in us pursues its ends by the light of knowledge, but here, in the weakest of its manifestations, only strives blindly and dumbly in a one-sided and unchangeable manner, must yet in both cases come under the name of Will, as it is everywhere one and the same—just as the first dim light of dawn must share the name of sunlight with the rays of the full mid-day.[7]

The unceasingly striving, creative power at work everywhere in the universe—whether in the instinct of the animal, the life process of the plant, or the blind force of the physical world—this is merely the *will* that we know in our own experience and that underlies all existence, Schopenhauer insists. Actually, the separate existence of the individual merges into that of the species, the various species into the stream of life; and life itself is only will. What science has called the laws of nature are but our description of the principles by which the World-Will operates in the physical universe, as in animals it operates by instinct and in man by intelligence. In one instance after another Schopenhauer notes the truly remarkable function of instinct as an instrument of the will to live at the animal level: "the bird builds the nest for the young it does not yet know; the beaver constructs a dam the object of which is unknown to it; insects deposit their eggs where the coming brood finds future nourishment." The cause of human action, as we are immediately aware, is the dominant force of will. The final cause of all things is the same dominant but unconscious and groping World-Will.

In later life, Schopenhauer read widely in the field of science and sought in a number of essays to provide scientific support for his thesis. But it was not until the work of Henri Bergson, distinguished French philosopher of our own century, whose *Creative Evolution* (1907) is one of the outstanding works of modern philosophy, that Schopenhauer's insight was given influential scholarly validation. In the "Life Force," the *élan vital*, which Bergson sees as the creative driving force behind all human conduct and natural phenomena alike, one finds again the World-Will of Schopenhauer—described in theoretical rather than popular fashion, to be sure, but true nonetheless to Schopenhauer's original insight.

### Pessimism: The World as Evil

In popular usage, anyone who constantly looks on the dark side of life, who sees the world as gloomy, unhappy, and unappealing, is called a pessimist. In more accurate philosophical terms, a pessimist is one who finds life, despite its occasional bright moments, "so bad that it ought not to be," who sees evil, not good, as the ultimate fact of existence. So, also, the philosophical optimist is not simply one who looks on the bright side of things but one who finds this world, despite its obvious pain and unhappiness, to be "the best of all possible worlds," who sees good, not evil, as the ultimate fact in life.

Schopenhauer was a pessimist in the philosophical as well as the popular sense. The pleasures of life, in his opinion, are but passing shadows that throw the fundamental evil of the world into stronger relief. The pursuit of pleasure, to which man, dominated by will and desire, inevitably gives himself, in the end brings pain, not happiness. We have only to look at life as we see it around us, he maintains, to recognize that pain and suffering, not pleasure and happiness, are the constant lot of our fellows as well as of ourselves.

### Desire and Happiness

First, life is evil because will and desire are basic aspects of human nature. The very *will to live* itself engenders a ceaseless striving, a restless longing to satisfy our desires. The hedonist, in his naïveté, has assumed that if we get what we want, if our desires are fulfilled, we will be happy. It is quite obvious, Schopenhauer maintains, that such is not the case:

> All *willing* arises from want, therefore from deficiency, and therefore from suffering. The satisfaction of a desire ends it, yet for one desire that is satisfied there remain at least ten which are denied. Further, the desire lasts long, the demands are infinite; the satisfaction is short and scantily measured out. But even the final satisfaction is itself only apparent; every satisfied wish at once makes room for a new one. No attained object of desire can give lasting satisfaction, but merely a fleeting gratification; it is like the alms thrown to a begger that keeps him alive today that his misery may be prolonged till the morrow. Therefore, so long as we are given up to the throng of desires with their constant hopes and fears, so long as we are the subjects of willing, we can never have lasting happiness or peace.[8]

Getting what we want, then, does not make us happy. It simply makes it possible to want other things we do not have. Schopenhauer wrote at a time when the material comforts of life were denied to the mass of people, when want seemed almost universal in a period of postwar exhaustion. Had he lived in our country amid the prosperity of the mid-twentieth century, Schopenhauer would have smiled to himself as he saw his analysis of life so amply substantiated. A technological civilization makes available to us material possessions that far exceed the fondest dreams of our forefathers. Yet no generation has seemed less satisfied and happy. When we have one automobile, we want two. When we have one television set, we soon realize that we must have one for the younger as well as for the older members of the family, to obviate the conflict of desires for different programs that suit the tastes of each. If we have only a black and white set, we are dissatisfied with its old-fashioned and outmoded features and sure that only a new color model will make us happy. So we daily provide support for Schopenhauer's view of life. Advertising, which is the life of modern business, makes it a point to see that the gratification of one desire does not bring any lasting satisfaction. Ten more desires must at once be stimulated to take the place of the one that has been satisfied.

Even the complete fulfillment of desire, however, the getting of everything that we want, holds out no hope of happiness, according to Schopenhauer. Above the mass of the people, most of whose desires are unfulfilled, is that small, privileged group, known as the "jet set," which has the means to gratify every desire: leisure, travel, amusement, sex. No faintest passing fancy is denied its members. But instead of happiness, the result is actually *ennui*, boredom, Schopenhauer maintains. We are unhappy when we cannot have what we want. When we get it, we find that it no longer satisfies. None are so easily bored, he writes, as the "idle rich," who give all their thought and effort to enjoying themselves:

> As soon as want and suffering permits rest to man, *ennui* is at once so near that he necessarily requires diversion. The striving after existence is what occupies all living things and maintains them in motion. But when existence is assured, then they know not what to do with it; thus the second thing that sets them in motion is the effort to get free from the burden of existence, "to kill time," i.e., to escape from *ennui*. . . .
>
> As want is the scourge of the people, so *ennui* is that of the fashionable world. Thus between desiring and attaining all human life flows on. The desire is, in its nature, pain, the attainment soon begets satiety; the end was only apparent; possession takes away the charm; the desire, the need, presents itself under a new form; when it does not, then follows emptiness, *ennui*, against which the conflict is just as painful as against want.[9]

### Love and Happiness

There is that romantic period in youth when all of us are convinced that in love, as in nothing else, man's happiness is to be found. But even here the pessimism of Schopenhauer raises a serious question concerning the assumptions of hedonism. What we like to call love, Schopenhauer insists, is but the most subtle device of the *will to live*, its shrewdest method of achieving its end. And that end is the perpetuation of the species, not the happiness of the individual. Opposites attract each other, as we constantly observe, but the reason is that thus the species is improved. In every case of sexual appeal and romantic passion the subtle purpose of the will to live is the production of a hardy offspring. Such is the unconscious eugenics of love.

"Each one loves what he lacks," Schopenhauer maintains. Accordingly the most masculine man will seek the most feminine woman, and vice versa. Each one will regard as especially beautiful in another individual those perfections that he himself lacks—nay, even those imperfections that are the opposite of his own. Little men love big women; fair persons like those who are dark; intelligent women fall in love with strong but stupid men. The weaker a man is the more he will seek a strong woman; and the woman on her side will do the same. Everyone endeavors to neutralize by means of the other his own weaknesses and defects so that they will not perpetuate themselves. What guides us here, Schopenhauer insists, is an instinct that is directed toward the welfare of the species, not the happiness of the individual. The health of the race is the great work with which Cupid is occupied unceasingly. In comparison with the importance of this great affair, the concerns of individuals are very trifling. Nature is therefore always ready to sacrifice them without hesitation.

The passion of love depends, then, upon an illusion, the illusion that the satisfaction of desire will bring us happiness. With the fulfillment of desire, the individual discovers that he has been the dupe of the species. In reality, love is a deception practiced by nature for its own ends, and marriage is bound to be disillusioning:

> Nature can only attain its ends by implanting a certain illusion in the individual; on account of this that which is only good for the species appears to him as good for himself, so that when he serves the species he imagines he is serving himself. In accordance with the character of the matter, every lover will experience a marvelous disillusion after the pleasure he has at last attained, and will wonder that what was so longingly desired accomplishes nothing more. Because the passion depended upon an illusion, the deception must vanish after the attainment of the end of the species.
>
> Marriages from love are made in the interest of the species, not of the individual. Certainly the persons concerned imagine they are advancing their own happiness; but their real end is one which is foreign to themselves, for it lies in the production of an individual which is only possible through them. Brought together by this aim, they ought henceforth to try to get on together as well as possible. But very often the pair brought together by that instinctive illusion, which is the essence of passionate love, will in other respects be of very different natures. Accordingly, love marriages, as a rule, turn out unhappy; for through them the coming generation is cared for at the expense of the present. "Who marries for love must live in sorrow," says the Spanish proverb.[10]

Schopenhauer's essay *On Women* is one of the classics in the literature of misogyny, "that last recourse of the captured male." It is just in the physical charms of the young woman that the *will to live* presents its greatest temptation, he felt, to the man who is struggling to free himself from slavery to passion and desire. In his youth a man has not intelligence enough to realize how temporary and deceptive are the feminine charms that move him. When that realization comes, it is too late:

> With young girls, nature seems to have in view what, in the language of drama, is called a striking effect, as for a few years she dowers them with a wealth of beauty and is lavish in her gift of charm, at the expense of all the rest of their lives, so that during those years they may capture the fancy of some man to such a degree that he is hurried away into undertaking the honorable care of them, in some form or another, as long as they live—a step for which there would not seem to be any sufficient warrant if reason only directed man's thoughts.[11]

For Schopenhauer the pessimist, the less an intelligent man has to do with women, the better it will be for him. Let him never forget the snare of the *will to live* that lies hidden behind a woman's charms, the inevitable disillusion to which his desire for her must lead.

### The Evils of Life

At bottom, life is evil because life is strife. The restless *will to live* can beget only conflict, competition, and strife. The effort to get what we want leads us inevitably into conflict with others. The goods of the world are limited; the desires of men are infinite. On every hand we see evidence of the inevitable strife and conflict into which we are led by nature. Every kind of being fights for the matter, the space, and the time of another. "This strife may be followed throughout the whole of nature; indeed nature only exists through it," Schopenhauer writes, and provides an impressive account of the strife he sees as an essential aspect of the world of nature:

> Many insects lay their eggs on the skin and even in the body of the larvae of other insects, whose slow destruction is the first work of the newly hatched brood. The young hydra, which grows like a bud out of the old one, and afterwards separates itself from it, fights while it is still joined to the old one for the prey that offers itself, so that the one snatches it out of the mouth of the other. . . . Thus the will to live everywhere preys upon itself; and in different forms is its own nourishment, till finally the human race, because it subdues all others, regards nature as a manufactory for its own use. Yet even the human race reveals in itself with most terrible destructiveness this same conflict, this variance with itself of the will, and we find *homo homini lupus* (man is a wolf to man).[12]

In recent years there has been a new interest in human aggression and quite impressive support for Schopenhauer's view. For example, *African Genesis*, a popular work by Robert Ardrey, treats human aggression as the manifestation of an innate drive that man inherits from his killer-ape ancestors. And in his widely read book *On Aggression* Konrad Lorenz has this striking comment: "An unprejudiced observer from another planet, looking upon man as he is today, in his hand the atomic bomb, the product of his intelligence, in his heart the aggressive drive inherited from his anthropoid ancestors, which this same intelligence cannot control, would not prophesy long life for the species."[13]

As Schopenhauer surveyed the human scene in his own age, he everywhere found manifestations of the strife and conflict bred by will and desire. Strong nations preyed upon the weak, and then in turn became the victims of the conflict they had initiated. The imperious will of Napoleon urged him on from victory to victory; but none brought him lasting satisfaction and he fell at last before the combined forces of the nations he had oppressed. Austria, Prussia, and England at once sought to gain for themselves the power of the fallen conqueror, each at the expense of the others, and so aggression and strife continued unceasingly. As Schopenhauer witnessed this spectacle in the Napoleonic era, we witness it again today. The same weary cycle repeats itself again as the currently great powers compete for the domination of a world that is larger than Napoleon's but seems little changed for the better. A war to end wars breeds only a worse conflict in its place. Nations that unite to wage war victoriously fall immediately into conflict with one another when victory is won.

The world, then, is evil, not good, Schopenhauer concludes, finding the wisdom of the East, especially the Buddhist view of life, more convincing than the optimism of the West. Pain is the basic fact of human existence, and what we call pleasure is only the temporary cessation of pain. The total picture of life is too painful, indeed, for contemplation. We make it bearable only by closing our eyes to its real character.

Only the young, in their ignorance, think that happiness is possible. They think that willing and striving are joys only because they have not yet discovered the weary insatiableness of defeat. But with old age there comes disillusion—"for by that time the fictions are gone which gave life its charm; the splendors of the world have proved null and void, its pomp, grandeur and magnificence are faded," Schopenhauer concludes. "A man has then found out that behind most of the things he wants, and most of the pleasures he longs for, there is very little after all, and so he comes by degrees to see that our existence is all empty and void."[14]

### The Wisdom of Life

After such undiluted and thoroughgoing pessimism, one might well expect Schopenhauer to recommend suicide as the only possible escape from the suffering and disappointment he takes to be the general lot of mankind. But like most sensible pessimists he managed to find good reasons for avoiding this conclusion. What most impressed Schopenhauer as a philosopher was the futility of suicide. It was a gesture at which the World-Will could smile contentedly. Suicide may seem at first a triumph for the individual over will and desire. But in reality this is not the case; and even more important, in the species the *will to live* persists unhindered despite an occasional suicide. For every such deliberate death there are a thousand unplanned births: "Suicide, the willful destruction of the single phenomenal existence, is a vain and foolish act; for the thing-in-itself (the species, life, the will in general) remains unaffected by it, even as the rainbow endures however fast the drops which support it for the moment may change."[15]

The evil of life lies not in our own unhappiness; that is merely superficial. The ultimate evil consists in the fact that the game of life is played at all. Not the impotent pawn but the ruthless player, the brutal World-Will, must be killed.* It is the task of the philosopher to make a contribution to this larger end, not to retire from the game by a futile gesture of self-destruction. Thus Schopenhauer interprets his own role.

### The Contribution of Intelligence

With the hedonists Schopenhauer agrees that man is essentially self-centered by nature. Each of us is interested primarily in himself, in his own desires, needs, and ambitions: Each individual, Schopenhauer writes, "makes itself the centre of the world, has regard for its own existence and well-being before anything else; indeed from the natural standpoint, is ready to sacrifice everything else for this—is ready to annihilate the world in order to maintain its own self, this drop in the ocean, a little longer. Every one looks upon his own death as upon the end of the world, while he accepts the death of his acquaintances as a matter of comparative indifference if he is not in some way affected by it. This disposition is egoism, which is essential to everything in Nature. Yet it is just through egoism that the inner conflict of the will with itself attains to such a terrible revelation."[16]

To conquer the will and free ourselves from its domination, we must overcome the egoism so deeply embedded in human nature. This task, as Schopenhauer well realizes, is not easy, but it is not an impossible one, he feels, and he sets out to show how it can be accomplished. Despite his earlier emphasis upon the secondary place of intellect in human nature, Schopenhauer in the end cannot escape the conviction of all philosophy that intelligence must serve as a pathway to the good life. Man's intellect has been produced as the instrument and servant of the will to live, and for most of us it operates only in this capacity. It is possible, however, for reason in time to master the will that produced it. Desire can be moderated by knowl-

---

* In our own day, but for quite different reasons, a move to significantly limit the propagation of the human species has been supported by scientists and others deeply concerned with the population explosion. Schopenhauer's analysis of this problem is one to which those so keenly aware of the dangers to us all inherent in this situation might well give careful consideration.

edge; passion controlled by understanding: "Of ten things that annoy us, nine would not be able to do so if we understood them thoroughly in their causes, and therefore knew their necessity and true nature; but we would do this much oftener if we made them the object of reflection before making them the object of wrath and indignation. For what bridle and bit are to an unmanageable horse, the intellect is for the will in man; by this bridle it must be controlled."[17]

Our desiring and striving, our impatience with the conditions of life, arise for the most part from the fact that we regard our lot as a result of circumstances that might easily have been different. "We do not generally grieve over ills which are directly necessary and quite universal; for example, the necessity of age and death, and many daily inconveniences," Schopenhauer points out. When intelligence gains control over will, we are able to see clearly the necessity that exists in the nature of things. We realize that matters could not be otherwise than they are, "that pain as such is inevitable and essential to life, and that nothing depends upon chance but its mere fashion, the form under which it presents itself, that thus our present sorrow fills a place that without it, would at once be occupied by another which now is excluded by it."[18]

Life, when guided by intelligence rather than will, is then for Schopenhauer a life of self-control, of contemplation, of disinterestedness, to use an expressive term of Walter Lippmann's. It is a life freed from the desire and passion that self-interest breeds in us. Most men looking at the world see only objects of desire, and for them the intellect remains the tool of will. But the man in whom intelligence has finally overcome the domination of will is able to forget his own individual desires and ambitions. He sees objects of contemplation rather than of desire. It is in the disinterested pursuit of truth that such a goal is most completely achieved, Schopenhauer feels, and this is the ideal of pure science at its best. The great scientist is interested in truth for its own sake, not for what he can get out of it. A detachment of spirit, a freedom from individual ambition and self-interest, distinguishes such an individual and releases him from the pettiness and bitterness of ordinary life. In this enjoyment of knowledge for its own sake, reason in man achieves its full triumph over the *will to live*. "But, in fact, such a powerful control of reason over directly felt suffering seldom occurs," our pessimistic philosopher sadly admits. Among the vast multitude of human beings there are few who can expect to rise to such heights as this. The life of reason holds out little hope, therefore, for the common man.

### The Enjoyment of Beauty

Schopenhauer was as fond of music as he was of philosophy, and at noon each day he customarily found relaxation in playing for half an hour upon his flute. The enjoyment of art and music, he gradually came to realize, affords a deliverance from life's pain and strife more widespread and appealing than that which disinterested intelligence can provide. Both art and science enable man to forget his individual desires, ambitions, and frustrations, to overcome the limitations of self-interest, and to become aware of that which is universal. In this fashion both provide an escape from the pain and tragedy of life. The truth that science seeks is an abstract truth, however, and is gained only as the result of careful, rational thought. Great art, on the other hand, is the product of an immediate insight, in which a man of genius grasps the true nature of his subject without that long process of rational analysis upon which scientific knowledge depends.

In great art we find what Schopenhauer calls the "concrete universal"; that is, the poet or painter depicts a particular object with such insight that it reveals a universal truth. Thus the madonnas of Raphael portray not one woman but womanhood at its best, Schopenhauer writes.

> The nature of art is such that with it one case holds good for a thousand, for by a careful and detailed presentation of a single individual, person or thing, it aims at revealing the genus to which that person or thing belongs. . . . The true work of art should lead us from the individual fact, in other words, that which exists once only and then is gone forever, to that which always exists an infinite number of times in an infinite number of ways.[19]
>
> The abundance of natural beauty which invites contemplation and even presses itself upon us whenever it discloses itself suddenly to our view, almost always succeeds in delivering us, though it may be for only a moment, from subjectivity, from the slavery of the will. This is why the man who is tormented by passion, or want, or care, is so suddenly revived, cheered and restored by a single free glance into nature: the storm of passion, the pressure of desire and fear and all the miseries of willing are then at once in a marvelous manner, calmed and appeased. Happiness and unhappiness have disappeared; we are no longer individual; the individual is forgotten; we are only pure subject of knowledge . . . Thus all differences of individuality so entirely disappear that it is all the same whether the perceiving eye belongs to a mighty king or a wretched beggar.[20]

Being especially fond of music and conscious of its immediate appeal to all sorts of people, Schopenhauer suggests that it must be given a place by itself among the arts. "The effect of music is stronger, quicker, more necessary and infallible," he writes. "It stands alone, quite cut off from all the other arts." We have only to look at our own experience to find ample confirmation of Schopenhauer's position. To develop "college spirit" among its students, to unite them in a common cause, colleges and universities have traditionally made use of the song which has become the "alma mater." To make its soldiers forget themselves and become part of a larger whole, an army turns to martial music. And countless men and women have been able to forget themselves, for a brief time at least, as they enjoy a great symphony rendered by one of the outstanding orchestras of the day. Thousands of young people today, to whom college songs and martial or traditional music no longer appeal, likewise respond in similar fashion to rock concerts like that at Woodstock.

In the enjoyment of beauty, then, we may forget our pain and suffering for a time at least. But even here there is no permanent escape from evil for the pessimist. Even the artist is inexorably called away from his vision of beauty by the urge of appetite, if not of ambition. Ordinary men and women can hope at best for only brief moments of this higher joy, for but a fleeting escape from the pendulum of life that swings relentlessly from pain to ennui and back to pain. Soon "the magic is at an end and we are again abandoned to all our woe."[21]

Schopenhauer's analysis of the appeal of art and music may also help one to understand the widespread appeal of marijuana on college campuses today. Many have found here an accessible escape from the frustration and disillusionment of modern life, or even from the boredom of college classes. In this way their consciousness of individuality, their self-consciousness and self-interest, is removed and a sense of shared well-being achieved. As Schopenhauer points out, however, this is at best a temporary experience. It provides no permanent answer to life's problems.

### The Pessimist's View of Religion

Schopenhauer's youthful reaction to religion was quite critical. In the Christian churches of his day he was impressed only by the ecclesiastical organization, the theological argument, and the hypocrisy and self-deception that he saw. In later years, however, he realized that the Christian view of life was in some ways remarkably similar to his own. Orthodox Christianity has always maintained that man's state in this world is "both exceedingly wretched and sinful," he points out. It has condemned the quest for earthly goods together with all human selfishness, and urged man to think of his neighbor as himself. With none of this does Schopenhauer have any quarrel. Christianity, he declares, is actually "a profound philosophy of pessimism." "Certainly the doctrine of original sin (assertion of the will) and of salvation (denial of the will) is the great truth which constitutes the essence of Christianity, while most of what remains is only the clothing of it, the husk or accessories," he writes. "That in recent times Christianity has forgotten its true significance, and degenerated into dull optimism, does not concern us here."[22]

The deepest insights of the Christian gospel Schopenhauer finds in such well-known teachings of Jesus as "Do for others what you want them to do for you"; "Love your neighbor as yourself"; "Sell all that you have and give the money to the poor." It is human selfishness and sinfulness that leads a man to make a distinction between his own interests and the interests of others. The highest religious vision leads him to see that he is one with all men. He ceases to want for himself anything that others cannot also have. He "recognizes in all beings his own inmost and true self."[23]

The most profound interpretation of religion, Schopenhauer came to feel, is found in the disenchanted wisdom of the Orient, not in the eager ambition of the Western world. It is not in the Christianity of Europe and America but the Buddhism of India and China. The Buddhist recognizes specifically, as the Christian does not, that all individual distinctions are transitory and unreal. He accepts as the major goal of the religious life not love of others and involvement in their circumstances, but rather the complete extinction of will and desire in Nirvana. In the Buddhist ideal of asceticism Schopenhauer finds the surest road to salvation and the blessedness of Nirvana:

"By the term asceticism, which I have used so often," he writes, "I mean in its narrower sense this intentional breaking of the will by the refusal of what is agreeable and the selection of what is disagreeable, the voluntarily chosen life of penance and self-chastisement for the continual mortification of the will." Since he who has attained to this point "denies the will which appears in his own person, he will not resist if another does the same, i.e., inflicts wrong upon him. Therefore every suffering coming to him from without, through chance or the wickedness of others, is welcome to him, every injury, ignominy and insult. He receives them gladly as the opportunity of learning with certainty that he no longer asserts the will. Therefore he bears such ignominy and suffering with inexhaustible patience and meekness, returns good for evil without ostentation, and allows the fire of anger to rise within him just as little as he does that of the desires. If at last death comes, which puts an end to this manifestation of that will whose existence here has long since perished through free denial of itself, it is most welcome and is gladly received as a longed-for deliverance."[24]

That this prospect of the complete denial of all desire has held so little attraction for most Westerners is simply evidence of the power that the *will to live* still exercises upon us, in Schopenhauer's opinion. He would no doubt be pleased to know that in this country the religious thought of the East as well as its music now has a rather widespread appeal.

### The Blessedness of Nirvana

By those who have been freed from the domination of the World-Will and from the mirage of happiness that it holds before our eyes—by those alone is a deeper satisfaction and lasting escape from life's pain and frustration known.

He who has attained to the denial of the will to live, however poor, joy-less, and full of privation his condition may appear when looked at externally, is yet filled with inward joy and the true peace of heaven. Nothing can trouble him more, nothing can move him, for he has cut all the thousand cords of will which hold us bound to the world, and as desire, fear, envy, anger, drag us hither and thither in constant pain, he now looks back smiling and at rest on the delusions of this world, which once were able to move and agonize his spirit also, but which now stand before him as utterly indifferent to him as the chessman when the game is ended, or as in the morning, the cast-off masquerading dress which worried and disquieted us in the night in carnival. Life and its forms now pass before him as a fleeting illusion, as a light morning dream before half-waking eyes, the real world already shining through it so that it can no longer deceive, and like this morning dream they finally vanish alto-gether without any violent transition.[25]

### Pessimism and Hedonism

What shall we say of such a disillusioned view of human life? Is it enough to make the easy comment that to those who wear dark glasses the world always looks dark? Can we explain the unpleasant conclusions to which Schopenhauer's analysis of life led him merely by pointing to the circumstances in which his own life was cast, to the man himself and the age in which he lived? This has been done. "The natural response to such a philosophy is a medical diagnosis of the age and of the man," writes Will Durant in his *Story of Philosophy*. "Pessimism is an indictment of the pessi-mist. Given a diseased constitution and a neurotic mind, a life of empty leisure and gloomy *ennui*, and there emerges the proper physiology for Schopenhauer's philosophy."[26]

Such a statement, as appealing as it is to some who read Schopenhauer for the first time, is too easy an escape from the task of facing squarely the issues raised by his disturbing analysis of human nature and human life. It is an escape so easy, indeed, that once we accept it we can never find any dependable ground for distinguishing the true from the false. If Schopen-hauer's pessimism is dismissed as simply the inevitable consequence of the individual and social influences that shaped his life, then we can legitimately claim no more than this for optimism or high idealism. Once we admit that the conclusions of the human mind are but the reflection, the inevitable product, of those circumstances and surroundings in which it is set, we surrender all hope of establishing any enduring truth. That is certainly too high a price to pay, if it can be avoided, for an easy answer to the pessimism of Schopenhauer. The innate confidence in the ability of man's mind to distinguish the true from the false is one of our most prized possessions, one without which there is little hope of building a dependable and satisfying philosophy.

The unpleasant and disagreeable aspects of his own life undoubtedly served to open Schopenhauer's eyes to the widespread tragedy of human existence, but just as surely those aspects of life that he found so tragic were not simply the products of his own imagination. If his insight is limited and partial, it is also penetrating and disturbing. Too much that he has to say rings true in our experience, too much of his philosophy anticipates more recent movements of wide influence—such, for example, as Freudian psychology or the philosophy of Henri Bergson—to be easily dismissed as only the product of a neurotic mind or a diseased constitution. The problems Schopenhauer raises must be dealt with honestly and convincingly by every thoughtful student of philosophy. His emphasis upon the primary place of will in human life has found influential expression in our own age. In the thought of both Nietzsche and William James, as well as in the philosophy of the existentialists, we shall meet this point of view again and deal with it more directly.*

For our present consideration, however, the significance of Schopenhauer's pessimism is to be seen primarily in the questions that it raises. The questions raised about the validity of hedonism are so serious as to make that philosophy increasingly difficult to accept. Schopenhauer does, to be sure, agree with the basic assumption of hedonism—that man naturally gives himself to the pursuit of pleasure and the satisfaction of desire. But his searching analysis of human experience convinces him that hedonism is actually self-refuting. The pursuit of pleasure, the effort to get what we want when we want it, brings not happiness but pain, suffering, and disillusion. All life, as Schopenhauer sees it, swings like a pendulum from the pain of desire unsatisfied to the boredom and satiety of desire that is satisfied, *when life is lived upon hedonistic premises.*

Should not the intelligent student of life then question the assumptions upon which this pessimistic philosophy rests? It may well be, as many able philosophers both ancient and modern maintain, that there are other, more adequate and appealing ends in life than the pursuit of pleasure, the satisfaction of appetite and desire. Such, at least, is the claim made by exponents of that philosophy known as rationalism, to which we now turn. Here the life of reason, to which Schopenhauer himself was in fact eventually led, is not seen as the last hope of the pessimist, weary of life and anxious to escape its trials and hardships. It is seen rather as the philosophy of men seeking to live in a way that is truly and uniquely human and thus to enjoy the lasting satisfaction that understanding alone can bring to human life.

* See Parts Three and Four.

# Two
## THE LIFE OF REASON

Men are disturbed not by things, but by the view they take of things.

EPICTETUS

Life itself is neither good nor evil, but only a place for good and evil.

MARCUS AURELIUS

It is written in many languages, and in the idiom of many cultures, that if a man is to find happiness, he must reconstruct not merely his world, but, first of all, himself.

WALTER LIPPMANN

through all of this I see the idea that "goodness" is not something of its own, or something natural to man; rather, it is something which man must strive to achieve. Morality may be a product of man's control over himself.

## CHAPTER 5

# Rationalism for the Layman

## *The Stoic Philosophy*

As our examination of hedonism has moved beyond the urbane and sophisticated essays of Lin Yutang to the disillusioned pessimism of Schopenhauer, the adequacy of the pursuit of pleasure as a satisfying philosophy of life becomes increasingly open to question. Among critics of hedonism, the most forthright and uncompromising are the Stoics, early exponents of rationalism, who propose to develop a philosophy that they believe to be more genuinely human in outlook and spirit. In the life of reason alone, the Stoic philosophers asserts, lies our one dependable avenue to meaning and purpose in human experience. We are in the world, so these early rationalists maintain, not to live pleasantly but to acquit ourselves like men. Only by thus acting in accord with our true nature can we hope to derive lasting satisfaction.

In every age the insights of the rationalists have had enduring appeal. This was as true of the young Athenians who twenty-five hundred years ago gathered to hear Socrates declare that the unexamined life is not worthy of a man as of the young men and women of England and America who a generation ago discussed Bertrand Russell's popular essays on philosophy. As we examine the thought of the hedonists, we find that they themselves in almost every case also covertly return to reason as the *sine qua non* of the good life. Neither the prudence urged by Epicurus nor the enlightened self-interest of the Utilitarians can be achieved unless reason controls man's immediate and "natural" desire for pleasure. And Schopenhauer's proposal that we adopt the self-denial of the ascetic to escape the pervasive ills of life demands an even more complete domination of desire by reason. In the hedonistic philosophy, however, reason is at best but a helpful guide in the pursuit of pleasure. At worst, as for Schopenhauer, it is a refuge from the inevitable disillusion that comes in the wake of desire and passion. For the Stoics, on the other hand, the life of reason is not merely a means of securing the basic satisfactions; it has intrinsic worth and value in its own right.

*The School of Cynics*

Historically, the forerunners of the Stoics were a group of early Greek philosophers known as Cynics. Providing a connecting link between the teaching of Socrates and that of the Stoics, these early Cynics developed a way of life rather than a system of philosophy. Their ideal of the good life differs surprisingly little, as a matter of fact, from that of Schopenhauer. Antisthenes, the founder of the school, was an Athenian about twenty-five years younger than Socrates. His first introduction to philosophy seems to have been in the lectures of the Sophist orator Gorgias, and from the Sophists he learned to think of natural law, not human convention, as the proper foundation of morals and social life. But Antisthenes soon became an ardent admirer and disciple of Socrates, from whom his deepest philosophical insights were derived.

Something of the influence of Socrates on the youth of his day is to be seen in the tradition that every morning Antisthenes walked forty furlongs (about five miles) from his home outside Athens in order to hear the master. He is mentioned also as being in the group who was with Socrates till the end on the day he drank the hemlock. Not long after Socrates' death, in 399 B.C., Antisthenes set up a school of his own in Athens, meeting his disciples in a gymnasium known as the Cynosarges. It was for this reason that the group became known as Cynics. The unconventional behavior and biting sarcasm of the followers of Antisthenes helped give the term "cynic" its later definition.

Antisthenes accepted the Socratic principle that reason provides the only foundation for morality and the good life. But Socrates' complete lack of interest in the material things of life made an even greater impression on Antisthenes. When a friend on one occasion poked fun at Socrates because of his frugal circumstances and the absence of material pleasure from his life, Socrates is said to have replied: "You, Antiphon, would seem to suggest that happiness consists in luxury and extravagance; I hold a different creed. To have no wants at all is, to my mind, an attribute of godhead."[1] This Socratic dictum became the cornerstone of the Cynic philosophy. With Schopenhauer, Antisthenes agrees that the pursuit of pleasure does not lead to happiness but rather drives man into a slavery to desire and to external circumstances beyond his control. To Antisthenes, indeed, is attributed the statement, "I would rather go mad then feel pleasure," strong language even for a pessimist like Schopenhauer.

"Ridding himself not only of all artificial wants which complicate and enervate life, but of all ties whatsoever that bind him to the rest of the world," the Cynic set out to live "according to nature" in the most radical sense of that phrase. In the midst of Athenian civilization he adopted a way of life that in some ways reminds one of those who advocate the "new naturalism." <u>Since the external world is beyond his control, the wise man will free himself completely from dependence upon it, the Cynic taught.</u> He will be concerned about neither the material goods of life nor the attitude of his fellow men toward him. He will rather <u>master himself</u>, controlling his desires so that nothing outside can disturb him. In time, this philosophy led the followers of Antisthenes to a rigorous asceticism, quite Schopenhauerian in outlook, and certainly much more extreme than the "natural life style" adopted by communal groups of today.

The spirit of the Cynic is well exemplified in the life of Diogenes, one of Antisthenes' best-known disciples. Wandering about Greece with no other shelter than a tub, Diogenes, upon noticing a child drinking with its hands, threw away his cup as a final unnecessary luxury. On another occasion, as Diogenes sat upon his tub enjoying the sun, the great King Alexander chanced to ride by and stopped his horse to converse with the rather notorious and eccentric old philosopher. Impressed by his independence of spirit in the presence of a king, the impetuous monarch is said to have exclaimed, "Ask anything you wish of me, and I will grant it." "Then be so good," replied Diogenes, "as to stand out of my sunlight."

Thoroughgoing individualists themselves, the Cynics carried their contempt for conventional order and propriety to lengths that shocked their contemporaries. It is not hard to understand how the word "cynic" has come to denote a contempt for all the accepted conventions of social life. In their independence of mind, their indifference alike to the comforts and the inconveniences of life, their insistence that a man must master himself, the Cynics provide a good introduction to the philosophy of the Stoics, the earliest recognized exponents of rationalism. That the Cynics themselves exemplify the life of reason at its best, however, is open to serious question.

## The Abler Exponents of Stoicism

### Zeno and the Early Stoa

Like so much of our philosophical heritage, Stoicism had its origin in Athens. It is cosmopolitan, however, rather than distinctively Greek in spirit and outlook. Zeno,* the founder of the Stoic school (ca. 335–263 B.C.), was the son of a merchant of Cyprus, and in his view of life the influence of his Phoenician heritage is quite apparent. While it is not possible to harmonize all the later stories about his conversion to philosophy, we may accept as historical the tradition that he first came to Athens on some mercantile enterprise, probably bringing a cargo of purple, a commodity in which his father dealt.

---

* Not to be confused with Zeno, the Eleatic philosopher, who is famous for his riddle of Achilles and the hare.

At Athens a new world opened for the young merchant. Here people were discussing matters much more important than commercial gain and loss, and soon Zeno was moving enthusiastically from one school of philosophy to another. The atmosphere of Athens at that time, the late fourth century B.C., was still alive with the philosophic spirit engendered several generations earlier by Socrates. The disciples of both Plato and Aristotle were busy spreading the ideas of these two great masters of ancient philosophy, and the rivalry between the two schools was still keen. Zeno seems to have listened with interest to all points of view but to have been attracted most strongly by the teaching of Crates of Thebes. The pupil and successor of Diogenes as head of the Cynic school, Crates, like his more famous predecessors, had trained himself to bear hunger and thirst, heat and cold, flattery and abuse, with equal indifference, and had abandoned all his possessions as impediments to the philosophic life.

Pictured as rather unassuming and not especially attractive, Zeno nevertheless was a man of marked ability, moral earnestness, and good will, and he earned the respect and admiration of his contemporaries. By about 300 B.C. he had formulated views of his own, distinctive and appealing enough to attract disciples, and like Epicurus at about the same time he also established a school in Athens. Gathering at the *Stoa Poikile* (Painted Porch) for informal discussions of the problems of philosophy, his followers soon became known as Stoics, or "men of the porch."

During the latter part of his life Zeno was one of the prominent and influential figures in Athens to whom the leaders of the city turned for advice in political emergencies. So great was his fame as a philosopher that large numbers of people were drawn to Athens to hear him, and even the tradesmen seem to have been pleased at the crowds. To honor so distinguished a citizen Athens voted Zeno a golden crown and a bronze statue. The public citation read on that occasion indicates how successfully he avoided the difficulties into which a devotion of philosophy had led Socrates a little over a century earlier.

Of the books that Zeno wrote nothing survives but the titles and a few detached phrases. While still associated with the Cynic school, he completed the work that is most widely associated with his name, his *Republic*. The Stoic school in Athens continued under Zeno's direction for about forty years, and during these years he gathered about him a group of able disciples. Then at an advanced age he suffered a minor injury; he regarded this as an indication of the divine will, and accordingly in 262 B.C. he put an end to his own life, saying to the gods; "I am coming of my own accord. Why then do you bother to call me." His immediate successors as head of the school in Athens, Cleanthes and Chrysippus, carried forward effectively the work he had begun until the Stoic philosophy became by far the most influential intellectual and moral force in the Graeco-Roman world.

Cleanthes, known in antiquity as a man of strong character but rather limited intellect, was the theologian of early Stoicism. Belief in God, which for Zeno was essentially a rational conviction, becomes in the verses of Cleanthes almost an ardent faith. His great *Hymn to Zeus** is easily the most important document that has come down to us from the early Stoics. Chrysippus, on the other hand, was a logician and a bit impatient with the poetic approach to philosophy adopted by Cleanthes. His principal contribution was organizing Stoic doctrine and defending it by dialectic. Like Zeno, he made large use of the syllogism, and he is now considered one of the great logicians of the ancient world. Commonly regarded as the second founder of Stoicism, he wrote some 750 books, covering almost every important aspect of philosophy (if the list of titles given by Diogenes Laertius can be trusted).†

A precise historical treatment of Stoicism distinguishes the Early, the Middle, and the Late Stoa. In each period a particular philosophical outlook and emphasis is apparent. The Early Stoa, which flourished in Athens during the third century B.C. under the leadership of Zeno and his immediate successors, was largely political and religious, as opposed to the more individualistic outlook of Epicurus and his followers in the Athens of that age. This initial concern, however, was in time largely replaced by the outlook of the Middle Stoa, influential primarily during the second century B.C., with its center in Rhodes. Posidonius, its best known figure, was largely responsible for equating the Stoic political philosophy with the imperial rule of Rome.

By 150 B.C. the teaching of the Stoics had gained great popularity and influence in Rome, and the Late Stoa had its center there during the first two centuries of the Christian era. Their political concern was still important in this period, but the major interest of the Stoic philosophers shifted more directly to ethical questions. There was much in Stoicism that would have a natural appeal to the typical Roman during the vigorous days of the Empire. Such distinguished Roman citizens as Cicero and Cato were numbered among its adherents; Epictetus, Seneca, and Marcus Aurelius, the major exponents of the Stoic philosophy during this third and final period, all lived in Rome.

The enduring influence of the Stoic moral philosophy is even now, as a matter of fact, still apparent. The kind of admonition about character and conduct that young people have traditionally received from their parents as they were growing up is to a large extent in keeping with the teaching of the Stoics. This point of view now seems to some a bit old-fashioned and moralistic, not quite in touch with the spirit of the age in which we live.

---

* See page 118.

† The comment in a recent book on Stoic logic is quite interesting. "Without doubt [Chrysippus] was the best student the Stoic professors ever had. While in training he thought of so many skeptical arguments against Stoicism that he was accused by later Stoics of supplying Carneades [one of their ablest early critics] with ammunition for attacking them." (Benson Mater, *Stoic Logic*. Berkeley: University of California Press, p. 7.)

Whether those who feel this way can examine Stoicism with desirable objectivity is, of course, somewhat doubtful. But its importance as one of the influential philosophies men live by requires us to make the effort.

### Epictetus

In many ways the most significant figure among the Stoic philosophers in Rome was Epictetus (ca. A.D. 55–135), Greek slave in the household of a Roman soldier. Certainly the Stoic doctrines of rational self-control and obliviousness to the ills of life come better from the lips of such a teacher than from the pen of Seneca, a wealthy Roman senator, or from the Emperor Marcus Aurelius. Relatively little is known of the early life of Epictetus. He first appears as a slave in Rome. But the young slave must have showed signs of unusual intellectual ability, for he was permitted to attend lectures by the distinguished philosophers of the day.

Epictetus' early life could not have been very enjoyable, however. The Stoic philosophy to which he was attracted provided much more for him that a mere theoretical system. It offered a way of living designed to meet the uncertainties in a household ruled by a hard and often irresponsible soldier of fortune. Tradition has it that at one time, when his master in a fit of anger was having Epictetus' leg twisted, Epictetus pointed out to him that under such treatment one's leg would break and, when it broke, his only comment was, "You see, it is as I told you." Since there is good evidence that Epictetus was lame in his youth, the story is probably apocryphal. But there were occasions enough in the life of a Roman slave where the Stoic obliviousness to pain and suffering was an invaluable asset.

When Nero was forced to flee from Rome, Epictetus' master, who was captain of the royal guard, accompanied him. He later aided the tyrant in taking his own life and for this act was himself put to death by Nero's successor. Epictetus was then able to obtain his freedom. He had already achieved some renown as a philosopher, and he soon established himself as a teacher in Rome. Independence in thinking is never welcome to a despot, however, and shortly thereafter all philosophers were expelled from Rome by order of the new emperor. Epictetus was forced to leave the city, but about A.D. 90 he opened a school not far away in Nicopolis, where he was able to teach until he was quite an old man. Distinguished more as a lecturer and speaker than as an author, Epictetus wrote nothing that has been preserved, but one of the group of enthusiastic followers who gathered about him fortunately copied down his lectures on philosophy and edited them in eight volumes. Four of these volumes now survive, known as the *Discourses of Epictetus*.

In his *Discourses* Epictetus urges young men, and even young women, to the study of philosophy. His belief in the power of reason over men's minds is strong, and he is convinced that the remedy for the ills of mankind lies in philosophy. Without philosophy it is impossible, he maintains, to live a virtuous life. His concept of philosophy is quite practical. The aim of the philosopher is the practice of the good, not merely a knowledge of its nature. Practice has much greater efficacy, also, in instructing others than does mere talk about the good life. We learn by doing, Epictetus avers, not by listening (a principle of which colleges and universities even today often seem unconvinced). Every habit and faculty is maintained and increased by the corresponding action, he points out. The ability to run is achieved by running. If you would be a good reader, read; if a good writer, write.

It is the duty of philosophers, Epictetus declares, "to superintend as far as they can all mankind and see what they do, how they live, what they neglect contrary to their duty." He who speaks to all men about what is right and what is wrong, about slavery and freedom of the spirit, about the enduring purpose of life, is doing a greater service to the state than if he took public office and carried out its routine activities. Until a man learns to control himself, however, it is unwise, Epictetus warns, for him to undertake to admonish others. This conviction, indeed, underlies all Stoic philosophy.

### Lucius Annaeus Seneca

In the writing of Seneca and Marcus Aurelius, one a distinguished Roman senator, the other ruler of the Roman Empire, there is ample evidence that Stoicism also had large appeal for those more favored by circumstance. Born in Cordova about 4 B.C. of a wealthy and illustrious Spanish family, Seneca had all the things that should make life enjoyable—if the Epicureans are to be believed. He had cultured companions, leisure, ample means to satisfy every desire. His father, who was himself an influential author as well as a Spanish gentleman of means, educated Seneca for the legal profession in the expectation that he would hold public office. Seneca not only achieved outstanding success as a lawyer but rose rapidly in the public life of Rome and gradually amassed a huge fortune. His large estates were partly inherited from his father, partly given him by the emperors he served, but partly also acquired by legal practices that we today would regard as unethical. Critics both ancient and modern have been somewhat disturbed, as a matter of fact, by the marked discrepancy between Seneca's energetic pursuit of wealth, at times by rather dubious means, and his repeated advocacy of the simple life in which all such externals have no value. It has been well suggested that "cleavage between profession and practice is a common phenomenon, but seldom is the gap so yawning because Seneca was an artist both in his preaching and his malefactions."[2]

The Empress Agrippina made Seneca the tutor of her son Nero, and he became a close advisor to the young prince in his better days. The bene-ficient administration during the first five years of Nero's reign can be attributed largely to his influence. Unfortunately, it was not long before Nero's true nature emerged, and relations between the two became increas-ingly strained. In A.D. 62, at the age of sixty-six, Seneca offered his enormous fortune to the emperor and retired voluntarily to his own private estate.

Three years later the suspicious and vacillating Nero, imagining that his former counselor was implicated in one of the plots against his life, determined to have Seneca killed. The description of Tacticus (*Annals* 15.62) of the last scene in Seneca's life reveals a theatrical quality perhaps not unlike that of the tragic heroes in Seneca's plays, but also a fortitude more in keeping with his Stoic philosophy than with some aspects of his own previous life:

> Seneca calmly requested tablets for making a will. Upon the Centurion's refusal, he turned to his friends and declared that as he was prevented from showing them the gratitude they deserved he would leave them the possession he valued most, the pattern of his life. If they heeded this, they would win a reputation for good character and the reward of stead-fast friendship. At the same time he led them, first by persuasion and then by rebuke, from tears to fortitude, asking them repeatedly, "Where are those philosophical precepts and where the logic that you have studied so long for just such an event?"

Whatever we may think of some less exemplary aspects of his conduct, Seneca's interest in literature and philosophy was perhaps as enduring, and certainly in the long run more rewarding, than his desire for political recog-nition or economic gain. As a young man he attended the lectures of the Stoic teachers of his day and later became the associate of the ablest of these philosophers. His friends in places of prominence looked to him for advice and counsel on the nature of the good life, and he found time, even during his active involvement in social and political life but especially during his periods of retirement, to write a large number of essays and letters, many of which have come down to us. Among these the essays *On a Happy Life*, *On Tranquility*, *On the Shortness of Life*, and *On Providence* provide the fullest statement of his Stoic philosophy.*

* Equally interesting for the general reader is the collection of 124 letters addressed to Lucilius. There is no reason to doubt that these are genuine letters, although written with a view to publication near the end of Seneca's life when he had retired finally from political activity. "Few Roman writings transport readers to the Roman scene so effec-tively," according to a distinguished contemporary scholar. "But the homiletic tone persists throughout. The letters read, in fact, like the midweek chats of a skillful and alert modernist preacher. In his relaxed mood, especially in the earlier letters, Seneca can so far abate his Stoicism as to include, with high approbation, choice tidbits from

*Marcus Aurelius Antoninus*

The Emperor Marcus Aurelius (A.D. 121–180) ranks among the outstanding men of the Roman Empire, among the finest individuals indeed of any age. Every Roman of his day, it is said, was anxious to possess his portrait. Recent experience with such "personality cult" leaders as Hitler, Mussolini, and Stalin may make us somewhat suspicious of this practice, but in the case of Marcus Aurelius the desire seems to have reflected genuine admiration as well, no doubt, as a measure of political prudence.

As a youth, Marcus Aurelius showed high promise in philosophy as well as in such manly sports as wrestling and boar hunting. His education was decidedly not that of the typical prince, but more in line with Plato's proposal for his philosopher-kings. The guardians of the young man gathered about him the most distinguished teachers of his day, and he early became acquainted with the Stoic philosophy. When only twelve years old he assumed the simple garb of the Stoic disciple and accustomed himself to sleep upon a plank bed. In the first book of his *Meditations,* Aurelius expresses his debt to these early Stoic teachers in interesting fashion. From one, he writes, he learned to avoid listening to slander; from another to despise superstition and to practice self-denial; from a third, undeviating steadiness of purpose and the uncomplaining endurance of misfortune; from a fourth, "not continually to excuse the neglect of ordinary duties by alleging urgent occupations." Throughout his life Aurelius adhered with sincerity to the practical precepts of Stoicism. In its more theoretical doctrines he seems never to have had any great interest.

For many years Marcus Aurelius lived quietly either at Rome or at the villa of his foster-father (the then emperor Antoninus Pius) on the seacoast about twelve miles from the capital, hunting, fishing, wrestling, and continuing his studies. A not too happy matrimonial venture was perhaps the one disturbing event of these years. In A.D 161, when Marcus Aurelius was forty, his foster-father became critically ill. Summoning his councilors, the emperor ordered transferred to Marcus's room the little god of fortune whose statue was kept in the private bedchamber of the ruler as an omen of public prosperity. In this instance the charm had little potency, however. Almost immediately a veritable deluge of misfortune descended upon the state, and along the borders of the empire revolts broke out among the fierce barbarian tribes in one section after another. Despite his own disinclination to do so, Marcus Aurelius was forced to spend most of his time and energy as emperor quelling such uprisings and restoring order in the empire. During

---

the Epicurian school." (Moses Hadas, *The Stoic Philosophy of Seneca,* p. 13). Among the attractive and informative letters included in this volume are letters on friendship, slaves, moderation, the happy life, old age, suicide, and immortality.

these military campaigns his *Meditations* were written, largely as a private diary and with no thought of publication. The calmness of spirit and the insight into human nature found here reflect the calmness of the emperor's mind, not that of the world in which he lived. In these *Meditations*, indeed, one sees ample evidence that the life of reason can enable a man to master external circumstance, no matter what its nature.

There were occasions enough upon which Marcus Aurelius, emperor though he was, was called upon to practice the philosophy he professed. Perhaps the clearest expression of Marcus Aurelius' spirit is to be seen, however, in his attitude toward the revolt of Avidius Cassius, a general he trusted and admired. While Aurelius himself was busy with wars in the west, Cassius set himself at the head of the army in the east and proclaimed himself a ruler there, alienating many of the eastern provinces from their loyalty to Marcus Aurelius. As the emperor was gathering a force to quell the rebellion, Cassius was assassinated by his own officers and the disaffection quieted. Aurelius thereupon requested the Senate to pardon the family of the rebellious general and journeyed in person through the provinces that had revolted, showing the greatest forbearance and clemency in dealing with all those implicated in the affair. Almost immediately upon his return from this mission, Aurelius had to leave Rome again to oppose barbarian forces in Germany. During this campaign he contracted a contagious malady and died in camp near Vienna in A.D. 180. Amid widespread grief among his subjects, his ashes were carried to Rome, where he received the honor of deification. Those who could afford it had his statue or bust placed among their *Dei Penates* (household deities).

It is only, so Plato insists, when kings become philosophers that justice will prevail in the state. Marcus Aurelius went far to substantiate the Platonic dictum. Seen in the light of the life he lived, the nine rules Marcus Aurelius drew up for reflection before dealing with an offender become all the more impressive. These rules succinctly summarize the Stoic philosophy that permeates his *Meditations* as a whole. Remember, Aurelius writes, that:

1.  Men were made for each other.
2.  Invincible influences act upon men and mold their opinion and their conduct.
3.  Sin is mainly error and ignorance, an involuntary slavery.
4.  We ourselves are feeble and by no means blameless.
5.  Our judgments are apt to be very rash and immature.
6.  Man's life is only for a moment and after a short time we are all laid out dead.
7.  No wrongful act of another can bring shame upon us.
8.  Our own anger hurts us more than the acts of others.
9.  Benevolence is invincible, if it be not affected or acting on our part.[3]

## The Stoic View of Life

### Man the Master of His Fate

Stoicism as a practical philosophy of living was most fully developed during its final period of influence in Rome. Primary emphasis is placed upon the doctrine that the character of life is determined from within, not from without. In every sense that matters, man is the captain of his soul, the master of his fate. It is our responsibility, as well as our opportunity, to see that we make of life something worthwhile. This emphasis is to be seen with equal clarity in the lives and in the teaching of the great Stoics of this period. "Men are disturbed not by things, but by the view which they take of things," Epictetus writes. "Thus death is nothing terrible else it would have appeared so to Socrates. But the terror consists in our notion of death. . . . The origin of perturbation is this, to wish for something and that this should not happen. Therefore, if I am able to change externals according to my wish, I change them, but if I cannot, I am ready to tear out the eyes of him who hinders me."[4]

Little reflection is needed, according to the Stoic, to recognize that external circumstances in themselves do not really matter. They affect us only as we let them. It is our own attitude that counts. Whether a particular situation is good or evil, whether beneficial or harmful, depends on how we take it—on what we make of it—and that depends entirely upon ourselves. For all the great Stoics Socrates provides the example of how life should be lived and hardship encountered. His attitude toward his accusers at his trial, his calmness in the face of death, his contention that those who are guilty of injustice harm themselves more than their victims, his complete indifference to the material advantages for which men customarily strive—all these expressed perfectly the Stoic philosophy.

The world in which we live is neither good nor evil; it is simply a place for good and evil. This conviction the Stoic philosophers never tire of repeating. "No man finds poverty a trouble to him but he that thinks it so; and he that thinks it so, makes it so," Seneca writes. "He that is not content in poverty, would be so neither in plenty; for the fault is not in the thing but in the mind. If anyone be sickly, remove him from a kennel to a palace; he is at the same pass, for he carries his disease along with him." "No man shall ever be poor who goes to himself for what he wants, and that is the readiest way to riches." "The thing that matters is not what you bear but how you bear it."

It is, the Stoics would insist, the student who must work his way through college who usually gets the most out of an education. Only a person who has hard work to do develops the character and determination needed to succeed in later life. "No tree stands firm and sturdy if it is not buffeted by constant wind," Seneca writes; "the very stresses cause it to stiffen and stand firm." To have everything we want given to us by fond parents is hardly the way to develop the stamina and self-control required for great achievement. Frequently, also, a physical handicap or misfortune serves as a stimulus to greater determination or concentration of effort, whereas those of us with comparatively good health may spend life at the level of mediocrity. Deafness does not necessarily produce a Helen Keller or an Edison, nor poliomyelitis send one to the White House for four terms. But physical ailment is not in itself an evil. The typical ills that affect life are all capable of being turned to our own advantage. It is our attitude that determines whether or not we find the means of surmounting difficulty and making life worthwhile.

An appealing statement of the Stoic point of view is found in Seneca's essay *Of a Happy Life*:

> There is nothing in this world that is more talked of or less understood than the business of a happy life. It is every man's wish and design, and yet not one of a thousand knows wherein that happiness consists. We live, however, in a blind and eager pursuit of it; and the more haste we make in the wrong way, the farther we are from our journey's end. The great blessings of life are within us and within our reach. Tranquility is a certain state of mind, which no condition of fortune can either exalt or depress. . . . He that is perfectly wise is perfectly happy; nay, the very beginning of wisdom makes life easy to us. Wisdom instructs us in the way of nature and in the government of life; not to make us live only, but to live happily. She allows nothing to be good that will not be so forever; no man to be happy but he that needs no other happiness than he has within himself; no man to be great or powerful that is not master of himself. A wise man in whatever condition he is will still be happy, for he subjects all things to himself and himself to reason. . . . He that would be truly happy must so live with men as if God saw him, and so speak to God as if men heard him.[5]

### Rational Self-Control and Universal Law

(Feeling and emotion, the Stoics contend, are signs of weakness.) For the Stoics, as for Schopenhauer, the rational life involves a complete control of emotion and appetite by the dictates of reason. With entire freedom from emotion and with reasoned calmness, the man who is master of himself will look unperturbed upon the world about him. Desire and emotion indeed seem to the Stoics much like a disease. Given ever so slight a foothold in our lives, they soon spread like a contagion to control us. Even the sorrows and misfortunes of others must not be allowed to disturb the calmness and serenity of spirit that is the goal of the rational life. We should help others as reason demands, to be sure, but we should do it without letting ourselves be led into feelings of pity or sympathy.

Epictetus does not shrink from the uncompromising logic of this view of life:

> When you see a person weeping in sorrow, whether when a child goes abroad, or when he is dead, or when the man has lost his property, take care that the appearance does not hurry you away with it as if he were suffering in external things. But straightway make a distinction in your mind, and be in readiness to say, it is not that which has happened that afflicts this man, for it does not afflict another, but it is the opinion about the thing which afflicts the man. So far as words go, then, do not be unwilling to show him sympathy, and even if it happens so, to lament with him. But take care that you do not lament internally also.[6]

Seldom has the position advocated here by the Stoic been expressed with more dignity and simplicity than by Seneca:

> I will look upon death or upon comedy with the same expression of countenance. I will despise riches when I have them as much as when I have them not. Whether fortune comes or goes, I will take no notice of her. I will view all lands as though they belonged to me, and my own as though they belonged to all mankind. I will so live as to remember that I was born for others and will thank nature on this account; for in what fashion could she have done better for me? Whatever I may possess, I will neither hoard it greedily, nor squander it recklessly. I will think that I have no possessions so real as those which I have given away to deserving people. I will do nothing because of public opinion, but everything because of conscience.[7]

In the life of reason, then, as portrayed by the Stoic, self-control is given primary place. The rational man is the master of circumstances because he is master of himself, not the creature of emotion and desire. But the Stoic philosophy does not stop here; indeed, it cannot stop here. The question still remains, in accord with what principles shall the rational man direct his life? Self-control in itself is but an empty formula. If human life is to make sense and have meaning, it must be seen as but part of a larger whole. Rational self-control is good and desirable because it brings human conduct into conformity with the laws of the universe itself, the Stoics maintain. In the life of reason man rises above the strife and pettiness of human desire to the orderliness and certainty of universal law. He lives in accord with the law of nature, which is the law of God.

For the Stoic philosophers of every age physics, or metaphysics, is the necessary foundation of ethics. Only as a man understands the nature of the universe can he hope to understand himself. As this deeper note in the Stoic philosophy becomes clear, rational self-control assumes greater significance. The intelligent—that is, the rational—man is aware of the fact that the order and law of the universe, the Divine Reason, is both universal and necessary.

It is not only foolish, it is useless, to try to disobey its dictates and escape its consequences. One brings upon himself only unnecessary anxiety and suffering by attempting to disregard universal law. When a man can see, moreover, that the dictates of reason in his own life are but an expression of the rational law of the universe, he can gladly accept such universal law as his own and direct his life accordingly. In the words of Epictetus,

> Remembering then this disposition of things, we ought to go to be instructed, not that we may change the constitution of things—for we have not the power to do it, nor is it better that we should have the power—but in order that, as the things around us are what they are and by nature exist, we may maintain our minds in harmony with the things which happen.[8]

Thus the wise man is content. He has what he wants because he has learned to want what is in conformity to the laws of the universe. "To be instructed is this, to learn to wish that everything may happen as it does," Epictetus writes.

### Reason and Religion

Nor did the Stoics hesitate to use the word God for this enduring rational order, governing at once the universe of nature and the life and destiny of man. Stoicism was thus monotheistic, or, perhaps better, pantheistic, in tendency, and far more rationally appealing than the current polytheism of that period. Among the finest expressions of the religious thought of Stoicism is the *Hymn to Zeus*, written by Cleanthes, Zeno's successor as leader of the Stoic school in Athens. This hymn, the only important document from the early period of Stoicism to be preserved in full, is quite comparable in its religious spirit with the Hebrew and Christian scriptures:

> O King, most High, nothing is done without Thee,
> Neither in heaven or on earth, nor in the sea,
> Except what the wicked do in their foolishness.
> Thou makest order out of disorder,
> And what is worthless, becomes precious in Thy sight;
> For Thou hast fitted together good and evil into one,
> And hast established one law that exists forever.
>
> But the wicked fly from Thy law, unhappy ones,
> And though they desire to possess what is good,
> Yet they see not, neither do they hear, the universal law of God.
> They go astray, each after his own devices,—
> Some vainly striving after reputation,
> Others turning aside after gain excessively,
> Others after riotous living and wantonness.

Nay, but O Zeus, giver of all things,
Deliver men from this foolishness,
Scatter it from their souls and grant them to obtain wisdom,
For by wisdom Thou dost rightly govern all things.
Nor is there, for mortal men or for the gods, greater thing than this—
Rightly to adore the universal law.[9]

No conflict exists, then, for the Stoic philosophers between reason and religion. They recognize the enduring order in the universe as the expression of a Divine Reason that permeates the whole. In inner nature, man and God are essentially akin, and man's chief responsibility is to measure up to his divine heritage. As Epictetus puts this Stoic doctrine:

You are a distinct portion of the essence of God, and contain a certain part of him in yourself. Why then are you ignorant of your noble birth? Why do you not consider whence you came? You carry a God about with you, poor wretch, and know nothing of it. Do you suppose I mean some god of gold or silver? It is within yourself that you carry him, and you do not observe that you profane him by impure thought and unclean actions. If the mere external image of God were present, you would not dare to act as you do; and when God himself is within you, and hears and sees all, are you not ashamed to act thus,—insensible of your own nature, and at enmity with God.[10]

### The Problem of Evil

Among the more serious philosophical problems faced by the Stoic philosophy is the so-called problem of evil. If we maintain with the Stoic that the character of life is determined from within, that each man can make of life what he chooses, then how shall we explain the large amount of suffering and pain in life? Surely if a Divine Reason orders the universe in which we live, there should be more to justify our hope for a better world. In times like ours, when awful weapons of mass destruction are used even by our own nation to inflict untold misery and suffering upon millions of helpless civilians, and when the total destruction of all that is good in our civilization is an ever-present danger, the problem of evil becomes especially acute. Can the Stoic hope to meet adequately the issues raised here?

Initially, of course, Stoic philosophers insist repeatedly and emphatically that hardship and suffering, poverty, sickness—the ills of life that are usually called evils—are actually necessary to bring out our best qualities. Strong character can be developed not by a life of softness and ease but only by facing danger and enduring hardship. As a teacher gives the most difficult tasks to those students who have the most ability, so God deals with the noblest men and women in this life, Epictetus points out: "It is difficulties that show what men are. Therefore, when a difficulty confronts you, remember that God, like a trainer of wrestlers, has matched you with a rough young man." The dangers and hardships that men and women confront in times of war tend to confirm this. In such times deeds of moral heroism become commonplace. The courage of many a man, which in times of prosperity and ease was never suspected, now comes to the surface. Instead of the selfish and petty interests so widely characteristic of us all in times of peace and prosperity, we see high qualities of courage exhibited on the battlefield by jungle fighters and helicopter crews; quiet heroism on the part of doctors, nurses, and chaplains. And in our recent involvement in Vietnam it may well have taken more courage on the part of some young men to refuse to fight in a war they believed to be wrong than to face the dangers of military service.

We must look beneath surface appearance, then, the Stoic points out, before deciding that any particular hardship, deprivation, or danger can justly be called evil. Upon examination, many of these so-called ills of life turn out to hold more promise of good than of evil. Yet all evil cannot be thus accounted for. There are situations that certainly require further explanation, and Seneca, in his essay *On Providence,* is concerned to provide this. "I shall show," he writes, "that what seem to be evils are not actually such: in the first place, they benefit the individuals to whose lot they fall, and, in the second place, they benefit the whole body of mankind, for which the gods are more concerned than they are for individuals; . . . further these things are destined, and befall good men by the same law that makes them good."[11]

The typical ills of life, that is, can be divided into several classes. There are evils that we bring upon ourselves; there are evils that others bring upon us; and there are evils that befall us as a result of the forces of nature. As each is examined, its justification in the total scheme of things can be supported, the Stoic argues. Insofar as we bring hardship and pain upon ourselves, we recognize the justice and even the desirability of suffering the consequences of our own misdeeds. The child who plays with fire gets his fingers burned. The student who does not prepare the work assigned, as a rule, fails the course he is taking (or at least most of us feel that he should). Thus by experience each person learns the necessity of intelligence and hard work for successful living. Only as cause and effect operate dependably in our own conduct is the development of character and understanding possible.

Moreover, the Stoic points out, man is but a part of a larger whole, and what seems evil to an individual may actually prove necessary for mankind as a whole. Only as nations, like men and women, suffer the consequences of their misdeeds and injustices will they learn the necessity of a higher, more reasonable, and juster social ideal. War is certainly the gravest of all social ills, bringing destruction and death upon thousands of innocent men and women. But if we in the United States, for example, failed to gain wisdom from the efforts of the industrial nations of Western Europe to impose an alien political system upon the peoples of Africa and Asia, then we perhaps inevitably found ourselves involved in the failure of a somewhat comparable attempt in Vietnam. Only thus at terrible cost to all concerned could we learn—let us hope once and for all—that the world is a community in which each people must work out its own way of life or with the rest of humanity suffer the consequences in international strife and hatred.

A universal law of social life operates in this fashion, if the Stoic point of view is adopted, to commit the nations of the world to a higher moral ideal. When this law is not observed, the righteous and the guilty suffer alike, the weak as well as the strong. Nations, to be sure, are not as rational as individuals. The group mind (if such there be) is as yet largely emotional; and national self-interest is easily disguised as the highest patriotism. Yet as each man is rational by nature, so mankind itself may become rational. Indeed, so mankind *must* become rational in its collective life, the Stoic insists, if it wishes to escape the suffering that inevitably follows the breaking of these universal moral laws at work in our larger human relationships. It may be that only the destructiveness of atomic warfare, or the perils of widespread pollution and global overpopulation, can teach us this lesson, but it is a lesson that it seems the world must learn if mankind is to survive.

Finally, what is true for the individual and for society is also true, the Stoic maintains, in our relation to the physical universe. The suffering that comes to us from action of the forces of nature results from the operation of dependable rational laws. Yet it is clearly far better that we live in a dependable universe governed by rational law than in a universe at the mercy of the changing whims and fancies of an inscrutable fate. It is true that famine in India or China may wipe out the lives of thousands of helpless victims year after year, while automobile accidents, airplane crashes, and disastrous floods also kill thousands every year in our own country. But it is also true that the mind of man is capable of grasping the laws at work in the world of nature. Airplanes can be built and personal trained capable of flying more safely. The safety of persons in automobiles can be vastly improved, if Ralph Nader, for example, is given credence. Ways can be devised to control floods, to irrigate arid desert land, even to limit population growth.

In modern science the mind of man has an instrument able to shape the forces of nature to meet the needs of human life to an almost unbelieveable degree. But this is possible only because the forces of nature are governed by consistent law rather than by chance. If water boiled today when heated but froze under the same conditions tomorrow, if the forces of gravity operated today but could not be counted upon tomorrow, it is easy to see how completely impossible life as we know it would be. Individuals may suffer at times from the forces of nature, but mankind as a whole is immeasurably benefited by the dependable operation of universal laws of nature that bring rain or sunshine upon the just and the unjust alike.

It is in general this interpretation of evil that is adopted by Seneca in his essay *On Providence* and by Epictetus in his *Discourses*. Upon each of us, as rational men and women, falls a responsibility to help in removing the ills of life, the Stoic maintains, whether they spring from individual, social, or natural causes.

### Man the Captain of His Soul

Ultimately, only that is evil which we regard as such and allow to affect us undesirably, the Stoic philosophers repeatedly insist. Our own attitude toward an external fact determines its character. "External things touch not the soul, not in the least degree." "Life is neither good nor evil but only a place for good and evil." "It is not possible that any evil can befall a good man." Here we meet the most characteristic of the Stoic doctrines regarding the problem of evil. The essence of virtue is integrity of character; it is rational self-control. The good man can be good no matter what the circumstances of his life, for there is no circumstance that can take his integrity from him. That this is a philosophy by which a man can live nobly and courageously was convincingly demonstrated by the great Stoics whose lives we have examined. Nowhere has their conviction been more movingly expressed than in the familiar lines of William Ernest Henley's "Invictus":

> Out of the night that covers me,
>   Black as the Pit from pole to pole,
> I thank whatever gods may be
>   For my unconquerable soul.
>
> In the fell clutch of circumstance
>   I have not winced nor cried aloud.
> Under the bludgeonings of chance
>   My head is bloody, but unbowed.
>
> It matters not how strait the gate
>   How charged with punishments the scroll,
> I am the master of my fate;
>   I am the captain of my soul.[12]

### Popular Rationalism in Our Age
### *Walter Lippmann's* Preface to Morals

Despite the hedonistic spirit that has accompanied our increased prosperity in America, the philosophy of the Stoics has continued to be ably and persuasively advocated. It is a philosophy to which men turn when strength and fortitude are needed to face the hardships and dangers with which life so insistently confronts us. Among contemporary philosophers, Bertrand Russell has (more explicitly, perhaps, than any other major figure) advocated certain Stoic attitudes as both acceptable and desirable. A disturbing, widely read early essay of his, *A Free Man's Worship* (1909), presented in striking fashion the attitude of the Stoic as the only spiritual refuge for the thoughtful man who really understands the scientific picture of the world. The universe that modern science portrays does not support the Stoic interpretation, as Russell sees it. Rather it is purposeless and void of meaning. Man is the product of causes that had no awareness of the end they were achieving. Our hopes, our fears, our loves, and our most cherished beliefs are but the outcome of an accidental collection of atoms. No heroism, no intensity of thought or strength of conviction, can preserve an individual life beyond the grave.

> All the labors of the ages, all the devotion, all the inspiration, all the noonday brightness of human genius, are destined to extinction in the vast death of the solar system, and the whole temple of man's achievements must inevitably be buried within the debris of a universe in ruins —all these things, if not quite beyond dispute, are yet so nearly certain that no philosophy which rejects them can hope to stand. Only within the scaffolding of these truths, only on the firm foundation of unyielding despair, can the soul's habitation henceforth be safely built. . . .
>
> Blind to good and evil, reckless of destruction, omnipotent matter rolls on its relentless way; for man, condemned today to lose his dearest, tomorrow himself to pass through the gate of darkness, it remains only to cherish, ere yet the blow falls, the lofty thoughts that ennoble his little day; disdaining the coward terrors of the slave Fate, to worship at the shrine that his own hands have built; undismayed by the empire of chance, to preserve a mind free from the wanton tyranny that rules his outward life; proudly defiant of the irresistible forces that tolerate, for a moment, his knowledge and his condemnation, to sustain alone, a weary but unyielding Atlas, the world that his own ideals have fashioned despite the trampling march of unconscious power.[13]

One does not have to agree with such a position as this in order to admire the courageous spirit reflected in it, remarkably similar, of course, to that in Henley's *Invictus*. Russell himself is, however, by no means a consistent advocate of Stoicism. The most appealing popular statement of such a philosophy for our age is to be found, as a matter of fact, not in the work of professional philosophers like Bertrand Russell but in a provocative work by Walter Lippmann (1889–    ), entitled *A Preface to Morals*. Lippmann is not known primarily as a philosopher, but rather as one of the ablest interpreters of the twentieth-century economic and political scene. His syndicated column, "Today and Tomorrow," appeared for many years in the best newspapers throughout the country. Over some fifty years he also published more than twenty-five influential studies of current economic and political issues.*

Lippmann has always been more than a commentator on current events. He has approached the social problems of our age with a clear-cut philosophy of his own and consistently raised issues more fundamental and more searching than those found in the usual newspaper columns. His philosophical interests went back indeed to his college days at Harvard University where, as a member of the illustrious class of 1910, he majored in philosophy during the years when Josiah Royce, William James, and George Santayana made Harvard the most distinguished center of philosophy ever known in America. In 1913, when only three years out of college, he published his first book, A Preface to Politics, which soon became the unofficial bible of the young liberals of that day.

A Preface to Morals is unique among Lippmann's books. In it he turned aside from his professional writing, as it were, to formulate his own personal philosophy of living. Here is an account of that in which he believes, an interpretation of the philosophy upon which he feels a man must base his life if he hopes to find any enduring meaning and satisfaction. The book is not the creed of a professional philosopher but the philosophy of a professional journalist, of a man whose life has been spent in observing and interpreting the course of human affairs. As such, it has an appeal and a practical value for ordinary men and women greater than that of the works of many eminent contemporary philosophers. As Lippmann himself sums up his career, "I have lived two lives, one of books and one of newspapers. Each helps the other. The philosophy is the context in which I write my columns. The column is the laboratory or clinic in which I test the philosophy and keep it from becoming too abstract."[14]

Actually his Preface to Morals provides a thoughtful twentieth-century statement of the position adopted and given wide popularity two thousand years ago by the Stoic philosophers. Like Seneca in particular among the early Stoics, Lippmann here interprets rationalism for the intelligent laymen in able and, for many at least, persuasive fashion.

### The Hedonistic Fallacy

Published well over a generation ago (1929), A Preface to Morals was in part the expression of a reaction against the hedonistic spirit of the 1920s. In that age of jazz and bootleg whiskey, it was widely believed not only by

* Among these The Method of Freedom (1934), The Good Society (1937), U. S. Foreign Policy (1943), and The Public Philosophy (1954) are perhaps the best known and more significant. In the library of Yale University there is already a Lippmann room that contains, in addition to the books he has published, 288 articles by Lippmann, 72 articles about him, 122 reviews of his books, 10 volumes of his "Today and Tomorrow" syndicated column, and 120 portraits, photographs, caricatures, and cartoons. (See also Walter Lippmann and His Times, edited by Marquis Childs and James Reston, 1959.)

the younger generation but by many of their elders as well that the road to happiness lay in a perpetual round of indulgence and excess, a Cyrenaic pursuit of pleasure of the most blasé and uninhibited sort. In vigorous opposition to a hedonism such as this, Lippmann insisted that only a philosophy of living based upon reason could meet the tests of experience and common sense, and in discerning fashion he undertook to present such a philosophy. Many of the specific problems with which he deals are now dated, of course, but his major ideas are remarkably true to the spirit of the Stoics.

The central issue that confronts every man and woman in personal life, as Lippmann sees it, is a choice between the immediate satisfaction of desire and the life of reason. "It is a deep conviction that happiness is possible," he writes, "and all inquiry into the foundation of morals turns ultimately upon whether man can achieve this happiness by pursuing his desires, or whether he must first learn to desire the kind of happiness that is possible." In recent years those who call themselves liberals in politics and in morals have taken the position that if only the external circumstances are favorable, happiness can normally be achieved. The root of evil, from this liberal point of view, lies in not recognizing that in an economy of abundance the fruits of such abundance must be widely distributed. The need is for good jobs for all, with wages high enough to provide a decent standard of living and the basic comforts of life for all men and women whatever their color or creed. This has been the ideal of the reform movements in our American social and political life in the present century, whether termed the Fair Deal, the New Deal, or the Great Society. It is not the reform of desire but the provision of greater opportunities for the fulfillment of desire that these liberal programs have consistently advocated. Interestingly enough, much this same philosophy is also accepted by Philip Slater in *The Pursuit of Loneliness* as the dominant emphasis in the "new culture" of the younger generation today. It is simply "the direct, immediate and uncontaminated bodily and sensory" gratification of our desires that makes possible the cultivation of joy and beauty in which the meaning of life consists, Slater writes.[15]

Those who accept this so-called liberal point of view, and hope that man will find happiness in the pursuit of pleasure and the satisfaction of appetite and desire, ignore the testimony not merely of their maiden aunts but also, Lippmann maintains, of the great teachers of wisdom through the ages: "It is written in many languages, and in the idiom of many cultures, that if a man is to find happiness, he must reconstruct not merely his world but, first of all, himself."

Our age has reacted vigorously against the attitudes and morals that are customarily called Puritan. We now praise frankness, openmindedness, and freedom in our social conduct. Indeed, these have become for many young men and women the essential principles of morality. As a result, the deep wisdom deposited in our traditional moral ideals has been obscured, and it is very hard, especially for young people, to realize that virtue is really good and sin really evil:

"Morality has become so stereotyped, so thin and verbal, so encrusted with pious fraud," Lippmann points out; "it has been so much monopolized by the tender-minded and the sentimental, and made so odious by the outcries of foolish men and sour old women, that our generation has almost forgotten that virtue was not invented in Sunday Schools but derives originally from a profound realization of the character of human life."[16]

### The Meaning of Maturity

The trouble with most men and women is simply that they fail to grow up. They never attain that maturity of spirit upon which the success or failure of life depends, Lippmann feels. We all grow older, to be sure, but too frequently we do not grow up. The achievement of maturity in this sense has little to do with the acquiring of factual information. A college degree, possession of accurate scientific knowledge, is no guarantee of maturity: "The critical question is whether childish habits and expectations are to persist or are to be transformed." Maturity involves "the acquiring of a different sense of life, a different kind of intuition about the nature of things."

When a childish disposition is carried over into an adult environment, the symptoms are fairly evident. Life seems to such an individual a kind of conspiracy to make him happy or to make him miserable. He has a deep feeling "that life owes him something, that somehow it is the duty of the universe to look after him, and to listen sharply when he speaks to it." "The childish pattern appears also as a disposition to believe that he may reach out for anything in sight and take it, and that having gotten it nobody must under any circumstances take it away."[17] Finally, this childish pattern becomes a deep preference for not knowing the truth, a habitual desire to think of the world as one prefers it, a determination that the facts shall conform to his wishes, and a deep resentment when they do not.

Only as we discover that our wishes have little or no authority in the world, only as we see the necessity that is in the nature of things, do we begin to approach maturity, Lippmann maintains. When we begin to see that the external world no longer obeys our wishes, we realize, if we are mature, that we cannot let our wishes become too deeply involved in specific attractions. When we can no longer count on possessing whatever we may happen to want, we must learn to want what we can possess. The mature man is the one who has ceased to expect anything of the world that it cannot give. He has what he wants because he has learned to want what he can have. He has learned to possess things not by grasping them for himself but by *understanding them*.

*The Political Philosophy of a Rationalist*

In popular usage there is a vague distinction between two very common words, *politician* and *statesman*. To call a man a statesman is a high compliment; to call him a politician is, if not an insult, at least in some degree disparaging. Lippmann's effort to clarify these implications, which are dimly to be seen in the popular mind, throws a good deal of light upon the meaning of rationalism as a political philosophy. The politician he defines as a man who seeks to gratify the particular interests and wishes of the people who elect him, a man dominated by desire and emotion rather than by reason or disinterested inquiry.

> When we think offhand of a politician we think of a man who works for a partial interest. At worst it is his own pocket. At best it may be his party, his class, or an institution with which he is identified. We never feel that he can or will take into account all the interests concerned, and because bias and partisanship are the qualities of his conduct, we feel, unless we are naïvely afflicted with the same bias, that he is not to be trusted too far.[18]

When, then, does a man cease being a mere politician and begin to be a statesman? When he stops trying merely to satisfy the momentary wishes of his constituents, Lippmann suggests, and sets out instead to help them realize that their interests must fit the facts of the political order and be harmonized with the interests of others. When a man, that is, gives up a kind of naïve political hedonism and moves over into the life of reason in politics, he begins to manifest the spirit of the statesman.

> The politician says: "I will give you what you want." The statesman says: "What you think you want is this. What it is possible for you to get is that. What you really want, therefore, is the following." The politician stirs up a following, the statesman leads it. The politician, in brief, accepts unregenerate desire at its face value and either fulfills it or perpetrates a fraud; the statesman reeducates desire by confronting it with the reality, and so makes possible an enduring adjustment of interests within the community.[19]

Few can quarrel with the political implications of rationalism as outlined so effectively by Lippmann. As recent developments have made abundantly clear, we certainly need leaders for whom reason, not desire, is the guiding principle. Yet Lippmann himself is forced to admit that the way of such a statesman is difficult in a democracy. When all the adult population has the right to vote, it is not certain that anyone can be elected to office without employing some of the tricks of the politician. "It may be," Lippmann writes, "that statesmanship, in the sense in which I am using it, cannot occupy the whole attention of any public man. It is true at least that it never does."* Whether the appeal of such presidential candidates as Eugene McCarthy and George McGovern to so many young people was a tribute to their statesmanship or to their skill as politicians, each reader must judge for himself. Certainly, however, Watergate has led us all to see that the devices of the politician cannot be allowed to assume control of the office of the president.

### Love as the Rationalist Sees It

Politics may seem unlikely soil in which to cultivate the spirit of reason, but one must admit that Lippmann is remarkably successful here in building a social philosophy upon the foundations of rationalism. Love and sexuality, however, appear an even less promising area. It is worth noting, therefore, that many critics at the time it was published saw the section in A *Preface to Morals* devoted to "Love in the Great Society" as the best thing in the book.

Lippmann himself admits that never before our age has hedonism had conditions so favorable for its success as a principle governing the relation of the sexes. This situation, he points out, has arisen largely because of circumstances inherent in our modern ways of living. Accepting what they considered to be the logic of birth control, the advocates of hedonism a generation ago contended that sexual expression made its main contribution to our lives in the pursuit of pleasure. Their actual proposals were given a variety of names at that time—free love, trial marriage, companionate marriage, and the like. But when these proposals are examined, it is evident that they all took the ready availability of contraceptive methods as their major premise, and then deduced from that fact some or all of the logical consequences. It was Bertrand Russell who stated clearly the conclusion implicit in their position:

> My own view is that the state and the law should take no notice of sexual relations apart from children, and that no marriage ceremony should be valid unless accompanied by a medical certificate of the woman's pregnancy. But when once there are children, I think that divorce should be avoided except for very grave cause. I should not regard physical infidelity as a very grave cause and should teach people that it is to be expected and tolerated but should not involve the begetting of illegitimate

* In a recent work, *Adlai Stevenson: A Study in Values* (Harper and Row, 1967), Hubert J. Muller provides additional support for Lippmann's doubt about the practical effectiveness of pure statesmanship in our democratic society.

children—not because illegitimacy is bad in itself, but because a home with two parents is best for children. I do not feel that the main thing in marriage is the feeling of parents for each other; the main thing is co-operation in bearing children.[20]

Russell's position is more widely accepted today, of course, than when this was written some fifty years ago. In its attitude toward sexual freedom the new naturalism of our day is perhaps not as new as some of its critics suggest. It is at this point, moreover, that Lippmann believed the hedonism of his day to be most vulnerable. "It is, I think, to the separation of parent-hood as a vocation from love as an end in itself that the moralist must address himself," he writes. "For this is the heart of the problem: to deter-mine whether this separation, which birth control has made feasible and which law can no longer prevent, is in harmony with the conditions of human happiness."[21]

If you start with the belief that love is no more than the pleasure of the moment, is it really surprising, Lippmann asks, that it yields only a momentary pleasure? The trouble with this type of hedonism, as with all hedonism, lies in its failure to read aright the nature of human life and the conditions of human happiness, he maintains. Love, when it is genuine, is supposed to stimulate and liberate all our finer activities, both physical and psychic.

I take this to mean that when a man and a woman are successfully in love, their whole activity is energized and victorious. They walk better, their digestion improves, they think more clearly, their secret worries drop away, the world is fresh and interesting, and they can do more than they dreamed that they could do. In love of this kind sexual intimacy is not the dead end of desire as it is in romantic or promiscuous love, but a periodic affirmation of the inward delight of desire pervading an active life. Love of this sort can grow. It can grow because it has something to grow upon and to grow with; it has for its object not the mere relief of physical tension, but all the objects with which the two lovers are concerned.[22]

What most men and women are necessarily concerned with is earning a living, building a career, managing a household, rearing children, finding recreation. If the art of love is to stimulate and enrich their lives, it is these prosaic activities that it must stimulate, Lippmann points out. If you make parenthood a separate vocation, isolate love from the hard realities of living, and say that it must be spontaneous and carefree, what have you done?

You have made love spontaneous but empty, and you have made home-building and parenthood efficient, responsible and dull. Lovers who have nothing to do but love each other are not really to be envied; love and nothing else very soon is nothing else. The emotion of love, in spite of the romantics, is not self-sustaining; it endures only when lovers love many things together, and not merely each other. It is this understanding that love cannot successfully be isolated from the business of living which is the enduring wisdom of the institution of marriage.[23]

It would be foolish to underestimate the enormous difficulty of achieving successful marriage under the conditions that exist in modern life. This Lippmann readily admits. Too many young people have been disillusioned about marriage as they see what has happened to their own parents or to many other married couples they know. The high divorce rate in our country suggests that it is not only the young who find the institution of marriage less satisfactory than it once was piously said to be. Even so, Lippmann's analysis of what is essential for happiness in love is certainly not without value.

In the understanding that love cannot successfully be isolated from the business of living lies the enduring wisdom of the institution of marriage. This is the heart of Lippmann's position. The convention of marriage will survive in the modern world, "not as a rule of law imposed by force, for that has now, I think, become impossible," Lippmann concludes. "It will not survive as a moral commandment with which the elderly can threaten the young. They will not listen. It will survive as the dominant insight into the reality of love and happiness, or it will not survive at all. That does not mean that all persons will live under the convention of marriage. As a matter of fact in civilized ages all persons never have. It means that the convention of marriage, when it is clarified by insight into reality, is likely to be the hypothesis upon which men and women will ordinarily proceed. There will be no compulsion behind it except the compulsion in each man and woman to reach a true adjustment in his life."[24]

## Popular Rationalism: An Evaluation

As portrayed by the abler Stoic philosophers, whether past or present, the life of reason certainly commends itself. We may not always agree with the Stoic, but we cannot help admiring his spirit and his conviction. In times of crisis, whether in the life of an individual or in a nation, the Stoic philosophy sounds a note of courage and of heroism. In the uncertainties of our age, as in the turbulent circumstances of the Roman Empire, this spirit is surely needed. It is not too much to say perhaps that no mature philosophy of living is possible without a Stoic strain in its fabric.

Even the most skillful advocates of popular rationalism, however, whether among the Stoics or as ably interpreted by Lippmann, have not been successful in making rationalism a widely held philosophy among ordinary men and women. A person under the influence of the new naturalism will hardly find in the life of reason as here portrayed an acceptable philosophy of living. Critics of Stoicism see its portrayal of the good life as a rather cold and impersonal affair. All other values are subordinated to the intellectual. Modern psychology, on the other hand, has demonstrated beyond any question that one's feelings and emotions play as essential a role as reason in the full development of human personality. A satisfying philosophy of living, the critics of Stoicism maintain, cannot accept so determined a repression of man's emotional life as the Stoic recommends.

The Stoic philosophy likewise approves too readily an acceptance of life as it is, some of its critics insist. Its injunction seems to be: "Learn to take things as they come," rather than "Seek to make the world a better and more desirable place in which to live." As a result, Stoicism is for these critics too fatalistic in spirit to provide an acceptable basis for life at its best. In youth especially there is a desire for action, a conviction that the evils in life should be eradicated, not calmly or passively accepted. Stoicism may well appeal to those who have felt the disillusionment or the bitterness that age too frequently brings, but will those who are young, eager, and hopeful find it satisfying?

Walter Lippmann has done an impressive job of interpreting the insights contained in the philosophy of the Roman Stoics and applying these to the problems of our age. But he also has made even clearer a major problem to which the critics of rationalism point. In the end he recognizes explicitly that, for his own philosophy as for every completely consistent rationalism, the only enduring value in life is the understanding of life. This fact stands out unmistakably in the final paragraphs of A *Preface to Morals*, where Lippmann draws for us his most graphic picture of the life of reason:

> And so the mature man would take the world as it comes, and within himself remain quite unperturbed. When he acted, he would know that he was only testing an hypothesis, and if he failed he would know that he had made a mistake. He would be quite prepared for the discovery that he might make mistakes, for his intelligence would be disentangled from his hopes. The failure of his experiment could not, therefore, involve the failure of his life. For the aspect of life which implicated his soul would be his understanding of life, and, to the understanding, defeat is no less interesting than victory. . . .
>
> Since nothing gnawed at his vitals, neither doubt nor ambition, nor frustration, nor fear, he would move easily through life. And so, whether he saw the thing as comedy, or high tragedy, or plain farce, he would affirm that it is what it is, and that the wise man can enjoy it.[25]

Can such a view of life as this really satisfy the deeper needs and aspirations of the human spirit? Can rationalism, even with its obvious sources of strength, prove acceptable as a satisfying philosophy to live by? Before finally answering this question, let us look carefully at the thought of Benedict Spinoza, one of the great philosophers of all time, whose interpretation of rationalism helped make it the dominant point of view during the early decades of modern philosophy.

## CHAPTER 6

# Scientific Rationalism

*Benedict Spinoza*

In the history of Western thought the seventeenth century is customarily termed the Age of Reason. The outlook and the achievements of science had by that time begun to influence appreciably the general climate of opinion. Thoughtful men in every walk of life looked to human reason, especially as reflected in the outlook of science, as the one really dependable source of knowledge and guide to conduct. The conflict between science and religion, as we have come to know it, had its beginning during this century. A new understanding of the nature of the solar system was provided in the work of Galileo, Copernicus, and Kepler, and the old Aristotelian astronomy, around which the medieval church had woven its Christian cosmology, was gradually discredited. The ideas of Copernicus, like those of Galileo, were condemned by the Church but the "truth," as science portrayed it, could not be suppressed for long.

The changed outlook in philosophy that resulted was equally significant if somewhat less dramatic. Not only a new account of the nature of the universe and of man's place in the natural order, but also a new theory of human knowledge, became necessary. This was magnificently accomplished by two great seventeenth-century philosophers, René Descartes and Benedict Spinoza. Descartes, a distinguished French philosopher of the early seventeenth century (1596–1650), is generally considered the founder of modern philosophy. He is the first original thinker of high philosophical ability whose outlook had been profoundly affected by the new physics and astronomy. More than any other individual Descartes marks the intellectual transition from the Middle Ages to the modern world. He is responsible in large measure for establishing rationalism as the dominant point of view in the early period of modern European philosophy.

For Descartes, as for his contemporaries, human reason provided the only dependable key to knowledge of the universe. Through the speculation of Copernicus, Kepler, and Galileo, in the scientific genius of Newton, human reason was gradually forcing the natural universe to reveal its ways of behavior. And Nature's laws when discovered proved to be so precise and dependable, so capable of exact mathematical formulation, that mathematics easily ranked as the queen of the sciences. Here reason expressed her insights with perfect clarity and inescapable logic, and upon this foundation Descartes built his philosophy.

His younger contemporary Benedict Spinoza (1632–1677) completed with remarkable success what Descartes began. Spinoza is not only one of the great figures at the dawn of modern philosophy; he ranks among the three or four ablest philosophers in the entire history of Western thought. In his philosophy there is not only an impressive portrayal of the life of reason, but also a point of view that has had lasting influence upon modern thought.

## The Development of Spinoza's Philosophy

The course of our study so far has made it increasingly apparent that a man's life and his philosophy are not separate and unrelated but rather are aspects of one larger whole. In some cases this relationship is quite obvious; in others its exact nature must remain largely a matter of conjecture. Spinoza's case is one of those in which the underlying principles of his philosophy are as apparent in the life he lived as in the pages of his great treatise *Ethics*. All that he reasoned out so logically and objectively was a product as well of his own spiritual travail. As one of his biographers aptly puts it, "Spinoza's philosophy was more than a delicate bloom nurtured in the forcing-house of his mind; it was a virile and luxuriant tree rooted in the depths of his soul."[1] If fate seems to have conspired to make of Schopenhauer a pessimist, the tides of life just as surely moved to turn Spinoza toward the rationalism of Descartes and the Stoics, equipping him to bring to full fruition the cardinal insights upon which this philosophy rested.*

During the sixteenth century, a colony of Spanish and Portuguese Jews, seeking to escape persecution by the Spanish kings, had made their precarious way to Holland, the haven of refuge for the persecuted of that day. Into this colony, about a century later (1632), Baruch Spinoza was born. His father, Michael D'Espinoza, was a fairly well-to-do merchant and a man of some authority and influence in the local Jewish congregation. He expected that in time his son would take over the mercantile business.

---

* Perhaps the fact that Spinoza is much more than a disciple of Descartes should be emphasized here. As Stuart Hampshire points out in his able study of Spinoza: "Great divergencies between Descartes' and Spinoza's thought and purpose will emerge at every stage in this exposition; to treat Spinoza primarily as a follower and disciple of Descartes, as he has often been treated, is, I believe, largely to misconstrue and misrepresent him." (*Spinoza*, Penguin Books, rev. ed., 1962, p. 21.)

Spinoza early distinguished himself as a studious youth, but with a greater taste for learning than for business. As a boy he received a thorough education covering all aspects of Judaism. It was not long before he passed from his study of the Bible itself, the basic curriculum of the synagogue, to an examination of the Talmud, which contained the writing of later rabbis. But the commentaries of great teachers such as Abraham Ibn Ezra and Moses Maimonides raised in his mind more perplexing questions about his ancestral faith than they answered. Instead of settling down to the life of a successful Jewish merchant, Spinoza began to make friends outside Jewish circles and took up the study of Latin as a gateway to the intellectual world of his day.

During this period, he read widely in philosophy. He knew Socrates, Plato, and Aristotle, but among the ancients he preferred the great Stoic philosophers, and above all he was attracted by the thought of Descartes, who was just then at the height of his influence. Quite soon Spinoza decided to terminate his engagement in the mercantile business. But until he was twenty-four he held a responsible position in his father's business, and actually managed its affairs for several years after his father died.

### Excommunication

As the religious creed of his fathers proved unequal to the demands made upon it by his growing scientific knowledge, Spinoza was drawn increasingly to the rationalism of Descartes. In the spirit of Descartes he began to doubt the reasonableness of many of his former beliefs. "I confess," he is reported to have said, "that I can perceive no valid objection to the belief that God has a body. As for angels, it is certain that Scripture does not say they are real and permanent substances, but mere phantoms. And as for the soul, it would be vain to search for a single passage in support of its immortality."[2]

Speculation of this sort is always apt to be dangerous. In Holland during the seventeenth century it was particularly so, as the Jews could ill afford to offend the Protestants who had given them political protection in Holland. Word of the young scholar's scientific speculation and his doubts about the orthodox Jewish faith in time reached the elders of the synagogue. They called Spinoza before them and offered him a substantial annuity if he would refrain from spreading his ideas. This arrangement Spinoza flatly refused. The synagogue decided, therefore, upon excommunication, and on July 27, 1656, when he was but twenty-four years of age, Spinoza was formally accused of heresy and officially cut off from all further contact with his own religious group. The writ of excommunication, which is still preserved in the archives of the Amsterdam Synagogue, left no doubt about the completeness and finality of this break:

With the judgment of the angels and the sentence of the saints, we excommunicate, curse, and cast out Baruch de Espinoza, the whole of the sacred community assenting. Let him be accursed by day and accursed by night; let him be accursed in his lying down and accursed in his rising up; accursed in going out and accursed in coming in. May the Lord never more pardon or acknowledge him. May the wrath and displeasure of the Lord burn henceforth against this man, load him with all the curses written in the Book of the Law, and blot out his name from under the sky; may the Lord sever him from all the tribes of Israel, weigh him with all the maledictions of the firmament contained in the Book of the Law and may all ye who are obedient to the Lord your God be saved this day.

Hereby then are all admonished that none hold converse with him by word of mouth, none hold communion with him by writing; that no one approach within four cubits length of him, and no one read any document dictated by him, or written by his hand.

The young philosopher took his excommunication calmly. It was nothing more than expected, he said. Changing his name from Baruch to Benedict (its Latin equivalent), he took a room just outside Amsterdam with Gentile friends who were members of a pious but tolerant Mennonite sect known as Collegiants (because their congregations were called "collegia" rather than churches in order to avoid possible religious persecution). Spinoza reputedly began grinding and polishing lenses for a living. This occupation, in which he was perhaps already interested as a student of the new science, was well established and quite lucrative in Holland at the time.

The years that followed were quiet but fruitful. Spinoza worked at his trade by day and at his books in the evening, coming down occasionally to smoke a pipe in the peace of the evening with his host and hostess or for a friendly discussion of the Sunday sermon they had just heard. This provided almost the only contact with his fellows that he desired at the time. Cut off as a Jew from the rest of the world, from his family, who had disinherited him, and from the people of his own religion, who now shunned him, Spinoza was forced to find a philosophy adequate for the needs of his spirit. His love of knowledge seemed the only love left to him, and to this consuming passion Spinoza gave himself unstintingly. Often, indeed, he became so absorbed in his work that he would remain in his room for two or three days at a time, having his meals brought upstairs to him.

### Influence of the Mennonites

Because of his habit of life during these years Spinoza has often been pictured as a rather lonely recluse, and his political philosophy as largely intellectual speculation. Recently it has been made abundantly clear that nothing of the sort was true. Spinoza lived at a time of war and political revolution, of the age of Cromwell in England, of Jan de Witt in Holland, and of Louis XIV in France. It was an age when democracy and liberalism were struggling to be born and the absolute monarch seeking to protect his power. Spinoza was inevitably caught up in the political struggle of his time. He worked closely with the political leaders of the day in Holland, especially with the republican group associated with de Witt, and he shared their deep commitment to the political ideals of democracy and freedom. It is perhaps not an exaggeration to say with one of his admirers that Spinoza is the founder of the philosophy of political liberalism, "the first political philosopher of modern times to avow himself a democrat."[3]

Following the unpleasant experience of excommunication, his early years were of withdrawal from public life. They were spent largely in association with his Mennonite friends. After living for several years in the suburbs of Amsterdam, Spinoza decided to leave the city and went to live in Rijnsburg, a quiet village not far from Leyden. Rijnsburg was the center of a group of Collegiant Mennonites who had adopted a sort of Utopian communist philosophy, and Spinoza found the serious and friendly life among his Mennonite friends most congenial. His early work *On the Improvement of the Understanding*, although never completed and not published until after his death, was written in 1662 while he was living in Rijnsburg. Intended to provide a background and introduction to his thought, it is by far the most revealing and readable introduction to the philosophy he lived by. While still in Rijnsburg, Spinoza in 1663 published his first book, *The Principles of Cartesian Philosophy*. Dictated originally as the basis for his instruction of a young student who roomed with him at the time, the work attracted much favorable attention among his friends in Amsterdam, and at their insistence Spinoza agreed to publish it.

### Political Philosophy and Activity

As stimulating as were his philosophical studies, and as fond as he was of his Mennonite friends, Spinoza became increasingly discontent with their ethic of withdrawal from political life and activity. As he approached the age of thirty, he felt more and more strongly the need to participate actively in the political debates of the day and to support the republican leaders of his country. In April 1663, he packed his belongings, left his cottage in Rijnsburg, and moved to Voorburg, a suburb of The Hague, capital city of Holland. Here began the second stage in the evolution of his philosophy, that of the practical political philosopher.

No longer was Spinoza a recluse. Once it became known in The Hague that he now lived in the neighborhood, a steady stream of visitors came out to see him. Most important among these was Jan de Witt himself, for many years the head of the Dutch government, and a man of learning as well as a liberal statesman. De Witt was genuinely devoted to the brilliant young philosopher and probably arranged a small pension from the state for Spinoza to help support him during these years. With such connections and interests Spinoza soon became an important figure in the political life of the day.

Unfortunately it was not long before a strong reaction against the liberal policies pursued by de Witt's government occurred. Spinoza at once joined those who rallied to support de Witt. He laid aside his more scholarly studies and began a *Treatise on Theology and Politics*, an undertaking that gradually grew far beyond his original intent. When finally published in 1670, it had become a political analysis of the problems of democracy set in a scriptural framework.

Shortly before Spinoza was ready to publish his book, one of his close friends was imprisoned for expressing ideas very similar to his own, and was so brutally treated in prison that within a year he died. Spinoza was outraged. In the preface to his *Treatise* he loses for a time the calm objectivity of the life of reason, and condemns in indignant terms those reactionary groups that had brought about the death of his friend. "Doomed indeed is any land," he writes, "where opinions are put on trial and condemned as crimes, and where those who avow them are sacrificed, not to public safety, but to the hatred and savagery of their enemies. Deeds alone should be made the grounds of criminal charges, and speech should be utterly free. Every man should be allowed to think what he likes and to say what he thinks; without such freedom there cannot be any peace or true piety."

Fortunately, the *Treatise on Theology and Politics* was published anonymously. Even in comparatively tolerant Holland, its unorthodox religious outlook and liberal spirit created quite a furor. Almost immediately the book was banned by the Church and its sale forbidden by the civil authorities. Despite the furor caused by the *Treatise*, Spinoza himself was not molested, however, even after his authorship of the book became generally known.

## The Philosopher in an Age of Reaction

Spinoza published nothing more after the *Treatise*, but continued his study and writing. For some time he had been at work on his *Ethics*, the book that was to establish his place among the great philosophers of all times. Just as he was writing the final section in 1672, disaster befell the republican government of his friend Jan de Witt. The army of Louis XIV of France invaded the Netherlands, and the country was saved from complete defeat only by cutting the dikes and flooding a large region. De Witt's enemies made good use of his defeat, stirring up the people against him to such an extent that they turned upon de Witt and his brother and brutally murdered them both.

The political optimism of Spinoza was to a large extent destroyed by the bloodshed and by the reactionary spirit of the mob. The third and final stage of his life was marked by an intellectual crisis, a spirit of melancholy and a readiness to accommodate himself to existing conditions both in practice and in philosophical theory. In these later years we find adequate foundation for the image of Spinoza, the retired solitary scholar, that so impressed his early biographers. Although by no means wealthy, Spinoza now had as much of this world's goods as he desired, for money possessed no greater attraction for him than did fame or social position. When one of his friends and admirers, Simon de Vries, a rich merchant of Amsterdam, offered him a substantial gift of money, Spinoza without hesitation refused it.

Most flattering to him, certainly, was the offer which Spinoza received in February 1673 of a professorship in philosophy at the University of Heidelberg. This generous offer moved him greatly. For a whole month he debated the question, sitting alone in his small attic. Karl Ludwig, the ruler of the Palatine and sender of the offer, was no ordinary German prince. He was famed throughout Europe for his liberalism. The University of Heidelberg was a center of learning that would tempt any scholar; its faculty contained some of the ablest men of the day. Yet at the end of the month Spinoza wrote a courteous letter to the Councilor of the Prince, declining the post. As it turned out, Spinoza's decision was a wise one for reasons other than those stated in his letter. The following year Heidelberg was captured by the French armies and the university was closed, while Spinoza continued his writing in Holland undisturbed.

### Spinoza's Ethics

In 1675, after working on it for twelve years, Spinoza finished his *Ethics*. It is the book in which the essential ideas of this greatest exponent of rationalism find their clearest and most explicit expression. Looking at the finished product, built theorem upon theorem with geometrical precision, its author remarked: "I do not claim to have found the best philosophy. But I know this—that I think it the true one. If you ask me how I know this, I can only answer: in the same way that you know that the three angles of a triangle are equal to two right angles."

Conscious of the furor created by his *Treatise on Theology and Politics*, Spinoza for some time made no effort to publish the *Ethics*. When at last he did contemplate publishing it, a rumor spread to the effect that a book of his was about to appear that endeavored to prove that there was no God. A complaint was lodged with the authorities against him, and at the advice of friends he determined to await a more favorable time to publish his masterpiece. Such a time did not arrive. When Spinoza died in 1677, the *Ethics* was still carefully locked in his writing desk. To be sure that the book would not be lost, however, he had made arrangements to have the manuscript transmitted after his death to his publisher in Amsterdam.

Spinoza's last work was an unfinished *Treatise on Politics,* designed to show how "government can be so organized that it will escape tyranny, and be compatible with the peace and ability of the citizens." It was to be the work of a secular political scientist, without the religious spirit of his early *Treatise on Theology and Politics.* Having dealt first with monarchy and then with aristocracy, Spinoza came to his chapter on democracy. But that was as far as he got. He was now too ill to go on.

Although he was only in his early forties, a familial tendency had developed into active tuberculosis as Spinoza worked at the grinding and polishing of lenses or at his writing desk. He knew that the end of his life was now at hand, but true to the spirit of his philosophy he was not disturbed. He had lived as he desired, had done the work upon which his heart was set, and he calmly made ready for death. Going through his manuscripts, he destroyed those he felt to be of no consequence. Locking the rest in a desk drawer, he arranged to have them forwarded to his publisher in Amsterdam upon his death. The only instruction he gave was that when the *Ethics* was published, his name should not appear on the book. Its truth, he felt, should be self-evident to the intelligent reader. It needed no other endorsement, and he saw no reason to seek further fame or denunciation for himself.

One Sunday afternoon in February 1677, when the family with whom he lived was at church, Spinoza passed quietly away. Only his friend and physician, Dr. Schuller, was at his bedside. Four days later he was buried. Despite the rain that fell steadily on that inclement February day, many distinguished men in the Dutch capital attended his funeral. Those who opposed his ideas sought in vain to destroy the dead philosopher. A hundred years later, the enduring significance of Spinoza's thought was widely recognized in literary and philosophical circles throughout Europe. Two hundred years after his death a statue in his honor was erected in The Hague. Today he ranks among the two or three ablest and most significant figures in the history of modern philosophy.

### On the Improvement of the Understanding

The philosophy to which he gives allegiance is clearly outlined in Spinoza's early essay *On the Improvement of the Understanding.* His interest in philosophy, as described here, is actually quite practical. He is seeking, he tells us, to discover "an absolute and unchanging good that will never fail or disappoint us." And, with Descartes and the Stoics, Spinoza puts his confidence unhesitatingly in the life of reason as the only path to such enduring satisfaction. A revealing account of the considerations that led him to this conclusion is found in the opening pages of his essay. Its Stoic note is unmistakable:

After experience had taught me that all the usual surroundings of social life are vain and futile, seeing that none of the objects of my fears contained in themselves anything good or bad, except in so far as the mind is affected by them, I finally resolved to inquire whether there might be some real good, which would affect the mind singly, to the exclusion of all else; whether, in fact, there might be anything of which the discovery and attainment would enable me to enjoy continuous, supreme and unending happiness. I say, "I *finally* resolved," for at first sight it seemed unwise willingly to lose hold on what was sure for the sake of something then uncertain. I could see the benefits which are acquired through fame and riches, and that I should be obliged to abandon the quest of such objects, if I seriously devoted myself to the search for something different and new. I perceived that if true happiness chanced to be placed in the former I should necessarily miss it; while if, on the other hand, it were not so placed, and I gave them my whole attention, I should equally fail.[4]

Riches, fame, and the pleasures of the senses, the three sources to which men ordinarily turn in search of happiness, did tempt him at times, Spinoza admits. But careful examination revealed to him the deceptive character of such pursuits. He was convinced, as was Schopenhauer a century and a half later, that none of these holds promise of any enduring satisfaction. In the case of riches and fame, the more we have the more we want. The gratification of appetite brings with it only satiety and boredom or remorse and repentance, depending upon the nature of the pleasures indulged in. If, on the other hand, our desires and hopes are frustrated, we are plunged into the deepest disappointment and sadness.

This does not mean that riches and fame, or the pleasures of the senses, are in themselves evil. Spinoza is too consistent a Stoic to reach that conclusion. The terms "good" and "evil" are only relative, he points out. Nothing external is either good or evil in itself; its worth for us is determined by how we use it. So wealth, fame, and even pleasure, when not sought for their own sake but used instead as means to a good end, are quite desirable. But the only enduring good in human life, Spinoza concludes, lies in the development of character. The good man is the man of mature and disciplined character. He has achieved the kind of maturity of spirit that Lippmann in his *Preface to Morals* finds so essential for the good life. Spinoza's rationalistic philosophy is quite apparent as he describes such maturity of character:

What that character is we shall show in due time, namely, that it is the knowledge of the union existing between the mind and the whole of nature. This, then, is the end for which I strive: to attain such a character myself, and to endeavor that many should attain it with me. In other words, it is part of my happiness to lend a helping hand, that many others may understand even as I do . . . and also to form a social order such as is most conducive to the attainment of this character by the greatest number with the least difficulty and danger.[5]

Maturity of spirit and disciplined character, then, depend ultimately upon the development of reason and understanding. In order to achieve the good life, one must first be intelligent. On this point Spinoza is quite specific. It is his primary concern in this early essay:

> Before all things, a means must be devised for improving the understanding and purifying it, so that it may apprehend things without error, and in the best possible way. The more the mind knows, the better it understands its forces and the order of nature; the more it understands the order of nature the more easily it will be able to liberate itself from useless things; this is the whole method.[6]

### The Rationalist's View of Knowledge

Three essential and closely related aspects of Spinoza's rationalism should be distinguished: first, his confidence in the ability of reason, and reason alone, to supply us with accurate and dependable knowledge (epistemology); second, his conviction that the universe itself is governed by rational law, that by proper use of reason we comprehend an eternal, rational order in the nature of things (metaphysics); and finally, his certainty that reason is the one acceptable guide to living, that in the life of reason alone man can hope to find enduring satisfaction (ethics).

In accord with Descartes, Spinoza unhesitatingly puts his confidence in human reason as man's only dependable avenue to knowledge and truth. And, as with Descartes, this is a complete confidence. When an idea is entirely clear and self-evident, when there can be no possible doubt of its truth, then it can be accepted as reliable knowledge. This rationalistic theory of knowledge is proposed in Spinoza's early essay, *On the Improvement of the Understanding*. It is developed carefully and fully in his *Ethics*. Accepting the rationalist tradition that originated with Plato, Spinoza distinguishes three levels of knowledge.*

Knowledge derived wholly from sense perception is assigned to the lowest level, and (as in the Platonic tradition) is called "opinion." Such knowledge is of some value but is obviously neither entirely trustworthy nor coherent. We see the sun rise in the east each morning and set in the west each evening. Yet modern science has long ago convinced us all that these particular perceptions of our senses, like other sensory experiences, do not provide an accurate understanding of what is actually happening.

A second level of knowledge, therefore, is to be found in rational, scientific ideas and judgments. At this level each individual idea becomes part of a whole system of necessary and logically related ideas. The relation of the sun and the earth to each other, for example, is only fully understood

---

* Four types of knowledge are suggested in the early essay, but these are later combined in the *Ethics* into three major levels.

in the science of astronomy. Here we are no longer dealing with unreliable sense perceptions but with what Spinoza calls "adequate ideas," ideas that are clearly conceived, logically related, and about which we have complete certainty. Mathematics in general, and geometry in particular, provided for Spinoza, as for his contemporaries, a system of *logically necessary* judgments that were unquestionably true. Once we see that six is to three as four is to two, we know that this is true; that it *must* be true. It will always be true. There can be no possible doubt about it. In mathematics, then, Spinoza finds the *method* of right reasoning, the method that will always secure dependable knowledge. And this method must be used, he feels, not only in science but also in philosophy, if we hope to secure dependable "philosophical knowledge."

The third and highest level of knowledge Spinoza terms scientific intuition (*scientia intuitiva*). It is the most difficult to define accurately and correctly, the easiest to misinterpret. Such intuition can only come to those who have mastered scientific knowledge, which it then enables them to transcend. Spinoza clearly does not have in mind what we frequently refer to as a woman's intuition. Rather he is identifying insights such as those of a Darwin or a Freud—those that enable all great scientists to see possibilities that lie beyond the realm of scientific knowledge, and to find answers to difficulties of which the ordinary individual is not even aware. For Spinoza, the true, or "adequate," idea of the Universe as a single comprehensive system, governed by rational law, is grasped only in such "intuitive knowledge" at the highest level. The philosopher who possesses such knowledge sees immediately that he himself and everything around him are necessary parts of the whole structure of Nature. Such insight also makes possible for Spinoza that "intellectual love of God" in which is found man's highest and fullest relation to the Universe.

Albert Einstein, the symbol of scientific greatness in our century, not only admired Spinoza but at this point tends to agree with him. "The most beautiful and most profound emotion we can experience is the sensation of the mystical," Einstein wrote. "It is the sower of all true science . . . To know that what is impenetrable to us really exists, manifesting itself as the highest wisdom and the most radiant beauty which our dull faculties can comprehend—this knowledge, this feeling is at the center of religiousness."[7]

### God and Natural Law

Among the impressive characteristics of Spinoza's philosophy are its clarity and depth of insight. Writing some three hundred years ago, when modern science was in its infancy, Spinoza saw quite clearly what the scientific interpretation of the universe in terms of natural law must involve. Only after another two hundred years did his position become the accepted outlook of those trained in science. And with equal clarity he saw what religion must mean to men committed to the scientific viewpoint regarding the universe. It is perhaps not too much to say that if a reconciliation of science and religion is possible—within the framework that accepts science "as a closed system of rational law"—then it is to be found in Spinoza's philosophy. Later treatments of the subject have done little more than popularize or develop his essential insights. If in the last few decades our thinking about the relation of science and religion has taken a somewhat different turn, it is not because of inadequacies in Spinoza's understanding of Newtonian science. Rather, a revolution in the field of science itself has brought into question much that formerly seemed essential to the very existence of the scientific enterprise.*

## Concerning Miracles

The most serious conflict between science and popular religion Spinoza found in the interpretation of miracles. To many religious men in his day, the miracles recorded in the Bible were taken to be man's clearest evidence of the presence and activity of God. This seemed to Spinoza a fundamental misunderstanding both of religion and of the nature of God. It showed how inadequately most people understood the meaning of science and the scientific picture of the universe. Such people, Spinoza writes, "think that the clearest possible proof of God's existence is afforded when nature, as they suppose, breaks her accustomed order, and consequently they believe that those who then explain or endeavor to understand phenomena, or miracles, through their natural causes are doing away with God and His providence. They suppose, forsooth, that God is inactive so long as nature works in her accustomed order, and vice versa, that the powers of nature and natural causes are idle so long as God is acting."[8]

It was just this kind of separation between God and the rational order of nature that did violence, in Spinoza's opinion, to religious faith as well as to the new science. God was here pictured as a kind of oriental monarch who intervened, when he felt like it, with the work of nature. What science had revealed unmistakably to Spinoza was the law-abiding character of the universe. It was not whimsical but dependable. It could be counted on to act in accord with certain principles that were rational. And he was convinced that in this fact, not in the performance of miracles, was to be found

* See Lincoln Barnett, *The Universe and Dr. Einstein*: "before the turn of the past century certain deviations from [Newton's] laws became apparent; and though these deviations were slight, they were of such a fundamental nature that the whole edifice of Newton's machine-like universe began to topple. The certainty that science can explain *how* things happen began to dim about twenty years ago. And right now it is a question whether scientific man is in touch with 'reality' at all—or can ever hope to be." (1957 rev. ed., p. 8.)

the clearest indication of the providence of a rational deity. "Nothing, then, comes to pass in nature in contravention to her universal laws, nay, there is nothing that does not agree with them and follow from them," he writes, "for whatsoever comes to pass, comes to pass by the will and eternal decree of God." The "providence of God," in its deepest sense, "means nothing but nature's order following necessarily from her eternal law."[9]

If this is not the case, we are left with the conclusion that the laws of nature are actually opposed to the will of God. This then would not be the kind of universe God would like it to be but one that operates in some way against His will. Such a conclusion, Spinoza points out, is no more satisfactory for religious faith than for scientific thought. Thus, the popular belief in miracles actually turns out to be religiously unacceptable as well as scientifically untenable:

> It is plain that the universal laws of nature are decrees of God following from the necessity and perfection of the Divine nature . . . If anyone asserted that God acts in contravention to the laws of nature, he *ipso facto* would be compelled to assert that God acted against his own nature—an evident absurdity. Therefore miracles, in the sense of events contrary to the laws of nature, so far from demonstrating to us the existence of God, would, on the contrary, lead us to doubt, where, otherwise, we might have been absolutely certain of it, knowing that nature follows a fixed and immutable order.[10]

### Science and God

Every age has its typical ways of defending religious faith, its characteristic arguments for proving to unbelievers the existence of God. Spinoza felt the need of interpreting the nature of God in terms adequate to do justice to the new universe that science was discovering. The old concept of God was clearly inadequate. It had been developed by men who lived before the modern, scientific picture of the world had been formulated. The real danger, as Spinoza well realized, was that thoughtful people would give up their belief in God altogether, when actually what they disbelieved in was an old and inadequate concept of God.

This, as a matter of fact, still happens to many young people today. They find that the early concept of God, which they accepted at home or in Sunday School, does not fit the new world of modern science with which they are becoming acquainted. There is no place any longer for a benevolent and venerable old gentleman with white hair sitting on a throne somewhere up in the sky. And too frequently, instead of realizing that a new conception of God adequate to their new knowledge must replace this earlier, inadequate one, such disillusioned youths simply discard belief in God completely. Spinoza undertook to do for the more thoughtful men of his generation what still needs to be done for many today: that is, to restate the idea of God in terms adequate to do justice to the new knowledge of modern science.

The real problem, as Spinoza sees it, is not to prove that God exists but rather to find out what God is like. His first step, therefore, is a simple but very effective one. He defines God in such a way as to make his existence no longer debatable. God, Spinoza affirms, is that eternal order of things of which both the physical universe and man himself are but partial expressions. That such an eternal order did exist, no philosopher touched by the new scientific spirit of Spinoza's day would have thought of denying. The problem, then, was simply one of determining somewhat more accurately than before the nature of that enduring order of the universe. As a good rationalist, Spinoza is confident that this can be done by human reason. And in such an undertaking science will be of as much help as religion. It is not necessary, Spinoza argues, to rely upon any special revelation to find out what God is like. The nature of God is clearly revealed to the eyes of reason in the picture science draws of the universe. Here we find the only revelation that the rationalist can accept.

### God and Nature

Spinoza's concept of God is certainly among the more difficult aspects of his philosophy. Deeply imbued with the spirit of the new science of his day, he did not question the underlying unity of the laws of nature that science was gradually but surely managing to catalog. The rational order of the universe, he believed with the scientists of that age, was the expression of one consistent principle, a principle eternal and unchanging. The scientific picture of the universe could not be denied. It was the surest result of man's reason. Nor could a God exist somewhere apart from the universe that science pictured. Spinoza saw the childishness of the suggestion made by some of his contemporaries that God, like a man, had created the world and then gone off to do something else. No—in the eternal rational order of the universe, God was present. There could not be two conflicting or unrelated powers at work in the universe. If science and reason were trustworthy, there could be only one. What science revealed to man, then, was just what religion also was trying to discover.

Spinoza's most careful discussion of his idea of God is found in the first book of the *Ethics*. There it is set in the geometrical framework that he felt to be most compelling for human reason, and now Spinoza is no longer concerned to use the traditional language of religious faith. God he defines as the *substance* upon which all things in the universe ultimately depend. The term "substance," however, is somewhat misleading today. The English word has a meaning quite different from the Latin *substantia* used by Spinoza. *Substantia* is literally that which "stands under" and gives support—or, better still, "being"—to everything else. For Spinoza, the rationalist, this underlying "substance" of all things is not primarily physical or material but rather that rational order by which the nature of all things is determined.

Spinoza's point of view may be made somewhat more intelligible if we think of the point of view of an engineer concerning the structure of a great bridge. Most of us take the steel and stone to be its "substance." But for the engineer the underlying reality is the system of mathematical laws in accord with which the bridge is constructed and without which it is impossible to have a bridge. The steel and stone that we see and to a great extent depend upon are, to be sure, one aspect or dimension of the reality of the bridge. Without these also there would be no bridge. It is the system of rational laws, however, and not the steel and the stone, that actually determines the nature of the bridge. And these laws are grasped by human reason, not by the senses.

In some such fashion as this, then, Spinoza defines God as the "Substance" of all things, and he goes on to give us his scientific picture of the divine nature. "All things are in God and everything takes place by the laws alone of the infinite nature of God," he writes. "Whatever is, is in God, and nothing can either be or be conceived without God. . . . In nature there is nothing contingent, but all things are determined from the necessity of the divine nature to exist and act in a certain manner. Therefore things could be produced by God in no other manner and in no other order than that in which they have been produced. . . . From the infinite nature of God all things have necessarily flowed, or continually follow, by the same necessity as it follows from the nature of a triangle from all eternity that its three angles are equal to two right angles."[11]

From this severely scientific point of view, moreover, freedom in the popular sense of the word is simply a confused idea. Thus it is clearly impossible for God to do anything that is not in accord with his own nature. "There are some who think that God is a free cause because He can, as they think, bring about that those things which follow from His nature should not be, or should not be produced by Him," Spinoza writes. "But this is simply to say that God could bring about that it should not follow from the nature of a triangle that its three angles should equal to two right angles, which is absurd." The necessity by which God acts is the necessity of reason, Spinoza believes; God's freedom must be understood in the only sense that freedom is possible in the universe which modern science depicts: "God alone is a free cause for God alone exists from the necessity alone of His own nature and acts from the necessity alone of His own nature. Therefore He alone is a free cause."[12]

Spinoza's God is far different, then, not only from the anthropomorphic deity of popular religion, but also from the God of the Christian faith. God, as portrayed by our philosopher, is not a person, very human in character but much more powerful than any man. Any such anthropomorphism Spinoza specifically rejects. "There are those who imagine God to be like a man, composed of body and soul and subject to passions," he writes; "but it is clear enough from what has already been demonstrated how far all men who believe this are from the true knowledge of God." God is rather to be known in that eternal rational order which finds expression in the natural universe and in human life and thought.


### The Rejection of Dualism

One of the most serious problems in the philosophy of Descartes was its inability to find a satisfactory relationship between matter and spirit, God and nature, or, in man, mind and body. The Cartesian philosophy was left finally with a dualism that recognized two separate and independent aspects of reality. This position Spinoza emphatically rejects, and his way of dealing with the problem is one of the significant and original aspects of his philosophy.

The one enduring "Substance" by which all nature is conditioned is infinite, he maintains, and may have an infinite number of attributes. But there are only two such attributes or aspects of reality of which we are aware—Thought and Extension. These two characterize all nature. We are immediately aware of these in man's mind and his body. In the larger universe of nature, Spinoza in the same way distinguishes what he terms *natura naturans* and *natura naturata*—the active creative principle at work in all nature, and the established system of created things (what is usually meant by nature in most philosophical thought other than Spinoza's).

As interpreted by Spinoza, *natura naturans* and *natura naturata* merely describe two different approaches to, or ways of understanding of, the same reality. They are but two different aspects of the Substance of reality, ways in which its attributes of Thought and Extension find expression. It is correct, then, to speak of God as the eternal creative principle in nature, *natura naturans*, but also to see God in the created world of nature, *natura naturata*. Indeed, it is not only correct but necessary that this be done. For these are two essential expressions of one reality, just as mind and body, the mental and the physical, are two necessary dimensions of one human nature.

"From what has gone before," Spinoza writes, "I think it is plain that by *natura naturans* we are to understand that which is in itself and is conceived through itself, or those attributes of substance which express eternal and infinite essence, that is to say, God in so far as He is considered as a free [creative] cause. But by *natura naturata* I understand everything which follows from the necessity of the nature of God, or any one of God's attributes, . . . in so far as they are considered as things which are in God, and which without God can neither be nor be conceived."[13]

For Spinoza, then, the one entire system of reality, whether termed God or Nature, can be interpreted equally well as a system of "extended," that is, physical and material things, or as a system of "thinking," that is, creative or spiritual reality. In man as in nature, for every chain of mental activities there is a corresponding sequence of physical or material relationships. The same determined cause-and-effect relationships appear in the order of Nature under whichever attribute it is seen. The one reality is simply comprehended under two different modes of expression. "Whether we think of Nature under the attribute of Extension or under the attribute of Thought or any other attribute whatever," Spinoza writes, "we shall discover one and the same order or one and the same connection of causes."[14]

The experience of physicians as well as psychotherapists has provided interesting support for Spinoza's theory of the relationship of mind and body. Not only has the restoration of the body to health and wholeness been reflected in a similar improvement in the mind, but the restoration of the mind to health has likewise been reflected in an accompanying health of the body. Consequently the importance of a psychosomatic understanding of illness is now generally recognized.

### An Immanent Deity

In this fashion, Spinoza disposed of the difficulties that characterized the Cartesian dualism. For him spirit and matter, mind and body, God and nature, are not two separate and independent orders of reality, each with its own different principle of operation. Everything in the universe falls within one single intelligible causal system. It is as impossible to conceive of a Creator apart from and essentially other than his creation as to separate man's mind from his body. Spinoza is then a pantheist rather than a theist. God has his being and moves in and through the natural universe. There is no transcendent Creator, beyond and above the world of Nature.*

When he was quite naturally accused by his enemies of identifying God and nature, however, Spinoza indignantly denied the charge. Writing to a close friend he said:

* ". . . in Spinoza's use the word 'God' is interchangeable with the word 'Nature,' " in Stuart Hampshire's view. "To say that God is the immanent cause of all things is another way of saying that everything must be explained as belonging to the single and all-inclusive system which is Nature, and no cause (not even a First Cause) can be conceived as somehow outside or independent of the order of Nature. Any doctrine of a transcendent God, since transcendent simply means 'outside the order of Nature,' or any doctrine of God as Creator distinguished as transcendent cause from his creation, involves this impossibility; for it introduces the mystery of an inexplicable act of creation, an act which is somehow outside the order of events in Nature. God, or Nature [is] the eternal cause of all things and of itself." (*Spinoza*, p. 44.)

I hold that God is the immanent, not the extraneous cause of all things. I say that all things are in God and move in God, thus agreeing with Paul and perhaps with all the ancient philosophers. It is a complete mistake on the part of those who say that my purpose is to show that God and nature, meaning by the latter a certain mass of corporeal matter, are one and the same. I had no such intention.[15]

What we are justified in saying, perhaps, is that for Spinoza the nature of God as free and creative spirit is revealed in the eternal rational processes of the universe rather than in the kind of independent creative acts portrayed in the book of Genesis. His God is a lineal descendant of the Divine Reason of the Stoic philosophers, but where the Stoic belief was vague and undeveloped, Spinoza gives exact, rational statement to this concept. Alexander Pope, representative poet of the Age of Reason, later phrased the contemporary pantheism as follows:

> All are but parts of one stupendous whole,
> Whose body Nature is, and God the soul . . .
> To Him no high, no low, no great, no small;
> He fills, he bounds, connects, and equals all.[16]

If Spinoza could have read these lines of Pope's, his one objection might well be in the separation suggested here between body and soul, Nature and God. Just as a man's body is an essential part of the man himself, a necessary means of expressing his creative spirit, so for Spinoza the world of nature, the physical universe about us, is as essential an aspect of the reality of God as is the rational spirit that unifies and shapes its existence. For Spinoza both are aspects of one eternal reality.

### Human Nature and Conduct

In his treatment of God and the universe, Spinoza had undertaken to provide for his readers a completely rational, objective, and scientific account. When he came to the discussion of human nature and conduct, he proposed to handle this subject in similar fashion. "I shall consider human actions and desires in exactly the same manner as if I were concerned with lines, planes, and solids," he writes.[17] Here, of course, Spinoza anticipated the outlook and efforts of the linguistic philosophers of our own day. He was as anxious as they are to remove all emotional overtones and connotations from the philosophical vocabulary. Long before the era of modern "scientific" psychology, Spinoza recognized that if the rational laws of science are universal, they are as applicable to human life and thought as to the physical universe of which man is a part.

Before we can have a scientific ethics, he sees that we must develop a scientific psychology. Self-preservation is in a very real sense the first law of our nature. It is the tendency in every individual being to try to preserve its own existence. "Everything, insofar as it is in itself, endeavors to persist in its own being; and the endeavor wherewith a thing seeks to persist in its own being is nothing else than the actual essence of that thing," Spinoza writes in quite contemporary spirit. Man is no exception to this rule. Hence, a reasonable ethics must be based upon a recognition of this fact of human nature. "Since reason demands nothing against nature, it concedes that each man must love himself, and seek what is useful to him, and desire whatever leads him truly to a greater state of perfection; and that each man should endeavor to preserve his being so far as in him lies."[18] In Spinoza's view, a philosophy of living that proposed conduct contrary to this basic principle of human nature would be foolish as well as ineffective.

Ethics becomes then largely a matter of applied psychology. The virtuous man is not one who lives in accord with moral commandments imposed upon him by some external authority. "Virtue means nothing but acting according to the laws of our nature," Spinoza writes; "and happiness consists in this—that a man can preserve his own being." The foundation of virtue, of genuinely moral conduct, is the effort to act in accord with our true nature, and this for the rationalist means to guide our conduct by reason. Thus for Spinoza rationalism, in ethics as in metaphysics, provides the truest statement of naturalism.

### Of Human Bondage and Freedom

It makes only for confusion to talk of chance or accident in human conduct, of a free will by which man may change the direction of his life as he likes, Spinoza is convinced: "All our efforts or desires follow from the necessity of our nature in such a manner that they can be understood either through it alone or in so far as we are a part of nature." There is no more escape from the laws of cause and effect in human conduct than there is in the behavior of the world of nature, of which man is an essential part. We too readily think that we are free because we find at times that we are able to do what we want to do. Actually there is no freedom in doing what we want to do. What we want is as completely determined by other preceding causes as any other aspect of experience:

> Thus the infant believes that it desires milk of its own free will, the angry child that it is free in seeking revenge, and the timid that he is free in taking flight. So also an insane man, a garrulous woman, a child, and very many others of the sort, believe they speak of their own free will when nevertheless they are unable to control their im-

pulse to talk. Thus experience itself shows, no less clearly than reason, that men think themselves free only because they are conscious of their actions and ignorant of the causes that determine them. The passions of hatred, anger, envy and so on, considered in themselves, follow from the same necessity of nature as other things; they have certain definite causes through which they are to be understood.[19]

In terms of this thoroughly "scientific" view of life Spinoza conducts his examination of human conduct; and he finds, as Schopenhauer also so vigorously insisted, that most of us are in bondage to our passions and emotions. Our thought and conduct are largely controlled by external circumstance. Life is dominated from *without* rather than *within*. "The impotence of man to govern or restrain the emotions I call bondage," Spinoza writes; "for a man who is a prey to his emotions is not his own master but he is at the mercy of fortune, so much as that he is often compelled while seeing that which is better for him to follow that which is worse."[20]

An emotion is treated by Spinoza simply as a "confused idea." Our emotions are the product of a lack of clear understanding of the situation that confronts us. We feel strongly because we understand dimly. Only an immature individual kicks the chair he stumbles over; yet we are all equally immature in blaming our troubles upon the government, the opposite sex, and the like. Our anger at other people is simply the result of our failure to understand the forces that make them act as they do. When we understand their action, and see the necessity that caused them to do as they do, we cease to be angry with them. "A passion ceases to be a passion as soon as we form a clear and distinct idea of it," Spinoza writes, "and the mind is subject to passions in inverse proportion to the number of adequate ideas it has."[21]

We escape from the bondage of passion, then, not by doing what we want to do but by learning to act in accord with reason. It is the man who knows what he is doing, and why he is doing it, for whom alone freedom is possible in the only meaningful sense of the word. The free man is the man who controls himself, the man whose conduct is controlled by reason:

We readily see the difference between a man who is led solely by emotion or opinion, and a man who is led by reason. The former, whether he wants to or not, does those things of which he is entirely ignorant; but the latter is his own master and only does those things which he knows are of greatest importance in life and which he therefore desires above all else. I call the former, therefore, a slave and the latter a free man. . . . A free man is one who lives according to the dictates of reason alone; he is not led by fear but directly desires what is good. In other words, he strives to act, to live and to preserve his being in accord with the principle of seeking his own true advantages.[22]

## Spinoza and Freud

There is a rather striking similarity between Spinoza's interpretation of human nature here and that later developed by Freud. Both find in man's emotional life the expression of unconscious drives. Both maintain that any frustration in the expression of these unconscious drives manifests itself in some painful disturbance in our conscious life. And both emphasize the necessity of understanding these unconscious complications before any improvement in a man's conscious life is possible. There are important differences, of course, between Freud's conception of the *libido* and Spinoza's *conatus* (the basic drive of every individual to preserve its own existence), but the psychological operations of these two drives as described by Freud and Spinoza are more than superficially parallel.

Both of these great Jewish thinkers insist, for example, that human nature must be studied as a biological organism within Nature and that only in this way can man hope to understand his actions and emotions. For both, moral praise or blame in dealing with any particular desires is quite irrelevant. Like Spinoza, Freud sees moral problems as essentially clinical problems, which are only confused, not helped, by the use of approval or disapproval, praise or blame. Because of this more objective and scientific, and less "moral," approach to man's individual and social conduct or misconduct, Spinoza was widely condemned in his day as Freud was in his. As aptly put by Stuart Hampshire in his able study of Spinoza, both were condemned for "the grave, prophetic, scrupulously objective tone of voice in which they quietly undermined all the established prejudices of popular and religious morality."[23]

In his philosophy Spinoza also proposes a technique of mental therapy that clearly anticipates the method of Freudian psychotherapy of our day. An intelligent man will seek to understand the causes of his emotions, that is, bring the unconscious determinants of behavior into clear consciousness, Spinoza points out. When he understands the causes of irrational behavior, the irrational motives lose their force and he can then act rationally in accord with desires that are clearly understood. This, of course, is much the same technique that has been employed by the disciples of Freud with marked success in treating emotionally disturbed individuals in our own day.

## Good and Evil

In Spinoza's completely determined universe, good and evil must be recognized as purely relative terms. They describe our reaction to the circumstances of life, not the enduring nature of things. When viewed in a total perspective and under the aspect of eternity (*sub specie aeternitatis* is Spinoza's favorite Latin phrase), good and evil are human prejudices that an eternal reality cannot recognize. Spinoza agrees with the great Stoic philosophers that things in themselves are not good or evil; they are simply necessary. It is our own reaction and attitude that determines the quality of our experience: "It is plain, that in no case do we strive for, wish for, long for or desire anything because we deem it good, but, on the contrary, we deem a thing good because we strive for it, wish for it, long for it, or desire it."[24]

Pain is a fact, of course. We cannot escape it entirely, and we cannot deny its existence when it has taken hold of us. But we can prevent the bitterness of spirit that the ignorant exhibit when they suffer. For pain is one thing and hate is another. "Let the pain of life teach you to understand and you will not hate life, but in the joy of understanding, you will love it." This is the burden of Spinoza's philosophy wrung out of the depth of his own experience. The way to kill hate in our hearts, that is, is to connect the individual fact that is painful with the whole order of nature, which makes this fact, like every other, equally necessary. Thus Spinoza meets the problem of evil.

### The Life of Reason

As Spinoza portrays the manner of life to which reason leads a man, one can hardly fail to appreciate its appeal. Knowledge and understanding give life poise, perspective, and power. It is the nature of reason to perceive things under the form of eternity (*sub specie aeternitatis*). The reasonable man understands the laws at work in the universe and his own place in the vast cosmic scheme of things. He sees how trivial are the events that once disturbed him, how absurd the ambitions that agitated him and brought him into conflict with others. He recognizes that his own good is inextricably bound up with the welfare of others. "Hence men who are governed by reason —that is, who seek what is useful to them in accord with reason—desire for themselves nothing which they do not also desire for the rest of mankind, and consequently are just, faithful and honorable in their conduct," Spinoza writes. "Therefore, men in so far as they live according to the dictates of reason, necessarily live always in harmony one with another."

Clearly Spinoza is here providing strong support for that spirit of understanding and good will upon which many groups of young people today are undertaking to build a creative community life. Indeed, reason at its best leads him to accept love and good will as the only power strong enough to overcome evil. "Minds are not conquered by force but by love and generosity," he points out. "He who lives according to the dictates of reason, endeavors, as far as possible, to repay the hatred, anger or contempt of others towards him with love and kindness. Hatred is increased by being reciprocated and can only be quenched by love."[25]

Such an attitude exemplifies not only the life of reason at its best but also for Spinoza the essence of religion. True religion consists in the knowledge we possess of our oneness with the eternal, rational order of the universe and the willing acceptance of our place therein. In this union of ourselves with Nature through reason and understanding, we find the only lasting satisfaction and happiness that life can provide. Here the mind rises to "the high serenity of contemplation which sees all things as parts of an eternal order." We learn not only to love life but also to love God. We are freed from the struggle and strife that beset the ignorant man and we enjoy at last the "blessedness" that all men in their hearts desire. To this attitude, which combines at once the best in science, in morality, and in religion, Spinoza gives the name "the intellectual love of God."

"I have completed all that I intended to show regarding the power of the mind over the emotions, and the freedom of the mind," Spinoza writes in summarizing his philosophy:

> From what I have said it is evident how much stronger and better the wise man is than the ignorant man, who is driven only by lust alone. For the ignorant man, besides being agitated in many ways by external causes without even gaining true satisfaction of the spirit, lives as it were without consciousness of himself, of God, and of things, and just as soon as he ceases to suffer, he ceases to be. The wise man, on the contrary, is little disturbed in spirit, but conscious of a certain eternal necessity in himself, in God, and in things he never ceases to be, but always possesses a true satisfaction of spirit. If indeed the way I have shown to lead to this seems exceedingly difficult, it may nevertheless be discovered. And clearly it must be very hard since it is so seldom found. For how could it be that salvation is neglected practically by all if it were close at hand and could be found without difficulty? But all things excellent are as difficult as they are rare.

With this calm and hopeful passage Spinoza's *Ethics* comes to an end. Here the essential spirit of the book and the philosopher find eloquent expression.

## The Appeal of Spinoza

Estimates of Spinoza have been almost unbelievably diverse. He was in his own time widely condemned as an atheist and enemy of religion. Yet by later critics his thought has been taken to be so fundamentally religious in spirit that he was described as "God-intoxicated." Is he the cold and remorseless fatalist whose philosophy undermines the established foundations of religious faith, or is he the saint whose humility and gentleness of life hold charm and comfort for all who are burdened or outcast? To this question each reader must find the answer for himself. And the appeal of Spinoza's philosophy will in large measure be determined by that answer.

Certainly the philosophy of Spinoza provides what is perhaps the noblest effort of the human mind to derive a satisfying way of life entirely from the spirit of reason and conclusions of natural science. Whether dealing with human conduct or with religious faith, Spinoza finds the scientific view of human life and destiny the only acceptable one. He has developed a thoroughly scientific morality and a completely scientific religion, and he will have us make no compromises, no concessions to human hope, frailty, or need. *To be good, to be blessed, to be free*—all mean one and the same thing. They are the outcome of a life that is lived entirely in accord with the insights of reason, a life that understands the rational laws at work in the universe, gladly conforms to them, and in so doing finds the contentment and happiness we all desire. There seems little reason to think that from the point of view of a strictly scientific rationalism any improvement upon Spinoza's position can be expected.

There are thoughtful critics of Spinoza, however, who do not feel that he has met difficulties to be seen also in the popular rationalism of the Stoics. Between his ethics and his metaphysics, these critics see an unresolved contradiction that Spinoza himself does not recognize. As he pictures the universe, all things are the necessary outcome of an eternal, rational order. In a favorite phrase of his, all things flow from the nature of God with the same necessity that the angles of a triangle equal two right angles. Nothing could possibly be other than it is. The misdeeds of the sinner are just as necessary and as completely determined as are the achievements of the saint. The sinner could not be other than he is, nor could the saint.

Yet it is the major aim of Spinoza's ethics to show that the way of the saint, the man who has brought his life into conformity with the rational laws of God, is far better and more desirable than the way of the sinner, whose life is torn by conflict and unfulfilled desire. The wise man should certainly seek to achieve the blessedness of the life of reason rather than remain in ignorant bondage to desire and passion. In presenting his ethical ideal, Spinoza clearly assumes, his critics argue, that man has the freedom to obtain knowledge, and thus escape his bondage to ignorance and suffering. However, upon Spinoza's own premises, is not what we know just as completely determined as what we do, so that nothing could be other than it is? Thus, as one critic suggests, about his moral philosophy as a whole Spinoza's metaphysics seems to cast a shadow of make-believe.[26]

Other critics feel that in his effort to reconcile science and religion, Spinoza has actually surrendered the fundamental convictions of religious faith to the rationalism of science. Although Spinoza uses the term God to describe the eternal order of the universe upon which man's life and destiny depend, this rational order certainly has little in common with the religious man's idea of God, these critics point out. At the heart of Spinoza's universe one finds no concern for the moral ideals that man takes to be so essential in life at its best, nor any sympathy for suffering human beings who desperately need help.

For Spinoza, as definitely as for Lippmann, "the aspect of life which implicates the soul is the understanding of life." But is it perhaps not also true that Spinoza only portrays in a more appealing fashion Lippmann's view of the life style of the consistent rationalist?—"Since nothing gnawed at his vitals, neither doubt nor ambition, nor frustration, nor fear, he would move easily through life." "And so, whether he saw the thing as comedy, or high tragedy, or plain farce, he would affirm that it is what it is, and the wise man can enjoy it."[27] In such a view of life there is none of the warmth and affection that most psychologists feel essential for human happiness and well-being.

There is ample evidence today, one must admit, that Spinoza's rationalism might well not have the appeal for youth that it had in the Age of Reason. In Spinoza's deterministic philosophy one does not find the kind of motivation for the making of a better world that proved so attractive to many in the political philosophy of Eugene McCarthy, Robert Kennedy, and George McGovern. A widespread reaction against the domination of life by reason, and by the scientific world view closely associated with it, has also been recognized by major spokesmen for the philosophy of the younger generation. In *The Greening of America*, for example, this generation is described as "deeply suspicious of logic, rationality, analysis" and convinced that the life of reason misses too many valuable aspects of experience. Central in the outlook of the counter-culture, Theodore Roszak believes, is "a radical rejection of science and technological values. The good, the true, and the beautiful are now being sought through the nonintellectual capacities of human personality, not through reason."[28] This situation in no way, of course, detracts from Spinoza's greatness or his significant contribution to modern philosophy. It does mean, however, that the appeal of his philosophy for young men and women today could well be more limited than the soundness of its insights justifies.

## CHAPTER 7

# Rational Idealism

*Plato*

That intelligence is necessary as a guide to successful living, few would deny. In the philosophy of the consistent rationalist, however, only the satisfactions provided by the understanding find a meaningful place; and in the understanding alone one can hardly expect to discover the full meaning of life. Human life at its best has always felt the compelling force of an ideal that somehow lifts a man above the ordinary and commonplace and gives to his effort an enhanced significance in the nature of things. Consideration must be given, therefore, to philosophies that develop this insight adequately. Among the exponents of idealism Plato has certainly been the most successful in combining the approach of the rationalist with the insights of the idealist. His rational idealism may well prove to be our most appealing and satisfying expression of rationalism as a philosophy of life.

## On Idealism and Realism

In recent years it has been common for the more sophisticated and cynical—those who pride themselves on being realists—to speak with amusement of anything that goes under the banner of idealism. Who, they ask, can be an idealist, but the most naïve and unlearned beginner in philosophy? Isn't the barest acquaintance with the hard facts of life, whether in business or in politics, enough to disillusion youth of its brave ideals? Isn't a year at the university usually enough to make of an idealistic freshman, if not a permanent drop-out, at least a hardened and sophisticated sophomore? As Dorothy Parker has so aptly put it:

> When I was young and bold and strong,
> Oh, right was right, and wrong was wrong!

My plume on high, my flag unfurled,
I rode away to right the world.
"Come out, you dogs, and fight!" said I,
and wept there was but once to die.

Now I am old; and good and bad
Are woven in a crazy plaid.
I sit and say, "The world is so;
And he is wise who lets it go.
A battle lost, a battle won—
The difference is small, my son."[1]

Many and varied, of course, are the philosophies that lay claim to the title of idealism. Most significant for the philosopher is the idealism of the *metaphysician*, who maintains that reality itself is basically such stuff as ideas are made of, that the rational is the real, and the real in some sense is rational. According to the proponents of metaphysical idealism, it is to the mind of man rather than to the world of nature that we must turn for an understanding of what our universe at heart is really like. Unfortunately, the defense of idealism as a metaphysical theory easily becomes abstract and theoretical—a scholarly and necessary debate among professional philosophers, yet too often a fruitless one for the ordinary reader—but that this need not be the case, Plato clearly demonstrates.

Equally important, but quite different in spirit and emphasis, is the *ethical* idealism that finds direct expression in the philosophy by which one lives. It is only in the highest ideals of the human spirit, in his moral and religious aspirations, the ethical idealists maintain, that a man can find the full meaning of life and so enjoy enduring happiness. Only as he guides his life by such ideals can he achieve complete self-realization. In ethical idealism one actually finds no fanciful flight from the hard facts of life and reality, its defenders claim. Rather one finds an awareness of those elements in reality that alone can save us from cold and barren weariness, from the disillusion and pessimism to which those who pride themselves upon being completely realistic are so frequently driven.

It may well be, indeed, that the *realist*, so-called, does not actually comprehend the enduring and sustaining realities of life. Too often he sees in experience only the unpleasant, the grim, and the sordid. He grasps only one side of life—its darker side—as any thoughtful observer recognizes at once as he reads the pages of such classic "realistic" interpretations of life as John Steinbeck's *Grapes of Wrath* or Richard Wright's *Native Son*. And this fact is even clearer in books like *The Autobiography of Malcolm X* and E. Cleaver's *Soul on Ice*.

Anyone who goes to the opposite extreme and sees in human experience only the bright, the pleasant, and the honorable is, of course, equally unrealistic. But if he sees alongside or beneath the ruthless, the base, and the callous, those aspirations and achievements that reveal the high ideals and courageous hopes of the human spirit, he perhaps can claim to have a more adequate and satisfying view of life as it *really* is. Let us turn, then, to a philosopher who recognizes the compulsion of the rational ideal in human life and undertakes to interpret it in this spirit.

## Plato and *The Republic*

No other figure in the history of philosophy is so definitely identified with idealism as Plato, and in no single book is there so influential a statement of a man's philosophy as in Plato's *Republic*. This book has stood through the ages as the greatest single masterpiece in the literature of philosophy, with no serious rival to date. Until one reads and masters *The Republic*, he has not really begun the study of philosophy. In our concern for what is immediate and practical, we too easily overlook the lasting pattern that underlies the passing scene. We forget that there may be enduring principles to which any sound design for living must conform. These principles *The Republic* presents in appealing as well as convincing fashion.

*The Republic* is the work of Plato's mature years. It breathes the spirit of Socrates, but the spirit of Socrates remade by the genius of Plato. No other influence upon the thought of Plato was so pervasive and formative as that of Socrates. Nor has any scholar been able to say with authority just where Socrates stops speaking and Plato begins, for Socrates is the central figure and spokesman in all but the latest of Plato's dialogues. By the time he wrote *The Republic*, however, Plato was speaking as a philosopher in his own right, not simply as the most distinguished pupil of a great master. And into his mature view of life had gone the best that the brilliant Athenian civilization of the fifth century B.C. had to offer. In this chapter, therefore, we will give our attention primarily to Plato's philosophy as presented in *The Republic*.

### Plato's Youth

In 427 B.C., the year in which Plato was born, Pericles, the greatest leader that Athenian democracy produced, had been dead but two years and the dreary Peloponnesian war between Athens and Sparta had just begun. Athens itself at this time was little more than an armed camp. Plato grew to manhood amid the dangers, the turmoil, and the hatreds bred by war. War is never healthy for democracies, and during these years the Athenian democracy began to crack under the strain. In 404 B.C. Athens capitulated. Plato was just twenty-four when this occurred.

As is so frequently the case, defeat in war brought revolution. An aristocratic regime in Athens overthrew the democratic government and, with the aid of Sparta, established itself in power. Plato was a member of one of the most distinguished families in the city. His father was descended from Codrus, reputedly the last king of Athens; his mother belonged to the family of Solon, the great Athenian lawgiver. In aristocratic circles, during Plato's youth, democracy was only another name for mediocrity and corruption. Plato grew up in an atmosphere of intrigue as his family and friends laid their plans to wrest control of the government from the democratic leaders, whom they considered both incompetent and unworthy.*

Despite the political turmoil, Plato was raised in comfort, perhaps in wealth. He read Homer with eagerness and enthusiasm, as did the abler Greek youth of his day, and he early displayed the mind and the interests of a poet. His association with Socrates, however, proved the turning point in Plato's life. Nothing so fascinated him as to behold this master of dialectic at work in the Athenian marketplace, puncturing intellectual pretense and questioning outworn dogmas. Under such stimulus Plato gave himself unreservedly to philosophy—to the love of wisdom and the search for its full meaning as a guide to life and truth. For eight years he was in almost daily association with the intrepid and invigorating mind of Socrates, and he could not help absorbing the central concerns that dominated the life of the master.

The tragic death of Socrates, at the hands of the democratic government soon after it regained power in Athens, had an effect upon Plato as powerful as did their years of association together. It made him thoroughly skeptical of democracy as he knew it. Any form of government that could condemn and destroy its ablest and choicest spirit was obviously incompetent and undesirable, Plato felt. His own aristocratic lineage and breeding had certainly not predisposed him favorably toward the democratic ideal. What sympathy he might have had was finally destroyed on the day that Socrates was forced to drink the hemlock. Central among his interests in *The Republic* is Plato's desire to fashion a society in which the rule of the wisest and best might replace mob rule, which seemed to him forever to condemn democracy to mediocrity.

### Years of Travel

After the execution of Socrates in 399 B.C., there was every reason for a man with Plato's aristocratic connections to be under suspicion. He also had been among those active in the endeavor to save Socrates from the democratic leaders who sought his death, and he was perhaps the most influential exponent of the Socratic doctrines. Never could a man find a time more propitious for travel. Plato bade Athens farewell and set out to see the world.

For twelve years he traveled. Unfortunately there is no reliable account of his activities during the years that immediately followed Socrates' death.

---

* This aspect of Plato's youth is given special significance by R. H. S. Crossman in his criticism of Plato's philosophy. See his *Plato Today*, pp. 91–92.

He is known to have visited Italy, Sicily, and Egypt, however, and to have returned at least once to Athens. He spent time in Megara with Euclid, the great mathematician and the father of geometry, and he was also much impressed by the doctrine of the Pythagorean philosophers who in the rational order of mathematics caught something of the harmony and the order of the universe. Perhaps his most fateful journey was one he made in 388 B.C. to Syracuse, the thriving commercial city of the Mediterranean world. Here he became the friend and teacher of Dion, a brother-in-law of Dionysius, the dictator (*dictator* was not then a term of abuse) in that city, and laid the foundation for an experiment in statecraft that almost ended as tragically as did the patriotic mission of Socrates in Athens.

### The Academy in Athens

Finally, at the age of forty, Plato returned to Athens to establish his own school of philosophy. Taking its name, the Academy, from the suburb northwest of Athens in which it was located, this school soon became the center of the intellectual world of that day. Following the fashion of the day, Plato had it incorporated as a religious association dedicated to the Muses who were the patron deities of philosophy. Not only from Greece, but from Macedonia, Sicily, and Asia Minor, orators, statesmen, and artists, as well as mathematicians and philosophers, came in increasing numbers to discuss philosophy with Plato.

The method of instruction adopted at the Academy naturally followed the precedent set by Socrates. Friendly association between teacher and disciples, and informal talk interrupted by occasional questions and answers, constituted the normal order of life. Mathematics and science were also among the subjects stressed. According to tradition a motto over the shrine in the garden dedicated to the Muses read: "Let no one ignorant of geometry enter here," and among the early members of the group were numbered almost all the ablest mathematicians of the day. Within the Academy itself, teacher and pupils enjoyed a thoroughly democratic fellowship together and ate at a common table. But it is recorded that Plato did not frequent the Athenian marketplace and the public meetings of the city, as Socrates had. There seems to have been an aristocratic flavor in his bearing as in his philosophy.

Plato believed deeply, however, in the political philosophy he was developing, and he wanted to see it at work in practice. Twice at least he left the quiet groves of the Academy to enter the turbulent affairs of political life. When Dionysius II became ruler of Syracuse, Plato's old friend Dion, the uncle of the new king, urged Plato to return to Syracuse as political advisor to the young ruler. "Now, if ever," Dion wrote, "is there a good chance that your own ideal can be realized, and true philosophy and power over a great dominion be united in the same person." Despite Plato's personal distaste for this venture—he was now almost sixty years old and also quite successful in his work in the Academy—he did not feel that he could reject this opportunity. "And so," he says, "I followed reason and justice as far as a man may, and went."[2]

Unfortunately the situation at Syracuse did not work out as Plato had hoped. His friend Dion was eager to inaugurate the kind of reforms to which Plato himself was committed; but a powerful party was arrayed against him at court, a group of conservatives intent upon maintaining the old order. These men soon gained the support of the young ruler, and four months after Plato's arrival Dion was expelled from Sicily as a dangerous agitator. The young king himself also refused to undertake the serious study of philosophy that Plato proposed, and a new war was threatening. In these circumstances Plato felt it wise to return to Athens and resume his activities as head of the Academy. He kept in touch with affairs at Syracuse, however, and his personal relations with the young Dionysius remained quite friendly.

When Dionysius himself some time later wrote Plato a long letter urging him to come back once more, the philosopher agreed to do so. But this visit was no more successful than the earlier one. Affairs went from bad to worse and soon the reactionary group persuaded the king to confine Plato to his house under constant guard. The old philosopher was happy to be able to regain his freedom through the efforts of friends and returned to Athens once more, where he spent the remaining years of life. Finally, in 347 B.C., at the age of eighty, he died quietly one night after attending the wedding of one of his disciples—or so tradition has it.

### The Dialogues of Plato

The most influential products of Plato's years at the Academy were his philosophical dialogues. These seem to have been written not primarily for the members of the Academy itself but rather for the enlightened public of that day. There is, especially in the early dialogues, a liveliness and vitality about them that make them far more effective in revealing the spirit of philosophy to the average reader than other great classics in this field. Their effectiveness and influence even in Plato's day is well attested. *Gorgias*, so Aristotle tells us, was read by a Corinthian farmer, who was so deeply moved by it that he sold his property and came to Athens to study philosophy at the Academy.

As far as scholars can tell, all or almost all that Plato wrote has been preserved. The earliest of his works are the so-called Socratic dialogues. Included here are the *Euthyphro, Charmides, Lysis,* and *Laches*—dialogues in which Socrates carries on eager but inconclusive discussions of the meaning of virtue and the good life. To this early group also, of course, belong Plato's two best-known dialogues on the trial and death of Socrates, the *Apology* and *Crito*. There is good reason to believe that in these early dialogues

Plato is primarily a dramatist and a disciple of Socrates, portraying effectively the spirit and teaching of the master.*

Then there is a transitional group of dialogues, in which the spirit of Socrates is still to be seen but in which Plato is evidently going beyond the limits of the Socratic philosophy of life and beginning to propose his own answers to the problems he inherited from his revered teacher. Early in this group belong the dialogues that bear the names of the two ablest Sophists, the *Gorgias* and *Protagoras*. Three other well-known works of plato are also found here: his argument for the immortality of the soul in the *Phaedo*; his theory of knowledge as recollection in the *Meno*; and the famous portrayal of Platonic love in the *Symposium*. The *Republic* follows this transitional group. A comprehensive statement of Plato's own position, it covers all fields of philosophical inquiry: psychology, education, ethics, politics, metaphysics, theology, theory of art; and upon them all Plato sheds the light of his genius. Scholars usually date the *Republic* between 385 and 375 b.c.

In a large and important group of later dialogues, Plato undertakes a more careful and systematic statement of his thought. Here the dramatic quality of the early works is sacrificed to the mathematical precision of the scholar as Plato deals with more difficult issues in ethics, epistemology, political philosophy, philosophy of religion, and metaphysics. Finally there is the *Laws*, that rather extensive work of Plato's old age. Here a more practical and conservative spirit has appreciably modified the uncompromising rational idealism of the *Republic*. Let us then examine the *Republic*, not merely as a classic to be admired but also as a possible guide to the problems that face us in our own day.

## On the Nature of Morality

A major concern of the *Republic*, as its title clearly indicates, is the building of the good society, but Plato's social philosophy is neither narrow nor compartmentalized. For the Greek mind of his day, the good society and the good life are almost synonymous terms, and moral issues must always be examined in their larger social context. In the *Republic* we find Plato facing squarely the issues that have perplexed us thus far in our study of philosophy. Whether it be the moral relativism of the Sophists, the hedonists' concern with the pursuit of pleasure, or the emphasis of Socrates, and much later of Spinoza, upon the essential role of intelligence in morals—all are considered in the pages of the *Republic*. No matter how venerable a tradition or custom, or how well established a precedent, is challenged, Plato discusses each

---

* There is an excellent, nontechnical discussion of Plato's relation to Socrates in these dialogues in Francis M. Cornford's *Before and After Socrates*, Ch. III. Other points of view are defended by able scholars, however. See Chapter 1, page 16.

question without fear or hesitation and seeks to find the answer that reason itself would give.

The first book of the *Republic* is a little dialogue of its own, with all the characteristics of the early Socratic dialogues. It may well have been among Plato's first literary efforts, later used as an introduction to the main body of his thought in the *Republic*. As the dialogue opens, Socrates is discussing with his friends the nature of morality* and examining with his usual dialectical skill current views on the subject. An initial definition, one sanctioned by custom and common sense, is proposed by Cephalus, a wealthy and friendly old merchant: The essence of morality is simply paying one's debts and telling the truth. This everyone ought to know and ought to do. Thus Cephalus expresses the common-sense point of view.

*Can we count on common sense in morals?* This is the initial question raised by Plato. Is it enough to know that we ought to tell the truth and pay our debts, to be satisfied with conscience as our guide in morals? Or must we know also when to tell the truth and when not to? Here is a friend who is critically ill and could be hurt by our fearful assessment of truth. He is in no condition mentally or physically to stand the shock of disaster. "A friend ought always to do good to a friend," Socrates points out; yet telling him the truth as we see it in this case may do him harm.[3] Our debts should be paid, of course. But what do we really owe to those who have befriended us, or to our parents, or to society? Can we ever repay debts such as these? We must know more about what is right and what is wrong than the dictates of conscience and common sense reveal to us, Plato insists. Common sense is apt to be confused, or to have no word of direction for us just when we need it most. The consciences of equally good men disagree fundamentally upon the most important decisions in life. Clearly we must be able to distinguish between what really *is* right and what merely *seems* to be right. This is the first requirement in the moral life, and this obviously requires knowledge. Without understanding, what is right and what is wrong cannot be determined. We must look, therefore, beyond common sense and conscience for a satisfactory definition of morality.

### Does Might Make Right?

Plato next examines the interpretation of morals that we have come to associate with the philosophy of Nietzsche. In the *Republic* this position is

* The customary translation of the term used here by Plato is "justice," but justice has come to have primarily a court-of-law connotation that is too narrow to express Plato's meaning. Nor is "righteousness" a desirable term, although it is preferable in some ways to "justice." What Plato has in mind is "the whole sphere of moral action, both external and internal," as B. A. G. Fuller points out. (*History of Greek Philosophy*, Vol. II, p. 214.)

adopted by the Sophist Thrasymachus. What we call right is nothing but the interests of the strong, of those in positions of power and authority, Thrasymachus maintains.[4] Anyone who doubts that might makes right has only to look about him and observe the situation that actually exists, he argues. Whether in a democracy, an aristocracy, or a dictatorship, the interests of the strong in each case are what prevail and are accepted as right. Thus, as we can readily see today, when a landed and titled gentry was for generations in power in Great Britain, the laws of Britain established as morally right the interests and privileges of this group. In America, a wealthy middle class early established itself in power, and our democratic customs and institutions have given sanction to the rights of private property and free enterprise. In Russia, however, and more recently in China, a proletarian revolution has achieved for members of that class the same moral and legal rights.*

Now what, forsooth, Thrasymachus argues, is *right* in each case but the interest of the most powerful, and what makes it right but the *might* of those who have established themselves in power? Let us have no more of this naïve idealism, which suggests that some things are always right and others always wrong, when only a glance around us is enough to disprove so foolish a proposition. As Nietzsche insisted over two thousand years later, beyond good and evil lies the will to power; by that, and that alone, all morality is conditioned.

Such is the contention of Thrasymachus; but Socrates, after some argument, manages to confound the blustering Sophist with words out of his own mouth. For Thrasymachus is forced to admit, under skillful questioning, that the use of power for the benefit of those who possess it necessarily requires knowledge and understanding. Thus a dictator frequently forces upon his subjects policies that are really injurious to his own interests. Not too long ago, for example, Mussolini forced the Italians to join the Germans in a war that they did not want. As a result, Italy came under German domination; dissension was produced among his own followers, and Mussolini himself was finally overthrown and killed. Here obviously not the interest of the strong man but his downfall was promoted by his unwise use of power. Much the same fate also befell such dictators as Hitler in Germany and Ngo Dienh Diem in South Vietnam. How, then, can we say that might necessarily makes right? Actually, knowledge is essential, even to those who have power, before they can further their own interests. And, as Plato

---

* Plato raises this same question and deals with it in much the same way in another dialogue, *Gorgias*. There the Sophist Callicles, rather than Thrasymachus, is spokesman for the position that might makes right. Socrates is pictured as rejecting the arguments of Callicles upon essentially the same grounds that he uses here to refute Thrasymachus. This position of the Sophists was, of course, restated much more convincingly in economic terms by Karl Marx and has become an essential aspect of the Marxian philosophy. (See Chapter 10.)

goes on to point out, with such knowledge we may well find that what is right for one may be right for all, and vice versa. But what is right can be known only by the man who possesses wisdom. No matter how great his power, an ignorant man cannot escape wrong-doing.

### Is Morality Only Social Convention or Enlightened Self-Interest?

No sooner, however, has the position of Thrasymachus been rejected as untenable than another current interpretation of morality has to be faced. Is it not true, asks one of Socrates' friends, that the pressure of social convention forces us to do what is accepted as right and wrong, rather than our own moral insights or convictions?

Suppose, for example, that we had complete freedom from all the penalties that social convention imposes upon those who defy its dictates, what, then, would our conduct be like? Plato places this issue squarely before his readers in the fable of the ring of Gyges. Gyges, a shepherd in the service of the king of Lydia, was caught in a great storm while tending his flock. An earthquake opened a cavern before him, in which he found a dead body with nothing on it but a gold ring. He placed the ring upon his own finger, returned to his flock, and later rejoined the other shepherds of the king. To his surprise, he found that when the stone of the ring was turned inside his hand he became invisible. Thereupon he contrived to be chosen one of the messengers sent to the royal court, where he seduced the queen and with her aid overthrew the king and took the kingdom for himself.[5]

Now, says Plato, can you really imagine anyone possessing a ring with such marvelous power and still always doing what is right? What would you do, for example, if such a ring were on your own finger? Let us look about us a moment before replying with complete certainty. On a small college campus or in a small town, a person does as a rule behave fairly well. Everybody knows him, and he cannot get by with anything contrary to the prevailing social conventions without having it immediately known and talked about. The pressure of public opinion and convention keeps moral standards fairly high. But let this same individual leave the small-town campus for a large university, or his home community for a visit to New York, Chicago, or Paris, and observe the results. When in New York or at a major state university where no one knows or cares what he does, will he follow those same moral principles that he followed at home or at college? Or does this situation seem like the time for a little—just a little—"moral holiday"?

If there is still a question in your mind, look at what goes on today at the typical state university or at the annual convention of almost any political or military organization. It is easy enough to see what happens to our conventional morals when the restraints of accepted social convention are removed. Does it not begin to appear, Plato asks, that morality is really a matter of keeping up appearances, and when appearances do not matter, then morals do not seem to matter much either?

Nor is this the only problem we must face. When we examine our motives more carefully, Plato suggests, do we not find that one of the strongest incentives to do what we call right is the reward we can get by doing so? We say that "honesty is the best policy," but what does this mean? Surely that it *pays* to be honest. We get ahead faster, there is less chance of getting in trouble if we are honest than if we are dishonest. But suppose the conditions were reversed. Then would not dishonesty become the best policy and an enlightened self-interest cause us to discard the moral ideals that we now accept? Surely our own experience with the Watergate affair offers strong confirmation of the point of view Plato is discussing here.

Look even at the moral precepts of religion, and what do you find? Men are urged to high moral endeavor in order to get to Heaven. They are warned of the tortures of Hell that await the sinner. The broad path of easy living is assumed to be the pleasanter and the more desirable; the straight and narrow path of moral idealism a much less appealing one. The plea of religion is actually made to an enlightened self-interest. Who would not choose to give up the pleasures of a few years on earth for the eternity of bliss that rewards the righteous man? It is not what is right in itself that appeals to us, it seems, but the rewards that right conduct brings. "No one praises morality except with a view to the glories, honors, and benefits that flow from it," one of Socrates' friends remarks.

### Virtue Its Own Reward?

This issue, then, is Plato's major concern in the early pages of *The Republic*. Is right conduct right for its own sake? Are our moral ideals enduring and universal principles, or are they simply the dictates of enlightened self-interest, the pressures of social convention, the interests of the powerful? One can hardly deny that in this discussion Plato has faced the issue squarely. He has marshaled all the evidence against his own position, and presented it in uncompromising fashion. He has not set up a straw man to be knocked down at will, as we too often do when presenting arguments with which we disagree. Virtue must be stripped of all external rewards— indeed, it must even be dressed in the usual garments of vice and immorality —and still be shown to be preferable to vice, Plato insists. Only then can we be sure that virtue is its own reward, that right is right for its own sake.

How, then, does Plato go about providing convincing support for this position? In what at first seems a surprising and disconcerting move, he shifts the discussion sharply from the question of personal morals to a consideration of social philosophy, and justifies this by saying that the state is but the individual writ large. Is it intelligent, he asks, for a man to strain his eyes to read very fine print when the same information is right before him in large letters on an inscription? Let us first examine the nature of social morality, of justice in the state. Then the nature of personal morality will become clear, Plato promises us.[6]

Perhaps we should not reject this analogy too hastily. There are many and obvious differences between the individual and the state, but the basic premise of Greek political thought seems sound: it is impossible for an individual to live the good life alone. Man is a social being and must find the good life in a good society. There is an essential relationship between personal and social morality. Plato's approach here is without question superior to one in which either of these aspects of human life is considered in isolation from the other. With this, many people who are attempting today to work out satisfying personal relationships in small experimental groups obviously agree. Let us give Plato the benefit of the doubt at this point, and see how well he succeeds in treating the problem that he has set for himself.

### A Functional Analysis of the State

Plato begins his social philosophy by asking a few simple but searching questions: What is a state good for? What needs does it meet? How can it best meet these needs? Let us look at the state in its simplest terms, in terms of origin and function, he suggests. Only in such terms, in terms of needs met and functions performed, can we talk intelligently about right and wrong in the life of either the state or the individual.

"A state arises out of the needs of mankind," Plato writes; "no one is self-sufficient but all of us have many wants. Now the first and greatest of necessities is food, which is the condition of life and existence. The second is a dwelling, and the third clothing and the like."[7] As an ordered society develops, a specialization of function inevitably appears. The herdsman, the husbandman, the carpenter, the smith, the baker, the merchant, and the tradesman gradually form a natural class of citizens engaged in supplying these common needs. These citizens who supply the basic needs of mankind in the state Plato calls *artisans*:

> Let us consider first of all, what will be their way of life, now that we have thus established them. Will they not produce corn, and wine, and clothes, and shoes, and build houses for themselves? And when they are housed, they will work, in summer, commonly, stripped and barefoot, but in winter, substantially clothed and shod. . . . And they and their children will feast, drinking of the wine which they have made, wearing garlands on their heads, and hymning the praises of the gods, in happy converse with one another. And they will take care that their families do not exceed their means; having an eye to poverty or war.[8]

This idyllic and simple life is but a passing phase, however, in the development of the state. Man's desire for things, for wealth and luxury, soon produces an expanding economy. New needs must be met by additional activities. Poets, actors, dancers, even doctors and servants, will be required in this enlarged and more affluent society. Even more significant, as Plato clearly saw and as every age including our own has convincingly demonstrated, will be the conflict between one nation and another that this expanding economy will bring. "Then we must enlarge our borders; for the original healthy state is no longer sufficient," he writes; "a slice of our neighbors' land will be wanted by us for pasture and tillage, and they will want a slice of ours if, like ourselves, they exceed the limit of necessity, and give themselves up to the unlimited accumulation of wealth. And so we shall go to war."[9] Thus another important class of men is required in the state—the *warriors*, who defend it from its enemies without and maintain order within its own boundaries.

As society becomes increasingly complex, and man's relation to his fellows more difficult to arrange, a third need becomes urgent. There must be a class of rulers, or *guardians*, as Plato calls them, whose function it is to direct the life and destiny of the state. In doing so, their attention must be directed to the common good of all citizens, thus avoiding the confusion and anarchy that accompanies the effort of each man to follow his own desires without regard for the interests of others.

These, then, are the three basic needs to be met in the state: it must be *nourished*; it must be *defended*; it must be *governed*. Likewise three classes of citizens must be distinguished, each performing an essential function as it meets one of the enduring needs of the state. There must be *artisans* to nourish the state; *warriors* to defend it; and *guardians* to rule it.*

### The Cardinal Virtues

On the basis of this functional approach, it is not difficult to determine what constitutes the just state or the good society: it is the state or society that functions well, the state whose basic needs are well met. With the Greek world of his day, Plato identifies four cardinal virtues: wisdom, courage, temperance, and justice. These virtues will be found alike in the life of the good society and of the good man, Plato believes, and their meaning in each case will be essentially the same. Thus *wisdom* is found in the state only when it has rulers who know what is needed for its welfare and are devoted to the common good. The wisdom that good rulers must have is the posses-

* Initially Plato groups the warriors and rulers together, using the term "guardians" to apply to both. Later the warriors are distinguished from the rulers and given the name "auxiliaries." (Book III, §414B.)

sion, Plato argues, only of the philosopher. He alone sees things whole, understands what is needed for the common good, and is willing to work for its achievement. We do not find wisdom in a state, therefore, until it has rulers with such philosophic vision and insight. Plato makes this the cornerstone of political philosophy, the dominant principle of his *Republic*. "Until philosophers are kings," he writes in a famous passage, "or the kings and princes of this world have the spirit and power of philosophy, and political greatness and wisdom meet in one, and those commoner natures who pursue either to the exclusion of the other are compelled to stand aside, cities will never have rest from their evils—no, nor the human race as I believe."[10]

As wisdom is the virtue of the rulers of the good state, so *courage* is the virtue of its warriors. Courage is found in the state, however, not when its army is powerful or even fearless but only when its military leaders know what to fear and what not to fear, what things to fight for and what are not worth fighting for, Plato maintains. This higher form of courage is nearer what we would call "moral" courage.

*Temperance*, the third of the cardinal virtues, is normally taken to be "the ordering or controlling of certain pleasures and desires," Plato points out. For the individual, it is a matter of self-control. Similarly, in the state temperance will mean that self-mastery in which the wisdom of the rulers controls and directs the power of its military forces as well as the ambition of the businessmen. Unlike courage and wisdom, which are virtues of one class only, temperance "extends to the whole and produces a harmony of the weaker and the stronger and the middle class, whether you suppose them to be stronger or weaker in wisdom or power or numbers or wealth, or anything else," Plato writes.[11]

And now we will have not only wisdom, courage, and temperance but likewise justice itself in our state, Plato concludes. For justice is not distinct and separate from the other virtues. It is constituted by these virtues and consists in them: the just state, that is, is the state in which wisdom, courage, and temperance are found. In its larger social context, justice is essentially a matter of the proper functioning of each part for the good of the whole. It may be defined, then, as that harmonious functioning of the whole in which each class performs effectively the activity for which it is fitted and thus the good of the whole is achieved. It follows, then, that in simplest terms, injustice for Plato results from the failure of any social group to do its own job well, or the effort of any such group to usurp the functions of another or to put its own welfare above the common good.*

* "When the cobbler, or any other man whom nature designed to be a trader, having his heart lifted up by wealth or strength or the number of his followers, or any like advantage, attempts to force his way into the class of warriors, or a warrior into that of legislators and guardians, for which he is unfitted; or when a man is trader, legislator, and warrior all in one, then I think you will agree with me in saying that this interchange

*Plato Today*

Let us make Plato's social philosophy somewhat more specific than we have by drawing an analogy with our own situation today. Justice, he would point out, is not found in the state when organized labor uses its power to control the industrial life of the nation for its own benefit with no regard for the common welfare. Most of us have felt this rather keenly when coal miners, steel workers, or railroad unions have called strikes that seriously endanger the economic life of the country and deprive thousands of people of goods or services they badly need. But neither can justice be found in the state when the owners of industry make the profits of business their exclusive concern and show no interest in the welfare of workers or consumers. In Ralph Nader we have at present, of course, a staunch advocate of this aspect of Plato's social philosophy. And the widespread interest in ecology is also an effort to ensure that the pursuit of immediate or short-run profits for one group does not cause industry to neglect the common welfare by heedless pollution of the streams or the air of the nation.

Nor do we find justice, as Plato defines it, in a state where politicians are interested primarily in what they can get out of political power. Plato would not only condemn politicians who profit from crime and vice, but also congressmen and senators who can see no interests other than those of their own constituents or their own section of the country. Walter Lippmann's helpful distinction between the politician and the statesman is essentially Platonic in spirit. But injustice also prevails, Plato feels, in a state in which the ablest and most gifted young men do not want to be of service in government, but "leave politics to politicians" and seek instead to make private fortunes for themselves in business and industry. And this is equally true if they are content to develop their own special intellectual or scientific interests without any real concern for what happens to the nation.

This, says Plato in effect, is what we mean by social immorality, by injustice in the state. Nor is it difficult to recognize injustice of this sort when it appears today. When powerful military establishments for a time almost completely dominated the state in Germany and in Japan, it was apparent to all that this created not only injustice in the states involved but danger to the world as a whole. For Plato a similar social immorality would have been found in Communist Russia when the leaders of the proletariat siezed control of the state and dominated its operations for the interests of one class alone. There are many today, indeed, who see the domination of a

---

and this meddling of one with another is the ruin of the state," Plato writes. "This then is injustice; and on the other hand when the trader, the auxiliary [warrior], and the guardian each do their own business, that is justice, and will make the city just." (*Republic*, IV, §434B.)

white middle class in the government of the United States for some two hundred years as the source of a social injustice that most of them until quite recently failed to recognize.*

### Human Nature and Goodness

As Plato's interpretation of social morality is directly dependent upon his "sociology," so in like manner his moral ideal for the individual is based on his "psychology." That is to say, for Plato as for Spinoza, there is a necessary rational or scientific foundation for morality. Plato accordingly begins his discussion of moral conduct with a consideration of human nature. There are, he points out, three basic aspects of human nature that correspond surprisingly well with the threefold functional division of the state. First, there is *appetite,* the biological aspect of human nature that expresses itself in eating, drinking, and mating.[12] Its function, like that of the artisans in the state, is to nourish and preserve human life, and to perpetuate it by reproduction.

Second, we find in human nature a rational principle whose function, like that of the guardians of the state, is to distinguish the desirable from the undesirable and so to provide guidance and direction for human life. *Reason* is that aspect of human nature so dear to the heart of most philosophers, especially to rationalists like the Stoics and Spinoza, who see in the life of reason all that is worthwhile in human experience. Although he obviously leans in the same direction, Plato does not quite yield to this temptation.

A third aspect of human nature must also be distinguished, Plato feels. This he terms *spirit.*[13] It is that dominant drive in the self which expresses itself in ambition, in self-assertion, in the desire to get ahead. In human life, spirit or ambition has much the same function as do the warriors in the life of the state. It is seen in man's effort to master others and to move toward a place of leadership in the group. It is seen also, Plato points out, in our indignation at suffering and at injustice, and it moves us to strive to right the wrongs that we find about us, whether they be inflicted upon us or upon others. Centuries later this aspect of human nature so impressed Nietzsche that he took the will to power to be man's dominant drive.

In terms of such an analysis, it is not difficult to anticipate Plato's concept of the good man. An individual achieves goodness, he maintains, in exactly the same way that the state achieves justice; the cardinal virtues in each case are the same. *Wisdom* belongs only to the man who has an

* The strong criticism of Plato's social philosophy by scholars who see the aristocratic spirit in his political thought as basic and quite antagonistic to democracy should be pointed out, and is dealt with on page 185. Concern with this issue, however, should not lead one to overlook the insight found in Plato's analysis of the nature of social and individual morality with which our present discussion is primarily concerned.

understanding of life and a willingness to let reason guide his conduct. "And him we will call wise who has in him that little part which rules," Plato writes; "that part too being supposed to have a knowledge of what is for the interest of each of the three parts and of the whole." The man of *courage* resolutely devotes himself to this rational ideal: "And he is to be deemed courageous whose spirit retains in pleasure and in pain the commands of reason about what he ought and ought not to fear."[14] For Plato there can be no courage without intelligence.

The man who is *temperate* orders and controls his appetites and his ambitions in accord with his own best interests, the welfare of the self as a whole. Such a man is master of himself because the highest principle in the self has the other two under control. Whenever appetite or ambition has its way, heedless of the permanent interests of the self as a whole, we find intemperance. For Plato, a man cannot be temperate, then, unless he knows what he is doing. Temperance does not mean simply smoking a little less, drinking a little less, or not working quite so hard. For some men and women, drinking, or even smoking, at any time may well be intemperate, but not necessarily for all. The same, of course, is true of spirit or ambition. Excessive ambition can easily destroy a man's health, lead to the breakup of his home, or disillusion his children.

What, then, is the meaning of moral conduct? We have, Plato affirms, not only defined wisdom, courage, and temperance but made clear the nature of morality as well. Morality is just that *inner harmony*, that *organic unity* of the *human* soul, in which each basic aspect of human nature—reason, spirit, and appetite—functions effectively for the good of the self as a whole. Clearly Plato has in mind something much like the well-adjusted personality upon which contemporary psychology has laid so much stress. The moral man, he writes,

> . . . sets in order his own inner life, and is his own master and his own law, and is at peace with himself; and when he has bound together the three principles within him, which may be compared to the higher, lower and middle notes of the scale,—when he has bound all these together, and is no longer many, but has become one entirely temperate and perfectly adjusted nature, then he proceeds to act, if he has to act, always thinking and calling that which preserves and cooperates with this harmonious condition, just and good action, and the knowledge which presides over it, wisdom.[15]

### Does It Pay to Be Good?

We are now in a position, Plato believes, to return to the problem with which he began his consideration of morality: Is virtue its own reward? And the answer is now so clear that no further argument is necessary. Our old question of the comparative advantage of morality and immorality "has now become ridiculous," he writes. "We know that when the bodily constitution is gone, life is no longer endurable though pampered with all kinds of meats and drinks, and having all wealth and power." But as health is the harmonious functioning of the human body, so goodness is the harmonious functioning of the human spirit: "Virtue is the health and beauty and well-being of the soul, and vice the disease and weakness and deformity of the same."[16] A man will want to be good, when he understands the meaning of goodness, as naturally and inevitably as he will want to be healthy. Only ignorance can lead anyone to immoral conduct. This fundamental doctrine of Socrates Plato has now demonstrated to his own satisfaction.


## Building the Good Society

The desirability of justice in society is likewise so obvious, once we understand justice to be the harmonious working together of all groups for the common good, that further argument in its support is unnecessary. The question we face today, as did the Greeks in the age of Pericles, is not whether we want a just society but how we can get one. Plato's effort to answer this latter question leads him to his most radical social theories, and the major part of *The Republic* is devoted to this practical problem.

Achieving the good society is, of course, not an easy task. It requires a number of things. Among these, Plato argues, are the intelligent use of eugenics, of education, of religion, and, to a limited extent, even of communism. The role of each is discussed in surprisingly contemporary fashion in *The Republic*. We talk of equal opportunity for all in education, but Plato outlines a program that goes well beyond anything we have attempted, even in the generous provisions of our most enlightened social legislation. We still argue with some renewed heat, as a matter of fact, the question of freedom and equality for women. Plato, as confirmed a defender of equal rights for women as any member of the Women's Liberation movement, holds that women should have every opportunity given to men—in education, in government, even in the army. We are much concerned today with communism, Marxian or otherwise. Its dangers and its sources of strength are analyzed, not only in the arenas of politics and the college classroom, but from the pulpit and at the dinner table as well. Plato felt the appeal of communism, or something much like it, centuries before Marx and Lenin, and he may well have fallen victim also to some of the illusions that afflict contemporary Communists. In our more sober moments, we also wonder with Plato whether democracy may not encourage mediocrity, putting into office the best vote-getter but not the ablest man. "To devise a method of barring incompetence and knavery from public office, and of selecting and preparing the best to rule for the common good": such is the avowed aim of the *Republic*.

*Education for Citizenship*

In building the good society, the most important instrument in Plato's mind, without question, is education. Here he is thoroughly modern. John Dewey himself, influential American exponent of educational reform, did not surpass Plato in emphasis upon the social significance of education. For both, the building of a better society is the undergirding purpose of the whole educational system, and development of a common loyalty to the welfare of the group is the initial step. Plato's proposals for accomplishing this, however, are quite different from those recommended by Dewey.

How is it to be done? First, in very realistic fashion, Plato points out that we must get rid of all people who are over ten years of age. As long as young people are subjected to the conservatism, the outworn antagonisms, and the prejudices of their elders, we can expect to get nowhere with the ideals that reason prescribes. Those in charge of building the good state "will begin by sending out of the country all the inhabitants who are more than ten years old," Plato writes, "and will take possession of their children, who will be unaffected by the habits of their parents. These they will train in their own habits and laws, and in this way the State and the constitution of which we were speaking will soonest and most easily attain happiness."[17]

Plato's proposal is hardly as drastic as was the action of the Russian Communists, who, upon gaining control of the government in 1917, either killed or bundled off to Siberia those who opposed their regime. But the principle is the same. We must start with a clean slate if our new society is to escape the constant criticism and opposition of those whose habits of thought and life have been already fixed along other channels. When given this chance, the ideal we seek may become a reality. "The state, if once started well, moves with accumulating force like a wheel," Plato points out. "For good nurture and education implant good constitutions, and then good constitutions taking root in a good education improve more and more, and this improvement affects the breed in man as in other animals."[18]

During their early years, the youth in Plato's Utopia will receive a thorough training in the humanities. Literature, music, and religion—these are the disciplines by which the young and plastic mind is molded. The important thing in these formative years is the development of taste, not the acquisition of information. At this stage what a youth admires is of more significance than what he knows. His early training must give him an admiration for noble deeds and noble character. Of the youth in his program of general education, Plato writes, "We mean them to honor the gods and their parents and to value friendship with one another." Lin Yutang is right: the educated man is the man who has the right loves and hatreds.

The ideal good, Plato recognizes, must likewise be made appealing at this stage. The books a youth is given to read must be interesting, the music he hears must be moving, the gods he worships must be good. "Bodily exercise when compulsory does no harm to the body; but knowledge which is acquired under compulsion obtains no hold on the mind," Plato writes. "Then, my good friend, let early education be a sort of amusement; you will then be better able to find out the natural bent. For no one will love that which gives him pain, and in which after much toil, he makes little progress."[19] Even the proponents of progressive education could ask for no more forthright statement than this.

At times, it is true, Plato almost becomes a propagandist, as the liberal of our day will immediately point out. But his guiding principle is clear— and sound. Our thinking in later years is done in terms of the values and ideals we actually possess. Thinking does not occur in a vacuum, but always in a specific situation in which there are some elements that we desire and admire, others that we detest. Even for Plato, human reason is no transcendent arbiter, unmoved by the scene in which it operates. And our values are shaped for us by all those unconscious influences that play upon our lives during the first formative years, before reason has developed its critical faculties. The movies we see, the television programs we watch, the songs we sing—these are the influences at work in educating modern youth. Parents today might do well to take Plato to heart. Even college students may well find that the popular songs of the day, rather than their textbooks on ethics, best express the philosophy of life current in their generation. He who has been educated aright, Plato points out, "will justly blame and hate the bad, now in the days of his youth, even before he is able to know the reason why; and when reason comes, he will recognize and salute the friend with whom his education has made him long familiar."[20]

An inner harmony of spirit, a personality integrated by its devotion to the common good; this is the aim of Plato's program of general education, as well as of his theory of morals. Plato has no intention of producing weaklings, however, or youths without stamina and fortitude. Following the instruction in the humanities, he seems to have had in mind about two years of universal military training, designed to provide physical strength and courage in all youth, and also to lay the foundation for a strong army. There is a Spartan note in his educational philosophy at this point that suggests an admiration for the customs he observed among his neighbors to the south.

### Education for Women

Thus far nothing has been said about the opportunities open to women in the educational program. And in the Greek world of Plato's day this would not have seemed strange. A respectable woman's place was in the home; no other career was open to her. But Plato finds no sound reason for this position. There is nothing in a woman's nature, he argues, that assigns her necessarily to such a life. Actually she should have every educational opportunity that a man has, whether in the study of the humanities or in gymnastics.

Plato's proposals here are, as a matter of fact, in keeping with our own recent practice. So far as gymnastics go, he advocates what has now taken place. Let the program of physical education for women include what it does for men. There need be no segregation of the sexes either on the athletic field or in the classroom. Even the athletic costumes need not be different, Plato feels. Women need not be bundled up in cumbersome garments while men perform freely and gracefully on the athletic field. A generation ago these ideas seemed quite radical. Today with Plato we accept most of them as dictates of reason and common sense.

But what about the waging of war? Should women not be debarred from military life? And surely the rulers of the state must be men; for politics is no fit field for a woman? Not at all, says our philosopher. Women differ as individuals, just as men do. Some women have the temper of warriors, some of statesmen, some of philosophers. Some may make good doctors, some good musicians. Give equal opportunity to all. The first principle in our social philosophy is that each one is to do the work suited to his or her own nature.[21] Let any job open to men be open to a woman as well. Our own recent experiences are pushing us rapidly in Plaot's direction. Women now take their place in the army and the navy, and we have congresswomen and female members of the president's cabinet. American males have at times agreed to this hesitatingly, grudgingly, as a matter of necessity, perhaps, but we move nevertheless steadily and surely toward Plato's goal.

### Plato's Philosopher-Kings

At the age of twenty, a thorough and comprehensive examination is necessary to determine those prepared to go ahead as well as those whose formal education should be ended. What kind of men and women has our educational program produced? What is the important question, Plato believes, if able and dependable rulers of the state are to be discovered. Let us note among our youth not only those with the greatest ability but also "those who in their whole life show the greatest eagerness to do what is for the good of their country, and the greatest repugnance to do what is against the best interests of the nation. Those are the right men," Plato declares.[22]

Those who do not survive Plato's first progress test now take their place in the economic and industrial life of the nation. They become the businessmen who produce the material necessities without which the good society is impossible. And according to Plato, it is important to note, this is what they are fitted to do and want to do. For them it is the natural and desirable thing. They have shown neither the ability nor the interest to go further in formal education. Like the great majority of youth in every generation, they are now eager to marry, get jobs, earn a living, and raise a family. In other words, they will consider this no hardship, no mistreatment. They are not resentful or rebellious at such a policy. Indeed, one intention of this whole program of general education, Plato points out, is "that in the case of the citizens generally, each individual should be put to the use for which nature intended him, and then every man would do his own business and so the whole city would be one and not many."[23]

For the outstanding youths, both men and women, who have successfully met his first series of tests, Plato proposes a severe ten-year discipline in mathematics and the sciences. And those who show the greatest promise in this study will be fit candidates, for the final stage of higher education—a five-year course in philosophy. The study of philosophy demands maturity, Plato believes. Care must be taken in introducing our promising youth to reflection of this sort.* When rightly pursued, however, philosophy enables a man to distinguish the true from the false, and to understand the nature of the good as it is in itself rather than as it appears in various embodiments. This is the kind of wisdom that our ablest youth must have. Until a person "is able to define rationally the idea of the good, and unless he can run the gauntlet of all objections, and is ready to disprove them, not by appeals to opinion, but to absolute truth, never faltering at any step of the argument —unless he can do all of this," he is not the person Plato is seeking as the philosopher-king.[24]

At thirty-five, the formal education of our future rulers is at last completed, but one final test awaits them. Knowledge by itself is not enough. A good ruler must be able to use his knowledge successfully in the practical affairs of life. Hence for another fifteen years the ability of our doctors of philosophy to deal with men and affairs—their practical leadership—must be tested. They will be given a sort of internship in government and sent out to undertake political or military tasks for which they are qualified. Finally, those who demonstrate their ability in meeting successfully the conflicts of life itself automatically become the rulers of the state.

### Communism and Eugenics

One might think that Plato's rulers, so carefully prepared by education, are ready at last to usher in the good society. But the social resources of reason are not yet exhausted. Plato saw clearly the importance of heredity,

---

* "There is a danger lest they should taste the dear delight too early," Plato writes; "for youngsters, as you may have observed, when they first get the taste in their mouths, argue for amusement, and are always contradicting and refuting others in imitation of those who refute them; like puppy-dogs, they rejoice in pulling and tearing at all who come near them. And when they have made many conquests and received defeats at the hands of many, they get into a way of not believing anything which they believed before, and hence, not only they, but philosophy and all that relates to it is apt to have a bad name with the rest of the world." (*Republic*, VII, §539B.)

and he recognized that the social situation in which a man lives shapes his character and conduct as much as do his heredity and training. What, Plato asks, tends most quickly to corrupt a man and overrule his loyalty to the common good? Most quickly the love of money; then the love of a woman and the love of one's children, Plato feels. Power always enhances the appeal of wealth and luxury. When a man might perhaps resist temptation himself, he has a natural desire to provide security and the comforts of life for his wife and family. A feeling of this kind could easily overshadow that concern for the common good which Plato took to be essential in the lives of the rulers of the state.

How, then, is this situation to be avoided? Plato is as direct and radical in attacking this problem as any other. In order to devote themselves wholly to the common welfare, our rulers must be freed from all the temptations of avarice, luxury, or power for themselves or their families:

> In the first place, none of them shall have any property of his own beyond what is absolutely necessary; neither should they own a private house; their provisions should be only such as are required by trained warriors, who are men of temperance and courage; they should agree to receive from the citizens a fixed rate of pay, enough to meet the expenses of the year and no more, and they will go to mess and live together like soldiers in a camp. Gold and silver we will tell them they have from God; the diviner metal is within them, and they have therefore no need of the dross that is current among men, and ought not to pollute the divine by any such early admixture; for that commoner metal has been the source of many unholy deeds, but their own is undefiled. And they alone of all the citizens may not touch or handle silver or gold, or be under the same roof with them, or wear them, or drink from them. And this will be their salvation, and the salvation of the state.[25]

As important features in this common way of life, Plato also introduces a program of eugenics and a community of wives and children. Any good breeder of dogs knows that to provide the finest breed and offspring, the best and strongest should be mated, and the weak and sickly eliminated. The rulers of the state should recognize the same principle in handling the marriage of young men and women, Plato argues. Marriage and reproduction are of primary importance to the welfare of the state. Like education and religion, both must be controlled for the common good, not left to the passing fancy or irrational desire of the individual. On this point we have traditionally in America disagreed quite vehemently with Plato. As dangers to the future of civilization in the population explosion become more apparent, however, not only our scientists but even some politicians are beginning to advocate this Platonic principle.

The procedure proposed by Plato to achieve his purpose does not as yet have significant support today. Among the most gifted young men and women "the best of either sex should be united with the best as often, and the inferior with the inferior, as seldom as possible," Plato writes.[26] Certain festival times are to be appointed each year when the prospective brides and bridegrooms shall be brought together, and the brave and abler youths will as a reward for valor and achievement be given as mates the best members of the opposite sex. All children of such unions shall be taken at once to the community nursery, where they are cared for in separate quarters by nurses especially appointed for this office.

The rulers of the state will now have all things in common: their wealth, their wives, their children. Each man and woman will think of all children born in a certain period as their own. Each child will consider all men and women wedded on a certain date as his parents. This Plato concludes, will do away once and for all with the distinction between what is *mine* and what *not mine*, that causes so much dissension in our present society. The common welfare will be the common concern. There will be no rugged individualism, no disrupting self-interest to undermine the good of the whole.

Not too long ago these proposals of Plato were dismissed as thoroughly communistic or as no more than pleasant fancies at best, despite the desirable ends he hoped to achieve. Recent fundamental changes in our sexual morality have made a rethinking of this attitude more acceptable. In *Future Shock*, for example, Alvin Toffler sees the distinct possibility of a "corporate" family, "in which from three to six adults adopt a single name, live and raise children in common and legally incorporate to obtain certain economic and tax advantages."[27] This suggestion, with other possibilities Toffler discusses, makes Plato's proposals seem no longer so fanciful.

Here, in any case, is Plato's Utopia. Beside it even some of the more radical social programs of our own day still appear mild and conservative. But Plato, let us remember, set out resolutely to establish a concern for the common good as the dominant ideal in society. He has let nothing stand in his way thus far, and he has not yet finished his task. To be completely equipped for their work, the rulers of the state "must raise the eye of the soul to the universal light which lightens all things, and behold the absolute good; for that is the pattern in accord with which they are to order the State and the lives of individuals, and the remainder of their own lives also."[28] At this point we are led in our study of Platonism from the good society to the Idea of the Good itself.

## Plato's Theory of Ideas

No aspect of the rational idealism of Plato is more basic or more generally associated with the Platonic philosophy than his so-called "theory of ideas." It is here that Plato develops the metaphysics upon which his moral philosophy rests. Without this enduring foundation in the nature of things, our moral ideas would lose for Plato that eternal validity which makes them true and right, whether any individual men and women happen to discover and accept them or not. The theory of ideas takes us into that aspect of rationalism discussed already in the philosophy of Spinoza, but instead of the pure rationalism of Spinoza, Plato proposes a more inclusive rational idealism.

### The Allegory of the Cave

In the *Republic*, a dramatic and popular statement of Plato's position is presented in his well-known "Allegory of the Cave." The condition of human beings, he here suggests, is like that of prisoners who live in an underground cave. The cave has a large opening through which the light comes in and a broad wall at the back upon which shadows are reflected. Outside the mouth of the cave a fire is blazing, and between the fire and the cave there is a raised pathway over which all sorts of objects pass back and forth. All their lives these prisoners in the cave have been chained, with their legs and necks made fast, so that they can see only the broad wall at the back of the cave, on which are reflected the shadows of objects that pass back and forth outside. And in the cave an echo makes all sounds seem to come from its back wall rather than from its mouth.

In such circumstances, Plato asks, what would the prisoners take to be the real world? The shadows on the wall, of course. For they have never seen or known anything else. And what would happen if one of the prisoners were able to break his chains, turn toward the mouth of the cave, go outside, and see there the real objects that were reflected within? He would at first be blinded by the light, confused and uncertain; but in time he would come to know things as they truly were. Let him, however, return to the prisoners in the cave and try to explain matters to them. In the dim shadows there, those who were prisoners would be quite at home while he alone would be confused and uncertain. They would laugh at his story of "the real world," would say he had lost his sight, and his good sense, and would refuse to allow him to lead them out of their prison house. Indeed, let him try hard enough and they might even have him put to death.[29]

Such, in a parable, says Plato, is the story of our lives as human beings. What does it mean? It is Plato's attack upon our deep-seated materialism. The world of sensory experience, which we take so much for granted, is for Plato much like a world of shadows. The material and physical objects, which appeal to us as real because we touch and taste them, have no permanence, he maintains. They are merely reflections of a deeper, enduring reality that we can come to know only by reason. Reason alone can free us from the chains that imprison us in the world of sensory experience and disclose to us the real world beyond. The plight of ordinary individuals is portrayed by the prisoners in the cave. Like prisoners, most people are from birth chained by the senses to a world of physical and material things. They never discover the world of real and enduring values that philosophy reveals to the more enlightened.

Most of us, as Plato here recognizes, do live in the world of sensory experience. What is real for us is the things that we can feel and see, substantial objects that occupy space. A real supper means steak, apple pie, and ice cream. The new automobiles, the warm sand and sunshine on the seashore—certainly these are real, we feel, if anything is. Yet, if we consider a moment, we will see that we do not completely accept this materialistic philosophy. We speak, for example, of a *real* friend, a *real* man. Obviously we are not here referring to anything that can be seen or touched, anything physical or material. But there is something beyond the senses, something grasped only by reason, in idea, that identifies the real friend and discloses the pretense of one who merely appears to be a friend. Or consider a scientific law, such as the law of gravity. This is not something that can be touched or seen. Yet it is not, for most of us, merely an intellectual concept, something in the human mind. It describes a reality of some kind beyond the physical and material objects, a reality analyzed only by reason and presented to us in idea, a level of reality which we cannot fully comprehend as long as we live only in the world of sensory experience.

### Science and Plato's World of Ideas

An earlier illustration will help us understand Plato's position: Engineers today built great suspension bridges over rivers and bays that were once impassible on foot. As the ordinary individual crosses such a bridge, he assumes without much question that the steel cables and concrete reinforcements he sees and touches, which support his automobile in safety, constitute the real bridge. But to Plato this is simply the opinion of a prisoner in the cave, one who mistakes the shadows for the reality. The real bridge, he maintains, is to be found in the mathematical laws and formulas used by the engineers in the construction of this specific suspension bridge. Without a knowledge of those laws, it would have been impossible to build a bridge at all. Unless this structure is an expression of those laws, it will soon not be a bridge but simply a tangled mass of steel and concrete piled up in the river bed below.

Several important aspects of Plato's rational idealism become clear in this illustration. It is apparent at once that reality for him is known only by reason. It is grasped in the minds of the mathematically trained engineers. Those of us who do not understand mathematics will never be able to know the real bridge. We can know only what appears to our senses in this particular structure. Furthermore, the real bridge—that is, the mathematical laws and principles that constitute its reality—is an indestructible and eternal thing. It has always existed. Otherwise it could not have been grasped by the mind of the engineer. Likewise, it cannot be destroyed. A great flood may wash away the particular structure that we build, but the mathematical laws and principles that constitute the real bridge are entirely unaffected by this occurrence. Plato's world of "ideas"* is not then something within the human mind. It is rather an eternal and unchanging world of rational patterns or forms, which constitute the structure of reality and which human reason at its best is capable of apprehending.

Developments in the physical sciences, particularly in the field of nuclear physics, have provided unexpected scientific support for Plato's philosophy in recent years. The old, hard, substantial material world has gradually melted away in the hands of the physicists. The taste, color, hardness, and softness of material things are all supplied by our own senses, not found in the objects we see and touch, the scientists tell us. When attempting to describe the reality that science finds in the atom, the physicist today, like Plato, is led to mathematical formulas. All that we can know about the atom is a complicated mathematical equation. That is what it is in the only sense that science can comprehend its real nature. As Werner Heisenberg, distinguished nuclear physicist, points out, "physics and chemistry—driven we hardly know by what force—have continuously developed in the direction of a mathematical analysis of nature. . . . *All* the qualities of the atom in modern physics are derived; it has no *immediate and direct* physical properties at all."†

## The Idea of the Good

Able and distinguished scientists of our day do, then, agree with Plato that dependable insight the real and enduring nature of things is provided by mathematical principles rather than by the physical and material qualities we see and touch. Plato, however, does not stop at this point. His rational idealism leads him further than the contemporary scientist is willing to follow. Among the rational forms or principles by which reality is constituted, the most basic and fundamental, Plato holds, is not a mathematical principle but an ethical or moral principle. This he terms "the idea of the good."

* "There can be no doubt that in Plato the word 'idea means primarily 'form' or 'figure,' and it will save a very great deal of confusion if we drop the word 'idea' altogether in discussion of this doctrine." (J. Burnet, *Platonism*, p. 41.)

† *Philosophical Problems in Nuclear Physics* (London: Faber and Faber, 1952), pp. 38, 39. In a popular work, *The Mysterious Universe*, written a good many years earlier (1935) by Sir James Jeans, British astronomer and physicist, there is even more explicit agreement with Plato. "The essential fact is simply that *all* the pictures which science now draws of nature, and which alone seem capable of according with observable fact, are *mathematical* pictures," Jeans wrote. (p. 150; see also pp. 165–187.)

Something can be called good, he maintains, only when it accomplishes the purpose for which it is intended. Thus, a good ship is one that sails well. If it cannot do this, it is not a *good* ship. Likewise a good shipbuilder is one who builds a ship in such a way that it will sail well. He fashions the parts and puts them together in the order necessary to accomplish this end. Unless a man knows what a ship is like and what its function is, he cannot build a good ship. Thus, it is quite literally true from Plato's point of view that every detail of the shipbuilder's work is determined by an "idea of the good"—that is, by what the ship in itself is intended to be and to do.[30]

In similar fashion, unless we understand what human nature is like and how a man must act in order to achieve the best life, it is impossible for us to do what is right or good. The idea of the good may well be likened to the sun, Plato suggests, in concluding the "Allegory of the Cave." Just as the sun throws its light upon the world and enables us to see, so the idea of the good enables us to see the meaning and purpose of the universe as a whole and to understand the part we play in it:

> You have often been told that the idea of the good is the highest knowledge, and that all other things become useful and advantageous only by their use of this. Do you think that the possession of all other things is of any value if we do not possess the good? Or the knowledge of all other things if we have no knowledge of beauty and goodness? . . . My opinion is that in the world of knowledge the idea of the good appears last of all, and is seen only with an effort, and when seen, is also inferred to be the universal author of all things beautiful and right, parent of light in the visible world, and the immediate source of reason and truth in the intellectual; and that this is the power upon which he who would act rationally either in public or private life must have his eye fixed.[31]

### Plato Put into Practice

We now have before us, in broad outline at least, Plato's Utopia and the philosophy upon which it is based. Again and again his insights have been confirmed. During the Middle Ages, for example, Europe was controlled for a thousand years by the Catholic Church in a fashion strikingly like that envisioned by Plato in the *Republic*. The priesthood formed an order of guardians, dedicated, as Plato would have them, to the common good rather than to self-interest or personal power. Leadership was based upon ability clearly demonstrated in a long and arduous process of education and a period of practical activity, much as Plato recommends, and positions of leadership were open to any who demonstrated such ability. The clergy likewise were freed from all ties to family as well as to possessions, practicing a sort of Christian communism that unquestionably did achieve results of the kind Plato had in mind. A clear-cut division existed also between the three main classes in society: the artisans, who were tillers of the soil; the warriors, who spent their time and energy in seeking the rewards and the spoils of combat; and the spiritual rulers of mankind, who in principle devoted themselves without thought of self to a service of the ideal good.

In the common life of all men one found indications of the kind of order and purpose, the sense of unity and harmony, that Plato took to be the foundation of morality. Even the theology of the Church had manifest similarity to Plato's doctrine of Ideas. Man's spiritual concerns were generally recognized as possessing an enduring reality. To the physical and material realm was attributed only a very passing and unsubstantial existence.

Most of us today do not desire a return to the Middle Ages. Whenever a small and dedicated group establishes itself in a position of power, however, we do see again the familiar outlines of Plato's social philosophy reappearing. In the early years of Russian Communism, for example, the group that ruled Russia was held together by its dedication to the common good as these revolutionary communists interpreted it. And the party demanded of its members much the sort of denial of all lesser personal ties and family loyalties that Plato took to be essential for the rulers of his state. In more recent social experimentation in Israel, dedication to the common good in the *kibbutz* again replaces individual self-interest, and family life is modified in the direction that Plato at least suggests.

### Totalitarian or Democrat?

As our age has seen the results of totalitarian policies (such as those of Hitler in Germany, of Stalin in Russia, and of Mao in China), the grave dangers that face every democratic society have become increasingly apparent. This has led to a strong reaction against Plato. Critics have attacked his philosophy vigorously, castigating him as essentially a totalitarian and a dangerous enemy of our democratic social order. "I believe that Plato's political program, far from being morally superior to totalitarianism, is fundamentally identical with it," writes one of the more extreme among Plato's critics. By Plato, "equality, freedom, self-government—all are condemned as illusions which can be held only by idealists whose sympathies are stronger than their sense," in the opinion of another.*

* R. H. S. Crossman, *Plato Today* (London: Allen & Unwin, rev. ed., 1959), p. 39. A British Socialist and a Labour Member of Parliament, Crossman wrote one of the earlier popular attacks upon Plato's philosophy. Karl R. Popper, Professor of Logic at the University of London, supported Crossman's position in a detailed analysis of Plato's dialogues in *The Open Society and Its Enemies*, Chs. 6–8 (1950). This issue has attracted enough attention to justify a volume of essays, entitled *Plato: Totalitarian or Democrat?* (1963), edited by Thomas L. Thorsen. This volume contains not only ample selections from Crossman and Popper but also selections from equally notable philosophers and political scientists defending Plato. The first of the quotations above is from Karl Popper, the second from R. H. S. Crossman.

Plato, of course, was neither a democrat nor a totalitarian, as we understand these terms today. He was fundamentally opposed, to be sure, to the irresponsible democracy he knew in Athens during the late fifth century B.C., and he accepted an essentially aristocratic political philosophy. But he insisted that ability and intelligence rather than birth or ancestry should determine who would hold and exercise political power. Plato saw quite clearly the serious limitations in both democracy and totalitarianism, and he sought to formulate a political philosophy that would provide adequate safeguards against the dangers in both these types of government.

History has shown repeatedly and convincingly, however, that any dominant group, whether an established aristocracy or a dictatorship, does in time tend to lose its concern for the common good and become interested almost entirely in its own privileges and power. This happened quickly to the group of Communist leaders who now rule Russia. It happened more slowly but no less surely to the British aristocracy, as its power was extended over America, India, and the Near East. It happened in time even to the dominant hierarchy of the Catholic Church, as the ignorance, squalor, and wretchedness of the medieval serf make abundantly clear. One of the surest insights of democracy, it seems, is that if the common good is to be achieved, power and privilege must somehow be equitably distributed among all men and not left completely in the hands of an entrenched minority. This point of view Plato was never quite willing to accept. The provisions that he proposes in *The Republic* to safeguard the interests of all its citizens do then need careful examination.

## Plato's Dualism

Able critics of Plato also find an apparent dualism, both in Plato's social philosophy and in his metaphysics, that presents a serious problem. This dualism is to be seen, they argue, in the conflict between the social order he outlines and the ideal of the good life for the individual that he proposes. As Plato recognizes early in the *Republic*, life at its best demands an inner harmony of spirit in which the three basic elements in human nature—appetite, reason, and ambition—all find adequate as well as harmonious expression. Yet, his critics maintain, in the Utopia he sets up Plato in effect denies to everyone the kind of full self-realization he has proposed.

The artisans, for example, are assigned a life in which man's basic biological appetites and desires are dominant. Home, family, and sufficient possessions are theirs, but the spirit of adventure, of leadership, of ambition, is given little room for expression in the life that is allotted them. Nor are the satisfactions of self-government open to them. And, despite the superior social status accorded to the warriors and the rulers in this society, Plato provides for them, too, only a very limited opportunity for full self-development. A home and family and possessions that are one's own: these are the normal foundations for stable personal development as well as for a sound society. Few men or women are capable, perhaps, of such self-denial and exclusive loyalty to the common good as Plato envisions. None, perhaps, can find in a life devoted entirely to military duty or even to intellectual reflection that well-developed and balanced personality that Plato himself recognizes as the desirable moral ideal for the individual. This, at least, is the argument of philosophers who are critical of Plato.

The difficulty he faces in ethics, Plato also faces in metaphysics. His concern to establish the enduring reality of the world of rational forms and ideals is so great that he is led to separate this transcendent world almost completely from the physical and material world around us. The world of the senses, of the things we see and feel, becomes only a world of shadows, lacking genuine reality, his critics insist. The importance of the rational ideal in human experience must be established, they maintain, without destroying the obvious worth of the natural, of the physical and the material things in life. Each student will certainly have to face this question in his own evaluation of Platonism.

In concluding our consideration of Plato, however, let us not forget the enduring insights that characterize his philosophy as a whole. He was keenly aware of every problem with which philosophers have wrestled since his day. He raised the major questions that needed consideration, and upon them all his genius shed significant light. In the words of Alfred North Whitehead, one of the ablest and most discerning philosophers of our century: "The safest general characterization of the European philosophical tradition is that it consists of a series of footnotes to Plato." It will be our task to see if these footnotes enable us to resolve more satisfactorily some of the questions that have been raised concerning Plato's philosophy. And clearly the place to begin is with Aristotle—the greatest of those who were drawn to Plato's Academy.

# Three

## THE VISION OF NATURALISM

Man is a political creature, designed by nature to live with others. The happy man then, since he will possess all naturally good things, must have friends.

ARISTOTLE

Democracy has many meanings, but if it has a moral meaning, it is found in resolving that the supreme test of all political institutions shall be the contribution they make to the all-around growth of every member of society.

JOHN DEWEY

From each according to his ability, to each according to his need.

KARL MARX

## CHAPTER 8

# Classical Greek Naturalism

*Aristotle*

The rational idealism of Plato stirs in us healthy discontent with the world as it now is and suggests possibilities that undoubtedly have genuine appeal. Yet Plato, a good many feel, does not quite have his feet on the ground. His idealism is not firmly enough established in the nature of things. And those who have enjoyed the freedom and opportunity that democracy at its best affords see serious limitations in his social philosophy. Not only is this the reaction of Plato's critics today; it was in large measure the reaction of Plato's ablest pupil in the Academy—an unusually promising young Macedonian named Aristotle. Although greatly influenced in his earlier thought by the rational idealism of Plato, Aristotle felt it essential that philosophy become more practical and down-to-earth.

He was especially well equipped both by nature and background to accomplish this task. Whereas Plato was an Athenian aristocrat, naturally suspicious of the outlook of the masses, Aristotle came from a provincial, middle-class background. His interest lay in understanding the world as it was, not in trying to see with Plato what it would be like if men's actions were completely in accord with reason. And Aristotle succeeded so well in his undertaking that he became known to a later age as *the* philosopher, the greatest and most discerning of all those who sought to make understanding and wisdom their guide in life. It has been said, indeed, that all men can be divided into two classes: those who are Platonists and those who are Aristotelians, so penetrating was the insight of these two great Greek philosophers.

## Historical Background

Aristotle was born in 384 B.C. in Stagira, a Macedonian town some two hundred miles north of Athens. His father, Nicomachus, was a prominent physician in Stagira, and a man of considerable reputation throughout Macedonia. Soon after Aristotle's birth, his father was offered the post of court physician by the Macedonian king, and the family moved to Pella, the Macedonian capital. There Aristotle spent his childhood; little more is known of his youth. It is not unreasonable, however, to trace his interest in science, and above all in biology, to his father's profession. Physicians frequently trained their sons in medicine, and it is quite possible that Aristotle even as a boy may have helped his father in his work.

We next hear of Aristotle when at eighteen he appeared in Athens as a student at Plato's Academy. Here he seems to have made a marked impression, not entirely favorable. Tradition has it that he quite openly regarded himself as intellectually superior to his associates. Despite the fact that he was correct about this, his demeanor as a whole seems hardly calculated to make him popular with other members of the Academy. There is ample evidence of Plato's regard for Aristotle's ability, however, and of Aristotle's respect for the great philosopher.

Plato died in 347 B.C. Aristotle was then thirty-seven and naturally had ambitions to succeed to the headship of the Academy. When Plato's nephew Speusippus was selected as his successor, Aristotle was bound to be irked. Not only was he a far abler man that Speusippus, but he was particularly unsympathetic with Plato's tendency in his later years to "turn philosophy into mathematics," as Aristotle himself phrased it, which was the point of view adopted by Speusippus and his associates.*

In these circumstances Aristotle was happy to accept an invitation from two of his former friends and colleagues at the Academy to join them in the city of Assos in Asia Minor. Hermias, the ruler of the province, was a self-made man who had established himself there as overlord and had persuaded the Persian government to recognize him as a "prince." Like Dion at Syracuse, he seems to have been intrigued by Plato's idea of the philosopher-king, and he was quite pleased to have Aristotle establish in Assos a school like that of Plato's in Athens. Soon also a very genuine attachment developed between Hermias and Aristotle, and the philosopher later married Pythias, a niece or adopted daughter of the ruler. An alliance of this sort with a woman of independent means naturally had its appeal to Aristotle, but he seems to have been genuinely fond of his wife.

### Aristotle and Alexander

Five years after Aristotle left Athens, Philip of Macedonia offered him the position of tutor to his son Alexander. Philip was posing as a champion

---

* For a better understanding of the relation of Aristotle to Plato and of the development of Aristotle's own thought, scholars today are largely indebted to Werner Jaeger's *Aristotle, Fundamentals of the History of His Development* (Oxford University Press, Eng. trans. 1934). Jaeger's position is a highly controversial one, however, and has led to greatly increased interest during subsequent years in the nature of the Aristotelian manuscripts. A helpful, nontechnical discussion of Jaeger's book is available in Marjorie Greene's *Portrait of Aristotle* (University of Chicago Press, 1963), pp. 17–37.

and protector of Hellenism against the Persian "barbarians," and a man of Aristotle's prestige in Greek intellectual circles certainly would appeal to him as a member of the royal household. Nor would the prospect appear undesirable to Aristotle himself. Philip was now the most powerful of the Greek monarchs, and Alexander was the successor to his throne. Like Plato, Aristotle no doubt felt that the proper education of a future ruler, especially one with so much power, was an important task for the philosopher. In any case he now returned to Pella, the capital city of Macedonia, which he had left as a boy some thirty years before.

Aristotle soon won the affection and confidence of his pupil, the young prince, but the extent to which he succeeded in influencing Alexander is a matter of dispute. In any case, Aristotle did not have many years to work with Alexander. It was not long before all Greece was at the feet of the victorious Macedonian king; but shortly thereafter, at the wedding of one of his daughters, Philip was assassinated and his son became king. Alexander's days of study were now definitely over, and Aristotle's work as tutor was done.

### The Lyceum at Athens

In 334 b.c., just thirteen years after leaving Plato's Academy, Aristotle returned to Athens. Now fifty years old, he was ready to establish his own school of philosophy, and Athens, despite its political reverses, was still the cultural center of the Greek world. Its climate also appealed to Aristotle far more than the harsh winters in Macedonia. He rented some buildings—as an alien he could not buy them—in a park northeast of Athens. The place, formerly a favorite spot with Socrates, was dedicated to Apollo Lyceus and known as the Lyceum. Here Aristotle began to meet informally with disciples, discussing philosophical problems as they walked together in the colonnade. This led to a nickname for his group, the Peripatetic Philosophers,* a term that stuck and later became widely used as a designation of Aristotle's entire system of philosophy.

With impressive energy and thoroughness, Aristotle, during the twelve years that he conducted the Lyceum, devoted himself to developing and clarifying his own thought as well as to teaching. He seems to have had an insatiable curiosity, a thousand irons in the fire, and scientific research under way on almost every subject. Our contemporary idea of the "specialist" did not then exist. Every important area of human knowledge—mathematics, physics, astronomy, biology, anatomy, politics, ethics, logic, rhetoric, art, metaphysics—was of concern to Aristotle. Never before had one man so thoroughly mastered the whole body of existing knowledge. Never again would it be possible for a single individual to do so.

There is a good deal of speculation as to just how Aristotle managed to finance his various undertakings. One major work, a digest of 158 political

---

* It is now generally agreed that it was the covered walk, περιπατος, not the practice of *walking about*, to which this designation referred.

constitutions, suggests considerable secretarial assistance, although the first of these, *The Constitution of Athens*, Aristotle seems to have written himself as an introduction to the work as a whole. He collected hundreds of manuscripts on scientific and philosophical subjects, and set up a museum of specimens to illustrate his lectures on natural history. His was the first great university library, the model for later libraries at Alexandria and Pergamum. As the center of all this research and scholarly activity, the Lyceum became an increasingly important and busy institution. It soon overshadowed the Academy, which was still in operation but since the death of Plato and the departure of Aristotle had not retained its prestige.

### Later Years and Death

Aristotle did have enemies, however. He was by now thoroughly identified in the popular mind with the Macedonian party and was a close friend of Antipater, the Macedonian governor in Athens, whom he had known at the court of Philip. He was also still the advisor of Alexander. In this position he could not escape suspicion and criticism, especially in Athens, which was intensely patriotic and never quite reconciled to its position as a vassal state.

Upon the death of Alexander, the patriotic party in Athens immediately sounded the call to revolt against the Macedonian rule. Demosthenes, the great Athenian orator, was the leader of the patriots, and feeling in the city ran high. Most of those associated with the Macedonian party fled from Athens, and Aristotle, even though he had refrained from active participation in politics, could not escape. An absurd charge of atheism, based upon a hymn and epitaph he had written for his friend Hermias, was brought against the philosopher. Remembering the fate of Socrates, Aristotle very wisely decided to depart from the city before it was too late, not wishing, he remarked, "to give the Athenians a second chance of sinning against philosophy."

Leaving one of his long-time associates, Theophrastus, in charge of the Lyceum, he retired a safe distance to a country estate inherited from his mother. He had been in ill health himself for some time, however, and now his malady took a turn for the worse. In the summer of 322 B.C., just a year after the death of Alexander, Aristotle himself died at the age of sixty-two.

In addition to his outstanding intellectual power, Aristotle possessed a very genuine human sympathy. The will that he made during the last year of his life is more revealing in this regard, perhaps, than is his influential volume on ethics. Fortunately it was preserved for us by Diogenes Laertius in his *Lives of Eminent Philosophers*.

### Intellectual Achievement

For sheer intellectual achievement, Aristotle stands with Plato, unequaled in the ancient world and perhaps not surpassed in the modern. In the field of *logical inquiry*, Aristotle's accomplishment was outstanding. The very development of logic as a separate discipline owed its origin and impetus in large measure to him. His various treatises on logic were put together in one volume at least as early as the sixth century A.D., and became known as the *Organon*, or instrument of knowledge. The thinking of the later Middle Ages was shaped almost entirely by this Aristotelian *Organon*, and it likewise provided the foundation for the formal logic of a later day.

Aristotle's contribution to *natural science* was equally impressive. His books on physics and astronomy as well as his studies in biology and psychology were both extensive and influential. His pioneer work on *Metaphysics*, or the first principles of philosophy, contains a discussion of fundamental concepts and principles that has served as the foundation of metaphysical study ever since. His *Politics* is equally able, and his *Poetics*, the standard analysis of literary form for generations, is still a work of primary importance.

Despite these important contributions to science, to metaphysics, to logic, and to aesthetics, Aristotle's greatest achievement was in the field of ethics. Of all his works, the *Nicomachean Ethics* has had the most profound and lasting influence. Here we find what for many years provided the Western world with its clearest ethical insights as well as its most mature and balanced discussion of man's moral problems. Of the *Nicomachean Ethics* a discerning interpreter writes:

> It is still the most important book on the subject. Its general points of view are those to which modern writers are increasingly turning. This is not because of its perfect adequacy or finality on any subject. But the importance of its fundamental principles becomes more and more impressive when one realizes how they are based upon an extraordinarily high ideal of human life and conduct, as well as upon views of nature (within and without) which derive their forces from the evidence of science and history.[1]

Although they have had such wide and continued influence, the works of Aristotle have not come down to us in good condition. Their style is choppy and unfinished; loose clauses often appear in the middle of a sentence and there are many seemingly unnecessary repetitions. As a result, Aristotle is neither as interesting nor as easy to read as Plato. It is clearly not enough simply to call Plato a poet and Aristotle a scientist. The manuscripts Aristotle prepared at the Lyceum were undoubtedly more in the form of lecture notes and revisions of his earlier writing than finished works like Plato's *Dialogues*. According to the story told by Strabo, an ancient geographer, Aristotle's manuscripts also went through a succession of unhappy adventures that helps in some measure to account for their present condition.

When he was forced to flee from Athens in 323 B.C., Aristotle left his library and manuscripts at the Lyceum. Some thirty-five years later, they were buried in a cellar, and for one hundred and fifty years, so the story goes, these manuscripts lay hidden in the damp cellar. By now in terrible condition, they were mildewed, worm-eaten, torn, and disarranged. When Greece was overrun by the Roman general Sulla and Athens was conquered, Aristotle's manuscripts were taken to Rome along with other choice spoils of war. There a systematic edition of his works was made and later published about 50 B.C. by Andronicus of Rhodes. It is from this edition that the works of Aristotle as we know them today largely come.

## Science and Metaphysics

Aristotle's approach to philosophy in general and his disagreements with Plato in particular can be understood most easily in terms of the divergent scientific views of the two men. Plato, as we have seen, was interested primarily in mathematics. Aristotle, on the other hand, was deeply influenced by the natural sciences, especially biology. As a mathematician, Plato thought in terms of laws and principles that are rational and universal: two plus two has always equaled four and always will. The laws of gravity are not something we see but something we discover by reason. Reality, as the mathematician conceives it, is rational, unchanging, eternal. By contrast, Aristotle as a biologist was aware, first of all, of change and development. To be alive, a thing has to grow, change, develop. And as a scientist, Aristotle recognized also the necessity of patient observation, analysis, and experimentation if one hoped to gain knowledge. It is not the univeral but the particular, the concrete, and the specific that must be examined, described, classified. A fundamental difference in philosophical spirit and outlook results then from the fact that Plato saw the world through the eyes of a mathematician, whereas Aristotle saw life and reality largely as a biologist sees it.

Aristotle, of course, made important contributions to science in every field. His works on astronomy, meteorology, and physics were quite extensive and were for centuries considered authoritative. But it was in biology that his scientific interests centered. Here he conducted an extensive and painstaking inquiry, collecting data on five hundred or more kinds of animals and investigating in detail examples of at least fifty species that covered the whole range of the animal kingdom. His studies in the growth of chicken embryos, accomplished by breaking hens' eggs at various stages of incubation, comes close to scientific method as we know it today, and his description of the development of the chick is still regarded with admiration by embryologists. His discussion of the mechanism of sexual reproduction was also careful and thorough, as was his study of the facts of heredity. He pointed, for example, to the peculiar genetic problem illustrated by the children of a woman of Elis who married a black: the children of this union were all white, but blacks reappeared in the second generation. In this study Aristotle anticipated some of the findings of modern genetics, although in general his conclusions are more fanciful and open to error here than in other areas.*

### The Doctrine of Entelechy

Aristotle's study of biology led him directly to psychology and metaphysics. His work in science was patient, impressive, and thorough, but essentially he was a philosopher. Change, growth, development—these were the most important aspects of life at whatever stage he saw it, whether animal, vegetable, or human. Life was everywhere dominated by an inner urge to grow, to become something greater. This process of development in the living organism in fact provided Aristotle with his answer to the major dilemma he saw in the philosophy of Plato.

The world of rational law (his world of *Ideas*), Plato set apart too completely from the material, physical universe; and he never successfully brought the two together again, Aristotle felt. Neither world is complete without the other, however, nor can the two really be separated. There is, Aristotle points out, within all living things an inner form or pattern that guides their growth and development. Rational form is not a separate reality grasped only by the human mind, as Plato suggests. It is an inner necessity, Aristotle insists, that molds the material world in accord with the end or design of the living organism. To this inner creative force he gives the name *entelechy*.† This is for Aristotle the most significant aspect of life and of nature, and provides the key to his philosophy as a whole. Development is not haphazard or accidental. Growth does not take place at random. Every living organism is guided naturally by a creative force within itself, its *entelechy*. "For we call anything 'natural' when by virtue of a principle inherent in itself it progresses continuously toward some goal," Aristotle writes. "Such principles do not all make for the same goal, but each inner principle always makes for the same goal of its own, if nothing interferes."[2]

A good illustration of the Aristotelian *entelechy* is afforded by studying an acorn. One cannot understand what an acorn really is simply by analyzing its physical or chemical components. By far the most important thing about an acorn is the creative force within it, which given the proper conditions will enable it to become an oak tree. In the very structure of the acorn there is the pattern or form of an oak which guides and directs its growth: This is its

---

* Among the more important of Aristotle's works on science, the following are usually included: *On the Heavens, Meteorology, Physics, The History of Animals, On the Parts of Animals, On Motion in Animals,* and *On the Generation of Animals.* A number of other books and monographs on science are included in the twelve-volume translation of Aristotle published by the Oxford University Press between 1928 and 1952, but these are generally attributed to Aristotle's associates at the Lyceum.

† The Greek term εντελεχεια means, literally, having its end or purpose within itself.

*entelechy*. This inner form is not something physical or material, as Aristotle sees it, but it is nevertheless very real—the most significant thing about the reality of the acorn. It is not, however, the only important aspect of the acorn's reality, Aristotle recognizes. To produce a great oak tree, the acorn must have good soil, water, and sunshine. Without these, it will still grow, but it will become only a small, insignificant oak—a scrub oak, not a great tree. What is true of the acorn is true of all living creatures. The egg of the hen is so *designed* that it will become a chicken, not a robin or a duck. The young gorilla will grow to be an animal; the young child in time will become a human.

In his theory of *entelechy*, Aristotle modified the philosophy of Plato in terms of insights later stressed by John Dewey. Plato was deeply impressed with the rational form or pattern without which a thing could not be what it was; Dewey was equally impressed with the process of growth and development fundamental to life and achievement. Each, however, was in a measure unimpressed by the aspect of reality so important to the other. Aristotle sees both, and the necessity of both. Life is a process of growth and development, but it is growth in a definite direction, toward a clearly defined end or goal. The rational forms that Plato recognizes are not, then, something apart from the world of matter. They are the guiding and directing principles by which the physical and material growth of the living organism is controlled.

It is with the dualism inherent in Plato's thought that Aristotle disagreed fundamentally in building his own philosophy. Plato, he felt, was too out of touch with the world of nature, and he missed the most important aspect of reality, the individual thing. A bridge, for example, is not a *real* bridge so long as it is only a rational pattern, existing apart by itself, Aristotle insists. It becomes a real bridge only when the pattern is realized or actualized in a specific, individual bridge. Reality, that is, involves both *form* and *matter*. The rational form Aristotle takes to be essential. Without it there could be no bridge. But the material, the steel and concrete, that is used to give body and substance to the form is equally necessary. Without this there could also be no bridge. Plato had set off the world of rational ideas or forms too completely by itself, Aristotle felt, ascribing to it an independent reality that it did not possess.*

* It is in this context that Aristotle develops his well-known doctrine of the "four causes." Seeking to discover the different conditions necessary to explain the process that produces any concrete individual thing, he identifies four of these conditions—answering the questions: What is it? Out of what is it made? By what agent? And for what end or purpose? When Cicero translated Aristotle into Latin several centuries later, he used the Latin term *causae* to translate Aristotle's Greek word, and Aristotle's four conditions have been known ever since as the *formal* cause, the *material* cause, the *efficient* cause, and the *final* cause.

In the illustration mentioned above, for example, the concept *bridge* is the formal cause, steel and concrete are the material causes, an engineer and his workmen are the efficient cause, and its use to provide a crossing for a river is the final cause. These are

*The Nature of the "Soul"*

Christian thought, more influenced by the dualism of Plato than by the naturalism of Aristotle, has tended in similar fashion to separate the soul almost completely from the body. For Aristotle, however, soul and body cannot be treated as separate entities, but, like form and matter, they are two inseparable elements in a single reality. His position here is in general accord with the "new naturalism" of our day: Cultivation of the soul involves a corresponding cultivation of the body, not its neglect—as both neo-Platonism and the medieval Church unfortunately maintained.

"The soul," Aristotle writes, "is the 'determining principle' of the living body." It is "the essential and enduring character of a body possessing the capacity of life," the inner form which guides the life and development of the whole organism—in short, its *entelechy*: "Nature, like mind, always acts for a purpose, and this purpose is its end. In animals the soul is such an end (*telos*). That it should be so is according to nature; for every part of a living body is an organ of the soul. Evidently then all such parts are for the sake of the soul, which is their natural end."[3]

It is necessary, therefore, to enlarge our concept of the soul, in Aristotle's view, and recognize not only a human soul but also an animal and a vegetable soul. "The nutritive soul must be possessed by everything that is alive," he writes, "and every such thing is endowed with soul from its birth to its death. For what has been born must grow, reach maturity and decay." It is the "soul" of the carrot or the acorn—that is, its *entelechy*—that within rather narrow limits shapes its destiny and provides for the ongoing of its species. Similar functions are performed by the animal soul, but it has wider activities and higher powers as well. Animals not only live, they have sensations, they feel, and they move about at will. Movement, moreover, is not entirely haphazard. The animal moves toward certain things and away from others. Its movements are directed, Aristotle suggests, by inner desires and needs that we now call instincts.[4]

The soul of man, the rational soul, is for Aristotle the highest order of being in nature. It has the properties of both the vegetable and the animal souls, but its powers far exceed theirs. The power of rational thought is possessed by the human soul alone. In significant fashion, Aristotle points out, the rational capacity of the human soul distinguishes man from the animals.

---

for Aristotle the four kinds of explanation, the four necessary conditions for understanding the process that produced the bridge. In order to make this process, or any other, fully intelligible, we must know all four. Only one of the four, however, the efficient cause, the agent involved (the engineer in this case), is a "cause" in the popular use of this term today. Aristotle clearly is interested in a more comprehensive and adequate interpretation of the conditions at work in causation than our usage today suggests. (See J. H. Randall, Jr.: *Aristotle*, Columbia University Press, 1960, p. 124.)

Man is able to shape his own destiny in a way that is not possible for the animal or the vegetable soul. There is nothing that the carrot or the acorn can do about its development, about its future. Given good soil and climate, the seed will grow well. Without these, it will wither away and die. The animal can do a little more to fulfill its destiny, but not much. The hungry dog can seek food; the bird can migrate from north to south to find better climate. But in both cases, the destiny of the animal is determined almost completely by forces within or without it over which it can exert no effective control.*

In human conduct, however, intelligence may supplant instinct or appetite as the guiding and directing force. Though prompted by desire and appetite, intelligent men "do not yield to their inclinations but follow reason," Aristotle writes. The human soul has its destiny in a very real sense within its own power. By the use of practical reason, a man can not only understand the end or purpose of his life as a human being, but also in large measure determine that end and so shape his development.

Thus, after examining his own abilities and interests and analyzing the needs of his community, one young person may well decide to become a doctor, another an engineer, a third a social worker. If one is influenced by the "new naturalist" philosophy, he may well decide to devote himself to the political reform of society, or perhaps to sever his ties with the established social life entirely and become a member of an experimental commune. In each case, however, the life of the individual is significantly altered as he intelligently chooses the conduct that will enable him better to achieve the ends decided upon. Thus the *entelechy* that shapes the growth, the purpose, and the end of the human life is within man's control in a way that sets him apart fundamentally from the animal world. His intelligence gives man freedom—in the only sense that freedom is possible. It is easy to see why for Aristotle reason is the crowning glory of man, why man's distinctive excellence lies in the development of intelligence.

### The Compulsion of the Divine Ideal

As with his treatment of the soul, Aristotle's discussion of the nature of God is naturalistic and scientific rather than religious in spirit. His theology is, in fact, largely an extension of his physics, or better perhaps of his metaphysics. No study of the universe is complete, he maintains, unless it produces an adequate explanation of its cause. What made it as it is? For Aristotle the over-all process of growth and development, or movement, toward a given end throughout the universe must have an explanation. It cannot be taken for granted. And for an explanation he turns again to his basic concept of

* It is true that some natural scientists in their experimental work with dolphins and their kin have identified a type of intelligence and certain social relationships that impress them greatly. But Aristotle's central point about human potentiality still appears a valid one.

*entelechy*. As the growth of every living organism is determined by its *entelechy*, an inner form or purpose, so Aristotle argues, the initial impulse to movement as well as the continued development of the universe as a whole, must be seen as the result of an inner creative cosmic purpose or *entelechy*. This we call God. Aristotle's God is both the goal toward which all things move and the drive and purpose within things. Thus for him God is the final as well as the first cause of nature.[5]

Aristotle's analysis of form and matter led him to see that these were in one sense relative terms, not fixed or final ways of interpreting reality. However perfectly any object achieved its own particular form, it might still be only the material for some further and more developed form. The great oak is the form toward which the acorn grows and which it may finally realize. But then the oak itself may become the matter from which sturdy chairs and tables are made. And these chairs and tables, once completed, are not ends in themselves but are used as the materials from which a schoolroom is designed. And even the school, however perfect in itself, is but one of the components that go to make up a well-planned community. So Aristotle is led to look, finally, for some pattern that shapes the nature and direction of the universe as a whole, a design in which human society, life below the human level, and the physical universe itself are all component parts. That design, of course, is for him what is meant by God.

God, however, must be an "unmoved mover," Aristotle insists, coining a famous phrase. He must be the cause of motion, of change and development within the universe, without himself being involved in this change. God, that is, must be pure form. Everywhere else both form and matter are essential for reality, Aristotle argues, but not in God.* The divine nature must be absolutely perfect, not marred, as is human nature, by imperfections or failure to achieve its purposes. Hence the imperfections of human life and society cannot be a part of God. Evil and error must have another explanation.[6] God's perfection is obtained then by separating God from the material and physical world in a way in which the soul is not separate from the body.

How can such a God, removed from all involvement in the struggle of life, serve as the *entelechy*, the end and creative purpose, of the whole universe? To meet this difficulty Aristotle makes use of poetic rather than scientific language. "God moves the world as the beloved object moves the lover," he writes. "The object of desire and the object of thought move in this way; they move without being moved."[7]

The relation of Aristotle's God to the universe may be more clearly understood, perhaps, by a romantic analogy. At a homecoming football game an unsophisticated young freshman sees the current beauty queen introduced,

---

* Aristotle does rather surprisingly, however, at one point accept as a fact that rational mind in its intuitive aspect is independent of the body in a way that the "soul" is not, and so is immortal and imperishable (*De Anima*, III, 5).

strikingly beautiful and appealing. He falls in love with her on sight and vows to himself to become worthy of her. His whole life is changed. A new ideal moves him, guides his conduct, remakes his life. But—and this is the tragedy of Aristotle's theology—despite the profound impact of this experience upon him, the freshman is never able to meet the girl who has exerted so significant an influence upon him. She remains completely unconscious even of his existence. The struggles through which he goes, his achievements and his disappointments, affect her not at all. In such an analogy as this, we see the God of Aristotle exemplified. As the ideal goal toward which all things move, God is the first and the final cause of the universe, its inspiration and guiding principle. But in his perfection God is completely unmoved by the toil, the effort, and the failures of mankind.

## On the Nature of Happiness

The moral philosophy of Aristotle, like his study of natural science, is empirical and practical in spirit. The function of ethics, as he describes it, is to deal with the activities that improve human life. Reflecting the viewpoint of a physician, he sees ethics as concerned with the health of the soul, just as medicine is concerned with the health of the body. Aristotle has been called the first great humanist, and his moral philosophy provides an important expression of the vision of naturalism. As he interprets morals, there is no conflict between the natural and the ideal in human life. The moral ideal is not something artificial or arbitrary, imposed upon men who are at heart antagonistic to it. Instead, as Santayana has suggested, for Aristotle "every ideal has a natural basis, and everything natural has an ideal development." Excellence of all kinds, both intellectual and moral, has its roots in nature, Aristotle writes: "We are just, temperate, courageous, and the like from our very birth, natural moral states exist even in children and lower animals. . . . It is neither by nature nor in defiance of nature that virtues arise in us. Nature gives us the capacity, and that capacity is perfected by habit."[8]

### The Truth and the Error in Hedonism

The mistake of many moralists lies in trying to force men to be good. A brief examination of human conduct is enough to demonstrate that it is not goodness for its own sake but happiness that men desire, Aristotle points out. Goodness and happiness must not be opposed to each other; the essential dependence of one upon the other must be demonstrated if we want men to be good. In accord with Plato's tripartite analysis of human nature, Aristotle identifies three more or less generally accepted views of the good life: (1) the life of enjoyment, (2) the life of honor, and (3) the life of contemplation. But in each case he finds that happiness is actually the aim of life.

This is what men hope to achieve whether they seek it through pleasure, through ambition, or through philosophy:

> Now happiness above all else appears to be absolutely final in this sense, since we always choose it for its own sake and never as a means to something else; whereas honor, pleasure, intelligence, and excellence in its various forms, we choose indeed for their own sakes (since we should be glad to have each of them although no extraneous advantages resulted from it), but we also choose them for the sake of happiness, in the belief that they will be a means to our securing it. But no one chooses happiness for the sake of honor, pleasure, etc., nor as a means to anything whatever other than itself.[9]

This is as far as Aristotle's agreement with the hedonists goes, however. All men want happiness, but few know how to obtain it. To say that happiness is the chief good in life, then, is something of a platitude. A clearer account of what it is is still necessary. The hedonists in particular have misled men, Aristotle feels, by their emphasis upon the pursuit of pleasure as the way to achieve happiness. Hedonism is correct, to be sure, in insisting that all men naturally seek pleasure and desire happiness. But the hedonist does not understand the nature of pleasure, nor the relation of happiness to the business of living well.[10]

The hedonist, Aristotle suggests, is like a man who, coming into a cool room and noticing that the thermometer registers only 60°F., raises the mercury to 76°F. by blowing his warm breath on the bulb and then is surprised to find that he is no warmer. In similar fashion the advocates of hedonism, in his judgment, from Aristippus and Epicurus to Omar Khayyam and Lin Yutang, have gone on raising their own emotional temperature by the pursuit of pleasure. But they never succeed in achieving enduring happiness because they do not understand its cause.

The initial error of hedonism lies in treating pleasure as an independent emotional state or an end in itself. Careful psychological analysis shows us that this is not the case, Aristotle points out. Pleasure is actually a by-product; it is the mark and the completion of an activity that is functioning properly. "Pleasures are not really processes, nor do they result from the process of acquiring our faculties, but from their exercise." Pleasure accompanies the "unimpeded activity of our natural state."[11] Defined more exactly, *pleasure is the emotional accompaniment of the healthy exercise of function.* When we are hungry and eat a good meal, we enjoy it. That is, we find marked pleasure in the experience. And the same is true of all normal human functions. A game of tennis when we need exercise, conversation with friends when we are lonely, reading a good book in the evening—these activities are all accompanied by pleasure. One might well term pleasure the sign and seal of such healthful exercise of function. And in this sense obviously pleasure is desirable.

> An activity is augmented by the pleasure that belongs to it, since those who work with pleasure always work with more discernment and with greater accuracy—for instance, students who are fond of geometry become proficient in it, and similarly lovers of music, architecture, or the other arts, make progress in their favorite pursuit because they enjoy it.[12]

Pleasure and life are inseparably united, however; pleasure cannot be pursued successfully as an end in itself. As Walter Lippmann observed, lovers who have nothing to do but love each other are not to be envied. Love and nothing else is soon nothing else. We must live a life with all our capacities in healthful and well-proportioned exercise to enjoy the pleasure that all men naturally desire. For activities, when not healthful, do not bring us pleasure. To anyone who has just eaten a large Christmas dinner, food has no appeal. If he eats again, eating will bring not pleasure but pain. The athlete who has just played a strenuous football game will not find a game of tennis appealing or pleasant. The student who is devoting eight or ten hours a day to serious study will not do much additional reading for pleasure:

> No human activity is capable of uninterrupted activity, and therefore pleasure also is not continuous, because it accompanies the activity of our faculties. Each sense has a corresponding pleasure, as also have thought and contemplation, and its activity is pleasantest when it is most perfect, and most perfect when the organ is in good condition and when it is directed to the most excellent of its objects; and the pleasure perfects the activity like the bloom of health in the young and vigorous.[13]

### Pleasure and Happiness

What, then, about happiness? Has it become simply a matter of the enjoyment of pleasure when properly understood? Not at all, Aristotle maintains. There are some important distinctions still to be made in arriving at our definition of happiness. Aristotle saw clearly, as did John Stuart Mill many centuries later, that mere quantity of pleasure is not the important thing. There are different kinds of pleasure, some unquestionably better than others. A little pleasure of one kind is far more appealing to us than a great deal of pleasure of another kind. And these higher pleasures can easily be distinguished from lower pleasures, Aristotle suggests, in terms of the particular activities or functions that the pleasures accompany.

To make this point clear we might perhaps make use of Plato's threefold analysis of human nature in terms of appetite, spirit, and reason, which parallels Aristotle's life of enjoyment, life of honor, and life of contemplation. The pleasures that accompany the healthful functioning of the appetite, the will to live, are well known and appealing to us all. "As the pleasures of the body are the ones which are most often met with, and as all men are capable of these, they have usurped the family title; and so men think them the only pleasures that exist, because they are the only ones which they know," Aristotle points out.[14]

Once men know both types of pleasure, however, it is clear that they place a higher value upon the pleasures that accompany the healthful exercise of ambition, the life of honor, in all its various manifestations. Thus when college athletics was still essentially nonprofessional, star athletes felt it no real deprivation to give up tempting food, late hours, and other indulgences in pleasures of the senses, in order to condition themselves for victory. The enjoyment that accompanied such success proved to be far more appealing than the pleasures of the physical senses. Similarly, the candidate for political office or the ambitious businessman will work strenuously day after day, depriving himself of ordinary pleasure and driving himself without hesitation, in order to achieve success in business or in politics, which he expects to bring pleasures far more satisfying.

In like manner, the pleasures of rational activity in its broadest sense, intellectual, aesthetic, moral, and spiritual—what Aristotle calls the life of contemplation—certainly have had greater appeal to the gifted than any other type of pleasure. The scientist, the scholar, and the artist have been willing to deny themselves all the ordinary pleasures of the senses, and likewise those of ambition and the exercise of power, in order to attain the enduring satisfactions that accompany the healthful exercise of man's rational faculties.[15] It was Anatole France who remarked, by no means facetiously, that if Napoleon had been as intelligent as Spinoza, he would have written four books and lived in a garret. In the pleasures that accompany the satisfying exercise of his reason, man certainly can come very close to happiness, and Aristotle at times does identify the two:

> Now the activity of philosophical reflection or wisdom is admittedly the most pleasant of excellent activities; at all events it is held that philosophy or the pursuit of wisdom provides pleasures of marvelous purity and permanence, and it is reasonable to suppose that those who possess knowledge pass their time more pleasantly than those who seek it. If accordingly the attributes of this activity are found to be self-sufficiency, leisureliness, such freedom from fatigue as is possible for man, and all the other attributes of blessedness, it follows that it is the activity of reason that constitutes complete human happiness—provided it be allowed a complete span of life. If reason is something divine in comparison with the rest of human nature, so also is the life of reason in comparison with human life as a whole.[16]

Aristotle, then, is apparently willing to define happiness as the enjoyment of those pleasures that accompany the life of contemplation. He recognizes clearly the enduring appeal of a more practical exercise of reason, but cannot quite bring himself to admit its superiority. Thus in the *Politics* he writes:

Even those who agree in thinking that the life of excellence is the most desirable, raise a question whether the life of business and politics is or is not more desirable than one which is wholly independent of external goods, I mean than a contemplative life, which by some is maintained to be the only one worthy of a philosopher. For these two lives—the life of the philosopher and the life of the statesman—appear to have been preferred by those who have been most keen in the pursuit of excellence, both in our age and in other ages. Which is the better is a question of no small moment: for the wise man will necessarily regulate his life according to the best end.[17]

### The Values of Friendship

While Aristotle in theory does generally give precedence to the life of contemplation, it is the spirit of practical wisdom that actually pervades his ethical system as a whole. This undoubtedly constitutes his deeper insight into moral conduct. He is particularly eloquent, as a matter of fact, on the rewards of friendship. Friendship, he writes,

> . . . is indispensable to human life. No one would choose to live without friends, even though he possessed all other blessings. For what is the good of prosperity if there is no one with whom to share it? On the other hand, in poverty and other such adversities friends may serve as our refuge. In our youth they help us correct our faults; in old age they wait upon us and perform those necessary tasks for which weakness has incapacitated us, and in the prime of life they stir us to noble deeds: "going shoulder to shoulder," they inspire us to think and to act.[18]

Indeed, in friendship between men of character and ability Aristotle finds the highest type of human relationship. As he looked at love, at women, and at children from the point of view of his own day and age, friendship seemed to him more rewarding than marriage. Friendship may, of course, be based upon notions of utility or expediency, when we seek to gain some advantage for ourselves from the others. But friendship that is genuine, enduring, and rewarding in the best sense must for Aristotle be between men of virtue, who seek only to be of service to their friends.[19]

Is complete happiness possible without friends? Aristotle answers in the negative. "It is ridiculous to suppose that the happy and fortunate man is a recluse," he writes. "No one would choose to have every conceivable good thing on condition that he remain solitary, for man is a political creature, designed by nature to live with others. The happy man, then, since he will possess all naturally good things, must have friends."[20] Quite obviously Aristotle's recognition of the essential place of friendship in a happy life is in accord with that of the "youth culture" of our day. Here friendship that is genuine, and not self-seeking, is accepted as necessary for enduring happiness.

In such popular songs as "You've Got a Friend," "Lean on Me," and "Bridge over Troubled Waters," this feeling is given forthright and eloquent expression.

### Happiness as Self-Realization

In life at its best, then, the intelligent man will achieve a nice balance or harmony of his various interests and activities.* When Aristotle's philosophy is interpreted in this more comprehensive fashion, it clearly agrees with the high value given personal growth and development by the psychology of our day. The happy man is the man who develops to the full those capacities and potentialities that he has as a rational human being. He is the man who, to use Aristotle's earlier terminology, fulfills the inner purpose or ideal (the *entelechy*) by which his life is inspired and guided. If some more exact formulation is helpful, we may define happiness in Aristotelian terms as *the felt awareness of self-realization*. Happiness of this sort is qualitatively distinct from pleasure, just as pleasures of the higher kind are distinct from lower pleasures.

What one needs to do, therefore, is to understand the cause of happiness, and the effect will follow. In order to be happy, we must take advantage of those opportunities that will enable us to develop fully our capacities as human beings, and so to realize our *entelechy*. A college education, for example, is usually seen as one step along the way to full self-realization. So also is the shared enjoyment of art and music, and the opportunity to do work that is creative and socially beneficial. As a social animal man is likely also to find happiness only with congenial friends, and in helping to create a pleasant home and family, or perhaps in the shared life of a communal group.

### Ends and Means

If we are to achieve the happiness that accompanies self-realization, it is toward such goals as these that our lives must be directed. But how are these ends to be accomplished? Again Aristotle speaks with practical wisdom. It is impossible to live the good life without the means necessary to do so, he maintains. The material, the physical, and the economic aspects of life are as necessary a part of self-realization as are intellectual and spiritual achievement. In fact, the two cannot be separated:

Happiness plainly requires external goods, for it is impossible, or at least not easy, to act nobly without some furniture of fortune. There

---

* Certainly B. A. G. Fuller is correct when he writes that for Aristotle "reason, in the interests of its freest, most detached, and most scientific use, bids the human being in whom it is lodged to assert the unity of his composite organism and to make the most and best of all his functions." (*History of Greek Philosophy*, III, p. 255.)

are many things that can be done only through instruments, so to speak, such as friends and wealth and political influence, and there are some things whose absence takes the bloom off our happiness, as good birth, the blessing of children, personal beauty. Happiness, then, seems to stand in need of this kind of prosperity.[21]

The larger and more worthwhile our ends in life, the more ample, indeed, our means must be. The president of a great university, the editor of a great metropolitan newspaper, the ambassador of our nation to a great foreign power, all must have adequate resources available if they are to accomplish successfully the tasks they have undertaken. It is in this connection that Aristotle develops his well-known doctrine of virtue as the desirable mean between extremes. Since our needs vary with different circumstances and different purposes, no one right course of action for all people can be prescribed. What is right is just what is needed to accomplish our purposes in any specific situation, no more and no less.*

The Aristotelian doctrine of the mean is, however, a general rather than a specific guide in conduct. Its real value lies in identifying the desirable ethical attitude as "what is fitting." But it also requires intelligent decisions to fit each situation rather than blind obedience to social convention or tradition. It leaves room for continuous growth in insight; it provides the needed flexibility for different conditions and different individual needs. It forces one to deal with specific and concrete situations, not to be content with abstract principles or vague aspirations. In what is known today as "situation ethics," the importance of this aspect of Aristotle's philosophy has been recognized, and a general ethical theory based upon it.

Conduct that is right for one man in one set of circumstances may well be wrong for another in different circumstances. What is good is something quite specific and always relative to the particular person and situation. At this point we find Aristotle in accord with the underlying principle of all Greek moral philosophy: a man cannot be good unless he is intelligent. Before he can achieve moral excellence of any kind, he must know what he is doing, and how self-realization is being furthered thereby.

---

* "By the mean relative to us I understand that which is neither too much nor too little for us; and that is not the same for all," Aristotle writes. "For instance if ten be too large and two be too small, if we take six, we take the mean relative to the thing itself, or the arithmetical mean. But the mean relative to us cannot be found in this way. If ten pounds of food is too much for a given man to eat, and two pounds too little, it does not follow that the trainer will order him six pounds; for that also may perhaps be too much for the man in question, or too little; too little for Milo [a famous wrestler], too much for the beginner. And so we may say generally that a master in any art avoids what is too much and what is too little, and seeks for the mean and chooses it—not the absolute but the relative mean. So that people are wont to say of a good book, that nothing could be taken from it or added to it, implying that excellence is destroyed by excess or deficiency, but secured by observing the mean." (*Ethics*, II, 6.)

### The Magnanimous Man

There is then for Aristotle an essential relationship not only between self-realization and happiness; the relationship of goodness and happiness is equally important. "Each man has just so much of happiness as he has of virtue and wisdom, and of virtuous and wise action," Aristotle writes. "The happy man lives well and does well; for we have practically defined happiness as a sort of good life and good action."[22] The man whose life and conduct exhibits moral excellence Aristotle calls "magnanimous"—one who possesses greatness of spirit or high-mindedness. His oft-quoted description of the magnanimous or high-minded man provides a concrete, but at times unfortunately a somewhat disappointing, portrayal of Aristotle's idea of the man of high moral principle:

High-mindedness, as its very name suggests, means to be occupied with great things. A person is thought to be high-minded who regards himself as worthy of great things and who is worthy of them. The high-minded man will be the best of men, for the better a man is the more he deserves, and he that is best deserves most. Therefore the truly high-minded man must be a good man. . . .

The high-minded man does not run into danger for trifling reasons nor is he fond of encountering dangers, as there are few things he values enough to endanger himself for them. But he will face danger in a great cause, and in the hour of danger will be ready to sacrifice his life knowing that there are conditions under which life is not worth having. . . .

He will, of course, be open in his hatreds and his friendships, as secrecy is an indication of fear; and he will care more for the truth than for what people think. . . . He will not be a gossip; he will not talk much about himself or about anybody else, for he does not care to be praised himself or to get other people censured; he will not speak evil of others, even of his enemies, except when he deliberately intends to insult them. . . . He is the kind of person who would rather possess what is beautiful, although it does not bring in profit, than what is profitable only, as such a preference indicates his self-sufficiency.[23]

### Political Philosophy

Aristotle's political philosophy, like his ethics, is concrete, empirical, and practical. His concern is with the specific and the individual, not the abstract or the general. Plato in his *Republic* begins with the state and then seeks to fit the individual into a larger social framework. Aristotle, on the other hand, in general agreement with our American democratic point of view, maintains in his *Politics* that the purpose of the state is to make possible the good life for the individuals who compose it. "The good of man must be the aim of the science of politics," he writes. "He who would properly inquire about the best form of state ought first to determine what is the most acceptable life; while this remains uncertain the best form of the state must remain uncertain."[24]

Political philosophy, then, provides the larger social dimension of ethics, and the *Nicomachean Ethics* was designed by Aristotle as the introduction to his own later work on political philosophy. For him politics is "the master science." "To secure the good of one person is better than nothing, but to secure the good of a nation or state is a finer and more godlike achievement."[25] In order to accomplish this task successfully, the political philosopher must have a good understanding of human nature. He must not only know the conditions under which happiness is achieved but he must also know why men act as they do.*

A sound psychology reveals to us that human personality is a social product, that man is by nature "a political animal," Aristotle consistently maintains. The state thus is so essential a part of man's full social development that we can properly speak of the state as "a creature of nature, originating in the bare needs of life, and continuing in existence for the sake of a good life":

> The individual, when isolated, is not self-sufficing. He who is unable to live in society or who has no need to do so because he is so self-sufficient, must be either a beast or a god. A social instinct is implanted in all men by nature, and he who founded the state was the greatest of benefactors. For man, when perfected, is the best of animals, but, when separated from law and justice, he is the worst of all.[26]

### Reactions to Plato's Republic

It is easy to understand, of course, why Aristotle, with his concern for the happiness of the individual and his more empirical, practical approach to politics, did not find the specific proposals in Plato's *Republic* appealing. A communistic ownership of goods and property such as Plato advocates for his rulers seemed to Aristotle particularly undesirable. Such a scheme simply will not work, writes our practical philosopher. What belongs to everybody will be

---

* "Now if this is so, it clearly behooves the political philosopher to have some acquaintance with psychology," Aristotle writes, "just as the physician who is to heal the eye, or other parts of the body, must know anatomy. Indeed a foundation of science is even more requisite for the philosopher in as much as political philosophy is a higher and more honorable art than medicine. The student of political philosophy, therefore, as well as the psychologist, must study human nature." (*Ethics*, I, 13.)

cared for by nobody. "Everyone thinks chiefly of his own, hardly ever of the public interest; and then only when it concerns him as an individual."

Aristotle also observes, with some sarcasm, that Plato does not go far enough when in the *Laws* he proposes that the wealthiest citizens of the state can possess only five times the amount possessed by the poorest. In such a situation, Aristotle points out, "the legislator who fixes the amount of property should also fix the number of children; for if the children are too many for the property the law will be broken." As Plato's *Republic* plainly shows, once the regulation of life by the state is begun it cannot be stopped short of complete regimentation. Aristotle concludes: "Such legislation may have a specious appearance of benevolence; men readily listen to it, and are easily induced to believe that in some wonderful manner everybody will become everybody's friend, especially when someone is heard denouncing the evils now existing, which are said to arise from the possession of private property. These evils, however, arise from quite another source—the wickedness of human nature."[27]

### The Good Society

To find the form of government most likely to achieve the good life for its citizens, Aristotle examines carefully the relative merits of monarchy, aristocracy, and democracy. True to the spirit of his empirical approach, he does not accept any one form of government as best for all people in all circumstances. Monarchy and aristocracy have both good and bad features, he points out. The best form of government for an undeveloped people will not be the best for an abler group, more capable of self-government. This matter of good government must be dealt with in concrete, scientific fashion: "for the best is often unattainable, and therefore the true statesman ought to be acquainted not only (1) with that which is best in the abstract, but also (2) with that which is best relative to the circumstances."[28] It is this kind of practical insight that is essential for dealing intelligently with the problems of political philosophy, Aristotle points out. It is an insight, moreover, that we as Americans have frequently lacked in our insistence that our own democratic form of government was suited for all other people, no matter what their stages of political and social development.

Where conditions are such as to make it practical, a constitutional government based on law seems the most desirable alternative, in Aristotle's judgment. The rule of law provides the kind of mean between the extremes of tyranny on the one hand and anarchy on the other that naturally appeals to him. The rule of law, moreover, is preferable to that of any individual, for in good laws we have reason unaffected by desire: "He who bids the law rule may be deemed to bid God and reason alone to rule, but he who bids man rule adds an element of the beast; for desire is a wild beast, and passion perverts the minds of rulers, even when they are the best of men." Dictatorship, common in Aristotle's day and unhappily also in our own, is clearly the worst form of government. It does away entirely with the rule of law and rests upon the unchecked ambition and desires of one individual.*

### The Influence of Aristotle

The philosophy of Aristotle has had understandable and enduring appeal throughout the ages. Perhaps it is a bit too much to say, with one of his contemporary admirers, that it provides the most influential system of thought ever put together by any single mind. But every later age has drawn upon Aristotle's philosophy for insight and stimulus. His *Organon* shaped the thinking of the medieval world; and, if the *social order* of the Middle Ages was largely a reflection of the philosophy of Plato, the medieval *mind* was as clearly dominated by Aristotle. During that period his works came to be for European philosophy what the Bible was for theology—an almost infallible guide to the solution of every problem. As *The Canterbury Tales* of Chaucer describes the outlook of the theological student at Oxford University in the fourteenth century:

> . . . he would rather have at his bed's head
> Some twenty books, all bound in black and red,
> Of Aristotle and his philosophy
> Than rich robes, fiddle, or gay psaltery.

For another three hundred years, as a matter of fact, the *Ethics* and the *Politics* of Aristotle were the texts used at Oxford to fashion the outlook of the ruling British mind. Even in our own country not so long ago, Aristotle's philosophy provided the foundation for a vigorous movement of reform in higher education, in which Robert M. Hutchins and Mortimer Adler at the University of Chicago were the moving spirits.

In logic and science Aristotle has understandably not fared so well in recent years. The modern inductive and empirical approach in logic, for example, has tended to discredit Aristotle's formal and deductive approach. "Any person in the present day who wishes to learn logic will be wasting his time if he reads Aristotle," Bertrand Russell has written.[29] This statement is no doubt too extreme, but it reflects quite clearly the recent reaction against Aristotelian logic. Of Aristotle's work in the physical sciences, Russell has no

---

* "Tyranny is just that arbitrary power of an individual which is responsible to no one, and governs all alike, whether equals or betters, with a view to its own advantage, not that of its subjects, and therefore against their will. No freeman, if he can escape from it, will endure such a government." (*Politics,* IV: 10, 8.)

higher opinion. "Every significant intellectual advance has had to begin with an attack on some doctrine of Aristotle," he maintains.

For our present study Aristotle has much to offer, however. His interpretation of happiness as the state of mind that accompanies self-realization contributes significantly to a better understanding of the enjoyment of life. While aware of the error in hedonism, he nevertheless clarifies that aspect of the pursuit of pleasure which has given to hedonism its persistent attraction in every age. Likewise, long before John Dewey's recognition of the fact, Aristotle pointed out that growth and development are essentials of the good life—that only as one is moving ahead, achieving more fully what he is capable of, can he hope to find happiness and enduring satisfaction. And, without sacrificing its essential insights, Aristotle was able to free Plato's rational idealism from the dangers of asceticism and mysticism that too frequently rendered the Platonism of later ages unacceptable.

In concluding our discussion of Aristotle, we must ask whether he does justice to the moral and spiritual resources upon which human life at its best has so often relied. Bertrand Russell, one is rather surprised to find, has criticized Aristotle at this point in quite specific fashion: "There is an emotional poverty in the *Ethics* which is not found in the earlier philosophers," Russell writes, ". . . all the more profound aspects of the moral life are apparently unknown to [Aristotle]. He leaves out, one may say, the whole sphere of human experience with which religion is concerned."[30]

Upon the base of Aristotle's able, empirical analysis of human nature and conduct, it is certainly possible, however, to develop a more adequate concept of self-realization than his picture of the "magnanimous man" provides. If his naturalism can be strengthened at its weaker points, there is good reason to see in it a philosophy of living that is not only concrete and practical, but quite appealing as well. The testimony of the past suggests as much, and the rise of the "new naturalism" provides contemporary confirmation.

## CHAPTER 9

# Naturalism and Humanism

*John Dewey*

During the more than twenty centuries between Aristotle's day and our own, naturalism has had many able advocates, and the new naturalism of today indicates its continued appeal. Modern exponents of naturalism, however, frequently have been accused of picturing the forces at work in nature as in direct conflict with, or at least as completely without concern for, man's highest ideals and values. For example, in the decades following the publication of Darwin's *On the Origin of Species* (1859), Thomas Henry Huxley, one of Darwin's ablest disciples, saw as inescapable a conflict between nature "red in tooth and claw" and a human society based upon good will, cooperation, and mutual understanding. Bertrand Russell's widely read essay, "A Free Man's Worship," already mentioned in Chapter 4, gave classic statement to the view that the forces of nature inevitably doom man's highest values to destruction in the debris of a universe in ruins. More recently W. T. Stace, in his essay "Man Against Darkness" (1948), forcefully restated Russell's point of view.

More directly than any other philosopher in this century, John Dewey sought to refute this image of man and nature in fundamental conflict. In the spirit of Aristotle he undertook to bridge the gap between naturalism and humanism, and to restore an awareness of the bond that makes man one with nature, turning as Aristotle did to the biological sciences as the foundation for an empirical naturalism. Human nature can only be understood, Dewey insists, when man is seen as an integral part of the larger universe of nature: "Man's home is in nature; his purposes and aims are dependent upon natural conditions." Separated from these conditions man's aims become empty dreams or idle fancies.

By background and early experience, as well as by temperament and training, Dewey was unusually well fitted to express the empirical and scientific spirit of twentieth-century America. Circumstances left nothing undone to prepare him as an able spokesman of the deep-seated American belief in democracy and progress. In his philosophy we find what is certainly the most influential American effort to base logic, morals, and education directly upon human experience and scientific method. As Aristotle was the spokesman of classical Greek naturalism, so Dewey became the spokesman of the naturalistic philosophy of our century. As Aristotle came to naturalism after a period of commitment to the idealism of Plato, so Dewey reached naturalism after an initial commitment to Hegelian idealism. And this early philosophical outlook significantly influenced the mature positions of both men.

### Formative Influences on Dewey's Thought

John Dewey was born in Burlington, Vermont, on October 20, 1859, the third son of a local grocer, whose literary tastes far exceeded his formal education. None of the Dewey family had a college education until John and an older brother attended the University of Vermont, which was near at hand and charged little tuition. Although the Dewey family was never in financial need, its resources were always quite limited, and the boys shared as a matter of course in the household responsibilities as well as in simple agricultural activities.

On the other hand, John Dewey and his friends were bored with their school work. What they were given to read was of little interest or use to them as far as they could see. Their only pleasure came when an occasional teacher encouraged discussion of topics outside the prescribed school curriculum. Such boyhood experiences played a large part in forming Dewey's later educational theories. He never forgot that the most important parts of his own early education were obtained outside the classroom, and his caustic comments on the stupidity of the ordinary school recitation reflect in no small manner the memory of the dull hours he spent in school as a youth in Burlington.

Dewey's early contacts with nature were also such as to enhance the appeal of a life that was natural and spontaneous. Set on a hill rising from Lake Champlain, Burlington possessed an unusual natural beauty. Across the lake to the west were the Adirondacks; on the horizon to the east were the Green Mountains. John and his brother tramped through the Adirondacks. They also outfitted their rowboats with a tent, blankets, and cooking utensils, and explored Lake Champlain from one end to the other. Later they took longer trips up the St. Lawrence and into the beautiful lakes of French Canada, where they found use for the French they had picked up at home.

### University Education and Early Philosophy

When John Dewey entered the University of Vermont in 1875 it was a small institution. His graduating class four years later had only eighteen members. The students were well acquainted with each other and with the entire faculty of eight professors. Little in the way of class distinction or prejudice existed. The year of Dewey's birth (1859) was also the year in which Darwin's *On the Origin of Species* was published. Dewey early became familiar with the theory of evolution as taught in his courses in geology and zoology at the University, and discussions of this new theory interested Dewey more than did his regular courses in philosophy.

However, encouraged by his professor of philosophy at Vermont, Dewey decided to undertake graduate work in this field. In the fall of 1882 he entered Johns Hopkins University in Baltimore, and two years later he received his doctorate. The intellectual atmosphere of the new university was stimulating, and the years at Johns Hopkins proved to be both pleasant and rewarding. During these years Dewey came into contact with many of the men who took a leading role in American education for the next three or four decades.

When Dewey entered Johns Hopkins he had no very clear philosophical convictions. When he left two years later he was a confirmed Hegelian. This was due in large measure to the persuasive presentation of Hegelian idealism by Professor George Sylvester Morris, at that time professor of philosophy at Johns Hopkins and later Dewey's colleague at Michigan. As Dewey himself later described this experience: "it was impossible that a young and impressionable student, unacquainted with any system of thought that satisfied his head and heart, should not have been deeply affected to the point of at least temporary conversion by the enthusiastic and scholarly devotion of Mr. Morris."[1] Looking back upon the experience from this later perspective, Dewey felt that Hegel's philosophy also offered him at the time a welcome intellectual escape from the unhappy dualisms that were a part of his New England cultural heritage—the separation of body and soul, nature and God, the self and the world.

Upon leaving Johns Hopkins in 1884 Dewey accepted a position on the faculty at the University of Michigan. These were the years during which President James B. Angell was making Michigan one of the great universities of the Midwest. In addition to emphasizing creative scholarship, Angell fostered a genuinely democratic spirit among both students and faculty and encouraged the freedom and individual initiative that are essential for meaningful educational achievement. Dewey's early unconscious faith in democracy gradually became a strong conviction that underlay much of his later thought.

Perhaps the most important influence on Dewey during his early years at Ann Arbor came, however, from another source. During his first winter there he lived in a boardinghouse in which two co-eds also had rooms. That his interests were not all academic is indicated by the fact that one of them became Dewey's wife two years later. A native of Michigan, Alice Chipman had grown up in a home in which memories of pioneer days and the spirit of adventure were still strong. She had courage, energy, intellectual integrity, and a clear mind, which cut through sham and pretense to the heart of a problem.

Her influence on the young philosopher from the conservative East was stimulating and far-reaching. Having developed a critical attitude toward accepted social attitudes and injustices, she helped turn Dewey's concern from historical and theoretical philosophy to the issues of contemporary life. She also had a deeply religious spirit but did not accept the doctrines of any specific church. Her husband gradually came to share her belief that the religious attitude is a natural aspect of human life which theological doctrine and ecclesiastical institutions more frequently weaken than promote. In view of his own experience, it is not difficult to understand why Dewey became an early and enthusiastic advocate of coeducation.

### Dewey at Chicago

In 1894 Dewey was offered the chairmanship of the Department of Philosophy and Psychology at the recently established University of Chicago. In his work at Michigan he had gradually come to see that existing educational practice, especially in the elementary schools, was not in harmony with what psychologists knew about normal development and learning. Even then he was turning over in his mind the idea of starting an experimental school in which the best psychological principles of learning could be put into practice. One of the things that led him to accept the position at Chicago was the inclusion of pedogogy in the department of philosophy and psychology. Within a few years he got together a group of parents interested in an educational experiment that very much appealed to him. With their financial aid he started a Laboratory School at the university. For many years, this school, which was popularly known as the "Dewey School," supplied a powerful impetus to the critical examination and improvement of educational philosophy and practice.

Some of Dewey's most widely popularized work was done in connection with this Laboratory School at Chicago. The year it was founded he published an article, "Interest and Effort," which was perhaps his first distinctive contribution to educational psychology. Education, Dewey here maintains, must grow out of self-directed interests of students, interests that develop naturally and inspire their own effort. Interest and effort are not two different things, he argues, but are simply different aspects of the same ongoing activity. This was revolutionary in 1896. In some quarters it still is today.

The following year Dewey published a small monograph, *My Pedagogic Creed*, which was even more unorthodox and disturbing. Here he stated for the first time his fundamental thesis that education "is a process of living and not a preparation for future living." The school, therefore, must represent real life, allowing the child to learn by his own guided experience. "There is no succession of studies in the ideal school curriculum," Dewey writes. "If education is life, all life has, from the outset, a scientific aspect, an aspect of art and culture, and an aspect of communication. It cannot, therefore, be true that the proper studies of one grade are mere reading and writing, and that at a later grade, literature or science may be introduced. The progress is not in the succession of studies, but in the development of new attitudes towards, and new interests in, experience."² It is the social life of the child that supplies the curriculum, not history, or geography, science or literature, Dewey maintains.

At the University of Chicago Dewey gradually gathered together a group of able and distinguished men in psychology and philosophy. In 1903 this group published a volume of essays entitled *Studies in Logical Theory*, which they dedicated to William James, at that time the most influential philosopher in America. James hailed the volume as marking the birth of a Chicago school of logic in general accord with his own pragmatic philosophy. The rewarding personal friendship between Dewey and James that began then lasted until James' death in 1910. Dewey had been much influenced by James's *Principles of Psychology* when it came out in 1890. When James's major work *Pragmatism* appeared in 1907, Dewey published a long and quite sympathetic review of the book, indicating his own general acceptance of James's position as well as some important differences between his philosophy and that of James.

### Social Philosophy

In 1905 Dewey joined the faculty of Columbia University. For more than forty-five years he was connected with that institution, first as professor of philosophy, then as head of the department, and finally as professor emeritus. His years at Columbia were remarkably productive, both in scholarship and in active support of causes that promised to promote a better social life. In this new environment his own social philosophy also gradually matured. During his early years, Dewey shared the common faith of his contemporaries that American democracy in its normal evolution would in time do away with serious economic injustice as well as with political inequality. Residence in New York hastened a change in his outlook that had already begun before he left Chicago. He found it impossible to keep alive, in that eastern center of American financial interests, his earlier Midwestern faith in the manifest destiny of democracy. Active effort was necessary to make political and social democracy a reality, Dewey now realized, and he gave himself unhesitatingly to those causes that held most promise in this regard.

His long support of the women's suffrage movement was based on the belief that the enfranchisement of women is a necessary part of political democracy. For a number of years he was chairman of the League for Independent Political Action, which seemed to offer an opportunity for bringing intelligence more actively into politics. He interested himself in the democratic administration of schools and universities and helped organize the

Teachers Guild, which, as part of the American Federation of Teachers, is now affiliated with the American Federation of Labor. He was active also in founding the American Association of University Professors, and was its first president.

Social philosophy, Dewey came to believe, is not a separate area of philosophy but rather the goal and culmination of all philosophical thought. His philosophy as a whole became social in intent and direction. It is the function of philosophy, he writes, "to free men's minds from bias and prejudice and to enlarge their perceptions of the world about them." Philosophy should clarify men's "ideas as to the social and moral strifes of their own day," and should "become so far as is humanly possible an organ for dealing with these conflicts."[3] With this in mind Dewey consistently works out the social and political implications of his philosophy in every area.*

Trips to the Orient and to Russia also played an important part in the development of Dewey's social philosophy. In 1919 he was invited to lecture at the Imperial University at Tokyo and had an opportunity there to become acquainted with the more liberal elements of Japanese life and culture. His Tokyo lectures, entitled *Reconstruction in Philosophy* (1920), provide one of the clearest general statements of his own philosophy.

In 1928 Dewey spent a short time in Russia. His contacts there were also in the main with educators, and his visit to Russia was too short for any investigation of economic or political conditions. But he did meet a large number of Russian men and women, both students and teachers, who were enthusiastically engaged in building a new and better world for themselves and their countrymen. Although there was much political propaganda in the schools in Russia, Dewey also found at that time an impressive cooperative endeavor among the Communist leaders to promote the common good of all people. The sympathy he expressed for the Russian experiment led him to be branded as a "red" by the conservative press in America when he returned home.

An increasing regimentation of the schools under the Stalin regime, however, and their use as tools by the politicians, in time disillusioned Dewey. Gradually he became convinced that by their very natures violent revolution and dictatorship are incapable of establishing a desirable social order, no matter what set of leaders is in power. A careful study of the revolutionary movement in Russia completely confirmed his own early belief "in the inti-

---

* In *Democracy and Education* (1916), Dewey develops the larger significance of his philosophy of education. In *Human Nature and Conduct* (1922), one of the classics in this field, he outlines the principles of social psychology upon which his discussion of all social issues is based. In *The Public and Its Problems* (1927) he develops in concrete fashion the political implications of his philosophy. *Characters and Events* (1929), composed largely of articles written for the *New Republic*, provides direct application of Dewey's philosophy to vital and concrete issues of that day.

mate and indissoluble connection of means used and ends reached." He now became as unalterably opposed to revolutionary Bolshevism as to Fascism, and was called a reactionary by the left-wing press.*

### Other Interests

Throughout his long life Dewey was deeply interested in problems of morals and in the principles by which human conduct should be directed. In *Reconstruction in Philosophy* (1920), *Human Nature and Conduct* (1922), and *The Quest for Certainty* (1929), his empirical approach to morals is developed and its implications worked out in detail. The need in morals, Dewey came to believe, as in the natural sciences, is to clarify particular situations and problems, not to formulate moral commandments. Hence an empirical and inductive logic is as essential in the field of ethics as it is in every other branch of philosophy.

By far the most practical and widely read of Dewey's studies in logic was *How We Think* (1910), a volume that established problem-solving as the only "respectable" method of educational thinking. For more than forty years he continued to publish works in this field. Finally, in *Logic: The Theory of Inquiry* (1938), when almost eighty years old, Dewey drew together the whole of his penetrating analysis of logical theory in what is certainly one of the more significant works of his long career. Before he died in 1952 at the age of ninety-three, he had gained an influence and prestige throughout the world accorded to no other American philosopher.

### The Influence of Darwin on Philosophy

Dewey's mature approach to philosophy is, like that of Aristotle, essentially biological and naturalistic in spirit. But his naturalism is shaped by Darwin's theory of evolution, which led him to a fundamental revision of Aristotle's point of view. The appearance of *On the Origin of Species* in 1859, the year Dewey was born, marked a revolution in the intellectual outlook of the modern world. Within a decade almost everyone was talking about evolution. During the next half-century men looked more and more to the biological sciences rather than to physics or mathematics for an understanding of nature, and a vigorous reaction set in against rationalism and determinism in the realm of philosophy. The universe portrayed by Darwin was no impersonal, rational order like that of Spinoza and the mathematicians, moving eternally in accord with principles that never change. It was a universe in which life, struggle, and development were the characteristic features.

* The conclusions reached by Dewey as a result of this investigation appeared in two books, *Not Guilty* and *Freedom and Culture*. His own strong condemnation of Communism is to be found in his *Liberalism and Social Action*.

Evolution meant growth, progress, achievement. The urge of progress appealed to men with new force, and to this rather than to the life of reason they turned with increasing enthusiasm.

What particularly distinguishes Dewey among philosophers of his age is the undisguised completeness with which he adopts the evolutionary hypothesis. His starting point in every field is Darwinian, and with unusual insight he undertakes the reconstruction in philosophy he believed to be necessary as a result of Darwin's theory of evolution. Both Herbert Spencer and Nietzsche, it is true, each in a different fashion attempted this same task. But in the far-reaching implications of Darwin's theory Dewey saw, far more clearly than either Spencer or Nietzsche, constructive suggestions for educational and social philosophy as well as for logical theory. He developed these implications over a full life of remarkable achievement with a thoroughness and insight that even Spencer's renowned volumes on the philosophy of evolution cannot rival.

The significant impact of Darwinian evolution upon Dewey's thought is quite apparent in the volume of essays published in 1910, soon after he came to Columbia University, entitled *The Influence of Darwin on Philosophy*. These essays make it clear that the empirical temper of Dewey's philosophy as well as his naturalistic outlook are direct outgrowths of the Darwinian revolution in the field of science. He wrote:

> That the publication of the *Origin of Species* marked an epoch in the development of the natural sciences is well known to the layman. That the combination of the very words origin and species embodied an intellectual revolt and introduced a new intellectual temper is easily overlooked by the expert. In laying hands upon the sacred ark of absolute permanence, in treating the forms that had been regarded as types of fixity and perfection as originating and passing away, the *Origin of Species* introduced a mode of thinking that in the end was bound to transform the logic of knowledge, and hence the treatment of morals, politics, and religion. No wonder, then, that the publication of Darwin's book, a half century ago, precipitated a crisis.[4]

These implications of Darwin's position were concealed for a time by the religious controversy that the theory of evolution aroused. In Dewey's opinion, however, the battle between science and religion over the Biblical account of Creation had relatively little significance for philosophy. But the Darwinian principle of natural selection revolutionized the philosophy of science generally accepted in that day. Prior to Darwin, philosophical knowledge was taken to involve an understanding of a purpose that lay behind and beyond the processes of nature. This was variously portrayed as the Christian idea of God, the Absolute of Hegel, or the *entelechy* of Aristotle. The Darwinian principle of natural selection, however, cut straight into the heart of this essentially Aristotelian philosophy. There was no longer need for an intelligent design or purpose outside the world of nature to account for change and development. The principle of natural selection was all the explanation needed.

When considered in this Darwinian fashion, the evolutionary process reveals no transcendent design or purpose that points beyond Nature, Dewey maintains. It is true that all the goods of life arrive, so to speak, as natural results of evolution, but so also do all the evils of life and all the various grades of good and evil. It is our own human preferences that lead us to select the good and to fight for it, not some transcendent design. There is for Dewey only a natural process at work in this whole evolutionary development. Indeed, the outlook of his own naturalistic philosophy is already clearly apparent here:

> It is putting the cart before the horse to say that because Nature is so constituted as to produce all types of value, therefore Nature is actuated by regard for values. Nature, till it produces a being who strives and who thinks in order that he may strive more effectively, does not know whether it cares more for justice or for cruelty, more for the ravenous wolf-like competition of the struggle for existence, or for the improvements incidentally introduced through that struggle. Literally it has no mind of its own.[5]

Man, as a conscious organism, in time becomes aware of what Nature and evolution provide, both good and bad. He begins to prefer the good and to battle for his preferences, picking out what is favorable to his aims and what is hostile. "Then and there Nature has at last achieved significant regard for good," Dewey writes. "Not, then, when Nature produces health or efficiency or complexity does Nature exhibit regard for value, but only when it produces a living organism that has settled preferences and endeavors. When Nature produces an intelligence—ah, then, indeed Nature has achieved something. Not, however, because this intelligence impartially pictures the nature which has produced it, but because in human consciousness Nature becomes genuinely partial."[6]

### The Mission of Philosophy

The nature and task of philosophy then must be restated, Dewey feels, in the light of this radical change in our point of view. While in past centuries philosophy often sought only to discover some absolute truth far removed from human need and experience, this was not its original spirit and purpose. "Wherever philosophy has been taken seriously, it has always been assumed that it signified achieving a wisdom which would influence the conduct of life." Almost all ancient schools of philosophy, the Epicurean and the Cyrenaic, the Stoic and the Cynic, also taught organized ways of living.

_[margin handwriting: Nature has created intelligence]_

Those who accepted their doctrines were committed to certain distinctive modes of conduct. This suggests a more adequate concept of the task of philosophy, Dewey points out: "Philosophy is thinking what the known demands of us—what responsive attitude it enacts. It is an idea of what is possible, not a record of accomplished fact. Hence it presents an assignment of something to be done—something to be tried. Its value lies not in furnishing solutions but in defining difficulties and suggesting methods of dealing with them."[7]

When we let the facts of human life just stare us in the face, we find a multitude of goods about us, but also, unfortunately, a multitude of evils—and pretty much all grades of both. It is the task of philosophy to deal with the social and moral ills from which humanity suffers, to concentrate its attention upon the causes and the exact nature of these evils, and to develop a clear and practical concept of the better society that we are now able to achieve for all men and women. When rightly understood, "its aim is to become as far as is humanly possible an organ for dealing with these conflicts." Its outcome should be a contribution to man's attainment of "a more ordered and intelligent happiness."[8]

## Education as a Way of Living

Dewey's philosophy of education holds a central place in his thought as a whole. It is this aspect of his philosophy with which he was initially concerned at Chicago and which was generally known and most widely influential. It provides needed insight into the meaning of his naturalism as a whole. Perhaps it is not too much to say that until a person understands his philosophy of education he does not understand Dewey—and that when he does understand this he has the key to the rest.

In Dewey's opinion, wherever any philosophy is alive and vital, it is always connected with some concrete program of social living. When a philosophy makes no difference in the way men live, it can be dismissed as merely verbal or artificial, at best only a sentimental indulgence for a limited few. Thus it is easy to see the necessity of intimate connection between philosophy and education. For it is through the process of education that a person's social ideals and practices are developed. It is here, Dewey feels, that we meet philosophical problems "where they arise and thrive, where they are at home, and where acceptance or rejection makes a difference in practice. Education is the laboratory in which philosophic distinctions become concrete and are tested."[9]

"Although a book called *Democracy and Education* was for many years that in which my philosophy, such as it is, was most fully expounded, I do not know that philosophic critics, as distinct from teachers, have ever had recourse to it," Dewey noted in 1930. "I have wondered whether such facts signified that philosophers in general, although they are themselves usually teachers, have not taken education with sufficient seriousness for it to occur to them that any rational person could actually think it possible that philosophizing should focus about education as the supreme human interest in which, moreover, other problems, cosmological, moral, logical, come to a head. At all events this handle is offered to any subsequent critic who may wish to lay hold of it."[10]

### The Social Function of Education

When he published *Democracy and Education* in 1916, Dewey was primarily concerned with the social function of education. His analysis here of the nature of education is one of the classic statements of educational philosophy. Civilization can exist only insofar as the beliefs, the ideals, the hopes, and the practices of one generation are passed on to the next, he points out. Every individual, whether in a modern city or in a savage tribe, is born immature, helpless, without language, beliefs, or social standards. In our highly complex civilization the gap between the achievements of the well read or scientifically trained and those of an uneducated person is tremendous.

"Beings who are born not only unaware of, but quite indifferent to the aims and habits of the social group have to be rendered cognizant of them and actively interested," Dewey points out.[11] Education, in its broadest sense, is the means by which this is accomplished. Hence education cannot be seen as a luxury for a privileged few. It is a matter of social necessity.

Understood in this sense, most education is, of course, informal and thoroughly natural. It is the very process of living together that educates. Among primitive peoples, children naturally and inevitably learn the customs of the adults, and at the same time acquire their emotional reactions and stock of ideas, *by sharing in what the elders are doing.* But as civilization becomes more complex, it is no longer possible for a child to be educated only by his parents and companions. In the development of Western culture teaching was gradually delegated, therefore, to a special group of persons, and schools and courses of study became necessary. Formal education of this kind is essential, of course. But there is likewise a very real danger that this change may undermine the effectiveness and vitality of the educational process. Learning in school easily loses the personal and vital quality of informal education. The material of formal education is isolated from the immediate concerns of life. It is stored up in books and easily becomes of interest only to the schools. Students do not see any use for most of what they learn. "Thus we reach the ordinary notion of education, the notion which ignores its social necessity, and which identifies it with imparting information about remote matters and the conveying of learning through verbal signs: the acquisition of literacy."[12]

## The Influence of Environment

Even after education has become largely a matter of "going to school," however, much of our learning still takes place outside the classroom and in a quite natural fashion. It is impossible for a normal human being to live without taking into account at every turn the activities, the expectations, the approval, and the condemnation of others. We have to get along with our family. We want the social approval of our contemporaries—our gang or our peer group. We do what they do, and we think as they think, without being aware that we are doing so or why we are doing so. Man's social environment, then, becomes as important and as natural a factor in the intellectual growth of the human individual as is the physical environment in the growth of the biological organism at an earlier stage. And, as we see clearly here, we learn most effectively from what we see other people do and what we ourselves are called upon to do.

Our social environment shapes our lives, then, by engaging us in activities that arouse and strengthen certain impulses and, at the same time, inhibit others. A child growing up in a white middle-class suburb naturally and inevitably develops an entirely different outlook on life and pattern of values from that of a child who grows up in a black ghetto. Each one does different things; believes in different principles; has different desires. "We rarely recognize the extent to which our conscious estimates of what is worthwhile and what is not, are due to standards of which we are not conscious at all," Dewey writes. "But in general it may be said that the things which we take for granted without inquiry or reflection are just the things which determine our conscious thinking and decide our conclusions. And these habitudes which lie below the level of reflection are just those which have been formed in the constant give and take of relationships with others."[13]

The only way, then, in which the kind of education that children get can be controlled is by controlling the environment in which they act, and hence think and feel. It is impossible to educate children directly by urging them to believe certain assertions or to act in certain ways that we think they should. They can only be educated indirectly, by means of the social environment in which they are placed. This, unfortunately, is an insight that parents have difficulty in recognizing and even greater difficulty in putting into practice.

It is the responsibility of the school, however, to create the kind of environment in which desirable growth and development will take place, Dewey feels. This can be done only by enabling an individual to participate in the common activities of the group that will in quite natural fashion inculcate the skills, insights, and attitudes desired. We learn by doing, and by doing with others what appeals to us as worthwhile, Dewey repeatedly insists. Such a theory of learning, of course, necessitated very radical changes in the whole traditional system of education. These changes Dewey set out resolutely to accomplish. The "Progressive Education" movement, which looked to him as its founder and which significantly modified public schools throughout America, was one of the influential results of Dewey's ideas and efforts.

## Education as Growth

As Dewey examines human life from his evolutionary point of view, he agrees with Aristotle that the most important characteristic of man is his capacity for *growth*. To be alive, a thing must grow in some way. Otherwise it soon ceases to live. Life is essentially development and growth, and, conversely, to develop and grow is to live. From this viewpoint, then, the central concern of education must be with growth—the growth of a human individual who has the natural capacity to develop. And its major aim should be to provide the conditions under which native endowments and capacities will develop naturally and fully.

Such a concept of education not only involves a drastic revision of our accepted educational procedures; it also gives us a sound basis for determining when teaching is successful and when it is a failure. The task of education is not to provide students with an abundance of information, as some teachers have seemed to believe. The possession of knowledge is never an end in itself. It is valuable only as a means to greater growth in intelligent behavior. Formal education, to be successful, must become a way of living that stimulates and inspires learning by active participation in group activity as naturally as does informal education, Dewey insists. Only in this way will growth of the right sort—growth that involves the full development of all the natural capacities of the individual—take place.

The fallacy of the old concept of education as essentially a period of preparation, of getting ready for something that still lies in the future, is at once apparent. This traditional point of view has had a most undesirable effect upon education, in Dewey's opinion. Youth lives in the present, he points out, not in the future. To be constantly told to get ready for something in which one is not particularly interested destroys the motivational power of learning. It places a premium on procrastination. The future is a long way off. Plenty of time will intervene before it comes. Why be in a hurry to get ready for it? There are so many more interesting things to be done now. These are the natural reactions of students to an educational program that undertakes to prepare them for life in the future rather than to offer them a stimulating way of living in the present.

It is this reaction that has led to the creation of our vicious system of artificial rewards and punishments in formal education, Dewey points out. When a pupil can see no value in what he is told to do, his mentors try to stimulate effort by rewarding him with a good "grade" if he does it well. There is small wonder that students soon become more interested in grades than in education. When diplomas and degrees take the place of the satisfactions that should come from genuine intellectual and social achievement, education loses its natural appeal and vitality. It is not surprising that students in college and university rebel against the meaninglessness of the conventional grading system—and not only when they get poor grades. Such grades, they insist, provide no satisfactory measure of the value to them of their work in a particular field.

### The Nature of Intelligence

Dewey's emphasis upon growth as the end and aim of education does not mean, however, that he was less concerned than were the traditional schools with the cultivation of intelligence. Actually this emphasis leads him to a greater concern with this important aspect of education, he maintains, because he understands better what it involves. Being intelligent has little to do, as a rule, with possessing a vast amount of information, or even with getting good grades or advanced degrees.

Dewey's interpretation of the nature of mind and intelligence is a direct outcome of his philosophy of evolution. Man's mind was produced by nature as the biological organism sought to adjust itself better to its environment. "Mind is not a name for something complete in itself; it is a name for a course of action in so far as that is intelligently directed; in so far, that is to say, as aims, ends, enter into it, with selection of means to further the attainment of ends," Dewey writes.[14]

When seen in this functional fashion intelligence simply means the capacity to deal successfully with the concrete situations that we face in living. It means the ability to make intelligent choices, to think and to act intelligently. It is a practical thing—which one learns from experience and not from books except quite indirectly. The major responsibility of a school or college is to develop this capacity in its students, Dewey insists. When it fails to do this, it fails to educate them, no matter how much information they may acquire.

There are then for Dewey no subjects that are inherently "intellectual," none that possess any magical power to train the mind. The worth of any subject depends upon its relevance in a particular situation to the needs and abilities of the particular students, as well as upon the way in which it is taught. Students cannot be given a liberal education merely by making them take a prescribed course of studies, no matter what these studies may include. Liberal studies are studies that liberate the minds of those studying them. "Accordingly, any subject, from Greek to cooking, and from drawing to mathematics, is intellectual, if intellectual at all, not in its fixed inner structure," Dewey concludes, "but in its function—in its power to start and direct significant inquiry and reflection. What geometry does for one, the manipulation of laboratory apparatus, the mastery of musical composition, or the conduct of a business affair, does for another."[15]

Because they do not understand the nature of intelligence, the traditional schools, in Dewey's judgment, too frequently turn out students who are trained to accept ideas imposed upon them by others rather than students capable of thinking for themselves when faced with perplexing individual or social problems. There is a widespread feeling among the younger generation today that our schools and colleges have become channels of propaganda. They are seen as agencies being used by the Establishment to indoctrinate students with ideas and beliefs that serve to perpetuate the status quo, not as institutions designed to develop intelligence or stimulate freedom of thought. This feeling, of course, provides a measure of confirmation for Dewey's criticism.

## Intelligence and Morals

As he began to consider seriously the pressing moral problems of his day, and to examine critically what had been taught about ethics, Dewey could find no moral philosophy that he felt an intelligent man could accept. None seemed to him in keeping with the scientific, democratic, and technological forces at work in contemporary life. So he set himself the task of developing a clear and consistent moral philosophy in keeping with the evolutionary and democratic point of view by which his own thought was shaped. And he began by examining with some care moral theories of the past.

### The Necessity of Intelligence

The early Greek philosophers saw clearly that man's chief business is pursuit of the good, and that intelligence is an essential factor in this quest. It was Socrates who brought philosophy down to earth and taught that morals and philosophy are one and the same thing, "namely a love of that wisdom which is the source of secure and social good," Dewey points out. And in Plato's *Republic* philosophy achieved some sense of its social basis and mission, for Plato recognized that the organization of a just social order is the chief business of the philosopher. But in Dewey's opinion this was about as far as philosophy progressed for many centuries. It soon got lost in dreams of another world.

After Aristotle, the essential function of intelligence in morals was completely lost sight of for almost twenty-five hundred years, Dewey feels. The task of philosophy was taken to be the discovery of an ultimate moral good or an eternal moral law. Hedonists, for example, from Epicurus and Aristippus to John Stuart Mill and Lin Yutang, insisted that pleasure was the supreme good, and a life of pleasure man's natural and right aim in life. Rationalists, from the Stoics to Spinoza and Walter Lippmann, urged upon men a devotion to the life of reason as the only path to the good life. The authoritarians in morals held that loyalty or obedience to a higher power, whether the will of God, laws of the state, or the dictates of conscience, was the one acceptable principle of moral conduct.

On the surface these moral theories seem to differ rather sharply from one another. Actually they all agree, Dewey points out, in assuming that there is one single, fixed, and final good. They disagree only in their idea of what it is. It is just at this point that Dewey, as a naturalist and an empiricist, challenges the whole traditional approach to morals. The only way out of the moral conflict and confusion of our day, he feels, lies in rejecting this idea that traditional moral theories have had in common, that there is one fixed and final moral good.

What we actually find in experience is a large number of changing, individual goods and aims in the moral life. For some men in some situations health is the most important thing in life; for others honesty or temperance is essential in meeting successfully the temptations of modern life. For the university student the development of his mental capacities may well be the primary concern. "We cannot seek or attain health, wealth, learning, justice or kindness in general. Action is always specific, concrete, individualized, unique," Dewey insists. "To say that a man seeks health or justice is only to say that he seeks to live healthily or justly. These things, like truth, are adverbial. They are modifiers of action in special cases. How to live healthily or justly is a matter which differs with every person. It varies with his past experience, his opportunities, his temperamental weaknesses and abilities. Not man in general but a particular man suffering from some particular disability aims to live healthily, and consequently health cannot mean for him exactly what it means for any other mortal."[16]

"If we still wish to make our peace with the past," Dewey writes, "and to sum up the plural and changing goods of life in a single term, happiness is certainly the most apt. But we should again exchange free morals for sterile metaphysics, if we imagine that 'happiness' is any less unique than the individuals who experience it."[17]

To assert bluntly that every moral situation is unique and different from every other situation may seem not merely blunt but preposterous, Dewey admits. Let us, however, follow the pragmatic rule and, in order to discover the meaning of an idea, ask for its consequences. Then, surprisingly enough, it turns out that what we have done is to transfer the weight and burden of morality to intelligence. A man cannot do what is right unless he is intelligent—unless he examines the particular situation and acts in such fashion as to meet its requirements, Dewey points out in agreement with Socrates. Should a doctor tell his patient that he is about to die, when the truth will almost certainly seriously upset him? Should a college student devote his time largely to study or give his major attention to social or political activities? The right action in such cases is not self-evident. There are conflicting desires and different apparent goods for each individual. What is needed is to find the right course of action and the best results in each particular situation.

This means, of course, that we cannot do what is right simply by following approved social conventions or traditional moral standards: "Morals are not a catalogue of acts nor a set of rules to be applied like drugstore prescriptions or cook-book recipes. The need in morals is for specific methods of inquiry and of contrivance: methods of inquiry to locate difficulties and evils; methods of contrivance to form plans to be used as working hypotheses in dealing with them."[18]

### Growth and Morals

"The absurdity of applying the same standard of moral judgment to savage people that is used with civilized groups will be apparent," Dewey writes. "No individual or group will be judged by whether they come up to or fall short of some fixed result, but by the direction in which they are moving. The bad man is the man who no matter how good he *has* been is beginning to deteriorate, to grow less good. The good man is the man who no matter how morally unworthy he *has* been is moving to become better. Such a conception makes one severe in judging himself and humane in judging others."[19]

The process of growth, of improvement and progress—rather than the static outcome and result of what we do—is then the significant thing in morals. The "good" man is not one who lives according to certain specific moral standards, no matter how desirable these may be. A person becomes good by constantly improving himself—in whatever ways he most needs to improve. It is to this end that he must use his intelligence and direct his conduct. "Growth itself is the only moral 'end,'" Dewey writes.[20] An empirical account of morals thus makes it clear that the process of education and the moral process are one and the same. For the moralist, as for the educator, growth is the aim and the end of life. There is no way in which education can escape a concern with morals. This, indeed, is its major concern. In an empirical moral philosophy the relation between goodness and happiness also becomes clear. Goodness without happiness would be intolerable in Dewey's opinion: "Happiness is found only in success, but success means succeeding, getting forward. It is an active process, not a passive outcome."[21] The man who is growing, who is accomplishing what he wants to do in worthwhile activity, is not only a good man. He is also the only man who is really happy, Dewey concludes, in general agreement with Aristotle.

### The Moral Meaning of Democracy

Dewey is never willing to define growth in any specific or final fashion. Growth necessarily means something different to each person in terms of his own capacities and needs as well as in terms of the particular situation in which he happens to be. It means one thing to the young and vigorous, something else to those who are mature and more experienced. For those who are fortunate and comfortable, growth involves achievements quite different from what is feasible for those who must live in the slums or the ghetto.

When he is discussing democracy, however, Dewey does give us an appealing description of what growth means to him. Actually he is one of the relatively few great philosophers who has championed democracy with enthusiasm. Democracy is the best form of government, he believes, not because it is the most efficient. Dictatorships are too frequently more efficient, as we have learned to our sorrow. In a democracy we often make mistakes. We fail to act promptly and decisively when we should. We frequently elect the wrong men to public office, and we tolerate both stupidity and graft on the part of our public officials. [But by democracy alone can we provide for all men and women the freedom and opportunity for the kind of growth that is essential to the good life.]

Democracy means much more to Dewey than a special form of government. Democracy is a way of life, both social and individual. And the opportunity that the democratic way of life offers to every mature human being to take part in determining the conditions under which he must live is, for Dewey, its most significant feature.* For it is this opportunity that makes possible the growth of all men and women in a democracy as in no other form of government. The foundation of democracy is, then, faith in human intelligence, faith in the capacity of men to grow, faith in their ability to meet the demands that are made upon them if they have the opportunity to do so, Dewey points out. And here lies its greatest source of strength, in the opinion of our philosopher.

> Government, business, art, religion, all social institutions, have a meaning, a purpose. That purpose is to set free and to develop the capacities of human individuals without respect to race, sex, class or economic status. And this is all one with saying that the test of their value is the extent to which they educate every individual into the full stature of his possibilities. Democracy has many meanings but if it has a moral meaning, it is found in resolving that the supreme test of all political institutions and industrial arrangements should be the contribution they make to the all-around growth of every member of society.[22]

### Naturalism and Humanism

Dewey's philosophy as a whole is thoroughly naturalistic: man is a product of the natural forces at work in the process of evolution. Human intelligence developed in this evolutionary process as naturally as did man's arms or

---

* This point is given particular emphasis by J. Ratner in *Intelligence in the Modern World: John Dewey's Philosophy*, p. 400.

his hands, and for precisely the same reason. It provided the biological organism with improved means of meeting its needs, of getting done what primitive man wanted to do. The higher values of human life were realized in essentially the same fashion. This evolutionary approach leads Dewey to insist, therefore, that the usual opposition between humanism and naturalism is a false one. "In truth, experience knows no division between human concerns and a purely mechanical physical world," he writes. "Man's home is in nature; his purposes and aims are dependent for execution upon natural conditions. Separated from such conditions they become empty dreams and idle indulgences of fancy. This philosophy is vouched for by the doctrine of biological development which shows that man is continuous with nature, not an alien entering her processes from without."[23]

A humanistic philosophy is one committed to achieving what is best in human life and best for human welfare, Dewey feels. It is marked by a greater sensitiveness to social well-being and greater use of human intelligence to promote that well-being. Darwin's concept of evolution, when properly understood, makes clear the fallacy of the old antitheses between man and nature, between human values and their natural setting, between reason and experience, between science and morals. True humanism, then, must be a naturalistic humanism, a view of man and of human values that emphasizes the close relationship of both to their source in nature.

The new humanism must be scientific as well as naturalistic in spirit. Human progress and well-being have become more and more dependent upon scientific knowledge and control of the forces of nature. Every step forward in the social sciences, every advance in furthering the public good intelligently, illustrates the direct dependence of our important social concerns, and of the human values that lie behind them, upon the methods and results of the natural sciences. "When the consciousness of science is fully impregnated with the consciousness of human value, the greatest dualism which now weighs humanity down, the split between the material, the mechanical, the scientific and the moral and ideal will be destroyed."[24] And the vexatious and wasteful conflict between naturalism and humanism will then be terminated, Dewey hopefully concludes.


## The American Scene since Dewey

The impact of Dewey's philosophy, not only in America but throughout the world as well, has already been noted. His books on education—translated into a dozen or more languages of foreign countries—were widely read and used. School systems in all these countries at one time or another have undergone, to some extent at least, a reform of traditional practices along lines suggested by Dewey. In America the Progressive Education movement became one of the powerful forces in reshaping our secondary education.

Dewey's work in logic and ethics, although not so obviously successful in shaping contemporary thinking, also had large influence.

Rarely has one man during his own lifetime seen his ideas become so influential. To celebrate Dewey's seventieth birthday in 1929, the American Philosophical Association met at Columbia University and devoted its program to papers eulogizing Dewey and his philosophy. To celebrate his eightieth birthday in 1939, the Association again met at Columbia University. The papers read on this occasion, however, while speaking in the highest terms of Dewey the man, almost all took occasion to point to limitations in his philosophy. On the occasion of his ninetieth birthday in 1949, no such celebration was planned. By this time John Dewey had outlived his own position as an influential spokesman of contemporary thought, and few younger philosophers accepted his point of view without reservation.

To understand this situation we should perhaps look briefly at what has happened to philosophy in America since the 1920s. Four major trends are apparent, and each raised a fundamental question about Dewey's position. First, in the field of logic, the movement known as "logical positivism," or, at times, "logical empiricism," became increasingly influential in the United States during the 1930s. This movement originated in Europe with a group known as the "Vienna Circle," and in 1936, Rudolf Carnap, a member of the Vienna Circle, was appointed professor of philosophy at the University of Chicago. He soon became the recognized spokesman for this movement in America. While superficially akin to Dewey's empirical philosophy in its emphasis upon science and experience, logical positivism flatly rejected any philosophical significance in man's concern with moral and spiritual values. Thus it raised serious question about the foundation upon which the moral dimension in Dewey's naturalism was based.

Second, the point of view of the logical positivists was given increased influence in this country by the somewhat later movement known as "linguistic analysis" or "analytic philosophy." This had developed marked strength at Cambridge University in England, and the key figure in the movement, Ludwig Wittgenstein, came from the Continent to Cambridge in 1929. From the analytic point of view, philosophy's major function is to describe and clarify. When the nature and meaning of the language used in our value judgments is made clear, the philosopher's task is complete. He cannot legitimately undertake the kind of reconstruction of experience and of moral values with which Dewey was concerned. With the building of a sound philosophy of life, a pattern of values by which human life is made more fruitful and satisfying—with this task the philosopher as such is not concerned, according to the linguistic and analytical school.*

* An excellent and sympathetic presentation of this point of view is found in Morton White's *The Age of Analysis*—a Mentor paperback (New York: New American Library, 1955).

A growing acceptance of existentialism in certain philosophical and religious circles provided the third significant trend in American thought in the post-Deweyan period. Existentialism also was European in origin. It became a major philosophical movement in France and Germany with the moral and social disintegration that accompanied the rise of the Nazis to power. Paul Tillich and Reinhold Niebuhr, both of German extraction, were the most influential spokesmen for religious existentialism in America a decade or two later. Dewey's optimistic faith in the ability of human intelligence to cope successfully with man's moral and spiritual problems as well as with the complexities of social life seemed both shallow and unrealistic to these existentialist thinkers. Their major concern was with man's "tragic sense of life" and with the existential commitment needed to give human life meaning and direction. These were aspects of experience, however, about which Dewey's philosophy provided no helpful insight.

A fourth major development in American thought was the reappearance of speculative metaphysics, stimulated by the philosophy of Alfred North Whitehead. Whitehead came to Harvard from England in 1924 at the age of sixty-three, and until his death in 1947 exerted a strong if limited influence upon philosophy in this country. His students have been America's ablest metaphysicians. With as thorough a commitment to modern science as that of Dewey, they have been critical of Dewey's failure to develop even the limited metaphysical implications of his own philosophical naturalism.*

These four developments, each in its own area of concern, raise questions about Dewey's philosophy that need to be faced in any serious consideration of its adequacy and validity. There has also been an interesting change in educational philosophy since Dewey. With the gradual winding down of the war in Vietnam, accompanied by a major reduction in the space program, thousands of well-trained scientists and engineers in the early 1970s suddenly found themselves without jobs and with no further demand for their skills. This clearly indicated the necessity of rethinking the scientifically motivated educational philosophy developed after the initial success of the Russians in orbiting the earth.

Such a rethinking soon got under way. It was made inescapable by the dissatisfaction of thousands of college and university students with the kind of academic experience being provided for them. This dissatisfaction was expressed not merely in mild protests and demonstrations, but in the occupation and even destruction of university buildings and the actual shutting down of several institutions. The tragedies at Kent State, Jackson State, and Southern University in Baton Rouge, which resulted from clashes between students and the police and National Guard, were perhaps the most publicized of

---

* *Science and the Modern World* (1925), *Process and Reality* (1929), and *Adventures in Ideas* (1933) provide the clearest expression of Whitehead's philosophical point of view.

such student demonstrations. In addition to a reaction against the Vietnamese war, it is quite clear that educational principles emphasized earlier by Dewey were also significantly involved in these demonstrations.

Basic student demands—"non-negotiable demands," as student leaders sometimes naïvely insisted—almost always called for reforms of the sort proposed by Dewey: (1) More relevance in academic programs was demanded— that is, the introduction of courses more clearly related to student experience or more honest in dealing with racial tensions and minority cultures. (2) More opportunity to participate in the decision-making process was insisted upon—that is, a more genuinely democratic educational experience. (3) A new approach to morals was apparent—symbolized by more freedom from social restrictions and by such changes as co-ed dormitories and open visiting hours for both men and women. In all these demands students were clearly seeking to shape their educational experiences along lines that Dewey emphasized as essential for meaningful intellectual and moral growth.

The new naturalism of today involves a life style that provides a great increase in freedom also for the individual from yesterday's rigid mores. This finds expression in various ways—in much more general acceptance of casual dress, in a more open relation between the sexes, in the open advocacy of use of marijuana together with a hard look at alcohol and other traditional narcotics. A situation has been created which, if it is to become a constructive aspect of American life, obviously demands the kind of mature intelligence in moral and social experience that Dewey so strongly advocated.

## CHAPTER 10

# Historical Materialism

*Karl Marx*

There are few professional philosophers whose thought has had such wide influence, and certainly no nineteenth-century writer who numbers so many men and women in our age among his professed followers, as Karl Marx. In his later years, it is true, Marx thought of himself primarily as a social scientist rather than a philosopher. His major concern was with an objective analysis of capitalistic society, designed to reveal its ends and inevitable destruction. And *Das Kapital*, his greatest single work is, today one of the classics in this field.

It has become increasingly apparent, however, that a purely economic approach to the thought of Marx is much too limited. With the success of the Russian revolution in 1917, and the gradual rise of a powerful Communist state under Lenin's leadership, the Marxist political philosophy became, if anything, more important than his economic theories. This trend received added confirmation, of course, with the recognition of the People's Republic of China as one of the three or four most powerful nations of the world.

For our purposes, the fact that Marxian communism is one of the influential philosophies that men live by today—indeed, it may well be the most influential—is especially significant. Its widespread influence is immediately apparent, of course, as one thinks of the vast population of China as well as of Russia and its statellites, all under Communist domination. The appeal of Communism to the peoples of India and southeast Asia as well as of Africa and Latin America is equally impressive. Nor should the intense and uncompromising commitment of the avowed Communist to the Marxist beliefs he professes be overlooked.

Under these circumstances it is disturbing to realize that in our own country until quite recently the philosophy of Marx "has not been taken seriously enough to be seriously studied," as a thoughtful critic of Marxism points out. We can certainly agree also that "it is no longer sufficient for Americans to be against a doctrine which they have not taken the trouble to study or understand."[1] Our discussion here is designed at least in part to meet this criticism.

## The Development of Marx's Thought

Marx is, of course, a controversial figure. Not only his ideas but even his life and character easily lend themselves to quite contradictory interpretations. To those who consider themselves his disciples he appears a far different person than to those who see him as the evil genius of his day as well as of our own. It is quite impossible to portray either Marx the man or the major aspects of his philosophy in a fashion acceptable to both of these widely divergent groups. One can only attempt to be as objective and factual as circumstances permit, avoiding any conscious or deliberate misrepresentation for polemical purposes.

Karl Marx was born on May 15, 1818, in the old Rhineland city of Trèves (modern Trier) where his father, Heinrich Marx, was a respected and moderately successful lawyer. Both of Marx's parents were Jews, and a grandfather as well as a great-grandfather had been prominent rabbis in the Rhineland. His father, however, gradually separated himself from the Jewish community and the synagogue. He changed his surname from Levi to Marx, and built a growing legal practice among his German associates. Quite early, also, he realized that in Karl he had not only an unusually bright but also a difficult and stubborn son. The boy soon exhibited a voracious, almost ungovernable, intellectual curiosity, and, unfortunately, often antagonized people whom his father felt to be important to his own success as well as that of his son.

### Education and Early Influences

At the age of seventeen Marx enrolled as a student in the faculty of law at the University of Bonn. There for one year he seems to have lived the gay and carefree life of the typical German university student of that period. He joined one of the university societies, wrote romantic poems, got into debt, fought a duel, and was arrested at least once for riotous behavior. This was not the kind of life, however, that appealed at all to his more serious father, who was paying for his education. After a year at Bonn, his father insisted that Karl transfer to the University of Berlin, then the intellectual and cultural center of Germany.

Among the influences upon Marx's intellectual development, none was more critical than his years at the University of Berlin. Berlin was a large, ugly, and modern city. It was the center of the Prussian bureaucracy but also the meeting place of the radical and discontented intellectuals who were seeking to destroy the government's power and influence. Marx here confronted urgent social and intellectual issues quite different from those he had encountered in the small provincial town where he grew up.

The dominant intellectual influence in all the major German universities at that time was the Hegelian philosophy, and the University of Berlin was its most important center. Hegel himself taught here as professor of philosophy during the most influential years of his life, from 1818 until his death in 1831, and in all areas the intellectual outlook of the university was shaped by his ideas and point of view. Repelled at first by Hegelian idealism, Marx found himself unable to discover an acceptable alternative. He therefore undertook an exhaustive study of Hegel, reading night and day in his customary intense fashion, until he had covered all the available material. At the end of three weeks he was a complete and enthusiastic convert.


### The Young Hegelians

Marx now joined an association of free-thinking intellectuals at the University who met regularly in Berlin beer cellars to argue endlessly the fine points of Hegelian philosophy. He soon became on intimate terms with the half-dozen young men who in later years were leaders of the left or more radical wing of Hegelian thought. During this period Marx also completed work for his doctorate in philosophy at the University of Jena with a conventional thesis on Democritus and Epicurus, treating them as forerunners of Hegel. He might well have gone ahead to become a scholarly university professor of philosophy, a position he then was seeking, but for two sudden changes in his fortune.

Marx's father, upon whom he was still financially dependent, died at about this time, leaving barely enough money to support his widow and younger children. And the Prussian Ministry of Education, alarmed at the radical ideas of the young Hegelian intellectuals, decided to refuse university appointments to any members of that group. With the possibility of a university career closed, and no other means of support, Marx was happy to accept an offer from Moses Hess, a liberal Jewish publisher in Cologne. He moved to Cologne to assist Hess in editing the *Rheinische Zeitung*, a recently established and outspoken democratic journal in that city.

The impression that Marx made upon Hess, an enthusiastic Hegelian and something of a radical himself, is quite revealing. In a letter to a friend, Hess said of Marx: "He is the greatest, perhaps the one genuine philosopher now alive and will soon draw the eyes of all Germany. Dr. Marx is still very young (about twenty-five at most) and will give medieval religion and politics their *coup de grace*. He combines the deepest philosophical seriousness with the most biting wit. Imagine Rousseau, Voltaire, Holbach, Lessing, Heine, and Hegel fused into one person—I say fused, not thrown in a heap—and you have Dr. Marx."[2]

At about this time Marx read with great interest an article on Hegel by Ludwig Feuerbach that led him to modify fundamentally his early Hegelianism. Hegel had placed great emphasis upon the *Zeitgeist*, the spirit of an age or culture. In this unique *spirit of the age* Hegel saw the determining influence that shaped the Greek genius, the Roman character, the age of the Renaissance, and accounted for their particular characteristics. Feuerbach, who was a materialist, maintained in his *Theses on the Hegelian Philosophy* that the motivating force in history was not a vague rational spirit or idea of the sort Hegel accepted. It was simply the sum of the concrete material conditions at any one period. These material conditions determined the way men thought and acted as well as the way they lived, and so accounted for the differences in each age. Human history is then actually the history of the way in which his material environment produces changes in man's life and thought, Feuerbach argued.

As he read Feuerbach, Marx was writing editorials in the *Rheinische Zeitung* on the poverty and exploitation of the vine-growing peasants in the Moselle valley. In these editorials he viciously attacked the landlords, who preserved their wealth and power by harsh laws that severely punished any effort of the peasants to ameliorate their own poverty. It was Feuerbach rather than Hegel, Marx now came to feel, who was in touch with the realities of man's social life.

## The Years in Paris

A series of Marx's editorials, fiercely condemning the Russian government as the chief obstacle to European liberty, happened to be seen by the Russian Emperor at about this time. The Emperor's angry reaction led the Prussian government, which was anxious not to offend him, to suppress the *Rheinische Zeitung* without warning in April 1843. In this same month Marx married Jenny von Westphalen, the attractive daughter of a distinguished neighbor who had befriended him as a boy in Trier. Now without means of support in Germany, and no longer in sympathy with his old Hegelian associates in Berlin, Marx with his wife decided to emigrate to France.

The two years he spent in Paris, 1843–1845, are among the most decisive of Marx's life in shaping his thought and future activity. In the mid-nineteenth century Paris was the major center of social, political, and artistic activity in the Western world. Poets and painters, radicals and reformers, intellectuals of all varieties, were drawn there and found an acceptance and a freedom not elsewhere available. The enthusiasm and the hopes of political radicals and revolutionary writers were at their height; the intellectual atmosphere was exciting and stimulating. Although this had not been Marx's primary reason for coming to Paris, he was soon caught up in the life and spirit of the city.

He became well acquainted with a group of radical intellectuals who supported the theories of Saint-Simon, and he found their ideas most appealing. A landed nobleman ruined by the French revolution, the Comte de Saint-Simon (1760–1825) not only shifted his allegiance to the new bourgeoisie but also sought to account adequately for its rise to power. Economic forces, he came to believe, are the determining factor in history. And he interpreted historical development as essentially the result of a conflict between economic classes—between those who possess the major economic resources at any given period in history and those who lack such resources.

Marx also developed a close association with several revolutionary groups of German workers who were much influenced by communist agitators. Now for the first time he came to see the proletariat as an economic class with concrete needs and hopes of the sort suggested but not developed by Saint-Simon. Gradually he worked out the philosophy to whose development and application he devoted the rest of his life. In it he significantly modified his early Hegelianism with new insights, gained from Feuerbach and Saint-Simon in particular as well as from his own wide reading and experience in Paris.*

### Marx and Engels

Friedrich Engels (1820–1895) was an able young German intellectual whose father was a wealthy cotton manufacturer in the Rhineland. Engels had submitted some critical articles on the English economists to a journal Marx was editing, and he came to Paris to talk with Marx about these articles. This meeting had a profound and lasting influence upon both men. It was the beginning of a remarkable friendship and professional collaboration that lasted the rest of their lives.

Engels was only twenty-four when he came to see Marx. Tall, fair, and rather elegant, he had a marked taste for such bourgeois pleasures in life as fencing and riding to the hounds, as well as for the best wines—pleasures his father's wealth easily enabled him to satisfy. As a young man he also had some interest in and quite a gift for poetry. But his father, a devout Calvinist as well as a successful manufacturer, had no sympathy for poets and sent his son off to Bremen to learn the export business. At the docks in Bremen, however, young Engels took more interest in the plight of the workers than in

---

* These influences upon Marx are carefully examined and documented by Isaiah Berlin in *Karl Marx—His Life and Environment*, Chapters Five and Six. Marx's philosophy, he writes, "is a wide and comprehensive doctrine which derives its structure and basic concepts from Hegel and the young Hegelians, its dynamic principles from Saint-Simon, its belief in the primacy of matter from Feuerbach, and its view of the proletariat from the French communist tradition. Nevertheless it is wholly original; the combination of elements does not in this case lead to syncretism but forms a bold, clean, coherent system. . ." (p. 157.)

his father's business. He began to read radical literature and at the age of twenty-two was converted by Moses Hess to communism. Later he went to Manchester in England to enter his father's textile business in that city. But before long he was busy exploring the city slums that were hidden behind Manchester's prosperous façade. There he found a stunted population, living in filth and finding in gin and evangelism their only escape from poverty and hopelessness.

Engels now turned from radical poetry to journalism. Exploring the slums of Manchester until he knew every hovel as well as the ills of its inmates, he published a powerful indictment of English industrialism, entitled *The Condition of the Working Class in England in 1844*. He wrote clearly and easily, with unusually shrewd insight and a talent for recognizing the practical aspect of ideas and theories. Soon he began a new series of essays designed to show that the well-known English economists of the day were really apologists for the existing capitalistic society. These were the essays he came to discuss with Marx in Paris. Marx at once felt that here was the one man among the communists who really understood the economic issues and forces at work in modern society. Engels found in Marx a powerful personality of great intellectual ability whose insights and theories he accepted almost without question.

Engels had, in fact, arrived at a point of view much like that being developed by Marx. He had no particular philosophical ability, however, and was immediately attracted by what he felt to be Marx's genius, insight, and originality. For the rest of his life he was happy to provide for Marx a rich supply of concrete information about conditions in the English industrial communities, and to give an easier and more lucid expression to the economic and political theories that Marx too often expressed in clumsy and obscure fashion.

For forty years he and Marx collaborated in almost everything that Marx undertook. For many difficult years in London, Engels also provided almost the only financial support that kept Marx and his family alive during periods of desperate poverty. When Marx died in 1883, Engels became the guardian and interpreter of the orthodox Marxist economic philosophy.

### Marx's Early Philosophy

During the years in Paris, and shortly thereafter, Marx did some significant philosophical and political writing. Until fairly recently his well-known later works, *The Manifesto of the Communist Party* (later, and now universally, known as *The Communist Manifesto*) and *Das Kapital*, have been taken as the clearest expression of Marx's revolutionary philosophy. Within the last twenty-five years, however, there has been a revival of interest in his earlier thought. A somewhat different interpretation of Marx's later economic and political philosophy is now being supported, as a matter of fact, in the light of this earlier point of view. It has turned out that the most significant writings of Marx during this period are four brief essays written in 1844. These were not published in a full and accurate version until 1932, however, and were not available in English until 1959. Translated as Marx's *Economic and Philosophical Manuscripts,* these essays are now reshaping the current interpretation of his philosophy.*

Marx had by now clearly formulated his own revolutionary philosophy. He was a committed communist, convinced that armed revolt of the proletariat was necessary to establish communism and that the workers must be organized and prepared specifically to play their part in the coming revolution. With this end in mind he set out to create an international revolutionary organization of workers. The most encouraging response came from a group of German workers in London who had formed a federation called the Communist League. Under Marx's guidance the League grew rapidly. Now for the first time he was in the kind of position he desired, the organizer and leader of an active and growing revolutionary movement.

In 1847 the Communist League asked Marx to write a definitive statement of the beliefs and aims to which it was committed. This provided him with just the opportunity he needed to state in clear and explicit fashion his own social philosophy. Early the following year he sent to London the brochure that was published under the title *The Manifesto of the Communist Party.* This *Manifesto,* the joint work of Marx and Engels, is generally ranked among the most influential revolutionary documents in existence.

The year 1848, when the *Manifesto* was published, was one of revolutionary fervor in Europe. Indeed, it looked for a time as if the old order might be abolished. In the ominous but accurate words of the *Communist Manifesto*: "A spectre is haunting Europe—the spectre of communism." Marx meanwhile had gone to Cologne to help incite the German masses to revolt, and published there a series of highly inflammatory articles in the *Neue Rheinische Zeitung,* which he helped to establish.

Gradually, however, the revolutionary enthusiasm began to fade, first in Paris and then in Germany, and the conservative forces slowly regained power. Expelled by the Prussian government, Marx left the Rhineland and returned to Paris. Although not quite thirty-two at the time, he was generally recognized as an influential and dangerous revolutionary leader, and the new government soon ordered him to leave.

---

* Erich Fromm, the well-known psychologist, has been perhaps the most active scholar in America to reinterpret the Marxist social philosophy in terms of this earlier point of view. Particularly significant among the books by Erich Fromm are *Marx's Concept of Man* (1961) and *Beyond the Chains of Illusion* (1963). Fromm has also edited *Socialist Humanism,* the papers read at a symposium on Marxist philosophy (1965). Two books by Robert C. Tucker of Princeton, which place particular emphasis upon this early thought of Marx, should also be mentioned: *Philosophy and Myth in Karl Marx* (1961) and *The Marxian Revolutionary Idea* (1969).

*Exile in London*

In only one country in Europe could Marx now expect to be allowed to live and write. In August 1849, one month after his return to Paris, friends provided funds that enabled him to leave for London. His family joined him there shortly thereafter.

When Marx arrived in London, he expected to stay a few months at most. He was there the rest of his life. The next ten years were mostly spent at work in the reading rooms of the British Museum; his contacts were confined in the main to his family, to Engels, and to a small circle of close friends. Marx now lived in desperate poverty, hardly knowing from day to day where he would find food or shelter for himself and his family. Three of his children, two sons and a daughter, died during these years largely as a result of the conditions the family faced. They moved from one dilapidated dwelling to another, unable to pay the rent, buy food for themselves or medicine needed for the sick children. On one occasion they were forcibly evicted, their possessions confiscated to pay their bills, and were left cold and shivering in the street without even beds to sleep on.

Interestingly enough, by 1860 Marx—at forty-two—was already thought of as an old man. He was seen as a leading agitator—now exiled and destitute —of a former generation, with his influence confined to a narrow circle of German radicals and exiles in London. This situation was changed significantly, however, with the rise of a new and militant party of socialist workers in Germany. As German Social Democracy grew, the party turned to Marx for economic and political ideas. He was consulted on all questions of theory and accepted as the unquestioned authority on socialist philosophy. Once again he attained a position of importance in Europe and was rescued from the relative inconspicuousness and poverty that characterized his first fifteen years in London. His influence was further increased when the International Workingmen's Association was established in 1864 by groups of French and English workers. For many years Marx dominated the general council of the International (as it came to be called). Here he demanded undeviating adherence to his policies, and systematically crushed all opposition by any means that were necesssry.

During these years Marx's major thought and effort, however, was given to writing *Das Kapital*, the work that was to establish his reputation securely. This three-volume work is certainly his single greatest achievement. The first volume appeared in 1867, and was an event of great significance not only for Marx himself but also for the progress of international socialism. Its fame and influence grew slowly at first, but gradually *Das Kapital* acquired a symbolic significance for Communists quite like that of the scriptures of the world's great religions. For Marx himself *Das Kapital* created a new reputation as an outstanding scholar and intellectual.

*Last Years and Death*

Despite his greatly improved circumstances, Marx's health now began to decline rapidly. Overwork and a life of poverty had undermined his strength. He became more and more preoccupied with his own health, and gave less and less time to work on the later volumes of *Das Kapital*.* His family and Engels were his only close associates.

In 1881 his wife Jenny died of cancer after a long and painful illness. This left Marx broken in health and disconsolate. He lived for two more years, but his strength was virtually exhausted. On March 14, 1883, he died peacefully while asleep in the armchair of his study. Three days later he was buried in Highgate Cemetery beside his wife. Only members of his family and a few friends attended the funeral. Engels's moving address on the occasion aptly described Marx's achievement as seen by his closest friend:

> Just as Darwin discovered the law of development of organic nature, so Marx discovered the law of the development of human history: the simple fact that man must first of all eat, drink, have shelter and clothing, before he can pursue politics, science, art, religion, etc.; that therefore the production of the immediate means of subsistence, and consequently the degree of economic development of a given epoch, form the foundation on which state institutions, legal conceptions, art and even religious ideas have evolved and in the light of which they must, therefore, be explained.
>
> Marx was before all else a revolutionist. His real mission in life was to contribute, in one way or another, to the overthrow of capitalistic society, and to the liberation of the proletariat, which he was the first to make conscious of its own position and needs. Fighting was his element. And he fought with a passion, a tenacity and a success few could rival.
>
> His name will endure through the ages, and so also will his work.[3]

## The Communist Manifesto

The cooperative work of Marx and Engels, *The Manifesto of the Communist Party*, is without question the most significant of all socialist pamphlets. A document of great dramatic force, when written in 1848 it provided for Marx an opportunity to express in brief compass the central features of his revolutionary philosophy. "As an instrument of destructive propaganda, it

---

* These he never completed. The second and third volumes of *Das Kapital* were edited and published by Engels after Marx's death. They required much editorial work and are greatly inferior in insight and analysis to the first volume. A fourth volume was later edited by K. Kautsky from posthumous material.

has no equal anywhere; its effect upon succeeding generations is unparalleled outside religious history; had its author written nothing else, it would have insured his lasting fame." This is the judgment of Isaiah Berlin, one of the ablest of Marx's biographers.*

As Engels stated in his funeral tribute, "Marx was before all else a revolutionist." He began his adult life as a revolutionist against the political establishment of his day. He wrote and fought as a revolutionist. He was exiled from one country after another because of his revolutionary activities. His reputation as a revolutionist has become almost legendary throughout the world today—in capitalist as well as socialist nations. An accurate portrayal of Marxist social philosophy must then make clear its revolutionary character, recognizing this as the central aspect of Marx's thought. For such an interpretation The *Communist Manifesto* provides an excellent basis. Here Marx's revolutionary thesis is more directly and explicitly expressed than in any other single work. Here we have a revolutionary document, designed not primarily to inform but rather to incite the proletariat to armed revolt. Here, also, the central feature in Marx's theory of social revolution, an inescapable class conflict, is presented in dramatic and emotional fashion.

"The history of all hitherto existing society is the history of class struggles," Marx writes in beginning his *Manifesto*.† In all such struggles the oppressor and the oppressed, whether master and slave, lord and serf, or patrician and plebeian, have placed themselves in opposition to each other and have carried on an uninterrupted conflict, hidden or open, that has led time after time to the revolutionary reconstitution of society at large.

### The Bourgeoisie‡

The present age is interpreted by Marx as the age of the bourgeoisie, the commercial and banking class in the cities. It is an age in which modern capitalists, the owners of the means of industrial production and the employers of wage-labor, have gained economic power and control of the democratic state as well. In the *Manifesto* Marx describes in some detail the long course

---

* *Karl Marx—His Life and Environment*, p. 169. In his preface to an authorized English translation of the *Manifesto* in January 1888, forty years after its first publication, Engels states that the fundamental ideas expressed here came from Marx and contain his social philosophy. Engels also mentions the fact that during these intervening forty years the *Manifesto* had been translated into all the major European languages: into French in 1848; into English first in 1850 in London, and then in New York in 1872; into Russian about 1863; then a new Danish translation in 1885; a new French translation in 1886 from which a Spanish translation was also made in the same year; and a Polish translation that appeared earlier.

† All quotations are from the authorized 1888 English translation of the *Manifesto*.

‡ Originally the tradesmen in the towns, the middle class, as contrasted with the feudal nobility on the one hand and the serfs on the other (from the French *bourg*, fortified town).

of economic development, and with it the series of revolutions in modes of production, that in time created modern capitalism and gave it almost unlimited power. Each step in the economic advance of the bourgeoisie was accompanied by a corresponding increase in its political influence and power. With the establishment of the modern industrial system and the world market, the bourgeoisie gained exclusive political power and complete control of the so-called democratic state. "The executive of the modern state is but a committee for managing the common affairs of the whole bourgeoisie," Marx declared in one of his provocative phrases.

The central evil of bourgeois society and capitalism, as Marx describes it in the *Manifesto*, is the exclusive concern with the making of money that displaced and corrupted all other values. Capitalism, he states, put an end to the "idyllic relations" of feudal society. It left only man's naked self-interest to replace "the most heavenly ecstasies of religious fervor, of chivalrous enthusiasm, of Philistine sentimentalism. . . . In one word, for exploitation veiled by religious and political illusion, it has substituted naked, shameless, direct, brutal exploitation."

In a capitalistic society, every occupation hitherto honored and revered has been stripped of its former values. Personal values have been replaced by property values. The physician, the lawyer, the priest, the poet, even the man of science, has been converted into a paid wage-laborer who measures success in terms of the money he makes. The family also has lost its sentimental meaning and become largely a mere money relationship. Such at least is Marx's description in 1848 of the bourgeois or middle-class society created by capitalism.

This analysis of the rise of the bourgeoisie to power reveals several points that are central in Marxist philosophy. There is, as described in the *Manifesto*, a historical process at work in which the economic forces in each age— more specifically, the modes of production and exchange—bring to positions of power and influence those classes that control and profit most from these economic conditions. An inescapable conflict exists between the ruling and privileged class in each age and the classes that are oppressed and exploited. But the nature of this historical process is such, Marx believes, that the economic forces that establish a privileged class will in time also inevitably produce its downfall.

The mercantile economy, for example, which produced the bourgeoisie, was generated in feudal society. At a certain stage in its development the feudal economy, based upon agriculture and the feudal property relations that went with it (the serfs and the lords of the manor), become no longer compatible with the developing modes of production and distribution in mercantilism: "They became so many fetters. They had to burst asunder; they were burst asunder," Marx points out. Gradually free competition took the place of the feudal economy. And with free competition there emerged in the towns and cities a new social and political order of tradesmen and bankers compatible with the new economy. Thus, in Marx's judgment, the economic and political domination of the bourgeois class was actually created by the changed modes of production.

"A similar movement is going on before our own eyes," he wrote in 1848. "Modern bourgeois society, a society that has conjured up such gigantic means of production and of exchange, is like a sorcerer who is no longer able to control the powers of the nether world which he has called up by his spells." The same historical process that created capitalism and brought the bourgeoisie into power was now moving to destroy what it created. The complex industrial order developed by the bourgeoisie no longer supported bourgeois property relations (the private ownership of the means of production and the accumulation of wealth and power by a few privileged individuals). Instead, the economic and social conditions of bourgeois society had themselves now become fetters, hindrances to further economic progress, as was the feudal system when capitalism first emerged. Hence capitalism could no longer survive. "But not only has the bourgeoisie forged the weapons that bring death to itself," Marx concluded; "it has also called into existence the men who are to wield these weapons—the modern workingclass—the proletarians."

### The Proletariat

This new class of proletarians is described in the *Communist Manifesto* in terms that clearly reflect Engel's picture in *The Conditions of the Working Class in England in 1844*. Composed of modern industrial workers, who are wage laborers, the proletariat possesses the means of livelihood only so long as its members can find work. These wage laborers have become a commodity in the market, to be bought like any other commodity, and so are exposed to all the vicissitudes of competition and fluctuations of the market. The extensive use of machinery has gradually taken all individual character, all charm and human meaning, from the work of the proletarian: "He has become an appendage of the machine, and it is only the most simple, most monotonous and most easily acquired knack that is required of him," the *Manifesto* declares. To make matters worse, "As the repulsiveness of the work increases, the wage decreases."

Masses of laborers are crowded into factories and into intolerable living conditions. "Not only are they the slaves of the bourgeois class and of the bourgeois state, they are daily and hourly enslaved by the machine, by the overseer and, above all, by the individual bourgeois manufacturer himself." The more fully modern industry develops, the less skill or strength is required and the more men are superseded by women. Both men and women, however, are simply instruments, commodities, more or less expensive to use and to replace.

The proletarian is without property. All his family ties are torn asunder. His wife and his children are transformed into commodities, articles of commerce and instruments of labor. His home and family life has lost even those values still seen in bourgeois family life. In fact, the capitalistic economy no longer assures the worker of the ability to support himself. The state has to feed him instead of being fed by him.

Since it is no longer compatible with society's needs and development, however, this bourgeois capitalistic system can no longer survive, Marx concludes: "the development of modern industry cuts from under its feet the very foundation on which the bourgeoisie produces and appropriates products [that is, the private ownership of the means of production]. What the bourgeoisie therefore produces above all else are its own grave diggers. Its fall and the victory of the proletariat are equally inevitable."

### The Goals of Communism

"The theory of the Communists may be summed up in a single sentence: abolition of private property," Marx writes. But he makes it quite clear that by this he means the private ownership of the means of production and distribution—which is for him *bourgeois* private property. Personal property that is acquired as the fruit of a man's own labor, hard-won, self-earned property that is the foundation of personal freedom, activity, and independence— that kind of private property Marx does not seek to abolish. In fact, the development of industrial capitalism has to a great extent destroyed it already for nine-tenths of the population, he feels. The wage he receives for his labor does not create any property for the laborer. Indeed, it barely keeps him alive.

The Marxist "labor theory of value," an important revolutionary and propaganda principle, is suggested in the *Manifesto* but developed more fully in *Das Kapital*. The actual value of any article, Marx believed with many other economists of his day, is created by the amount of socially necessary labor that goes into producing it. But the worker does not receive the full value of the work he has put into the product. He is paid only the going wage —the amount needed to maintain his bare existence. The remainder is kept by the capitalist as profit, and thus provides an increase in his capital. Capital, then, is really a social product. From Marx's point of view what the owner takes as profit should rightfully belong to the workers, not the capitalist. The private ownership of the means of production thus enables the bourgeoisie to steal from the proletariat what is rightfully theirs.

Under leadership of the communists, the proletariat will be made fully aware of this situation. It will be effectively organized as a political body and will then by revolutionary action overthrow the bourgeoisie and establish itself as the ruling class. The old conditions of production—that is, the private ownership of the means of production—will be swept away, and thus the basis of class antagonism and of class distinctions in general will be destroyed. Then, Marx concludes in the optimistic spirit that always characterizes his comment on this development: "In place of the old bourgeois society, with its classes and class antagonism, we shall have an association in which the free development of each is the condition for the free development of all."

> The Communists disdain to conceal their views and aims. They openly declare that their needs can be attained only by the forcible overthrow of all existing social conditions. Let the ruling classes tremble at a Communist revolution. The proletarians have nothing to lose but their chains. They have a world to win.
> Working men of all countries, unite!

With this emotional plea the *Communist Manifesto* and the initial statement of the Marxist revolutionary philosophy conclude.

## Philosophy of History

His philosophy of history is a major aspect of Marx's revolutionary thesis and of his social philosophy as a whole. He accepts the Hegelian position that there is at work in world history a "dialectical" process that produces inevitable changes in human society. But, as clearly indicated in the *Manifesto*, Marx saw this historical process as shaped by economic forces, not by rational understanding or moral conviction. Material changes in man's economic and social situation determine the development of human society as well as the values and convictions of individual men and women in any particular period. Although it is not a term that Marx himself ever used, *historical materialism* has become the generally accepted designation of his position. Nor does Marx ever use "dialectical materialism" or "scientific socialism" to describe his point of view, although these terms also have been frequent designations for his philosophy.*

Actually, Marx accepted a naturalistic philosophy. He believed man to be an integral part of the natural order and explicitly rejected any supernatural activity or other causal factors beyond human experience and natural law. Reliable knowledge, he maintained, was to be achieved only by scientific method. This approach Marx considered "scientific," and, in theory at least, he did not support the high hopes and dreams of the Utopian socialists of his day, who looked to social reform for the making of a better world. He was

---

* Lenin is responsible for the popular use of "dialectical materialism" to describe the orthodox Marxian philosophy. Recent scholarship has accepted this as actually the position of Engels, developed most explicitly in a work of his generally known as *Anti-Dühring*, and not a position that Marx ever adopted in anything he himself wrote. "Scientific socialism" is also first used by Engels in his *Anti-Dühring*, and in a later reprint of a part of this work entitled *Socialism—Utopian and Scientific*, to describe the Marxian position as he interpreted it. A careful examination of all the relevant material is provided in Z. A. Jordan's *The Evolution of Dialectical Materialism* (London: Macmillan, 1967).

interested in a descriptive and purely objective analysis of the economic and materialistic forces shaping social institutions and of the laws controlling their development.

### Marx's "New" Materialism

The materialism that characterizes Marx's mature thought consists essentially in his view that human life and thought are shaped by what he calls "the material conditions of production." This term he uses to describe the complex of economic and social forces (including available raw materials, race, climate, and population, as well as the specific mode of production) that determine the nature of any given culture. These material and economic conditions, Marx argues, shape not only every particular social situation, but also human nature as well, determining the thought and feelings of individual men and women.

It takes no deep intuition, he states in the *Manifesto*, "to comprehend that man's ideas, views and conceptions, in one word, man's consciousness, changes with every change in the conditions of his material existence, his social relations, and his social life." Those of us who enjoy the material benefits of a capitalistic society, for example, naturally believe private property and free competition to be desirable and right. Those who live in slums and ghettos and enjoy no such material benefits just as naturally believe these principles to be evil.*

While he accepts materialism in this sense, Marx explicitly rejects the more traditional scientific materialism of his day. In it human nature was seen as completely subject to the scientific laws that govern the physical and material universe. Man became little more than a mechanism whose behavior was reducible to physiological, or chemical and physical, changes in the human organism. Marx recognizes only a natural process at work in human society, to be sure, and is quite willing to agree that "circumstances make men as much as men make circumstances." But he insists that in all social development there is a genuine give-and-take relationship. It is a dialectical process in which the conscious thought and activity of men shape external circumstance quite as genuinely as external circumstances shape human thought and conduct. "The distinctive character of social development as opposed to the natural processes of development," he writes, "lies in the fact that human consciousness is involved." Human beings, although conditioned by society,

---

* "The way in which men produce their means of subsistence," Marx writes, "is a definite form of activity of these individuals, a definite form of expressing their life, a definite *mode of life* on their part. As individuals express their lives, so are they. What they are, therefore, coincides with their production, both what they produce and how they produce. The nature of individuals thus depends on the material conditions determining their production." (*The German Ideology*, p. 7.)

are enabled by conscious activity to change both society and themselves. *"Intelligent social action is creative action. . . . By acting on the external world and changing it, man changes his own nature."*[4]

In Marx's judgment orthodox materialism failed to recognize the important part played by human consciousness, by man's insights and ideas, in shaping social developments. His own point of view, therefore, he calls the "new" materialism. Engels later calls it "dialectical materialism." This position avoids the dangers of a complete philosophical determinism, Marx feels, which if accepted would destroy the significance of all conscious and deliberate action on the part of educators and reformers. "The materialistic doctrine that men are products of circumstances and a changed upbringing, forgets that it is men that change circumstances, and that the educator himself needs educating," he maintains.[5] Obviously people are not easily motivated to undertake revolutionary activity when their conscious effort makes no difference in the outcome, a fact that Marx did not overlook.

In his own position there is a unifying synthesis of the sound insights in both the materialism of Feuerbach and the idealism of Hegel without the limitations of either, Marx maintains. Hence, at least in his earlier thought, he feels "naturalism" to be the preferable designation for his philosophy. "We see here," he writes in his *Economic and Philosophical Manuscripts*, "how consistent naturalism or humanism is distinguished from both idealism and materialism, and at the same time constitutes their unifying truth. We see also that only *naturalism* is able to comprehend the process of world history."[6]

### The Marxian Dialectic

Among the Hegelian ideas that influenced Marx's mature philosophy, the interpretation of historical development as a *dialectical* process is perhaps the most significant. Although Marx modifies the Hegelian concept in important respects, he finds in the dialectical process a sound explanation of historical development. It not only adequately accounts for changes in social life and thought, Marx feels, but also recognizes the creative element in human thought and behavior, and thus avoids the dilemma of a purely deterministic philosophy.

The Hegelian dialectic accepts a dialectical conflict of ideas as the logical process by which man's rational insight develops. This dialectical process Hegel describes quite specifically: Every idea (*thesis*) inevitably breeds its opposite (*antithesis*) through a sort of internal contradiction. Then from the conflict of these two points of view there emerges a third position (*synthesis*), which resolves the conflict through a creative combination of the conflicting insights. This famous anatomy of the dialectical process—thesis, antithesis, and synthesis—has become the best known aspect of the Hegelian logic. Not only is Hegel's analysis of logical dialectic more precise than that of earlier thinkers; he also goes much further than they do in its application. All development—in society and in history as well as in logic—is rational and can be understood only as a dialectical process, Hegel maintains.

In contrast to the broad sweep of the Hegelian philosophy, Marx made use of the dialectic only in the interpretation of human history and social development. As he sought a guiding principle to interpret the enormous complexity of social life, the Hegelian dialectic provided the needed answer. In the conflict of economic ideas and in the historical development of economic institutions Marx found clear and convincing expression of Hegel's dialectic. Thesis, antithesis and synthesis, each followed the other here in approved Hegelian fashion. For example, recognizing feudalism, with the landowner as its central economic principle, to be such a thesis, Marx pointed to capitalism, with the industrial employer, as the antithesis, which economic developments in feudalism itself necessarily produced. Then socialism, with the wage-earner as its basic economic component, became for Marx the synthesis that will inevitably emerge from the economic forces that capitalism itself has produced.

In accord with the Hegelian philosophy of history, Marx accepts this as the necessary result of the economic forces at work in the historical process. The triumph of socialism over capitalism is as certain, he believed, as was the emergence of capitalism from the mercantile economy of the feudal system.*

### The Economic Interpretation of History

Despite his recognition of the important place of human ideas in social development, Marx does definitely identify the economic forces at work in any given period as the determining influence. The economic structure of

---

* "At a certain stage in their development, the material productive forces of society come in conflict with the existing relations of production or—what is but a legal expression for the same thing—with the property relations within which they have been at work hitherto," Marx writes. "From forms of development of these productive forces, these relations turn into fetters. Then begins an epoch of social revolution. With the change of the economic foundations the entire immense superstructure is more or less rapidly transformed. In considering such transformations a distinction should always be made between the material transformation of the economic conditions of production, which can be determined with the precision of natural science, and the legal, political, religious, esthetic, or philosophic—in short, the ideological forms, in which men become conscious of the conflict and fight it out.

"No social order ever perishes before all the productive forces for which there is room in it have developed; and new higher relations of production never appear before the material conditions of their existence have matured in the womb of the old society itself. Therefore mankind always sets itself only such tasks as it can solve; since, looking at the matter more closely, it will always be found that the task itself arises only when the material conditions for its solution already exist, or are at least in the process of formation." (*Critique of Political Economy*, in *Marx and Engels: Selected Works*, Vol. I, pp. 362–364, abridged. Moscow: Foreign Languages Publishing House, 1955.)

society not only produces class distinctions and class conflict but it also determines the accepted property rights. Private property, the private ownership of the means of production, is for Marx certainly the most important aspect of a capitalistic social order. And private property rights are but the legal expression of a capitalistic economy. That is, the law is simply an instrument that provides ownership and control of the fruits of production for the class that has political as well as economic power.*

The large social significance of this Marxist poistion is, of course, easy to see. It helps explain, for example, why some persons who, as members of proletarian groups or racial minority groups, feeling themselves exploited, refused to accept the laws and property rights in a capitalistic society as valid. "Law and order" to them simply means a commitment to maintaining economic and political privileges that they do not accept as just. Thus to them the policeman becomes the symbol of enforced exploitation—exploitation by the capitalist to the Marxist proletarian, exploitation by the white man to the black Marxist.

The class with economic power controls the state, the schools, the Church, the press (today the television), and other means of communication as well as the economic structure of a given society, Marx points out. Its ideals and values become accepted as "right" and desirable, while the ideas and aims of an oppressed class are seen as dangerous, evil, revolutionary. "The ideas of the ruling class are in every epoch the ruling ideas," he writes: "That is . . . the class which has the means of material production at its disposal, has control at the same time over the means of mental production."[7]

The Marxist social philosophy has stimulated a whole school of historians who have applied Marx's economic interpretation to the rewriting of history. Among American historians Charles A. Beard has been an especially influential member of this group. In this spirit, all phases of American history have been reinterpreted from this Marxist point of view: The Civil War has become a conflict between the agrarian South and the industrial North. The American Constitution was written by and designed to benefit an early Seaboard aristocracy. In our day we recognize the enormous political power of what President Eisenhower called the "military-industrial complex," of which critics see recent presidents and the Pentagon as dangerous agents. This economic point of view has become so generally accepted, indeed, in the writing of history that its Marxist origin and spirit have been almost forgotten.

---

* In the preface to his *Critique of Political Economy*, Marx states as specifically as anywhere his acceptance of economic determinism. "In the social production of their subsistence men enter into determined and necessary relations with each other which are independent of their wills—production relations which correspond to a definite state of development of their natural productive forces," he writes. "The mode of production of the material subsistence conditions the social, political and spiritual life process in general. *It is not the consciousness of men that determines their social existence, but on the contrary it is their social existence that determines their consciousness.* (*Loc. cit.*, trans. N. I. Stone, p. 11. Emphasis added.)

### The Marxist Utopia

As already pointed out, recent English translations of Marx's early *Economic and Philosophical Manuscripts* have led to renewed interest in his philosophy and to quite a changed emphasis in its interpretation. European history, as pictured there, is not only the account of a progressive economic and industrial expansion; it is also the story of an increasing "alienation" in human experience. Marx is now credited not only with having anticipated the existentialists' analysis of the human condition, but likewise with providing here as elsewhere a provocative economic interpretation of the situation.

In the work that one does, in his creative and productive activity, Marx finds man's most meaningful relationship to nature, to society, and also to himself. It is only here that he fulfills himself, that his life gains significance and meaning. Marx's *fundamental* criticism of capitalism, then, is not that it is unjust in the distribution of wealth, though he certainly accepts this as an evil in his "labor theory of value." It is in the area of production, however, rather than of distribution, that he sees the central evil of capitalism: it turns the work that men and women do in industry, on the assembly line, into forced, monotonous, and meaningless labor. Marx attacks capitalism, then, *not primarily* because it has robbed the working man of his share of wealth (that is, because of an economic exploitation), but because it has robbed him of his self-respect. The meaningfulness of a man's work, his opportunity for self-realization, has been destroyed by capitalism. It has, in fact, led to an increased *alienation* in human life.

"There is no greater misunderstanding or misrepresentation of Marx than that which is to be found, implicitly or explicitly, in the thought of the Soviet Communists, the reformed socialists, and the capitalistic opponents of socialism alike," writes Erich Fromm, "all of whom assume that Marx wanted *only* the economic improvement of the working class, and that he wanted to abolish private property so that the worker would own what the capitalist now has. *Marx's central criticism of capitalism is not the injustice in the distribution of wealth; it is the perversion of labor into forced, alienated, meaningless labor, hence the transformation of man into a 'crippled monstrosity.'* "[8]

### Man's Alienation in Modern Industrialism

In the industrial order created by modern capitalism what most disturbed Marx was its progressive dehumanization or "alienation" of man. *Alienation* was, in fact, a Hegelian concept, and one taken over by the more radical young Hegelians—the idea that in his social experience man is not what he potentially could be. As it was put by Erich Fromm: "that he is not what he ought to be, that he ought to be that which he could be."[9] In a capitalistic economy, the wage-laborer is treated simply as another commodity, Marx points out. As a result the work a man does loses its character as an expression of the worker's creative ability. Labor and its product assume an existence separate from and over against the individual worker. The clearest and most specific description of man's alienation, as Marx sees it in a capitalistic economy, is found in his early *Economic and Philosophical Manuscripts*:

> What constitutes the alienation of labor? First, that the work is external to the worker, that it is not part of his nature; and that, consequently, he does not fulfill himself in his work but denies himself, has a feeling of misery rather than well-being, does not develop fully his mental and physical energies but is physically exhausted and mentally debased. . . . His work is not voluntary but imposed, forced labor. It is not the satisfaction of a need, but only a means for satisfying other needs. Its alien character is clearly shown by the fact that as soon as there is no physical or other compulsion, it is avoided like the plague . . . . Finally the external character of work for the worker is shown by the fact that it is not his own work but work for someone else, that in work he does not belong to himself but to another person.[10]

Like Freud and other more recent psychiatrists, Marx sees creative work as an essential aspect of self-realization. Only as a man is productively creative can he find meaning in his work and thus enjoy life. When his work makes possible an adequate expression of his mental as well as his physical powers, Marx feels, labor provides the means for man's fullest self-expression, the full development of his potentialities.* Thus a man's work is not only—indeed not primarily—a means to an end, the finished product. *Work is actually an end in itself*, the meaningful expression of man's creative energy and so the avenue of self-realization. Initially Marx did speak of "the abolition of labor" as an aim of socialism, having in mind the kind of situation that he felt capitalism had produced. But later, after differentiating more clearly between free creative labor and alienated labor, he saw the aim of socialism as the "emancipation" rather than the "abolition" of labor.

In the modern industrial system we arrive, Marx maintains, at the result in which man (the worker) feels that he is freely active only when eating, drinking, and procreating—his animal functions—or at most in his home life and personal adornment. In what should be his most genuinely human

---

* "Labor is in the first place, a process in which both man and nature participate, and in which man of his own accord starts, regulates and controls the material reactions between himself and nature," Marx writes in *Das Kapital*, when describing a man's work that is *meaningful*. "By thus acting on the external world and changing it, he at the same time changes his own nature. He develops his slumbering powers and compels them to act in obedience to his sway. At the end of every labor process, we get a result that already existed in the imagination of the laborer at its commencement. He not only effects a change of form in the material on which he works, but he also realizes a purpose of his own that gives the law to his *modus operandi* and to which he must subordinate his will" (*Capital*, Vol. I, pp. 197–198, abridged).

function—creative and productive work—he is reduced to the animal level: "the animal becomes human and the human becomes animal." In this dehumanizing process man not only feels himself alienated from nature or the external world, Marx argues. Man is alienated from himself as a creative and productive human being; and he is also alienated from other men, since in "alienated labor" he comes to regard other men in accord with the same standards and evaluation by which he judges himself.*

Speaking as a psychologist, Erich Fromm accepts Marx's analysis as fundamentally sound.

> There is only one correction which history has made in Marx's concept of alienation. Marx believed that the working class was the most alienated class, hence that the emancipation from alienation would necessarily start with the liberation of the working class. Marx did not foresee the extent to which alienation was to become the fate of the vast majority of people, especially the ever-increasing segment of the population which manipulate symbols and men, rather than machines. If anything, the clerk, the salesman, the executive, are even more alienated than the skilled manual worker. . . . They all crave for things, new things, to have and to use. They are the passive recipients, the consumers, chained and weakened by the very things which satisfy their synthetic needs. They are not related to the world productively, grasping it in its full reality, and in this process becoming one with it; they worship things, the machines which produce the things—and in this alienated world they feel as strangers and quite alone.[11]

### The Classless Society

Marx and Engels have been criticized at times for not describing in greater detail the economic and political features of the new society to be achieved by communist revolution. This has made it possible, unfortunately, for Lenin, Stalin, Mao, and any number of professed Marxists to provide their own working models of a Communist dictatorship. It is now apparent that Marx's major concern for the new communistic society was not political or even economic as such. Even more surprising, his central concern, it now seems, has actually been lost sight of in most present-day Communist states.

---

* In his mature analysis of capitalism (in *Das Kapital*), Marx reemphasizes this early point of view: "Within the capitalistic system, all methods for raising the social productiveness of labor are brought about at the cost of the individual laborer, all means for the development of production transform themselves into means of domination over and exploitation of the producers; they mutilate the laborer into a fragment of a man, degrade him to the level of an appendage to the machine, destroy every remnant of charm in his work and turn it into a hated tool; they estrange him from the intellectual potentialities of the labor process." (*Capital*, Vol. I, p. 701.) Our concern in this discussion is, of course, with Marx's major philosophical ideas, not his economic analysis of capitalism as such. An excellent popular discussion of this latter topic is provided in R. L. Heilbroner's *The Worldly Philosophers*, Chapter VI.

The major aim of socialism for Marx only becomes clear, in fact, as it is related to his concept of alienation. The revolution of the proletariat and the establishment of communist society was designed to free the worker from the dehumanizing effect of the capitalistic industrial order, and to make possible his full self-realization in a new type of economy. The socialized economy was not expected to produce more things, a more abundant economy—that had been achieved well enough under capitalism. Nor was it designed primarily for a fairer distribution of the wealth produced, although Marx did see that as one desirable outcome. The fundamental objective of communism for Marx was the production of new human beings: men and women who for the first time would be able to achieve full self-realization in the work they did. The abolition of "private property"—that is, the private ownership of the means of production—was then only the first step in the social revolution. "It is of the utmost importance to note that Marx views the abolition of private property entirely as a means for the abolition of alienated labor, and not as an end in itself," writes Herbert Marcuse, perhaps the ablest contemporary Marxist in this country.[12]

Communism, Marx himself said in a most significant statement, meant "the positive abolition of private property, of human self-alienation, and thus the real appropriation of human nature through and for man. It is, therefore, the return of man to himself as a social, that is, a really human being, a complete and conscious return which assimilates all the wealth of previous development. Communism as a fully-developed naturalism is humanism and as a fully-developed humanism is naturalism. It is the definitive resolution of the antagonism between man and nature and between man and man. It is the true solution of the conflict between existence and essence."[13]

### The State and Revolution*

A basic tenet of Marxism, of course, is the necessity of a revolutionary overthrow of the bourgeois state. Without this the new communist social order, and the opportunity for man's full self-development, could not be established. In his economic interpretation of politics, Marx saw the state as primarily a weapon of class conflict, an instrument of the ruling class used to preserve its power and control. "Political power, properly so called, is merely the organized power of one class for oppressing another," he wrote in the *Communist Manifesto*. Or, as Lenin later phrased this in provocative fashion: "Marx grasped the essence of capitalistic democracy splendidly, when, in analyzing the experience of the Commune, he said that the oppressed are allowed once every few years to decide what particular representative of the oppressing class should represent and repress them."[14]

* This is the title of Lenin's well-known and perhaps most influential volume, published in 1917. It contains his own interpretation of Marx's political philosophy.

Marx was uncompromisingly committed, therefore, to the overthrow not only of capitalism, but also of the "democratic" state that consolidates its power. But he was not especially concerned with the *political* details of the communist order that would then emerge victorious. His major interest, as already pointed out, was in the changed social conditions that the new economic order would make possible. One political comment of his, however, has had far-reaching and unfortunate consequences: "Between capitalist and communist society lies a period of the revolutionary transformation of the one into the other," he pointed out, and went on to say: "There corresponds to this also a political transition period in which the state can be nothing but the *revolutionary dictatorship of the proletariat*." Lenin later seized upon this suggestion and built around it the political theory that has guided the development of Communism not only in Russia but in most other Communist states as well.*

Despite his lack of interest in the specific political structure of the new communist state, Marx does state very clearly its central significance as he sees it:

> In a higher phase of communist society, after the enslaving subordination of the individual to the division of labor, and with it the antithesis between mental and physical labor, has disappeared; after labor has become not only a means of life but also the primary necessity of life; when with the all-around development of the individual the production forces have also increased and all springs of cooperative wealth flow more abundantly—only then can the narrow horizon of bourgeois right be fully left behind and society inscribe upon its banner: From each according to his ability, to each according to his needs.[15]

When this desirable condition is reached, the state, as organized and centralized political power, will no longer be necessary, and, to use an expressive phrase of Engels's, will simply *wither away*. In this situation, "when people will have become so accustomed to observing the fundamental rules of social intercourse and when their labor is so productive that they will voluntarily work *according to their ability*," there will be no further need, so Lenin assures us, for "*the special apparatus* for compulsion which is called the state."[16]

Here then are the major features of the Marxist Utopia—"the good society" that social philosophers since the time of Plato have portrayed in a variety of ways, depending on their differing ideals and values.

---

* Robert L. Heilbroner, in his stimulating discussion in *The Worldly Philosophers*, makes this pertinent comment: "Marx, it must be kept in mind, was not the architect of communism. That task fell to his successor Lenin. *Das Kapital* is the *Doomsday Book* of Capitalism, and in all of Marx there is almost nothing which looks beyond the Day of Judgment to see what lineaments paradise may present." (*Op. cit.*, New York: Simon and Schuster, rev. ed., 1961, p. 156.)

### The Appeal of Marxism

Without question the Marxist philosophy has had and continues to have wide appeal. Obviously its appeal is strongest among classes and nations that feel themselves exploited, or unable under present conditions to participate in the abundance of material benefits that a capitalistic economy has made possible for the more privileged industrialized nations in the Western world. But Marxism also has had a very genuine appeal to concerned and sincere individuals among the more privileged. Many of these people are also deeply conscious of the suffering and injustice that does accompany our present urban and industrial social order.

The significant contribution made by Marx to a realistic social philosophy is too obvious to need additional emphasis. The outlook of the historian and the social scientist has been much influenced by the Marxist economic interpretation of history, as already suggested. Marx's contribution here is well described by Sir Karl Popper, one of his most vigorous critics: "He opened and sharpened our eyes in many ways. A return to pre-Marxian social science is inconceivable. All modern writers are indebted to Marx, even if they do not know it. This is especially true of those who disagree with him, as I do."[17]

### The Religious Quality of Communism

All who examine with some care the appeal of contemporary Communism also point to an unmistakable religious quality in the attitude and experience of its converts. "Marxism clearly fulfills one of the simple requirements of religion," writes Crane Brinton in his *Shaping of the Modern Mind*: "It has its sacred books, its authoritative scripture in the writings of Marx and Engels with the comments, exegesis, and additions brought by Lenin and, to a much less extent, Stalin."[18]

While all interpreters of Marxism do not, of course, use such specific religious terminology, almost all are impressed by marked similarities they find between much that Marx wrote and did and the Jewish prophets of the Old Testament. These prophets were political as well as spiritual leaders. They not only denounced man for sins, social as well as personal, and announced the punishment to come; they also showed him a vision of what society should be like, and could be like, if his faith were strong enough. And in their teaching it was through the processes of history that all this would be brought about. These are characteristics that are quite apparent in Marx's philosophy.

It is true, of course, that Marx saw the orthodox Christianity of his day, whether Catholic or Protestant, as but one of the many dimensions of the social order shaped by capitalism. The Christian Church was simply an institution used to support and justify the capitalistic economy. In Marx's provocative phrase, religion (including Christianity, of course) was "the opiate of the people," that is, a device used by the privileged to drug the thought of the oppressed away from the injustices they suffer in this world by visions of the glories awaiting them in the next.

What a closer examination of Marxism as a philosophy of life seems to reveal quite clearly, however, is that its appeal is more largely religious in spirit than economic or philosophical. Its appeal is based on values that give life meaning and direction, values that are emotional rather than intellectual, as Koestler has portrayed so vividly in *The God That Failed*.* This today makes Marxism perhaps the most influential of any philosophy to which men and women give their allegiance.

### Does the End Justify the Means?

Most of those familiar with the thought of Marx, and especially with the earlier statements of his philosophy, acknowledge, as a matter of fact, that the major aims of communism as Marx describes them are quite desirable. In agreement with both Dewey and Aristotle, Marx is simply seeking a way to insure the full development of human personality, the realization of man's potentiality. He wants to achieve this, moreover, not only for the more fortunate but for those who have so far benefited least from our social order.

When discussing Marx's philosophy, it is essential, of course, to distinguish his own position from policies and actions of the official Communist Party, outside as well as inside the Soviet Union. No intelligent Marxist who is not an official member of the Party will undertake to defend the deceit, the misrepresentation and downright dishonesty, the character assassination and tyranny, that have frequently characterized the action of Communist leaders in Russia as elsewhere—or the repeated purging and heartless punishment of all deviation from the official position of those in power.

But the question is raised, and raised quite honestly, by all critics of Marxism: Does not Marx's insistence upon armed revolution involve an

---

* That the appeal of Marxism to the convert is essentially religious in quality is given quite explicit expression by Arthur Koestler, one of the more gifted of the writers who have renounced their faith in Communism. Koestler's essay in *The God That Failed* provides penetrating psychological analysis of the "conversion" experience that made a Marxist of him. "A faith is not acquired by reasoning," he writes. "One does not fall in love with a woman, or enter the womb of the church as a result of logical persuasion. Persuasion may play a part in a man's conversion; but only the part of bringing to its full and conscious climax a process which has been maturing in regions where no persuasion can penetrate. A faith is not acquired; it grows like a tree. . . . In December 1931, at the age of twenty-six, I joined the communist party in Germany. I became converted because I was ripe for it and lived in a disintegrating society thirsty for faith. I was ripe to be converted as a result of my personal history; thousands of other members of the intelligentsia and the middle classes of my generation were ripe for it, by virtue of other personal case histories." (*Op. cit.*, New York: Bantam Books, 1952, pp. 13–14).

inevitable destruction of those values that a democratic society has come to recognize as essential for that full self-development of the individual? Armed class conflict, civil war, and dictatorship, along with the intolerant, even fanatical, spirit that always accompanies a war psychology, produce, in the judgment of all Marx's critics, greater evils than those that Communism seeks to eliminate. No doubt it is too easy for those of us who benefit from the opportunities and privileges of a democratic society to agree with such a conclusion. Certainly the political establishment in our own country has not preserved man's freedom nor removed the inequality and injustice in our society as it should have. But there is certainly ample objective evidence available to provide the thoughtful student with a sound evaluation of the dangers as well as the appeal of Marxism.

Most non-Communist writers now recognize that *Das Kapital* provides a penetrating analysis of the capitalistic economy that Marx and Engels knew in nineteenth-century Europe. But they seriously question that it reveals the inevitable and unchanging laws of historical development that Marx thought he had discovered. As Reinhold Niebuhr points out, an open society in twentieth-century Europe has taken "innumerable steps to guard the rights and the essential humanity of the person," steps Marx thought impossible without a revolution.[19] Even in America our social institutions are being significantly modified by democratic methods to provide increasing equality of opportunity for all citizens, whether middle-class or proletarian, white or black. This process may well be too slow. But Marx's contention, that only by armed revolution can the economic privilege and political power of the ruling capitalist class be overthrown, no longer appears so convincing.*

### Truth and Freedom of Thought

Serious philosophical problems as well as questions of political strategy are, of course, raised by Marxism. Two of these should perhaps be mentioned. As one critic quite pointedly suggests, "In the place of the abstract conception of man as a free agent capable of remaking his attitudes in accordance with the dictates of reason, Marx developed the concept of man as grouped in social classes which set the premises of his attitudes and restricted the role of reason to that of discovering and advancing the interest of his particular class."[20] There is no question, of course, that for Marx economic forces are largely responsible for bringing about changed conditions and changed ideas and beliefs. The only question is whether or not the sequence of events and ideas in a given culture is completely determined.

---

* It is true that both Marx (in 1872) and Engels (in 1886) recognized the possibility of a peaceful social revolution in England and America. But they also were never willing to accept the fundamental revision of their philosophy that this possibility involved.

Able American philosophers who have accepted the Marxist point of view, men like Sidney Hook and Herbert Marcuse, for example, insist that Marx does not accept complete economic determinism. In his dialectical approach to historical and social development they feel that he recognizes the creativity, and by implication the freedom, that is essential for valid rational insight and truth. In view of Marx's general emphasis upon economic determinism, such arguments have not proved convincing to the non-Marxists. On this point each student must wrestle with the issues involved and reach the conclusion that he finds acceptable.

A second philosophical problem is posed by Marx's acceptance of the communist society as the culmination of the dialectical process in history. It has been asked: does not the static nature of the classless state posited by Marx's secular eschatology contradict his own dynamic view of history? Marx argues, of course, that class conflict will be abolished in the classless society that communism creates. If one assumes, however, that Marx's dynamic view of history is valid, there is reason to question the adequacy of this explanation. Interestingly enough, Hegel, in his interpretation of historical development, saw the dialectical process culminating in the Prussian state of his day, which he greatly admired. This Hegelian view Marx found quite unacceptable. It is perhaps understandable that Marx's own position is equally unconvincing to those who do not share his admiration for the Communist society.

Despite the difficulties to which its critics call attention, however, the appeal and influence of Marxism today is perhaps greater than in any previous period. The comment made some years ago by Sidney Hook, one of the abler American philosophers attracted by the thought of Marx, cannot be lightly dismissed: "The social philosophy of Karl Marx exerts a stronger influence upon the present age than the social theory of any of our contemporaries. A new philosophy of life, avowedly Marxian in inspiration, is slowly emerging to challenge the dominant attitudes and values of Western and Oriental cultures."[21]

# Four
## THE DOMINANCE OF WILL

There is nothing either in the world or out of it that is good without qualification except the good will.

IMMANUEL KANT

If your heart does not want a world of moral reality, your head will assuredly never make you believe in it.

WILLIAM JAMES

The world seen from within, the world defined and designated according to its intelligible character—would simply be "Will to Power" and nothing else.

FRIEDRICH NIETZSCHE

## CHAPTER 11

# The Moral Imperative

## *Immanuel Kant*

The great philosophers have with remarkable unanimity stressed the importance of human reason in achieving the good life. From Plato and Aristotle to Spinoza and John Dewey, they have consistently maintained that, if intelligence and virtue are not completely identical, at least there is an essential relationship between the two: only as a man is intelligent, only as he knows what he is doing, can he hope to do what is right. Despite this impressive consensus, however, it is difficult to escape an uneasy suspicion that, in the world today as in the past, the "good" people are for the most part not the more learned or those of superior intelligence. Goodness seems somehow much more the concern of the ordinary and unsophisticated. It is certainly not something upon which the clever and well-informed have a monopoly.

Of this fact one distinguished philosopher, at least, has been well aware. Immanuel Kant, influential eighteenth-century German philosopher, has taken it as the point of departure for his discussion of morality, and around man's awareness of the compulsion of the moral ideal he has built what has been perhaps the most influential ethical system in modern thought. Although in analyzing moral conduct he emphasizes the importance of "good will" rather than of intelligence, Kant is not always included among those responsible for the contemporary disparagement of reason. He himself, no doubt, would have vigorously denied that this was his aim. As we examine the implications of his *Critique of Pure Reason*, however, and observe also the central place in his moral philosophy of man's will rather than his reason, it becomes quite clear that Kant should be included among those responsible for the point of view of both the pragmatists and the existentialists.* Let us look then at Kant, and more directly at his moral philosophy.

* A comment by William Barrett on Kant's influence is quite relevant: "Kant can justly be called the father of modern philosophy, for out of him stem nearly all the still current and contending schools of philosophy: Positivism, Pragmatism and Existentialism." (*Irrational Man*, p. 162.)

### The Man and His Mission

Immanuel Kant, greatest of German philosophers, was born on April 22, 1724, in Königsberg, a city of East Prussia not far from the Russian border. In this city almost all his long life was spent, and there in 1804 he died. As we look at the lives of such men as Spinoza or Schopenhauer, we discover circumstances that enable us better to understand the philosophy that they adopt and defend with such ability. In the case of Kant, there is hardly a ripple on the quiet and regular current of his life as it flowed on day after day for eighty years.

Kant's father was a saddle-maker, and young Immanuel was the fourth of nine children. Poor in the goods of this world, both Kant's parents were deeply religious. Kant's early training, both at home and at school, was deeply colored by the spirit of Pietism. Although he later reacted against the narrowness and dogmatism of the religion of his youth, he never ceased to feel the effects of this early moral and religious instruction. Nor was his respect for the simple faith of his parents ever destroyed. "People may say what they will of Pietism," he wrote in his old age. "Those in whom it was sincere were worthy of honor. They possessed the highest thing that man can have—the quiet, the content, the inner peace, which no suffering can disturb."[1]

At sixteen, Kant matriculated at the small university in Königsberg, which had at the time about 300 students, and there spent the next six years. An uncle seems to have given him some financial assistance, but in the main he had to support himself. He did this largely by coaching his more well-to-do fellow students, but to some extent also, one is rather surprised to learn, by his regular winnings at billiards and cards, in both of which he excelled.

### Career as University Professor

Kant completed his doctorate at Königsberg when he was about thirty, and was given a post there as private lecturer—approximately the status of instructor in an American university today. From the very beginning his lectures were popular and unusually well attended, and his writing soon made him the most distinguished man at Königsberg. The university was so poor, however, that for fifteen years he was not promoted. Even at the age of forty-two, Kant could write, "I have the fortune to be a lover of metaphysics but my mistress has shown me few favors so far." Gradually, however, he was becoming better and better known. Finally, at the age of forty-five, he was made professor of logic and metaphysics at Königsberg. This post he held until he retired thirty years later.

Kant's life during these years was uneventful enough. A portrait of the philosopher at forty-four shows him to be small, spare, and rather insignificant looking. He was just over five feet tall and as he grew older he became little more than a shadow of a man, retiring more and more into the recesses of his own mind. Of frail health, he was seldom ill but was very careful about his food and his habits of life. There is a tradition that he twice considered matrimony. In each case, however, he deliberated so long about the merits of the young lady in question and the hazards of married life in general that the issue was settled for him. One lady accepted the advances of a bolder suitor; the other moved away from Königsberg before the philosopher had made up his mind.

The unvaried routine of Kant's life, indeed, became a byword. In a well-known passage, the poet Heine has left us the following description of the philosopher:

> The life of Immanuel Kant is hard to describe; he had indeed neither life nor history in the proper sense of the words. He lived an abstract, mechanical, old-bachelor existence, in a quiet, remote street in Königsberg. . . . I do not believe that the great cathedral clock of this city accomplished its day's work in a less passionate and more regular way than its countryman, Immanuel Kant. Rising from bed, coffee-drinking, writing, lecturing, eating, walking, everything had its fixed time; and the neighbors knew that it must be exactly half past four when they saw Professor Kant, in his gray coat, with his cane in his hand, step out of his housedoor, and move toward the little lime tree avenue, which is named after him, the Philosopher's Walk. Eight times he walked up and down that walk at every season of the year, and when the weather was bad, or the gray clouds threatened rain, his servant, old Lampe, was seen anxiously following him with a large umbrella under his arm like an image of providence.[2]

This caricature of the typical university professor should not blind us, however, to the fact that Kant was an excellent teacher. According to the reports of students, his lectures were not only interesting but even entertaining. For a time it was quite fashionable for the more cultured townspeople of Königsberg to attend Kant's lectures on anthropology, which were particularly popular.

He disliked especially to have students carefully copy down unimportant remarks he made. "You will not learn philosophy from me, but how to philosophize—not thoughts to repeat, but how to think," he is reported to have said in the spirit of Socrates. "Think for yourselves, inquire for your selves, stand on your own feet." There are still a good many in university circles today, unfortunately, who do not share Kant's understanding of the meaning of education.

### The Problem Raised by Modern Science

The events that made a difference in Kant's life were not the external happenings—these to him were unimportant. The important things were the influences that affected his thought. Especially significant in shaping his philosophy were his introduction to Newton and the spirit of modern science, when he was still a student at the university, and his first reading of Rousseau when he was about forty. (The only time Kant missed his regular after- noon walk, so the story goes, was the day he became so absorbed in Rousseau's *Émile* that he completely forgot it.) His contact with British empiricism and the philosophy of David Hume, at about the same time, woke him "from his dogmatic slumbers," Kant says, and caused him to modify drastically the rationalistic metaphysics that he had until then accepted without serious question. And finally, when he was about forty-five, a profound revolution in his own thought led him to formulate afresh the central problem of meta- physics and to begin work on a new "critical" interpretation of philosophy. From the time of this revolution in his own outlook, Kant was a man with a mission. To this mission he devoted all his energies and efforts. Nothing else really mattered.

But by far his most important early achievement was a volume pub- lished in 1755, entitled *The General Natural History and Theory of the Heavens*. This book is chiefly remembered because Kant here suggests that all planets have been or will be inhabited, and proposes a nebular hypothesis to account for their origin. It was this theory that Laplace later developed with greater scientific precision. More important in Kant's own development, however, is the clear insight into the nature of modern science that this volume reveals. Kant stands with Spinoza at the beginning of our age in recognizing clearly the broader implications of modern science, long before these had been spelled out by psychologists and sociologists in words that all could understand. And he saw more clearly than did Spinoza the central problem for moral philosophy raised by science: how is it possible to reconcile the thoroughgoing mechanical view of the universe adopted by modern science with the belief in human freedom and responsibility that is essential for any genuine moral conviction and purpose in life?

"Two things fill the mind with ever new and increasing admiration and awe, the oftener and more steadily we reflect upon them," Kant wrote: "*the starry heavens above and the moral law within*." If he accepted without reservation a scientific philosophy based upon the Newtonian physics, how- ever, there would be little left, he recognized, of the moral idealism and religious faith of his youth.

## The Influence of Rousseau

Surprisingly enough it was the French philosopher Jean Jacques Rousseau who suggested to Kant the approach to human freedom and to religious faith upon which he later built his own philosophy. No two men seem less alike than Kant and Rousseau—the one careful, meticulous, and respectable; the other brilliant but wayward. Kant saw in the philosophy of Rousseau, how- ever, more than mere romantic charm. He discovered there a new appreciation of the worth of ordinary men and women, people like his own parents. Until he read Rousseau, Kant had, with the rationalists, been accustomed to take great pride in his own superior intellectual attainments. At forty, he wrote:

> I am myself by inclination a seeker after truth. I feel a consuming thirst for knowledge and a restless passion to advance it, as well as satisfaction in any forward step. There was a time when I thought that this alone could constitute the honor of mankind, and I despised the common man who knows nothing. Rousseau set me right. This blind prejudice vanished. I learned to respect human nature, and I should consider myself far more useless than the ordinary working-man if I did not believe that this view could give worth to all others to establish the rights of man.[3]

What appealed especially to Kant was Rousseau's convincing contrast between the mask that civilization places upon a man's countenance and the actual man underneath. The truly permanent aspect of human nature, Kant came to see as he read Rousseau, is not what man appears to be but what he ought to be, what he knows in his heart he can be. This insight, that the "real man" is found in man's moral convictions and not in his physical nature, Kant credits to Rousseau. It proved a crucial turning point in his own development.

Just as he himself was becoming aware that neither morality nor religion could be described by a thoroughly scientific philosophy, Kant found Rousseau also recognizing this fact and pointing to conscience rather than reason as the true source and foundation of religious faith. The duties of morality are the essentials in religion, Rousseau maintained. A just heart is the true temple of God, and faith is the natural outcome of the moral life. When Kant, late in life, came to write his own philosophy of religion, these were the views that he accepted, and he developed them much more fully than Rousseau himself was ever to do.

### Kant's Philosophical Mission

The chief error in the old rationalistic metaphysics, Kant felt, was that men too quickly accepted human reason as a valid instrument of knowledge. Thus Spinoza talks unhesitatingly of an eternal substance that is God, and of the rational laws by which the order of nature is directed. We are not in a position to describe the nature of the world outside us, Kant maintained, until we know how the human mind itself works. We must understand ourselves before we can understand the universe or God. Kant undertook, therefore, to provide a penetrating and comprehensive analysis (or "critique") of human reason that would become the foundation for all future metaphysics. In doing so he unintentionally initiated an undermining of rationalism and a loss of confidence in rational speculation that has culminated eventually in the existentialism and anti-intellectualism of our own day.

The first, and in many ways the most famous, volume of Kant's critical philosophy is his *Critique of Pure Reason*, his philosophy of science, published in 1781. The initial reaction to the book was a sort of dazed wonder and incomprehension. His *Critique* was termed a dangerous book. Many felt that Kant had destroyed science, not saved it. Almost everyone complained bitterly of Kant's obscurity and his almost incomprehensible terminology. Ever since Kant published his volume, moreover, critics have disagreed about its complications—and they continue to do so today.

Gradually, however, people began to see more clearly what Kant was attempting. German universities took up the *Critique*, and it soon became prescribed reading for all students of philosophy. By the beginning of the nineteenth century it was generally recognized that no one could hope to understand philosophy until he had mastered Kant.

Turing from the philosophy of science, the modest author of this revolutionary work devoted himself more directly to a consideration of the problems of morality and religion. In 1785 he published the *Fundamental Principles of the Metaphysic of Morals*, and in 1788, the *Critique of Practical Reason*. These works contain a searching analysis of moral conviction and conduct, comparable to Kant's treatment of scientific knowledge in the *Critique of Pure Reason*. Finally, in two other works, the *Critique of Judgment* and *Religion Within the Limits of Reason Alone*, Kant completed his study of the activities of the human mind with an examination of aesthetic and religious experience. It had taken him twenty years and five impressive, closely reasoned volumes to state the "critical" philosophy to his own satisfaction. But his place among the great philosophers of all time was now securely established.

Kant's energy was now exhausted. He was almost seventy-one and his work was done. The following year he did publish a monograph on *Everlasting Peace*, which contains a remarkable anticipation of the principles upon which the League of Nations was organized. Shortly thereafter he retired from his professorship at the University of Königsberg. Gradually his mind began to fail, and finally in 1804, as he was approaching eighty, the distinguished old philosopher died as quietly and peacefully as he had lived.

### The Categorical Imperative of Duty

The new provinces of the mind that modern science had opened up, the concern of the scientist to increase the extent of human knowledge, and the scientist's devotion to truth as he saw it—all these made a deep impression upon Kant. But Kant also recognized, more clearly than did his contemporaries, that modern science made a new approach to moral and religious philosophy necessary. He saw the two concerns he believed to be most important in human life apparently at war with one another. Belief in scientific determinism and in moral responsibility appeared to be both necessary and irreconcilable. A continuing effort to preserve the independence and the integrity of both science and morals pervades Kant's entire system of philosophy.*

In his brief but closely reasoned *Fundamental Principles of the Metaphysic of Morals*, Kant undertakes to make clear the nature of morality and its claims upon the human spirit. None of Kant's books makes easy reading. Even his *Fundamental Principles of the Metaphysic of Morals* assumes more than a beginner's knowledge of the highly technical terminology he employs to express his own position. But certainly this volume on morals is the place for the student of philosophy to begin his reading of Kant. For here Kant hopes to write not so much for the philosopher as for the intelligent layman. "A metaphysic of morals, in spite of its forbidding title, can be in a high degree popular and suited to the ordinary intelligence," he says in explaining the purpose of his volume.[4] This aim is always before him, no matter how far he falls short at times·of accomplishing it.

### Man's Ordinary Moral Conviction

To understand the nature of morality, we must begin with "the pure, unspoiled moral mind of man," Kant maintains.[5] The influences of modern civilization tend to corrupt us. Two years in the army, even a year or two in a fraternity house or a college dormitory, is usually enough to play havoc with such simple, unspoiled moral conviction. If we want a sound basis for our analysis of the moral life, however, we must go back, Kant insists, to that simple and unsophisticated moral conviction which he believes all of us normally possess.

Upon examining this *unspoiled* moral outlook, we find in every case the certainty that *we can be good if we want to.* Morality, we are convinced, is within our grasp in a way that nothing else in life is. Not everyone can be a great scientist such as Einstein; not everyone can be an outstanding artist or a successful musician; not everyone can be wealthy, or famous, or even happy But everyone can be *good* if he really wants to. This each of us knows immediately and surely as the firm conviction of the moral consciousness. A course or two in psychology or sociology, it is true, will often produce the kind of rationalization that places upon circumstances about us rather than upon ourselves the blame for our own wrongdoing. But unless we have become thoroughly sophisticated, or corrupted by the social life of our day,

---

* In both America and Germany philosophers have been primarily interested in Kant's epistemology, and consequently have placed major emphasis upon his *Critique of Pure Reason*. In British circles, on the other hand, until quite recently Kant's moral philosophy was given a much more central position. The present interpretation follows the traditional British approach.

we know well enough that when we do what is wrong it is our own fault and not anyone else's.

As a contemporary interpreter aptly puts it, Kant's moral philosophy springs from a very human motive. It is, in its essence, a philosophy for the ordinary man: "Some things in the world, it says, are doubtless destined to be enjoyed only by the gifted and the privileged. Whether we shall be happy, influential, successful, or what not, depends always to a great extent on matters beyond our control—on natural gifts, inherited temperament, congenial circumstances." But this is not so of every kind of accomplishment. There is one achievement that is as open to the ordinary individual as it is to the man of genius or the child of fortune. "*Only in certain circumstances can you be happy; but you can always be good.* For to be good you need only to want to so be. If you wholly want to be good then you are so."[6]

## Motives vs. Consequences

In Kant's judgment, it is the motive, not the consequence, that determines what is right or wrong; and for our motives we alone are responsible. The outcome of conduct does not provide a means of judging its moral worth, he insists. A good mother or father is the parent who wills to do what is right by a child. Circumstances may prevent such a parent from giving his child the opportunities for education and culture he would like, but he does the best he can notwithstanding. Another parent with ample means may provide abundantly for all his children's needs, but only perhaps to satisfy his own self-esteem or desire for social respectability. In Kant's judgment, it is the former, not the latter, who is really a "good" parent. Goodness lies not in intelligence or in shrewdness; it lies in a deep disposition of the heart. "Be good, sweet maid, and let who will be clever," the poet admonishes. Between goodness and cleverness there is a fundamental contrast.

But how can we formulate a moral philosophy that does justice to this basic conviction of the moral life that a man can be good if he wants to? This is Kant's initial problem, and a careful examination convinces him that morality has to do with man's will, not his intellect. In the well-known opening passage of his essay on morals, he writes:

> There are many things which in one sense or another may be called good; talents, such as understanding, wit or judgment; temperamental gifts, such as courage, decision, resoluteness; gifts of fortune, such as power, honor, riches, health, happiness. But all of these are good only conditionally. They are good if they are used well, but not otherwise. Closely scrutinized, it is not they that are good; it is the will behind them. *There is nothing either in the world or out of it which is good without qualification except a good will.*
>
> It is only in his will, ultimately, that a man can be either good or

bad. On the other hand, if he is good there, he is good. There is nothing further to be said in the matter. Nothing else in that case can make him bad. Want of power, want of opportunity, or any other misfortune may interfere with the accomplishment of a good man's designs. But it cannot qualify his goodness so long as his will is good. Even if it should happen that, owing to a special disfavor of fortune . . . with its utmost effort [this will] still accomplishes nothing, and only good will is left (not, to be sure, as a mere wish but as the summoning of all means in our power), then, like a jewel it would still shine by its own light as a thing which has its whole worth in itself.[7]

### The Categorical Imperative of Duty

Even if we agree, tentatively at least, that moral conduct and character are determined by the good will and by the good will alone, we are still left, of course, with the problem of determining just what the good will is. What are the motives that can be accepted as right? Amiability, generosity, unselfishness—all of these have been highly prized by good men, but none, Kant maintains, will serve as our criterion. At the very heart of the moral life, we find an inescapable sense of obligation to do what is right, no matter what the consequences. To this unique moral conviction, the awareness that we *ought* always to do right, Kant gives a formidable name—the categorical imperative of duty.

The only right motive, he maintains, is the motive of duty. The only right act, as we know well enough when we examine our own moral life, is the act done in conformity with this imperative of duty. It is when we do what is right because it is right, and for no other reason, that our conduct is moral. Upon this Kant insists with unrelenting logic. Many things we do may happen to be *in accord* with our sense of duty, but unless a thing is done *for the sake of duty* and for that reason alone, it cannot be accepted as morally right, he insists. There is, then, for Kant a fundamental distinction between acting prudently and doing what is right. Honesty may well be the best policy in most if not all situations. And a prudent man will therefore, as a rule, be honest. But such action has no moral value, in Kant's judgment. Even the most benevolent and unselfish conduct cannot be accepted as morally good, he maintains, unless the action is done *only* because it is right:

To help others where one can is a duty, and besides this, there are many spirits of so sympathetic a disposition that, without any further motive of vanity or self-interest, they find an inner pleasure in spreading happiness around them and can take delight in the contentment of others as their own work. Yet I maintain that an action of this kind, however right and however amiable it may be, has still no genuinely moral worth. . . . for its maxim lacks moral content, namely, the performance of such actions, not from inclination, but *from duty*.[8]

This approach to morals enables us to understand the Christian teaching about love, Kant points out—teaching that otherwise is not really intelligible.

> It is in this way, undoubtedly, that we should understand those passages of Scripture which command us to love our neighbor and even our enemy. For love, as an inclination, cannot be commanded. But kindness done from duty, also when no inclination impels it and even when it is opposed by a natural and unconquerable aversion, is practical love, not pathological love. It resides in the will and not in the feeling, in principles of action and not in tender sympathy; and it alone can be commanded.[9]

### The Function of Moral Philosophy

<u>When a man knows that moral conduct consists in doing his duty, and when he undertakes uncompromisingly to follow the dictates of conscience, he needs no further philosophical insight in order to be good. His own common sense is enough</u>, Kant believes:

> It would be easy to show how human reason, with this compass in hand, is well able to distinguish, in all cases that present themselves, what is good or evil, right or wrong . . . and how in consequence there is no need of science or philosophy for knowing what man has to do in order to be honest and good, and indeed to be wise and virtuous.[10]

In view of the complex and conflicting issues that face us in life today, this statement sounds a bit overoptimistic. Questions about our involvement in Vietnam, for example, or about the use of drugs, divided people sharply for a decade or more. Even those who are quite conscientious easily became confused about what actually constitutes their duty. President Lyndon Johnson, in facing the trying decisions he confronted early in Vietnam, is reported to have said, "It is not hard to do what is right. The real problem is knowing what is right."

A young student may leave home with well-established standards of right and wrong, but he soon faces conflicting demands made upon him in a college or university situation. Many of his friends, who seem quite able and sincere, differ with him about what is right and wrong. In view also of the inescapable sophistication that comes with higher education, as well as with wider experience in business or politics, there is certainly need for a sound moral philosophy to make clear what a consistent and reasonable morality involves. Despite his earlier statement, Kant does recognize that such a need  should be met. "Innocence is a splendid thing, only it has the misfortune not to keep well and to be easily misled," he writes.*

---

* "On this account," Kant continues, "wisdom itself—which in any case consists more in doing and not doing than in knowing—does require science as well, not in order

### The Nature of Conscience

Among the most helpful insights provided by Kant's moral philosophy is a better understanding of the nature of conscience. As he points out, the common reason of mankind—that is, the simple, unspoiled moral mind of man—causes us to recognize an immediate obligation to *do* what is right. But in the complexities of modern life we easily become confused as to just what *is* right. We begin to see that conscience is not infallible; if a given person had grown up in a city slum instead of on a family farm, in China instead of the United States, his conscience would certainly have operated quite differently. He would now have entirely different moral standards. From premises of this kind, moral relativists in our day, like the Sophists in Athens many years ago, conclude that there are no universally valid moral principles: "our duty" is merely what we have been taught in our youth, and morals are but the customs and conventions of society. Unless our moral convictions are quite strong, it is easy to accept the position of the moral relativist and adopt some purely personal or pragmatic standard to guide our conduct.

Kant not only rejects irrevocably any such moral relativism; he also provides a discerning explanation of the circumstances that produce this skeptical attitude. In all knowledge, whether it be the theoretical knowledge of science or the practical knowledge of morality, Kant identifies two elements: an empirical content, which comes from our own experience, and a rational principle of interpretation, which is supplied by the mind itself and not by experience. We can see both of these elements clearly in the operation of conscience, he feels. The content of conscience, the *specific behavior* that we take to be right or wrong, is the product of our experience, and consequently will always vary with the experience and background of each individual. Those who have been reared in a relatively strict moral environment will believe that such acts as gambling and drinking are wrong. Those reared in more liberal homes may well accept these practices without serious question. Those of us who grow up in America will normally believe in a human right to freedom and the right of each individual to direct his own life. Young people in a Communist country will just as naturally accept the right of the state to regulate men's lives more completely.

Now the content of one's conscience in such situations provide what Kant calls "an empirical morality." Like everything else based upon experience, it is necessarily relative and subject to change. The moral relativists are entirely correct about this fact. What they are pointing out is that the con-

---

to learn from it, but in order to win acceptance and permanence for its own precepts. In this way the *common reason of mankind* is impelled, not by any need for speculation (which never assails it so long as it is content to be mere sound reason) but on practical grounds, to leave its own sphere and take a step into the field of practical philosophy." (*Metaphysic of Morals*, trans. by H. J. Paton, pp. 72–73.)

crete *content* of a person's conscience is the product of his specific social environment. But where they are wrong, from Kant's point of view, is in assuming that a valid moral ideal is to be found in such an empirical morality. They fail to understand the true nature of morality, of right and wrong, because their analysis of conscience is deficient and superficial.

Conscience contains not only this specific *empirical* content, which is relative and changing. It contains also a *rational* or formal principle, which is universal—and which is not the product of experience at all, but is an essential aspect of human reason, according to Kant. This universal moral principle is expressed in man's sense of obligation to what is right: the conviction that we ought to do our duty no matter what the consequences. This is Kant's categorical imperative of duty. However much men may disagree about *what* they take to be right, they all agree that there is a fundamental difference between right and wrong, and that a man *ought* to do what is right, Kant insists. On this point there is actually no disagreement between the black witch doctor born into an unsophisticated African society and the white Christian missionary who has come there to give his unselfish service to others. The disagreement is only on *what* a person ought to do.

This moral imperative, the sense of obligation to do what is right, does not come from experience, however, Kant maintains. It is here that he disagrees fundamentally with the moral relativist as well as with most modern sociologists. The moral imperative is for Kant an essential aspect of human reason itself. We as rational human beings bring this to experience; we do not find it anywhere in our experience. Such a principle Kant terms *a priori* to distinguish it from all insights that do come from experience.

## The Moral Law

How can we escape the dangers of moral relativism and build a morality that is valid for everyone, everywhere, regardless of circumstances? To do so, we must derive our moral principles entirely from the moral *a priori*, the categorical imperative of duty, Kant maintains. We must get away from anything that is based simply on our own experience or training. When we do this, we will have a morality, he believes, that makes the same necessary and universal claims upon men's minds as does mathematics.

Now the one basic and universal categorical imperative of duty that is completely independent of all experience, Kant believes, is this: *Always act on that maxim which can at the same time be made a universal law of conduct.*[11] This is the principle that lies at the heart of a valid morality. The real test of moral conduct does not consist in its value to us, Kant points out. We cannot discover whether an action is right or wrong by finding out how well it works for us. In order to find out whether our conduct is actually right, right for everyone, we must universalize our principles of behavior. That is, we have to ask what would happen if everybody did as we are doing, and if everyone knew we were doing it? These are the questions that enable us to determine whether our conduct conforms to the moral law.

Kant suggests a simple example to make this point clear: A man finds himself driven to borrowing money because of need:

> He well knows that he will not be able to pay it back; but he sees too well that he will get no loan unless he gives a firm promise to pay it back within a fixed time. He is inclined to make such a promise; but he still has enough conscience to ask, "Is it not contrary to duty to get out of difficulties in this way?" Suppose, however, that he did resolve to do so, the maxim of his action would run thus: "Whenever I believe myself short of money, I will borrow money and promise to pay it back, though I know that this will never be done."
>
> Now this principle of self-love or personal advantage is perhaps quite compatible with my own future welfare; only there remains the question "Is it right?" I therefore frame my question thus: "How would things stand if my maxim became a universal law?" I then see straight away that this maxim can never rank as a universal law and be self-consistent, but must necessarily contradict itself. For the universality of a law that everyone believing himself to be in need may make any promise he pleases with the intention not to keep it, would make promising itself, and the very purpose of promising, impossible, since no one would believe that he was being promised anything, but would laugh at utterances of this kind as empty shams.[12]

Dishonesty, then, is clearly unacceptable morally because (1) dishonesty is effective only when it is believed to be honesty—a lie is of value to us only when taken to be the truth. Hence dishonesty is essentially self-contradictory. And (2) dishonesty is useless when everyone practices it. It cannot be universalized. The same defects will be apparent, Kant feels, in all other morally unacceptable actions.

A second formulation of the moral law is also possible—not quite as general as the first, perhaps, but also universal and equally valid. Human beings, because they alone are rational and capable of high moral achievement, have a dignity and worth of their own which it is wrong to transgress, Kant points out. Hence no behavior can be universally adopted—and so accepted as morally right—that deprives others of the opportunity to develop their own capacities as fully as they can. In Kant's language, persons are ends-in-themselves. His second formulation of the moral imperative is as follows: "*Act in such a way that you always treat humanity, whether in your own person or in the person of another, never simply as a means but always at the same time as an end.*"[13]

We have only to examine our traditional practices in industry, in racial relations, in war and politics, to see the significance of this way of stating the moral law. Are we not guilty, again and again—and often quite unconsciously, of treating other persons as means only? They may be workers in an automobile factory, members of an underprivileged minority, or the people of a backward and exploitable country. Too often, it seems, we seek to get what we want in life, careless and unaware of the effects upon others.

### The Enlightened Conscience

As one considers Kant's analysis of conscience and his discussion of the moral imperative, it becomes clear that his moral philosophy goes well beyond the pure, unspoiled moral insights of the innocent or naïve individual. Only as our conscience is educated, and educated in terms of the moral principles that Kant outlines, can we hope to do what is right. His primary emphasis is upon the place of will—and the good will—in moral conduct, to be sure. But "practical reason" is essential as well in determining what is right and wrong. To do what is right in the complexities of modern life, a man must follow the dictates of his conscience, but only an enlightened conscience can enable him to escape the limitations and inconsistencies of an empirical morality.

In every instance the dictates of conscience must be examined in the light of Kant's two principles. We must ask ourselves quite honestly: can this action of mine be made a universal law of conduct? Would I be willing to see everyone, under all circumstances, act in this way? Does this involve using other people simply as *means* for my own purposes? Questions such as these can prove quite searching. But they reveal also that the consequences of our behavior as well as our motives are actually involved in Kant's moral philosophy, when seen in its entirety.

It becomes at once obvious, of course, why dishonesty is wrong when tested in this fashion. Disloyalty to one's friends, or the failure to do what one can to assist them, proves to be equally immoral. What about one's relationships with members of the opposite sex? Can what we generally take for granted as acceptable here meet both these Kantian tests successfully? It is certainly easy to *use* other persons for our own ends. When this is done consciously we all recognize its immorality. But does it not happen far too often in ways of which we are not immediately aware?

As a matter of fact, when we examine the appeal to some of life in the small commune, is it not obvious that Kant's moral imperative is being recognized? Among other things, there is clearly a deep concern here to see that people are not treated as things, not used and discarded, but are given the opportunity to be persons in their own right.

### Kant and the Christian Moral Ideal

Kant's formulation of the moral law agrees also in large measure with two popular statements of the Christian moral ideal: do unto others as you would have them do unto you, and treat all men as brothers. Here are earlier expressions of the categorical imperative of duty, which through the centuries have impressed Christians at least as possessing those qualities of necessity and universality that Kant finds in the moral law.

Kant himself, indeed, was quite satisfied to see in his *Fundamental Principles of the Metaphysic of Morals* just such a clear understanding and accurate statement of man's enduring moral conviction. "A critic who wished to say something against that work really did better than he intended when he said that there was no new principle or morality in it but only a new formula," Kant wrote some years later. "Who would want to introduce a new principle of morality and, as it were, be its inventor, as if the world had hitherto been ignorant of what duty is or had been thoroughly wrong about it? Those who know what a formula means to a mathematician in determining what is to be done in solving a problem without letting him go astray, will not regard a formula which will do this for all duties as something insignificant and unnecessary."[14]

The primary task that Kant undertook in his *Fundamental Principles of the Metaphysic of Morals* has now been accomplished. He has shown how morality is within the grasp of the ordinary man, that a man can be good if he wants to. He has outlined the basic principles of the moral law, and indicated the essential relationship of the good will to the categorical imperative of duty. He has defended the universality and necessity of the moral ideal against the attacks of the moral relativists. In his judgment these are the things that moral philosophy should do.

## Moral Conviction and Religious Faith

Kant's careful study of the methods and findings of modern science convinced him that the endeavor to reconcile science and religion was an impossible one. Science, by its very nature, must interpret human behavior, like the behavior of the universe, as completely determined; cause and effect must apply everywhere with equal finality. "If it were possible to have so profound an insight into a man's mental character as to know all its motives and likewise all the external occasions that can influence them, we could calculate a man's conduct for the future with as great certainty as a lunar or solar eclipse," Kant writes in describing the scientific point of view.[15]

Science, then, cannot be used to support religious faith in God or immortality, and it is a mistake to try to use scientific knowledge for this purpose. For scientific knowledge deals only with the world of sensory experience; it is an interpretation of the physical and material universe, not of man's moral or spiritual experience.*

---

* "It is impossible by means of metaphysics to progress from knowledge of this world to concepts of God and a proof of his existence through cogent inferences . . . The concept of God is one which belongs originally not to physics, but to morals." (*Critique of Practical Reason*, pp. 240–242.)

What can be shown, Kant maintains, and what he therefore sets out to show, is that religious faith is morally necessary. That is, in order to make sense of the moral life and the categorical imperative of duty, we *must* believe in God, in freedom, and in immortality. But for Kant these beliefs are matters of faith, not of verified knowledge, as religion has always maintained. What the Church should do, then, is not to argue about belief in God or immortality but to deepen its members' moral insight and sense of duty. Once a man becomes inescapably aware of the moral imperative of duty, he will find faith in God and in freedom of the will a necessity, Kant maintains.

### Freedom of the Will

The categorical imperative of duty for Kant is an inescapable fact of the moral life. Every day there are actions that we know we *ought* to do, not because we can prove logically that they are necessary but because of an inner moral sense of obligation to do what is right. But there is obviously no sense in talking about right or wrong if everything one does is the necessary result of environment or past training. Such scientific determinism takes away completely the moral significance of conduct. For my act to be right or wrong, it is essential that I be responsible for my own choice. Here Kant deals directly with the chief problem raised by the scientific ethics of Spinoza.

We see clearly enough, for example, when a gangster forces a bank teller to hand over $10,000 at the point of a gun, that the teller is not held responsible for what he does in this situation, and his action is not considered wrong, because circumstances almost completely determine his conduct. But if the teller falsifies his books and takes the $10,000 to pay for a new Cadillac for his wife, he is held to be both morally and legally responsible, and when caught he is punished by society. Now the convictions "of that marvelous faculty within us called conscience are in complete agreement" with this way of looking at things, Kant points out.

> A man may dissemble as much as he will in order to paint his unlawful behavior as an unintentional error, as mere oversight, which can never be avoided, as something to which he is carried along by the stream of natural necessity, and in this way to make himself out as innocent. But he finds that the advocate who speaks in his behalf cannot silence the accuser in him when he is conscious that at the time when he committed the wrong he was in possession of his freedom.[16]

In our inescapable certainty of obligation and of duty there is included, then, an awareness of freedom, Kant maintains. Duty and freedom are not two separate facts as much as two ways of looking at the same moral experience. This conviction Kant states in the famous dictum: *I ought, therefore I can.* That is, it makes no sense at all to feel that we ought to do something if we cannot do it. A world of this sort would not be intelligible or meaningful. In order to make sense of conscience, we must believe that we have the freedom to do what is right as well as what is wrong.

Look at human conduct, Kant goes on to say, and you will see that all men do regard themselves as free. This is the assumption upon which we always act, whenever we make a rational choice. We deliberate upon several alternatives, choose one, and act upon it. Such behavior makes no sense if our conduct is already completely determined.

## Kant's Dualism

As soon as we face honestly the problem raised by this belief in moral freedom, we see that man is a creature who lives in two worlds, Kant points out. One is the spiritual, or *intelligible*, world, the world of moral law and of religious faith. The other is the *sensible* world, the physical and material world of sensory experience with which the natural sciences deal. Moral freedom and responsibility are essential aspects of the spiritual world. In the world of nature, the sensible world, on the other hand, everything is completely determined in accord with the laws of cause and effect. This is a dualism that Kant sees no way to escape. It is forced upon us by the scientific interpretation of the universe, on the one hand, and the imperatives of the moral life, on the other. The Kantian position was well summarized a generation ago by Rufus Jones, the distinguished American Quaker philosopher:

> Moral obligation, therefore, for Kant is significant not so much for the specific deeds it leads to as for the fact that it reveals a deeper universe to which the moral man belongs. Through the forms of reason which are native capacities in us we cooperate in building up the world of science but as moral beings, obedient to commands of duty, we discover a world of wholly different order, which rests for its stability and for its ultimate triumph on a permanent and unvarying good will grounded in the deepest nature of the universe itself. We can live in either world equally well—the world ruled by fixed mechanical causation or the world of ends under ideals, in the world of space and time or in the world of the spirit where personality comes full into play.[17]

## Faith in God and in Immortality

It is as impossible, Kant argues, for a genuinely moral man to reject belief in God as to fail to believe in freedom of the will. Both of these convictions are necessary aspects of the moral life. There has been some criticism of the way in which Kant states his moral argument for God, but there can be no misunderstanding of his forthright conviction in the matter. The moral imperative, he points out, demands that we promote the highest good we know without question or hesitation. In order to do this rationally, however, we must believe not only that we are free to act as we should, but also that this moral ideal to which we devote ourselves can actually be achieved. The moral man then cannot accept as final the scientific picture of a universe of natural law in which human ideals and purposes are of no consequence. For if he does, he denies the validity of conscience and of morals. "Therefore it is morally necessary to assume the existence of God," Kant concludes.[18]

The heart of Kant's position here is simply that the presupposition of all genuine moral effort is the belief that we are not living in the kind of world that nullifies such effort. The man who has committed his life to high moral endeavor believes inescapably that what he is doing is in accord with the deeper purposes of the universe, that somehow he has the universe behind him, no matter how circumstances may appear to contradict this. In other words, the moral man is led necessarily to believe in a divine moral order and purpose in the fabric of the universe. He cannot rest content with belief in a universe that is hostile or indifferent to ethical endeavor.

Kant's statement of the case for belief in immortality many find less convincing than his argument for belief in moral freedom and in God. He is content to describe the immortality of the soul as a legitimate hope, not a necessary belief. But even so his approach here is far superior morally to the popular religious idea that immortality is a reward for being good.

The imperative of duty sets before us a moral perfection of which no human being is capable in this world, Kant points out. After a long life of moral endeavor, we realize that we have made only a beginning toward what we ought to become. We see that an infinite moral progress will be necessary for us before we can reach this high ideal. Yet we know that such moral perfection is something we *ought* to strive for. We are led, therefore, to believe in immortality, not as a reward for goodness, but as an opportunity to achieve the moral ideal.* Otherwise we would be in the contradictory position of believing we *ought* to achieve an ideal that we could never hope to achieve.

### The Moral Ideal and Practical Religion

Man's faith in God, in freedom, and in immortality is in Kant's judgment then dependent in the final analysis upon the deep moral conviction of the human spirit. The moral imperative provides not only the best but the only *proof* religion is capable of. Religion at its best must be concerned, therefore, with high moral endeavor, not with the details of rational theology. Like his ethics, Kant's view of religion is designed to meet the needs of the com-

---

* "One who is conscious of having persisted from legitimate moral motives to the end of a long life in a progress to the better, may well have the comforting hope, though not the certainty, that he will be steadfast in these principles in an existence continuing beyond this life," Kant writes. "This infinite progress is possible, however, only under the presupposition of infinitely enduring existence and personality of the same rational being; this is called the immortality of the soul." (*Critique of Practical Reason*, Beck trans., pp. 227n, 226.)

mon man. The essence of religion lies in "the recognition of all our duties as divine commands," he writes.[19] The voice of conscience is our best guide to the will of God. Genuine religion is to be found not in reciting the creed, not in church attendance nor ecclesiastical ceremony, but in high moral endeavor. Churches and creeds have value only insofar as they inspire us to a better life, and they should be judged by this standard, Kant insists in his last major work, *Religion Within the Limits of Reason Alone*.

As he looked around in his own day, however, Kant saw the Christian Church emphasizing creed and ritual rather than love and brotherhood. Men measured religion by church attendance or theological belief instead of by deep moral conviction and unselfish way of life. It was high time, Kant maintained, that the essential moral content of religion be clearly recognized and made central in Christianity again. Today many young people still find this Kantian point of view thoroughly sound and convincing.

## Philosophy of Science

When the sciences portray a world of natural law in which every event, whether in the physical universe or in human life, is completely determined, how can we believe in a moral universe, in freedom of the will, in God, and perhaps in immortality, no matter how necessary such faith may be for man's moral life? In Kant's judgment, the central issue with which philosophy must deal is posed by this question. The *Critique of Pure Reason* is his answer. He seeks to provide here an interpretation of scientific knowledge and the scientific endeavor that recognizes the validity of science and yet does not invalidate the moral imperative or religious faith. Kant gave eleven years to writing this *Critique* before he was satisfied. But this task had to be accomplished, he felt, before he could go ahead with his moral philosophy. Unfortunately, many interpreters of Kant have been so intrigued by the *Critique of Pure Reason*—or in some cases so baffled by it—that they never get to the moral philosophy for which it prepared the way.

### The Kantian Revolution in Philosophy

Kant's philosophy of science can be understood only when one sees clearly the problem he faced. As a young student he had taken for granted with Newton that the natural sciences give us dependable knowledge of the physical and material world around us. But from this "dogmatic slumber," as he called it, Kant was awakened by the philosophy of David Hume, the Scottish skeptic who pushed British empiricism to its logical conclusion.

If we believe only what we can see, as some empiricists naïvely insist, we find very little that we can believe, Hume points out in his *Treatise on Human Nature*. Examine experience carefully and we discover, for example, that it contains no awareness of cause or natural law. We see the sun rise in the east day after day and conclude that it must do so, but in no instance do we actually observe any such necessity. Necessity is not a fact of experience. It is merely an inference that we ourselves make. We see one billiard ball strike another. We see them together for an instant, and then we see them move apart. But we never *see* anything that we can justly call causation. The fact that we see this happen a hundred times rather than once does not justify us, as empiricists, in concluding that it must always occur. That conclusion is not justified unless we can actually observe the necessity of a particular event. And necessity is something that we never observe.

As a young philosopher Kant was given a rude jolt by the scepticism of Hume. He realized that he had been taking for granted a number of assumptions about scientific knowledge that he could not prove. On the other hand, he was sure that the Newtonian science, which he knew so well, provided him with dependable knowledge that the empiricists could not satisfactorily explain. Hume had convinced him that the kind of knowledge science then claimed to have—knowledge that is universal and necessary for all rational beings—can never be derived from experience. Yet we do have such knowledge in the natural sciences, Kant believed.* It was this achievement of Newtonian science that so impressed him. Could it perhaps be that the rational principles or "laws," which science uses in interpreting the physical universe, actually come from the mind itself, and not from our experience of external objects at all?

When this possibility first struck him, the "critical philosophy" to which Kant devoted the rest of his life was born. Philosophy, he came to believe, must begin with the reflection of the mind upon its own nature and its own operations, rather than upon the nature of things outside the mind. This basic principle he stated quite simply:

> Hitherto it has been assumed that all our knowledge must conform to objects. But all attempts to extend our knowledge of objects by establishing something in regard to them by means of concepts have, on this assumption, ended in failure. We must, therefore, make trial whether we may not have more success if we suppose that *objects must conform to our knowledge*.[20]

### The Work of the Mind

The first problem that Kant deals with in the *Critique of Pure Reason* provides the key to his whole philosophy of science. How, he asks, is mathematical knowledge possible? According to the empiricism of Hume, it is impos-

---

* As pointed out in the discussions of Spinoza and Plato, there has been a revolution in scientific thought in our own century that has changed the outlook of the scientist. The natural scientist now thinks in terms of probability rather than absolute necessity, and of symbols rather than objective reality. See pages 143n., 183.

sible to find in experience either *necessity* or *universality*. Yet, as a matter of fact, in mathematical knowledge both necessity and universality are unmistakably present. Two plus two will always and necessarily be four. The mind cannot entertain any other possibility, no matter what the situation. Upon closer examination we discover, then, Kant points out, that in mathematics the universality and necessity come from the mind itself and not from experience. It is because the mind works as it does that we can always be sure that $2 + 2 = 4$. Experience merely provides the occasion for the use of certain fundamental principles by which the mind works. It does not supply these principles.

Here we have the insight, Kant maintains, that will enable us to understand how scientific knowledge is possible and what it is like. The mind is not a blank tablet, as John Locke had suggested, upon which experience writes and thus gives us our knowledge of external objects. The human mind is, rather, an active agent at work collecting and organizing the data of experience according to certain principles inherent in its own nature. The mere apprehension of facts never gives us scientific knowledge. Facts must be put together, organized, and made intelligible before we get any knowledge; and this is the work of the mind itself.

At the heart of Kant's philosophy is a new interpretation of the mind's creative activity. The work of the mind might well be compared to that of the managing editor of a great newspaper like *The New York Times*. From all over the world there comes to the editor's desk information about what is happening: news flashes, feature articles, routine dispatches, weather reports, political cartoons, sports results. He has far more at his disposal than he can use. What he has does not by itself make sense. It lacks the order and arrangement necessary for a coherent and informative newspaper or news report. This the editor himself must provide. He must supply the pattern, the principles of organization and interpretation, that make of this mass of unrelated data a coherent whole, a meaningful picture for the reader of the newspaper. He eliminates what he cannot use, and fits what he feels most significant into the pattern that he himself creates. And then, whether we like it or not, as we read the paper at breakfast the next morning, or listen to the news that evening, we see the world through the pattern that the editor himself has provided.

Not only does this analogy portray clearly the active function of the mind in ordering the rough data of experience. It indicates also another equally important aspect of Kant's critical philosophy: no knowledge is possible until we have the data of sense experience to organize and interpret. Without the work of the editor there would be no coherent newspaper. But likewise there could be none without the mass of data that came to his desk from the outside world. In similar fashion, the mind by itself can give us no knowledge of the world, Kant maintains. It is equipped to organize and interpret what we see and hear, using certain fundamental categories of its own.

### A Priori Knowledge

Those principles of interpretation which the mind contributes to our knowledge of the world Kant calls *a priori*. That is, they exist in the mind *prior to* all experience, and it is only as they arrange and order the data of the senses that experience as we know it becomes possible.* It is not difficult to distinguish the *empirical* from the *a priori* or purely rational elements, Kant is convinced. As Hume so successfully argued, necessity and universality could never be derived from experience. Hence, whenever we find knowledge that is necessary and universal, we can be sure that it is *a priori*:

> Experiences tell us what is, but not that it must be necessarily what it is and not otherwise. Secondly, experience can never tell us that a judgment is always and universally true, only that it is here and now valid. Necessity and strict universality are, therefore, sure criteria of *a priori* knowledge, and are also inseparably connected with each other.[21]

### The Limits of Scientific Knowledge

In this fashion Kant rescues scientific knowledge from the uncertainty that Hume's empiricism had cast upon it. The creative activity of the human mind itself is the cornerstone upon which his philosophy of science is built. It is here that we must look for the sure foundations of our scientific knowledge. The validity, the necessity, the universality that have given to science such prestige and influence are all supplied by the human mind, Kant maintains. They are not discovered in the external world of nature.

If Kant can be said, however, to have saved scientific knowlege from the skepticism of Hume, he certainly did not rescue it undamaged. His philosophy of science is quite different from that accepted by most scientists of his century. For if Kant is correct, the world as we know it in the natural sciences is not the world as it "really" is. It is rather a world we ourselves have built by fashioning the data of the senses in accord with a pattern our own minds provided. We might perhaps illustrate the difference by contrasting a photographer's picture of a landscape with an artist's painting of the same scene. The photographer reproduces the landscape as it actually looks to our eyes, we say. The artist gives us his creative interpretation of the scene, based upon actual facts to be sure, but given a new meaning and beauty by the

---

* "By *a priori* knowledge we shall, therefore, in what follows understand, not such knowledge as is independent of this or that experience, but such as is absolutely independent of all experience," Kant writes. "Opposed to it is empirical knowledge, or that which is possible only *a posteriori*, that is, by experience" (*Critique of Pure Reason*, Intro. § 1).

genius of the artist. In the philosophy of Kant the scientific picture of the universe turns out to be more like the creative work of the artist than like the optically faithful reproduction of the photographer.

As thus interpreted, science does not, and cannot, give us knowledge of reality itself, of whatever is as it really is. Scientific knowledge is knowledge of a world that we ourselves have built in accord with the pattern supplied by the human mind. This Kant calls the phenomenal world, to distinguish it from the world as it exists regardless of human recognition. The realm with which morality and religion is concerned, however, the realm of God and the human spirit, of freedom of the will and immortality, lies beyond the phenomenal world of science. It can never be brought within the domain of scientific knowledge. When science attempts to go beyond the limits of the physical world, and to provide knowledge of God or spiritual reality, it immediately falls into unresolvable dilemmas, Kant points out. We cannot prove the existence of the soul nor its immortality. But we cannot disprove either of these beliefs by scientific data, since it is impossible to use the categories of science (such as space, time, cause, substance) beyond the limits of sensory experience.* Moral conviction and religious faith, on the one hand, and the world of scientific knowledge, on the other, simply cannot be make to coincide or be commensurate, Kant concludes, in agreement with the dualism that he finds inescapable. Only as we recognize this dualism can the conflict between scientific determinism and religious faith be resolved. "I have therefore found it necessary to deny *knowledge* of God, freedom and immortality, in order to find a place for *faith*," he writes in the preface to his first *Critique*.[22]


## What Kant Accomplished

In the field of moral philosophy Kant stands in a place by himself. He introduces a dimension of morals not recognized in the thought of Plato or Aristotle, nor in that of Spinoza or Dewey. And he portrays the compulsion of the moral ideal with a conviction found nowhere else in the history of philosophy. His position, if accepted, effectively rescues man's moral life from the intricacies and uncertainties of moral relativism. He skillfully defends the validity of freedom of the will and of moral conviction against the determinism of scientific thought. And he commits himself without equivocation to faith in God and the moral order of the universe as a fundamental tenet of the philosophy by which a moral man must live. It is not difficult, therefore, to

---

* Kant calls these insoluble dilemmas, where science tries to go beyond experience, "the antinomies of pure reason." Among such antinomies he includes questions such as whether the world is finite or infinite in space, whether it had a beginning in time or is eternal. An endless chain of cause and effect is inconceivable, Kant feels, but a First Cause that had no cause is equally inconceivable.

understand the large appeal of Kant's moral philosophy to men of good will in earlier generations as well as our own.

There are difficulties, of course, in Kant's position. His ethical theory, in the judgment of his critics, oversimplifies the actual nature of moral conduct. The problems that perplex us, as a rule, are not in choosing between loyalty or obvious disloyalty to family, to friends, to country, or to religion. In such situations we usually find that we can tell what is right and what wrong without serious difficulty. Actually our perplexing moral choices come when these basic loyalties conflict. It is when we have to choose between two courses of action both of which are good in themselves that we need help. When loyalty to family seems to ask of us conduct that conflicts with loyalty to country, or when loyalty to country demands of us action that is in conflict with a higher loyalty to God or to our fellow man, Kant's moral philosophy, in the opinion of his critics, has little insight to offer us.

His position, these critics maintain, is too *formalistic*. It does not tell us concretely enough what the positive goods of life are. Kant's conception of morality is in marked contrast here, for example, to that found in naturalism. As is clearly to be seen in the philosophy of Dewey and Aristotle, naturalism places little emphasis upon duty and obedience but portrays the "good life" as one of concrete achievement, joy, and self-realization. Kant, we may well agree, provides us with an excellent test for moral conduct: always act in accord with a principle that can be made a universal law. But this general principle does not provide the insight needed to determine the concrete achievements and satisfactions that make up the good life for each of us.

The principle that we ought always to treat every person as an end, and never as a means only, desirable though it be, does create serious legal and political difficulties, in the judgment of so discerning a social philosopher as Reinhold Niebuhr. This principle does not help us reach the *right* decision, for example, when the interests and welfare of two persons or two groups of people genuinely conflict, Niebuhr feels. While both *should* be treated in this way, sometimes both cannot be. Nor can the common good, the welfare of the community, be adequately protected upon Kant's principle. War in any circumstance is certainly undesirable, but there are times when justice is a higher social goal than peace, Niebuhr argues. He is finally led to accept the conclusion, therefore, that the Christian ethic, which is essentially Kantian in spirit, is of much greater significance in the life of the individual than in dealing with the problems of social morality.[23] Can we escape the same conclusion concerning the Kantian moral philosophy?

Our examination of Kant's philosophy has indicated, however, that the scope and validity of scientific thought may well also be limited. When man is seeking direction in the conduct of life, when he seeks some dependable insight into the meaning of human existence and into the enduring nature of the universe itself, it is not to reason and science but to his moral experience and conviction that he must go, if Kant's point of view is accepted. In this fashion his philosophy strikes a mortal blow at man's unqualified confidence in reason.

It is true that recent developments in science do not lend support to Kant's theory of *a priori* knowledge nor the details of his philosophy of science. But through the door that he opened such philosophers as Arthur Schopenhauer, Friedrich Nietzsche, and William James proceeded to a much more direct and vigorous attack upon reason and science, and to an emphasis upon will as the dominant factor in shaping human life and conduct. In our own day the existentialists have carried even further this movement for which Kant was initially responsible. Jean-Paul Sartre and Martin Buber both accept the Kantian position that man is a creature of two worlds, the world of rational analysis and scientific thought, on the one hand, and the world of immediate moral awareness and deep personal experience, on the other. And with Kant they turn to the second of these two worlds for man's deepest insight into the meaning of life.

## CHAPTER 12

# Pragmatism

## *William James*

William James was the first great American philosopher. In the history of American thought there are other figures before him of unquestioned distinction—such men as Jonathan Edwards in theology and Emerson in literature—whose achievement was philosophical in the larger sense of the word. And there are numerous lesser figures in the field of philosophy proper. In recent years Charles S. Peirce, a contemporary and friend of James, has also been recognized as a philosopher of more than ordinary ability. But James was the first American to be accepted in England and in Europe as a philosopher of stature comparable to that of his illustrious contemporaries in these countries. He was the first American to develop a philosophical point of view that took its place among the positions bidding for the allegiance of scholars as well as laymen both in America and abroad.

While James's pragmatism was essentially American in spirit, his sympathies and the formative influences that shaped his thought were more than provincial or national. The broad evolutionary and anti-intellectual forces at work in the late nineteenth century touched his mind and were caught up in his pragmatic philosophy as surely as they were in the thought of Friedrich Nietzsche in Germany and Henri Bergson in France. It was in large measure, indeed, because James gave clear and forceful expression to the inner spirit of the age that he achieved popularity and influence such as no American philosopher had known before him and as none has since, with the possible exception of John Dewey.

The appeal of James's thought for the ordinary reader is greatly enhanced also by the way in which it is presented. James writes not with the scholarly detachment or the formidable technical vocabulary of Spinoza or Kant but with the force and directness of the popular speaker. Except for his influential two-volume work on psychology, most of his books are made up of lectures or essays, which were first read to university and lay audiences. And James, true to his own principles, was convinced that a lecture, to be good, must succeed —that is, people must understand it and be moved by it. The major concern of his pragmatic approach, as a matter of fact, is to make philosophy practical, usable in everyday life. Only that which will work when put into practice, only that by which men can live successfully, is entitled to be called good or true, James insists.

## The Education of William James

Among the philosophers we have considered thus far, some were child prodigies and many were men whose genius came to expression early and easily. John Stuart Mill was reading Latin and Greek when he was eight. Schopenhauer published his volume *The World as Will and Idea* when only twenty-eight. Both Spinoza and Nietzsche had completed their contributions to philosophy before the end of their forty-fifth years. William James, on the other hand, was well past thirty before he reached any kind of certainty concerning his major work in life. His early years, however, were rich in breadth of experience and in maturing insight. Indeed, education was for William James, more obviously than for most men, a matter of the kind of life he lived and the interests and associations he pursued rather than a formal experience to be cataloged in terms of years of study or degrees taken in one institution or another.

### Early Years at Home and Abroad

James's father was a restless man. Life somewhere else always seemed to hold charms greater than those at hand. Much of William James's youth was spent in periodic trips to Europe or in efforts by his father to find a more congenial spot for the family home in America. The most prominent characteristic of his education was constant change. As the James family grew in size—eventually there were four sons and one daughter—their father became increasingly dissatisfied with the New York schools, as well as with the "shocking bad manners" the boys picked up in the streets of the city. There seemed to him something very desirable about the schools of Europe that American schools as yet did not possess. So in June 1855 the whole family sailed for Europe, and by early August, William and his younger brothers were nicely established in private schools in Geneva. But the Swiss schools in the abstract looked much better than the Swiss schools in the concrete. By October their father had become so unhappy that the family was on its way to England for the winter.

The next year was spent in much the same way. In the summer of 1857 the family moved to Boulogne, a French seaside resort on the English channel. Here William, now sixteen, attended the local college, and for the first time had a solid year of sound and uninterrupted instruction. His chief interest lay in the sciences, especially in biology. As he wrote to a young friend at the time, "If I followed my taste and did what was most agreeable to me, I'll tell you what I would do. I would get a microscope and go out into the country, into the dear old woods and fields and ponds. There I would try to make as many discoveries as possible."[1]

He had little opportunity, however, to develop this inclination. The following spring, as by now had become its custom, the whole family moved bag and baggage, this time back to Newport, Rhode Island. William had been eager to attend Union College at Schenectady, where his grandfather had been a trustee and his father had graduated. But he found his father much opposed to the idea of his going to any American college. "He says that colleges are hot-beds of corruption where it is *impossible* to learn anything," William wrote a friend in disappointment. After a year and a half at Newport, Henry James again settled on Switzerland as the ideal spot to educate his "ingenuous" boys.

The following summer William decided that what he really wanted to study was art rather than science. To his father art seemed frivolous and narrow when compared with the glory of religion or the usefulness of science. But he was discerning enough in his views on education not to interfere when his son was convinced that his talent and interest lay in art. After studying painting for a year, however, William found that his interest in art was much less compelling than he had imagined. He turned from art to science without further question and without regret.

### Harvard University and Later Studies

In the fall of 1861, William James began the study of chemistry in the Lawrence Scientific School at Harvard. For the next forty-six years Harvard University played an important role in his life. He soon passed from the study of chemistry to biology and anatomy. Here he wrestled with the problem of evolution, just then being given great prominence by the work of Darwin and by Herbert Spencer's philosophy. And he also came under the influence of Louis Agassiz, at that time the most distinguished figure at Harvard in science. A few years later James joined an expedition to Brazil that Agassiz headed. But eight months in the Amazon away from all contact with civilization convinced him that he had little desire to spend his life in collecting and classifying fish or in natural history as such. He felt the need of people, of friends and family, of religion, philosophy, love, and the like. He wrote to friends at Harvard, "When I get home I'm going to study philosophy all my days."

When he did get back, however, he went ahead with the studies in the Harvard Medical School that he had begun some years before his expedition with Agassiz. Upon completing the necessary work for his medical degree in 1872, when thirty years old, James began his teaching career at Harvard as instructor in physiology. When three years later he was promoted to an assistant professorship, he was definitely established professionally. His commitment to Harvard became one of the important aspects of his life as gradually but surely he began working his way from physiology through psychology to philosophy. Writing to his brother Henry a good many years later, James noted that nowhere in Europe "did I see a University which seems to do for all its students anything like what Harvard does."

The year 1878, when James was thirty-six, in many ways marks a turning point in his life. Perhaps the most important event of that year was his marriage to Alice Gibbens, an attractive young woman distinguished in both character and common sense. James's wife brought into his life a composure and a steadying sense of purpose that his high-strung and mobile nature greatly needed. She cared for his health with untiring devotion; and she protected him time after time from the consequences of his own rash generosity.

A few months before his marriage, James had signed a contract with Henry Holt and Co. to write a textbook on psychology. It was twelve years before this work was actually completed, but the commitment initiated one of his most fruitful and influential undertakings. His *Principles of Psychology* appeared in 1890, when the author was forty-eight years old. The book immediately attracted wide attention and marked James as one of the gifted and original scholars in the field. The ease with which James wrote and the richness of concrete illustration in his book added to its appeal. *The Principles of Psychology* was unique in its day, and even today, after more than eighty years, it remains one of the more instructive and readable discussions of the subject.

### Commitment to Philosophy

Upon the publication of this text, James experienced a profound sense of relief, the feeling of a job completed. The year 1890 actually marks the culmination of his active interest in psychology. His major concern and achievement henceforth were to center in philosophy. He did not, to be sure, become a philosopher overnight. His interest in philosophy had been deep and abiding through most of his life, but philosophy was never for him a detached and dispassionate inquiry or a mere academic theory. It was rather a matter of personal conviction. The need James felt was for a philosophy that would enable him to overcome the periods of discouragement and depression to which he was so frequently subjected.

In a very real sense the moral philosophy that he developed was not so much the philosophy he lived by as the kind of philosophy he needed to make life worthwhile. The paradox between James the man and James the philosopher is a revealing one. Put another way, this is the contrast between what James saw himself to be and what he wanted to be. Much like Nietzsche, he identifies danger, "strenuousness," intensity, as essential to give life vitality and meaning. He contrasts the tough- and the tender-minded and, in an essay that attracted wide attention, *The Moral Equivalent of War*, finds in the heroism that war inspires the kind of tough-mindedness that he admires.[2]

But, as his diary makes quite clear, this was not the kind of man James saw himself to be. He was plagued by anxiety, despondency, and discouragement. He was often ill. Much like his father, he found it difficult to make up his mind or continue steadfastly in any one course of action. His very moves from biology, to psychology, to philosophy, were one expression of such uncertainty and indecision. Clearly also to James this was essentially a matter of will. It was at this point that philosophy, to be useful, must contribute.

For many years he brooded upon the nature of the universe and the destiny of man. In the scientific picture of the universe, with its acceptance of a complete determinism, he could find no ongoing purpose to inspire him, and for a while life did not seem worthwhile to the young student. His experience was actually much akin to that later given such prominence by the existentialists. During this time, however, he read the *Essays* of Charles Renouvier, a celebrated French philosopher, and from them he gained a new sense of freedom and a faith in free will. "My first act of freedom will be to believe in free will," James asserted. Thereafter he never relinquished his will to believe. It became the permanent foundation of his own philosophy of living.

Because of his own deep personal commitment to the faith he lived by, James doubted the wisdom of making the teaching of philosophy his profession. "Philosophical activity as a *business* is not normal for most men, and not for me," he wrote, during his early years on the Harvard faculty:

> My strongest moral and intellectual craving is for some stable reality to lean upon, and as a professed philosopher pledges himself publicly never to have done with doubt on these subjects, but every day to be ready to criticize afresh and call in question the grounds of his faith of the day before, I fear the constant sense of instability generated by this attitude would be more than the voluntary faith I can keep going is sufficient to neutralize.[3]

This fear, however, proved to be exaggerated. James became not only a professional philosopher but also a most successful teacher. His students enjoyed their contacts with him, both in class and at his pleasant house not far from the campus. Some of them were later quite famous; interestingly enough, two of the more famous, Theodore Roosevelt and George Santayana, were among the few whom James actively disliked.

## Mature Achievement

It was not until 1897, when James was fifty-five, that his first book in philosophy, *The Will to Believe and Other Essays in Popular Philosophy,* was published.* Running through these essays is a moral earnestness, a conviction that, if there is to be anything valuable in living, it must come as one is free to believe in a moral ideal and to serve it without enervating doubt.

The following year James was invited to deliver the Gifford Lectures in Edinburgh, a signal distinction that has come to few American philosophers. His Gifford lectures were published immediately upon delivery (in 1901–1902) under the title *The Varieties of Religious Experience,* and the book is one of James's best. Like his *Principles of Psychology,* it has continued to hold the interest of thoughtful people today, old and young alike.

On New Year's Day in 1906, James left Cambridge for California to become Visiting Professor of Philosophy for the spring term at Stanford University, and he was in Stanford at the time of the great San Francisco earthquake of 1906. His article describing his own reactions on that occasion is one of the classic psychological accounts of such an experience. Soon after returning from Stanford, James delivered at Harvard the lectures on "Pragmatism" that provide the most direct popular statement of the philosophy for which he has become famous. These lectures were repeated the following spring at Columbia University, and were published in 1907 in the volume entitled *Pragmatism.* The audience at Columbia University numbered more than a thousand persons, and James's book attracted widespread attention. James himself felt that he was now giving the most effective statement to his philosophy and was greatly heartened by its reception. "I shouldn't be surprised," he wrote his brother Henry about the volume, "if ten years hence it should be rated as 'epoch-making,' for of the definitive triumph of that general way of thinking I can entertain no doubt whatever—I believe it to be something quite like the protestant reformation."[4] To another friend, James wrote: "I want to make you all enthusiastic converts to 'pragmatism.'" It is the "philosophy of the future." "Every sane and sound tendency in life can be brought under it."

James's influence, in Europe as well as in America can hardly be overestimated. He was constantly called upon to speak, both to university and to

* The title of his essay, "The Will to Believe," offered to critics of James's philosophy an inviting opportunity to attack his position. One critic suggested that it should be called "the will to make-believe," and James later said he was sorry he had not used "the right to believe" as a title. Actually, however, it is the dominant place of will rather than reason that characterizes James's philosophy, as correctly indicated here. The effort by Douglas C. Macintosh, for many years a distinguished professor in the Yale Divinity School, to restate James's position more precisely is quite interesting: "We have the right to believe as we must in order to live as we should, if we can logically and psychologically do so."

lay audiences, and he continued to write and publish frequently. The pragmatic approach, if not the principles of pragmatism, characterized American philosophy for a generation after James's lectures on pragmatism were delivered. Although he did not by any means make pragmatists of all the younger philosophers in this country, he gave effective expression to a spirit and point of view that simply became a part of popular American thought.*

The year *Pragmatism* was published, James retired from teaching at Harvard. He was sixty-five and, although his teaching responsibilities had been quite light for some years, his health and strength were gradually failing. He was now anxious to devote all his remaining energy to the more systematic statement of his philosophy while there was yet time to do so. Two years later he published *The Meaning of Truth*, a collection of essays developing this aspect of pragmatism, and *A Pluralistic Universe*, lectures given at Mansfield College in Oxford in 1908.

In these volumes James was striving to provide the kind of scholarly and systematic statement of pragmatism that none of his earlier and more popular works contained. With the growth of his reputation and influence, he became increasingly conscious of the criticism directed against him on this score, and he was anxious to meet it. "I live in apprehension lest the Avenger should cut me off before I get my message out," he wrote to his brother Henry. "I hate to leave the volumes I have already published without their logical complement." But he was aware, also, that he never quite managed to accomplish his aim successfully. He died with the task incomplete; perhaps it was an impossible one. As the final comment in the last essay he published, James himself had written his own last word in philosophy—a revealing and characteristic comment: "There is no conclusion. What has concluded that we might conclude regarding it? There are no fortunes to be told and there is no advice to be given. Farewell."

## James as Moral Philosopher

Philosophy, for William James, was always a very practical matter. It was never a detached or dispassionate search for some "abstract" truth, never a pastime or form of amusement, but rather a serious existential concern. As a young man James felt a continuing need to work out for himself a satisfying philosophy to live by, a creed that would give his life purpose and direction.

---

* One of the clearest evidences of this is to be found in the legal philosophy of Justice Oliver Wendell Holmes, James's friend at Harvard and colleague there as a member of the Law School faculty before his appointment to the United States Supreme Court. In his classic book *The Common Law* Justice Holmes explicitly adopted a pragmatic position that clearly shaped his celebrated opinions during a long service on the Supreme Court. (See Lloyd Morris, *William James*. New York: Scribners, 1950, pp. 84–85.)

"There are some people—and I am one of them—" he observes with G. K. Chesterton, "who think that the most important and most practical thing about a man is still his view of the universe. We think that for a landlady considering a lodger it is important to know his income, but still more important to know his philosophy." As James sees it:

> [T]he philosophy which is so important in each of us is not a technical matter, it is our more or less dumb sense of what life honestly and deeply means. It is only partially got from books; it is our individual way of just seeing and feeling the total push and pressure of the cosmos. It works in the minutest crannies and it opens out the widest vistas. It "bakes no bread," as has been said, but it can inspire us with courage; and repugnant as its manners, its doubting and challenging, its quibbling and dialectics often are to common people, no one of us can get along without the far-flashing beams of light it sends over the world's perspectives.[5]

As a consequence of this approach, a moral earnestness permeates James's philosophical thinking. The major issue we face in life, he feels, is the conflict of good and evil; and he is eager to discover a moral ideal that one can not only *believe in* but also follow. He has a strong distaste, therefore, for anything that seems superficial, mediocre, decadent. James is also a vigorous exponent of the contemporary. There is something to be done *now* to make the world better. This is well illustrated by his reactions to travel in Italy. A brief visit was enough. "Italy is a very *delightful* place to dip into but no more," he wrote to his sister from Rome. "The weight of the past world here is fatal,—one ends by becoming its mere parasite instead of its equivalent. The ancients did things by doing the business of their own day, not by gaping at their grandfathers' tombs,—and a normal man today will do likewise."[6]

### What Makes Life Worth Living?

This is a question with which James was deeply concerned, and his own answer is direct and clear. It is not what you find in life, but what you put into it, that gives it meaning. Danger, courage, struggle—in a word, heroism—are necessary to make life significant. What is needed is a "real fight," actual risks and genuine obstacles. If one feels that the risks and difficulties are put there merely for their moral effect, however, the spirit of adventure and achievement is lost. There must be genuine conflict with evils that are real and dangerous. No more apt portrayal of this point of view is to be found than James's vivid description of a week he spent at the religious Assembly Grounds on Lake Chautauqua, a place well known a generation or two ago both for its commitment to rather rigid moral standards and also for what Karl Marx would have seen as an ideal expression of the bourgeois life-style. James wrote of it:

The moment one treads that sacred enclosure, one feels one's self in an atmosphere of success. Sobriety and industry, intelligence and goodness, orderliness and ideality, prosperity and cheerfulness, pervade the air. It is a serious and studious picnic on a gigantic scale. . . . You have magnificent music—a chorus of seven hundred voices, with possibly the most perfect open-air auditorium in the world. You have general religious services and special club-houses for the several sects. . . . You have culture, . . . you have equality, you have the best fruits of what mankind has fought and bled and striven for under the name of civilization for centuries. . . .

I went in curiosity for a day. I stayed for a week, held spell-bound by the charm and ease of everything, by the middle-class paradise, without a sin, without a victim, without a blot, without a tear.

And yet what was my own astonishment, on emerging into the dark and wicked world again, to catch myself quite unexpectedly and involuntarily saying "Ouf! What a relief! Now for something primordial and savage to set the balance straight again. . . . this goodness is too uninspiring. This human drama without a villain or a pang; this community so refined that ice-cream soda-water is the utmost offering it can make to the brute animal in man; . . . this atrocious harmlessness of all things,—I cannot abide them. . . .

Such was the sudden right-about-face performed for me by my lawless fancy. There seemed to be a paradox and self-contradiction somewhere, which I, as a professor drawing a full salary, was in duty bound to unravel and explain, if I could. . . . And I soon recognized the element that gives to the wicked outer world all its moral style, expressiveness and picturesqueness—the element of precipitousness, so to call it, of strength and strenuousness, intensity and danger. What excites and interests the looker-on at life . . . is the everlasting battle of the powers of light with those of darkness; with heroism, reduced to its bare chance, yet ever and anon snatching victory from the jaws of death.[7]

This strenuous quality in human life, its intensity and danger, is unfortunately absent also, as James had discovered, in the academic enterprise. There is something too tame and conventional about university courses that limits their appeal and effectiveness for the typical undergraduate, he felt, and that often makes intercollegiate athletics seem much more significant. While he was on the Harvard faculty, a proposal was made to shorten the time required for the B.A. degree from four to three years. This plan James championed with characteristic spirit. Writing in the *Harvard Monthly*, he pointed out that most university students, although probably intelligent, are not interested primarily in what is *theoretical*. Although the analogy he uses is not too popular today, the point he makes is still supported:

These excellent fellows need contact of some sort with the fighting side of life, and with the world in which men and women earn their bread and butter and live and die; there must be the scent of blood, so to speak, upon what you offer them, or else their interest does not wake up. The blood which is shed in our electives fails to satisfy them very long. The A.B. degree should be accommodated to the needs of students of this second category and for them the three-year course is long enough.*

## The Moral Equivalent of War

In general agreement with Friedrich Nietzsche, James condemned mediocrity, passivity, failure to meet squarely the moral issues of the day. Even the martial spirit, which so appealed to Nietzsche, now seemed to James also akin to the qualities he took to be essential in the good life. But James saw, as Nietzsche did not, the limitations and dangers in the naked will to power. He set himself therefore to find a moral equivalent that would preserve what he felt to be ethically valuable in war, but that would avoid the bloodshed, destruction, and horror of modern warfare. The heroic struggle to which we must give ourselves in life should be a struggle with evil and the forces of evil, not a battle of the strong to conquer and subdue the weak.

In 1910, James published an essay, *The Moral Equivalent of War*, in which he developed this position. It was immediately popular in a way that would hardly be the case today. Thousands of reprints were distributed, and it was twice republished in popular magazines. Men in nonacademic circles, among them many army officers, were attracted by its obvious masculine prejudices. The dangers of war "are a cheap price to pay for our rescue from a world of clerks and school teachers, of coeducation, associated charities and feminism," James wrote. "No scorn, no hardness, no valor any more. Fie upon such a cattle-yard of a planet."

But the purpose of the essay was to support the cause of peace—to secure the moral fruits of war, which looked so appealing to James, without its horror and destruction. To this end James proposed a conscription of the youthful male population to form an army "to conquer Nature for the good of society." The insights of the ecologists and the widespread concern to safeguard the beauty and the balance of nature as well as the influence of the Women's Liberation movement would today require a basic restatement of James's proposal. James, of course, was simply looking for a worthwhile social endeavor through which "the military ideals of hardihood and discipline could be brought into the growing fibre of the people, without the callowness, cruelty and degradation that are the inevitable accompaniment of war."[8]

* Ralph Barton Perry, *The Thought and Character of William James*, p. 243. James would be pleased, no doubt, to find that in a number of colleges today winter term courses organized around the outward-bound concept are quite popular. These clearly provide the kind of strenuous quality, psychological as well as physical, that James felt to be essential if College courses were to become appealing for most students.

As James recognized clearly, however, it is the cause for which one fights that ultimately determines the value of the fight, not simply the combat itself. "We are all ready to be savage in some cause," he writes. "The difference between a good man and a bad one is the choice of the cause."

## The Will to Believe

The causes to which we give ourselves, James feels, are the important things in life. These choices, however, are not the result of abstract, rational reflection. They are the outcome of our own needs and experiences. Most Americans do not believe in Buddhism, for example, but we probably would had we grown up in certain parts of the Orient instead of in America. "If one should assume that pure reason is what settles our opinions, he would fly in the teeth of the facts," James writes. "As a rule we disbelieve all facts and theories for which we have no use," and we customarily find reasons for believing what we want to believe. The will comes first, not the intellect, James concludes in agreement with Schopenhauer.

> If your heart does not *want* a world of moral reality, your head will assuredly never make you believe in it. Some men (even at the student age) are so naturally cool-hearted that the moralistic hypothesis never has for them any pungent life, and in their supercilious presence the hot young moralist always feels strangely ill at ease. The appearance of knowingness is on their side, of naïveté and gullibility on his. Yet, in the inarticulate heart of him, he clings to it that he is not a dupe, and that there is a realm in which (as Emerson says) all their wit and intellectual superiority is no better than the cunning of a fox.[9]

Two attitudes toward belief are possible. We can resolve not to believe anything unless we have sufficient evidence to make it completely certain. This is the position of science: "Believe nothing, keep your mind in suspense forever, rather than by closing it on insufficient evidence to incur the awful risk of believing lies." James is emphatic in insisting that the scientist, who is dealing with nature and can wait as long as necessary before making a decision, should accept only those beliefs for which he has such convincing evidence. But there are other situations in life in which decisions must be made, in which we must accept one alternative or another, whether we are entirely ready to do so or not. A judge, for example, must usually decide whether a man is guilty or not in the light of the evidence at hand. He cannot simply postpone the matter indefinitely as can the scientist who may —indeed, who often must—wait years before making up his mind just how the atom can be smashed or how a manned flight to the moon can be achieved.

Now the moral and religious decisions we have to make in life are, in the main, matters about which a decision has to be made one way or the other, James points out. They are what he calls *forced options*. But in such moral and religious decisions, what we believe actually helps determine the future facts. The man who says to himself, "I will have no friends until I am absolutely sure of the worth and loyalty of my acquaintances," will have no friends. But the man who shows himself a friend to others will *make* friends of them. If you *will* believe well of your fellow men, you may well create the good you believe in. This was a favorite maxim of James's, which he practiced as well as preached. As a result, his presence usually raised the general temperature of good will in any company.

> There are, then, cases where a fact cannot come at all unless a preliminary faith in its coming exists. And where faith in the fact can help create the fact, that would be an insane logic which should say that faith running ahead of scientific evidence is the "lowest kind of immorality" into which a thinking being can fall. Yet such is the logic by which our scientific absolutists pretend to regulate our lives. . . .
>
> I, therefore, for one cannot see my way to accept the agnostic rules for truth-seeking, or willfully agree to keep my willing nature out of the game. I cannot do so for the plain reason that a rule of thinking which would absolutely prevent me from acknowledging certain kinds of truth if those kinds of truth were really there, would be an irrational rule. . . . If we had an infallible intellect with its objective certitudes, we might feel ourselves disloyal to such a perfect organ of knowledge in not trusting to it exclusively. But if we are empiricists, if we believe that no bell in us tolls to let us know for certain when truth is in our grasp, then it seems a piece of idle fantasticality to preach so solemnly our duty of waiting for the bell. Indeed we *may* wait if we will,—I hope you do not think I am denying that—(we ought, on the contrary, delicately and profoundly to respect one another's mental freedom) but if we do wait, we do so at our own peril as much as if we believed.[10]

Thus it becomes quite clear that for James a man cannot maintain the role of a disinterested spectator in attaining the truth that is of most value to him. The knower is not merely an observer, he is an active participant in the process of knowing, James maintains, quite in agreement with the later point of view of the existentialists.*

### The Dilemma of Determinism

James's doctrine of the "will to believe" assumes, of course, that there is genuine freedom in human thought and conduct. To the belief in freedom James commits himself with characteristic vigor and candor. "I disclaim openly

---

* "The knower is an actor and a co-efficient of the truth on one side," James writes, "while on the other he registers the truth which he helps to create. Mental interests, hypotheses, postulates, so far as they are bases for human action—help to *make* the truth which they declare." (*Collected Essays and Reviews*, Longmans, Green and Co., 1920, p. 67.)

on the threshold all pretension to prove to you that the freedom of the will is true," he writes in a discerning essay, *The Dilemma of Determinism*. "The most I hope is to induce some of you to follow my own example in assuming it to be true, and acting as if it were true." The very fact of freedom of thought implies, indeed, that no conclusive demonstration of freedom is possible, James observes. Otherwise, we would *have* to believe in it, and we would not then be free!

What does determinism really mean? It means, as Spinoza so clearly pointed out, "that those parts of the universe already laid down absolutely appoint and decree what the other parts shall be. The future has no ambiguous possibilities hidden in its womb." Everything that happens must happen as it does; it could not be otherwise. As the translator of the *Rubaiyat* aptly expressed the idea poetically:

> With Earth's first clay They did the Last Man knead,
> And there of the Last Harvest sowed the seed:
>     And the first Morning of Creation wrote
> What the Last Dawn of Reckoning shall read.

It is this position that James finds unacceptable. Picking up the morning newspaper, he reads in it the account of a cruel and wanton murder: a husband kills his wife, seemingly untouched by her cries for mercy, and hacks her body to pieces. What man in his right senses is not moved by a profound sense of *regret* as he reads of this deed? James asks. Yet look at what such regret involves for the determinist. "The judgment of regret calls the murder bad. Calling a thing bad means, if it means anything at all, that the thing ought not to be, that something else ought to be in its stead. Determinism, in denying that anything else can be in its stead, virtually defines the universe as a place in which what ought to be is impossible,—in other words, as an organism whose constitution is afflicted with an incurable taint, an irremediable flaw."[11]

Those who are determinists cannot legitimately regret the murder, James points out. "It is absurd to regret the murder alone. It could not be different." What one should regret, if he accepts determinism, is the whole frame of things of which the murder is only one member. But does this not lead the determinist inevitably to pessimism? For it means that world is not and cannot be the kind of world it ought to be. Even his pessimism, however, poses for the determinist a curious logical predicament, if James is right. His philosophy should lead the determinist to call judgments of regret wrong, because they imply that what is impossible ought to be. "But how then about the judgments of regret themselves? If they are wrong, other judgments, judgments of approval, ought to be in their place. But as they are necessitated, nothing else could be in their place; and the universe is [for the determinist] just what it was before;—namely, a place in which what ought to be appears impossible."[12]

What James is here so skillfully displaying, of course, is the moral paradox that so impressed Kant. Genuine moral conviction, our inner certainty of right and wrong, has no place in the kind of completely deterministic universe long accepted by modern science and so ably depicted by Spinoza. Our moral convictions, along with everything else, must necessarily have been produced in such a universe. Yet they are senseless and absurd in a completely deterministic scheme of things. The rationalist who accepts determinism is thus led to accept a universe that is essentially irrational, and so in the end refutes his own position, James maintains. The moral life demands for its very existence a belief in freedom and indeterminism, and this belief for James is essential in a sound philosophy:

> What interest, zest or excitement can there be in achieving the right way, unless we are enabled to feel that the wrong way is also a possible and a natural way,—nay, more, a menacing and an imminent way? And what sense can there be in condemning ourselves for taking the wrong way, unless we need have done nothing of the sort, unless the right way was open to us as well. I cannot understand the belief that an act is bad, without regret at its happening. I cannot understand regret without the admission of real, genuine possibilities in the world.[13]

Here, of course, James is in full agreement with the moral philosophy of Kant, although his approach is quite different. With Kant he sees clearly the moral nihilism of a philosophy that accepts complete determinism in human life and thought. He undertakes, therefore, to demonstrate its fundamental inconsistency without resorting to the dualism to which Kant is led.

Life, then, offers us *real* possibilities for good as well as for evil. It is one of James's fundamental convictions that this proposition is essential for any genuine moral conduct. His emphasis upon the "will to believe" is an outgrowth, indeed, of his acute awareness of the difficulties we face when we try to find the *right* direction in life. Our predicament, together with the existential "leap of faith" it necessitates, he describes in the following graphic fashion:

> Each man must act as he thinks best; and, if he is wrong, so much the worse for him. We stand on a mountain pass in the midst of whirling snow and blinding mist, through which we get glimpses now and then of paths which may be deceptive. If we stand still we shall be frozen to death. If we take the wrong road we shall be dashed to pieces. We do not certainly know whether there is any right one. What must we do? "Be strong and of a good courage." Act for the best, hope for the best, and take what comes.[14]

### Pragmatism as James Interprets It

This quest for what is morally desirable, as well as practical, dominated James throughout his life. He wanted a philosophy that would redeem him from abstractions and double-dealing, from carrying on his bookkeeping in two accounts, like Sunday Christianity. He wanted to restore to philosophy something of the empirical temper of science and of practical life. He wanted a philosophy concerned with the present as well as the future, a philosophy of concrete achievement and progress. It was this concern that led him to become a pragmatist.

The word "pragmatism" is derived from the Greek term $\pi\rho\alpha\gamma\mu\alpha$, meaning "action," the same word from which "practice" and 'practical" come. Both the name and the philosophical method were suggested to James by an article Charles S. Peirce published in 1878 in *Popular Science Monthly*, entitled "How to Make Our Ideas Clear." To find the meaning of an idea, we must examine the consequences to which it leads in action, Peirce there maintains. These consequences are its concrete and positive significance. If we want to understand the meaning of democracy, look at what we do in America, not what we say. If we want to understand Christianity, follow the same procedure. (This, of course, may cause us to change our minds somewhat about these terms. But at least we shall know what we are talking about.) This is the principle of pragmatism, as Peirce first stated it, and upon this principle James develops a full-blown philosophy.

### *The Pragmatic Method*

Pragmatism was for James first of all a method, a method primarily of getting away from metaphysical abstractions and bringing philosophy back into close contact with life and with conduct. If a philosophical dispute is serious, if it has real meaning for our living, it ought to make some practical difference whether one side or the other is right. The pragmatist, James points out, simply insists that in every argument we ask what difference in practice it makes if this notion rather than that notion is true. He insists that we try a formulation out, act upon it, and see what happens. If no differences whatever in practice can be discovered between two notions, then the alternatives mean *practically* the same thing, and all dispute is idle.

It is astonishing, James observes, to see how many philosophical disputes collapse into insignificance the moment you subject them to this simple test of tracing the concrete consequences involved. Here is a person who professes to be a Christian, here is one who is a Buddhist. Here is a man who claims to be an advocate of democracy, here is one who is said to be a communist. Examine the concrete conduct to which each of these beliefs leads and you will find its positive meaning for the individuals concerned. What anything means, as a matter of fact, is, to the pragmatist, an individual and positive thing, a matter of experience. There is no such thing as general and universal meaning. We let ourselves be too easily deceived by names, by words, by ideas. It is a kind of unconscious pragmatism, indeed, that has led many members of the younger generation to a distrust not only of conventional Christianity but also of our democratic political institutions. Even college and university administrators have come in for some rather severe criticism as a pragmatic philosophy forces them to look honestly and concretely at what they do, not what they say.

His pragmatic approach was not new in philosophy, James pointed out. As a subtitle for his own volume *Pragmatism* he chose "A New Name for Some Old Ways of Thinking." Socrates had used the pragmatic method constantly and adeptly. Aristotle had seen its importance. The British empiricists, Locke, Berkeley, and Hume, had developed some of its implications. James believed that pragmatism would enable philosophy to profit from what is most important in scientific thought: its experimental method, its tentativeness, its concern with the concrete and specific. At the outset, at least, pragmatism stood only for a method. "It has no dogmas and no doctrines save its method," James writes. "No particular results then, so far, but only an attitude of orientation—the attitude of looking away from first things, principles, 'categories,' supposed necessities; and of looking towards last things, fruits, consequences, facts. . . . All that the pragmatic method implies then is that truth should have practical, *i.e.* particular, consequences."[15]

### The Meaning of Truth

Actually, however, the philosophical implications of pragmatism are by no means completely to be seen in its method alone. There is, as a matter of fact, an entirely different view of truth from that accepted by the rationalist involved in the philosophy of the pragmatist. As he examines human experience, the pragmatist finds that ideas are themselves but parts of his experience, James points out. When he asks what "truth" means in a pragmatic sense, he sees that ideas are true for him just insofar as they help him get into satisfactory relation with other parts of experience: "Any idea upon which we can ride, so to speak; any idea that will carry us prosperously from any one part of our experience to any other part, linking things satisfactorily, working securely, simplifying, saving labor, is true for just so much, true in so far forth, true instrumentally."[16]

The important thing for James as a pragmatist is that ideas *become* true for us. We do not accept a new opinion as true when we first meet it. Indeed, we are often shocked by the idea. But in time we find that we have come to regard this opinion as true. James's description of how any individual settles into new opinions is an excellent example of his acute psychological insight:

The process here is always the same. The individual has a stock of old opinions already but he meets a new experience that puts them to a strain. Somebody contradicts them; or in a reflective moment he discovers that they contradict each other; or he hears of facts with which they are incompatible; or desires arise in him which they cease to satisfy. The result is an inward trouble to which his mind till then had been a stranger, and from which he seeks to escape by modifying his previous mass of opinions. He saves as much of it as he can, for in this matter of belief we are extreme conservatives. So he tries to change first this opinion, and then that (for they resist change very vigorously), until at last some new idea comes up which he can graft upon the ancient stock with a minimum of disturbance of the latter, some idea that mediates between the stock and the new experiences and runs them into one another most felicitously and expediently.

This new idea is then adopted as the true one. It preserves the older stock of truths with a minimum of modification, stretching them enough to make them admit the novelty, but conceiving that in ways as familiar as the case leaves possible. An *outrée* explanation, violating all our preconceptions, would never pass as a true account of a novelty. We should scratch around industriously till we found something less eccentric. The most violent revolutions in an individual's beliefs leave most of his old order standing.[17]

One has only to look at this process at work in the minds of students in the early years of their university education to recognize the accuracy of James's description. Coming from varied backgrounds, with different ideals and convictions, their reactions to the new ideas and changed situation of university life are equally varied and individual. Some accept with little difficulty new scientific, moral, and political ideas they find defended by their friends or discussed in their classes. For others such views cause too much of a shock to underlying religious or social convictions to function as "true" in their thinking. Some make compromises to suit their needs. Others refuse steadfastly to do so, keeping their religious, moral, and scientific ideas in separate, watertight compartments as long as possible. But everywhere new ideas *become* true as a result of the way they work, James points out. They help each of us relate more satisfactorily the various aspects of our total experience. They satisfy needs, intellectual or social, that are deeply felt.

### Truth as Human Value

"Purely objective truth, truth in whose establishment the function of giving human satisfaction in marrying previous parts of experience with newer parts plays no role whatever, is nowhere to be found," James concludes. Examine the most ancient truths we know: "They also once were plastic.

They also were called true for human reasons. They also mediate between still earlier truths and what in those days were novel observations. . . . *The reason why we call things true is the reason why they are true, for 'to be true' means only to perform this marriage-function.*"[18]

The rationalist, to be sure, argues that truth is independent of our own subjective needs and desires. In his judgment we "find" truth; we do not help create it. Truth is not the servant of human need but the arbiter of human destiny. But the truth with which the rationalist is concerned turns out upon examination to be only "the dead heart of the living tree," James insists. All this supposedly independent and objective truth came into being in just the same fashion as ideas now become true—to meet human need, to bring order and unity into human experience—that is, because of its value in enabling men to live more satisfying or successful lives. For James, the conclusion to which this points is clear: "truth is one species of good, and not, as is usually supposed, a category distinct from good and co-ordinate with it. The true is the name of whatever proves itself to be good in the way of belief, and good, too, for definite assignable reasons." "Truth is *made*, just as health, wealth and strength are made, in the course of experience."

Writing in this vein, James is led to his most relativistic comment upon the nature of truth: "The true is only the expedient in our way of thinking, just as 'the right' is only the expedient in our way of behaving. Expedient in almost any fashion; and expedient in the long run and on the whole, of course; for what meets expediently all the experiences in sight won't necessarily meet all further experiences satisfactorily."[19]

Philosophy, as a rule, has been rationalistic, James recognizes. Each philosopher has insisted upon the reasonableness and truth of his own position; but there have been few who were able to agree with one another.

Of whatever temperament a professional philosopher is, he tries when philosophizing, to sink the fact. Yet his temperament really gives him a stronger bias than any of his more strictly objective premises. It loads the evidence for him one way or the other, making for a more sentimental or a more hard-hearted view of the universe, just as this fact or that principle would. He *trusts* his temperament. Wanting a universe that suits it, he believes in any representative of the universe that does suit it. He feels men of opposite temper to be out of key with the world's character, and in his heart he considers them incompetent and "not in it," in the philosophic business, even though they may far excel him in dialectical ability.[20]

This simply confirms James in his empiricism, his denial of any one absolute and unchanging truth. Pragmatism, he feels, is experimental and tentative, empirical in spirit rather than rationalistic. The pragmatist sees no infallible way to tell *that* we do know the truth or *when* we know it. It is this spirit, he insists, that philosophy must cultivate in order to meet the practical demands of our day and become a guide to successful living.

### Pragmatism and Religion

Religious experience and religious faith were always matters of deep concern to James, but he was especially interested, of course, in the more practical aspects of religion. Religion, he felt, was good and desirable when it did something for the individual, when it enriched his life, gave him greater strength and courage to meet more successfully the demands of living. The common man has always believed in a God who does things. Both the Bible and the sacred writings of non-Christian religions are full of accounts of divine intervention in human life. Perhaps, James shrewdly suggests, the reason why many people today do not believe in God is that God is not doing anything in their lives.

It was in this spirit that he approached his writing of *The Varieties of Religious Experience*. Here the empirical and pragmatic character of his philosophy of religion is clearly apparent. How do we determine the value, the significance, indeed the *truth* of religious insight and experience? "It is the character of inner happiness in the thoughts which stamps them as good," James writes; "or else their consistency with our other opinions and their serviceability for our needs, which makes them pass for true in our esteem." "It is either because we take an immediate delight in them; or else it is because we believe them to bring us good consequential fruits for life." Or as he later phrases it, "*immediate luminousness*, in short, *philosophical reasonableness*, and *moral helpfulness* are the only available criteria."[21]

In accord with this pragmatic point of view, James then accepts the religious man's belief in God as meaningful because his faith in God does make a concrete and discernible difference in human experience. James's own idea of the nature of the supreme reality does differ from that of conventional Christianity, but he finds no difficulty in using the word of God to describe this reality:

The practical needs and experiences of religion seem to me sufficiently met by the belief that beyond each man and in a fashion continuous with him there exists a larger power which is friendly to him and his ideals. All that the facts require is that the power shall be other and larger than our conscious selves.

God is the natural appelation, for us Christians at least, for the supreme reality, so I will call this higher part of the universe by the name of God. We and God have business with each other; and in opening ourselves to his influence our deepest destiny is fulfilled: . . . God is real since he produces real effects.[22]

## Implications of James's Pragmatism

Without question, James performed a lasting service to the cause of philosophy. He urged the philosopher to come down from his ivory tower and deal with the practical realities of life in terms that the average man could understand. He made it clear that until a philosophy would work successfully it could not hope to gain or hold the allegiance of mankind. He turned the major attention of the philosopher to the concrete consequences of what he believed rather than to the logical consistency of his ideas. Philosophy in his hands became a program of action, not primarily a source of intellectual or aesthetic satisfaction.

James was interested above all in avoiding the life-destroying agnosticism that seemed to him the outcome of nineteenth-century rationalism. He was seeking a practical philosophy to live by. As a discerning psychologist, he recognized the fundamental place of faith in life, and he refused to allow the nerve of faith to be severed by the skeptical spirit of science. His pragmatism takes its place with Bergson's doctrine of creative evolution and Nietzsche's emphasis upon human freedom as a necessary reaction against the rationalism, as well as against the scientific determinism, of the late nineteenth century.

James frankly recognized also the basic place of will in human nature and human life. He agreed enthusiastically with Schopenhauer and Nietzsche in their revolt against rationalism. As they all insist, our beliefs and convictions, as surely as our conduct, are motivated by will and desire rather than by reason. And this is true of the philosopher as surely as of the ordinary man or woman.

### What Is Truth?

In dealing with the nature of truth James is especially provocative. His description of the way in which our beliefs are accepted as true shows rare psychological insight. Perhaps, indeed, it is as a psychologist rather than as a philosopher that James here makes his greatest contribution. We reach our conclusion that certain beliefs are true out of our own experience and in the light of our general body of convictions. There is no other standard by which we can judge. James's analysis reveals clearly the fallibility of all our beliefs, even the most precious, and in highly effective fashion he warns us against undue dogmatism.

It is James's pragmatic theory of truth, however, that has occasioned the most serious criticism of his philosophy. He is guilty here, his critics claim, of confusing the truth of an idea with our knowledge of its truth. An idea, if it is true, must provide for us, these critics insist, some valid understanding of a reality beyond ourselves and independent of our desires. We can find out whether or not it is true only by acting upon it, by fitting it into our body of established convictions, to be sure. And our knowledge of truth can never be absolute. This James saw so clearly that he vigorously opposed absolutism in every form. But truth itself, the goal toward which we are moving but never quite achieve, provides a knowledge that is objective, independent, and enduring, in the judgment of those who reject the pragmatist's position.

It is not unfair, certainly, to apply to the philosophy James developed his own criterion of truth and value. Will pragmatism work as a practical guide to life, or does the suspicion of subjectivity that it arouses actually tend to undermine the strength of one's belief? Suppose we think that our reason for believing in God, for example, is simply that this belief is of value to us (rather than that it is *true*); will not the belief lose its conviction and its value for us? As Professor D. C. Macintosh of Yale, one of James's admirers, regretfully pointed out, we find in the end that the pragmatic doctrine of truth "fails to work except in the direction of destroying our practically necessary conception of truth."[23] We are thus faced with the strange situation, Macintosh maintains, in which an idea can become true for us pragmatically only if we disbelieve in the pragmatic theory of truth. Yet is this not the dilemma, he asks, in which pragmatism places us? Only a nonpragmatic view of truth seems to offer an escape.

Despite the large influence of James's pragmatic philosophy upon American life and thought during the first half of this century, there are now few philosophers who accept his position without qualification. James's philosophy may well turn out to be not so much a final answer to our moral and personal problems as a stimulating and helpful suggestion about how to face them. James urges us to meet life as an eager participant who feels deeply about the important issues, one who courageously supports what he considers right, and whose attitudes and choices make a real difference in the world he helps to create. These are surely valuable insights and suggestions that his pragmatism can contribute to an acceptable and influential philosophy of living.

### James as an Early American Existentialist

Until quite recently it was customary to see in the philosophy of John Dewey, and in the pragmatism of other American philosophers who accepted his point of view, the most significant development of the thought of William James. It was always quite clear, however, as both Dewey and Charles S. Peirce pointed out, that pragmatism did mean something quite different to James than it did to either of them. Later pragmatists have usually been at some pains to disassociate themselves from the extreme subjectiveness of some statements in James's philosophy. With the advent of existentialism in the past several decades, it has now become apparent that William James has much more in common with the existentialists than with the positions developed by Peirce and Dewey. This is well put by William Barrett in *Irrational Man*, one of the discerning introductions to existentialism:

Of all the non-European philosophers, William James probably best deserves to be labeled an existentialist. Indeed, at this date, we may very well wonder whether it would not be more accurate to call James an Existentialist than a Pragmatist. What remains of American Pragmatism today is forced to think of him as the black sheep of the movement. Pragmatists nowadays acknowledge James's genius but are embarrassed by his extremes.[24]

As a matter of fact, one finds in James's philosophy all the major convictions of the existentialist. There is a clear recognition that psychology takes precedence over logic where the two are in conflict. No one is more passionate than James in condemning a rationalistic philosophy that gives reason rather than personal experience the deciding voice in one's conviction. As vigorously as any of the later existentialists, James insists upon the necessity of personal decision and conscious choice in determining what the facts of life are and what the destiny of the individual will become. He, like all existentialists, reacts with vigor and passion against a scientific position that portrays the universe as a unified rational system in which human life and experience is completely controlled and determined. And with the existentialists he emphasizes repeatedly the reality of human freedom in the choices that men face.

For most people belief in free will, in moral freedom and responsibility, is not a matter of deep personal and fateful concern. But it was for William James. For him this was no mere abstract philosophical problem. It was an existential concern upon which the very meaning and purpose of human life depended. It occasioned an existential crisis in his life, and was resolved by an experience of commitment and faith quite comparable to those described by the later existentialists.

In *The Varieties of Religious Experience* (Chapter VII) James describes in vivid and concrete detail the dark existential moments of melancholy and despair in his own life.* And his diary contains frequent references to his own desperate despair and actual contemplation of suicide, which accompanied repeated periods of ill health. Such experiences were almost always related to James's inability to find a convincing escape from the deterministic philosophy that for many years his scientific training made him feel to be the only reasonable position. So serious was this concern, as a matter of fact, that James at times wondered how so many other people would continue to live unconscious of "that pit of insecurity beneath the surface of life." Gradually, however, he worked out "a kind of crude existentialist philosophy," he tells

---

* James's personal experiences at this time are well described in G. W. Allen's *William James* (New York: Viking Press, 1967), the only full-length biography of the philosopher. Also included is James's statement to his son that the experiences described on page 160 in *The Varieties of Religious Experience* are descriptions of his own experience. (*Op. cit.*, p. 165.)

us, based upon his deliberate commitment to an active faith in freedom.* It was this that gave new meaning and purpose to his life, and finally overcame the pessimism and moral despair that belief in scientific determinism made unavoidable for James.

* "Today, I about touched bottom, and perceive plainly that I must face the choice with open eyes," James records in his diary on February 1, 1920: "Shall I frankly throw the moral business overboard, as one unsuited to my innate aptitudes, or shall I follow it and it alone, making everything else merely stuff to it?" He was at that time rereading the French philosopher Renouvier, and several months later (April 30) he wrote in his diary: "I think yesterday was a crisis in my life. I finished the first part of Renouvier's 2nd Essay and saw no reason why his definition of free will—'the sustaining of a thought *because I chose to* when I might have other thoughts'—need be the definition of an illusion. My first act of free will shall be to believe in free will. For the remainder of the year I will abstain from mere speculative & contemplative *Grübelei* [musing, meditation] in which my nature takes most delight, and voluntarily cultivate the feeling of moral freedom, by reading books favorable to it, as well as by acting." (G. W. Allen, *op. cit.*, pp. 164, 168.)

## CHAPTER 13

# The Will to Power

## *Friedrich Nietzsche*

Friedrich Nietzsche (1844–1900) is one of the more provocative as well as controversial figures in modern philosophy. Like William James and John Dewey, his influence beyond academic circles has been impressive. Indeed, until quite recently it was largely such nonphilosophical disciples that Nietzsche attracted. Because his thought is so radical and so disturbing, Nietzsche was to a large extent distrusted in more conventional philosophical circles, and his earliest followers were all intellectuals whose battles were academic and apparently had little practical significance.

With the advent of existentialism, however, Nietzsche like Søren Kierkegaard assumed a significant role as forerunner and prophet of that influential contemporary movement, and this has led to a quite different interpretation of his thought. Distinguished German philosophers have published substantial volumes examining his works in detail. Less academic writers see him as the prophet of an atheistic existentialism whose central problem is posed by Nietzsche's assertion that God is dead. The "God is Dead" controversy, in somewhat different context to be sure, has also become a significant issue in American theological thought. Today, Nietzsche not only speaks directly to the more disturbing moral and social issues of our age; he is the most forthright and radical philosophical spokesman for the contemporary revolt against reason.

### Development of Nietzsche's Thought

Nietzsche was born in Prussia, in the little village of Röcken, on October 15, 1844. This happened to be the birthday of the reigning king of Prussia, Frederick William IV. Nietzsche's father, pastor of the Lutheran Church of the village, was moved to joy by this coincidence, and christened his new son Friedrich Wilhelm. The boy grew up as Fritz to his family and friends. In later life he called himself Friedrich Nietzsche. When Nietzsche was only four years old, his father died after a year of illness. The boy was left in the care of five women, his grandmother, his mother, his two aunts, and his sister Elizabeth. Fritz, as the only man left in the house, was adored and petted with all the fervor that German women feel for the man of the family.

## University Life

At Easter in 1861, when he was sixteen, Nietzsche was confirmed and looked forward to entering the Lutheran ministry. But in another year or two something began to go wrong. The model pupil lost interest in his classes; he was disturbed by doubts about the existence of God. He even slipped off one Sunday and got quite drunk on beer, for which he contritely begged his mother's forgiveness in a long letter. At the age of twenty, Nietzsche matriculated at the University of Bonn, and there he made a determined effort to be one of the boys. Revolting against the high seriousness of his childhood and the long domination of the womenfolk, Nietzsche set out to sow his wild oats.

Beer, song, and young love, with the manly touch of the duel, gave the university its romantic appeal in Nietzsche's day, and he tried his best to find such experiences satisfying. He joined a student corps—the Franconia—at Bonn; he drank beer with his fellow students at noisy gatherings, and even made one pathetic attempt to fight a fuel. But beer, women, and tobacco actually disgusted him. As time went on, he more and more frequently dropped out of the jolly excursions of the Franconia. Finally he admitted that all he could see in them was a "coarse, Philistine spirit, reared in this excess of drinking, of rowdyism, of running into debt." Bonn became unbearable, and Nietzsche experienced here the first of a number of emotional crises that shaped his life and thought. Composing a somewhat too self-righteous letter of resignation from the Franconia, he turned his back forever on the pleasures of the senses and left Bonn for the University of Leipzig.

At Leipzig the study of classical philology absorbed his interests, and an able university professor, Friedrich Ritschl, challenged his best intellectual effort. For three years he devoted himself with industry and unquestioned ability to his studies. He became the favorite pupil of Professor Ritschl and a very promising young philologist, deepening and broadening his knowledge of Greek literature and philosophy. But, equally important for the development of his thought, soon after entering Leipzig, Nietzsche discovered Schopenhauer.

## The Influence of Schopenhauer.

During his early years religion had been the very center of Nietzsche's existence; then he lost his faith in the God of his fathers. The pursuit of pleasure he also found vain and futile. Life for him now seemed empty and meaningless. In one of his many autobiographical comments Nietzsche describes how, while rummaging in a Leipzig book shop during the lonely and disillustioned days after he had broken with his comrades of the Franconia, he came across Schopenhauer's *The World as Will and Idea*, took the book home, and read every word of it with increasing excitement:

> It seemed as if Schopenhauer were addressing me personally. I felt his enthusiasm, and seemed to see him before me. Every line cried aloud for renunciation, denial, resignation. Here I saw a mirror in which the world, life, my own mind were reflected in fearful grandeur. Here the wholly disinterested and heavenly eye of art looked at me; here I saw illness and salvation, banishment and refuge, hell and heaven.[1]

Schopenhauer provided the young student with what was then for him the one acceptable philosophy. At twenty-one Nietzsche became a pessimist. It is impossible, he decided, to make sense of human life. Will—the blind striving of millions of living creatures—and not reason, is what really makes life what it is. And it is cruel, stupid, futile. All that is left for a thoughtful man is resignation and renunciation—the extinction of the will to live, which is the source of the evil of life.

Such pessimism did not interfere, however, with the seriousness of Nietzsche's studies. He was a candidate at Leipsig for the degree of doctor of philosophy when, in 1868, a chair in classical philology at the University of Basel, in Switzerland, fell vacant. Ritschl managed to have his brilliant young student appointed to this chair as associate professor of Greek without benefit of the doctorate. Leipsig hurriedly awarded him the degree.

## Nietzsche and Bismarck

As a university professor, however, Nietzsche unhappily was not a success. He took his position quite seriously and hoped at first to inspire his students with a devotion to the ancient Greek culture that would open a new world to them. But his lectures were uneven and frequently too involved for university students. Soon only a few disciples came to hear him. Teaching gradually became a burden and a waste of time in his eyes. Nor did he get along well with his collegues. Life at Basel from the beginning was lonely and harassed, brightened only by his writing, his ambitions, and a few close friendships. Chief among his friends was Franz Overbeck, who joined the faculty at Basel as professor of Church history a year after Nietzsche's appointment there. To those who knew him casually Nietzsche seemed an over-sensitive young professor, timid and just a bit peculiar. Even Overbeck, who remained his friend for the rest of his life, found him a difficult person to get along with.

In 1870, Bismarck led Germany to war with France. At first Nietzsche held himself proudly aloof from the struggle in which his country was engaged. But soon the call to take part in "the redemption of the Teutonic race from Latin vice and rationalism" stirred him too deeply. When the state calls, he wrote, "our souls become forgetful of themselves; at its bloody appeal the multitude is urged to courage and uplifted heroism."

In a few months Bismarck brought a once-powerful Austria to her knees and humbled a proud France, where the legend of Napoleon still persisted. He likewise fused all the little German principalities into a mighty empire with Prussia at its head. Bismarck thus became the symbol of a new morality of strength and power, and Nietzsche more clearly than anyone else saw its meaning and undertook to give it effective statement. Here was a man who faced the realities of life, who said bluntly that "there is no altruism among nations," who set out to decide issues not by votes and rhetoric but by "blood and iron."

From Schopenhauer Nietzsche had learned that life is strife, and so brings pain, hardship, and suffering. For a time this left him a pessimist, with only a sense of the meaninglessness and futility of all the pain and suffering he saw. But Darwin's concept of evolution, which was now beginning to influence philosophical thought, and Bismarck's will to power, rescued him from the pessimism of Schopenhauer. Life indeed is strife and suffering, as Schopenhauer saw so clearly. But, as he had not seen, it is a struggle in which the fittest and strongest survive. This fact gives it meaning and purpose; saves it from futility. Pessimism now seemed to Nietzsche a sign of decay; optimism a sign of superficiality. "Tragic optimism" is the mood of the strong man, he writes—the man who seeks to live fully and intensely. He is delighted to accept strife as the law of life because in this strife he sees the will to power at work, and out of strife and suffering new strength and greatness emerging.

### Nietzsche and Wagner

Nietzsche's first and only complete book was *The Birth of Tragedy out of the Spirit of Music*. The interpretation of Greek culture that had gradually been taking shape in his mind is here stirred by a new passion—his friendship and admiration for Richard Wagner. Of all the personal relationships of Nietzsche's life, that with Wagner was in many ways the most significant.

Soon after coming to the university, Nietzsche learned that Wagner and his wife Cosima were living at the nearby Swiss village of Tribschen. He went at once to call on the great man, whom he had met earlier at Leipzig. Wagner had not yet fully established himself, even in Germany, and welcomed a new disciple who could lend to his cause something of the prestige that goes with scholarship and the universities. Soon the young professor was spending most of his spare time at Tribschen, listening to Wagner's music, discussing the magnificent synthesis of Western culture that Wagner was creating, running errands for the household, and falling in love in his own awkward way with Cosima.

In *The Birth of Tragedy* Nietzsche undertook to interpret Greek life and Greek art as a conflict between two contrasting forces. On the one hand, he saw the primal strength of nature, the turbulent instincts and passion that drive men to conquest, to love, to mystic ecstasy—symbolized by Dionysus, the god of wine and revelry. On the other was man's attempt to find peace, harmony, and repose in aesthetic order and philosophical understanding— symbolized by Apollo, the god of reason, of wisdom, of beauty.

Originally, the Dionysian element was clearly dominant in both Greek art and Greek life. The days when the Dionysian mood begot the Homeric epic, the drama of Aeschylus, and the pre-Socratic philosophy were "the tremendous days of Greece," Nietzsche maintains. Gradually, however, the spirit of Apollo triumphed over that of Dionysus, and its victory was too conclusive. The living strength of Dionysus was destroyed. Greek culture became restrained, reasonable, beautiful—and *dead*. The critical philosophy of Socrates and Plato replaced the philosophical poetry of the pre-Socratics. Science replaced art; intellect replaced instinct. On the temple of Apollo at Delphi were inscribed those words of passionless wisdom: "NOTHING IN EXCESS." Socrates and Plato taught that intelligence is the only virtue, and Aristotle praised the golden mean. In the strength of its youth the Greek spirit produced mythology and poetry. In the decadence of its old age it produced science and philosophy. So, at least, Nietzsche argues.

But perhaps the spirit of Dionysus may be reborn, our philosopher suggests. Did not Schopenhauer stress once more the deep and moving power of instinct and the superficiality of reason? And is not Richard Wagner another Aeschylus, restoring in his music the tragic myth of the Greeks, and uniting music and drama in the creative spirit of Dionysus? The German spirit had too long been content to reflect the Apollonian art of Italy and France, Nietzsche declares. In Wagner he saw a new expression of the Dionysian root of the German spirit, a new creative power that had nothing in common with the rationalistic spirit of a decadent culture. Let the German people realize that their own instincts are sounder than these decadent cultures: "in some inaccessible abyss the German spirit still rests and dreams, undestroyed, in glorious health, profundity, and Dionysian strength, like a knight sunk in slumber."[2]

Quite understandably, *The Birth of Tragedy* was praised by the disciples of Wagner. But the general public paid it little attention and Nietzsche's colleagues in the field of philology condemned it almost unanimously. It expressed, as they pointed out, the enthusiasm of the prophet and the unverified assertions of the propagandist, not the exact scholarship of the philologist. Although greatly disappointed, Nietzsche was deeply conscious even then of a sense of mission, a mission to do something great, something of lasting impact upon mankind. He projected a series of lectures on all the important issues of the day, and actually published four such essays in a volume that he called *Meditations Contrary to the Spirit of the Age.** Everything in the late nineteenth century now seemed wrong to Nietzsche. The age was vulgar, corrupt, materialistic. All greatness of mind and spirit was lost in the mediocrity bred by democracy. European civilization was doomed to perish unless such forces could be successfully challenged. The aim of life, as he now saw it, was "not the betterment of the majority, who taken as individuals are the most worthless type," but "the creation of genius, the development and elevation of superior personalities."[3]

The least scholarly of his four essays, entitled "Richard Wagner in Bayreuth," was intended originally as a campaign piece. It hailed Wagner's music-drama as the greatest of the arts, and called on the German people to support a magnificent Wagner festival at Bayreuth. By the time Bayreuth was completed in 1876, however, and the first festival opened, Nietzsche's enthusiasm had already cooled considerably. Wagner, instead of proving superior to the spirit of the age, was succumbing to it. Coming to Bayreuth with high purpose, Nietzsche found there only a summer resort, a watering place for the idle rich. "I should be insane to stay here," he wrote. "I await with terror each of these long musical evenings. . . . I can bear no more." Without a word to Wagner, who was in the midst of his greatest triumph, Nietzsche fled. The friendship between the two could not survive such a blow. They never met again on the old terms. In letters to his friends and finally in two brief monographs, *The Wagner Case* and *Nietzsche contra Wagner* (1888), Nietzsche attacks his old friend with unrestrained vehemence.

### The Decade of Outstanding Achievement

When only thirty-four, Nietzsche retired from his post at the University of Basel because of ill health. He had twenty years of life still ahead of him— a decade of extraordinary literary activity, during which all his greatest works were written, and a decade of hopeless invalidism which he spent mostly in bed, completely broken in mind and body. His great decade was spent in Italy and Switzerland, with an occasional brief visit to Germany. The long winters he spent on the Italian Riviera.

Three volumes of short epigrams, *Human, All Too Human* (1878), *The Dawn of Day* (1881), and *The Gay Science* (1882), celebrate Nietzsche's emancipation from teaching, his new enthusiasm for the brilliant wit of the French, and his discovery of the warm sunshine of Italy. The first of these is dedicated to Voltaire. The other two, the most cheerful of Nietzsche's books,

---

* The official English translation in the edition of Oscar Levy is entitled *Thoughts Out of Season. Untimely Meditations* is Walter Kaufman's translation. Brinton uses *Considerations Contrary to the Spirit of the Age.* The German title is *Unzeitgemässe Betrachtungen.*

were composed during the year when his spirit was being warmed also by the company of Lou Salome, a bright young Jewish intellectual in whom he saw the kind of disciple he most desired and with whom he also briefly fell in love. Lou Salome wrote a "Hymn to Life," which Nietzsche considered magnificent and set to music. In the end, however, Lou Salome found Nietzsche much too difficult a person to get along with. When she left him for another man, his old bitterness, loneliness, and intensity returned.* Loving neither man nor woman, he fled to the Swiss Alps and there received the inspiration for the volume that was to become his best-known work, *Thus Spake Zarathustra* (1885). It is an enigmatic book, a collection of parables, sermons, and poems, written in a sort of poetic prose. But it proclaims the gospel of the great prophet who brought to mankind a new gospel of salvation.

That his volume on Zarathustra was an inspired one Nietzsche had no doubt. Few men have spoken with a stronger sense of cosmic direction. Nietzsche later gives this account of the writing of *Thus Spake Zarathustra*:

> If one had the smallest vestige of superstition in one, it would hardly be possible to set aside completely the idea that one is the mere incarnation, mouthpiece or medium of an almighty power. The idea of revelation in the sense that something becomes suddenly visible and audible with indescribable certainty and accuracy, which profoundly convulses and upsets one—describes simply the matter of fact. One hears—one does not seek; one takes—one does not ask who gives; a thought suddenly flashes up like lightening, it comes with necessity, unhesitatingly —I have never had any choice in the matter.[4]

The gospel of *Thus Spake Zarathustra* was Nietzsche's gospel, but for an appropriate mouthpiece he turned back to the old Persian prophet whom we know in English as Zoroaster. His explanation of this choice is a revealing one:

> Zarathustra was the first to see in the struggle between good and evil the essential wheel in the working of things, Zarathustra *created* the most portentous error, *morality*; consequently, he should also be the first to *perceive* that error, not only because he has had longer and greater experience of the subject than any other thinker . . . the more important point is that Zarathustra was more truthful than any other thinker. In his teaching alone do we meet with truthfulness upheld as the highest virtue . . . The overcoming of morality through itself— through truthfulness . . . that is what the name Zarathustra means in my mouth.[5]

* About ten years later Lou Salome realized that Nietzsche was a much more important person than she had thought. She published several articles about her relations with him and with Paul Rée, the Jewish writer whom she had found so much easier to live with. These articles she later expanded into a book, *Friedrich Nietzsche and His Work*, published in 1894.

*Zarathustra* was Nietzsche's message to the world; his later works are largely commentaries upon it. In them he set himself the task of bringing its poetry down to earth. His next two books, *Beyond Good and Evil* (1886) and *The Genealogy of Morals* (1887), are undoubtedly the most lucid and convincing statements of his philosophy. Like his earlier works, they are composed of short essays and aphorisms, but they are built around a clear and definite thesis. Nietzsche is here seeking to destroy the conventional morality of the masses and to establish his new aristocratic ideal.

### The Final Years

Nietzsche's final years were lonely ones. He had quarreled with almost all his friends. Innkeepers, servants, and a few casual acquaintances provided Nietzsche's only contact with his fellows. "For the lonely one, even noise is a consolation," he wrote to Overbeck. "If I could give you an idea of my feeling of loneliness! I have nobody among the living or among the dead, to whom I feel related. This is indescribably horrible." A few years earlier Nietzsche had composed what he called "the talks of the last philosopher with himself": "I call myself the last philosopher because I am the last man. Nobody talks to me but myself, and my voice comes to me like that of a dying person. . . . Through you I conceal my loneliness from myself—the terrible loneliness of the last philosopher!—and make my way into the multitude and into love by lies, for my heart cannot bear the terror of the loneliest loneliness and compels me to talk as if I were two."[6]

Left thus alone, Nietzsche gave himself unsparingly to intense literary activity. Undoubtedly the intensity of his effort, his unremitting battle against the mediocrity of his age, his increasing loneliness and sense of being unappreciated, all helped bring on a mental breakdown. Disease and approaching blindness may well have contributed. During his last year of sanity he produced a series of small volumes, *The Wagner Case, The Twilight of the Idols, The Anti-Christ,* and *Ecce Homo.* Unmistakable signs of mental derangement are seen in these books by most readers. Walter Kaufmann's comment here is a judicious one: "Some will, no doubt, see Nietzsche's final catastrophe as the last act in which the Devil claims his own, while to the more extravagant disciples it appears as a transfiguration. Less spectacular . . . but juster perhaps, is the assertion that few men have fought more heroically against illness and agony, seeking to derive insight from their suffering, utilizing their talents to the last, and making their misery a stepping stone to new and bolder visions."[7]

In January 1889, Nietzsche suffered a paralytic stroke in Turin, and broke down completely. His terrified landlord was about to turn him over to the Italian authorities when Overbeck arrived to rescue him. Soon his aged mother took him back to Germany with her. Upon their mother's death, his sister moved Nietzsche to Weimar, which she planned to make his shrine. After all, had not Goethe and Schiller already given the place the right atmosphere for such genius? Here in a large, airy room, looking out on the sunset, Nietzsche's remaining years were spent. The paralysis that had struck him at Turin now incapacitated his whole right side. He simply lay for hours looking out the window. A statue of him in Weimar shows the once restless and brilliant philosopher now quiet, broken, and resigned. Perhaps Nature v̟as kind to him when she brought peace to his restless spirit. He died in Weimar on August 25, 1900.

"My time is not yet; only the day after tomorrow belongs to me," Nietzsche prophetically wrote in 1888. "It is not impossible that I am the foremost philosopher of this age, indeed perhaps even a little more, something decisive that stands between two milleniums." His faith in himself, when no one else would believe, has now been amply justified.

## The Death of God and Its Significance

Nietzsche's thought is highly poetic and symbolic, yet beneath and throughout all his writing, a single consuming idea seems to be at work, moving slowly toward full expression.* With Kierkegaard and the contemporary existentialists, Nietzsche is deeply and personally involved in a search for the meaning of human existence. Man's greatest task is to discover who he is and what his meaning is as a human being. Without any question this need was made more urgent for Nietzsche, as is the case for most existentialists, by his own personal history. Nietzsche's life was by and large a violent process of tearing himself loose from his own moral and spiritual roots at the same time that Western man was suffering the same fate. But, while Western civilization was still largely unaware of this fact, Nietzsche was acutely conscious of it. He was seeking desperately to understand this experience and to find for himself new and dependable values to replace those that had been destroyed.

### God Is Dead

As his own religious convictions were gradually uprooted, Nietzsche was cut off more and more completely from normal human fellowship and social life. The problem of human existence and the search for new values thus

---

* Martin Heidegger claims that Nietzsche, when properly understood, is a thoroughly systematic thinker—certainly a difficult position to demonstrate convincingly. The analogy of Karl Jaspers appears more discerning: "It is as though a mountain wall had been dynamited; the rocks already more or less shaped, convey the idea of the whole. Concealed within the vast heap of fragments lies the enigma of Nietzsche's being and thinking. [Or again it] is as though an unknown power had exploded the substance and, at the same time, had attempted to force the fragmented rocks to form a building, though without any prospect of success, so that now fragments of rock and building blocks lie all around. The task [of understanding Nietzsche] seems to demand a search through the ruins for the building, even though the latter will not reveal itself to anyone as a complete, single and unambiguous whole." (*Nietzsche, An Introduction to the Understanding of His Philosophical Activities*—Eng. trans. University of Arizona Press, 1965, pp. 3–4 condensed.)

became an increasingly acute concern for him. It was not until his years as a professor at the University of Basel, however, that he began to work out his mature philosophy. Then the full meaning of what had happened became apparent to him. Without God human life seemed threatened with complete loss of significance. It was this sense of the utter bleakness of life, the "disvaluation" of all man's higher moral and spiritual values, that first impressed Nietzsche as he dealt in his own poetic fashion with the discovery that God is dead.

At the time Nietzsche wrote, science and technology were making spectacular advances. Germany's political supremacy was being established on the continent of Europe and the British empire was giving peace and prosperity to much of the rest of the world. Material improvements, comforts, and even luxuries were an accepted aspect of Western civilization. A spirit of optimism was widespread. Yet to Nietzsche these material values had little appeal; rather they disgusted him. Only one thing really mattered; and it was incomprehensible that the people around him were unaware of this fact. "God is dead"—and we have killed him.

This theme, which pervades all Nietzsche's later writing, was first stated as a parable in *The Gay Science*, one of the books published shortly after Nietzsche had given up his professorship at Basel:

*The Madman*
Have you not heard of that madman who lit a lantern in the bright morning hours, ran to the marketplace, and cried incessantly, "I seek God! I seek God!" As many as those who did not believe in God were standing around just then, he provoked much laughter. Why, did he get lost? Said one.—Or is he hiding? Is he afraid of us? Has he gone on a voyage? Or emigrated? Thus they yelled and laughed.

The madman jumped into their midst and pierced them with his glances. "Whither is God," he cried. "I shall tell you. *We have killed him*—you and I. All of us are his murderers. . . . Whither are we moving now? Away from all suns? . . . Are we not straying as through an infinite nothing? Do we not feel the breath of empty space? Has it not become colder? Is not night and more night coming on all the while?

"God is dead. God remains dead. And we have killed him.* What was holiest and most powerful of all that the world has yet owned has bled to death under our knives. Who will wipe this blood off?"

Here the madman fell silent and looked again at his listeners; and they too were silent and stared at him in astonishment. At last he threw his lantern on the ground, and it broke and went out. "I have come too early," he said then; "my time has not yet come. This tremendous event is still on its way—it has not yet reached the ears of man."[8]

* In a lecture given in 1938, Jaspers develops in some detail the thesis that for Nietzsche it was Christianity that was responsible for the death of God. Since the "values offered by Christianity are mere fictions, the moment of their exposure must plunge man into a nothingness whose equal has never before been felt in all human history." (*Nietzsche and Christianity*, Henry Regnery Co., Gateway edition, 1961, p. 15.)

The symbolism in Nietzsche's parable is striking. Prophetically he pictures himself as madman: to have lost God means madness. With the death of God, man's dignity as man is gone. The values that give meaning to his life are gone. It has become colder; the night is closing in. Mankind is not yet mad only because the death of God has not been discovered. "Do we not wander through an endless Nothingness," Nietzsche asks? Then effectively he pictures the agony and misery of a godless world—and his own loneliness as he realizes that no one else has as yet discovered man's predicament. "Right up to the end those who somehow managed to have a god for a companion never experienced what I know as 'loneliness,'" he writes. "Today my life consists in the wish that all things could be quite different from the way I see them to be, and that someone could cause my 'truths' to become incredible." "A profound man has to have friends unless he still has his god, but I have neither god nor friends."[9]

The central issue in Nietzsche's existential philosophy now becomes clear. Can mankind meet this awful challenge of becoming adult and godless? Can man make human life meaningful without God? Man's supreme act of courage must be the process of tearing loose from his old roots. He must learn to live without any comforting religious or metaphysical illusions. If it was humanity's fate to become godless, it was his own destiny, Nietzsche saw, to be the prophet who would give mankind the necessary example of honesty and courage. "Not a day goes by," he wrote in one of his letters," that I do not lop off some comforting belief." Because man is the most courageous animal, however, he will be able to survive even the death of his gods and give new meaning to his existence. This Nietzsche in time came to believe.

At this point in his spiritual life two aspects of Nietzsche's atheism become apparent. He was deeply aware, almost overwhelmed indeed, by the way in which the nonexistence of God threatens human life with complete loss of meaning and significance. As seen in the parable of the madman, this is clearly the initial impact upon him of the loss of his own religious faith. But he was likewise dimly aware that the loss of belief in God and in a divine providence might actually enhance the value and significance of human life. As the gospel of Zarathustra took shape in his mind and in his philosophy, the latter of these two dimensions of his atheism becomes increasingly important and prominent.*

### The Gospel of Zarathustra

Not only is *Thus Spake Zarathustra* Nietzsche's greatest book; it is also a unique work of self-revelation. While Nietzsche does not speak here in the first person, it is throughout his self-revelation. And it is a more significant

---

* "To escape nihilism—which seemed involved both in asserting the existence of God and thus robbing this world of ultimate significance, and also denying God and thus robbing *everything* of meaning and value—that is Nietzsche's greatest and most persistent problem." So Walter Kaufmann describes this aspect of Nietzsche's thought. (*Nietzsche*, p. 86).

revelation because of the stream of images, symbols, and visions that came unconsciously from the depth of Nietzsche's own soul. "All that I have thought, suffered and hoped is in it, and in such a way that my entire life appears now somehow vindicated," Nietzsche wrote in 1883. "Behind all these simple and strange words stands my deadly seriousness and *my entire philosophy*."[10]

*Zarathustra* begins where the parable of the madman ends. As Zarathustra the prophet goes down the mountain to bring his new message of salvation to mankind, he meets an old man in the forest, who asks him why he is doing this:

> Zarathustra answered: "I love mankind."
> "Why," said the saint, "did I go into the forest and the desert? Was it not because I loved men far too well?
> "Now I love God: man, I do not love. Man is a thing too imperfect for me. Love to man would be fatal to me."
> "And what does the saint in the forest?" asked Zarathustra.
> The saint answered: "I make hymns and sing them; and in making hymns I laugh and weep and mumble: thus do I praise the God who is my God. But what do you bring us as a gift?"
> When Zarathustra heard these words, he bowed to the saint and said: "What should I have to give you! Let me rather hurry hence lest I take aught away from you!"—and thus they parted from one another, the old man and Zarathustra, laughing like schoolboys.
> When Zarathustra was alone, however, he said to his heart: "Could it be possible! This old saint in the forest has not yet heard of it, that *God is dead*!"[11]

### What Is Man?

For Nietzsche, as has been pointed out, the death of God initially left life without meaning and purpose. Man was now alone in the universe. But a new understanding of human nature and destiny must then replace the traditional Christian view of man. In the latter half of the nineteenth century the problem of man's nature had, of course, assumed a new and radical form. Darwin's theory of evolution posed the new problem for the scientist. Gradually the philosopher also came to see that his own major task was to help man discover or rediscover who he was and what was the meaning of his life. It was Nietzsche's fate to face this task in a peculiarly personal fashion—indeed it may well be that his philosophy is "one of the great episodes in man's historic effort to know himself."[12]

Zarathustra's central concern, as he gives poetic and symbolic expression to Nietzsche's philosophy, is to make clear how thoroughly problematic man's nature is. Man is an animal, to be sure, but he can never be understood as only an animal. He is *"the animal that is still not fixed,"* to use Nietzsche's expressive phrase—a being whose essential nature is still to be determined. Having broken free of nature—and, for Nietzsche, of nature's God as well—man must now shape his own destiny.

Even in his early philosophy Nietzsche is moved by a discontent with man as he now is and a desire to see the realization of his full human possibilities. "Since man is a failure, let us continue onward and upward," he has Zarathustra remark.[13] Indeed, the heart of Nietzsche's view of man's nature and destiny is found in the early stanzas of Zarathustra's prophetic message:

> What is great about man is that he is a bridge and not a goal, what is lovable in man is that he is a *going-over* and a *going-under*.
> Man is a rope stretched between the animal and the Superman—a rope over an abyss.
> What is the ape to man? A laughing-stock, a thing of shame. And just the same shall man be to the Superman: a laughing-stock, a thing of shame.
> You have made your way from the worm to man, and much within you is still worm. Once you were apes, and even now man is more of an ape than any of the apes.
> All beings hitherto have created something beyond themselves; do you want to be the ebb of that great tide, and would you rather go back to the beast than surpass man?
> *I teach you the Superman.* Man is something that must be surpassed. What have you done to surpass man?
> Behold, I teach you the Superman!
> The Superman is the meaning of the earth. Let your will say: the Superman *shall be* the meaning of the earth.
> Thus spake Zarathustra.[14]

### Man as His Own Creator

Nietzsche now sees clearly that the aim and purpose of human life is found in man's creative ability. Only in creating does he express his authentic being, and this lies in the domain of will, not reason. "Our salvation does not lie in knowing but in creating," Nietzsche writes. "Our only happiness consists in creating." "As a creator you transcend yourself—you cease to be your own contemporary."[15] That man has the kind of ability that creativity requires, Nietzsche never doubts. It is creation rather than freedom with which he is primarily concerned. In the ordinary circumstances of life, Nietzsche agrees that the average man's conduct is generally determined, as Spinoza had pointed out. But man's creative achievements constitute the highest expression of human nature. There we see a dimension of man's conduct that rises above the commonplace and the conditioned. For Nietzsche, that is, creation *is* freedom in the only meaningful sense of the word. And with the uncanny insight that characterizes so much of his philosophy, Nietzsche sees this as the essential significance of the theory of evolution.

As creator man rises above the merely biological and psychological. Here he reveals himself as he really is. Or, as Nietzsche puts it in one of the paradoxical phrases in which his radical naturalism finds expression, he "becomes what he is." It is as his own creator that man truly expresses himself, and in such creative activity the few and rare men of genius, the gifted men, rise above the common run of mankind, in whom Nietzsche has little interest. These *superior men* are the ones who show what man is capable of. Goethe (whom Nietzsche greatly admired), Heine, Beethoven, Frederick the Great, Napoleon, even Wagner, despite his many shortcomings—here are the superior men. In such individuals Nietzsche sees nature's "attempt to reach a species that is higher than man."

> You superior men, learn *this* from me: In the market-place no one believes in superior men.
> "You superior men"—so blinks the populace—"there are no superior men, we are all equal; man is man, before God—we are all equal!"

> \*    \*    \*    \*    \*    \*    \*    \*    \*

> Before God!—Now, however, this God has died. You superior men, this God was your greatest danger.
> Only since he lay in his grave have you risen again. Only now comes the great noontide, only now does the superior man become— master!
> Well! Take heart, you superior men! Only now does the mountain of the human future travail. God has died: Now *we* desire—the Superman to live.[16]

### The Superman as Symbol\*

"Superman" is the symbol Nietzsche adopts to describe that goal of the creative evolutionary process that gives human life its meaning and direction. Upon this he founds the values that once derived their significance from belief in God: "God has died. Now we desire the Superman to live." "In spite of all, he must come to us sometime, this *redeeming* man . . . who gives the earth its purpose, . . . this victor over God and nothingness."

> The Superman lies close to my heart; *that* is my first and only concern— *not* man: not my neighbor, not the poorest, not the sorriest, not the best.
> The beauty of the Superman came to me as a shadow. Ah, my brethren, of what account now are—the Gods to me.
> Thus spake Zarathustra.[17]

---

\* Various efforts have been made to find a better translation for Nietzsche's *Übermensch*, but none have proved really successful. Despite what the comic strips have done to the superman image, it is still the best available English term and must simply be given Nietzsche's connotation rather than a less adequate or desirable one.

It is true that the image of the Superman is never completely clarified by Nietzsche. Since by definition it is to be realized only in the future, it is impossible to know its exact nature. "Up to now, no artist has risen to the task of representing the supreme man," Nietzsche writes, "that is, the one who is at once simplest and most complete. But it may be that the Greeks, in the ideal of Athena, have seen the farthest of anyone up to now."

Indeed, to believe that man can create a being higher than man—that we are able "to create beyond ourselves," constitutes faith of the highest sort. "Can you *create* a god," Nietzsche asks? "Then be quiet about all gods! But you are quite capable of creating the Superman." This urge shapes all man's significant activities and achievements: "As all meaningful volition presupposes a goal, so man presupposes a being which, while not yet existing, gives purpose and meaning to his existence." His own desire and hope in this connection Nietzsche expresses as follows: "But from time to time may I be granted a glance—only one glance—at something perfect, something that has attained its end, something happy, powerful, triumphant, . . . a glance at a man who justifies mankind, a complementary and redeeming fortunate instance of a man for whose sake one can stoutly maintain his belief in mankind."[18]

### Nietzsche and Darwin

While Darwin's evolutionary philosophy rescued Nietzsche from the pessimism of Schopenhauer and provided the foundation for his new gospel, Nietzsche apparently had no first-hand knowledge of Darwin's *On the Origin of Species*. But he knew enough about Darwin to know that Darwin's interpretation of evolution was all wrong. The theory had a suspicious British flavor about it: "struggle for existence" and "survival of the fittest" did not describe the manner in which the new man would come into being, Nietzsche was sure. Darwin's doctrine of evolution was no call to battle to prepare the world for a better and stronger race of men, or for new and superior individuals. It was rather a mild sedative that lulls one into inactivity with the belief that natural selection will ensure progress despite our own folly and weakness.

What the evolutionary hypothesis suggested to Nietzsche was simply that there is meaning and purpose in life's incessant struggle. Life's cruelty and strife is justified as the indispensable means to a higher goal—the goal of producing a new and stronger being, greater than any of those who take part in the process of bringing him into being. The survival of the fittest means that the struggle of life is leading to something better. If the superior can be produced only at the expense of the inferior, is there not in this sacrifice more than the wanton and senseless cruelty seen by the pessimist? Indeed, is it not actually good as well as necessary?

What Darwin failed to realize—but Nietzsche himself saw so clearly—was that human evolution is no objective process to be analyzed and dissected by "scientific method." It is not something to which man himself is external; but it is within and through man that human evolution proceeds. Neither environment nor chance shapes human life and the destiny of man, Nietzsche maintains. With Schopenhauer, he looks instead to the force at work within man himself—the will, the inner drive or compulsion that urges man ahead—for his explanation of the process of evolution.

It is not *the will to live*, however, as Schopenhauer suggested, nor is this a struggle for existence, as Darwin, with his middle-class English prejudice, had described it. The dominant, driving force behind life, behind the process that shapes the destiny of mankind, is *the will to power*. The will to power drives the animal world on to prepare the way for man. It lies behind the conflict of man with man, of race with race, the conflict out of which something greater than man as we know him is destined to come. And this process must be apprehended and portrayed by the poet and the prophet, who recognize new meaning and purpose in the struggle to which Darwin directed general attention.

"Here one must think profoundly to the very basis and resist all sentimental weakness," Nietzsche writes. "Life itself is *essentially* appropriation, injury, conquest of the strange and weak, suppression, severity, obtrusion of peculiar forms, incorporation, and at the least, putting it mildest, exploitation." Any organism that is living and not dying "will endeavor to grow, to gain ground, attract to itself and acquire ascendancy not owing to any morality or immortality, but because it *lives*, and because life *is* precisely Will to Power."[19]

### The New Morality

The conventional interpretation of morality, of good and evil, of the purpose of life itself, must be restated in terms of his new insight, Nietzsche sees clearly. As the will to power is fundamental in nature and in life, so it must be made central in our moral ideals. This was the foundation of his effort to revolutionize moral theory in terms of the doctrine of evolution. *Beyond Good and Evil* and *The Genealogy of Morals* are the two most carefully organized and sustained statements of Nietzsche's moral philosophy. Written in the years immediately following the publication of *Thus Spake Zarathustra*, they contain his most discerning criticism of the age in which he lived as well as the clearest presentation of his own position.

Nietzsche is now seeking to compel mankind to recognize a higher and more creative obligation—its obligation to attain "the greatest power, depth and splendor of which the human type is capable." This new philosophy of his was aptly designated "an aristocratic radicalism."* In it, Nietzsche with

* Georg Brandes, a professor at the University of Copenhagen, chose this term to describe Nietzsche's philosophy. The distinction of "discovering" Nietzsche probably belongs to Brandes, who was lecturing on Nietzsche's ideas to his philosophy classes at Copenhagen as early as 1888.

biting sarcasm attacks both the traditional Christian morality and the conventional democratic ideal. Both of these he finds to be in direct conflict with his own new gospel. Much of his criticism here reflects his penetrating insight and uncompromising honesty. The concrete details of the aristocratic moral ideal he proposes may well not prove as discerning or convincing, in fact, as does his insight in identifying modern man's moral predicament.

### The Genealogy of Morals

Moral ideals have a dual ancestry, Nietzsche points out. On the one hand, our notions of good and evil originated with a ruling aristocracy, pleasantly conscious of its own worth, of its superiority over those it ruled. This is the "morality of the masters"—the *Herrenmoral*. Here "good" and "bad" mean practically the same thing as "noble" and "despicable." The cowardly, the timid, the insignificant, those who think merely of utility, are despised as "bad." The noble man honors the man of power, the man who has power over himself as well as over others, who knows how to command, "who takes pleasure in subjecting himself to severity and hardness, and has reverence for all that is severe and hard." The morality of the masters, the aristocratic morality, accepts the principle that a man has duties only to his equals. He may act toward beings of a lower rank, toward all that is foreign, just as seems good to him, just as he desires.

Quite a different notion of morality, however, has come down to us from among the classes that were dependent and lived under subjection to others as slaves. Suppose, Nietzsche asks,

> . . . that the abused, the oppressed, the suffering, the unemancipated, the weary, and those uncertain of themselves, should moralize, what will be the common element in their moral estimates? The slave has an unfavorable eye for the virtues of the powerful; he . . . would fain persuade himself that the very happiness there is not genuine. On the other hand, those qualities which serve to alleviate the existence of sufferers are brought into prominence and flooded with light; it is here that sympathy, the kind, helping hand, the warm heart, patience, diligence, humility and friendliness attain to honor; for here these are the most useful qualities, and almost the only means of supporting the burden of existence. Slave-morality is essentially the morality of utility.[20]

In such slave morality Nietzsche sees the origin of the more conventional contrast between "good" and "evil." According to the morality of the masses (*Herdenmoral*), that which is powerful and dangerous is taken to be evil. The evil man arouses fear. According to the aristocratic morality, it is precisely the *good* man who arouses fear and seeks to arouse it. For the servile mode of thought the good man must be the *safe* man, the man who is "good-natured, easily deceived, perhaps a little stupid." Wherever the slave morality has gained ascendancy the words "good" and "stupid" tend to have much the same meaning, Nietzsche feels.

In marked contrast to this, the *essential* quality in a healthy aristocracy is "that it should accept with a good conscience the sacrifice of legions of individuals, who *for its sake* must be suppressed and reduced to imperfect men, to slaves and instruments. Its fundamental belief must be precisely that society is *not* allowed to exist for its own sake, but only as a foundation and scaffolding, by means of which a select class of beings may be able to elevate themselves to their higher duties, and in general to a higher existence."[21] In this mood of the healthy aristocracy, the *essential* nature of evolution and of life itself finds expression. The morality of the masters, of the powerful and noble, is not contrary to the pulse and movement of life, Nietzsche maintains, but is in fundamental accord with its inner spirit.

### The Morality of Our Age

As Nietzsche looks around the European world of his day, however, he sees that on every hand the slave morality has somehow managed to gain control of men's minds—and most completely in the democratic and Christian outlook of the age: "The gregarious European man nowadays assumes an air as if he were the only kind of man allowable; he glorifies his qualities such as public spirit, kindness, deference, industry, temperance, modesty, indulgence, sympathy, by virtue of which he is gentle, endurable and useful to the herd, as the peculiarly human virtues."[22] It is just here that Nietzsche finds himself so "contrary to the spirit of the age." Its mediocrity, its essentially herd-mindedness, its ignoble and mean character, must be attacked without compromise, he urges.*

The English with their ideas of democracy and utility have been largely to blame for the state of affairs, Nietzsche feels. But he has located a culprit even more guilty than the English of undermining the aristocratic spirit in modern Europe. Above all else it is the Church and Christian religion that has been responsible for the triumph of the slave morality of the herd. Christianity has reversed the aristocratic values of living and thus brought about the "deterioration of the European race." All the instincts that are natural to an aristocracy—the manly, conquering, imperious instincts, delight in beauty and in joy of the senses—have been broken down. In their place the Christian Church has made brotherhood and unselfishness, sympathy for the weak and for the suffering, its cardinal virtues. Thus it has helped preserve the sick and weak, whom nature through the evolutionary process would eliminate.

Feminism for Nietzsche is a natural corollary of democracy and Christianity, and a further unmistakable sign of the degeneracy of modern Europe. With another of his striking "transvaluations," he takes the position of Schopenhauer and reverses it. Woman at her best and by nature is a creature of emotion and passion. Although the "modern" woman now talks of inde-

---

* In the popular novels of Herman Hesse, especially in the gospel of *Demian* and *Steppenwolf,* Nietzsche's point of view is skillfully restated for our age.

pendence, and the feminist (today the Women's Lib) seeks the "emancipation of women" and claims her right to equality with men, there is nothing but stupidity in this movement, Nietzsche insists:

> . . . to neglect exercise in the use of her proper weapons; to emphatically and loquaciously dissuade man from the idea that woman must be preserved, cared for, protected and indulged, like some delicately, strangely wild and often pleasant domestic animal,—what does all this betoken, if not a disintegration of womanly instincts, a de-feminizing? . . . That which inspires respect in woman, and often enough fear also, is her *nature*, which is more natural than that of man, her genuine, carnivora-like cunning flexibility, her tiger-claws beneath the glove, her *naïveté* in egoism, her untrainableness and innate wildness, the incomprehensibleness, extent and deviation of her desires and virtues. . . . And all that is now to be at an end? And the *disenchantment* of women is in progress? The tediousness of women is slowly evolving?[23]

Actually there is by nature, and must always be, a profound antagonism between man and woman, Nietzsche insists. This "eternally hostile tension" makes all dreams of equal rights, equal training, equal obligations, but shallow-minded delusions. The only man a woman really admires is a *strong man*; only as she recognizes him as her master, and obeys him, does she find happiness. The whole movement to "enlighten" women is, therefore, a great mistake, Nietzsche feels. (And if he has not managed to enrage all his feminine readers by now, his concluding comments should do so.) Enlightenment has hitherto properly been man's concern. There is good reason to doubt that woman even wants enlightenment about herself:

> What does woman care for truth? From the very first nothing is more foreign, more repugnant, or more hostile to woman than truth—her great art is falsehood, her chief concern is appearance and beauty. Let us confess it, we men: we honor and love *this* very art and *this* very instinct in woman.

If this seems severe, look at what women think of each other, Nietzsche suggests. "Did a woman herself ever acknowledge profundity in a woman's mind, or justice in a woman's heart?" he asks. "And is it not true that on the whole, 'woman' has hitherto been most despised by woman herself, and not by us at all?"[24]

### The New Aristocracy

Despite the degeneracy of modern Europe—despite its capitulation to democracy, Christianity, and feminism, and its seduction by English Utilitarianism—Nietzsche saw unmistakably signs of a new age. And he considered himself the prophet of its coming, a voice crying in the wilderness. "The conditions of Europe in the next century will once again lead to the breeding of the manly virtues," he writes with prophetic insight, "because men will live in continual danger." Another process was also at work, Nietzsche pointed out, moving to produce the strong race, the "superman" whom he envisioned as the goal and justification of human strife and suffering. Democracy carried within itself the seeds of its own destruction:

> [W]hile the collective impression of future Europeans will probably be that of numerous, talkative, weak-willed and very handy workmen who *require* a master, a commander, as they require their daily bread, the *strong* man will necessarily in individual and exceptional cases become stronger and richer than he has perhaps ever been before. I mean to say that the democratizing of Europe is at the same time an involuntary arrangement for the rearing of tyrants—taking the word in all its meanings, even in its most spiritual sense.[25]

He is seeking, Nietzsche asserts, simply to bring man back to nature and to an understanding of the insights or truths that nature contains. If man is to achieve the greater possibilities of which human nature is capable—to restore its creative genius—we must "annihilate morality in order to liberate life," and "attempt to be as amoral as nature," he writes. "It is *the innocence of becoming alone* that gives us the greatest courage and the greatest freedom."[26] At this point Nietzsche's moral ideal is much like that of Goethe's *Faust*. There is a Faustian urge, a dynamic quality, in his picture of the morality of the masters, the new aristocracy. Both Goethe and Nietzsche recognize that dangers are involved in this moral ideal, but Nietzsche is less skillful than Goethe in presenting his point of view. Serious dangers are much more clearly apparent in Nietzsche's imagery.

Nietzsche turns to history for a symbol to describe the men of power, the old aristocracy, the master races of the past—and in doing so he reveals all too clearly what life shaped by "the innocence of becoming," and by the will to power, has actually meant. "The truth is hard," Nietzsche writes in one of his celebrated passages, but let us face it:

> Let us acknowledge unprejudicedly how every higher civilization hitherto has *originated!* Men with a still natural nature, barbarians in every terrible sense of the word, men of prey, still in possession of unbroken strength of will and desire for power, threw themselves upon weaker, more moral, more peaceful races (perhaps trading or cattle-rearing communities), or upon old mellow civilizations in which the final vital force was flickering out in brilliant fireworks of wit and depravity. At the commencement, the noble caste was always the barbarian caste: their superiority did not consist first of all in their physical, but in their psychical power—they were more *complete* men (which at every point also implies the same as "more complete beasts").[27]

Here then we find the "morality of the masters" and "the innocence of becoming" revealed in all its "purity and wickedness"! But is this an expression of the genuinely and distinctly creative element in human nature? Or is Nietzsche's "transvaluation of all values," his radical naturalism, actually perhaps an appeal to the jungle that lurks just beneath the surface of civilization rather than the expression of man's creativity at its best? At this point such a question seems unavoidable.

## The Prejudices of the Philosopher

Nietzsche is without question the spokesman among philosophers for the revolt against reason in contemporary thought. No one else has condemned rationalism so sarcastically nor championed anti-intellectualism so explicitly. No objective, rational truth is possible, Nietzsche maintains. Every great philosophy up to now has consisted simply of the confessions of its originator. It is a sort of involuntary and unconscious autobiography. Thus the Stoics, in their pride, talked of living "according to Nature," but actually, while pretending to read with rapture the laws of nature, they were dictating their own convictions to nature, insisting that nature shall be like the Stoics.

Even more clearly "the hocus-pocus in mathematical form," by means of which Spinoza tried to make the universe fit his own prejudices, gave expression actually to the "love of *his* wisdom, to translate the term fairly and squarely," Nietzsche writes. This is the old and everlasting story. It happened in the past; it happens again today. Behind all our logic are enduring values and beliefs that we accept because they are necessary for the maintenance of beings such as we are. As soon as a philosophy begins to believe in itself, it always creates the world in its own image; it cannot do otherwise. Philosophy is thus the most spiritual expression of the Will to Power; it is the will to "creation of the world." The reason that philosophers are regarded half distrustfully and half laughingly is not because they make mistakes so frequently and lose their way, Nietzsche observes. This happens to all men. But the philosophers refuse honestly to admit their dilemma:

> They all pose as though their real opinions had been discovered and attained through the self-evolving of a cold, pure, divinely indifferent dialectic; whereas, in fact, a prejudiced proposition, . . . which is generally their heart's desire abstracted and refined, is defended by them with arguments sought out after the event. They are all advocates who do not wish to be regarded as such, generally astute defenders, also, of their prejudices, which they dub "truths."[28]

An idea or belief is good if it succeeds, and this is the only sense in which it can be called "true," Nietzsche insists in complete agreement with the pragmatism later defended by William James. Any other use of the term is but a retaining of the old moralistic concept of truth as something objectively "good" or ideal. Nietzsche not only sees this implication of an evolutionary philosophy as clearly as did James and Dewey; he admits it gladly; and glories in the paradox that this view of truth involves:

> In spite of all the value which may belong to the true, the positive, and the unselfish, it might be possible that a higher and more fundamental value for life generally should be assigned to pretense, to the will to delusion, to selfishness and cupidity. . . . The falseness of an opinion is not for us any objection to it; it is here, perhaps, that our new language sounds most strangely. The question is, how far is an opinion life-furthering, life-preserving, species-preserving, perhaps species-rearing; and we are fundamentally inclined to maintain that the falsest opinions are the most indispensable to us; that without a recognition of logical fictions, man could not live—that the renunciation of false opinions would be a renunciation of life, a negation of life. *To recognize untruth as a condition of life*: that is certainly to impugn the traditional ideas of value in a dangerous manner, and a philosophy which ventures to do so, has thereby alone placed itself beyond good and evil.[29]

This much must be conceded, Nietzsche argues: there could have been no life at all except on the basis of semblance, of deception, of *fiction*. In truth, man only became "human" through an illusion and an indispensable error: "the basic view that man alone is free in a world of the unfree, that he is the eternal miracle worker, the super-animal, the demi-god, the meaning of creation, the one whose non-existence is unthinkable and who furnishes the key to the riddle of the cosmos." Indeed, may it not well be that the world as we portray it, the world in which we live, is actually such a *fiction?* Is not the "desire for Truth" simply one of man's desires, which must be dealt with like the rest of his desires? "It is nothing more than a moral prejudice that truth is worth more than semblance," Nietzsche writes: "it is, in fact, the worst proved supposition in the world."[30]

Behind all life, all effort and striving, beyond logic and beyond good and evil, there is for Nietzsche an ultimate force by which all these are conditioned. "Psychologists should bethink themselves before putting down the instinct of self-preservation as the cardinal instinct in an organic being," he writes. "A living thing seeks above all to *discharge* its strength—life itself is *Will To Power*; self-preservation is only one of the indirect and most frequent *results* thereof." Indeed, we have the right to define all active force in the universe unequivocally as *Will to Power*: "The world seen from within, the world defined and designated according to its 'intelligible character'—it would simply be 'Will To Power' and nothing else."[31]

### The Appeal of Nietzsche

It is not difficult, of course, to point to contradictions in Nietzsche's pragmatic view of truth, to question his exaggerated condemnation of conventional morality, or to show the serious limitations of his own aristocratic and naturalistic gospel. Despite this fact, his philosophy has had and continues to have an enduring appeal. Attacked as vigorously by some as he is deeply admired by others, he has established a place for himself as the philosopher of our age in a peculiar sense, the philosopher who accepted our *will to power*, our worship of power, as the basic fact of modern civilization and sought to interpret its meaning with no pretense or hypocrisy.

To his own generation Nietzsche appealed most strongly as an apostle of freedom. His was an age dominated by the tyranny of scientific determinism. A depressing chill was taking hold of men's minds, and they wanted an escape from it. Nietzsche, with all the vigor and boldness of the prophetic spirit, demands of his disciples originality, newness of life, creativity. He called upon men to reject the rational and coldly logical; to live as though nothing were inevitable; to live as masters of the universe, enslaved neither to custom nor to priest nor to philosopher nor to scientific dogmatist. It is not in logical or intellectual theory but in the free creativity of will and instinct that fullness of life and achievement is to be found, Nietzsche urges. In his attack upon reason and the scientific rationalism of the late nineteenth century, he gives his own expression to that larger movement of thought in which such philosophers as William James and Henri Bergson are also outstanding figures.

A second major source of appeal in Nietzsche's moral philosophy is its honest and uncompromising character. He speaks with bitterness but with sincerity. He will countenance none of the conventional hypocrisy and pretense with which so much religion and moralizing is wrapped up. He is a disturbing thinker, a rebel who cannot be lightly dismissed. Nietzsche calls upon us to look at life as it is and base our moral ideals upon this.

There is a realism here, an appeal to the heroic in man, that reminds one at once of William James. This could well be Nietzsche's significant ethical contribution. How many can find happiness or enduring satisfaction in the self-seeking mediocrity of hedonism? The tame and uninspired calmness of the life of reason is apt to pall upon the young and vigorous, as William James came to feel so strongly in his experience at Lake Chautauqua. Nietzsche calls us to something greater, something more deeply appealing in life than pleasure. This note of the heroic, this urge to create something superior, something greater than ourselves, this attack upon mediocrity and upon hypocrisy, will always have an appeal.

Ever since he wrote, moreover, Nietbsche's philosophy has held an undeniable charm for bright and sensitive young men and women who are just coming to see how dull, muddled, and mediocre their elders really are. Nietzsche brings to such emancipated spirits inspiration in the midst of a routine and conventional society. With delight they find in Nietzsche that freedom of spirit which is beyond good and evil. Secure in the transcendent wisdom of Zarathustra, such young nonconformists of every generation can look down serenely upon the browsing herd—among which they are apt, indeed, to find their teachers along with their families.

The wide popularity some years ago of *The Fountainhead* and *Atlas Shrugged*, two novels by Ayn Rand, has been seen with some justification as evidence of Nietzsche's contemporary appeal. Her contempt for mediocrity, for herd-mindedness, even for altruism and the traditional Christian virtues, is quite as deepseated as was Nietzsche's. For both only the heroic and the creative in man is worthy of admiration and respect. Even Ayn Rand's atheism in rather surprising fashion reminds one of Nietzsche. In her view, "the concept of God is insulting and degrading to man—it implies that the highest possible is not to be reached by man, that he is an inferior being," writes one of her committed followers. "She rejected the concept of God as *morally* evil."[32]

Despite these similarities, however, Ayn Rand is *not* an exponent of Nietzsche's philosophy. As a young university student in communist Russia (in 1921), she was initially attracted by *Thus Spake Zarathustra*. But Nietzsche's emphasis upon the will to power, especially power over other men, as the basis of greatness make her uneasy. When she later discovered Nietzsche's open denunciation of reason she knew that "in their basic premises" she and Nietzsche were "philosophical opposites." For Ayn Rand *reason* not power is "the only absolute," and man's creativity finds its highest expression in productive achievement (economic and industrial as well as artistic and intellectual), not in the exercise of power over others. It is to Aristotle, not to Nietzsche, that she looks for sound philosophical insight, and to American capitalism not to Nietzsche's Superman for the most acceptable social expression of the creative values in human life. "The New Intellectuals," she writes, "must fight for capitalism, not as a 'practical issue, not as an economic issue, but, with the most righteous pride, as a *moral* issue."[33]

### Nietzsche and the Nazis

Nietzsche, of course, has not been without critics. During the early years of World War I, critics both in England and the United States associated his philosophy with the policies of the German Kaiser. It was only with the rise of Hitler and the Nazis in the early 1930s, however, that Nietzsche was taken with complete literalness and the effort made to put his ideas into actual practice. The noblest dreams of the prophet sometimes look like nightmares when they are taken too literally. Crane Brinton makes this point in his detailed analysis of the use made by the Nazis of Nietzsche's philosophy:

Nietzsche called for the Superman. Mussolini and Hitler answered the call. It does not much matter that in all probability Nietzsche would have scorned them as perverters of his doctrine, would have opposed them bitterly. It does not even matter that had Nietzsche never written these men would in all probability have come to power much as they did. They have found a use for Nietzsche, a use he probably never intended his words to provide.*

It is not difficult to find in Nietzsche's philosophy almost all the tenets of the creed to which the Nazis subscribed. In their interpretation of Nietzsche, and in the use to which they put his philosophy, its dangers and limitations became quite obvious. These Nazi disciples simply took at face value Nietzsche's most violent and bitter attacks upon conventional morality, upon parliamentary government, upon the mediocrity that comes with democracy, and upon Christianity with its gospel of pity and kindness. They accepted Nietzsche's praise of war and of warriors as well as his suggestion that the new society should be authoritarian, militant, heroic, using without hesitation cruelty, hardness, and immorality for its purposes. And then they did what none of his other disciples had done—they actually put into practice those principles that suited their purposes.

Most interpreters of Nietzsche today claim that he did not really mean what the Nazis took him to mean. But if this is true, as it seems to be, one can hardly excuse Nietzsche and blame the Nazis for the misinterpretation. For in the end does Nietzsche's concrete description of the Will to Power portray what is most creative in the human spirit or what is fundamentally dangerous and destructive?

### Nietzsche as Philosopher

Until quite recently it was not the professional philosophers but rather literary men and intellectuals, and somewhat later, of course, the Nazi political propagandists in Germany, to whom Nietzsche's philosophy most directly appealed. With the advent of existentialism, however, this situation has changed significantly. Not only have influential books on the philosophy of Nietzsche been published,† but briefer accounts of his thought appear in

---

* Crane Brinton, *Nietzsche* (Harper Torchbook, 1965), p. 171. Hitler, as a matter of fact, visited the *Nietzsche Archiv* in Weimer several times, and had his picture taken beside the bust of the philosopher.

† Jaspers's substantial volume, *Nietzsche: An Introduction to the Understanding of His Philosophical Activity*, was published in 1936 but only translated into English in 1965. Heidegger's two-volume work, entitled *Nietzsche*, appeared in 1961, but is based upon lectures given in 1936 and 1940 at the University of Freiburg. It is not quite correct, of course, to overlook an early study by Hans Vaihinger, one of Germany's ablest philosophers, entitled *Nietzsche as Philosopher* and published in 1902. Vaihinger's own position, which he called the "philosophy of As If," was based in part on Nietzsche.

almost every volume in the growing body of literature dealing with existential philosophy. And in France Jean-Paul Sartre, the popular advocate of an influential atheistic existentialism, turns explicitly to Nietzsche for seminal ideas in his own philosophy.

The crux of the issue—one that Nietzsche's philosophy brings into clear focus—is simply this: What is power *good* for? What ends should it serve? In themselves, might and the will to power hardly seem self-sufficient. If there are good and bad uses of power, as Plato points out in The *Republic,* are there not moral standards other than success by which conduct must be judged? Nietzsche places great emphasis upon creativity, to be sure, and upon the values that creative effort contributes to human life. Yet, as his critics insist, power and creativity can surely not be identified, even upon Nietzsche's assumption that the Superman is the purpose and meaning of human life. Nietzsche has portrayed in bold and disturbing fashion the fundamental place of the will to power in human life and conduct. He has made it impossible for us to be as naïve as we once were in our personal or our political philosophy. He has made it clear that we cannot expect reason or good will to triumph easily over the will to power in either our personal or our social life. But is there adequate insight into the enduring values essential to the good life anywhere in Nietzsche's portrayal of the Superman? This is certainly a question that the thoughtful student must ask himself.

Of those philosophers today who undertake a sympathetic interpretation of Nietzsche's philosophy, Karl Jaspers is perhaps the most thorough and discerning. Jaspers himself emphasizes the fact that we should not expect to find in Nietzsche "an actual way of life nor a satisfying philosophy of life." "He does not show us the way, he does not teach us a faith, he gives us nothing to stand on," Jasper writes. "He grants us no peace, torments us ceaselessly, hunts us out of every retreat, and forbids all concealment."[34] Nietzsche's contribution to our philosophy is essentially an existential contribution.

It is not with a kindly farewell that Nietzsche leaves one. What he says sounds more like a rebuff: Everything finally is up to you. Genuine truth, truth for each person, is only what Nietzsche helps him bring out of himself.

# Five

## THE COMMITMENT OF THE EXISTENTIALIST

Life is nothing until it is lived. But it is yours to make sense of, and the value of it is nothing but the value you choose.

JEAN-PAUL SARTRE

In all seriousness of truth, hear this: Without *It* man cannot live. But he who lives with *It* alone is not a man.

MARTIN BUBER

What religion believes to be true is not wholly true, but ought to be true, and may become true by being resolutely believed.

REINHOLD NIEBUHR

## CHAPTER 14

# The Existential Christian

*Søren Kierkegaard*

No group of philosophers is more deeply concerned with the search for meaning and purpose in life than the existentialists. This concern, indeed, more than any other, gave rise to existentialism and helped to make it the most significant philosophical movement in Europe a generation or two ago. As has often been pointed out, existentialism developed in the first half of the twentieth century in large measure as an outcome of the European experience of catastrophe in two world wars, enhanced by the terror and repression of a totalitarian regime in France and Germany. In this country existentialism initially was associated with a kind of Bohemian spirit in Paris, which seemed a product of life in the French underground during the German occupation in the second World War. Its younger devotees in particular exhibited an interest in American jazz and a showy style of dress, and met for their discussions of philosophy in favorite night-club hangouts. All of this made interesting news for American journalists reporting on life in postwar Paris.

A genuine and growing interest—as well as curiosity—concerning this new and rather unusual intellectual phenomenon was soon apparent in America. For French existentialism was as much a literary as a philosophical movement, and its early leaders, Jean-Paul Sartre, Albert Camus, Simone de Beauvoir, were all gifted writers. It is true that the initial reaction of professional philosophers in this country was not especially friendly. Existentialism, as they saw it, was definitely a European movement, an expression of postwar disillusion and despair. Attitudes such as anxiety, dread, or concern with the "death of God" that characterized the existentialists were not normal or healthy. They might well disappear as life in Europe returned again to its more desirable prewar tempo—or so these American critics a bit prematurely predicted in the early 1940s.

We began instead to experience in this country something of the same disillusion with the material and technological advances of Western civilization that Europe knew. Interest in existentialism as a significant philosophical movement did not disappear, but soon increased markedly in both academic and nonacademic circles. The issues raised by the existentialists were perceived to be fundamental concerns of human life, not merely of a postwar generation in Europe. Sartre's plays and stories appeared in English translation in increasing numbers, and were widely read and discussed. Quite able and respectable German philosophers, men like Martin Heidegger and Karl Jaspers, became exponents of an influential existential philosophy, as impressive and formidable as German statements of philosophy usually are. And numerous works discussing the major figures in the existentialist movement began to appear in English in the early and mid-1950s. A new interest was also manifested here in the philosophy of Friedrich Nietzsche, who it now seemed had been the prophet of humanistic existentialism, as well as in the thought of that enigmatic Danish writer, Søren Kierkegaard, whose religious works had been translated into English a decade or two earlier by his American admirers. Existentialism had at last arrived in this country, and it soon gathered among its adherents a growing number of able younger American philosophers.

Today, a generation later, French existentialism as a cult has long been dead, and existentialism itself is no longer the latest fashion in intellectual circles. But during the rather grim decades of the Cold War no other movement generated a philosophy of living of comparable significance. The existentialists of that time were clearly the most influential and creative figures in man's continued search for meaning and direction in life, and their influence upon the thought of our age is still quite apparent. It can hardly be denied, of course, that these philosophers were also spokesmen of their own age, giving forceful expression to the spirit, the *Zeitgeist*, of the first half of the twentieth century. In this chapter and those that follow we shall look, then, with some care at existentialism in its various manifestations, examining its significance as one of the influential philosophies men live by. And certainly our discussion should begin with Søren Kierkegaard, that disturbing philosopher who was deeply concerned more than a century ago with all the major issues that characterized the existentialism of our own age.

A lonely and almost unnoticed figure in nineteenth-century Denmark, Søren Kierkegaard (1813–1855) became a central figure in the religious thought of Europe half a century later. While Kierkegaard's intense and paradoxical insights into human nature and the meaning of life have proved strangely contemporary in spirit, he is not an easy author to read. His flashes of genius are expressed in witty anecdotes, parables, and satirical essays as well as in complicated philosophical discourses. If the casual reader is not sympathetic with the author's point of view, he is more apt to be repelled than enlightened. Nor can one hope in a brief discussion to do justice to the range and depth of ideas—or the enigmatic genius—of this Danish Christian who considered himself also a disciple of Socrates.

In Kierkegaard's portrayal of the "existential" Christian, however, one finds all the cardinal ideas that have come to characterize existentialism. And, as for all later existentialists, his thought and his life cannot be separated—the two are but aspects of one organic whole.

## Formative Influences

The more significant experiences in Kierkegaard's life can perhaps best be portrayed in four basic relationships and activities, two private and two public: as son, as lover, as polemical writer, and as witness to truth.[1] Each provides insights that are essential for an understanding of his thought and his published works. As Kierkegaard himself once described the importance of the first two of these, "I owe everything that I am to the wisdom of an old man and the simplicity of a young girl."[2]

The youngest of seven children, Søren Kierkegaard was born in Copenhagen on May 5, 1813. The atmosphere of his home was marked not only by strict devotion to the orthodox Lutheran religion of Denmark, but by a somber and gloomy melancholy as well. Both were due directly to the spirit and attitude of his father, Michael Kierkegaard. While herding his sheep one bleak day on the Jutland Downs, Michael Kierkegaard as a boy was moved to curse the God of wrath whom he believed to be responsible for the misery of his young life. This act only deepened his gloom, however. He never forgave himself for what he had done. Even when in later life he moved to Copenhagen and became a successful merchant, he continued to brood on this youthful blasphemy. An act of sexual incontinence that occurred shortly after the death of his first wife further heightened the curse of sin that seemed to hang over the whole family.

For Søren the salvation of his soul was undoubtedly the most important concern during his early and impressionable years. A youth of marked intellectual ability, he spent much more time with his father than with companions of his own generation, and was clearly, as the son of his old age, his father's favorite. Unfortunately he absorbed the melancholy outlook on life as well as the deep religious faith of his father.

Because his father wanted him to prepare for the ministry, Søren did enroll in theology when in 1830, at the age of seventeen, he entered the University of Copenhagen. His academic interests were in literature and philosophy, however, and he soon became an enthusiastic student of the Romantic poets, of Shakespeare, of Plato, and of the current Hegelian philosophy. But he distinguished himself by his wit and his taste in fine food and drink more than in his studies, and, for a good many years at the university, he led the life of a Bohemian intellectual. He began to drink heavily and spent more time in the taverns and the theatre than in academic work. He had now broken with his father, and at least temporarily given up his interest in religion.

Although quite gifted and witty, Kierkegaard's sharp satire set him apart not only from his fellow students but from his Bohemian comrades as well. He was never fully accepted at the university, even though he spent some ten years there. Like Nietzsche, he remained a rather lonely figure, a person of strange contradictions and sudden shifts in moods. Despite his superficial commitment to the pleasures of social life, his sensitive conscience rebelled at such conduct. His own melancholy, like that of his father, deepened as time went on, and beneath the façade of gaiety and wit a deep seriousness pervaded his inner life even during these student years.

It was at this time that Kierkegaard began to record these inner conflicts in notebook entries, which were later to be published as his *Journals*. "What I really lack is to be clear in my own mind what I am to do," he wrote. "The thing is to understand myself, to see what God really wants me to do; the thing is to find a truth *that is true for me*, to find the idea for which I can live and die."[3] This youthful concern was to become the consuming passion of Kierkegaard's life, just as the search for a *personal* truth was to become a matter of abiding importance for all later existentialists.

### Kierkegaard and Regina Olsen

Michael Kierkegaard died in 1838 at the age of eighty-two. A short time earlier he and his son had become reconciled, and he had confessed to Søren the youthful sins that had so darkened his life. Søren was shaken, he says, as by "a great earthquake," and the memory of his father became almost as significant an influence upon him as their earlier association had been. Deciding now, at last, in penance perhaps, to concentrate on his theological studies, he passed his examinations *cum laude* in 1840, and in 1841 he preached his first sermon in a Copenhagen church. That year he also submitted a thesis, "The Concept of Irony," a study of the Socratic dialectic, for his master's degree at the university.

These two years also saw what was certainly his own deepest personal and emotional experience: his falling in love with Regina Olsen, the young and attractive daughter of a prominent government official in Copenhagen; and then his decision, soon after she had agreed to their marriage, to break the engagement with her.

Kierkegaard's reasons for breaking his engagement with Regina were quite complex, too complex perhaps ever to be fully understood.* Did he consider her to be too light-hearted and gay, a girl incapable of sharing the somber and melancholy life that he envisioned for himself? There are indica-

---

* For any who are interested in a fuller account of Kierkegaard's love for Regina and its pervasive influence upon his life and thought, the story is told in dramatic and moving fashion by Walter Lowrie in his *Kierkegaard*, Vol. I, Part Three. Lowrie's great work is also the most complete account of the relation of Kierkegaard's thought to the various aspects of his experience.

tions that this was the case. Was his breaking of the engagement a sacrifice he felt compelled to make for his own personal religious commitment? His use of the Old Testament story of Abraham's sacrifice of Isaac, his beloved son, suggests as much. Did he come to see celibacy as an indispensible condition of the unordained ministry to which he now felt himself called? This may well have been the case. In any event, he was deeply in love with Regina and, despite this decision to break their engagement, he never ceased to love her. "It was a time of terrible suffering to have to be so cruel and at the same time to love her as I did," Kierkegaard wrote in his *Journal*. "She fought like a tigress. If I had not believed that God had lodged a veto, she would have been victorious."[4]

The broken engagement stirred quite a furor in Copenhagen, and Kierkegaard was widely criticized as a scoundrel who had deceived an innocent girl. He stood the storm of criticism briefly, then after only two weeks departed for Berlin. Much of his time and thought in Berlin was given to writing his first significant work, *Either/Or, A Fragment of Life*. In his next work, entitled *Repetition: An Essay in Experimental Psychology*, Kierkegaard seems to have been considering the possibility of a reconciliation with Regina. But just as he was ready to publish the book, Regina's engagement to a former suitor was announced. Both surprised and distressed, he destroyed the last ten pages of this book and substituted a new ending.

### The Corsair Incident

Having inherited a sizable legacy from his father, Kierkegaard was now relatively well-to-do, and lived quite comfortably in the spacious family home in Copenhagen. Writing had become his chosen vocation and he committed himself to this task with single-minded devotion, letting nothing interfere with his intense literary activity. Within three years, between 1843, when *Either/Or* was published, and February 1846, the date of his *Concluding Unscientific Postscript*, he published fifteen books. As indicated by its title, Kierkegaard had thought of the last of these as his final literary work. He then looked forward to spending the remaining years of his life as a country pastor in the Danish Lutheran Church. But a most unfortunate journalistic dispute, for which he himself was in large measure responsible, caused a change of far-reaching significance in his plans.

In Copenhagen at that time a talented young Jewish publisher, Meyer Goldschmidt, edited a weekly scandal sheet, *The Corsair*, which the good people of the city publicly condemned but read with great relish. All Kierkegaard's acquaintances in literary circles were from time to time held up to ridicule in anonymous articles in its pages while he, curiously enough, was instead singled out for praise. After a most unpleasant controversy with one of the men who wrote for the paper, however, Kierkegaard himself was for almost a year ridiculed unmercifully in every issue of *The Corsair*. Accompanying these articles were insulting cartoons cruelly caricaturing his misshapen figure, his thin legs, the uneven length of his trousers, even the umbrella that he always carried.

Kierkegaard could now no longer appear in public without being laughed at or avoided. He was deeply hurt, and any illusions he had about human nature were completely destroyed. Gradually, however, he came to feel that this was God's way of showing him that he still had a mission to perform: the existential task of suffering for Christ and the intellectual task of making clear to all mankind the real meaning of Christianity. His own spiritual insight was certainly deepened by the suffering he went through, and a number of his important devotional works were written during this period.*

### Christian Apologist

At about this time Kierkegaard also published an essay entitled *The Present Age*, which contains his most penetrating attack upon the spirit of the age in which he lived. Much as Nietzsche did a generation later, Kierkegaard condemned the nineteenth century as an age of mediocrity. It was an age that exalted man in the mass but belittled the individual—an age that put a premium on conformity and had no use for genius or creativity. The increasing "alienation" of man Kierkegaard felt to be an inevitable consequence. In modern life man is "lost" in the crowd and is "at a loss" when not in the crowd. His life is empty. He is an anonymous, dependent being, only a fraction of a truly human person. While Kierkegaard was portraying the predicament of man in terms such as these, Karl Marx at about the same time was attributing man's "alienation" to more specific economic conditions.†

Increasingly during these years, Kierkegaard devoted his thought and energy to confronting men with the fact that institutional Christianity was not genuinely Christian. Real Christianity he set in vivid contrast to the pseudo-Christianity of the established Church and the age in which he lived. In successive years he published three books developing this point of view; *The Sickness Unto Death* (1849), *Training in Christianity* (1850), and *For Self-Examination* (1851). Somewhat to Kierkegaard's surprise, however,

---

* Books translated in English as *Purity of Heart, Works of Love, The Gospel of Suffering,* and *Christian Discourses* were written then, and have been widely read in this country.

† As William Barrett points out in his study of existentialism, Kierkegaard's essay *The Present Age* was to prove "brilliantly prophetic." This essay, Barret writes, "has been the source of nearly all the Existentialist criticisms of modern society—including those by Jaspers, Ortega, Berdyaev, and Marcel. So well has Kierkegaard's prophecy held up in fact that even contemporary efforts at journalistic sociology, like Riesman's *The Lonely Crowd* or Whyte's *The Organization Man,* are still repeating and documenting his insights." (*Irrational Man,* p. 173.) And even more recently, the criticism of our technological society in books like Roszak's *The Making of a Counter Culture* and Slater's *The Pursuit of Loneliness* clearly reflect Kierkegaard's point of view.

these attacks on the Danish Church attracted relatively little attention. Few people now read his books, and among those who did many no doubt considered these works predictable and opinionated.

Finally Kierkegaard came to feel that in order to make the true nature of Christianity unmistakably clear he must break with the Church completely and suffer a martyrdom much as Christ had done. Out of respect and genuine affection for Bishop J. P. Mynster, the venerable head of the Danish Church, who had been his father's friend and pastor, he seems to have postponed this final break for a time. When on January 30, 1854, Bishop Mynster died, Kierkegaard knew that the time for his attack had come. In a highly polemical article entitled "Was Bishop Mynster a Witness for the Truth?" he emphatically denied that this was the case. Instead, both by word and deed Mynster had actually borne witness not to true Christianity but to a pernicious error. The people of Denmark were shocked; the clergy was outraged, and the final battle to which Kierkegaard had looked forward was under way.

In a periodical that he published himself (*The Instant*), Kierkegaard developed his own position relentlessly. Nine issues appeared, and the tenth was complete on his desk when on October 2, 1855, he went to see Henry Lund, his brother-in-law and banker, to draw the last of his remaining capital. His money was now gone but his task was done. On the way home from the bank he collapsed on the street of Copenhagen and was taken to the hospital, paralyzed from his waist down. On November 11, now completely helpless and hardly able to speak, Kierkegaard died quietly at the age of forty-two.

His funeral service was held the following Sunday in the Cathedral Church in Copenhagen. His brother Peter, now a well-established figure in the Danish Church, delivered the funeral oration. The large church was packed with those who had been his foes as well as his friends. A vigorous protest by Kierkegaard's nephew, against the way in which the Establishment was taking advantage of a man who had consistently attacked it, interrupted the graveside services. But Søren Kierkegaard himself was at peace at last. A few years earlier, in prophetic fashion, he had written his own obituary:

The Martyrdom this author suffered may be briefly described thus: He suffered from being a genius in a provincial town. The standard he applied in relation to . . . disinterestness, devotedness, definition of thought, *etc.*, was on the average far too great for his contemporaries; it raised the price on them too terribly; it almost made it seem as if the provincial town and the majority in it did not possess *dominium absolutum*, but that there was a God in existence.

Yet it is true that he found also here on earth what he sought. He himself was *that individual* if no one else was, and he became that more and more. It was the cause of Christianity he served, his life from childhood on being marvellously fitted for such a service. Thus he carried to completion the task of translating completely into terms of reflection what Christianity is, what it means to become a Christian. . . .

But the grand enterprise he undertook did not infatuate him. . . .

he could not ascribe [it] to any man, least of all would he ascribe it to himself; if he were to ascribe it to any one, it would be to Providence, to whom it was in fact ascribed, day after day and year after year, by the author, who historically died of a mortal disease but poetically died of longing for eternity, where uninterruptedly he would have nothing else to do but to thank God.[5]

## The Stages on Life's Way

Much of Kierkegaard's early writing was devoted to an examination of life's three "stages"—the three spheres of human existence or types of life a man could choose. Each of these—the aesthetic, the ethical, and the religious —is portrayed with keen psychological insight in his two early works, *Either/ Or* and *Stages on Life's Way*. What Kierkegaard actually gives us is his analysis of man's achievement of genuine and authentic human *existence*, and this is now generally regarded as his most significant contribution to philosophical thought.

In his portrayal of the first two types of life, the aesthetic and the ethical, Kierkegaard wrote under various symbolic pen names: Johannes de Silento (John the Silent), Constan Constantius, Johannes Climacus, Frater Taciturnus, and the like. His ideas here are expressed in amusing anecdotes, parables, and other literary devices that appeal especially to the existentialist and indicate the inability of rational and logical analysis to get at the deeper truths of experience. In fact, in these aesthetic works it is not always easy to determine when Kierkegaard is expressing his own views, and when he is simply exploring all the possible implications of a position in traditional Socratic fashion.

For Socrates was Kierkegaard's lifelong philosophical hero, and he himself has been called the Danish Socrates. When he wrote his early M.A. thesis "The Concept of Irony," Kierkegaard was still under the influence of Hegel and somewhat critical of Socrates. He soon altered his estimate of both philosophers, however. Philosophy for Socrates was a way of life. It was an existential matter, not a matter of rational theory. Socrates was also the outstanding example of the reflective thinker who made clear "the creative function of doubt without himself being a doubter." Both these characteristics of Socrates appealed to Kierkegaard. In his own use of "the dialectical strategy of indirect communication," especially in his early aesthetic works, Kierkegaard felt that he was following the example and method of Socrates, not that of Hegel. By providing a head-on clash between opposing philosophies of life, by opposing every Yes with a No, he used the Socratic dialectic of confrontation and choice. This method, he hoped, would enable his readers to see for themselves the truth or falsity of the ideas under discussion, and so in time to recognize the validity of the position he was developing.

## The Aesthetic Stage

In *Either/Or* Kierkegaard included three essays with special meaning, he hoped, for Regina. These essays described three fictional victims of faithless lovers: Mozart's Donna Elvira and Goethe's Marguerite and Marie Beaumarchais. Detached from all moral concerns, as so well portrayed in Mozart's *Don Giovanni*, the "aesthetic man" gives himself freely to the pursuit of beauty and of pleasure. He seeks to find life's meaning solely in the pleasurable moments of experience. Proud of his refined techniques, he lives only for the present moment, constructing for himself a world of art rather than simply of passion. But, as Kierkegaard skillfully argues—and this is his criticism of the romanticism of his own age—the purely aesthetic experience is a dead-end route. It leads ultimately to boredom, disgust, and despair, depriving life of all enduring meaning.

Among the various moods in which romanticism found classic expression, Kierkegaard selects three—sensual immediacy, doubt, and despair—that in his judgment reveal the dialectic of the aesthetic life most clearly. Each of these moods he associates with a well-known literary figure that appeals to the imagination of the cultivated reader: sensual immediacy with Mozart's Don Juan; doubt with Goethe's Faust; and despair with Ahasuerus, the Wandering Jew.[6]

In the figure of Don Juan, Kierkegaard sees the exuberance and enthusiasm, the freshness of sensual experience that one finds in life before reflection sets in. This is the first phase of the aesthetic life. It begins innocently and pleasantly enough. But gradually sensuality builds a kingdom of the flesh in distinction from and finally in opposition to the kingdom of the spirit. Don Juan exemplifies quite well the first step on the road to spiritual disintegration. Here one's aesthetic experiences are taken to be not only primary but exclusive. Gradually the individual loses power over himself and becomes enslaved to the search for pleasure—but the pleasurable moment is never self-sustaining. Restlessness, boredom, *ennui*, are the inevitable results of the romantic hedonism symbolized by Don Juan. Such is Kierkegaard's conclusion, in complete agreement, of course, with Schopenhauer who, as a matter of fact, was developing his own pessimistic philosophy in Germany at about the same time.

The second phase in the aesthetic way of life is especially well portrayed in Goethe's *Faust*. Actually Kierkegaard had discovered in his own aesthetic experience a disturbing transition from confident joy to doubt and skepticism, and this transition he describes symbolically as the passage from Don Juan to Faust. Faust, as pictured by Goethe, is completely committed to the aesthetic way of life, and consequently is a lost soul. In his great dramatic work Goethe depicts clearly the futility of attempting to satisfy the human spirit with only the immediate pleasures of the senses. This way of life leads finally to skepticism about the worth of all pleasure. Or so at least Kierkegaard argues.[7]

In *Either/Or* Kierkegaard has an essay entitled "Diary of a Seducer," an essay that created quite a stir in Copenhagen when it was published. Unlike Don Juan, who found great sensual pleasure in his exploits with women, the Seducer makes of seduction an art in itself. The depths of such a person's unconcern for others, as seen here, reveals the low level to which the aesthetic life can sink. The cold and calculating inhumanity of the Seducer is enough to disillusion anyone, Kierkegaard feels.

In the despair of Ahasuerus, the Wandering Jew, the third and final step in the aesthetic dialectic is portrayed. Ahasuerus wanders endlessly through life, in dull indifference and completely without hope in God or man. Kierkegaard sees here an accurate picture of the outcome of the Romanticism of his own age. Silent despair inevitably follows the immediate joys, the doubt, and the skepticism, when aesthetic experience is taken to be in itself sufficient for man's spiritual needs. "So it appears that every aesthetic view of life ends in despair," he writes, "and that everyone who lives aesthetically is in despair whether he knows it or not."[8] Thus the analysis of the first, the aesthetic, stage in life is completed. Man must either pass beyond the aesthetic way of life, Kierkegaard maintains, or resign himself to an existence without purpose or meaning, a life of futility and despair.

### The Ethical and Religious Stages

An internal law of growth, an inner dialectic, should take a man beyond the ultimate despair of the aesthetic life, Kierkegaard believes, and bring him face to face with the demands of the ethical. In *Either/Or* he deals at some length with the relation of the aesthetic and the ethical as seen in a man's love for a woman: *Either* the erotic or aesthetic experience of love as an end in itself, *Or* the moral choice of marriage in which the purely aesthetic is transcended in love and devotion to something beyond oneself. This is the choice, he believes, that confronts every individual in his personal life, a choice that must be made, whether consciously or not.

Kierkegaard is not interested in a formal theory of ethics, and he sees little value in seeking to develop an abstract ethical system. The important thing for him is that the "ethical man" accepts moral obligation rather than pleasure as the guiding principle in his conduct. When confronted with alternatives he must commit himself to what he sees to be right. He is then no longer a mere spectator of life, uninvolved and indifferent. His life now has direction and purpose. It is in this choice and commitment, indeed, that man's freedom finds expression. He here becomes master of himself; he achieves genuine selfhood. In Kierkegaard's terms, he "creates" for himself the moral values that enable him to "exist as a man." Only in the ethical and the religious spheres, then, is there an "existential" awareness of life's meaning.

This act of choice and commitment is the heart of man's ethical experience. "The act of choosing is essentially a proper and stringent expression of the ethical," Kierkegaard writes. In the act of ethical choice man's freedom transcends the limits of the rational and temporal. The individual

> . . . chooses himself, not in a finite sense (for then this "self" would be something finite), but in an absolute sense; and yet, in fact, he chooses himself and not another. This self did not exist previously, for it came into existence by means of the choice, and yet it did exist, for it was in fact himself. For in case what I chose did not exist, but absolutely came into existence with the choice, I would not be choosing. I would be creating. But I do not create myself, I choose myself.* Therefore, as a free spirit I am born of the principle of contradiction, or born in the fact that I chose myself.[9]

In the ethical life, however, a man will always encounter situations where it is impossible to follow the moral imperative of duty. The moral man is then left in despair because he is unable to do what he knows he ought to do, Kierkegaard points out. He, of course, was especially conscious of this fact in his own experience when in love with Regina. In the major essay in his *Stages on Life's Way*, an essay entitled "Guilty/Not Guilty," he examines again his love affair with Regina, and makes clear his feeling that he faced there an impossible ethical dilemma. To marry Regina under the circumstances was wrong. To break the engagement with her was also wrong. In a situation such as this, as clearly seen in the account of Abraham's sacrifice of Isaac, the moral man is left in despair with a deep sense of guilt. That is, there are ethical dilemmas in human experience that cannot be resolved but must be transcended as man moves into the religious life.

It is in such crucial decisions as this that the ethically committed individual knows something of the anguish, the fear and trembling, which Kierkegaard identifies as an essential dimension of religion. No ethical man, he is quite certain, can make an uncompromising commitment to the will of God, when this requires that he abandon the moral imperative, without such feelings. Moreover, in such a "suspension of the ethical," the universal validity of the ethical is superseded by a religious recognition of the primary importance of the individual, Kierkegaard points out. It is this that characterizes a man's passage from the ethical to the religious sphere of existence. Religious commitments, then, are not decisions binding upon all men everywhere, as are the moral imperatives of duty. They are choices only for a particular individual in his unique awareness of God's will: "The paradox of faith is this," Kierkegaard writes, "that the individual is higher than the universal, that the individual determines his relation to the universal by his relation to the absolute, not his relation to the absolute by his relation to the universal."[10]

---

* It is interesting to compare Kierkegaard's description of this act of choice with Nietzsche's analysis of what man accomplished in creating himself, that is, "in becoming what he is." See pp. 325–326.

His favorite example, of course, is the Old Testament account of Abraham and Isaac. This story Kierkegaard examines with remarkable psychological insight in his work *Fear and Trembling*.* Only in anguish, in fear and trembling, can Abraham surrender his moral obligation to love, cherish, and preserve his beloved son, even when he believes the sacrifice of Isaac to be demanded by God (which is the point of view in Genesis). Perhaps indeed such a sacrifice was not God's will. How can one ever know for certain that one's deepest religious insights are valid, especially those that require a commitment—such, for example, as conscientious objection to war—that runs counter to generally accepted social values and ideals?

This dimension of religious experience Kierkegaard treats with rare comprehension, born certainly of his own inner struggles and travail. It is in such decisions as this that one must take a "leap of faith" and make the existential commitment, without which he can never hope to "exist" as a person in the full spiritual sense of the term. Only through *faith* was it possible for Abraham's sacrifice of his son to achieve its religious and existential meaning, and so enable Abram to become Abraham (Heb. 11:17). Thus the religious existentialist revises Descartes's famous dictum: I think, therefore I am, to become: I believe and act, therefore I am.

Kierkegaard's treatment of the Biblical account of Abraham's sacrifice of Isaac (Gen. 22:1–18) provides a vivid and dramatic portrayal of the "existential" character of that experience. It also is an excellent illustration of his literary skill. Four times he retells the story and each time suggests a new dimension that should be considered. Two of the more revealing of his narratives are included here:

> It was early morning, Abraham arose and had the asses saddled; he left the tent and Isaac with him, but Sara watched from the casement as they went down the valley until they disappeared from sight. For three days they rode in silence and on the morning of the fourth day, Abraham said not a word but lifted up his eyes and saw Mount Moriah afar off. He left his servants behind him and led Isaac by the hand as they climbed the mountain alone. But Abraham said to himself, "I cannot hide from Isaac where this path is leading him." He stood still, he laid his hand on Isaac's head in blessing and Isaac bowed down to receive the blessing. And Abraham's countenance was that of a father, his eyes gentle, his voice encouraging. But Isaac could not understand him. . . .
>
> Abraham climbed Mount Moriah but Isaac did not understand him. For a moment Abraham turned his face away from his son and when Isaac saw his face again, it had changed; his eyes were wild and he was terrible to look upon. He seized Isaac by the shoulders and threw him

---

* *Fear and Trembling* was written for the most part shortly after the announcement of Regina's engagement to her former suitor. The analysis of Abraham's sacrifice of his beloved son is Kierkegaard's way of showing that in what is clearly God's will, he also must surrender his beloved Regina.

to the ground and said, "Foolish youth, do you believe that I am your father? I am an idol worshipper. Do you believe it is God's command? No, it is my own pleasure."

Then Isaac cried out in terror. "God in Heaven, have mercy on me! God of Abraham, have mercy on me! I have no father on earth, be thou my father." And Abraham said softly to himself, "Father in Heaven, I thank Thee. It is better that he should believe me inhuman than that he should lose faith in Thee."

It was early morning, Abraham arose and kissed Sara, the young mother, and Sara kissed Isaac, her joy, her delight in all time. And Abraham rode away deep in thought, thinking of Hagar and the son he had sent into the wilderness. He climbed Mount Moriah, he drew the knife.

One evening when all was quiet, Abraham rode out alone and rode to Mount Moriah; he threw himself on his face, he prayed God to forgive him his sin, to forgive him for having wanted to sacrifice Isaac, to forgive him for having forgotten his fatherly duty towards his son. Frequently he rode his lonely way, but he did not find rest. He could not conceive that it was a sin to have wished to sacrifice to God his most precious possession when he would have given his life many times over for the sake of his son; and if this was a sin, if he had not loved Isaac in this way, then he could not understand that it would be forgiven. And could any sin be more terrible?[11]

## Christian Existentialism

### The Uniqueness of the Individual

The fact that each person is a uniquely existing individual was of utmost importance in Kierkegaard's view of religion. This was the basis of his intense criticism of the age in which he lived. The individual was lost in the crowd. Man became only a cipher, a fraction of a truly human person. Kierkegaard was in general agreement with Kant's formulation of the categorical imperative. Always treat human personality, whether in your own person or in others, as an end and never as a means only. But no category of behavior designed for humanity as a whole, even one as desirable as this, could provide adequate guidance for one's own unique needs, he was certain.

Thus for Kierkegaard the commitment of the individual to God's will makes a twofold contribution to man's search for life's meaning. It enables him initially to transcend his otherwise irresolvable moral dilemmas. But it also provides a relationship to God, to the absolute, that establishes the enduring worth of the person himself as a unique individual—accountable only to God.

Kierkegaard's disagreement with Kant does not consist in questioning the fundamental importance of moral obligation and the categorical imperative of duty. But he does not accept the absolute validity of the ethical upon which Kant insists. In the moral philosophy of Kant, moreover, man's sense of moral obligation provides the only solid foundation of religious faith. And with this Kierkegaard cannot agree. As he saw quite clearly, the Kantian moral philosophy implies that faith in a personal God, and religion as distinct from moral conviction, have no basis of their own in human experience. This he found to be completely contrary to his own existential religious experience, from which both moral obligation and religious faith ultimately derived.*

### Truth Is Subjectivity

It is in his attack on the Hegelian rationalism that Kierkegaard develops his central and best-known philosophical doctrine: our deepest knowledge of truth is found not in objective rational analysis but in subjective emotional awareness. In defending this position he clearly agrees in part with Kant's *Critique of Pure Reason*. The truth with which religion is concerned is not at all the kind of truth about man or the universe that science can provide. Nor is it found in the objective, rational propositions that are stated in the doctrines or creeds of the Church. Human intelligence can never remain outside of and unmoved by the emotional involvements and the crises of life, Kierkegaard maintains. Nor can a man look upon life as a spectator looks upon something outside of and unrelated to his own concerns. Our most rewarding concern is a passionate search for one's own truth, a search for life's meaning as revealed in our own deepest spiritual experience.

"Truth" is not, then, a system of intellectual propositions that the believer accepts because he knows them to be rationally and objectively true, as a system of geometry is true. Truth is a matter of personal insight and appropriation. Such existential truth is recognized intimately as a part of one's own existence. It is discovered by each individual for himself in the immediate process of living, and cannot be reduced to an objective intellectual generalization, equally true for all men. Something becomes true subjectively when a person believes it passionately, and has assimilated it into his whole existence. For Kierkegaard, "strictly speaking, subjective truth is not a truth that I have but a truth that I am."[12]

This distinction between scientific knowledge and religious truth, between the objective and the subjective, is a major tenet of Kierkegaard's religious epistemology. The *fact* of scientific or objective knowledge he never questions. It is its *significance* that he denies:

> The way of objective reflection leads to abstract thought, to mathematics, to historical knowledge of different kinds; and always it leads away from the subject, whose existence or non-existence, and from the

* This aspect of Kierkegaard's religious existentialism proved especially appealing to Reinhold Niebuhr: "The sense of obligation in morals from which Kant tried to derive the whole structure of religion is really derived from religion itself." (*An Interpretation of Christian Ethics*, p. 9.)

objective point of view quite rightly, becomes infinitely indifferent. . . . and while the subject and his subjectivity become indifferent, the truth also becomes indifferent, and this indifference is precisely its objective validity; for all interest, like all decisiveness, is rooted in subjectivity.[13]

"The psychologist generally regards it as a sure sign that a man is beginning to give up a passion when he wishes to treat it objectively," Kierkegaard points out. "Passion and reflection are generally exclusive of one another. Becoming objective in this way is always retrogression, for passion is man's perdition, but it is his exaltation as well."

The major fallacy in the philosophy of Hegel is simply that he mistakes the abstraction found in reflective thought for reality, Kierkegaard maintains: "If Hegel had written the whole of his logic and then said in the preface that it was merely an experiment in thought in which he had even begged the question in many places, then he would certainly have been the greatest thinker who ever lived. As it is, he is merely comic."[14]

Existence and a theory about existence are two quite different matters, no more alike than a printed menu and the food it describes. To emphasize the chasm between theoretical philosophy and the concrete expression of truth in life, Kierkegaard's favorite example is the college professor who builds a beautiful castle in his system of philosophical idealism but continues to live in his own miserable hut beside the castle. As he elsewhere writes, "The fact that philosophers talk about reality is often just as deceptive as when a man reads on a sign-board in front of a shop, 'Ironing done here.' If he should come with his linen to get it ironed, he would be making a fool of himself, for the sign-board was there only for sale."[15]

### Truth and Paradox

Despite the large existential significance to the individual himself of religious truth, Kierkegaard recognizes that it is extremely difficult, perhaps impossible, to formulate such subjective insights so that they can be communicated or shared with others. His most specific description of a religious truth indicates this quite clearly: "*An objective uncertainty held fast in an appropriation-process of the most passionate inwardness is the truth*, the highest truth for an existing *individual*."[16] As Kierkegaard points out, this is also an "equivalent expression for faith." And there cannot be faith without risk. If we could *know* God's nature objectively, then there would be no need of *faith*. It is precisely because we cannot know that faith is necessary. But religious faith—and the subjective truth upon which it rests—is made doubly difficult by the fact that we can only state the deepest religious truth as a paradox. Hence it must appear to human reason as *absurd*.

Let us try to make religious faith reasonable, intelligible—"almost probable, as good as probable, extremely and emphatically probable," Kierkegaard writes in characteristic fashion. Then we find that instead of our earlier faith, we now no longer *believe*, because we *almost* know, or as good as know, or extremely and emphatically know. But now obviously "religious truth" in its deeper existential significance no longer exists. The paradox of Christ is an enigma that reason cannot explain. It violates all the usual preconceptions and attitudes of our modern scientific age. No study of history or philosophy can make a man a Christian. Only an existential personal encounter with Christ can do so. "Christianity has declared itself to be the eternal essential truth which has come into being in time," Kierkegaard writes. "It has proclaimed itself as the *Paradox*, and it has required of the individual the inwardness of faith in relation to that which is an offense to the Jews and a folly to the Greeks—and an absurdity to the understanding."[17]

Since religious truth can only be known subjectively and by faith, an insistence upon objectivity merely repels the religious thinker. For him it implies a necessary distrust of the paradoxical and the absurd. "What now is the absurd?" Kierkegaard asks. "The absurd is—that the eternal truth has come into being in time, that God has come into being, has been born, has grown up, and so forth, has come into being precisely like any other individual human being, quite indistinguishable from any other individuals."[18] Among later existentialists, especially Sartre and Camus, Kierkegaard's recognition of the significance of the "absurd" proved quite influential. Even in the Theatre of the Absurd today there is continuing indication that the rational approach to life has serious limitations.

### What It Is to Be a Christian

Becoming a Christian is then an existential choice. Only as it is lived can the Christian faith be understood. This is the heart of Kierkegaard's message, and his attack upon institutional Christianity grew out of this conviction. To be a Christian one must be prepared to live like Christ; he must expect like Christ to be persecuted, lonely, "rejected of men." Only then can he know the "truth" of the Christian gospel. But now that everyone in Denmark was a nominal Christian, true Christianity had all but ceased to exist, Kierkegaard pointed out. The tragedy of Christendom, as he saw it, was that since all had become Christians, nobody was now a Christian. Christ's teachings had been watered down to a kind of thin conventional morality, a sort of polite respectability. The militant, demanding gospel of Christ no longer existed. The established Church had become a travesty. It no longer expected any genuine Christian faith and life in those who professed Christianity. In his characteristic paradoxical fashion Kierkegaard pointed out that it was now easier for a man to become a Christian if he was not a Christian than if he already (conventionally) was one.

This criticism of organized Christianity Kierkegaard depicts with his usual dramatic skill:

> The Parson (collectively understood) does indeed preach about those glorious ones who sacrifice their lives for the truth. As a rule the parson is justified in assuming that there is no one present in the church who

would entertain the notion of venturing upon such a thing. When he is sufficiently assured of this by reason of the private knowledge he has of the congregation as its pastor, he preaches glibly, disclaims vigorously, and wipes away the sweat.

If on the following day one of those strong and silent men, a quiet, modest, perhaps even insignificant-looking man, were to visit the parson at his home announcing himself as one whom the parson had carried away by his eloquence, so that he had now resolved to sacrifice his life for the truth—what would the parson say? He would address him thus: "Why, merciful Father in Heaven! How did such an idea ever occur to you? Travel, divert yourself, take a laxative." And if this plain-looking man were to fix his eye upon him with unaltered calm, and holding him with his glance were to continue to talk about his resolution, but with the modest expressions which a resolute man always uses—then the parson would surely think, "Would that this man were far away!"[19]

Thus Kierkegaard portrays the way in which the Christian Church itself has destroyed the spirit and the existential commitment of genuine Christianity. A generation later Nietzsche restated Kierkegaard's condemnation of institutional Christianity in his own more provocative fashion: "God is dead, and we have killed him."

Kiekegaard's message to the Church in his age is well summed up as follows: In an age filled with hypocrisy and pretense, *do not pretend*. Do not pretend to be religious if you are not. Do not pretend to be a Christian if you are not. Genuineness, integrity, commitment are the essential things. Genuine Christianity must find its expression in all that a man does, in what he is, not what he says or pretends to be.

Nor has Kierkegaard's message lost its relevance for our own day and age. He said quite effectively what many students are saying today, as they look to the Christian Church for guidance and moral leadership in the perplexities of modern life.

Theologians argue about *what* constitutes Christianity, what doctrine or creed is orthodox, what sacraments are Biblical, what institutions are historically correct. But none of these have anything to do with *being* a Christian for Kierkegaard. In his words: "The thing of being a Christian is not determined by the *what* of Christianity, but by the *how* of the Christian." It is the "inward appropriation" of Christian faith, what it means and does to the existence of the individual himself, to his existential self, that alone for Kierkegaard determines whether or not one is a Christian. It is such an experience as this indeed that for the existentialist determines whether or not an individual really "exists" as fully human, whether he has found *himself*.

### Kierkegaard's Importance

The rediscovery of Kierkegaard, first in Europe over half a century after his death in 1855, and then even later in America, had a marked influence upon religious thought during the first half of the twentieth century. Begin-

.ning about 1909, his forty-three esthetic, religious, and philosophical works were translated into German; then into French about twenty years later; and finally into English, beginning in 1936. The development of two significant twentieth-century movements—religious existentialism and the neo-orthodox or crisis theology of Karl Barth—was largely shaped by Kierkegaard's ideas and insights.

Several influences stand out as especially significant. Kierkegaard's analysis of the predicament of modern man is quite apparent in the thought of later existentialists. Indeed, the alienation of man in contemporary life became one of the bywords of existentialism. Kierkegaard's emphasis on the existential significance of choice, decision, and commitment has been equally influential. Upon this central insight Sartre in particular has built an impressive structure. The primacy of subjectivity, of inwardness, of existential moment-by-moment decisions, in shaping human life is another conviction of Kierkegaard's that later existentialists continued to emphasize.

Of wider significance perhaps is Kierkegaard's insistence upon the importance of the individual, and upon the destructive influence on man's humanity for which modern society is responsible. The influence of mass hysteria upon personal integrity Kierkegaard recognized as especially dangerous. And he made it clear that while the material benefits provided by modern science were in fact superficial, its spiritual dangers were enormous. Kierkegaard also rebelled against the excessive rationalism of Hegel and much nineteenth-century philosophy. Life, he insisted, is more than logic, and reason is not the surest key to reality. Without the existential insights of religion man is left to flounder in the poverty and falseness of the intellectual or the aesthetic life. Such recent American scholars as Reinhold Niebuhr and Paul Tillich, as well as the neo-orthodox school of Karl Barth and Emil Brunner, owe much to this aspect of Kierkegaard's thought.

Quite interesting also is the fact that the philosophy of the counter-culture, as portrayed by Roszak and Reich, is reemphasizing insights that we owe to Kierkegaard. In its concern for the worth of the individual, its awareness of the destructive influence of technology and science in modern life, its rejection of the objective scientific world view, and its emphasis upon subjectivity and upon "human" truth, Kierkegaard's point of view is quite apparent today.

## Some Disturbing Difficulties

Despite its continuing influence, Kierkegaard's existential philosophy is apt to leave us with serious questions unresolved. His emphasis upon the importance of the individual is so great, critics of his position insist, that he fails to do justice to the larger contribution of man's social life. Can a man find himself *only* by forsaking all friends, all personal relationships, and looking to God alone? Certainly this is not the generally accepted conclusion of those who examine human life. One easily sees this limitation in Kierkegaard's own experience. Neither with his father nor with Regina, the two persons who meant most to him, was he ever able to establish a fully meaningful personal relationship. Yet certainly, as philosophers from Aristotle's day to our own have recognized, here is found one of man's deepest and most meaningful sources of happiness.

Likewise Kierkegaard's emphasis upon the necessity of paradox and the absurd in stating the deeper truth of religious insight has its difficulties as well as its values. As is often pointed out, to repudiate logic and consistency in favor of contradiction and paradox does easily open one to self-deception and fanaticism. "Kierkegaard's central error," one of his critics writes, "is epitomized by his two epigrams: 'The conclusions of passion are the only reliable ones,' and 'What our age lacks is not reflection but passion.' "[20] Instead of providing a critique of reason, indicating what it can and cannot do, Kierkegaard seems to his critics to have "renounced clear and distinct thinking altogether." Such a course of action is hardly designed to strengthen his unequivocal rejection of rationalism. The anti-intellectualism and irrationalism found in much contemporary life certainly find support in the kind of emphasis upon subjectivity for which Kierkegaard is in part responsible. Can this be seen as a positive asset?

A question must likewise be raised about Kierkegaard's exclusive emphasis upon religion, and Protestant Christianity in particular, as the only avenue to man's discovery of himself and his achievement of selfhood. As important as mankind through the centuries has found spiritual life and religious insight to be, man has likewise found in other aspects of life essential ingredients for wholeness and happiness. It is a bit disturbing also in this connection to note how, for Kierkegaard, the religious life is forever pervaded by suffering. Certainly there are other important dimensions of historical Christianity, as well as of the religious experience outside the Christian tradition, that do contribute to a constructive philosophy of life.

Let us not forget, however, that in the spirit of Socrates, whom he so much admired, Kierkegaard was a religious gadfly who attacked the complacency of his age in the places where it most needed to be aroused. He spoke as a personal witness to the existential truth that he discovered in the depths of his own experience. And his influence upon the religious thought and the existential philosophy of the twentieth century has been not only creative and disturbing but almost unbelievably extensive.

## CHAPTER 15

# Humanistic Existentialism

## *Jean-Paul Sartre*

Of all the philosophers who are thought of as existentialists, two stand out in the popular mind in this country; Søren Kierkegaard and Jean-Paul Sartre. These two figures, fundamentally different in background, in outlook on life, and even in the ages in which they lived, have become intimately and inextricably associated with the philosophy of existentialism. In a very real sense they represent this philosophy for most laymen.

While Kierkegaard and Sartre have enough in common to justify their being termed existentialists, their differences are quite as significant as are their areas of agreement. Kierkegaard's existentialism is, of course, deeply religious. Sartre's existential point of view is the expression of an atheistic or, as he once maintained, a humanistic philosophy. The urbane and sophisticated atheism of Bertrand Russell is essentially a rational theory, to be discussed in objective and largely impersonal fashion. The atheism of Sartre is more somber and disturbing. It takes much of its mood from Friedrich Nietzsche, for whom, as we have seen, atheism was a matter of tragic personal experience.

Sartre is, to be sure, a philosopher in the French tradition. His work is distinguished by remarkable versatility. He was known for his novels, plays, and short stories before he became famous as a philosopher. In temperament and point of view, however, Sartre has been closer to Nietzsche and Heidegger, and more recently to Marx, than to his earlier French philosophers. In rather striking fashion he has combined significant aspects of French with German philosophical thought in his own humanistic existentialism.

### Personal History as Inevitable Change

"If a man is to have a history, it is necessary that he change, that the world change him as it changes, and that he change as he changes the world."[1] These words of Sartre's, written in 1952, are, like so much else that he wrote, a discerning comment on his own life and intellectual career. Change in his thought as he encountered new situations and new social forces is as significant as is his underlying existential point of view.

Jean-Paul Sartre was born in Paris on June 21, 1905. His father died when he was an infant and Sartre grew up in the home of his maternal grandfather, Charles Schweitzer, an uncle of the famous missionary doctor and theologian, Albert Schweitzer. Early life in his grandfather's home in Paris is described and analyzed in detail by Sartre in an autobiographical volume entitled *The Words*. Published in 1963, when he was almost sixty years old, this book actually provides a penetrating insight into Sartre's recent understanding of himself. Underlying his whole outlook on life and guiding its development, Sartre recognized, was "a deep childish revulsion against the sham façade of noble rectitude behind which his bourgeois family hid from itself, and from him, its real dereliction."[2] His grandfather became for him the symbol of bourgeois culture against which his childish spirit revolted.

By the time he was nine, he was firmly committed to becoming a writer, Sartre tells us. The books in his grandfather's library provided his only road to freedom and enjoyment. Unable to accept either the Catholic faith of his parents or the Lutheran faith of his grandparents, he found in writing the one means of establishing his identity as a person—of really discovering who he was. The earthly immortality of the printed page—of great books—fascinated him, even at this early age, and he undertook a number of youthful literary ventures of his own: "By writing, I was existing, I was escaping from grown-ups, but I existed only in order to write, and if I said 'I' that meant 'I who write.' . . . I was prepared at an early age to regard teaching as a priesthood and literature as a passion."[3]

Sartre attended the Ecole Normale Supérieure, an institution to which only the more able young Frenchmen are admitted by competitive examination, and in 1929 he took his degree there in philosophy. Then for ten years he taught philosophy in various French schools. Even at this time, however, he found conventional philosophy less than exciting. He became increasingly conscious of the discrepancy between life as he knew it at first hand and the ideals and values he had been taught at home and at school. The abstractions with which philosophy was too frequently concerned did not interest him, and its lack of relevance to the concrete details of ordinary life left him dissatisfied.

A friend of his, who had just returned from Germany, was quite enthusiastic about the new method of philosophizing being developed there by Edmund Husserl—a point of view known as phenomenology. Its emphasis upon the concrete and specific facts of experience, rather than upon abstract theory, appealed to Sartre, and he decided to find out for himself what phenomenology could do to vitalize philosophy. The academic year 1933–1934 he spent in Berlin studying with Husserl. This new way of looking at man and the world not only shaped Sartre's later existentialism but also helped him achieve his early ambition to become a recognized writer. His first novel, *Nausea*, was published in 1938. Its social realism, and the literary skill with which Sartre depicted those aspects of bourgeois life that he despised, brought him quick recognition in literary circles. This novel also reflected clearly his early existentialism.

### *Early Point of View:* Nausea

Three major stages in the development of Sartre's thought can be distinguished, or better perhaps three significant periods in his life that are reflected in his philosophy.[4] For with Sartre, of course, as with all existential thinkers, life and thought are essentially related and can be separated only for purposes of clearer analysis. In the first of these three periods he was interested primarily in working out for himself a philosophical point of view that would prove satisfying. He wanted a philosophy that deals with man in the concrete reality of life as it is actually lived, in a situation where a man has to face his destiny alone with no God to whom he could turn for guidance or assistance. His first novel, *Nausea*, provides initial expression of this early point of view; it reached its culmination a few years later in the French Resistance Movement.

The story of Roquentin, the hero of *Nausea*, is not told as an end in itself. Actually it expresses Sartre's own view concerning human existence. This story provides a descriptive or phenomenological account of a man's growing realization of the absurdity of human life in itself, and of his awakening to the fact that if a man's life is to have any meaning or purpose the individual himself must confer that meaning upon it. A sense of the absurd, the absurdity of life and of man himself, permeates Sartre's early existentialism. In *Nausea* he portrays this as an immediate insight in one's own experience. As he sat in a public park one day, staring at the long black roots of an old chestnut tree, Roquentin became acutely aware of the absurdity of his own existence:

> Absurdity was not an idea in my head nor the sound of a voice, it was this long, lean, wooden snake curled up at my feet—snake or claw or talon or root, it was all the same. Without formulating anything I knew that I had found the clue to my existence, to my nausea, to my life. And indeed everything I have ever grasped since that moment comes back to this fundamental absurdity.[5]

As Sartre later wrote, he himself was Roquentin, and those ugly roots, groping in darkness under the earth, were symbolic of life's nauseating absurdity. Nor is it too difficult perhaps to recognize an element of the absurd or irrational in nature and in life. Nature produces an enormous number of living beings, for example, most of which perish even before reaching their full development. Ultimately all of these, even the most able and creative, also perish and are soon forgotten. This absurdity inherent in the nature of things becomes even more apparent and forceful in a situation such as that faced by the French who lived under Nazi domination during the Second World War. It was a fact of experience, a fact soon brought home to Sartre himself.

One who contemplates the destructiveness and terror in a situation such as the recent one in Vietnam—created by the Vietcong and the Vietnamese, to be sure, as well as by American air power—may feel that man himself is clearly in danger of becoming absurd in Sartre's sense. His existence loses all meaning whatsoever. Indeed, in the minds of many this is what has happened in our time, and it is this dimension of human existence of which the existentialists have been acutely conscious. For them it poses the central problem with which a man must wrestle in seeking to make sense of life.

In the development of his own philosophy, Sartre was as yet concerned only with his personal "salvation," the attempt to create meaning in his own life through his writing. Some twenty-five years later in *The Words* he points out in his own dramatic fashion that in Roquentin he was describing his own early existentialism:

> I was Roquentin; I used him to show, without complacency, the texture of my life. At the same time I was *I*, the chronicler of Hell, a glass and steel photomicroscope peering at my own protoplasmic juices. Later I gaily demonstrated that man is impossible. I was impossible myself and differed from the others only by the mandate to give expression to that impossibility which was thereby transfigured and became my most personal possibility, the object of my mission, the springboard of my glory.[6]

### The French Resistance Movement

The years 1939–1945 were of major significance in shaping Sartre's thought. The experiences of these years radically altered his outlook and led him in time to the second stage in his existential philosophy. "It was the war which made the obsolete frames of our thought explode," he wrote, "the war, occupation, resistance, the years that followed."[7]

In 1939 Sartre was drafted into the French army. Captured by the Germans the following year, he spent nine months in a German prisoner-of-war camp, and was then returned to Paris because of ill health. There, with Albert Camus and Simone de Beauvoir, Sartre soon became a leader among the Paris intellectuals in the French Resistance Movement. The young men and women of France were at that time faced with what was soon known as an "identity crisis." Sartre and Camus in particular assisted many bewildered students who needed help in the moral and intellectual ordeal of growing up in a defeated and occupied country.

During these years Sartre wrote two of his most influential plays, *The Flies* (1943) and *No Exit* (1944). Certainly these are the plays to recommend to the student who wishes to feel the concrete spirit of Sartre's philosophy but has not the time or interest for his more elaborate and scholarly works. In both plays Sartre is dealing directly with the human predicament as reflected in the circumstances of the time. He was also, of course, formulating more clearly his own existential point of view. The suffering of the French under the German occupation made him acutely conscious of the concrete evil that man must face in life, an evil brought home to him and his compatriots in France in a way that most of us in America today have never known. "We have been taught to take Evil seriously," Sartre writes.

> It is neither our fault nor our merit if we lived in a time when torture was a daily fact. Chateaubriand, Oradour, the Rue des Saussaies, Dachau, and Auschwitz have all demonstrated to us that Evil is not an appearance, that knowing its cause does not dispel it, that it is not opposed to Good as a confused idea is to a clear one, that it is not the effect of passions that might be cured, of an ignorance that might be enlightened, that it can in no way be incorporated into idealistic humanism.[8]

Produced under the eyes of the Nazi censors, *The Flies* was presented in the form of the old Greek myth of Orestes and the Furies. It was understood generally by the French, however, as a statement of the spirit of the Resistance Movement. As a whole, the play gives expression to a passion and eloquence born of Sartre's own personal experiences and convictions. Orestes is the spokesman for Sartre's view of man's nature and destiny, and for his early existential philosophy as well. As pictured here, man actually has no God. Defiantly expressing his own ultimate freedom, he must choose his own destiny and accept full responsibility for that choice. At the end of the play in a superbly defiant speech before Jupiter, "the cosmic Gestapo chief," Orestes states this Sartrean conviction:

> Foreign to myself—I know it. Outside nature, against nature, beyond remedy, except what remedy I find within myself. But I shall not return under your law; I am doomed to have no other law but my own. Nor shall I come back to nature, the nature you found good. In it are a thousand beaten paths all leading up to you—but I must blaze my own trail. For I, Zeus, am a man, and every man must find his own way. Nature abhors man, and you too, god of gods, abhor mankind.[9]

*No Exit* is perhaps the most sensational of Sartre's plays. Here one sees his real talent as a writer expressed in the driving force of the play and in the passionate expression of ideas that are clearly his. Here also Sartre makes it quite clear that, having once chosen, man must live with the choice he makes. There is no exit. The three characters in *No Exit* are in Hell, where they are being punished by being given exactly what they have chosen. Sartre is actually dealing with the essence of evil in the manner of Martin Buber. His three characters have tried to treat man's being, his true humanity, as a *thing*. Now in Hell they have lost their genuine subjective being by identifying themselves with what they were in the eyes of other people; and they now have no other being than what each one has in the eyes of the others. In Buber's terms, only the *I–It* relation exists; the *I–Thou* has been destroyed.

More specifically, Sartre is pointing to such concrete evils in human life as hypocrisy and cowardice, sadism, and utter selfishness to make this clear. Each of these is portrayed by one of the characters in *No Exit*. And in each of these, human personality is treated as a thing, an *It* rather than a *Thou*. His three characters were actually dead before they died physically. They had, in fact, never been *alive*. They had never been able to use their freedom as human beings "to choose to live authentically." Their lives were always in the hands of others. They only played a role, and lived in a world of unreality.

### Man as Free and Heroic

In his war experiences, and in the danger and suffering, the daring and heroism of the French Resistance Movement, Sartre found a new answer to the meaning of existence. The Resistance Movement brought to him and to his generation a release from pettiness, boredom, and disgust, and a call to action and heroism. It was a decision that stretched man to the very limit of his being. Here individuals who were nothing became men—made men out of themselves. They rose above the selfishness and pretense of bourgeois society to a new contact with the realities of human life. It is necessary to emphasize this experience in order that we in America today can understand Sartre and the powerful appeal of his philosophy in the years following the Second World War. Sartre was in fact discovering for himself what William James had described many years earlier in his essay, *The Moral Equivalent of War*.

In *The Republic of Silence*, Sartre describes life in the French Resistance Movement as he knew it at first hand from 1940 to 1945. Here he strikes the note of heroism in human life, which is particularly impressive because in so much of his writing man is pictured as distinctly unheroic in nature. During these years not only did Sartre discover in the Resistance Movement the heroic in human nature; he also discovered the deeper meaning of human freedom. And this too became one of the essential features of his existential philosophy. In their time of greatest trial the French found a final, an irreducible freedom in their ability to say "No" to the might of the Nazi occupying forces. This was an existential freedom, an ultimate and final freedom that could never be taken from one. Sartre's view of human freedom as final and absolute, a view for which he has frequently been criticized, and which he actually later modified, derives from this experience. It is in this vein that he writes of life in the Resistance Movement:

> We were never more free than during the German occupation. We had lost all our rights, beginning with the right to talk. Every day we were insulted to our faces and had to take it in silence. Under one pretext or another, as workers, Jews, or political prisoners, we were deported *en masse*. Everywhere, on billboards, in the newspapers, on the screen, we encountered the revolting and insipid pictures of ourselves that our suppressors wanted us to accept. And, because of all this, we were free. Because the Nazi venom seeped into our thoughts, every accurate thought was a conquest. Because an all-powerful police tried to force us to hold our tongues, every word took on the value of a declaration of principles. Because we were hunted down, every one of our gestures had the weight of a solemn commitment.
>
> Exile, captivity, and especially death (which we usually shrink from facing at all in happier days) became for us the habitual objects of our concern. We learned that they were neither inevitable accidents, nor even constant and inevitable dangers, but they must be considered as our lot itself, our destiny, the profound source of our reality as men. At every instant we lived up to the full sense of this commonplace phrase: "Man is mortal!" And the choice that each of us made of his life was an authentic choice because it was made face to face with death, because it could always have been expressed in concrete terms: "Rather death than...." And here I am not speaking of the elite among us who were real Resistants, but all Frenchmen who, at every hour of the night and day throughout four years, answered NO.[10]

### Literature as a Mode of Action

During this first period in his thought Sartre was primarily concerned with man's life as an individual. He portrayed the aloneness and meaninglessness of man in the typical bourgeois society of the day, but he also emphasized man's existential freedom. By showing what the heroism displayed in the Resistance Movement enabled man to make of himself, he challenged every man to find his own way to salvation. In the second period in his life and intellectual career Sartre came to feel it essential that a man commit himself to the welfare and freedom of others. To be fully himself a man must become an involved member of a group committed to removing the injustices and exploitation present in social life.

Indications of this point of view are, of course, to be seen in his earlier thought. In *The Republic of Silence* Sartre wrote: "Thus in darkness and in blood a Republic was established, the strongest of Republics. Each citizen knew that he owed himself to all and that he could count on himself alone. Each of them, standing against the oppressor, undertook to be himself freely and irrevocably, and by choosing himself in liberty, he chose liberty for all."[11] *

In a significant essay entitled *What Is Literature?* (1947) Sartre stated his new point of view more concretely: Unless literature is committed—*engaged*, to use his term—it is of no real value. The engaged writer gives up the impossible dream of being uncommitted, impartial about political and social life. He not only deals realistically with the problems one faces in life, but writes so as to reveal the changes he wishes to bring into the world in which he lives. The prose writer should be an active participant in shaping the collective future of mankind. It is his function to become involved with the mass of humanity in their human adventure—"to go with his eyes open" where they were going. His one topic should be the freedom of all mankind. Wherever and whenever man's freedom is threatened, it is the obligation of the writer to protest.

It is clear that by the time he wrote *What Is Literature?* Sartre already felt the appeal of Marxism. He was as yet unwilling to accept the materialism and the economic determinism that characterized the orthodox Communist position. But he was by now convinced of the evils inherent in capitalism's exploitation of the workers, and he insisted upon the responsibility of the committed writer and philosopher to work for their freedom. It is a writer's duty so to influence the reader, Sartre feels, as to "provoke his intention of treating men in every case as an absolute end and, by the *subject* of his writing, to direct his intention upon his neighbors, that is, upon the oppressed of the world." He must make the reader feel deeply that "what he wants is to eliminate the exploitation of man by man."[12] Indeed, the writer who remains silent about the social injustices of his age is actually guilty of committing these injustices, since he has done nothing to prevent them.

The French existentialists have often been regarded as writers and poets, as literary men rather than professional or academic philosophers. The decade 1939–1948 was the "high tide" of Sartre's creative achievement. It was the period in which he published the first significant segment of his work: novels, short stories, plays, literary and political essays, and a major philosophical treatise. His reputation as a writer and an intellectual of world renown was by now unquestioned. Clearly, however, it was the *idea*, and especially the idea that leads to social action, that engaged Sartre in this mature period of his life and thought. He was in fact a social philosopher who made use of literature for his own ends.[13]

Sartre's political and philosophical goal during this second period in his life and thought was the achievement of a unified and idealized humanity, where all men could accept their own freedom only if all other men should be

---

* In her diary Simone de Beauvoir notes that Sartre at this time became aware of an important change in his thinking and realized that he could no longer remain aloof from political involvement. (See *Sartre: A Collection of Critical Essays*, ed. Edith Kern —Prentice Hall, Inc., 1962, p. 12.)

free. The interpretation of existentialism to which this led was stated by Sartre in a popular lecture he gave in 1945, entitled "Existentialism and Humanism."* His philosophy is presented here in much more interesting and less technical fashion than in his scholarly works. As a result the essay has been included in most of the English anthologies dealing with Existentialism, and has been widely read and discussed. It was for many years the best-known statement of Sartre's philosophy.

Existentialism, as interpreted here, "is nothing else but an attempt to draw the full conclusions from a consistently atheistic position," Sartre writes. Human nature is not something that exists ready-made, but "man is what he makes of himself." "Existence precedes essence." "We define man only in terms of his commitments." "As soon as there is a commitment, I am obliged to will the liberty of others at the same time as my own." "And in this willing freedom, we discover that it depends entirely upon the freedom of others and that the freedom of others depends upon our own."[14]

### The Convert to Marxism

Sartre had, of course, during all his mature life, been compelled by circumstance to confront Communism as a political force and Marxism as a philosophy. During the 1930s the tactics and the philosophy of the Communists had not interested him greatly, but during the war years he saw that he must master the Marxist social philosophy if he wished to deal with practical politics in France. With this in mind he and his friend Merleau-Ponty undertook a thorough study not only of Marx but of Hegel as well. As early as 1946, in an essay entitled "Materialism and Revolution," there is a clear indication of the increasing influence of the Marxist social philosophy upon Sartre. He was also quite well aware of the danger to his own existentialism that this involved.

"Young people today are uneasy," he wrote. "They no longer recognize their right to be young. It is as though youth were not an age of life, but a class phenomenon, a spell of irresponsibility accorded to the children of the well-to-do. The workers go without transition from adolescence to manhood." "I know that man has no salvation other than the liberation of the working class; I know this *before* being a materialist and from a plain inspection of the fact. I know that our intellectual interest lies with the proletariat." And then, in quite revealing fashion, Sartre asks: "Is that a reason for me to demand of my thinking, which has led me to this point, that it destroy itself?"[15]

In this essay, however, Sartre no longer stressed the radical freedom of

---

* In the earliest American translation by Bernard Frechtman, published in 1947, the essay is entitled "Existentialism Is a Humanism." This literal translation of the French title is somewhat awkward, however. The translation in England is entitled "Existentialism and Humanism," and in Germany, "Ist der Existentialismus ein Humanismus?"

each man to become what he wished to be. He now recognized that the individual worker could gain his own liberty only if his entire class was liberated, and he accepted with Marx the necessity of a revolution to overthrow the established bourgeois capitalistic order so that the freedom of the proletariat might be achieved. While not yet quite ready to accept Marxism as *the* philosophy, Sartre was willing to agree with Marx that the freedom open to any individual was definitely shaped by his particular situation in life. It was by no means absolute. Indeed in too many cases "the margin of choice left to him came very close to zero," Sartre admitted.[16]

By 1952 events in the world had brought Sartre to the place where he felt he could no longer temporize. In facing squarely his own responsibilities he must commit himself openly and explicitly to one side or the other. His "conversion experience" reminds one forcefully of that experienced by Arthur Koestler some twenty years earlier. "A faith is not acquired by reasoning," Koestler wrote. "Persuasion may play a part in a man's conversion—but only the part of bringing to its full and conscious climax a process which has been maturing in regions where no persuasion can penetrate."[17]

The occasion of Sartre's conversion was in itself quite insignificant. In May, 1952, General Ridgway arrived in Paris to take command of SHAPE, and the Communist Party called for an anti-Ridgway demonstration. When French security forces stopped the car of one of the protesting Communist leaders, they found two pigeons in it. They at once arrested the man and charged him with receiving orders from Moscow by carrier pigeon. The pigeons, as it turned out, had only been purchased for the evening meal; and Sartre himself was in Italy at the time. But this small incident was enough to bring to its conscious climax a process that had been at work below the level of consciousness long before the overzealous act of the Paris police took place.

"These sordid childish tricks [of the government] turned my stomach," Sartre wrote.

> There may have been more ignoble ones, but none more revelatory. An anti-Communist is a rat. I couldn't see any way out of that one, and I never will. People may find me very naïve, and, for that matter, I had seen other examples of this kind of thing which hadn't affected me. But after ten years of ruminating, I had come to the breaking point, and only needed one straw. In the language of the church, this was my conversion.[18]

The hypocrisy, the pretense and sham, the façade behind which his own class hid its real nature from itself, now struck him with overwhelming force, Sartre says: "In the name of the principles my class had inculcated in me, in the name of humanism and humanity, in the name of liberty, equality and fraternity, I swore a hatred of the bourgeoisie which will only die with me." "By contrast, what did begin to change me was the *reality* of Marxism, the heavy presence on my horizon of the masses of the workers, an enormous somber body which *lived* Marxism, which practiced it, and which at a distance exercised an irresistible attraction on petit bourgeois intellectuals."[19]

## The Political Imperative

Once he had committed himself to Marxism, not only Sartre's conduct but his comments on contemporary political and social situations as well were almost entirely predictable, "their force blunted by their monotony," in the words of a recent literary critic.* While he retained his right to criticize orthodox Communist philosophy and never became a member of the Party, Sartre's commitment to Marxism led him for a time to an almost undeviating agreement on political issues with the Communist Party line. Marxism actually defined his mental horizon during these years. What was done in and by the Communist dictatorship in Russia could always be explained as necessary and so ultimately right. What was done by the capitalists and imperialists, especially in the United States, was always contrary to the interests of the workers and so wrong.

In 1954 Sartre spent some time in the U.S.S.R., and upon returning from this visit he wrote: "The freedom to criticize in Russia is total. Contact is broad, open and easy as possible. In Russia a man is aware of the constant progress of his own life as well as social life. Intellectual and collective interests coincide."[20] He became more and more tolerant of the late Stalin; even the dictator's purge trials he now saw as justifiable in terms of the dialectic of history. Fidel Castro, Franz Fanon, and Patrice Lumumba became his heroes. In 1960 he visited Cuba, and in 1966 he wrote a preface to Fanon's *The Wretched of the Earth.*

Perhaps Sartre's most publicized rejection of any affiliation with bourgeois culture was his refusal of the Nobel Prize for literature in 1964. He also cancelled a series of lectures he had agreed to deliver at Cornell University. No dialogue was possible with Americans because of the Vietnam situation, Sartre felt. His appearance in the United States at that time would likewise be quite a disappointment to his Cuban friends, he pointed out. There was hardly a situation, national or international, significant or otherwise, on which he did not make a pronouncement that created a flurry of interest in the press.

## Sartre's Philosophical Pilgrimage

While it is easy to distinguish these three distinct periods in Sartre's activity and point of view, it is equally true that his intellectual and literary activity as a whole can be seen as a single story. There is here simply a stage-

* Germaine Brée, *Camus and Sartre* (New York: Dell Publications Co., 1972), p. 3. This book contains one of the more thoughtful but critical examinations of Sartre's 1952 commitment to Communism and its practical outcome.

by-stage development in his effort to achieve a fully responsible life. As a young student and teacher of philosophy he, like every Frenchman, felt a particular admiration for the thought of Descartes, that brilliant French-man who was the father of modern philosophy. Descartes had given new meaning to man's freedom—his freedom from the authority of the past, his freedom to doubt, to reject all beliefs no matter how appealing, until one's understanding itself was convinced without any external pressure. For Descartes the final and absolute authority is man's experience of his own existence.

The Cartesian point of view Sartre found completely acceptable, and Descartes's insight plays a significant role in his philosophy. As his point of departure Sartre writes:

> [T]here cannot be any other truth than this, *I think, therefore I am*, which is the absolute truth of consciousness as it becomes aware of itself. In order to define the probable, one must possess the truth. Be-fore there can be any truth whatever, there must be an absolute truth, and there is such a truth which is simple, easily attained and in the reach of everybody. It consists in one's immediate sense of one's self.[21]

But when Descartes, as a good Catholic, is led from his own existence to the existence of God, Sartre can find no convincing ground for this step. He is forced, initially at least, to ascribe to man himself the kind of absolute free-dom that for Descartes was to be found only in God. If there is no God, Sartre argues in the spirit of Nietzsche, man must take the place of God in making of himself and of his life whatever there is to be made.

### Human Nature

In his first major scholarly work, *Being and Nothingness* (1943), Sartre undertakes a systematic philosophical statement of this early existentialism. The philosophy that he accepts is expressed in much more interesting and appealing fashion in his novels and short stories, to be sure; but his more technical and scholarly philosophical statements must certainly be examined.

The central aim of *Being and Nothingness* is to describe man as he actually exists in various concrete situations, and thus to identify his "human" reality. Man alone of all beings in the universe possesses self-consciousness, an awareness of himself and of what is outside himself, Sartre points out. One always finds himself in a particular body and in a particular situation where he lives and works. His awareness of these findings makes up his conscious-ness. Take these away, and Sartre concludes that nothing is left of man. He is never aware of himself except in relation to something else. Hence man has no essence, no being of his own. *Man as such is Nothing*. He will become only what he makes of himself. Each man has his own idea of what he wishes to do and to become, his own project for the future. He always has the possibility of radically altering his view of himself and the world. Thus, Sartre maintains, he creates himself, his own nature, by acting on the world outside and beyond him. "The world changes him as it changes, and he changes as he changes the world." Man as such, then, never *is* but is always *becoming*.*

In order to understand the point of view that Sartre adopts here, we need to recall the actual situation in which *Being and Nothingness* was written. Sartre's involvement in 1943 with the Resistance Movement, together with his own war experiences, significantly shaped his thinking. A person who is faced every day with the threat of annihilation discovers that non-being, Nothingness, is a very real and permanent possibility. Non-being is "a perpetual presence in us as well as outside us," Sartre writes, "that is to say, Nothing haunts being."[22] *Being and Nothingness* expresses the feeling of an individual and a world threatened constantly by annihilation. Sartre's existential philosophy is clearly shaped by this experience. It can certainly be seen as a significant expression of the *Zeitgeist*, the spirit of the times, as well as a disturbing treatment of the perennial philosophical problem of Being and Non-Being.

Since man is what he makes of himself, and for Sartre only what he makes of himself, to understand man's nature we must examine this process of *becoming*. One obvious mode of becoming for man, Sartre points out, is found in what he possesses. We all seek to fulfill ourselves, to overcome the nothingness of the naked self, by the accumulation of things. Once they are mine, these things are no longer purely external. They in part now constitute myself. My car, my books, my home are a part of my personality, of myself. "The pen, the pipe, the clothing, the desk, the house—are myself. The totality of my possessions reflects the totality of my being. I *am* what I have," Sartre writes.[23]

Another favorite mode of becoming for Sartre is found in the various *roles* a man plays in the world. His example of the polished café waiter is a frequently cited example. As others see this man at work, he *is* a waiter. But he may and does play other roles. He may well play the roles of husband and father. He may also be known as a Communist or a Christian. Thus he is a man who transcends his roles even while he creates himself in and through them. "We are dealing with more than mere social positions," Sartre recognizes; "I am never any one of my atttitudes, any one of my actions."[24] Each individual recognizes himself as more than the roles he assumes, more than the objects he possesses, more than his body and his attitudes. Looking at himself from within, the waiter in the café knows that he is not a café waiter in the same way that an inkwell *is* an inkwell.

---

* In keeping with the general practice of philosophers, Sartre feels that he must create a technical vocabulary of his own to avoid confusing his ideas with commonly accepted connotations of ordinary terms. Thus *being-in-itself* is what we meet in immediate experience. The individual's own consciousness of himself Sartre terms *being-for-itself*.

Undoubtedly the most significant dimension of man, that which distinguishes him from all other beings, Sartre points out, is this ability to stand apart from the objects of his consciousness—to transcend them and in a real sense to transcend himself. I never wholly *identify* myself with what I possess, and what I happen to be doing in the present, or with my past activities, he believes. Indeed, as Sartre sees human nature, I am always looking to the future, projecting myself into what I wish to do or how I will change myself—what in fact I wish to *become*. Thus, "I am not the self I will be."

In the transcendence of the self Sartre finds the basis for man's most important characteristic—his freedom. If man is to choose the kind of person he is to become, and is responsible for this choice, he must have the freedom to choose and to act in the way he chooses. Of such freedom man is immediately conscious as a dimension of his self-transcendence, Sartre maintains. This freedom not only differentiates human reality from all other types of being. It is his freedom that makes it possible for an individual to create himself and thus become truly human. "Human freedom precedes essence in man and makes it possible," Sartre writes; "the essence of the human being is suspended in his freedom." "It is impossible to distinguish what we call freedom from the being of 'human reality.' "[25]

Once man recognizes the nature of this radical freedom—the fact that he is himself fully responsible for what he is—he cannot place any final blame for what he does upon heredity or external circumstance. Nor is there a God who shares this responsibility. It is for this reason that man's freedom is apprehended in anguish and dread, Sartre feels. "I am condemned to be free," as he expresses it. "This means that no limit to my freedom can be found except freedom itself or, if you prefer, that we are not free to cease being free." Nor is Sartre referring to any one major choice that shapes or determines life. Rather, in his view, we must constantly choose in each moment of life, by our actions, thought, feelings, and hopes, the kind of person we will become. We are free to determine what to make of our heredity and environment. These exist as facts of experience, of course, but they do not destroy our freedom to use them as we choose. There are, to be sure, many situations in which we feel that we do not choose. We let others choose for us; we let events shape our lives. Sartre's comment here is an arresting one: "Freedom is the freedom of choosing, but not the freedom of not choosing. Not to choose is, in fact, to choose not to choose."[26]

### Our Relations with Others

There is another important aspect of our immediate experience, of course: our awareness of other selves, other persons. This also Sartre analyzes in interesting fashion.* The relationship with other persons is a very present

---

* In the more technical terminology he employs here, Sartre terms these relationships *"being-for-others."*

and significant dimension of man's life, but the experience can be a disturbing one. Imagine yourself sitting on a park bench, Sartre suggests, when another person—a stranger—walks by and looks in your direction. Immediately you become, and you *know* that you become a body, an object, a thing to him. He annihilates your subjective reality in making you his object. Annoyed at becoming an object only, a thing like the park bench on which you are sitting, you in turn stare at the stranger in such a way likewise as to make him a thing for you. Thus, in striving to avoid being reduced to a thing in the eyes of the other, you in turn reduce him to an impersonal object, a thing, in your eyes.

It is this kind of relationship between two persons that Sartre emphasizes in *Being and Nothingness*. It is, of course, what Buber describes as the *I–It* relation. It is an essentially impersonal dimension in human life, and is a potential source of evil when persons treat one another in this fashion rather than in the affirmative *I–Thou* relation. In *No Exit*, for example, which was written just after the completing of *Being and Nothingness*, this threat that other people pose to one's subjective being is a central issue. As one character in the play aptly sums up its theme: "Hell is—other people."[27]

The attitude and emotion of love, which for many people provides Buber's ideal *I–Thou* personal relationship, Sartre sees as no exception to his own point of view. Love he interprets as essentially the desire to be loved. Hence what one wants is to be the object of another's devotion. Consequently one tends to *seduce* the other by making oneself as appealing and desirable an object as possible. If one is successful, the other person becomes again simply an object in one's relation to him. When what we call love is no more than sexual desire on the part of either or both persons involved, then the other person is even more clearly reduced to the level of an object of desire, a thing to be possessed. And the outcome, Sartre feels, is only self-disgust. Love, then, as he sees it here, is actually a never-ending conflict in which each person is attempting to annihilate the subjectivity, the inner self, of the other.*

In addition to such relations with other people as individuals, the individual also experiences himself as a member of a group, Sartre points out. In the light of his later Marxist point of view, his analysis here is of some interest. Owing to the class-consciousness of the proletarian, that is, his awareness of capitalists as employers and oppressors, Sartre finds, members of the working class experience themselves as a group of men who are collectively *alienated*, reduced to things, for the benefit of others. And, even this early, he recognizes

---

* "Thus ceaselessly tossed from being-a-look to being-looked-at, falling from one to the other in alternate revolutions, we are always, no matter what attitude is adopted, in a state of instability in relation to the other," Sartre concludes. "We pursue the impossible ideal of the simultaneous apprehension of his freedom and his objectivity. But we shall never place ourselves concretely on the plane of equality, that is, on the plane where the recognition of the Other's freedom would involve the Other's recognition of our freedom." (*Being and Nothingness*, p. 408.)

that in this situation each individual can no longer struggle simply to reassert his own subjective freedom. Rather, the oppressed class as a whole must seek to recapture its freedom from its oppressors.[28]

### Existentialism and Man's Social Responsibility

In the first phase of his existential philosophy, Sartre's major emphasis is upon *freedom*. Man has no essential nature, but he has the freedom necessary to make something of himself. Freedom itself is the only enduring value. To maintain this is always good; to abandon it is the one unforgivable evil. The free man creates himself from an existential nothingness; by his choices and his actions, he makes himself what he is. He is dynamic, ever creative. He chooses his own life style and accepts full responsibility for his choices. The unfree man, on the other hand, is always willing in "bad faith" to become something fixed and unchanging. He is a conformist, faceless, a member of the masses. *Bad faith* is one of Sartre's basic terms of condemnation. In bad faith a man tries to escape responsibility for his choices and his destiny. He claims that things could not be other than they are.

Sartre's study of Marx's social philosophy, however, made him increasingly conscious of serious difficulties in such extreme individualism. Obviously the freedom of the proletarian was in reality much more limited than he had recognized in such an essay as *The Republic of Silence*. An awareness of a man's social responsibility, his responsibility for the freedom of others, had been impressed upon Sartre by his experiences in the French Resistance Movement. His growing Marxist concern for the plight of the proletarian, especially his lack of any real freedom, made a further development of his existential philosophy essential. In his popular address, "Existentialism and Humanism," published in 1946, Sartre provides the clearest and most explicit statement of this second stage in his thought.

A basic principle of existentialism stated in *Being and Nothingness* is that existence comes before essence. This is not questioned, if anything it is reaffirmed more vigorously in "Existentialism and Humanism." By this concept "we mean that man first of all exists, encounters himself, surges up in the world—and defines himself afterwards," Sartre writes. "If man, as the existentialist sees him, is not definable, it is because to begin with he is nothing. Thus, there is no human nature. Man is nothing else but that which he makes of himself." In other words, "man is no other than a series of undertakings, he is the sum, the organization, the set of relations that constitute these undertakings. . . . That is the first principle of existentialism."[29]

A new dimension is now added to this first principle, however: "And when we say that man is responsible for himself, we do not mean that he is responsible only for his own individuality, but that he is responsible for all men. When we say that man chooses himself, we also mean that in choosing for himself, he chooses for all men."[30] This enables us to better understand the emphasis of the existentialist upon such feelings as anguish, abandonment, and despair, Sartre points out. When a man realizes that in the decisions he makes he is choosing not only for himself but for all mankind—in such a moment a man cannot escape a profound sense of anguish. For how can he know that this is the right decision? One excellent example of such anguish is to be seen, Sartre writes, in the experience of a military leader who orders an attack upon an enemy position, knowing that he is sending a number of men to their death. He believes it is the right thing to do under the given circumstances. But it is at bottom his own choice; he alone chooses. Even if the command comes from headquarters, he cannot evade his own responsibility, Sartre insists.

There are no objective standards, no eternal moral principles by which one's choices can be determined. "If I regard a certain course of action as good, it is only I who choose to say that it is good and not bad," he writes. As an atheistic existentialist, Sartre does not believe in God, but he "finds it extremely embarrassing that God does not exist," he admits "For there disappears with Him all possibility of finding values in an intelligible heaven." Nor are there any *a priori* moral principles of the kind Kant proposed: "Everything is permitted. . . . We have neither behind us nor before us a luminous realm of values." For the existentialist man's freedom is ultimate: "Man is free, man *is* freedom." "We are left alone, without excuse. That is what I mean when I say that man is condemned to be free," Sartre concludes.[31]

### The Social Dimension of the Self

In the second stage of his existentialism Sartre also reaches a point of view quite close to that of Buber's *I–Thou* relation, a position significantly different from that in *Being and Nothingness.* "Contrary to the philosophy of Descartes, contrary to that of Kant," he writes in "Existentialism and Humanism," "when we say 'I think,' we reach ourselves in the presence of the other, and we are just as certain of the other as we are of ourselves. Thus the man who discovers himself directly in the *cogito* also discovers all the others, and discovers them as a condition of his own existence. He recognizes that he cannot be anything (in the sense that one says one is spiritual, or that one is wicked or jealous) unless others recognize him as such. I cannot obtain any truth whatsoever about myself, except through the mediation of another. The other is indispensable to my existence and equally so to any knowledge I can have of myself."[32]

Not only, then, is man's knowledge of himself involved in this awareness of others. Even more important for Sartre, a man's own freedom is essentially conditioned by the freedom of others. This was an insight based, of course, upon his growing awareness of the situation of the Marxist proletariat: "We will freedom for freedom's sake, in and through particular circumstances,"

Sartre writes. "And in thus willing freedom, we discover that it depends entirely upon the freedom of others, and that the freedom of others depends upon our own."[33]

### Existentialism and Humanism

"I have been reproached," Sartre writes, "for suggesting that existentialism is a form of humanism." This criticism, however, reflects a failure to define the meaning of humanism accurately, in his opinion. A humanism "which upholds man as the end in itself and as the supreme value, . . . that kind of humanism is absurd," he writes. The essential characteristic of existential humanism is that "man is all the time outside himself: it is in projecting and losing himself beyond himself that he makes man to exist, . . . it is by pursuing transcendent aims that he himself is able to exist." But in this act of self-expression man "is himself the heart and center of his transcendence. There is no other universe except the human universe, the universe of human subjectivity."[34]

Morality from this humanist point of view is essentially creative. A comparison with the work of an artist is helpful in understanding its nature, Sartre points out: "There is this in common between art and morality, that in both we have to do with creation and invention." Thus when a Picasso paints a canvas, there are values that will appear in due course in the coherence of the painting. But no one can tell in advance what the painting will be like—not even Picasso. Yet the finished composition will be an expression of himself—part and parcel of his entire life.

In the same creative fashion man makes himself, Sartre contends. He does not appear with a ready-made human nature, but he makes himself by the choice of his morality—his values, his life style. When seen in this fashion, "to say that we invent values means nothing more nor less than this," Sartre writes: "Life has no meaning *a priori*. Life is nothing until it is lived; but it is yours to make sense of, and the value of it is nothing but the value you choose." And then he concludes with the rather surprising statement (in the light of his earlier point of view): "Therefore you can see that there is a possibility of creating a human community."*

### Existentialism and Marxism

The third and, so far as one can judge, the final stage in the development of Sartre's existential philosophy is found in *The Critique of Dialectical*

---

* "Existentialism and Humanism," pp. 49, 54 (trans. Philip Mairet. London: Methuen & Co. Ltd., 1948). In *Being and Nothingness,* Sartre concluded that the community of all mankind was "an empty concept," "although everyone keeps the illusion of being able to succeed in it by progressively enlarging the communities to which he does belong." (pp. 419–423.)

*Reason,* published in 1960. In this volume he explicitly recognizes Marxism as the philosophy of our age: "There was the period of Descartes and Locke," he writes, "then the period of Kant and Hegel, and since then there has been the period of Marx. Each of these three philosophies has been in turn the soil from which all individual ideas sprang and has formed the cultural horizon."[35] His own task, he feels, is to formulate an existential Marxism.

In doing so, he agrees with the central thesis of Marxism that man's existence is conditioned by his mode of economic production and by the social and moral structures built upon this economic base. He accepts Marx's contention that in all existing historical societies these economic forces have produced class structures and class conflict—that some classes are exploited and other classes the exploiters. He recognizes with Marx that an individual inevitably expresses the viewpoint of his class and that in any given period the prevailing ideas and values are those of the dominant class.

In the preface to *The Critique of Dialectical Reason,* however, Sartre points out that orthodox Marxism has now reached a dead end. In its emphasis upon class conflict and economic determinism it has lost that interest in the freedom and the welfare of the individual which should be its major concern. In its materialism, it has lost its awareness of the fundamental importance of the individual's self-consciousness, his subjective reality. A new emphasis is needed, therefore, which will restore the individual man as he actually lives his life in a particular situation to its central place in Marxism.

It is just such an emphasis that an existential approach to Marxism will provide, Sartre maintains. It will then accomplish the original aims of Marx himself, that is, the creation of a new man in the new communist society. And it will also, as Marx anticipated, inaugurate a new age that makes Marxism itself no longer valid. "As soon as there will exist for everyone a margin of *real* freedom beyond the production of life, Marxism will have lived its span," Sartre writes: "a philosophy of freedom will take its place. But we have no means, no intellectual instrument, no concrete experience which allows us to conceive of this freedom or this philosophy."[36] *

In describing the conditions of the worker in an industrial society, Sartre agrees with Marx that the proletarian is forced to work in a way that takes away his basic freedom and leaves him alienated—an object, a thing, rather than a person. Under these conditions, for the great majority of mankind,

---

* In both style and point of view *The Critique of Dialectical Reason,* unfortunately for most readers, resembles Sartre's early *Being and Nothingness* rather than the more popular statement of his philosophy in "Existentialism and Humanism." In the *Critique* he is concerned primarily with the social situations in which men live and act together. Sartre does not direct his attention as specifically as does Reinhold Niebuhr in *Moral Man and Immoral Society* to man's larger social groups, such as the structure of nations, of races, and social classes. But his analysis in 1960 of man's social and group attitudes does have much in common with that described by Niebuhr a good many years earlier (1932).

real freedom does not exist. The proletarian is forced to work or starve. Theoretically he is free to choose whether he will work or not, with whom he will work, and for what wages. Actually such freedom is an illusion. The proletarian must see himself as a member of the working class, accepting the attitudes and the situation of his class. It is quite clear, as Marx pointed out, that his real freedom depends upon the freedom of his class. This fact leads Sartre to agree also with Marx's early conviction: "It is not enough for philosophy to seek to understand the world, it must seek to change it."

The central importance of the individual, however, continues to be Sartre's major concern. Any group, he maintains, consists only of the individuals who have chosen to cooperate in order to achieve something they feel to be appealing or necessary. There are obvious differences, of course, between the group that stormed the Bastille and the group that composes the working class. But reality in both cases is for Sartre found in the concrete individuals who make up the group. He does not recognize any organic reality or metaphysical status of a group as such apart from the individuals who compose it. Thus he attempts to preserve the primacy of the individual that was central in his earlier existentialism, and that he felt was no longer recognized in orthodox Marxism. In the future society, to be ushered in by the revolution, the individual must always be treated as a human being, a person and not a thing, Sartre insists. While this principle is essentially Kantian, it is also quite in accord with Marx's point of view in his early *Economic and Philosophical Manuscripts*.

## Sartre and Existentialism: Some Disturbing Questions

An evaluation of Sartre's contribution to the thought of our day is a difficult undertaking. In the years immediately following the Second World War, he provided the youth of France with insights that were both appealing and of concrete assistance in the situation they faced. He gave to the choosing of one's own life-style a dramatic meaning rivaled only by the existentialism of Kierkegaard. He condemned social conformity, and interpreted an acceptance of the attitudes of the crowd as evading one's responsibility. Actually such conformity means choosing a life without significance or meaning —a life characterized by a lack of genuineness, Sartre insisted. But he pointed out that in thus choosing what he will be, the life he will live, man is responsible for making himself what he is. He can blame no one else, no outside circumstance. His humanistic existentialism likewise made quite clear the concrete implications of atheism for man's life. Deprived of any basis in the universe itself, or in human nature, by which his choices can be validly directed, man is left alone to face the results of what he makes of himself and his world.

This emphasis upon human freedom, upon the importance of the individual's own subjectivity and his accompanying responsibility, was especially timely. It came when both sociology and psychology were picturing human life as largely shaped by forces beyond man's control. In the social sciences, heredity and environment were seen as responsible for most of man's behavior. The Marxian economic determinism provided for many more a convincing explanation of human attitudes and values. The psychoanalysis of Freud pointed to unconscious forces shaping human life and thought in a way man had never before been willing to admit. Sartre's forceful presentation, especially in his plays and novels, of man's ultimate freedom and responsibility met a deep need of the human spirit. It gave meaning and significance to the decisions and commitments with which everyone was faced from day to day.

At this point he was only arguing for the fundamental importance of freedom, maintaining that when a man surrenders his freedom, he gives up what is most meaningful and worthwhile in life. This early "ethic of freedom" is a freedom without direction, however, a demonic freedom, much like Nietzsche's will to power, Sartre's critics insist. It seems open to the same objections that William James made so effectively. In pragmatic terms, what does man's freedom enable him to accomplish, what is it good for?

Sartre's later thought makes it quite clear that he himself was dissatisfied by this limitation in his early existentialism. Both in his comment upon the French Resistance Movement and his idea of an "engaged" literature, he emphasizes the importance of man's involvement in the welfare of others as well as his own. Whenever and wherever man's freedom is threatened, he says, it is the duty of the writer to protest: "As soon as there is a commitment, I am obliged to will the liberty of others at the same time as my own." The freedom of others, it is true, is of fundamental importance to one because one's own freedom is ultimately dependent upon theirs. But this recognition of an inescapable concern for others now becomes an essential aspect of Sartre's philosophy.

### Sartre and the Marxists

The questions raised thus far concern Sartre's existential philosophy. His Marxism must, of course, be judged upon its own merits. The criticism he makes of contemporary Marxism is a telling one, to be sure. Its lack of concern for the individual as a person in his own right is certainly disturbing. This has opened the way for the purges and terror of the Communist dictatorship, and so has weakened the appeal of Marxism for those not already committed to the Party orthodoxy. But Sartre is not as critical of Marxism as he might well have been. He does not see the fallacy in Marx's theory that the inner contradictions in capitalism would lead to a disinherited proletariat, and to the revolutionary overthrow of capitalism, in the judgment of Raymond Aron, one of Sartre's earlier friends and associates.

"The real revolution was quite different," Aron writes:

The repression of capitalism did not bring about a pauperization of the working class, but a rise in its standard of living. In the United States, the most capitalistic country today, the working class has the highest standard of living and the least desire for revolution. The only country where a revolution calling itself Marxist has succeeded is one where the objective conditions prescribed by Marx were not given.[37]

In his *Marxism and the Existentialists* Aron provides a thoughtful interpretation of the Communist refusal to accept Sartre's existential version of Marxism. The first reason, he feels, stems from the enormous prestige of science among the Communists, and their basic unwillingness to relinquish that claim that Marxism is based upon scientific truth. In the interpretation of Marxism provided by the existentialists, Marxism is no longer "scientific truth." Hence the existentialist point of view loses much of its appeal to the orthodox Marxist.

A second basic principle of orthodox Marxism, of course, is the inevitability of the revolution and the overthrow of capitalism. This is seen as a necessary result of the dialectical movement of history. It is also of great practical importance to the Marxist, for whom history has a progressive and creative meaning. Truth is established by history and revolution has a philosophical significance: "It is the realization of philosophy; it solves the enigma of history," Aron writes. For Sartre and the existentialists, however, man's commitment to the revolution to overthrow capitalism and free the proletariat from exploitation has its foundation in the subjective consciousness of the individual. It is one dimension of his commitment to the freedom of all men. To the Marxist this is hardly an acceptable substitute for the dialectic of history.

The conclusion reached by Aron in this discussion is a revealing one: "actually existentialism can never be carried as far as Marxism—that is, of course, without ceasing to be existentialist. In other words, if he remains an existentialist, one will never be a Marxist." "What will always prevent an existentialist from being a Marxist is that revolution will not solve his philosophical problem."[38]

### Sartre Today

In recent years Sartre has, in fact, become increasingly disillusioned with the Communist dictatorship in Russia. Speaking of his agreement with the official party line, he says, "That ended the moment the Russian tanks entered Budapest." He was equally critical of the manner in which all freedom of thought and opposition to the orthodox Russian point of view was stamped out in Czechoslovakia. Because of a growing disagreement with the oppressive policy of the Russian dictatorship, he goes on to say, "So, even before the incidents in Czechoslovakia, the U.S.S.R. was finished for me."

But this did not mean that Sartre gave up his allegiance to Marxism. He simply was disillusioned with the way in which the philosophy of Marx was being put into practice in Russia. "The way I understand it," he writes, "I am a Communist, but I believe the U.S.S.R. is destroying Communism. The real communist revolution, the way Marx foresaw it, must be accompanied in the beginning by a withering away of the State, whereas the Soviet system began by reinforcing the State."[39]

This change in his attitude to the Communist dictatorship in Russia, together with his association with radical students in Paris, led Sartre to see in Maoism the most promising expression of the Marxist philosophy. There were aspects of Communism in China that he did not find acceptable, of course. But in the Chinese Cultural Revolution Sartre saw a genuine and desirable expression of Marxism. Here the masses intervened to let the leaders know that they were becoming too bureaucratic. The power of the masses made itself felt. This is a powerful communist idea for Sartre: "it means moving in the direction of the withering away of the State," he writes. Also in China, "there is the idea that the intellectual and the masses must be one. Mao always believed this." The new-style intellectual must be a worker as well as a man who deals with ideas. So the Chinese student works six months in the field and six months in the University.[40]

These were aspects that Sartre found especially appealing in Maoism. In 1968 he championed the student uprising against the Establishment in Paris and became increasingly identified with the more extreme student groups in Paris. In April 1970, he accepted the editorship of *The People's Cause*, the newspaper of the Maoist faction of the revolutionary left.

It is always provocative, and sometimes even helpful, to see what a gifted individual with whom one may well disagree thinks of our own national attitudes and policies. The United States was early seen by Sartre as "the evil colossus of North American capitalism," the single greatest threat to the liberation of the masses. With our participation in the Korean War, American power became the greatest threat to the "salvation of mankind." By the time of the American intervention in Vietnam, Sartre had run out of words adequate to describe the depths of evil symbolized by the United States. To express his feelings, however, he participated actively in the tribunal, inspired by Bertrand Russell, on American war crimes in Vietnam (1966–1967).*

We might well conclude our discussion of Sartre by quoting recent comments by two French writers familiar with his thought. In the judgment of Germain Brée, a contemporary literary critic, Sartre is now actually a figure of the past. His recent Marxist pronouncements and activities have little influence upon the actual development of French politics. The affectionate

* It is of some interest also perhaps to note that Sartre does not see in the counter-culture in this country a movement of any great significance. In his opinion it is too involved with drugs and too dependent upon the capitalistic establishment. (*Esquire*, December 1972, pp. 280 ff.)

respect that his presence generally elicits from student groups stems largely "from a sense of his obdurate refusal to capitulate to common sense, his quixotic stance and unsparing labor. His intellectual authority is nonetheless a thing of the past."[41]

The suggestion of Raymond Aron, one of Sartre's former associates, is perhaps more constructive: "If Sartre hoped to succeed in revitalizing Marxist thought, he should have followed Marx's own example—that is, undertaken a careful examination and interpretation of the concrete capitalist and socialist economic and political structures of the twentieth century." In short, what is needed to revitalize Marxism, Aron feels, is a *Das Kapital* of the twentieth century, not a much too uncritical allegiance to the *Das Kapital* of the nineteenth.[42]

## CHAPTER 16

# Religious Existentialism

*Martin Buber*

Existentialism, even religious existentialism, is not a single well-defined philosophy. It is rather a particular approach to experience, a fundamental point of view about human life that initially found expression in the thought of Kierkegaard and Nietzsche and was later stated in somewhat different fashion by Sartre. "Existentialism," writes Paul Pfeutze, "(whatever else it may be) is in part the cry of men who move on the narrow edge of chaos and tragedy, groping for some value and meaning where none seems to be."[1] This underlying point of view brings together a number of philosophical positions that differ in other respects as markedly as they agree here.

No spokesman for religion in our day has developed an existentialist philosophy as popular and appealing as that of Martin Buber (1878–1965). Long before his death in 1965, Buber was recognized as the ablest and most distinguished Jewish philosopher of his generation. In striking fashion he seized upon one of the cardinal insights of existentialism—the personal dimension of existence—and made it the central aspect of a philosophy of living that has had wide appeal well beyond the boundary of professional philosophical circles. Buber's existential philosophy was given its most popular statement in a moving and creative book, *I and Thou*, a book that aroused genuine excitement among students and laymen as well as sustained interest among scholars. He seems the most appropriate spokesman for the religious existentialism of our age in a discussion of the philosophies men live by.

## Religious Heritage and Philosophical Development

Born in Vienna in 1878, Martin Buber lived until he was fourteen in Galacia with his grandfather. Solomon Buber was a distinguished scholar of the Jewish Enlightenment of that period, and as a boy Martin was absorbed in the world of Biblical and rabbinical thought. He learned classical Hebrew, and at thirteen he was confirmed as a member of the Jewish religious community. Within a few years, however, as was then so often the case among liberal and emancipated Jewish youth in Europe, he reacted against the strict Jewish spirit of his grandfather's home and soon ceased all formal religious observances.

### Early Influences

In 1904 Buber completed work for the doctoral degree at the University of Berlin. There he came into contact for the first time with the dominant intellectual currents of the late nineteenth and early twentieth centuries. Nietzsche and Dostoevski—and somewhat later, Kierkegaard—were among the writers who influenced him most during this period. The strong reaction in their thought against philosophical rationalism, against the dominance of scientific naturalism, and against the materialism of the age significantly shaped Buber's own philosophical development.

Nietzsche's dramatic style and prophetic fervor in *Thus Spake Zarathustra* also had marked appeal for Buber. *Thus Spake Zarathustra* literally "took possession of me," he later wrote. This book "worked on me not in the manner of a gift, but in the manner of an invasion which deprived me of my freedom, and it was a long time before I could liberate myself from it."[2] In *I and Thou* the poetic spirit of *Zarathustra* is clearly apparent, although in quite different guise. Not until some years later, when Kierkegaard was rediscovered and translated into German, did Buber become familiar with the religious existentialism of the great Danish writer. Here again he found a fresh and powerful source of intellectual and religious stimulation that also influenced him greatly.

When in later years he turned back to his own Jewish religious heritage, however, Buber did become increasingly critical of Kierkegaard's distinctly Christian outlook, as well as of his highly individualistic approach to religion and his deep pessimism about human nature. In the end, as a recent interpreter has well put it, he filtered Kierkegaard's existentialism through his own deeper and broader Jewish loyalties.

Upon completing his work at the University of Berlin, Buber decided to make Germany his home. There for a time he was deeply conscious of his own essential loneliness and "rootlessness." Although not unusual for young intellectuals, these feelings were intensified in Buber's case because he had broken with his Jewish heritage and found nothing to replace it. This sense of need led him gradually to an active participation in the Zionist movement, then in its infancy. It also stimulated a new interest in Hasidism, a popular mystical and communal movement quite influential among East European Jews during the eighteenth and nineteenth centuries. Turning away from all his other activities, Buber spent five years in careful study of this movement and became its ablest interpreter.

Despite the fact that he was still a relatively young man, Buber soon also became a leading spokesman of Zionism. With Chaim Weizmann, however, he saw the political state as only one aspect of Zionism, and supported a Jewish cultural renaissance as also essential. During this period Buber wrote and spoke extensively. The best statement of his early philosophy is found in *Daniel: Dialogues of Realization* (1913). But his greatest work was also gradually taking shape in Buber's mind. The first draft of *I and Thou* was completed in 1916, he tells us. Not until 1919, however, did it attain "decisive clarity" in his thought, and the finished work was published in 1923.

### Years of Mature Achievement

In 1923 Buber was appointed to the chair of Jewish Philosophy, later the History of Religions, at the University of Frankfurt. He held this important position for ten years until the rise of the Nazis to power in 1933 forced his resignation. Then he worked openly and fearlessly for another five years to aid his fellow Jews in Germany during the terrible persecution they suffered in those years. His courageous behavior won him the admiration and gratitude of his own people and kept him in constant danger with the Nazi police. Finally in 1938, at the age of sixty, Buber left Germany for Israel to accept the chair of Social Philosophy at Hebrew University in Jerusalem. There he inaugurated a period of significant social, religious, and philosophical activity in his new homeland.*

In Jerusalem Buber became a leading spokesman for those Jews who felt it essential to promote greater Jewish-Arab cooperation and friendship. He still retained his loyalty to the modified Zionism he had earlier advocated, but because of his liberal point of view Buber was never fully accepted in Israel. He belonged to no synagogue, and no rabbi or community in Israel adopted his teaching. Although in Western Europe and America Buber was considered a Jewish prophet, "in Israel he was surrounded by a wall of indifference, and we hardly listened to him," writes a prominent Jewish critic. "Our young people hardly knew he existed."[3]

The central importance of the Hebrew Bible in shaping Buber's thought should be mentioned. While still at the University of Frankfurt he had undertaken a new German translation of the Hebrew Bible in collaboration with Franz Rosenzweig, a gifted Jewish intellectual and close friend. During his years at the University of Jerusalem, much of his writing was on Biblical subjects. Buber also did a careful study of New Testament religion, entitled

---

* In three important works, *Israel and Palestine, Israel and the World: Essays on a Time of Crisis,* and *Paths in Utopia,* Buber formulated his mature social philosophy during his earlier years in Jerusalem. This philosophy is based upon the position developed in *I and Thou* but is deeply influenced also by the concrete life of the new Jewish community.

*Two Types of Faith*. He here contrasted the faith of Paul with the religion of Jesus, and reclaimed Jesus as a great Jewish prophet in a way that disturbed many of his more conservative Jewish colleagues. As he himself more than once points out, however, his philosophy is deeply rooted in the religious tradition of Judaism and in his Jewish Biblical heritage. "I must always be seen," he writes, "standing in the door of my ancestral home"—"nothing can separate me from the sacred history of Israel."*

### Retirement and Increased Recognition

Upon his retirement from active teaching in 1951 at the age of seventy-three Buber visited the United States, where he was invited to lecture at a number of leading universities and theological schools. The lectures given at Yale, Princeton, Columbia, and Chicago were published in 1952 under the title *The Eclipse of God*. Five years later Buber returned to America to deliver a series of lectures at the Washington School of Psychiatry. Then he came again the next year for a celebration of his eightieth birthday at Princeton.

A good bit of publicity was given to the fact that Dag Hammarskjöld, at that time the distinguished Secretary-General of the United Nations, was deeply impressed by Buber's social philosophy. In one of his major talks, Hammarskjöld made large use of Buber's ideas; he later visited the old philosopher in Jerusalem, and in 1959 nominated Buber for the Nobel Peace Prize.[4] At the time of his own tragic death, Hammarskjöld was beginning a Swedish translation of *I and Thou*.

On his eighty-fifth birthday (February 8, 1963) Buber was honored at a luncheon at Hebrew University and received congratulatory messages from all over the world. The following summer he was awarded the Erasmus Prize in Amsterdam. The cash award of approximately $28,000 he contributed to the improvement of Jewish-Arab relations in Palestine.

In the spring of 1965, now almost eighty-eight and something of a legendary figure throughout the Western world, Buber fell and fractured his hip. While he was in the hospital and weakening rapidly, with the end not far away, the Mayor of Jerusalem bestowed upon him a grant of the freedom of the city, its highest recognition of individual achievement. Unfortunately Buber was hardly conscious of this honor, and died shortly thereafter on June 13, 1965.

At his funeral the President and the Prime Minister of Israel, and the President of the University of Jerusalem, were among those who served as honorary pallbearers—a kind of recognition accorded too few philosophers. The eulogy on that occasion by the Prime Minister, Levi Eshkol, included the following comments:

* His *Teaching of the Prophet* appeared in 1942 (translated in English as *The Prophetic Faith*). Ten years later his great work *Moses* was published. Shortly thereafter he completed a discussion of the creation myth in Genesis, entitled *Images of Good and Evil*, as well as a brief book on the Psalms, *Right and Wrong*.

The Jewish people today mourns a man of thought and achievement who revealed the soul of Judaism with new philosophical force. All mankind mourns with us one of the spiritual giants of the century. I do not know whether there is anyone else in our midst, in the sphere of spiritual life, who was so much a part of the heritage of the entire world, but he was deeply anchored—to a depth that few could reach—in his Jewishness, in the Jewish people, in the resurgence of Israel and in the love of Jewry.[5]

### The Personal Dimension of Existence

With Kierkegaard and the religious existentialists in general Buber's philosophy falls in the tradition of "religious empiricism." Not only William James but also men like Friedrich Schleiermacher and Jonathan Edwards were great figures before him in this tradition. For Buber, moreover, as for all existentialists, the major concern of philosophy is not with abstract speculation, but is rather to aid the individual in achieving authentic selfhood. Philosophical insights are only meaningful as they are embodied in life itself.

Buber's experience in writing *I and Thou* was also quite typical of the existentialist. "When I drafted the first sketch of this book (more than forty years ago), I felt impelled by an inner necessity," he later tells us. "A vision which had affected me repeatedly since my youth, but had always been dimmed, had now achieved a constant clarity that was so evidently suprapersonal that I soon knew that I ought to bear witness to it."[6] He was reminded especially, he says, of Nietzsche's somewhat comparable experience in writing *Thus Spake Zarathustra*: "One hears—one does not seek; one takes —one does not ask who gives."

Probably no single small book in the literature of existential philosophy has had such popularity and influence as *I and Thou*. In this volume one encounters all the major characteristics of religious existentialism distilled to their essence and expressed in a sort of lyric prose.* Buber's approach to philosophy is one of passionate engagement, but—largely perhaps because of

---

* In an essay in the volume on Buber in the Library of Living Philosophers (Vol. XII, 1967), Walter Kaufmann raised a question about the translation of Buber's *Ich and Du* as *I and Thou* (the title of the English Translation by Ronald Gregor Smith). *Thou* has a "holy tone" in English today, Kaufmann pointed out, that is not found in the German *du*, a tone that Buber himself wanted to avoid. When requested to do so several years later, Kaufmann therefore undertook a new translation of Buber's book which was published in 1970. The title, *I and Thou*, was retained but through the book itself *du* was translated *you*, and a consistent effort was made to keep the English text closer to the original German than was the case in the earlier English version.

This increase in linguistic accuracy has been achieved, however, at the sacrifice of a poetic quality that gave to the initial English version much of its immediate appeal. (See the Translator's Preface to the second—1958—edition of Smith's translation, p. xi). Despite his unhappiness with the translation there of certain German terms, Buber himself had once said that he considered Ronald Gregor Smith his best translator. (See Kaufmann's *I and Thou*, p. 1.) At the request of the publishers of *I and Thou*, all quo-

his immersion in the religious tradition of Judaism—his thought does not have the anxious preoccupation with the sense of sin, the anguish and dread, that we find in Kierkegaard. His outlook is much more positive and hopeful. By comparison with the typical existential pessimism about man and the human predicament, Buber might even be called optimistic. His fusion of existential thought with the world-affirming spirit of Judaism is a significant philosophical achievement.

### The Twofold Nature of Experience

The world for man is twofold in accordance with his twofold attitude.
   The attitude of man is twofold in accordance with the two basic words he can speak.
   The basic words are not single words but word pairs.
   One basic word is the word pair *I–You.*
The other basic word is the word pair *I–It.* . . .
   Thus the *I* of man is also twofold.
   For the *I* of the basic word *I–You* is different from that of the basic word *I–It.*

These are the opening lines of Buber's best-known work. In the two fundamental ways identified here of relating the self to the world, the *I–You* and the *I–It* attitudes, he provides a fresh and more dramatic portrayal of the typical existential distinction between the detached intellectual approach to life, on the one hand, and the life of personal engagement and passionate participation, on the other. They vividly contrast the world of sensory experience with the world of personal relation.

The *I–It* attitude is the objective, detached approach ascribed to the scientific investigator. Here the world permits itself to be experienced, but has no concern in the matter. It does nothing to the experience, and the experience does nothing to it. That this attitude is a necessary and fruitful one in many human activities, Buber recognizes clearly. The scientific knowledge acquired by those holding such an attitude has provided man with a reliable perspective in dealing with the world of nature as well as giving him considerable control over it. The social scientists, adopting the same attitude, have likewise made an important contribution to the understanding of man's collective life. In itself, then, the *I–It* attitude is not an evil, and man neither can nor should seek to escape his relationships with the world of *It.*

The *I–It* attitude, the attitude considered characteristic of the scientist

---

tations from that book in the present discussion are from Kaufmann's 1970 translation. This does complicate matters somewhat, however, as the English version of Buber's other works still retain the phrase *I–Thou* with its somewhat different connotation. Also, as Paul Tillich has insisted, if God's relationship with man "is brought down to the level of a conversation between two beings, it is blasphemous and ridiculous" (*Systematic Theology* I, p. 127).

and the intellectual, however, as valuable as it is, does not provide man with his most meaningful human experience. "And in all the seriousness of truth, listen," Buber writes: "Without *It* a human being cannot live. But whoever lives only with that is not human."[7] Indeed, this attitude becomes a source of evil when an individual maintains it in situations where the personal relation is the desirable or appropriate one. This always occurs, of course, when another person is treated as an *It* rather than a *You*. Sartre, for example, portrays the evil of this situation dramatically in *No Exit*. And T. S. Eliot, in "The Love Song of J. Alfred Prufrock," has given us a classic poetic description:

> And I have known the eyes already, known them all—
> The eyes that fix you in a formulated phrase,
> And when I am formulated, sprawling on a pin,
> When I am pinned and wriggling on the wall,
> Then how should I begin
> To spit out all the butt-ends of my days and ways?[8]

It is then in the deeply personal *I–Thou* encounter, and not in the *I–It* experience, that the most significant and meaningful dimension of human life is to be found. And Buber's moving, almost poetic portrayal of this personal dimension of human existence gives his existentialism its large appeal.

In this relation the self is engaged by the other, affirms the other as it is in itself, and recognizes its being and worth as a concrete individual. "It is only when the individual recognizes the other in his very otherness, as a human being other than himself, and when on this basis he effects a penetration to the other that he can break the circle of his solitude in a specific, transforming encounter," Buber writes.[9] One may, in fact, find such genuine personal encounter, each in dialogue with the other, in a lively class session, which goes beyond the routine framework to a stimulating meeting of minds, as well as in the deeper personal relationships between a man and a woman. In these situations the encounter does not take place, Buber maintains, *in* each of the participants but *between* them, in a new dimension accessible to them alone.

Meaningful dialogue is an essential aspect of the *I–Thou* encounter for Buber.* It may be either spoken or unspoken. The essence of dialogue lies in the fact, not that something is said and responded to orally, but that "each of the participants really has in mind the other or others in their present and particular being and turns to them with the intention of establishing a

---

\* The development of Buber's thought falls naturally into three periods: an early period in which mysticism is especially apparent; a middle period in which the existential point of view is given primary emphasis; and finally his mature philosophy of dialogue. However, as Martin Friedman writes in his *Martin Buber: The Life of Dialogue* (1955): "Most of the ideas which appear in the early periods are not really discarded in the later but are preserved in changed form. Thus Buber's existentialism retains much of this mysticism, and his dialogical philosophy in turn includes important mystical and existential elements." (p. 27.)

living mutual relation between himself and them."[10] The essential element is this shared awareness of the other. In dialogue, then, one cannot be a mere observer; he must be a participant.

### The World of Personal Relation

The full meaning of such personal encounter cannot be stated rationally and conceptually, of course. It is just at this point that the personal dimension of experience differs fundamentally from the world of *I–It*. To understand the unique meaning of the *I–Thou* encounter, we can only look at concrete and specific moments of personal relation in our own experience and note their characteristics. These moments Buber describes as "inclusive" rather than exclusive. They always involve "experiencing the other side"; the other person must be recognized in the "actuality of his being." There is "first, a relation, of no matter what kind, between two persons; second, an event experienced by them in common, in which at least one of them actively participates; and third, the fact that this one person, without forfeiting anything of the felt reality of his activity, at the same time lives through the common event from the standpoint of the other."[11]

In his description of this deep personal relation Buber is quite close to Kant's second formulation of the categorical imperative: always treat another person as an end, of value in himself, and never only as a means to your own ends. But for Buber this sense of obligation to others grows out of immediate personal experience. It is not, as it is for Kant, the product of an abstract sense of moral obligation.

Understandably Buber sees the fullest realization of the *I–Thou* personal relation in love—not in the romantic view of love, of course, the heightened feeling of pleasure portrayed in Kierkegaard's aesthetic way of life. There the other person is simply an object to be enjoyed. In love as "experiencing the other side" in the full meaning of that phrase, Buber indeed comes very close to the *eros/agape* distinction of the New Testament. Love is much more than feeling. Feelings accompany love; they do not constitute it, he points out: "Feelings dwell in man, but man dwells in his love. This is no metaphor but actuality: love does not cling to an I, as if the You were merely its 'content' or object; it is between I and You. Whoever does not know this, know this with his being, does not know love. . . . Love is responsibility of an I for a You: in this consists what cannot consist in any feeling—the equality of all lovers."[12]

In the love of man and wife there is an opportunity, Buber feels, for the clearest expression of the *I–Thou* relation. Here one can find the bond of recognition, the affirming by each of the other in his or her uniqueness, the greatest degree of intimacy and sharing, the fullest revealing of each person to the other. Obviously marriage affords both the length of time and the intimacy needed for love of this kind. Yet the present dissatisfaction with conventional marriage that leads so often to divorce, and that now leads so many young people to prefer love without marriage, is indication enough that the deep personal relation Buber envisions is too frequently not achieved in modern marriage. As Buber himself well puts it, "But love without dialogue, without real outgoing to the other, reaching to the other, and companying with the other, love remaining with itself—this is called Lucifer."[13]

### Achievement of Authentic Selfhood

For Buber the *I–Thou* encounter does not simply relate persons who already exist independently. "Being spoken," it brings something into existence—the *I* of this relation. "There is no *I* taken in itself," he maintains, "but only the *I* of the primary word *I–Thou* and the *I* of the primary word *I–It*."[14] And the *I*, the self, in each case is different. However, "there are not two kinds of human beings, but there are two poles of humanity." Every man lives in the twofold *I*, the world of persons and the world of things:

> The *I* of the basic word *I–You* is different from that of the basic word *I–It*.
> The *I* of the basic word *I–You* appears as a person and becomes conscious of itself as subjectivity.
> Persons appear by entering into relation to other persons.
> Whoever stands in relation participates in an actuality, that is, in being that is neither merely a part of him nor merely outside him.
> Where there is no participation, there is no actuality.[15]

Authentic selfhood, then, is achieved by an individual only in personal encounter, in the *I–Thou* relation.* A man is not fully human, does not achieve complete selfhood, except as he enters into such genuine personal relation with another. "Where this self being turned toward the partner over against one is not lived, the sphere of man is still unrealized." Buber writes. "The human means the taking place from one time to another of that meeting which is latent in the being of the world."[16]

This relation for Buber is not limited, however, to the human sphere as we normally define it. There are three spheres in which the world of relation is experienced: our life with nature; our life with men; and our life with spiritual beings. The first "vibrates in the dark," beneath the level of language. The second is open and spoken. We give to and accept from the "other." The third is "wrapped in a cloud but reveals itself."[17] We perceive no *Thou*, yet we are addressed and we answer.

Three interesting examples of authentic selfhood are suggested by Buber, one in each of the three different spheres of personal relation which he recognizes:

1. "How beautiful and legitimate the vivid and emphatic *I* of Socrates

---

* Both the similarities and the differences in the descriptions of this creative experience by Kierkegaard, Buber, and Sartre are significant.

sounds," Buber writes. "It is the *I* of infinite conversation." The *I* of Socrates lives continually in such dialogue between man and man, whether in his daily contacts, before his judges in his trial, or in his last hours in prison. This *I* never questioned the reality of his fellowmen and in every circumstance went out to meet them in genuine dialogue.

2. "How beautiful and legitimate," likewise, the "full *I* of Goethe sounds. It is the *I* of pure intercourse with nature. Nature yields to it and speaks ceaselessly with it, she reveals her mysteries to it and yet does not betray her mystery. . . . and the friendship of the elements accompanies man into the calm of dying and rebirth."

3. And how powerful, how legitimate to the point of being self-evident is the *I* of Jesus. "For it is the *I* of the unconditional relation in which the man calls his *You* 'Father' in such a way that he himself becomes nothing but Son."[18] Here the authentic *I–Thou* relation in the world of the spirit is to be seen. Here the self is not limited in its reality to the human sphere alone, but raised by this personal relation to "unconditional being."

These are three examples suggested by Buber of "sufficient, true, and pure" personal dialogue. They illustrate the achievement of authentic selfhood by persons who, like Socrates, Goethe, and Jesus, have lived in different but genuine realms of full personal relation.

### The Nature of Truth

New insight and awareness of meaning is also, of course, an important dimension of genuine personal encounter. For Buber, as for all existentialists, science and scientific knowledge derived from the *I–It* experience can provide only practical understanding—a knowledge of means to be used not of ends to be chosen. In the world of personal relation alone can one hope to find meaning and direction in life. Buber is quite in accord also with his fellow religious existentialists in maintaining that the awareness of meaning in the *I–Thou* relation cannot be given rational, conceptual statement. "That meaning is open and accessible in the actual lived concrete does not mean that it is to be won and possessed through any type of analytical or synthetic investigation, or through any type of reflection upon the concrete," he writes. "Meaning is to be experienced in living action and suffering itself, in the unreduced immediacy of the moment. . . . Only he reaches the meaning who stands firm, without holding back or reservation, before the whole might of reality and answers it in a living way. He is ready to confirm with his life the meaning which he has attained."[19]

When we face the basic issues of human existence, we can only place our faith in the personal dimension of the immediate, concrete *I–Thou* relation and act upon it. As both Kierkegaard and William James insist, truth is expressed in a new quality of existence, not in an intellectual grasp of abstract ideas. Hence Buber prefers to speak of "human truth." Men *live* truth; they can never hope to express it adequately in conceptual terms:

"Human truth becomes real when one tries to translate one's relationship to truth into the reality of one's own life. And human truth can be communicated only if one throws one's self into the process and answers for it with one's self."[20]

In this approach to truth Buber, of course, accepts the essential principle of Kierkegaard that truth and subjectivity cannot be divorced. Both agree that, in contrast to scientific knowledge derived from an objective intellectual analysis of sensory experience, there is in the personal dimension of human experience a deeper and more meaningful awareness of moral and spiritual reality. Both agree, moreover, with Kant that man can and must live in two worlds—one, the world of sensory experience and scientific knowledge; the other, the world of personal relation and faith that is essentially religious. Buber goes further, however, than either Kant or Kierkegaard, and with William James recognizes man's active participation in establishing truth: "man finds truth to be true only when he stands its test."[21]

### Freedom and Determinism

The heart of the conflict between the scientific and the moral or religious view of the world and of man's destiny therein, is centered in one's belief about human freedom. In the world described by science, the world of *It* for Buber, causality has unlimited and universal reign. Not only every physical event perceived by the senses, but also every psychical event discovered in self-analysis, is the result of a necessary and determined causal chain. This fact, clearly seen and convincingly portrayed by Spinoza when modern science was in its infancy, is the foundation upon which the edifice of modern scientific knowledge was built.

In the "human" truth, however, of which man is immediately aware in the *I–Thou* relation, human freedom is quite as certain as is the reign of causality in the world of science. "It is only when reality is turned into logic, and A and non-A dare no longer dwell together, that we get determinism and indeterminism, a doctrine of predestination and a doctrine of freedom, each excluding the other," Buber maintains. "According to the logical conception of truth only one of two contraries can be true, but in the reality of life as one lives it, they are inseparable."[22]

Causality in the world of science does not then disturb the man who also lives in the world of personal relation. There he is assured of freedom as a matter of immediate awareness. "He knows that his mortal life swings by nature between *Thou* and *It*," Buber writes, and that he must cross this threshold again and again. He cannot remain permanently in the realm of personal relation, but causality does not weigh heavily upon him when he returns to the world of *It* bearing this deeper insight.

The sickness of our age, Buber believes, is like that of no other age because we have allowed the determinism of "quasi-biological and quasi-historical thought . . . to establish a more tenacious and oppressive belief in fate than has ever existed before." Whatever form this belief takes, it always means that man sees his life set in the frame of forces that he cannot escape and cannot control. The man who lives only in the world of *It*, who accepts the "dogma of immutable process," finds there at first a revealing understanding of experience. But in every truth he there discovers, he is enslaved only the more deeply to the world of *It*. The world of *Thou*, however, the world of personal relation, is open to all who will go out to it with complete commitment, with no reservation, Buber insists. Here our awareness of freedom is certain: "And to be freed from belief that there is no freedom is indeed to be free."

Despite the subjective certainty that characterizes this awareness of meaning in the *I–Thou* relation, Buber does not deny the objective uncertainty that one must face in accepting the approach to truth and the belief in human freedom he proposes—this way of life on "the narrow ridge." But this is a risk that one must be willing to take if he is to possess the sense of meaning that he must have for life at its best. As Buber describes the faith that is necessary in this situation—the "leap of faith" that Kierkegaard so strongly emphasized—one is reminded immediately of the risk that William James sees in "the will to believe."* "And if one still asks if one may be certain of finding what is right on this steep path, once again the answer is No, there is no certainty," Buber writes. "There is only a chance, but there is no other. The risk does not insure the truth for us, but it and it alone, leads us to where the breadth of truth is to be felt."23

### The Eternal Thou

Nowhere, of course, is the immediate awareness of meaning in the *I–Thou* relation more significant for Buber than in man's consciousness of the Eternal *Thou*. And no other aspect of the encounter is so little open to rational analysis. This is simply the most profound dimension of every genuine personal relation, Buber feels. In his Allegory of the Cave, Plato likens the Idea of the Good in the intelligible world to the sun in the world of sensory experiences. As the sun provides the light by which we see and recognize objects in the physical world, so the Idea of the Good for Plato provides the meaning that enables us to understand the world of Ideas. The Eternal *Thou* performs for Buber† a quite similar function in the realm of our deepest personal experiences:

> Extended, the lines of relationships intersect in the eternal You.
> Every single You is a glimpse of that. Through every single You the basic word addresses the eternal You.

* See page 303.
† It is important to note, however, that Buber sees a personal dimension in the experience which Plato does not recognize in the *Republic*. See p. 396.

> In every sphere, in every relational act . . . we gaze toward the train of the eternal You: in each we perceive the breath of it; in every You we address the eternal You.[24]

In all such personal encounter we are thus immediately aware of its larger dimension, Buber maintains. But such an awareness provides no basis for the kind of intellectual concept of God which the philosopher seeks. Here more so than in any other aspect of personal relation we are forced to proceed by faith. "The religious reality of the meeting with the Meeter, who shines through all forms and is himself formless, knows no image of him, nothing comprehensible as object," Buber writes. "It knows only the presense of the Present One."[25] And God, as known in such personal experiences, is a transcendent as well as an immanent reality: "Every sphere is compassed in the eternal *Thou*, but it is not compassed in them."

We naturally seek symbols to portray the meaning of this awareness of the presence of God, but one should be careful not to interpret these symbols literally. They are expressions of faith, not of conceptual knowledge, Buber insists. The imagery that Buber himself likes best is that suggested by Pascal in describing what he called his "second conversion" experience: "God of Abraham, God of Isaac, God of Jacob—not of the philosophers and scholars."

The use of personal terms in the portrayal of God is, of course, indispensable for Buber. The personal dimension of existence constitutes the central insight of his existential philosophy, and this dimension of reality is as essential in understanding God's nature as in man's. "All the enthusiasm of the philosophers for monologue, from Plato to Nietzsche, does not touch the simple experience of faith, that speaking with God is something *toto genere* different from 'speaking with oneself'; whereas, remarkably, it is not something *toto genere* different from speaking with another human being," Buber writes. "If to believe in God means to be able to talk about him in the third person, then I do not believe in God. If to believe in him means to be able to talk to him, then I believe in God."[26]

In his own thought God cannot be understood as a principle, as many philosophers hold, nor as an idea, not even Plato's Idea of the Good, Buber points out, but only as one who "whatever else he may be in addition, enters into a direct relation with us human beings through creative, revealing and redemptive acts, and thus makes it possible for us to enter into a direct relationship with him. This ground and meaning of our existence establishes each time a mutuality of the kind that can obtain only between persons. The concept of personhood is, of course, utterly incapable of describing the nature of God, but it is permitted and necessary to say that God is *also* a person."*

---

* *I and Thou*, p. 181. In this connection a comment made many years earlier by William James is of particular interest: "The universe is no longer a mere *It* to us, but a *Thou*, if we are religious; and any relation that may be possible from person to person might be possible here." ("The Will to Believe," included in *Essays in Pragmatism*, Ed. Alburey Castell, p. 106.)

The fact that his existential philosophy does remain so close to the immediacy of personal encounter can, of course, be seen as a limitation as well as a source of strength. Buber is clearly writing for those who are already aware in their own spiritual experience of personal encounter with the Eternal *Thou*. His approach will quite obviously not convince those in whose lives such experiences and insights have no place. Writing as an existentialist, however, Buber does not believe that we can ever have the kind of theoretical knowledge that would convince anyone who was not aware in his own experience of the presence of the Eternal *Thou*. He does not profess to be the creator of a philosophical system. In fact, he denies the possibility of embodying in any system of ideas living truth as it exists concretely in experience. It is his function, Buber feels, only to point to realities of which we are aware in the world of personal relation: "He who expects of me a teaching other than a pointing out of this character, will always be disillusioned."[27]

The reality of our encounter with the Eternal *Thou*, and the deeper meaning and insight that this provides, can then ultimately be verified only pragmatically, only in personal experience. Its truth is found in what it does in human life—and so should rightly be seen as "human truth." On this point Buber is in complete agreement with William James.

## The Social Dimension of Buber's Existentialism

An enduring concern for the realization of man's deepest religious and personal values in social and political life characterizes Buber's philosophy as a whole. This concern shaped his interpretation of Zionism, and it distinguishes his position markedly from that of Kierkegaard. For Kierkegaard the relation of the individual to God, and the responsibility of the existential Christian to exemplify in his own life the commitment and the suffering of Christ, were man's chief concerns. For Buber, on the other hand, "meeting with God does not come to man in order that he may concern himself with God, but in order that he may confirm that there is meaning in the world. All revelation is a summons and a sending." The man who limits himself solely to his personal relationship with God soon loses God as well, Buber insists: "God wants us to come to him by means of the Reginas* he has created and not by a renunciation of them."[28]

### Evil as Social and Existential

It has become increasingly apparent that the problem of evil in our age, a problem that deeply concerns the existential philosophers, can no longer be dealt with in the relatively simple fashion that the early Stoic philosophers found satisfying. The social and existential dimensions of the problem are now much more disturbing.

* The fiancée whom Kirkegaard felt it was God's will that he renounce.

Four main types or expressions of evil in modern life are easily identified: (1) the widespread *loneliness* of modern man in his contact with other men, men with whom he associates but whom he does not genuinely know. Of man's loneliness in this sense both Nietzsche and Kierkegaard were especially conscious. In his *Pursuit of Loneliness* Philip Slater identifies this as a basic problem for today's youth. (2) The increasing *alienation* that modern man faces in an industrial and scientific society. Ours is a social order in which man has become increasingly a slave to the technology he created, in which his own humanity and identity is increasingly being destroyed. This was, of course, the major criticism leveled by Karl Marx against the capitalistic economy of his day. Erich Fromm, among other able psychiatrists in our day, points to the corrosive effect of such alienation upon the lives of men and women in almost all walks of modern life, not only the Marxian proletariat. In current works such as *The Making of a Counter Culture* and *The Greening of America,* our technologically controlled environment is seen as a major factor in causing the disaffection of the younger generation in our own day. (3) The deliberate control and extensive *degradation* of human life within the totalitarian state. Obvious and distressing examples of this are to be seen in the persecution of the Jews during the Nazi regime in Germany and in the recurring liquidation by Communist regimes of all individuals and groups unwilling to accept complete conformity to state control. The most graphic extrapolation of this degradation of the individual in the totalitarian state is to be found, perhaps, in George Orwell's portrayal of life in *1984.* (4) Man's increasing sense of the *meaninglessness* of his existence in the kind of universe that modern science has depicted. A graphic picture of our human predicament as seen from the viewpoint of modern science was drawn by Bertrand Russell as early as 1909 in his widely read essay, "A Free Man's Worship." But Russell was still able at that time to find in the Stoic philosophy an acceptable response to the human situation as he saw it. Since then, however, secular existentialists, especially philosophers like Heidegger and Sartre, have come to see in man's "encounter with Nothingness" the central tragedy of human existence. And the scientific world view has clearly lost both its appeal and its certainty in the minds of the many thoughtful young men and women today.

### The Achievement of Community

As he analyzed the predicament of man in modern life, Buber identified man's own insecurity and alienation, on the one hand, and the tremendous collective power of the modern state, on the other, as its two major sources. He refused, therefore, to adopt either Kierkegaard's commitment to the religious redemption of the individual or the new pattern of society that Marx envisioned. Neither of these in his judgment provided an adequate resolution of man's predicament. The dilemma of *either* individualism *or* collectivism must be avoided, Buber insisted, and a creative third alternative proposed. Such an alternative would recognize *both* the personal wholeness of the individual *and* the reconstruction of society as essential. It would emphasize the necessity not only of meaningful I–*Thou* personal relationships but also the creative *We* of genuine community.

Buber was as committed as was Marx to the necessity of social restructuring. Our capitalistic economy is inherently destructive not only of creative personal relationships, but also of organic community, he believed. This fact, in his judgment, has become increasingly apparent. But the needed social restructuring will not come, as the Marxist believes, as the result of inevitable economic changes. There must be a conscious will and commitment to a new social order in which there is a much deeper awareness of community, Buber maintains. True socialism, in contrast to Marxian Communism, must have as its foundation the reality of community in the experience of a people itself. It cannot be imposed upon them from above. Communistic regimes, whether in Russia or elsewhere, have consistently subordinated the development of man's social relationships to political compulsion and domination, Buber points out. They have never genuinely attempted to realize the goal of Karl Marx in which the new social order would provide for the full self-realization of all individuals.

Genuine community is possible, in fact, only with an extension of the I–*Thou* relation, in Buber's view. This personal relation between individuals must become the basis upon which social life and social relationships are developed—"for only men who are capable of truly saying *thou* to one another can truly say *we* with one another." Through such an organic awareness of the *We*, and only through this, can the individual escape from the faceless, impersonal crowd: "A man is truly saved from the 'one,' not by separation but only by being bound up in genuine communion."[29]

Genuine community can only be achieved, moreover, in a concrete situation, Buber points out. It cannot be dealt with as an abstraction. For this reason, the movement to community must grow out of the needs of a given situation and be realized in that concrete situation here and now. It was in his contact with Hasidism that Buber first came to know the meaning and significance of community. Here, he says, somewhat debased to be sure but still unimpaired, he found "the living double kernel of humanity: genuine community and genuine leadership."[30] It is not surprising, indeed it was to be expected, that he would later see in the Jewish communes in Israel, the *kibbutzim*, a promising beginning of the social restructuring necessary for real community.

These communes are based, as Buber believed to be essential, on the concrete needs of each local situation rather than on abstract theory. They combine an economic need to provide support for the local group with ideal motives inspired by socialistic as well as Biblical teaching on social justice. And the members of these communes, especially in their early development, showed a genuine critical self-analysis together with the willingness to experiment with new and more promising forms of social relationship, Buber points out. Beneath all this, and essential to it, he writes, is "an amazing positive relationship" to "the inmost being of their commune," which amounts to a genuine faith.

The Jewish village communes then can provide valuable guidance in man's search for a new social structure, a structure in which groups of personally related individuals have the greatest personal autonomy and yet establish the greatest possible interrelationship with each other. "Nowhere, as far as I see, in the history of the Socialist movement," Buber writes, "were men so deeply involved in the process of differentiation and yet so intent on preserving the principles of integration." There is to be found in these Jewish communes not only an underlying sense of community and of social renewal but also, and of equal importance, the adequate meeting of an eternal human need: "the need of man to feel his own home as a room in some greater, all-embracing structure in which he is at home, to feel that the other inhabitants of it with whom he lives and works are all acknowledging and confirming his individual existence." *

In his philosophy of community Buber, of course, identified one of the major concerns of the counter-culture in our own country. In small cluster groups from Vermont and New Hampshire to California young people have sought to develop the relationships that Buber has identified as essential for genuine community. But it is also clear that this movement in America has never had the kind of political recognition and support that could perhaps enable the village communes in Israel to have a significant impact upon the political structure of that country.

## Hope for World Peace

The social implications of his philosophy of dialogue likewise provide the only basis for any real hope of world peace, Buber believes. Faith in dialogue, and commitment to the personal relation that underlies it, he sees as the only viable alternative to the present state of tension between nation and nation. Widespread distrust and fear today makes us see a people with an ideology different from our own as alien and dangerous. This leads us to feel that they must be destroyed in order that we may live in our kind of world—

---

* *Paths in Utopia*, pp. 139–140. Buber also recognized quite clearly that the rapid influx of refugees into Israel had caused a number of serious problems for the successful development of the social restructuring at work in the village commune. But he still felt that this movement held great promise for the future. When he was in America in 1952, he stated this quite pointedly in an address at the Jewish Theological Seminary in New York: "The coming state of humanity in the great crisis depends very much on whether another type of socialism can be set up against Moscow and I venture even today to call it Jerusalem." (Quoted by Friedman, *op. cit.*, p. 207.)

that is, a world dominated by our own social and political institutions. Dialogue between heads of government cannot remove this fear and distrust, Buber maintains. Summit diplomacy of the kind, for example, that appealed so much to Franklin Roosevelt and Richard Nixon can never accomplish the needed results.

The establishment of a positive and creative peace between peoples must be based upon dialogue between authentic representatives of the people themselves, Buber maintains, "independent persons with no other authority than that of the spirit." The men who can begin this needed dialogue between peoples "must have overcome in themselves the basic mistrust of their partners in dialogue." They must be capable of recognizing in such partners "the reality of their being."

"The representatives of whom I speak will each be acquainted with the true needs of his own people, and on these needs will be willing to stake themselves," Buber writes. "But they will also turn understanding to the true needs of other peoples, and will know in both cases how to extract the true needs from the exaggerations. Just for this reason they will unrelentingly distinguish between truth and propaganda within what is called the opposition of interests."[31]

Man's common destiny in today's world may perhaps, before it is too late, bring together those "who have in common the language of human truth" and enable them to rescue mankind from being devoured by political strife and domination: "Coming together out of hostile camps, those who stand in the authority of the spirit will dare to think with one another in terms of the whole planet. . . . The hope for this hour depends upon the renewal of dialogical immediacy between [such] men."[32]

Small wonder that Dag Hammarskjöld, when Secretary-General of the United Nations, found Buber's social philosophy appealing. If dialogue between peoples of the sort Buber described could have occurred at the United Nations, hope for world peace would certainly have been greatly enhanced. But, as Hammarskjöld's experience must have clearly indicated, it will be no easy task to replace the power politics of our day with Buber's proposed dialogue between "authentic representatives" of the people of the world. Perhaps in this poem in *Markings* Hammarskjöld expressed something of the meaning and appeal dimly visible to him in Buber's hope for world peace:

> Summoned
> To carry it,
> Alone
> To assay it,
> And free
> To deny it,
> I saw
> For one moment

> The sail
> In the sun storm,
> Far off
> In a wave crest,
> Alone,
> Bearing from land.
>
> For one moment
> I saw.[33]

### A Concluding Comment

Buber's *I and Thou* was published at a time when the concern of philosophy was becoming more and more impersonal and objective, when its attention was turning more and more exclusively to the world of *It*. It was a time when logical positivism and analytic philosophy were attracting wide interest. And beyond the realm of philosophy, technological advances were producing social developments that proved increasingly dangerous for the integrity and humanity of man. Buber's emphasis upon the *Thou* in human life—the personal dimension of existence—was especially valuable and timely. His philosophy provided a significant effort to safeguard man's integrity and identity, an aim now so basic in the counter-culture of our day.

As Buber himself came to recognize, his anthropology—that is, his interpretation of man and of human nature—occupies a central place in his philosophy. His significant contribution to contemporary thought is perhaps to be found in the fact that he put man's relation to his fellowman at the heart of human nature. This is the unique aspect of his philosophical anthropology. It is an insight that neither rationalism nor naturalism provides, and to which only Buber's existentialism in our day gives such importance. The sense of responsibility for the welfare of others, which he identifies as an essential—perhaps *the* essential—aspect of the *I–Thou* relation, provides one of the necessary foundations for genuine community. His insight is of particular importance in an age when numerous experiments in community life are being undertaken.

His critics indeed suggest that Buber may have been too exclusively concerned with this aspect of self-realization. Has he not, they ask, in his emphasis upon the social nature of the self and upon self-realization in the *I–Thou* encounter, neglected an adequate analysis of the reflective aspect of self-awareness and self-realization? Are not these, in fact, two necessary aspects of man's self-realization? And if so, must not both aspects of human nature be recognized and given comparable importance in treating man's full self-consciousness and self-realization?[34] It is this problem indeed that so troubled Reinhold Niebuhr and with which his own philosophical anthropology is so deeply concerned.

As a matter of fact, Buber does recognize this limitation of his thought in passing. "Certainly, in order to be able to go out to the other," he writes, "you must have the starting place; you must have been, you must be with yourself."[35] This aspect of human nature and experience is not developed by Buber, however. Perhaps it was inevitable that his deep and immediate awareness in experience of the *Thou*, the other person, would make unlikely adequate recognition and development of other aspects of selfhood.

In limiting the role of reason so largely to scientific thought and the world of *It*, Buber's philosophy, like that of other existentialists, does also leave itself open to rather serious criticism. For the existentialist, *truth* is an aspect of his own deep and meaningful experience. It cannot be communicated in rational terms to others, nor used to build a rational and consistent philosophical system. But, as his critics ask, is this a necessary and legitimate limitation of all philosophical thought? Has Buber gone as far as it is possible for the philosopher to go, when he interprets his role as follows: "I must say it again: I have no teaching. I only point to something. I point to reality. I point to something in reality that had not or had too little been seen. I take him who listens by the hand and lead him to the window. I open the window and point to what is outside."[36]

Few would question the significant contribution, however, that Buber in this fashion has made to our philosophy of living. He has certainly pointed to aspects of man's experience that badly needed to be identified and emphasized. But do these aspects of experience give us *no* dependable understanding of the world of *Thou*, the personal world revealed in man's moral and spiritual insights? This raises a fundamental question that each student can hardly escape in an adequate formulation of the philosophy he lives by. Writing in 1953, a German sociologist impressively described Buber's own achievement in the philosophy he lived by. One can hardly ask for anything more meaningful:

> Outside of Albert Schweitzer, I know of no one who has realized in himself a similar great and genuine identity of truth and life. This little, old man with the penetrating, incorruptible eyes has already today begun to project into the brokenness of our time like a legendary figure. He is living proof of what this life is capable of when it wills to fulfill itself fearlessly and only in responsibility. Buber has accomplished what we can say of a very few, he has reached the limits of his own being and through this has made the universal transparent.[37]

# SIX

# A WISDOM OF THE EAST: ZEN BUDDHISM

Existence is beyond the power of words to define. Terms may be used, but none of them are absolute.

LAO-TZU

One can tell for oneself whether the water is warm or cold. In the same way a man must convince himself about these experiences. Then only are they real.

I-CHING

When the Ten Thousand Things are viewed in their one-ness, we return to the Origin and remain where we have always been.

SENG-TS'AN

The great path has no gates,
Thousands of roads enter it.
When one passes through this gateless gate
He walks freely between heaven and earth.

MUMONKAN

# CHAPTER 17
## Zen Buddhism

During the past several decades Americans have had a steadily increasing interest in Eastern thought. This has been true not only of the philosopher and the psychiatrist but of the layman as well. In the ancient wisdom of the East they have discovered appealing insights that our traditional Western philosophy had failed to appreciate. It seems desirable, therefore, to conclude this examination of philosophies men live by with a brief discussion of one Eastern way of life that in recent years has been of particular interest to the West.

It would be impossible, of course, for even an accomplished Oriental scholar to provide in one brief chapter an adequate interpretation of Zen Buddhism. Dr. D. T. Suzuki (1870–1966), the distinguished Japanese exponent of Zen, has been more than any other individual responsible for making the appeal of this Eastern view of life widely known in the English-speaking world. And Suzuki has published a dozen books as well as countless essays in an effort to enable the West to gain some understanding of Zen Buddhism.* Obviously our endeavor here can only be to provide an introduction that will suggest some of the major insights of Zen and indicate its sources of appeal in the Western world today. If this should lead the thoughtful student to seek for himself a more adequate and satisfying understanding, it will have accomplished its major purpose.

---

* Suzuki's three-volume work, *Essays in Zen Buddhism,* was published in London and Kyoto, 1927, 1933, 1934. For the next twenty-five years, until he was over ninety, Suzuki continued every year to enlarge this initial effort to provide for Western readers an adequate interpretation of Zen.

## The Appeal of Zen

*East and West*

Western writers often note the basic difference between the Western view of life and that found in the Orient. As a rule their comments indicate how superior our Western point of view is. The industrial and technological progress of Western nations and the abundance of material comforts enjoyed in the West are customarily cited as evidences of this judgment. Our recognition of the worth and dignity of the individual, of human personality, is also frequently mentioned. It is of some interest, therefore, to have an Eastern writer as discerning as D. T. Suzuki give us his idea of how our Western view of life appears to the East.

There are, of course, in his description of Western thought a number of quite familiar characteristics. "The Western mind," he writes, "is: analytical, discriminative, inductive, individualistic, intellectual, scientific, conceptual, impersonal, legalistic, organizing, power-wielding, self-assertive, disposed to impose its will upon others. Against these Western traits, those of the East can be characterized as: synthetic, integrative, nondiscriminative, deductive, nonsystematic, dogmatic, intuitive, subjective, spiritually individualistic and socially group-minded."[1]

Western man, as Suzuki sees him, has a pair of sharp, deep-set penetrating eyes. With them he surveys the outside world much as does an eagle as he soars high in the sky. (In fact, the eagle is the national symbol of a certain Western power, Dr. Suzuki points out.) The high nose, thin lips, and general facial contour of the Western man all suggest a highly developed intellect and a readiness to act—rather comparable, in this case, to the lion. It is no accident then that the eagle and the lion are accepted symbols for Western nations.

As we are well aware, the scientifically minded West has used its intelligence to produce all kinds of gadgets that elevate our standard of living by saving us from unnecessary labor or drudgery. We have "developed" as fully as we can the natural resources available in our lands. Now, of course, there is reason to fear that we are exhausting these resources, and so face a crisis in continuing the way of life we have grown accustomed to. The East, on the other hand, has traditionally seemed quite satisfied with an "undeveloped" state of civilization. It does not object to being engaged in manual labor of all kinds. The East is not machine-minded. It does not want to turn itself into a slave to the machine.[2]

On this point Suzuki's view is interestingly like that of Karl Marx. The machine, as he sees it, is designed to finish the work in a hurry and produce the output for which it is made. The work that is being done has no value in itself. It is only a means to an end. Thus life for the worker loses its creativity and meaning. "Man is now a goods-producing mechanism." Western philosophers and politicians talk about the worth and dignity of the person, but as Suzuki looks at our highly industrialized and mechanized Western civilization, "the machine is everything and man is almost entirely reduced to thralldom," he feels. He recognizes, of course, that civilization cannot now abandon industrialism and return to a primitive handicraft stage. But we should all, in the West as well as the East, be aware of the evils that the mechanization of modern life has produced. And these evils result from an emphasis upon the intellect and upon technological progress at the expense of man's life as a whole.

"The Chinese and other Asiatic peoples love life as it is lived," Suzuki writes, "and do not wish to turn it into a means of accomplishing something else, which would direct the course of living to quite a different channel. They like work for its own sake, even though, objectively speaking, work means to accomplish something. But while working they enjoy the work and are not in a hurry to finish it. Mechanical devices are far more efficient and accomplish more. But the machine is impersonal and non-creative and has no meaning."[3]

As he looks at Western civilization today Suzuki sees a number of very undesirable results that analytical, scientific, impersonal, self-assertive technology has produced: the personal values in life have been almost entirely destroyed. The combination of the person and the machine involves a contradiction, he feels. In the machine-minded outlook, individual freedom and personal responsibility make no sense. Nor is there any real freedom in the Western way of life, as Suzuki sees it: "Freedom is another nonsensical idea." Not only does the machine limit man's freedom, but the social group of which he is a part provides an equally powerful limitation. All his movements, both mental and physical—what he thinks as well as what he does—are shaped by his social situation. Because of this fundamental contradiction in his civilization, Western man feels a deep psychological tension that is manifested in various ways in modern life. "Western man is from the beginning constrained, restrained, inhibited," Suzuki concludes. "The machine, behaviorism, the conditioned reflex, communism, artificial insemination, automation generally, vivisection, the H-bomb—they are each and all most intimately related, and form close-welded solid links of a logical chain."[4]

In this analysis of our way of life in the West, Suzuki is, of course, simply portraying from his Eastern point of view what has been described as the *alienation* of man in Western civilization. Philosophers and psychologists from Kierkegaard and Marx to Erich Fromm and the existentialists of our own day have been at pains to point to the same situation.

*Zen Buddhism\* and Recent Psychoanalysis*

Psychiatry is the popular method in the West, of course, of dealing with the spiritual crisis that Western man is facing. It is quite true that the majority of people in the West today are not consciously aware that they are living through a crisis in Western culture. Probably the majority of people in a radically critical historical period have never been consciously aware of the crisis in their civilization. But Fromm agrees with Suzuki that there are abundant indications of the existence and nature of such a crisis today. The impression that large numbers of people, especially in our major urban and industrial centers, depend upon the psychiatrist for their mental health is perhaps indication enough.

Both Zen and psychoanalysis embody theories concerning the nature of man, and both propose a method to achieve his well-being. One is a characteristic expression of Eastern thought, the other of Western thought. Because of its success in escaping the fragmentation and alienation that characterize so much of life in Western civilization, Zen proved of particular interest to two of the ablest psychoanalysts: Carl G. Jung, distinguished Swiss psychiatrist (1875–1961), and Karen Horney, influential German-born American psychiatrist (1885–1952). Both were much impressed late in their lives by the remarkable achievement of psychological wholeness and self-realization they saw in Zen. This held great attraction for them as practicing psychiatrists. Jung indeed wrote a quite interesting foreword, expressing this interest, for the 1949 edition of Suzuki's *Introduction to Zen Buddhism*. Erich Fromm has more recently deepened and sharpened the interest of the psychoanalyist in Zen that Carl Jung and Karen Horney originated.

In the East, especially in Taoism and Buddhism, the aims of the religious life have been preserved without a faith in an all-powerful, omniscient deity upon whom man is dependent for salvation. In these Eastern religions it is recognized as essential that a person overcome self-centeredness and make love, good will, and humility basic attitudes in his relation with others. But in Taoism and Buddhism the fact is accepted that man has no one to guide him in such an endeavor except teachers who are themselves "enlightened." That he can succeed in this endeavor, however, is assured because each man has within himself the capacity to awake, to be enlightened.

It is for this reason, Fromm feels, that Zen Buddhism, in which the

---

\* Zen Buddhism, as interpreted initially by Dr. Suzuki and more recently by numerous other Eastern and Western writers, is the way of life practiced by a quite influential Buddhist sect in Japan. The name Zen comes from the Japanese *Zazen*, which means to sit and meditate. (*Zazen* is the Japanese translation of the Chinese *ch-an*, which in turn is a translation of the Indian *Dhyana*—meditation.) Thus Zen is in origin a particular sect of Buddhism, one that placed its emphasis upon meditation. But in its development, first in China and then in Japan, it has radically transformed the traditional Buddhist and Western concept of meditation, as is indicated later in this chapter.

insights of Taoism and Buddhism are blended, has such appeal in the West today. "Zen Buddhism helps man to find an answer to the question of his existence," he writes, "an answer which is essentially the same as that given in the Judaeo-Christian tradition, and yet which does not contradict the rationality, realism, and independence which are modern man's precious achievements. Paradoxically, Eastern religious thought turns out to be more congenial to Western rational thought than does Western religion itself."[5]

### Zen and Western Philosophy

Schopenhauer was the first Western philosopher who found in Buddhism an insight and point of view that had marked appeal. Around its view of life, as he understood it, Schopenhauer built the pessimism that has distinguished his philosophy. This was a little over a century ago, and Western knowledge of Eastern thought at that time was quite limited. Great strides, however, have been made in Oriental studies since Schopenhauer wrote. Today there is much greater interest in as well as a better understanding of Oriental philosophy.

In the West, our view of life has in general been shaped by two major influences, the Hebrew and the Greek. Both are profoundly dualistic in spirit. The Hebrew dualism is moral and spiritual: God transcends the world of nature, and a sharp distinction must be made between God and nature, God and man, the spiritual and the material. The Greeks, on the other hand, made a division of reality along intellectual lines. Plato, "who virtually founded Western philosophy single-handed," as Professor William Barrett sees it, recognized a fundamental conflict between the world of the intellect and the world of the senses. Greek philosophy under his influence established the ideal of reason, of rationality, not only as the highest human achievement but as the very center of personal identity.* Christian philosophy in the modern as well as in the medieval period was largely shaped by its Greek and Hebrew heritage. The material world, the world of the senses, was not only sharply distinguished from the world of the spirit. It was usually seen as the source of evil in human life.

This dualistic approach to life was never accepted by the Orientals, however. For them intuition was superior to reason. At the center of human personality they found a spiritual unity in which the conflicting demands of the intellect and the senses, of the moral and the natural, were transcended. Recent Western thought has now also recognized the paradoxical nature of reason and its significant limitations. The inability of reason to provide a completely acceptable interpretation of the world of nature as well as of human nature is, of course, a fundamental conviction of the existentialists. Even in the sciences, advances in physics (Heisenberg) and in mathematics

* See *Zen Buddhism: Selected Writings of D. T. Suzuki*, ed. William Barrett (New York: Doubleday Anchor Books, 1956), p. ix. This is a very thoughtful and useful volume.

(Gödel) have indicated some apparently inescapable limitations in human reason. "Science in this century has at last caught up with Kant," Barrett suggests. Developments such as these in Western philosophy and science have undoubtedly given to Eastern thought a new interest and appeal.[6]

Zen, in fact, explicitly denies the dualism traditionally associated with religion and philosophy in the West. Its outlook and approach to life is entirely naturalistic and by healing the cleavage between man and nature, it enables man to feel at home in nature. Not only is American interest in Zen growing, but Zen may well have some affinity with what is distinctly American in modern philosophy.* Certainly one of the major aims of John Dewey's naturalism was to restore an awareness of the bond between man and nature, and to interpret human nature as an integral part of the larger universe of nature. But where Dewey turned to the theory of evolution and scientific thought to establish this view of man and nature, Zen sees this simply as a basic fact of experience. Zen is thus actually closer in spirit to the "new naturalism" of the younger generation in this country. In the view of life accepted there, the natural is desirable and good simply because it is found to be so. Man seeks to live close to nature, in harmony with nature, because in this way he finds life more appealing and satisfying. On this point there is genuine agreement with the teaching of the Zen masters.

Life, for the Zen disciple, is what it is felt to be in immediate experience. What counts is first-hand, day-by-day, moment-by-moment experience. If the great lesson of Zen is to be natural, its object is to enable one to become calm and free from all external pressures, to keep one's spirit undisturbed amid the haste and confusion of actual life. It is a need such as this that we in America are coming to feel more and more insistently. Under the pressures of our urban and technological society, the calmness and wholeness of spirit that Zen portrays does certainly become increasingly appealing.

## Brief Historical Background

As a sect of Buddhism, Zen traces its origin back to the founder of Indian Buddhism: Siddhartha Gautama, also known as Sakyamuni. Born about 560 B.C., Gautama was the son and heir of a wealthy rajah in a small province in what today is Nepal. According to legend, from birth the young prince was shielded from everything unpleasant or painful by an overprotective father

---

* This, for example, is the contention of Van Meter Ames. In his book *Zen and American Thought* (University of Hawaii Press, 1962), Ames provides a detailed account of some interesting agreements between Zen and the thought of such well-known Americans as Jefferson, Emerson, Thoreau, Whitman, William James, Peirce, Santayana, and Dewey. This is certainly an agreement in general aim rather than in specific method and point of view, however. None of these American writers could conceivably be seen as advocates of Zen Buddhism.

who hoped in this way to make his life happy and contented. As a young man, however, Gautama slipped out of the family palace for several secret and forbidden journeys into the outside world. There he saw three unhappy sights that altered his life completely: a destitute and abject beggar, a dead man surrounded by weeping mourners, and a hopelessly diseased cripple.

This experience raised fundamental questions in Gautama's mind about man's life and destiny. What, he asked himself, could be the meaning and purpose of life when suffering and disease are universal and when death is inevitable? Unable to endure the protection and luxury of the life he was leading as a young prince, Gautama finally decided he must leave the palace and seek some deeper insight into life's meaning. In the middle of one night, he stole away from his wife and young son, and for seven years he wandered from teacher to teacher seeking an answer to the questions that so disturbed him. None of the Hindu teachers, however, had answers that he found satisfying.

Then one day when sitting alone in deep meditation under the sacred Bo-tree he perceived for himself the answers he sought. This was his experience of "enlightenment." He became the Buddha, the Enlightened One, and for the next forty-nine years he spent his life teaching. He realized, however, that each man must find truth for himself. Gautama's aim was simply to assist his disciples in achieving for themselves the insight, the enlightenment, that so fundamentally changed his own life. His teaching is embodied in Buddhism's Fourfold Noble Truth and the Eightfold Path of Right Thought and Right Behavior.* It is essentially psychological, rather than religious in the Western sense of the word, and envisions a training in the discipline of mind and body designed to insure complete self-mastery and nonattachment to anything material or worldly. When properly followed, this discipline should enable one to rid himself of desire for possessions, of greed, of all attachment to objects or other persons. Finally it should bring complete freedom from all such worldly concerns and escape from the illusion of separation between the individual self and all reality. Thus the disciples of Gautama would attain *Nirvana*.

Buddhism soon split into two major divisions known as the Hinayana (Lesser Vehicle) and the Mahayana (Greater Vehicle). It was Mahayana Buddhism that spread northward into China during the sixth century A.D.

---

*The Four Certainties (the Fourfold Noble Truth): I. All life is sorrow, pain, and suffering. II. Desire, craving, thirst is the cause of pain and suffering. III. To find release from pain and suffering one must get rid of the desire, crush craving, deny thirst. IV. The Middle Way (Eightfold Path) is the way to rid oneself of desire, of craving, of thirst, and so to escape from the world of change, impermanence, and unreality. The eight steps or rules in the Middle Way are in outline: (1) Right Thought, (2) Right Aims, (3) Right Speech, (4) Right Action or Conduct, (5) Right Livelihood, (6) Right Effort, (7) Right Attitude, (8) Right Concentration. It was the Four Certainties of Buddhism, of course, that Schopenhauer found so appealing.

There what we now know as Zen developed as the strongest Mahayana sect, in which meditation (*ch'an*) in particular was emphasized. When in the twelfth and thirteenth centuries A.D. this sect reached Japan, it became known by the Japanese term for meditation (*zazen*), from which the name Zen is derived.

In the course of this pilgrimage, several important developments in the original Buddhist teaching took place. In China the prevalent Taoism gave to Ch'an Buddhism its naturalism and its unique spirit of "dynamic meditation," an attitude of full yet relaxed awareness. To the Chinese mentality, it was in the work of everyday life rather than through solitary meditation in the forest that a man found his deepest insights into life. In the Zen monastic communities master and disciples shared in all the work of supporting daily life— growing rice, cooking, chopping wood, keeping the place clean. The early Chinese masters were also steeped in Taoism. They saw every person and every experience as a part of the total interrelatedness of Nature, of the Tao. This view of man and nature enabled them to accept themselves and every- thing else as all naturally was, without the least need to alter or justify anything.[7] As Ruth Fuller, an American Zen Buddhist has said, "Zen is devel- oped Mahayana Buddhism as the Chinese mind, steeped in the Chinese world view and classical Taoism, realized it." When Ch'an Buddhism was later taken over in Japan (and *ch'an* translated *zazen*), an aesthetic and mystical spirit reshaped the dynamic meditation of the earlier movement. In his interpretation of Zen Buddhism to the Western world in the twentieth cen- tury, it is Buddhism as thus modified and enlarged through a pilgrimage of some twenty-five hundred years that Dr. Suzuki portrayed.*

### The Heart of Zen

Despite the widespread interest in Zen among philosophers and psycholo- gists in the West, it is not easy for the average person to grasp exactly what Zen involves. Properly speaking Zen is not a religion, nor is it a philosophy. It is a "way of life," but a way of life based upon certain fundamental insights and experiences that do have both religious and philosophical implications. All those who seek to interpret its meaning, to communicate to someone else what Zen is, stress the fact that this cannot be done by the use of words and concepts. "To know Zen—even to begin to understand it—it is necessary to practice it," they all warn us. This obviously presents those of us in the West with a serious problem. Dr. Suzuki writes:

* In the interest of accuracy, it should perhaps be noted that there are two main schools of Zen, the Soto and the Rinzai. It is the latter that Dr. Suzuki accepted and made known to Western scholars. Also, perhaps, the student should be aware that a distinguished Chinese scholar, Dr. Hu Shih, disagrees with Suzuki's account of the intro- duction of Buddhism into China and its early development there. Such scholarly dis- putes, however, do not in any way discredit Suzuki's portrayal of Zen Buddhism in Japan.

The essence of Zen Buddhism consists in acquiring a new viewpoint on life and things generally. By this I mean that if we want to get into the inmost life of Zen, we must forgo all our ordinary habits of thinking which control our everyday life, we must try to see . . . if our ordinary way is always sufficient to give us the ultimate satisfaction of our spiritual needs. If we feel somehow dissatisfied with this life, if there is something in our ordinary way of living that deprives us of freedom in its [highest] sense, we must endeavor to find a way somewhere which gives us a sense of finality and contentment. Zen proposes to do this for us and assures us of the acquirement of a new point of view in which life assumes a fresher, deeper, and more satisfying aspect.[8]

At a conference on psychoanalysis held in Mexico in 1957, Erich Fromm selected from Suzuki's description of Zen some characteristics that were especially appealing to the psychiatrist:

Zen in its essence is the art of seeing into the nature of one's being, and it points the way from bondage to freedom.

We can say that Zen liberates all the energies properly and naturally stored up in each of us, which are in ordinary circumstances cramped and distorted so that they find no adequate channel for activity.

It is the object of Zen, therefore, to save us from going crazy or being crippled. This is what I mean by freedom, giving full play to all the creative and benevolent impulses inherently lying in our hearts.

Generally we are blind to this fact, that we are in possession of all the necessary faculties that will make us happy and loving towards one another.[9]

### Enlightenment (Satori)

This desirable health and wholeness of the human spirit, the achievement of which Zen seeks, only comes, however, as one is enlightened. The experience of enlightenment (satori) is the major aim of Zen.* Fundamentally it is knowledge of one's own nature that is thus achieved. Hence Zen agrees with Socrates that man's chief concern is to "Know Thyself." This is not the kind of knowledge one gets as an observer, standing outside. It is rather the insight that comes in immediate experience to one who is inside. It is essentially the art of understanding oneself, of gaining an insight into human nature, the nature of one's own being, that liberates the individual

---

* "At all events there is no Zen without satori, which is indeed the Alpha and Omega of Zen Buddhism," Suzuki writes. "Zen devoid of satori is like a sun without its light and heat. Zen may lose all its literature, all its monasteries, and all its paraphernalia but as long as there is satori in it, it will survive to eternity." (Zen Buddhism, ed. Wm. Barrett, p. 84.)

from all the distractions and confusions that we as finite human beings usually experience in this world. As described by Dr. Suzuki, "Zen proposes to discipline the mind itself, to make it its own master, through an insight into its proper nature. This getting into the real nature of one's mind or soul is the fundamental object of Zen Buddhism. Zen, therefore, is more than meditation (*Dhyana*) in its ordinary sense. The discipline of Zen consists in opening the mental eye in order to look into the very reason of existence."[10]

Such an immediate insight and understanding is in nature similar certainly to the insights the existentialist emphasizes. To be enlightened as Zen understands it is to experience "the full awakening of the total personality to reality." This difference between intellectual, abstract, theoretical knowledge and experiential insight and understanding is basic. Hence the insights that accompany the enlightenment in Zen can never be conveyed to another person by intellectual concepts. His enlightenment must be an insight that comes to him in his own experience. "For a *satori* turned into a concept ceases to be itself," Suzuki points out, "and there will no more be a Zen experience."

In its initial form in India, prior even to the time Buddhism spread to China, the sect that later developed into Zen seems to have placed its major emphasis upon meditation. Gautama was in deep meditation under the Bo-tree at the time of his enlightenment. This figure of man in contemplation, seated cross-legged, with his hands in his lap and his eyes directed within, is portrayed frequently in Asian sculpture and painting. To the Eastern world it has much the same symbolic significance as does the figure of Christ on the Cross in the West.[11]

But for Zen in Japan the traditional idea of meditation is no longer acceptable. That is not the way to enlightenment (*satori*). As emphatically stated by Dr. Suzuki: "If there is anything that Zen strongly emphasizes it is the attainment of freedom, that is, freedom from all unnatural encumbrances. Meditation is something artificially put on; it does not belong to the native activity of the mind. No amount of meditation will keep Zen in one place. Meditation is not Zen. Zen wants to leave one's mind free and unencumbered; even the idea of oneness or allness is a stumbling block and a strangling snare which threatens the original freedom of the spirit."[12]

Enlightenment of this kind about life, and about man's own nature as well, is not easily gained, of course. There is a vast difference between *saying* the words about life and about oneself, and knowing them, feeling them to be real, in one's own experience. The training and discipline that Zen insists on is designed, therefore, to enable the disciple to achieve this insight, this enlightenment, as his own. In its method of instruction Zen is unique. There is no doctrinal teaching, no study of sacred scriptures, no formal program of spiritual development. Almost all records of Zen instruction consist of dialogues between the great Zen masters and their disciples and most of these at first sight appear to be nonsense.

## The Koan

That enlightenment can never come through logic or through intellectual understanding is a basic Zen conviction. Hence the method of Zen is to baffle, to puzzle, to make it clear initially that logic cannot provide the needed insight. The Zen master traditionally puts his disciple in a dilemma from which logic can never enable him to escape. It at once becomes apparent that some insight of a higher order is needed. One must see with the "eye of the spirit." It may take years of study, of meditation, of training before such insight is achieved. By the use of paradox and of apparent logical contradiction, Zen seeks to transcend the limitations of the intellect, of logical thought and analysis. It seeks to reflect life directly as lived—not as analyzed and abstracted. Comments such as the following are typical of the Zen masters:

> Empty-handed I go, and behold the spade is in my hand;
> I walk on foot, and yet on the back of an ox I am riding.

To most Westerners this stanza seems illogical and meaningless. By Zen disciples it is seen as "most refreshingly satisfying." "So long as we think logic to be final, we are chained, we have no freedom of spirit, and the real facts of life are lost sight of. Now, however, we have the key to the whole situation. We are master of realities; words have given up their domination over us."[13]

The term used for such statements as that quoted above by the old Zen masters is *koan*. The *koan* provides both a means of stimulating intuitive insight and also a way to test the depth of insight that has been achieved. No logical or rational explanation of the *koan* is possible, of course. In the early years of Zen in China there seems to have been a quite informal discussion between master and disciples. The disciple would raise questions about what he did not understand, and the master would then provide the kind of mental stimulation needed to lead the disciple to an experience of enlightenment.

In time there grew up a body of questions and answers of this kind, exchanged originally between masters and disciples. Then, as Zen training became more formalized in Japan, it was an accepted practice for the Zen teachers to make use of these statements by earlier and more creative masters. And the class of statements itself became known as the *koan*. A few examples are sufficient to indicate the paradoxical and puzzling nature of the *koan*. The following are some that are commonly given to the uninitiated:

> A monk asked Chao-chou, "What is the meaning of the First Patriarch's visit to China?" The master's answer: "The cypress tree in the front courtyard."

When Chao-chou first came to study Zen under Nan-chu-an, he asked, "What is the Tao (the Way)?" The master replied "Your everyday mind, that is the Tao."

A monk asked Tung-shan, "Who is the Buddha?" "Three *chin* of flax," was the reply.

A monk once asked, "All things are said to be reducible to the One, but where is the One to be reduced?" Chao-chou answered, "When I was in the district of Ch'ing I had a robe made that weighed seven *chin*."[14]

When asked, "What then is the Buddha's statement?" the master replied, "Have a cup of tea."

In comments such as these one is immediately aware indeed not only of paradox but also of a keen sense of humor, a rather startling irreverence and an unwillingness to be overserious about life. This is an aspect of Zen that has proved quite appealing to many who find the high seriousness and sense of tragedy in much conventional religion somewhat distasteful.

After being given such a *koan*, the pupil retires to meditate, thus seeking the insight needed to interpret the puzzling statement. He soon discovers, of course, that neither logic nor meditation in the ordinary sense of the term —keeping his mind fixed on the problem—is of any real value. It is with this in mind that Zen insists upon the necessity of "emptying oneself," clearing the mind of all thoughts, all specific efforts to concentrate. Then the needed illumination may come as a sudden, unsought intuitive insight. Thus Zen trains the mind "to see the meaning of life in the midst of life as it is lived." The desired insight may come as one is walking through the countryside, or as he is going about his usual daily work, or even as he is talking with a friend. Suzuki suggests it is comparable to Spinoza's concept of *intuition* as the highest form of knowledge. "Meditation" in the usual Western sense of the word is obviously not the right term to describe the *koan* exercise in Zen.*

A favorite statement by one of the Zen masters is included in almost all the accounts of enlightenment: "Before I was enlightened, the rivers were rivers and the mountains were mountains," the master is reported to have said. "When I began to be enlightened, the rivers were not rivers any more, and the mountains were not mountains. Now, since I am enlightened, the rivers are rivers again and the mountains are mountains."

* An experience reported by Aldous Huxley in *The Doors of Perception* will un-doubtedly be of interest to students. Huxley had been much perplexed by one of the classic *koans* as he turned it over repeatedly in his mind. In it a young novice asks his master "What is the Universal Mind or Godhead?" and gets the answer, "The hedge at the bottom of the garden." When conducting an experiment with carefully controlled doses of mescaline that relaxed the grip of the rational mentality, Huxley saw quite clearly with delight and amusement just what this Zen reply really meant. In this moment of freedom and illumination, he says, all life stood revealed to him as a totality, a great "One-ness." (Reported by Nancy Ross in *The World of Zen*, p. 12.)

In this Zen statement Erich Fromm sees a view of reality not unlike that in Plato's Allegory of the Cave. The unenlightened person sees only the shadows and mistakes them for reality. In the process of enlightenment he first recognizes that the shadows are not reality. But when he has become enlightened, when he has left the cave with its darkness for the light of truth, he sees reality as it actually is. He is now awake, and understands the difference between seeing the world as shadows and understanding it as reality.[15] This use of Plato's Allegory of the Cave in interpreting the Zen enlightenment is suggestive, perhaps even helpful. But the basic difference between the value and usefulness of reason in Plato's philosophy and in Zen must not be overlooked.

### Zen and Western Religions

Zen is clearly not a religion in the sense in which that term is customarily understood in the West. Zen has no God that one worships. It has no ceremonial rites to observe, no future heaven or hell to which the dead are destined. Nor is there a soul whose welfare and salvation should be one's primary concern. There are Zen monks and Zen temples, to be sure. The images of the various Buddhas and other images in Zen temples, however, are just so many pieces of wood and stone, if Dr. Suzuki's interpretation is sound. They are much like azaleas and camellias, he suggests. One can make obeisance to the camellia in full bloom; one can worship it as a beautiful expression of nature, if one likes. For the Zen Buddhist this is just as religious as bowing down to the various Buddhist deities—or just as irreligious.

"There are in Zen no sacred books and no dogmatic tenets," Suzuki writes, "nor are there any symbolic formulae through which an access might be gained to the significance of Zen. If I am asked, then, what Zen teaches, I would answer Zen teaches nothing. Whatever teachings there are in Zen, they come out of one's own mind. We teach ourselves; Zen merely points the way. Unless this pointing is teaching, there is nothing purposely set up in Zen as its cardinal doctrines or its fundamental philosophy."[16]

One who has not experienced the enlightenment that Zen emphasizes is clearly in no position to describe the insights that come with this experience. And all those who have experienced such enlightenment feel it quite useless to try to explain their insights to others. It seems certain, however, that at the heart of this central experience in Zen there is a new awareness of the unity and wholeness of all reality. The partition between the individual self and the universe itself is seen to be unreal. Man does become one with all nature in such an experience. He is caught up in a kind of Cosmic Consciousness (Suzuki prefers the term Cosmic Unconsciousness) that gives to all his experience a new quality and meaning. His view of life and his sense of values are transformed. As put by another Westerner to whom Zen has proved quite appealing: "Accepting oneself, not as one's apparently little self trying to maintain identity as a separate unity, but as part of all there is, all the flow and change going on, not at odds with it but at one with it, brings the peace of Nirvana in the midst of the world."[17]

An enlightenment of this sort is clearly comparable as a *psychological* experience to the conversion experience in traditional Christianity. It has even more similarity with the experiences described by the great Christian mystics. And it is not dissimilar psychologically to the *I–Thou* relation upon which Buber's existentialism is grounded. The obvious difference, of course, between the Zen experience and all such religious experiences is the fact that in the latter man's relation to God is the central feature. In Zen enlightenment there is no transcendent deity above and beyond the world of nature and of human nature.

This, as Suzuki suggests, is actually closer to the thought of Spinoza. As Spinoza describes the intuitive insight that enables man to rise above the level of logical thought and become aware of his own oneness with Nature, he seems to be more in accord with the outlook of Zen than with either Hebrew or Christian thought, even though he retains the word *God* to describe the whole of Nature, including human nature. In what Spinoza likes to call "the intellectual love of God," the mind rises to "the high serenity of contemplation which sees all things as parts of an eternal order." Man thus enlightened is freed from the struggles and strife that beset the ignorant man's life. He is aware of his oneness with the eternal order of Nature, and is content with his own place and part therein. He comes to love life, no matter what its content; he takes the world as it comes, and in himself is quite imperturbed.

One must remember, to be sure, that Spinoza, in approved Western fashion, insists that it is only after the fullest use of his reason that man is able to reach the enlightenment he seeks. At this point he disagrees directly with the Zen masters. But as far as one who looks from outside can judge, the experience of enlightment itself as Spinoza describes it is remarkably similar to that of the Zen master.

### The Elusiveness of Zen

The inner spiritual experience of the individual is, of course, the central fact of Zen. This is the foundation around which Zen constructs all the verbal and conceptual scaffolding that is found in its literature. Personal experience is everything; hence none of its ideas are genuinely meaningful to those who do not have the background in experience. Those of us in the West who have not been fortunate enough to experience the enlightenment so central in Zen cannot but find it extremely enigmatic and elusive.

Not only as an Oriental but as one deeply committed to Zen, Dr. Suzuki recognizes this as inevitable. No doubt even the comparisons suggested above with Christian mysticism and with Spinoza would be dismissed by the Zen disciple as deceptive. When you think you have grasped Zen, it is there no more, Suzuki maintains. It looks approachable but as soon as you come near where you thought it was, you find it even farther from you than before.

> Zen is a wafting cloud in the sky. No screw fastens it, no string holds it, it moves as it lists. Zen just feels fire warm and ice cold, because when it freezes we shiver and welcome fire. The feeling is all in all, as Faust declares. But "the feeling" here must be understood in its deepest and purest form. Even to say that "This is the feeling" means that Zen is no more there. Zen defies all concept-making. That is why Zen is difficult to grasp. . . . Zen perceives or feels, and does not abstract or mediate. Zen penetrates and is finally lost in immersion. Meditation, on the other hand, is outspokenly dualistic and consequently inevitably superficial.[18]

When Zen is described in terms like these, it is easy to see why reading or talking about Zen can give at best only a very superficial idea of what Zen really means: "Unless, therefore, you devote some years of earnest study to the understanding of its primary principles, it is not to be expected that you will have a fair grasp of Zen." This certainly is a warning we should heed.

## Zen and the West

Despite this rather formidable barrier that anyone in the West must confront as he seeks to understand Zen, its appeal has been remarkable. Members of New York's First Zen Institute have been meeting for more than three decades to practice Zen meditation exercises. During a number of summers Zen enthusiasts in Los Angeles have held a week of strict training in group meditation. Other interested Americans have spent long periods in study with Zen masters and in Zen monasteries. The most notable perhaps among these is Ruth Fuller Sasaki, a Zen Buddhist for over twenty-five years. At forty she began the study of Zen at a monastery in Kyoto, Japan, and later continued her study under a Zen master in America. Then she returned to Japan and for ten years lived in Kyoto, studying and practicing under a third Zen master. She now is virtually the abbess at a Zen temple in Kyoto, but says, "I have not yet completed my Zen study."[19]

### Beat Zen and Square Zen

A quite interesting discussion of the influence of Zen in America is found in a book by Alan Watts, entitled *Beat Zen, Square Zen and Zen.*\*

---

\*Published in San Francisco in 1959 by City Lights Books. Alan Watts is one of the first Western writers to be attracted by the philosophy of the East. A small book of his, entitled *The Spirit of Zen*, was published in England in 1935. It was dedicated to Christmas Humphreys, President of the Buddhist Lodge in London, who first introduced Watts to Dr. Suzuki and laid the foundation for his knowledge of Buddhism. The third edition of Watts's book, published in 1958, contains a helpful bibliography of works on Zen up to that time.

There is great appeal, Watts feels, in "a view of the world imparting a profoundly refreshing sense of wholeness to a culture in which the spiritual and the material, the conscious and the unconscious have been cataclysmically split."[20] But to make this growing interest in Zen of positive value, the Westerner who finds Zen appealing must understand his own culture thoroughly: "He must be free of the itch to justify himself." Otherwise Zen for him will become either "beat" or "square," either largely a revolt from his own culture and society or the effort to find a new form of stuffiness and respectability. When genuine, Zen is above all *liberation* of the mind from the conventional view of life, but this is something quite different from rebellion against convention, on the one hand, or adopting foreign ideas and conventions, on the other. "This is why the displaced or unconscious Christian can so easily use either beat or square Zen to justify himself. The one wants a philosophy to justify him in doing what he pleases. The other wants a more plausible authoritative salvation than the Church or the psychiatrist seem able to provide."[21]

The "beat" mentality for Watts is something more than the widely discussed way of life of the "hippies" in New York or San Francisco. It includes the revolt of the younger generation against participation in the orthodox "American Way of Life" as symbolized by the Establishment. This is a revolt, he feels, that does not seek to change the existing order but simply to escape from it—that seeks to find meaning "in subjective experience rather than in objective achievement." It is easy to see how Zen would appeal to a mentality such as this. "Beat" Zen, however, as Watts sees it, is a complex phenomenon: "It ranges from a use of Zen for justifying sheer caprice in art, literature, and life to a very forceful social criticism," which one may find in the poetry of Allen Ginsberg and in the prose of Jack Kerouac.

There is in Zen, it is true, an ultimate standpoint from which "anything goes." The world is seen to be beyond right and wrong from this ultimate standpoint. As one Zen stanza puts it:

> If you want to get the plain truth,
> Be not concerned with right and wrong.
> The conflict between right and wrong
> Is the sickness of the mind.[22]

Because of the sense of freedom from the accepted conventions and the established way of life implicit in Zen, there is always a danger that this freedom will be misused and become license. It is this mistake that characterizes "beat" Zen, in Watts's judgment. It is most unfortunate, he feels, to see Zen so misused as a pretext for license, when that involves such a fundamental misunderstanding of the genuine Zen view of life.

To some extent, however, this has happened in the "underworld" that attaches itself to legitimate artistic and intellectual groups. The Bohemian way of life in such groups is a natural outgrowth of the fact that artists and writers are so committed to their creative work that they lose allegiance to accepted social and moral conventions of their society. "But every such community attracts a number of weak imitators and hangers-on, especially in the great cities," Watts points out, "and it is mostly in this class that one now finds the stereotype of the 'beatnik' with his phony Zen."[23]

"Square" Zen is, of course, much disturbed by this spirit of license and lawnessness in "beat" Zen. Square Zen, as Watts defines it, "is the Zen of established tradition in Japan with its clearly defined hierarchy, its rigid discipline, and its specific tests of *satori*." It is the kind of Zen that Americans who study in Japan come to know and bring home. It can legitimately be called "square" because it is seeking the *right* or approved spiritual experience and will accept only that *satori* which receives the stamp of approval of established authority. "There will even be certificates to hang on the wall." The artistic expression of square Zen exhibits much these same characteristics, in Watts's judgment. It is often too studied, too "precious." "The student of *sumi*-painting, calligraphy, *haiku*-poetry, or the tea-ceremony can get trapped in a tiresomely repetitious affectation of styles, varied only with increasingly esoteric allusions to the work of the past." The creativity and freedom of genuine Zen is no longer present.[24]

There never has been a vital spiritual movement without its excesses and distortions, however, and Zen is no exception. Neither the extremes of beat Zen nor the spiritual thinness of square Zen should alarm the genuine Zen disciple, Watts concludes. "Indeed, it is possible that beat Zen and square Zen will so complement and rub against one another that an amazingly pure and lively Zen will arise from the hassle."

## Zen and the American Mind

The surprising appeal of Zen in recent decades and the similarities between the spirit of Zen and the thought of some of the more uniquely American writers is certainly impressive. A question must be raised, however, as to the larger significance of these facts. Is there a real possibility that Zen will take hold in America, as Van Meter Ames suggests—that there will develop an American Zen comparable to but different in important respects from the Japanese Zen that Dr. Suzuki has so ably portrayed?

Carl Jung's early response to the very genuine appeal he found in Zen is perhaps worth noting. "Zen is one of the most wonderful blossoms of the Chinese spirit," Jung wrote. But, he continues: "great as is the value of Zen Buddhism for the understanding of the religious transformation process, its use among Western people is very improbable. The spiritual conceptions necessary to Zen are missing in the West."[25]

One of the most basic of American attitudes, in fact, is the feeling that the conditions of life, wherever they are unsatisfactory, can and should be improved. When we in America want to make daily living more satisfying, this usually means making life better through better engineering, or control of the environment, or increased social services. We feel that floods should be prevented, poverty should be alleviated, racial discrimination should be eliminated. The victims of hurricanes, floods, or earthquakes should be aided—even when these are in Asian or Latin American countries. And our efforts to accomplish such concrete and practical results have certainly been among the finer expressions of the American spirit.

Even such an enthusiastic student of Zen Buddhism as Van Meter Ames is forced to admit that such an attitude as this is not to be found in Zen. Orientals are now rapidly coming to appreciate what science, industrialism, and social planning can do for them, he points out. Economic security can certainly assist one in living a full life instead of a meagre one. However, "this distinction is lacking in Zen literature," Ames writes, "and perhaps it is meaningless to one who can achieve Zen." But there are circumstances, he recognizes, where the acceptance of things as they are would be reprehensible: "It is admirable to have stamina and stoicism in adversity, but not to recommend Zen instead of trying to abolish poverty or oppression which no one should have to bear. . . . Zen would be inhuman if its effacement of self-concern meant unconcern for the troubles of other people." Some of the abler representatives of Zen should consider seriously, Ames concludes, the differences between the preindustrial conditions in which traditional Zen developed and social conditions in the modern world—with which Zen cannot be unconcerned.[26]

A comment on the significance of Zen by Martin Heidegger (1889—), the German existentialist whom many regard as the most original and influential European philosopher now alive, may well be noted, however, in concluding this discussion. A German friend has reported that when visiting Heidegger one day, he found him reading one of Suzuki's books. "If I understand this man correctly," Heidegger remarked, "this is what I have been trying to say in all my writings."[27]

Heidegger's remark, if accurately quoted, may well be an understandable exaggeration. His own philosophy, as Barrett points out, is "in its tone, its temper and its sources Western to the core." There is much in Heidegger that is not Zen and much in Zen that is not in Heidegger. The great error of Western philosophy for Heidegger, however, is to be found in its acceptance of an intellectual dichotomy that has cut man off from unity with Being and from unity in his own being. During some twenty-five hundred years in which Western philosophy has developed, Western man has in fact become the technological master of our planet. But in Heidegger's view this conquest of nature has served only to sharpen the dichotomy between man and nature, and to leave man estranged from Being itself. The Western tradition has come to the end of its cycle, he feels. Some new insights and new directions are essential if philosophy is to be meaningful. Are these perhaps now to be found in the wisdom of the East?

## A *Final Comment*

As human nature is examined by the philosopher and the psychologist, its inner contradiction is clearly apparent. Man is a creature of nature and at the same time is conscious of the fact that he transcends nature. In a unique sense, man is nature and life aware of itself. When he asks himself, as he must in his more thoughtful moments, what is the meaning of this fact and of his own existence, man becomes religious or he becomes philosophical. This existential concern indeed makes philosophy inevitable. Some try to evade such a concern by immersing themselves in the pursuit of wealth, of prestige, of power, of enjoyment; ultimately by trying to forget that they— that I—exist as a conscious self. But if an individual is deaf to this existential concern, if he does not seek a satisfying answer to it, he lives and dies like any other of the million things that he produces. To use Buber's favorite phrase, he lives only in the world of *It*, not in the world of *Thou*.

Our concern in the foregoing chapters has been to provide a broad overview of the philosophies that men have found appealing and satisfying, to enable the thoughtful student to examine with some care the philosophies men live by, and so to supply insights that may enable him to arrive at a more mature and dependable philosophy of his own. When discussing psychoanalysis and Zen Buddhism, Erich Fromm describes with rare insight the aim toward which one's philosophy of life should be directed. This aim he terms simply "well-being." It includes what earlier philosophers have called happiness, but identifies the concrete and specific aspects of such an experience in a fashion that also reminds one at once of Martin Buber and Jean-Paul Sartre:

Well-being is the state of having arrived at the full development of [human] reason: reason not in the sense of a merely intellectual judgment, but in that of grasping truth by "letting things be" as they are. Well-being is possible only to the degree to which one is open, responsive, sensitive, awake, empty (in the Zen sense). Well-being means to be fully related to man and nature affectively, to overcome separateness and alienation, to arrive at the experience of oneness with all that exists —and yet to experience myself at the same time as the separate entity *I* am, as the in-dividual.

Well-being means to be fully born, to become what one potentially is. It means to have the full capacity for joy and for sadness or, to put it still differently, to awake from the half-slumber the average man lives in, and to be fully awake. If it is all that, it means also to be creative; that is, to react and respond as the real, total man I am to the reality of everybody and everything as he or it is.

In this act of true response lies the area of Creativity, of seeing the world as it is *and* experiencing it as *my* world, the world created and transformed by my creative grasp of it, so that the world ceases to be a strange world "over there" and becomes *my* world.

Well-being means, finally, to give up greed, to cease chasing after the preservation and aggrandizement of the Ego, to be and to experience one's self in the act of *being*, not in having, preserving, coveting, using.[28]

No better basis than this could be suggested for judging the adequacy of the philosophy one lives by. Whether one's view of life is wholly Western, shaped by the philosophies discussed in the major portion of this volume, or whether it may have been influenced by insights derived from the wisdom of the East, to be finally acceptable it should enable one to achieve well-being as here described.

# Notes

## Chapter 1

**1.** See Reinhold Niebuhr, *Faith and Politics*, pp. 106–107, for a thoughtful discussion of this point of view. **2.** William Temple, *Nature, Man and God* (London: Macmillan, 1934), p. 35. **3.** *The Changing Values on Campus* (New York: Washington Square Press, 1972), p. 169. **4.** Charles A. Reich, *The Greening of America* (New York: Random House, 1970), Bantam ed., p. 284. **5.** B. A. G. Fuller, *History of Greek Philosophy* (New York: Henry Holt & Co., 1931), II, pp. 7–8. **6.** Plato, *Apology* (trans. Benjamin Jowett), § 23. **7.** *Ibid.* **8.** *Ibid.* **9.** *Ibid.*, § 30. **10.** Plato, *Phaedo* (trans. Benjamin Jowett), §§ 117–118. **11.** *Before and After Socrates* (New York: Cambridge University Press, 1932), p. 54.

## Chapter 2

**1.** *Op. cit.*, p. 376. **2.** A. J. Festugière, *Epicurus and his Gods*, Eng. trans. C. W. Chilton (Oxford: Blackwell, 1955), p. 29. **3.** R. D. Hicks, *Stoic and Epicurean* (New York: Scribners, 1910), p. 170. **4.** Norman W. DeWitt, *St. Paul and Epicurus* (Minneapolis: University of Minnesota Press, 1954), selections from pp. 188–193. Emphasis added. **5.** *Ibid.*, p. 190; see also R. D. Hicks, *op. cit.*, p. 172. **6.** Moses Hadas, *The Stoic Philosophy of Seneca* (Garden City, N.Y.: Doubleday & Co., Inc., 1958, p. 21. **7.** *Vatican Sayings*, 27, 28. **8.** R. D. Hicks, *op. cit.*, p. 171. **9.** *Ibid.* **10.** *Ibid.*, pp. 172–173. **11.** Norman W. DeWitt, *op. cit.*, p. 19. **12.** R. D. Hicks, *op. cit.*, pp. 189–190. **13.** Epicurus, *The Extant Remains*, Eng. trans. Cyril Bailey (London: Oxford University Press, 1926). **14.** A. D. Winspear, *Lucretius: De Rerum Natura* (New York: Harbor Press, 1956), Books II, III, selected passages. By permission of A. D. Winspear. **15.** Lin Yutang, *The Importance of Living* (New York: John Day, 1937), p. 126. **16.** *Ibid.*, p. 127. **17.** *Ibid.*, pp. 401–402 condensed. **18.** *From Pagan to Christian* (Cleveland, Ohio: World Publishing, 1959), pp. 14, 64.

## Chapter 3

**1.** Jeremy Bentham, *An Introduction to the Principles of Morals and Legislation* (Oxford: Clarendon Press, 1907), p. 2. **2.** *Ibid.*, p. 4. **3.** *Ibid.*, pp. 30–31. **4.** *Autobiography of John Stuart Mill* (New York: Columbia University Press, 1924), pp. 21–22. Emphasis added. **5.** *Ibid.*, pp. 93, 94–95, 97–98. **6.** John B. Ellery, *John Stuart Mill* (New York: Twayne Publishers, 1964), p. 31. **7.** *Autobiography*, p. 122. **8.** *Ibid.*, p. 179. **9.** *Ibid.*, pp. 180, 181. **10.** John Stuart Mill, *Utilitarianism, Liberty and Representative Government*. Everyman ed. (New York: Dutton, Inc., 1910), p. 6. **11.** *Ibid.*, p. 7 (abridged). **12.** *Ibid.*, pp. 8, 9. **13.** *Ibid.*, p. 16. **14.** *Ibid.*, pp. 15–16. **15.** *Ibid.*, p. 29. **16.** R. P. Anschutz, *The Philoso-*

*phy of John Stuart Mill* (Oxford: The Clarendon Press, 1953), p. 28. **17.** *Utilitarianism, Liberty and Representative Government*, p. 115. **18.** *Ibid.*, p. 73. **19.** *Ibid.*, p. 97. **20.** See J. Plamenatz, *The English Utilitarians*, pp. 123, 144; also R. P. Anschutz, *op. cit.*, p. 171. **21.** *Autobiography*, p. 100.


### Chapter 4

**1.** *The World as Will and Idea* (London: Kegan Paul, Trench, Trubner & Co., 1896), II, 361–362, 359–360. **2.** *Ibid.*, II, 416, 424, 427, 428 (abridged). **3.** *Ibid.*, II, 431, 432. **4.** *Ibid.*, I, 425. **5.** *Ibid.*, I, 339; III, 340–341 (abridged). **6.** *Ibid.*, III, 351, 343, 342 (abridged). **7.** *Ibid.*, I, 153. **8.** *Ibid.*, I, 253–254. **9.** *Ibid.*, I, 404. **10.** *Ibid.*, III, 345–346; 371–372. **11.** *Essays of Arthur Schopenhauer*, Eng. trans. T. Bailey Saunders (New York: A. L. Burt Company, n.d.), p. 435. **12.** *The World as Will and Idea*, I, 192–193. **13.** *Op. cit.*, Eng. trans. Marjorie Kerr Wilson (New York: Harcourt, 1966), p. 46. **14.** *Essays*, p. 200. **15.** *The World as Will and Idea*, I, 514, 515. **16.** *Ibid.*, I, 428. **17.** *Ibid.*, II, 426. **18.** *Ibid.*, I, 406, 407. **19.** *Essays*, pp. 281, 282 (condensed). **20.** *The World as Will and Idea*, I, 255–256. **21.** *Ibid.*, I, 256. **22.** *Ibid.*, I, 524. **23.** *Ibid.*, I, 489, 490, 491. **24.** *Ibid.*, I, 506, 493. **25.** *Ibid.*, I, 503–504, 504–505. **26.** *The Story of Philosophy* (New York: Pocket Books, Inc., 1954), p. 343.


### Chapter 5

**1.** Xenophon, *Memorabilia* i, 6. **2.** Moses Hadas, *The Stoic Philosophy of Seneca* (Garden City, N.Y.: Doubleday, 1958), p. 9. **3.** Marcus Aurelius, *Meditations*, Bk XI. See George Long's translation (New York: Putnam, n.d.), pp. 94–95. **4.** *Discourses*, Eng. trans. Thomas W. Higginson (Boston: Little, Brown, 1912), pp. 119–120. **5.** Seneca, *Morals*, Eng. trans. Roger L'Estrange (New York: Harper, 1917), pp. 92, 108 (abridged). **6.** *Manual*, § 16. **7.** *Dialogues*, VII, 20. **8.** *Discourses*, p. 47. **9.** Stanzas quoted in W. De Witt Hyde, *The Five Great Philosophies of Life*, pp. 98–99. **10.** *Discourses*, Bk II, Ch. 8. **11.** Moses Hadas, *op. cit.*, p. 32. **12.** Joseph M. Flora, *William Ernest Henley*, pp. 14–15 (v. 3 omitted). **13.** *Mysticism and Logic* (New York: Norton, 1929), pp. 47–48, 56–57. **14.** Marquis Childs and James Reston, Eds. *Walter Lippmann and His Times* (New York: Harcourt, 1959). **15.** Philip Slater, *The Pursuit of Loneliness* (Boston: Beacon Press, 1970), p. 90. **16.** *A Preface to Morals* (New York: Macmillan, 1929), p. 227. **17.** *Ibid.*, pp. 184, 185. **18.** *Ibid.*, p. 280. **19.** *Ibid.*, pp. 281–282. **20.** Judge Ben B. Lindsey and Wainwright Evans, *The Companionate Marriage*, p. 210. **21.** *A Preface to Morals*, p. 301. **22.** *Ibid.*, p. 296. **23.** *Ibid.*, pp. 306, 308–309. **24.** *Ibid.*, pp. 311–312. **25.** *Ibid.*, pp. 329–330 (abridged).


### Chapter 6

**1.** Lewis Browne, *Blesséd Spinoza* (New York: Macmillan, 1932), p. 280. **2.** Quoted in Lewis Browne, *op. cit.*, p. 107. **3.** Lewis Feuer, *Spinoza and the Rise of Liberalism* (Boston: Beacon Press, 1958), pp. 65, 101. Feuer's book provides an able treatment of Spinoza as an influential political philosopher, by no means a recluse.  **4.** *On the Improvement of the Understanding*, trans. R. H. M. Elwes (London: G. Bell, 1884), p. 3.  **5.** *Ibid.*, p. 6.  **6.** *Ibid.*, p. 7.  **7.** Lincoln Barnett, *The Universe and Dr. Einstein* (New York: Sloane, rev. ed., 1957), p. 105.  **8.** *Treatise on Theology and Politics*, trans. R. H. M. Elwes (London: G. Bell, 1883), pp. 91, 9.  **9.** *Ibid.*, p. 81.  **10.** *Ibid.*, p. 83.  **11.** *Ibid.*, p. 90.  **12.** *Ethics*, trans. R. H. M. Elwes (London: G. Bell, 1884), Part I, Prop. XV, XVI.  **13.** *Ibid.*, I, xvi, note.  **14.** *Ibid.*, II, vii, note.  **15.** *Letter XXI* (to Oldenburg).  **16.** *Essay on Man*, § I.  **17.** *Ethics*, III, Introduction.  **18.** *Ibid.*, III, vi; IV, xviii, note.  **19.** *Ibid.*, III, ii, note and Intro.  **20.** *Ibid.*, IV, Preface.  **21.** *Ibid.*, III, ix, note.  **22.** *Ibid.*, IV, lxvi, note; lxvii.  **23.** *Op. cit.*, p. 144. Cf. also pp. 142–144.  **24.** *Ethics*, IV, Preface; III, ix, note.  **25.** *Ibid.*, IV, xviii, note; xxxv; xlvi.  **26.** Edgar A. Singer, *Modern Thinkers and Present Problems* (New York: Holt, 1923), Ch. III. An unusually thoughtful discussion of the moral dilemma in Spinoza's philosophy.  **27.** *A Preface to Morals*, pp. 329, 330.  **28.** Charles A. Reich, *The Greening of America* (New York: Random House, 1970), Bantam ed., p. 278; Theodore Roszak, *The Making of a Counter Culture* (New York: Doubleday, 1959), Anchor ed., pp. 51, 205.

## Chapter 7

**1.** "The Veteran," in *The Portable Dorothy Parker* (New York: Viking, rev. ed., 1954), p. 101.  **2.** Quoted in G. C. Field, *Plato and His Contemporaries* (New York: Dutton, 1930), p. 20.  **3.** *Republic*, trans. Benjamin Jowett (London: Oxford University Press, 1892), Bk. I, § 332A.  **4.** *Ibid.*, I, § 338C.  **5.** *Ibid.*, II, § 359D ff.  **6.** *Ibid.*, II, § 368D, E.  **7.** *Ibid.*, II, § 369 B, D.  **8.** *Ibid.*, II, § 372A, B, C.  **9.** *Ibid.*, II, § 373B, D, E.  **10.** *Ibid.*, V, § 473D.  **11.** *Ibid.*, IV, § 430E, 432A.  **12.** *Ibid.*, IV, § 439D.  **13.** *Ibid.*, IV, §§ 439 E, 440, 441C.  **14.** *Ibid.*, IV, § 442C, B.  **15.** *Ibid.*, IV, § 443D, E.  **16.** *Ibid.*, IV, § 445A, 444E.  **17.** *Ibid.*, VII, § 541A.  **18.** *Ibid.*, IV, § 424A.  **19.** *Ibid.*, VII, § 536E, 537A.  **20.** *Ibid.*, III, § 402A.  **21.** *Ibid.*, V, §§ 451E; 452A, B.  **22.** *Ibid.*, III, § 412D, E.  **23.** *Ibid.*, IV, § 423D; cf. V, § 453B.  **24.** *Ibid.*, VII, § 534C.  **25.** *Ibid.*, III, §§ 416D, 417.  **26.** *Ibid.*, V, § 459D, E.  **27.** *Op. cit.* (New York: Random House, 1970), p. 245.  **28.** *Republic*, VII, § 540A.  **29.** *Ibid.*, VII, § 514-517.  **30.** This point is made in the *Gorgias*, § 503 E. See also R. L. Nettleship, *Lectures on the Republic of Plato*, p. 223.  **31.** *Republic*, VI, § 505A, B; VII, § 517C.

## Chapter 8

**1.** J. M. Warbeke, *The Searching Mind of Greece* (New York: Crofts, 1930), p. 345.  **2.** *Physics*, II, 8, trans. Philip Wheelwright, *Aristotle* (New York: Odyssey, 1951).  **3.** *De Anima*, II, 1, 4.  **4.** *Ibid.*, II, 1; III, 7-11.  **5.** *Metaphysics*, XII, 7.  **6.** *Ibid.*, VI, 2; V, 30.  **7.** *Ibid.*, XII, 7.  **8.** Reprinted by permission of the publishers from *The Nichomachean Ethics*, VI, 13; II, 1. Loeb Classical Library, H. Rackham trans. (Cambridge, Mass.: Harvard University Press, 1926).  **9.** *Ibid.*, I, 7.  **10.** *Ibid.*, I, 5.  **11.** *Ibid.*, VII, 12.  **12.** *Ibid.*, X, 5.  **13.** *Ibid.*, X, 4.  **14.** *Ibid.*, VII, 13.  **15.** *Ibid.*, X, 5, 7.  **16.** *Ibid.*, X, 7 (abridged).

17. *Politics*, VII, 2, W. D. Ross, Ed. (Oxford: The Clarendon Press, 1942).   18. *Ethics*, VIII, 1.   19. *Ibid.*, VII, 3.   20. *Ibid.*, IX, 9.   21. *Ibid.*, X, 8.   22. *Politics*, VIII, 1; *Ethics*, I, 8.   23. *Ethics*, IV, 3 (abridged).   24. *Ibid.*, I, 2; *Politics*, III, 9; VII, 1.   25. *Ethics*, I, 13.   26. *Politics*, I, 2.   27. *Ibid.*, II, 7, 5.   28. *Ibid.*, IV, 1.   29. *A History of Western Philosophy*, p. 202.   30. *Op. cit.*, p. 184.

## Chapter 9

1. "From Absolutism to Experimentalism," in *Contemporary American Philosophy*, W. P. Montague and C. P. Adams, Eds., p. 18. (New York: Macmillan, 1930).   2. Quoted in *The Philosophy of John Dewey*, P. A. Schilpp, Ed. (Evanston, Ill.: Northwestern University Press, 1939), pp. 462–463.   3. *Reconstruction in Philosophy* (New York: Holt, 1920), p. 26.   4. *The Influence of Darwin on Philosophy* (New York: Holt, 1910), pp. 1–2.   5. *Ibid.*, pp. 42–43.   6. *Ibid.*, pp. 43, 44.   7. *Democracy and Education*, pp. 380, 381. Copyright 1916 by Macmillan Publishing Co., Inc., renewed 1944 by John Dewey.   8. *Reconstruction in Philosophy*, pp. 26, 27.   9. *Democracy and Education*, pp. 383, 384.   10. "From Absolutism to Experimentalism," *loc. cit.*, p. 23.   11. *Democracy and Education*, p. 3.   12. *Ibid.*, p. 10.   13. *Ibid.*, p. 22.   14. *Ibid.*, p. 155.   15. *Reconstruction in Philosophy*, p. 169.   16. *Ibid.*, pp. 166–167.   17. *Influence of Darwin on Philosophy*, p. 69.   18. *Reconstruction in Philosophy*, pp. 169–170.   19. *Ibid.*, p. 176.   20. *Ibid.*, p. 177.   21. *Ibid.*, p. 179.   22. *Ibid.*, p. 186.   23. *Democracy and Education*, p. 333.   24. *Reconstruction in Philosophy*, p. 173.

## Chapter 10

1. Bertram D. Wolfe, *Marxism* (New York: Dial, 1968), p. xvii.   2. Quoted by Isaiah Berlin, *Karl Marx* (New York: Oxford University Press, 1939), p. 73.   3. "Karl Marx's Funeral," in Robert Payne, *Marx* (New York: Simon & Schuster, 1968), pp. 500–502 (abridged).   4. Quoted in Sidney Hook, *Towards the Understanding of Karl Marx* (New York: John Day, 1932), pp. 80, 81.   5. "Theses on Feuerbach, III." Reprinted in *Karl Marx and Friedrich Engels on Religion*, Reinhold Niebuhr, Ed. (New York, Schocken Books, 1964), p. 70.   6. *Economic and Philosophical Manuscripts*, Eng. trans. T. B. Bottomore, reprinted in Erich Fromm, *Marx's Concept of Man* (New York: Ungar, 1961), p. 181.   7. Quoted by Hook, *op. cit.*, p. 113.   8. *Marx's Concept of Man*, p. 42. Emphasis added.   9. *Ibid.*, p. 47.   10. *Economic and Philosophical Manuscripts*, *loc. cit.*, pp. 98–99, 95.   11. Erich Fromm, *op. cit.*, pp. 56–57.   12. *Reason and Revolution* (New York: Humanities Press, 1954), p. 282.   13. *Economic and Philosophical Manuscripts*, *loc. cit.*, p. 127.   14. *State and Revolution*, Ch. 5 (New York: International Publishers, 1943), p. 72.   15. *Critique of the Gotha Program*, in *Basic Writings on Politics and Philosophy*, Lewis S. Feuer, Ed. (New York: Doubleday, Anchor Books, 1959), p. 119.   16. *State and Revolution*, Ch. 5, pp. 74, 79, 80.   17. *The Open Society and Its Enemies* (Princeton University Press, rev. ed., 1950), p. 275.   18. Crane Brinton, *The Shaping of the Modern Mind* (New York: Mentor Books, 1953), pp. 203–204 (abridged). Cf. also R. C. Tucker, *Philosophy and Myth in Karl Marx*, pp. 21–27, 218–232.   19. *Karl Marx and Friedrich Engels on Religion*, Intro., p. xvi.   20. Gabriel A. Almond, *The Appeals of Communism* (Princeton University Press, 1954), p. 7.   21. Sidney Hook, *op. cit.*, p. 3.

## Chapter 11

1. Quoted in A. D. Lindsay, *Kant* (London: Oxford University Press, 1934), p. 2.
2. Quoted in Josiah Royce, *The Spirit of Modern Philosophy* (Boston: Houghton Mifflin, 1892), p. 108.   3. Quoted in E. Cassirer, *Rousseau–Kant–Goethe* (Princeton University Press, 1945), pp. 1–2.   4. *Kant's Groundwork of the Metaphysic of Morals*, Eng. trans. H. J. Paton (New York: Harper & Row, Torchbook, 1964), p. 59. Third edition.   5. This phrase is suggested by J. W. Scott, *Kant on The Moral Life* (London: Macmillan, 1924), p. 43.   6. *Ibid.*, p. 45. Emphasis added.   7. *Fundamental Principles of the Metaphysic of Morals*, I, § 1. Emphasis added.   8. *The Metaphysic of Morals*, Paton trans., p. 66.   9. *Ibid.*, Eng. trans. Lewis W. Beck (University of Chicago Press, 1949), p. 60.   10. *Ibid.*, Paton trans., pp. 71–72 (abridged).   11. See *ibid.*, pp. 70, 89, 104.   12. *Ibid.*, pp. 89–90.   13. *Ibid.*, p. 96.   14. *Immanuel Kant: Critique of Practical Reason and Other Writings in Moral Philosophy*, Eng. trans. Lewis W. Beck (University of Chicago Press, 1949), p. 123, note.   15. *Ibid.*, p. 204.   16. *Ibid.*   17. *Fundamental Ends of Life* (New York: Macmillan, 1924), p. 24.   18. *Critique of Practical Reason*, p. 228.   19. *Religion within the Limits of Reason Alone*, trans. by T. M. Greene, p. 142. Cf. also *Critique of Practical Reason*, Abbott trans., p. 226.   20. *Critique of Pure Reason*, 2nd ed., Eng. trans. Norman Kemp Smith (New York: Humanities Press, 1950), Preface, xvi. (Emphasis added.)   21. *Ibid.*, Intro., § 2.   22. *Ibid.*, Preface, xxx.   23. *Moral Man and Immoral Society* (New York: Scribner's, 1932), pp. 270–271.

## Chapter 12

1. Ralph Barton Perry, *The Thought and Character of William James*, Briefer edition (Cambridge, Mass.: Harvard University Press, 1948), p. 53.   2. This suggestion I owe to a discerning reader to whom the manuscript was submitted by the editorial staff at Holt, Rinehart and Winston.   3. Ralph Barton Perry, *op. cit.*, p. 136.   4. *Ibid.*, p. 300.   5. *Pragmatism* (New York: Longmans, Green, 1907), pp. 3, 4, 6.   6. Ralph Barton Perry, *op. cit.*, p. 220.   7. *Talks to Teachers* (New York: Holt, 1899), pp. 268–272 (abridged).   8. *Memories and Studies* (New York: Longmans, Green, 1911), pp. 287, 292.   9. *The Will to Believe and Other Essays* (New York: Longmans, Green, 1896), p. 23.   10. *Ibid.*, pp. 25, 28, 30.   11. *Ibid.*, pp. 161–162.   12. *Ibid.*, p. 163.   13. *Ibid.*, p. 175.   14. *Ibid.*, p. 31.   15. *Pragmatism*, pp. 54, 55.   16. *Ibid.*, p. 58.   17. *Ibid.*, pp. 59–64 (abridged).   18. *Ibid.*, p. 64. Emphasis added.   19. *Ibid.*, pp. 75–76, 143, 222.   20. *Ibid.*, p. 7.   21. *The Varieties of Religious Experience* (New York: Longmans, Green, 1902), pp. 15, 18.   22. *Ibid.*, pp. 525, 516–517.   23. D. C. Macintosh, *The Problem of Knowledge* (New York: Macmillan, 1915), p. 427.   24. *Irrational Man* (Garden City, N.Y.: Doubleday, Anchor Books, 1962), p. 18.

## Chapter 13

1. *The Birth of Tragedy*, Eng. trans. W. A. Haussmann (New York: Russell & Russell, 1964). Intro. p. xvii.   2. *Ibid.*, Chap. 24.   3. "Schopenhauer as Education," § 6, in *Thoughts Out of Season*, II. Eng. trans. Adrian Collins (New York: Russell & Russell, 1964).   4. *Thus Spake Zarathustra*, Eng. trans. Thomas Cotton

(New York: Russell & Russell, 1967), Modern Library ed., pp. 18–19 (abridged).
5. *Ibid.*, pp. 20, 21 (abridged).   6. Quoted in Karl Jaspers, *Nietzsche: An Introduction to the Understanding of His Philosophical Activity* (Eng. tr., Tucson: University of Arizona Press, 1965), pp. 87, 56.   7. *Nietzsche* (Princeton University Press, 1950), p. 59.   8. *The Gay Science*, Sec. 125 (abridged) in Walter Kaufmann, *The Portable Nietzsche* (New York: Viking, Inc., 1954), pp. 95–96.
9. Letters to Overbeck and to his sister, quoted in Jaspers, *Nietzsche*, p. 436.   10. Quoted in K. F. Reinhardt, *The Existential Revolt* (Milwaukee, Wis.; Bruce Publishing Co., 1952), p. 96.   10. *Thus Spake Zarathustra*, Prologue § 2 (abridged). Modern English added.   12. William Barrett, *Irrational Man* (Garden City, N.Y.: Doubleday, Anchor Books, 1962), p. 179.   13. Quoted in Jaspers, *op. cit.*, p. 167.   14. *Thus Spake Zarathustra*, Prologue, § 3, § 4 (selected stanzas).
15. Quoted in Jaspers, *op. cit.*, pp. 152.   16. *Thus Spake Zarathustra*, Part IV, LXXIII, §§ 1, 2.   17. Quoted in Jaspers, *op. cit.*, p. 167. See also *Thus Spake Zarathustra*, Part LXXIII, § 3.   18. Quoted in Jaspers, *op. cit.*, pp. 162, 126.
19. *Beyond Good and Evil*, IX, § 259. Eng. trans. Helen Zimmerin. (New York: Russell & Russell, 1964).   20. *Ibid.*, IX, § 260.   21. *Ibid.*, IX, § 258.   22. *Ibid.*, V, § 199.   23. *Ibid.*, VII, § 239.   24. *Ibid.*, VII, § 232.   25. *Ibid.*, VIII, § 242 (abridged).   26. Quoted in Jaspers, *op. cit.*, p. 149 (italics mine).   27. *Beyond Good and Evil*, IX, § 257.   28. *Ibid.*, I, § 5.   29. *Ibid.*, I, §§ 2, 4.   30. Quoted in Jaspers, *op. cit.*, p. 139; *Beyond Good and Evil*, II, § 34.   31. *Ibid.*, I, § 13; II, § 36.   32. Barbara Branden, *Who Is Ayn Rand* (New York: Random House, 1962), p. 162.   33. *Ibid.*, p. 192; *For the New Intellectual: The Philosophy of Ayn Rand* (New York: Random House, 1961), pp. 20, 39, 63.   34. *Nietzsche and Christianity* (Chicago: Regnery, Gateway ed. 1961), p. 104.


## Chapter 14

1. *Existentialism and the Modern Predicament* (Harper & Row, Torchbook, 1958), p. 30.   2. Quoted in Walter Lowrie, *Kierkegaard*, Vol. I, p. 229 (New York: Harper & Row, Torchbook Ed., 1962).   3. *The Journals of Søren Kierkegaard*, trans. Alexander Dru (New York: Oxford University Press, 1938), p. 22. Emphasis added.   4. *Ibid.*, p. 94.   5. *The Point of View*, Conclusion (abridged). *A Kierkegaard Anthology*, Robert Bretall, Ed. (Princeton University Press, 1946), pp. 337, 339.   6. *Journals*, pp. 26, 33. Kierkegaard's treatment of Romanticism is discussed in some detail in James Collins, *The Mind of Kierkegaard*, pp. 50–65.   7. *Journals*, pp. 41–43, 21. See also *Either/Or*, Vol. II, pp. 162–177.   8. *Journals*, p. 21.   9. *The Living Thoughts of Kierkegaard*, W. H. Auden, Ed. (New York: McKay, 1952), pp. 78–80 (abridged).   10. Quoted in Walter Lowrie, *op. cit.*, p. 264.   11. *Living Thoughts*, pp. 103–105 (the first and third narratives).   12. William Barrett, *Irrational Man*, p. 171.   13. *Living Thoughts*, p. 119 (order reversed).   14. *Ibid.*, p. 126.   15. In *Either/Or*, quoted in Walter Lowrie, *op. cit.*, p. 234.   16. *Concluding Unscientific Postscript*, Eng. trans. David Swenson (Princeton University Press, 1941), p. 182.   17. *Ibid.*, pp. 189, 191.   18. *Ibid.*, p. 188.   19. *Living Thoughts*, p. 210.   20. Walter Kaufmann, *Existentialism from Dostoevsky to Sartre* (New York: Meridian, 1956), p. 18.


## Chapter 15

1. *Saint Genet*, Eng. trans. Bernard Frechtman (New York: Braziller, 1963), p. 63.   2. Quoted in Germaine Brée, *Camus and Sartre* (New York: Dell, 1972),

p. 71. **3.** *The Words*, Eng. trans. Bernard Frechtman (New York: Braziller, 1964), pp. 25, 26. **4.** These three periods, implicit in most discussions of Sartre, are explicitly recognized and developed in L. J. Binkley's *Conflict of Ideals*, Ch. V. **5.** *Nausea*, quoted in Gabriel Marcel, *The Philosophy of Existence* (New York: Philosophical Library, 1949), p. 38. **6.** *The Words*, pp. 251–252. **7.** *Critique of Dialectical Reason* (Paris: Tallimard, 1960), p. 24. **8.** *What Is Literature*, Eng. trans. Bernard Frechtman (New York: Philosophical Library, 1949), p. 217 (abridged). **9.** *The Flies*, in *No Exit and Three Other Plays*, Eng. trans. Stuart Gilbert (New York: Vintage, 1955), p. 122. **10.** *The Republic of Silence*, A. J. Liebling, Ed. (New York: Harcourt, 1947), pp. 498–499. **11.** *Ibid.*, p. 500. **12.** *What is Literature*, pp. 275–276. **13.** See Germaine Brée, *op. cit.*, pp. 25–27. **14.** *Existentialism and Humanism*, Eng. trans. Philip Mairet (London: Methuen, 1948), pp. 51, 52, 56. **15.** "Materialism and Revolution," in *Literary and Philosophical Essays*, Eng. trans. Annette Michelson (New York: Collier Books, 1962), pp. 198, 220. **16.** Quoted in Simone de Beauvoir, *Force of Circumstance*, p. 199. **17.** *The God that Failed*, Richard Crossman, Ed. (New York: Bantam, 1952), pp. 13, 14. **18.** *Situations*, Eng. trans. Benita Eisler (New York: Braziller, 1965), p. 269. **19.** *Idem.*; see also *Search for a Method*, Eng. trans. Hazel Barnes (New York: Knopf, 1963), p. 19. **20.** *Liberation*, July 20, 1954 (quoted in Brée, *op. cit.*, p. 195). **21.** *Existentialism and Humanism*, p. 44. **22.** *Being and Nothingness*, Eng. trans. Hazel Barnes (New York: Philosophical Library, 1956), p. 46. **23.** *Ibid.*, p. 591. **24.** *Ibid.*, p. 60. **25.** *Ibid.*, p. 25. **26.** *Ibid.*, pp. 439, 481. **27.** *No Exit, loc. cit.*, p. 47. **28.** *Being and Nothingness*, p. 408. **29.** *Existentialism and Humanism*, p. 28. **30.** *Ibid.*, p. 29. **31.** *Ibid.*, pp. 31, 33, 34 (selected passages). **32.** *Ibid.*, p. 45. **33.** *Ibid.*, pp. 51–52. **34.** *Ibid.*, p. 55. **35.** *Critique of Dialectical Reason*, p. 27. **36.** *Ibid.*, p. 34. **37.** Raymond Aron, *Marxism and the Existentialists* (New York: Harper & Row, Inc., © 1959 by Raymond Aron in Eng. trans.), p. 39. **38.** *Ibid.*, pp. 30, 37; see also pp. 19–37. **39.** "What Is Jean-Paul Sartre Thinking Lately?" An interview with Pierre Bénichose, *Esquire*, December 1972, pp. 207, 208. **40.** *Loc. cit.*, p. 208. **41.** Germaine Brée, *op. cit.*, pp. 2–3. **42.** Raymond Aron, *op. cit.*, p. 176.

## Chapter 16

**1.** *The Philosophy of Martin Buber*, P. A. Schilpp and M. Friedman, Eds.; Library of Living Philosophers, Vol. XII (La Salle, Ill.: Open Court Publishing Co., 1967), p. 516. **2.** *Ibid.*, p. 12. **3.** Aubrey Hodes, *Martin Buber: An Intimate Portrait* (New York: Viking, 1971), pp. 74, 75, 85. **4.** Buber commented on his relationship with Hammarskjöld in a short essay, "Memories of Hammarskjöld," (in *A Believing Humanism*, pp. 57–59). In a biography of Hammarskjöld, *The Statesman and the Faith*, by Henry P. Van Dusen, the letter nominating Buber is reproduced. It was the Nobel Peace Prize, not the prize in Literature, as erroneously reported by some writers, for which Buber was nominated. **5.** Quoted in Roy Oliver, *The Wanderer and the Way* (Ithaca, N.Y.: Cornell University Press, 1968), p. 19 (abridged). **6.** *I and Thou*, Eng. trans. Walter Kaufmann (New York: Scribner, 1970), Postscript, p. 173. **7.** *Ibid.*, p. 85. **8.** T. S. Eliot, *Collected Poems*, 1909–1935, copyright 1936 by Harcourt, Brace and Company, Inc. and used with their permission and the permission of Faber and Faber, Limited. **9.** *Library of Living Philosophers*, Vol. XII, p. 42. **10.** Maurice Friedman, *Martin Buber: The Life of Dialogue* (New York: Harper & Row, Inc., Torchbook, 1960), p. 87. **11.** *Between Man and Man*, Eng. trans. R. Gregor Smith

(New York: The Macmillan Co.; London: Routledge & Kegan Paul, 1948), p. 97. **12.** *I and Thou*, p. 66. **13.** *Between Man and Man*, p. 21. **14.** *I and Thou*, p. 54. **15.** *Ibid.*, pp. 111, 112, 113, 114. **16.** *Library of Living Philosophers*, Vol. XII, pp. 35–36. **17.** *I and Thou*, p. 57. **18.** *Ibid.*, pp. 115–116. **19.** *Eclipse of God* (New York: Harper & Row, 1952), p. 35. **20.** *Israel and the World*, Eng. trans. Olga Marx (New York: Schocken Books, 1948), p. 46. **21.** *Between Man and Man*, p. 82. **22.** *Israel and the World*, p. 17. **23.** *Between Man and Man*, p. 71. **24.** *I and Thou*, pp. 123, 150. **25.** *Eclipse of God*, p. 45. **26.** *Between Man and Man*, p. 50; *Library of Living Philosophers*, Vol. XII, p. 24. **27.** *For the Sake of Heaven*, Eng. trans. Ludwig Lewisohn (Philadelphia: Jewish Publications Society of America, 1958), 2nd ed., Author's Foreword, p. xiii. **28.** *I and Thou*, p. 164; *Between Man and Man*, p. 52. **29.** *Paths in Utopia* (New York: Macmillan, 1950), pp. 140, 148. **30.** *Library of Living Philosophers*, Vol. XII, p. 20. **31.** *Pointing the Way*, p. 228. **32.** *Idem.* **33.** From *Markings* by Dag Hammarskjöld, Eng. trans. Leif Sjoberg and W. H. Auden (New York: Alfred A. Knopf, Inc., 1964), p. 211. **34.** See Philip Wheelwright's essay, *Library of Living Philosophers*, Vol. XII, pp. 69–95. **35.** *Between Man and Man*, p. 21. **36.** *Library of Living Philosophers*, Vol. XII, p. 693. **37.** Quoted in Maurice Friedman, *op. cit.*, p. 6 (abridged).

## Chapter 17

**1.** D. T. Suzuki, Erich Fromm, and Richard De Martino, *Zen Buddhism and Psychoanalysis* (New York: Harper & Row, 1960), p. 5 (abridged). **2.** *Ibid.*, p. 6. **3.** *Ibid.*, p. 7. **4.** *Ibid.*, pp. 8, 9. **5.** *Ibid.*, p. 80. **6.** *Zen Buddhism, Selected Writings of D. T. Suzuki*, edit. by William Barrett (New York: Doubleday Anchor Books, 1956), pp. ix–xi. By permission of Doubleday & Co., Inc., and Hutchinson Publishing Group, Inc. **7.** Alan W. Watts, *The Spirit of Zen* (New York: Grove, Evergreen Ed., 1960), p. 24; also "Beat Zen, Square Zen and Zen," in *The World of Zen*, ed. Nancy Ross, p. 340. **8.** Wm. Barrett, *op. cit.*, p. 83. **9.** D. T. Suzuki, *Zen Buddhism*, p. 3; quoted by Erich Fromm, *op. cit.*, pp. 114–115. **10.** D. T. Suzuki, *Introduction to Zen Buddhism* (London: Hutchinson Publishing Group Ltd., 1949), p. 40. Samuel Weiser, Inc., U. S. Distributor. **11.** See Nancy Ross, ed., *The World of Zen* (New York: Random House, Vintage Books, 1960), p. 9. **12.** *Introduction to Zen Buddhism*, p. 41 (abridged). **13.** *Ibid.*, p. 60. **14.** See Wm. Barrett, *op. cit.*, pp. 134–135. **15.** E. Fromm, *op. cit.*, p. 118. **16.** D. T. Suzuki, *Introduction to Zen Buddhism*, p. 39. **17.** Van Meter Ames, *Zen and American Thought* (Honolulu: University of Hawaii Press, 1962), p. 10. **18.** *Introduction to Zen Buddhism*, pp. 41–42 (abridged), p. 43. **19.** See Nancy Ross, *op. cit.*, pp. 4, 17, x. **20.** Alan Watts, "Beat Zen, Square Zen, and Zen," in Nancy Ross, *op. cit.*, p. 333 (quoted from *Beat Zen, Square Zen and Zen* [San Francisco: City Lights Books, 1959]). **21.** *Ibid.*, p. 340. **22.** Quoted by Watts, *loc. cit.*, p. 335. **23.** *Ibid.*, p. 338. **24.** *Ibid.*, p. 339. **25.** Foreword to Suzuki's *Introduction to Zen Buddhism*, p. 24. **26.** Van Meter Ames, *op. cit.*, p. 17. **27.** Wm. Barrett, *op. cit.*, pp. vii, xi. **28.** Erich Fromm, *op. cit.*, pp. 91–92 (abridged).

# Index